BELEAGUERED SUPERPOWER
Biden's America Adrift

BELEAGUERED SUPERPOWER
Biden's America Adrift

Steven Rosefielde
University of North Carolina, USA

Daniel Quinn Mills
Harvard Business School, USA

NEW JERSEY • LONDON • SINGAPORE • BEIJING • SHANGHAI • HONG KONG • TAIPEI • CHENNAI • TOKYO

Published by

World Scientific Publishing Co. Pte. Ltd.

5 Toh Tuck Link, Singapore 596224

USA office: 27 Warren Street, Suite 401-402, Hackensack, NJ 07601

UK office: 57 Shelton Street, Covent Garden, London WC2H 9HE

Library of Congress Cataloging-in-Publication Data
Names: Rosefielde, Steven, author. | Mills, Daniel Quinn, author.
Title: Beleaguered superpower : Biden's America adrift / Steven Rosefielde,
     University of North Carolina, USA, Daniel Quinn Mills, Harvard Business School, USA.
Description: USA : Word Scientific, 2021. | Includes bibliographical references.
Identifiers: LCCN 2021012130 | ISBN 9789811236181 (hardcover) |
     ISBN 9789811236570 (paperback) | ISBN 9789811236198 (ebook) |
     ISBN 9789811236204 (ebook other)
Subjects: LCSH: United States--Foreign economic relations--History--21st century. |
     United States--Politics and government--2021- | Biden, Joseph R., Jr.
Classification: LCC HF1455 .R6144 2021 | DDC 337.73--dc23
LC record available at https://lccn.loc.gov/2021012130

British Library Cataloguing-in-Publication Data
A catalogue record for this book is available from the British Library.

Copyright © 2021 by World Scientific Publishing Co. Pte. Ltd.

All rights reserved. This book, or parts thereof, may not be reproduced in any form or by any means, electronic or mechanical, including photocopying, recording or any information storage and retrieval system now known or to be invented, without written permission from the publisher.

For photocopying of material in this volume, please pay a copying fee through the Copyright Clearance Center, Inc., 222 Rosewood Drive, Danvers, MA 01923, USA. In this case permission to photocopy is not required from the publisher.

For any available supplementary material, please visit
https://www.worldscientific.com/worldscibooks/10.1142/12255#t=suppl

Desk Editors: Balamurugan Rajendran

Typeset by Stallion Press
Email: enquiries@stallionpress.com

Foreword

Beleaguered Superpower: Biden's America Adrift is the eighth book co-written by the authors on the closely connected themes of economics and American national security in the past 14 years. The subject matter has remained broadly the same, but our comprehension of the deep problematic has evolved and matured. This volume began as a treatise on rational choice Realpolitik before gradually broadening into an exploration of purblind international security management. Those interested in tracing the evolution of our thinking in response to a dramatically changing world should consult:

Masters of Illusion: American Leadership in the Media Age (Cambridge: Cambridge University Press, 2007).
Rising Nations: What America Should Do (New York: Amazon, 2009).
Democracy and Its Elected Enemies: American Political Capture and Economic Decline (New York: Cambridge University Press, 2013).
Global Economic Turmoil and the Public Good (Singapore: World Scientific, 2015).
The Trump Phenomenon and Future of US Foreign Policy (Singapore: World Scientific, 2016).
Trump's Populist America (Singapore: World Scientific, 2017).
Populists and Progressives: The New Forces in American Politics (Singapore: World Scientific, 2020).

Preface

This book is about military power, hard power, in today's world. Many prefer not to think about the matter, secretly hoping that not thinking about it will make it disappear, but it will not. Hard power unfortunately remains essential, in fact, irreplaceable by soft power or diplomacy for maintaining world peace. The Chinese, the Russians, and the Iranians do not hesitate to use military force. The Chinese in Tibet, the Russians in Ukraine, and the Iranians in mid-east against Israel and other states. Why then are they so hesitant to use it directly whenever the United States is involved? The answer partly must surely be that the time is not yet propitious; that the nuclear and conventional warfighting risks of being embroiled in prolonged hostilities today outweigh the expected benefits.

Preventing that time from arriving amid a simmering undeclared new Cold War (with altered ideologies) between imperially ambitious East–West superpowers is the primary strategic goal of the United States. What is required is keeping US hard power well ahead of its potential adversaries in weaponry and readiness. If they erode significantly, war becomes much more likely. Russia and China are better prepared today for aggression than they were two decades ago and both are fully capable of undertaking it. Global security depends upon America neutralizing these gains.

The danger is that perverse American domestic politics driven by patchwork coalitions of progressive and liberal self-seekers will cause the United States to over-reach (color revolutions) and simultaneously undercut Washington's commitment to continuing hard power dominance, compromising its war fighting capabilities. The threat is escalating rapidly because American progressives and liberals increasingly oppose or are

viii *Beleaguered Superpower: Biden's America Adrift*

disinterested in stout national security and militants are envenoming society. They devote their energies to assuring publics that authoritarian threats are manageable with less and less defense spending, or are figments of reactionary imagination. This book demonstrates that they are wrong on both scores by highlighting contemporary authoritarian perils, and debunking the canard that reducing Western hard power strengthens global security. It also tries to raise awareness of cognitive dissonance. Americans confronted with unwelcome evidence prefer to choose sides rather than make fully informed impartial assessments.

Reality is not binary. Classifying positions as hawkish or dovish, cruel or compassionate, Republican or Democratic, capitalist or socialist, or any other motive focused dichotomy is not a valid substitute for dispassionate international security policy analysis even though it has become the rule rather than the exception.

Beleaguered Superpower: Biden's America Adrift documents three intertwined threats imperiling America, and analyzes their implications for the world's future. All three threats are serious. One is internal. The others are external. The internal threat is a potent, and increasingly anti-patriotic American political current that prioritizes anti-competitive and anti-meritocratic social dependency. It privileges progressive causes and expanded welfare state spending over economic growth (entitlement over efficiency) and hollows military deterrence.

The external threats are the rising military power of Russia, China, North Korea, Iran, and the global jihadi, America's over-reaching support of "color revolutions" and an economic malaise punctuated with political and social strife spilling over from the West across the planet, dampening economic vitality, and sowing the seeds of discontent. The Russian, Chinese, North Korean, Iranian, and global jihadi challenges preceded the COVID-19 pandemic, and will outlast it. As authoritarians expand their spheres of influence and the West lapses into secular economic growth stagnation, new millennium synergies from globalization will reverse.

The external threats jeopardize the military, economic, and cultural dimensions of America's superpower, and imperil the peace and prosperity of the world's democracies. The danger is visible in plain sight, but few notice or appreciate that they should be concerned, especially generation X and millennials who harken to pied pipers. Most people are missing the forest for the trees because immediate personal concerns, perpetual political campaigning and media antics divert their attention from real external threats to their quality of existence. Many do not understand why

Preface ix

sane people contemplate war, shrug their shoulders and turn their attention to other matters, even though the historical record demonstrates the ever-present dangers of armed violence.[1]

They persuade themselves that because it is reasonable to disarm all nations will, even though disarmament efforts in the new millennium documented in this volume have been fruitless.

It therefore is important to appraise the portentous implications of Biden's America adrift with a dry eye. Authoritarianism, an undeclared new Cold War between East–West superpower rivals, secular global economic stagnation, and cultural decadence are greater menaces than COVID-19 and global warming.[2]

An Executive Summary succinctly states the present danger posed by America's waning superpower, pinpoints the causes, identifies the challenges, describes the difficulty of parrying Russian, Chinese, North Korean, Iranian, and global jihadi authoritarianism and assesses America's military and the globe's economic prospects.

Part I *Playing with Fire* describes the *zeitgeist* undermining America's economic vitality, military security, and responsible global leadership.

Part II *Authoritarian Regimes are Mounting a Serious Challenges* documents the burgeoning security threats posed by Russian, Chinese, North Korean, Iranian, and global jihadi authoritarianism.

Part III *Civic Discord on the Home Front is Crippling Us* parses the political, social, and economic factors hampering America's ability to parry the Eastern authoritarian threat amid an undeclared renewed Cold War between East and West superpowers, and limns the adverse consequences for globalization, American led supply chains, and worldwide prosperity.

---

[1] Charles H. Anderton and Jurgen Brauer, "Mass Atrocities and Their Prevention" (*Journal of Economic Literature*) forthcoming 2020. Charles H. Anderton and Jurgen Brauer, *Economic Aspects of Genocides, Other Mass Atrocities, and Their Prevention* (New York: Oxford University Press, 2016).

[2] James Traub, "The United States of America Is Decadent and Depraved," *Foreign Policy* (December 2019), https://foreignpolicy.com/2017/12/19/the-united-states-of-america-is-decadent-and-depraved/. "Perhaps in a democracy the distinctive feature of decadence is not debauchery but terminal self-absorption — the loss of the capacity for collective action, the belief in common purpose, even the acceptance of a common form of reasoning."

x   *Beleaguered Superpower: Biden's America Adrift*

Part IV *Trying to Manage the Threats* documents the ineffectuality of America policies designed to contain the security threats posed by Russian, Chinese, North Korean, Iranian, and global jihadi authoritarianism.

Part V *Rescuing a Beleaguered Superpower* assesses the state of play between rival American political forces hampering Washington's ability to neutralize the Eastern authoritarian challenge.

The message that stout defense deters aggression and achieving it necessitates sacrifices and competent implementation is a truism, but does not always govern security policy because leaders and political coalitions can deny incompetence, authoritarian aggressive ambitions, and claim that external threats are hobgoblins or resolvable with soft power. The contention that radicalism degrades global economic vitality is self-evident for those who understand general competitive theory, but progressives deny it, and liberals do not grasp yet that their policies menace prosperity.[3] Parts II and IV thoroughly document the present dangers. Readers who accept the premise that Russia, China, North Korea, Iran, and the global jihadi pose serious national security perils may wish to skim them. Those who are skeptical are encouraged to acquaint themselves more thoroughly with the evidence.

---

[3] Joseph Stiglitz, *People, Power, and Profits: Progressive Capitalism for an Age of Discontent* (New York: W.W. Norton, 2019). Paz Gómez, "Stakeholder Capitalism's Sleight of Hand," *Frontier Centre for Public Policy* (March 2020), https://fcpp.org/2020/03/13/stakeholder-capitalisms-sleight-of-hand/.

About the Authors

Steven Rosefielde, Professor of Economics, University of North Carolina, Chapel Hill. He received his PhD from Harvard University, and is a Member of Russian Academy of Natural Sciences (RAEN). His books include: *Democracy and Its Elected Enemies: The West's Paralysis, Crisis and Decline*, Cambridge University Press, 2013; *Inclusive Economic Theory* (with Ralph W. Pfouts), World Scientific, 2014; *Global Economic Turmoil and the Public Good* (with Quinn Mills), World Scientific Publishers, 2015; *Transformation and Crisis in Central and Eastern Europe: Challenges and Prospects* (with Bruno Dallago), Routledge, 2016; *The Kremlin Strikes Back: Russia and the West After Crimea's Annexation*, Cambridge University Press, 2016; *The Trump Phenomenon and Future of US Foreign Policy* (with Quinn Mills), World Scientific, 2016; *Trump's Populist America*, World Scientific, 2017; *China's Market Communism: Challenges, Dilemmas, Solutions* (with Jonathan Leightner), Routledge, 2017; *The Unwinding of the Globalist Dream: EU, Russia and China* (with Masaaki Kuboniwa, Kumiko Haba, and Satoshi Mizobata, eds.), World Scientific, 2017; *Putin's Russia: Economy, Defence and Military Foreign*, World Scientific, 2020; *Progressive and Populists* (with Quinn Mills), World Scientific, 2020.

Daniel Quinn Mills provides thought leadership in several fields including leadership, strategy, economics, and geopolitics. He has been a Director of publicly listed firms and is currently a Director of several closely held private corporations. He has published books about *Populists and Progressives: The New Forces in American Politics*, business activities, the media, American foreign policy, economic policy, and political processes. During the Vietnam War, Mills spent several years in Washington, DC helping to control inflation. For several years, he was in charge of all wages, prices, and profits in the construction industry (then fourteen percent of GDP). Simultaneously, he taught at MIT's Sloan School of Management. Thereafter he taught at the Harvard Business School. He has done consulting and speaking in the following countries: United States, Canada, the United Kingdom, Indonesia, Ireland, France, the Netherlands, Germany, Switzerland, Italy, Russia, Israel, China, Japan, Malaysia, Brazil, Columbia, Mexico, Singapore, South Africa, Kuwait, the United Arab Emirates, Saudi Arabia, Vietnam, and Australia.

Mills earned his MA and PhD from Harvard, both in economics. He received his undergraduate degree from Ohio Wesleyan. Throughout his career, Mills has been an influential author. His recent books are *Populists and Progressives*, World Scientific (with Steven Rosefielde), 2020; *The Trump Phenomenon and the Future of US Foreign Policy* (with Steven Rosefielde), 2016; *Global Economic Turmoil and the Public Good* (with Steven Rosefielde), 2015; *Shadows of the Civil War*, 2014; *The Leader's Guide to Past and Future*, 2013; *Democracy and Its Elected Enemies* (with Steven Rosefielde), 2013; *The Financial Crisis of 2008–2010*, 2010; and *Rising Nations* (with Steven Rosefielde), 2009. Previously he published *Masters of Illusion: American Leadership in the Media Age* (with Steven Rosefielde), 2007.

Acknowledgments

The authors thank Lisa Ji, Elizabeth Young, Stephen Blank, Bruno Dallago, Bowen Song, June Huang, and Minjoo Son for their valuable assistance.

Contents

Foreword		v
Preface		vii
About the Authors		xi
Acknowledgments		xiii
List of Figures		xvii
Methodology		xix
Executive Summary		xxi
Introduction		xxv
Part I	**Playing with Fire**	**1**
Chapter 1	The Biden–Harris Administration is Overreaching	3
Chapter 2	Resulting Security Morass	15
Part II	**Authoritarian Regimes are Mounting Serious Challenges**	**25**
Chapter 3	Russia	27
Chapter 4	China	71
Chapter 5	North Korea	101
Chapter 6	Iran	125
Chapter 7	Power of Their Collusion	143

xvi *Beleaguered Superpower: Biden's America Adrift*

Part III	**Civic Discord on the Home Front is Crippling Us**	**163**
Chapter 8	Non-Partisanship and Bi-Partisanship are Both Disappearing	165
Part IV	**Trying to Manage the Threats**	**187**
Chapter 9	Sanctions Are of Limited Use	189
Chapter 10	Assistance Can Be Too Costly	221
Chapter 11	Arms Control is Problematic	233
Chapter 12	Technology is Crucial	255
Part V	**Rescuing a Beleaguered Superpower**	**263**
Chapter 13	Rejecting Denial and Drift	265
Chapter 14	Shifting Power in America to Create Strength	279
Chapter 15	Security Lessons of COVID-19	285
Chapter 16	Prospects 2021–2030	293

Conclusion	301
Appendix: "Guns and Butter" Superpower	309
Bibliography	331

List of Figures

Figure 3.1	Soviet Institutional Foundations of Putin's Mixed Economy	51
Figure 8.1	Labor Force Participation Rate	174
Figure A1	Factor Space	313
Figure A2	Production Space	315
Figure A3	Distribution Space	319
Figure A4	Transfer Space	323
Figure A5	Quality of Existence Space	326
Figure A6	Price Adjustment Space	327
Figure A7	Quantity Adjustment Space	328
Figure A8	Maslow Hierarchy of Need	329

Methodology

Abram Bergson devised the evidence-based scientific methodology used by the National Intelligence Council (NIC) for assessing the economic and military potential of rival nations. He did this at Harvard in the 1930s, during World War II as director of the Russian Analysis Section of the Office of Strategic Studies (OSS), and as senior advisor to the CIA's Office of Soviet Analysis (SOVA).[1] He adjusted data for planned economies in accordance with neoclassical norms, pioneered the study of sources of economic growth, tested hypotheses econometrically, and inclusively interpreted outcomes in a broad social welfare framework.

---

[1] Abram Bergson, "A Reformulation of Certain Aspects of Welfare Economics," *Quarterly Journal of Economics* 52, no. 1, 1938: 310–334; Abram Bergson, "Soviet National Income and Product in 1937," Parts I and II, *Quarterly Journal of Economics* 64, nos. 2,3, 1950: 208–241, 408–441; Abram Bergson, "On Inequality of Income in the U.S.S.R.," *American Slavic and East European Statistician*, no. 3, 1951: 95–99. Abram Bergson, "Reliability and Usability of Soviet Statistics: A Summary Appraisal," *American Statistician* 7, no. 3, 1953: 13–16; Abram Bergson, editor and contributor, *Soviet Economic Growth: Conditions and Perspectives* (Evanston, Ill: Row, Peterson, 1953); Abram Bergson, "The Concept of Social Welfare," *Quarterly Journal of Economics* 68, no. 2, 1954: 233–253; Abram Bergson, *The Real National Income of Soviet Russia since 1928* (Cambridge, MA: Harvard University Press, 1961). Abram Bergson, "The Great Economic Race," *Challenge Magazine* 11, no. 6, 1963: 4–6; Abram Bergson, *The Economics of Soviet Planning* (New Haven, CT: Yale University Press, 1964); Abram Bergson, *Planning and Productivity under Soviet Socialism* (New York: Columbia University Press, 1968).

Abram Bergson, "Social Choice under Representative Government," *Journal of Public Economics* 6, no. 3, 1976: 171–190.

He shunned all forms of unfalsifiable speculative explanations because as Ludwig Wittgenstein proved propositional tautologies detached from objective reality are unscientific.[2]

This volume adheres strictly to Bergson's principles. It documents the supply side potential of rival economic systems, and assesses trends in the correlation of forces, always cognizant that policymakers are free to act impetuously. *Beleaguered Superpower* avoids the twin suppositions that leaders and patchwork coalitions (including the American Democratic Party) always act wisely or that universal reason eventually will compel them to do the right thing. Reason does not guarantee that American political coalitions will act in the nation's best interest or authoritarian states will become virtuous democracies.[3]

Although no methodology is infallible,[4] Bergson's approach has the virtue of transparency. It is not driven by a hidden agenda. There is nothing to deconstruct. The methodology creates credible "facts" for pragmatic analysis, discussion and debate without preconditions (see Appendix).

---

[2] David Redlawsk, Andrew Civenttini, and Karen Emmerson, "The Affective Tipping Point: Do Motivated Reasoners Ever 'Get It'," *Political Psychology* 31, 4, 2010: 563–593.

[3] Matthew Kovach, "Twisting the Truth: Foundations of Wishful Thinking," *Theoretical Economics* 15, 2020, 989–1022.

[4] Gerd Gigerenzer and Reinhard Selten, *Bounded Rationality* (Cambridge, MA: MIT Press, 2002).

Rom Harre with M. Krausz, *Varieties of Relativism* (Oxford: Blackwell, 1995). Rom Harre with J. Arson and E. Way, *Realism Rescued* (London: Duckworth, 1994). Rom Harré with Michael Tissaw, *Wittgenstein and Psychology* (Basingstoke, UK: Ashgate, 2005). Rom Harré, *The philosophies of science*, 2nd ed. (Oxford, GB: Oxford University Press, 1986). Rom Harré and P. Secord, *The Explanation of Social Behaviour* (Oxford, GB: Blackwell, 1973). Daniel Kahneman, "Maps of Bounded Rationality: Psychology for Behavioral Economics," *The American Economic Review* 93, no. 5, 2003: 1449–1475. Steven Rosefielde, "Operational Economic Theory in the Excluded Middle between Positivism and Rationalism," *Atlantic Economic Journal* 4, no. 2, May 1976: 1–8. Steven Rosefielde, "Post Positivist Scientific Method and the Appraisal of Nonmarket Economic Behavior," *Quarterly Journal of Ideology* 3, no. 1, Spring 1980: 23–33. Steven Rosefielde and Ralph W. Pfouts, *Inclusive Economic Theory* (Singapore: World Scientific Publishers, 2014). Ariel Rubinstein, *Modeling Bounded Rationality* (Cambridge, MA: MIT Press, 1998). Herbert Simon, *Models of Man: Social and Rational — Mathematical Essays on Rational Human Behavior in a Social Setting* (New York, NY: John Wiley and Sons, 1957). Clem Tisdell, *Bounded Rationality and Economic Evolution: A Contribution to Decision Making, Economics, and Management* (Cheltenham, UK: Brookfield, 1998).

Executive Summary

Russia annexed Crimea in 2014. China is contesting America in the South China Sea. North Korea has nuclearized, and Iran seems to be following Pyongyang's path. The United States used hard power, soft power, smart diplomacy, and global institutions to prevent these dangerous developments. It failed.

Eastern authoritarian states and the global jihadi have modernized their armed forces and are striving to make further advances. Some rivals are more powerful today than they were during the first Cold War 1947–1991 and intend to enlarge their spheres of influence and acquire new territories when opportunity knocks. There is clear and present danger that

(1) China may deny Western navies and merchant vessels free navigation in the South China Sea, usurp seabed resources, and seize Taiwan.
(2) Russia may annex additional territories in Novorossiya or conquer the Baltic States.
(3) Pyongyang may invade or otherwise subdue South Korea.
(4) Iran may attack and harass its neighbors and the global jihadi grab assets that imperil American and global security.
(5) Afghanistan will fall to the Taliban.

These developments are not coincidental. The likelihood that Eastern authoritarians will cross red lines is increasing for two reasons. First, America and European Union continue provoking Eastern authoritarians with their endorsement of "color revolutions" and "regime change."

Second, there has been an adverse shift in the correlation of forces abetted by the free world's refusal to match Russia's, China's, North Korea's and Iran's waxing military might.

The ability to deter Eastern authoritarian aggression today amid an undeclared new superpower Cold War, even as America continues over-reaching, grows more problematic with every passing day. Few expect a "bolt from the blue" like a Third World War. However, stumbling into World War III through losses in a series of small engagements is a possibility. Inadequate hard power might not only diminish American influence and inflict serious losses in local wars. It may become a corridor to global conflagration.

It would seem reasonable to suppose that America and the rest of the free world would mobilize to counter the Eastern authoritarian challenge, but they are not doing so. Western leaders while claiming to take appropriate countermeasures are betting on containment through weakness. They are paring hard power defense capabilities to increase domestic social spending, while continuing to instigate color revolutions and regime change.

The evidence compiled in *Beleaguered Superpower: Biden's America Adrift* suggests that the threats posed by Russia, China, North Korea, and Iran are more serious than Western governments publicly acknowledge. These threats although ominous, are manageable, if America restores its economic vitality, reins its over-reaching and funds robust deterrence.

The likelihood that America will do so anytime soon is slight. Opponents of stout defense believe that the United States can muddle through and eventually defang Eastern authoritarians. They insist that enhancing their brand of progressive-liberal social justice is more important to American security than faster economic growth and robust deterrence.

Some opponents of stout defense are prepared to tip their hats to hard power for electoral purposes, but refuse to do enough to deter Russia, China, North Korea, Iran, and the global jihadi from increasing their territories and spheres of influence. Likewise, progressives and liberals are willing to discuss initiatives to stimulate faster economic growth, but are not prepared to do enough to restore Western economic vitality, and forestall another global debt crisis. COVID-19 deficit spending is exacerbating the problem.

Proponents of stout defense do not have enough political influence to deter rising authoritarianism abroad, to restore merit-based economic competition, discipline incompetent Washington bureaucracies, reduce the national debt,[1] unify society, and restore bi-partisanship in the national interest. The progressive and liberal entitlement zeitgeist is too strong. For those who still remember the French "anything is possible" Popular Front, short-changing defense, undervaluing economic growth and instigating domestic agitation appear perilous games. Once upon a time, in the aftermath of the Soviet Union's demise, it seemed that American unipolar superpower would culminate in a golden age of global peace and prosperity, but this is no longer plausible. If progressive and liberal priorities prevent America from stemming the Eastern authoritarian tide, the United States risks becoming a fratricidal polity, an anemic zero-sum society at home,[2] a failed democratic free enterprise model abroad, and "paper tiger" in global affairs.[3] American influence abroad will wane. The domestic living standard may improve glacially, or even decline, alienating a large segment of the middle class. Liberalization and competitiveness in Asia, Europe, and much of the Third World will be in retreat and the global economy will atrophy.

America is losing the possibility of using its superpower to strengthen and sustain global security because of

(1) The rising security threats posed by "Eastern Authoritarians": Russia, China, North Korea, Iran, and the global jihadi.
(2) Washington's failure to provide a stout hard power (weapons) response to the "Eastern Authoritarian" challenge.
(3) The likelihood that progressive and liberal opposition will diminish America's hard power in the decades ahead.
(4) The likelihood that progressive policies and extravagant liberal welfare state spending will diminish GDP growth, foment partisan strife, and antagonize Russia, China, North Korea, Iran, and the global jihadi.
(5) The likelihood that progressive confrontation tactics will estrange allies and embolden adversaries.

---

[1] Steven Rosefielde and Quinn Mills, *Progressive and Populists* (Singapore: World Scientific Publishers, 2020).

[2] Lester Thurow, *The Zero-Sum Society* (Lexington: Basic Books, 1980).

[3] Mao Zedong, "U.S. Imperialism is a Paper Tiger," *Selected Works of Mao Zedong*, (July 1956), https://www.marxists.org/reference/archive/mao/selected-works/volume-5/mswv5_52.htm.

(6) The likelihood that America will not rein its "color revolution" over-reaching.

(7) The likelihood that foes will conclude that a divided and decadent America unwilling to defend itself is a "paper tiger."

Potent progressive and liberal opposition to competitive free enterprise impede the restoration of global economic vitality. It sparks internecine strife, precludes social harmony, and together with the Biden–Harris administration's aversion to hard power prevents Washington from bolstering American security amid the renewed East–West superpower Cold War.

This troublesome postscript to the United States' unipolar moment is avertable, but requires an improbable bi-partisan effort.[4] Biden's America is dazed, straitjacketed and adrift with little prospect for safely weathering the storms looming on the dark horizon.

---

[4]Steven Rosefielde and Quinn Mills, *Progressive and Populists* (Singapore: World Scientific Publishers, 2020).

Introduction

America became a superpower during World War II. It mobilized industries idled by the Great Depression, expanded them and introduced a new generation of technology that enabled it to defeat Germany and Japan. Washington used its industrial and financial muscle to support and bankroll post-war global recovery and development. President Harry Truman founded the International Monetary Fund (IMF) at Bretton Woods in December 1945, the World Bank in 1946.

The Soviet Union, although battered by Germany's invasion on June 22, 1941, also emerged from WWII as a military superpower, acquiring the atomic bomb in 1949 and the hydrogen bomb in 1955. It created satellite states in Eastern Europe and spheres of influence in North Korea and China. In Winston Churchill's ominous phrase, an "iron curtain descended over Eastern Europe" in 1946,[1] prompting America to adopt a policy of containment in 1947,[2] which led to the creation of NATO in 1949,[3] and other collective security pacts across the globe.

---

[1] Winston Churchill, "The Sinews of Peace ('Iron Curtain Speech')," Westminster College, Fulton, MO (March 5, 1946), https://winstonchurchill.org/resources/speeches/1946-1963-elder-statesman/the-sinews-of-peace/.

[2] George Kennan, "George Kennan's 'Long Telegram'," (February 22, 1946), https://digitalarchive.wilsoncenter.org/document/116178.pdf.

George Kennan, "Kennan and Containment, 1947," (1947), https://history.state.gov/milestones/1945-1952/kennan.

[3] "North Atlantic Treaty Organization (NATO), 1949," https://history.state.gov/milestones/1945-1952/nato.

American superpower thereafter until the Soviet Union collapsed provided stalwart military deterrence and containment of the USSR and its communist allies, and facilitated Washington-led economic globalization. These missions changed in the early post-Soviet age 1992–2010 when nuclear and communist threats diminished, and America pivoted to combating Islamic terrorism. A resurgence of Russian, Chinese, North Korean, and Iranian imperial ambitions, military and economic power 2010–2020 rekindled the need for authoritarian containment, but this time Washington choose to look the other way. It failed to counter Russia and China's successful military modernization drives, and Beijing's economic challenge. The Obama–Biden and Trump administrations took some notice, but their responses were inadequate. They did not stem the adverse turn in the correlation of forces,[4] because Washington could not adjust its politics to deal prudently with the new international authoritarian peril.[5]

America today consequently is a dazed and beleaguered superpower. The Biden-Harris administration faces the prospect of rising imperial military threats from China and Russia, and the disintegration of its global economic order, but cannot deal with it politically. Although, there are

---

[4] Julian Lider, "The Correlation of World Forces: The Soviet Concept," *Journal of Peace Research* 17, no. 2, June 1980: 151–171, http://jpr.sagepub.com/content/17/2/151.abstract. Allen Lynch, *The Soviet Study of International Relations* (Cambridge: Cambridge University Press, 1989).

The term correlation of forces, borrowed from physics, is a multi-factor version of the balance of power concept widely employed by Soviet and Russian security analysts.

[5] Cf. Richard J. Ellings and Robert Sutter, eds., *Axis of Authoritarians: Implications of China–Russia Cooperation* New York: NBR Books, 2018). Ash Carter, ed., "Shaping Disruptive Technological Change for Public Good," Belfer Center (August 2018), https://www.belfercenter.org/publication/shaping-disruptive-technological-change-public-good?utm_source=SilverpopMailing&utm_medium=email&utm_campaign=TAPP_ Ash%20Carter_Shaping%20Disruptive%20Technological%20Change%20for%20 Public%20Good%20(1)&utm_content=&spMailingID=20227006&spUserID=NTQ3OD k4MzgxNTgS1&spJobID=1340856526&spReportId=MTM0MDg1NjUyNgS2.

"I always said that as Secretary of Defense I was 'the Secretary of Defense of today' and also 'the Secretary of tomorrow.' Secretary of today meant standing strong against Russia and China, deterring and defending ourselves, allies, and friends from North Korea and Iran, and destroying ISIS and other terrorists in Iraq, Syria, Afghanistan, and around the world."

Introduction xxvii

solutions, the Democratic Party base will not tolerate an arms race,[6] and downgrading of its anti-meritocratic and anti-competitive social priorities. There is a Toynbee challenge, without any immediate prospect of a civilization saving response.[7] Biden's America is adrift.

Few appreciate the magnitude of the problem because they presume that America today is the same as it was yesterday. Washington responded appropriately in 1947 when the "iron curtain" fell, leading people to suppose that America will do so again if this becomes necessary. They do not adequately appreciate the political changes wrought by the Clinton and Obama–Biden administrations that have profoundly altered the rules of the game.

Today's West bears little resemblance to Samuel Huntington's "idea of the West,"[8] that is the competitive America that defeated Hitler, Mussolini, Hirohito, and won the Cold War. It idealizes those who progressives and liberals consider scorned, distains the middle class (bourgeoisie), disparages competitiveness, self-reliance, individual fulfillment and national security, except when hard power serves leftist purposes. The American Democratic Party has pivoted away from its 1930s working and middle class alliance toward progressivism,[9] anti-white nativism, socialism, and one world style internationalism. It has strengthened ties with Wall Street and Silicon Valley, embraced the philosophies of the "living constitution," "bigger the better" government, "cradle to grave" welfare state-ism, guaranteed minimum income, egalitarianism, comprehensive entitlement, affirmative action, and restorative justice, with some including Barack Obama and Joe Biden pressing for total nuclear disarmament and "giving peace a chance" conventional arms control.[10] Workers and

---

[6] Albert Wohlstetter, "Is There a Strategic Arms Race?" *Foreign Policy*, 15, Summer, 1974: 3–20. During the Cold War, Washington acknowledged Soviet military superpower, but refrained from engaging in an unrestrained arms race (claims to the contrary notwithstanding).

[7] Arnold Toynbee, *A Study of History* (London: Oxford University Press, 1987).

[8] Samuel Huntington was a member of the Greatest Generation. He was born in 1927 and served in the US army during WWII.

[9] Marianne Cooper, "The False Promise of Meritocracy," *Atlantic* (December 2015).

[10] Andrew Butfoy, "President Obama and Nuclear Disarmament," *Dissent* (August 2011), https://www.dissentmagazine.org/online_articles/president-obama-and-nuclear-disarmament; "Joe Biden: A Lifelong Champion of Nuclear Arms Control," https://livableworld.org/meet-the-candidates/joe-biden-a-lifelong-champion-of-nuclear-arms-control/.

small proprietors in the Democratic Party have become Ralph Ellison's invisible persons.[11] Wall Street and Silicon Valley and progressives have grown increasingly influential.

The Democratic Party has numerous factions including pro-working class socialists (Bernie Sanders), anti-capitalist radical progressives (Alexandria Ocasio-Cortez), pro-capitalist progressive reformers (Joseph Stiglitz), and big welfare state liberals (Joe Biden). It tilts toward an alliance blending "bigger the better" government, "cradle to grave" welfare state-ism (Biden faction), socially responsible competitive capitalism (Stiglitz), and radical progressive special issues (Alexandria Ocasio-Cortez, Elizabeth Warren).[12]

The "radical" in "radical progressive" indicates that a powerful minority of Democratic Party members favors top-down government micro-managed markets, nationalization of the health services industry, guaranteed minimum incomes for everyone, welfare state dependency, stakeholder capitalism,[13] anti-meritocratic attention to special needs,[14] anti-nativism,[15] and privileging revolutionary agendas like Black Lives Matter. Other "radical progressive" causes include "One World" transnationalism, open immigration (for non-whites and Moslems), fourth wave feminist empowerment, extreme environmentalism, homosexual marriage, anti-family attitudes and approval of consensual behavior incompatible with Adam Smith's concept of morally informed capitalism. Radical progressives seek to bend markets to their purposes or eradicate

---

[11] Ralph Waldo Ellison, *Invisible Man* (New York: Random House, 1952); Steven Rosefielde, "New Millennial Economic Systems: Paradox of Power and Reason," *Foresight and STI Governance* (*Journal of the National Research University of Higher School of Economics, Moscow*], Special Issue: "System Economics — Prospects of Development," (forthcoming 2020). William Haupt III, "Op-Ed: Defund Police Unions, Not Police Departments," *The Center Square* (June 15, 2020).

[12] Steven Rosefielde and Quinn Mills, *Progressive and Populists* (Singapore, World Scientific Publishers, 2020).

[13] Uri Friedman, "What Is a Nativist? And is Donald Trump one?" *Atlantic* (April 2017), https://www.theatlantic.com/international/archive/2017/04/what-is-nativist-trump/521355/.

[14] Sandel, Michael, *The Tyranny of Merit: What's Become of the Common Good?* (New York: Macmillan, 2020).

[15] Uri Friedman, "What is a Nativist? And is Donald Trump One?" *Atlantic* (April 2017), https://www.theatlantic.com/international/archive/2017/04/what-is-nativist-trump/521355/.

Introduction xxix

them more than pro-capitalist progressive reformers and liberals,[16] and tend to favor the "New Monetary Theory" that advocates unlimited money creation and national debt.[17] Radical progressivism is not a full-fledged ideology like Marxist-Leninism. It is a hodgepodge of politically correct causes,[18] including "cancel culture."[19]

All factions of the Biden–Harris Democratic Party coalition are anti-competitive,[20] and advocate curbing American military hard power in varying degrees regardless of the international environment. These cornerstones of the coalition's ideological United Front however constitute only half the problem of managing the Eastern authoritarian threat. Clinton–Obama–Biden Democrats all strongly support "color revolutions"[21] and "regime change" (that is pro-American coup d'etat) in

---

[16] Steven Rosefielde, "Stakeholder Capitalism: Progressive Dream or Nightmare?" *HOLISTICA — Journal of Business and Public Administration* (2021 forthcoming).

[17] Stephanie Kelton, *The Deficit Myth: Modern Monetary Theory and the Birth of the People's Economy* (New York: Public Affairs, 2020).

[18] Abram Bergson, "A Reformulation of Certain Aspects of Welfare Economics," *Quarterly Journal of Economics* 52, no. 1, 1938: 310–334. Abram Bergson, "The Concept of Social Welfare," *Quarterly Journal of Economics* 68, no. 2, 1954: 233–253. Abram Bergson, "Social Choice Under Representative Government," *Journal of Public Economics* 6, no. 3, 1976: 171–190.

The concept allows members to maximize utility without jointly optimizing wellbeing according to a single Bergsonian social welfare standard. Paretian and Bergsonian metrics are identical if individuals have common preferences and values. If everyone agrees then whatever the institutional order all select will be best. If members do not agree, some will necessarily be displeased and may try to harm others deliberately or inadvertently by exerting de facto regulatory power and imposing their "superior" values.

[19] Jesse Singal, "The Reaction to the Harper's Letter on Cancel Culture Proves Why It Was Necessary," *Reason* (June 8, 2020), https://reason.com/2020/07/08/the-reaction-to-the-harpers-letter-on-cancel-culture-proves-why-it-was-necessary/.

[20] Competitiveness has three aspects: (1) self- reliant individual competition in the market place, (2) pluralist social competition, and (3) stout national security. The outlook is consistent with Pareto competitive optimization theory in the economic, social and security spheres, but also accommodates cooperative action in defense, Keynesian macroeconomic regulation and basic social services.

[21] Color revolution is a journalist term for mass protests against the political elite that broke out in the post-Soviet region, a decade after the breakdown of the USSR. The most active, well-organized and successful "color revolutions" happened in Serbia (2000), Georgia (2003), Ukraine (2004), and Kyrgyzstan (2005). The concept was later extended to cover similar mast protests in the Middle East (Arab Spring). These protests were portrayed as spontaneous uprising by they were often given American aid and comfort. The word

xxx *Beleaguered Superpower: Biden's America Adrift*

Russia, China, North Korea, Iran, and other targets of opportunity. Rather than await peaceful evolutionary democratic advances, America has fought a series of wars in Afghanistan,[22] Iraq,[23] Yemen,[24] Libya,[25]

"color" highlights the importance of well-crafted and targeted political symbolism as a mass mobilization tool.

Anna Gawel and Aileen Torres-Bennett, "Academics Say U.S. Interventions to Force Regime Change Often Fail," *The Washington Diplomat* (May 20, 2020), https://wash diplomat.com/index.php?option=com_content&view=article&id=22460:academics-say-us-interventions-to-force-regime-change-often-fail&catid=1618:may-2020&Itemid=428; Steven Rosefielde, *Kremlin Strikes Back: Russia and the West after Crimea's Annexation* (Cambridge: Cambridge University Press, 2017).

[22] 2001–2014: War in Afghanistan: The War on Terror begins with Operation Enduring Freedom. On October 7, 2001, US Armed Forces invade Afghanistan in response to the 9/11 attacks and begin combat action in Afghanistan against Al Qaeda terrorists and their Taliban supporters.

[23] 2003–2011: War in Iraq: Operation Iraqi Freedom, March 20, 2003, the United States leads a coalition that includes the United Kingdom, Australia and Poland to invade Iraq with the stated goal being to disarm Iraq in pursuit of peace, stability, and security both in the Gulf region and in the United States. 2014–present: American intervention in Iraq: Hundreds of US troops deployed to protect American assets in Iraq and to advise Iraqi and Kurdish fighters. In August, the US Air Force conducted a humanitarian air drop and the US Navy began a series of airstrikes against Islamic State-aligned forces throughout northern Iraq.

[24] 2010–present: al-Qaeda insurgency in Yemen: The US has been launching a series of drone strikes on suspected al-Qaeda, al-Shabaab, and ISIS positions in Yemen. 2014: 2014 Yemen hostage rescue operations against al-Qaeda: On November 25, US Navy SEAL's and Yemeni Special Forces launched an operations in Yemen in attempt to rescue eight hostages that were being held by al-Qaeda. Although the operation was successful, no American hostages were secured. In the first attempt, six Yemenis, one Saudi Arabian, and one Ethiopian were rescued. On December 4, 2014, al-Qaeda in the Arabian Peninsula (AQAP) threatened to execute the Somers if the US failed to the unspecified commands. AQAP also stated that they would be executed if the US attempted another rescue operation. On December 6, a second operation was launched. 40 US SEALs and 30 Yemeni troops were deployed to the compound. A 10-minute fire fight occurred before the American troops could enter where the remaining hostages (Somers and Korkie) were being held. They were alive, but fatally wounded. Surgery was done in mid air when flying away from the site. Korkie died while in flight, and Somers died once landed on the USS Makin Island. No American troop was killed/injured, however a Yemenis soldier was wounded.

[25] 2011: 2011 military intervention in Libya: Operation Odyssey Dawn, United States and coalition enforcing UN Security Council Resolution 1973 with bombings of Libyan forces.

Pakistan,[26] Somalia,[27] Syria,[28] and Iran, none of which has ended positively.[29] Contemporary American progressives and liberals cannot restrain themselves from provoking Eastern authoritarians, but refuse to prepare adequately for the blow back.

Time of Troubles

Progressive and liberal social, economic, and security policies have led the United States into a "time of troubles."[30] America is no longer a

---

[26] 2011: Osama Bin Laden is killed by US military forces in Pakistan as part of Operation Neptune Spear.

[27] Drone strikes on al-Shabab militants begin in Somalia. This marks the 6th nation in which such strikes have been carried out, including Afghanistan, Pakistan, Iraq, Yemen, and Libya. 2013: Navy SEALs conducted a raid in Somalia and possibly killed a senior Al-Shabaab official, simultaneously another raid took place in Tripoli, Libya, where Special Operations Forces captured Abu Anas al Libi (also known as Anas al-Libi).

[28] 2014: 2014 American rescue mission in Syria: The US attempted to rescue James Foley and other hostages being held by ISIL. Air strikes were conducted on the ISIL military base known as "Osama bin Laden camp." Meanwhile, the bombings, Delta teams parachuted near an ISIL high-valued prison. The main roads were blocked to keep any target from escaping. When no hostage was found, the American troops began house to house searches. By this time, ISIL militants began arriving to the area. Heavy fighting occurred until the Americans decided to abandon the mission due to the hostages being nowhere in the area. Although the mission failed, at least 5 ISIL militants were killed, however 1 American troop was wounded. According to the reports, Jordan had a role in the operation and that one Jordanian soldier had been wounded as well. This was unconfirmed.

2014–present: American-led intervention in Syria: American aircraft bomb Islamic State positions in Syria. Airstrikes on al-Qaeda, al-Nusra Front, and Khorasan positions are also being conducted.

2014–present: Intervention against the Islamic State of Iraq and the Levant: Syrian locals forces and American-led coalition forces launch a series of aerial attacks on ISIL and al-Nusra Front positions in Iraq and Syria.

[29] 2015: April 30, 2015 US sends ships to the Strait of Hormuz to shield vessels after Iranian Seizure of commercial vessel: The US Navy deploys warships to protect American commercial vessels passing through the Strait of Hormuz from Iranian interference. Concerns were also raised that Iranian gunships were trailing a US container ship. Iran additionally fired shots over the bow, and seized, a ship registered in the Marshall Islands, part of a long-standing dispute between the two nations.

[30] "Time of Troubles, Russian Smutnoye Vremya, period of political crisis in Russia that followed the demise of the Rurik dynasty (1598) and ended with the establishment of the

unipolar superpower, although many deny this reality. The Biden–Harris administration and most Republicans still perceive America as the world's supreme economic powerhouse and the globe's indispensable nation.[31] They treat today's economic sclerosis (subpar economic growth verging toward secular stagnation), extreme over indebtedness, civic strife, and political turmoil as bumps along the road preceding a brighter tomorrow. Russian and Chinese great power resurgence, the North Korean, Iranian, and global jihadist challenges,[32] and divisions within allies like the European Union do not daunt them either.[33] Denying the reality or its importance, contemporary progressive and liberal leaders, think tanks and

---

Romanov dynasty (1613). During this period foreign intervention, peasant uprisings, and the attempts of pretenders to seize the throne threatened to destroy the state itself and caused major social and economic disruptions, particularly in the southern and central portions of the state," https://www.britannica.com/event/Time-of-Troubles.

[31] Shawn Donnan and Andres Schipani, "Obama Urges Trump to Regard US as An 'Indispensable Nation'," *Financial Times* (November 20, 2016), https://www.ft.com/content/643f6c9c-af84-11e6-a37c-f4a01f1b0fa1.

"The United States really is an indispensable nation in our world order," Mr. Obama told reporters at the conclusion of the 21-country Asia-Pacific Economic Cooperation summit in Peru." "US President Barack Obama wrapped up his final official trip abroad with a call for his successor Donald Trump to live up to America's responsibility as an "indispensable nation" in the world, and to bolster the international order it had helped create."

[32] Steven Rosefielde, Masaaki Kuboniwa, Satoshi Mizobata, and Kumiko Haba, eds., *The Unwinding of the Globalist Dream: EU, Russia and China* (Singapore: World Scientific, 2017).

[33] Zeeshan Aleem, "Why Europe is So Angry Over the Big Russia Sanctions Bill: The GOP's Effort to Tie Trump's Hands on Russia Looks Like It Could Be Very Costly," *Vox* (July 26, 2017), https://www.vox.com/world/2017/7/26/16034148/europe-russia-sanctions-bill-republicans-trump.

"Congress is close to passing a sanctions bill that would impose tougher measures on Russia for its meddling in the 2016 election while simultaneously restricting President Donald Trump's ability to lift them. The measure is popular at home, but unpopular in Europe, where some of Washington's closest allies are warning that it would harm their economies — and that they'd be willing to retaliate against the US in return." "The new bill would allow the US to sanction any company involved in the maintenance or development of Russia's energy export pipelines. That could cripple the construction of a colossal natural gas pipeline between Russia and Germany known as Nord Stream 2, which is owned by Russian energy giant Gazprom but also has European investors. "'If our concerns are not taken into account sufficiently, we stand ready to act appropriately within a

Introduction xxxiii

academicians spare themselves responsibility for the blame. They continue to insist that America can build down its military hard power, squeeze its productive classes,[34] and foment radical change while bending Eastern authoritarians to their will with consciousness raising, "smart diplomacy," soft power, identity politics, and media attitude management. The radical left, a significant component of the Biden–Harris coalition, is committed to revolutionary change from above (including street violence) against the open society, humanist and Enlightenment culture, political equality and *laissez-faire*;[35] an approach that cannot lead the nation out of today's economic malaise and security morass.

---

matter of days. 'America First' cannot mean that Europe's interests come last, EU chief executive Jean-Claude Juncker warned the US on Wednesday."

[34] The concept reflects two contestable premises. First, the only virtuous nation is one with an ethnic composition reflecting the global homogenized blend. Second, ethnically ideal nations are morally superior, that is, they hold the values espoused by America's progressive establishment.

These premises enabled Talbott and New Westers (shorthand for Global Nation evangelicals) to speak in the name of humanity. Like Lenin before them, they claimed to know what was best for the world, and sought to commit America as the future Global Nation to realizing their dream by transforming governance at home and abroad to their universal standard.

America's duty they contend is to perfect its multinational homogenized culture and make it the world's culture, replacing national government with one-world institutions that will secure peace, harmony and justice for all. Hence the double meaning of global nation. America will be the nation that is not a nation. It will be humanity's sovereign. As Mrs. Clinton put it during the 2016 election campaign, "America is great because it is good!"

New Westers believe that America is predestined to lead in the Global Nation's direction. They anticipate resistance on both domestic and foreign fronts, but also expect that they will prevail through the judicious use of "soft power." Dissenters will be shamed and sanctioned until they see the light, accepting the virtue of entitlement, egalitarianism, affirmative action and restorative justice at home, and transnationalism to bring these blessings to other shores. America will largely cede sovereignty in the process to global institutions, but this will not be problematic because the nation and globe are one-and-the-same-thing for the Global Nation.

Strobe Talbott, "America Abroad: The Birth of the Global Nation," *Time* (July 1992), http://channelingreality.com/Documents/1992_Strobe_Talbot_Global_Nation.pdf.

[35] Steven Rosefielde and Jonathan Leightner, *China's Market Communism: Challenges, Dilemmas, Solutions* (London: Routledge, 2018). Steven Rosefielde and Ralph W. Pfouts, *Inclusive Economic Theory* (Singapore: World Scientific Publishers, 2014).

xxxiv *Beleaguered Superpower: Biden's America Adrift*

Robust hard power is essential for deterring a "bolt from the blue," World War III, a catastrophe that appears improbable. Stout deterrence is also needed to keep the odds low of stumbling into World War III through losses in a series of small engagements, if

(1) China tries to block Western navies and commercial maritime trade from the South China Sea, seize its neighbors' seabed resources or conquer Taiwan,
(2) Russia tries to annex more of Novorossiya or conquer the Baltic States,
(3) Pyongyang invades South Korea,
(4) Iran attacks its neighbors, or
(5) The global jihadi seize assets threatening American and global security.[36]

Stout hard power is critical for winning World War III, if like World War I, great power adversaries stumble into it, and like World War II, American forces are unready.[37] There is no reliable substitute for robust hard power and readiness across all futures for winning serial small wars and World War III should deterrence fail. However, progressives and liberals steadfastly refuse to recalibrate their priorities. They are unwilling to temper their economic policies on the home front or procure the weapons and counter-cyber capabilities needed to support the projection of adequate hard power abroad for a secure global future. They have

---

Liberal Democracy is a term commonly used in the political economy literature to describe open societies that empower free individual competition in the private sector, and popular democratic control over public programs. The ideal is Pareto efficient for the production, distribution and transfer of private goods, and Arrow efficient in the production and distribution of public goods. The term however may cause confusion for some who conflate it with the Global Nation. Being liberal to New Westers means subscribing to the Global Nation. We alert readers to the problem by calling Liberal Democracy in the traditional sense "classical" Liberal Democracy.

[36] Jamie McIntyre and Travis Tritten, "Congressional Commission Cites 'Crisis of National Security,' Concludes Task of Rebuilding US Military Far From Complete," *Washington Examiner* (November 16, 2018), https://www.washingtonexaminer.com/congressional-commission-cites-crisis-of-national-security-concludes-task-of-rebuilding-us-military-far-from-complete.

[37] Loren Thompson, "If America's Military Loses World War III, Low Readiness Will Likely Be the Reason," *Forbes* (November 2018).

Introduction xxxv

forgotten — if they ever understood — that countervailing nuclear weapons today make the world free for conventional war.

Some Republicans consistent with their competitive philosophy have tried to save the day, but progressives and liberals have stymied them.

The ensuing chapters provide a detailed elaboration of this recipe for disaster and assess the likely consequences.

Part I

Playing with Fire

In this volume, we show that there has been an unheralded new millennium policy revolution in Washington inimical to the nation's interest and global security. Anti-capitalist and anti-competitive progressives and many liberals seek to re-engineer the society, the economy, and push a Third World authoritarian indulgent agenda without building the robust hard power needed to deal with the blowback.[1] They wrongly believe that fettering what used to be a competitive society, promoting post-colonialist atonement policies, and transnational networking will enable them to contain Russia, China, North Korea, Iran and the global jihadi; that strength through weakness is a shrewd idea.

The mindset is purblind and fraught with contradictions that are leading America into a global security morass where we can no longer successfully contain rising Eastern authoritarianism with our inadequate economic and military capabilities.

---

[1]Condoleezza Rice, *Democracy: Stories from the Long Road to Freedom* (New York: Hachette Book Group, 2017): 5. The establishment masks its social justice imperative by characterizing its mission as global democratization. Rice defines democracy on the first page of her first chapter as the content of the Universal Declaration of Human Rights adopted by the UN General Assembly in 1948. It is essentially an extended version of the American Bill of Rights. Democracy as she and the establishment see it is not a form of popular government, but a list of "social justice" rights on the "long road to freedom."

Part I
Playing with Fire

Chapter 1

The Biden–Harris Administration is Overreaching

The reining policy mindset in Washington today is not what it used to be.[2] It increasingly reflects the influence of an assortment of fashionable Democratic Party progressive and liberal attitudes that politicians consider crucial for acquiring and holding power. Leaders, special interest groups, bureaucrats overreach on behalf of constituencies committed to big government, radical social activism, and transnational networking, while claiming to be all things to the electorate ("We together").[3] They over-regulate, overspend, impair competitive efficiency, and depress

---

[2] Peter Gollwitzer, "Action Phases and Mind-sets," in E. Tory Higgins and Richard Sorrentino, eds., *The Handbook of Motivation and Cognition: Foundations of Social Behavior*, Vol. 2 (New York: Guilford Press, 1990): 52–92; Peter Gollwitzer, "Mindset Theory of Action Phases," in Paul Van Lange, Ari Kruglanski, and E. Tory Higgins, eds., *Handbook of Theories of Social Psychology*, Vol. 1 (Thousand Oaks: SAGE, 2012): 526–545; Robert French II and Heewon Chang, "Conceptual Re-Imagining of Global 'Mindset': Knowledge as Prime in the Development of Global Leaders," *Journal of International Organizations Studies* 7, no. 1, 2016: 49–62, http://journal-iostudies.org/sites/journal-iostudies.org/files/JIOS-ReviewEssay_GlobalMindset.pdf. A mindset is a set of assumptions, notions, and methods held by one or more people or groups of people that govern without critical rational management. It leads to "group think," mental inertia and a refusal to credence counter-evidence and disproof.

[3] Bureaucrats include the "deep state" and the "swamp." See Marc Ambinder and D. B. Grady (David Brown), *Deep State: Inside the Government Secrecy Industry* (New York: Wiley, 2013); Eric Bolling, *Corruption and Cronyism and How Trump Can Drain It* (New York: St. Martin's Press, 2017). The Chronicle of Higher Education leads the

4 *Beleaguered Superpower: Biden's America Adrift*

economic growth. They never miss a CARES (Coronavirus Aid, Relief, and Economic Security Act) opportunity to feather their nests,[4] while seeking to forge a progressive-liberal global empire.

Their outlook is incompatible with the Enlightenment values enshrined in the Constitution and at odds with the values of a large segment of Americans.[5] They favor transnational governance as a vehicle for spreading their economic, social, political, and environmental agenda across the globe, and many belittle patriotism.[6] The lure of Washington assisted, and subsidized windfall profits motivates big business. Wall Street, Silicon Valley, and American multinational corporations desire lucrative state contracts. They seek greater access to and control of foreign markets. They want to use immigration as a tool for containing domestic wage pressure. Their think tanks find transnational governance attractive because it reduces barriers to foreign market penetration. Nationalism for cosmopolitan progressives is secondary because they conflate it with "America First" "nativism" and many see one world government as an antidote for international conflict.[7]

---

education establishment. The Chronicle, based in Washington, D.C., is a major news service in United States academic affairs.

[4] US Congress, House, "Coronavirus Aid, Relief, and Economic Security Act" or the "CARES Act", March 19, 2020, HR 748, 116th Cong., 2nd sess., Congressional Record 131: S 3548, https://www.congress.gov/116/bills/s3548/BILLS-116s3548is.pdf. On March 25, 2020, the United States Senate passed the Coronavirus Aid, Relief, and Economic Security Act (CARES Act), aimed at providing financial relief to the American people and American businesses in response to the economic fallout from the fast-developing coronavirus (COVID-19) pandemic.

[5] Victor Davis Hanson, "Obama Won," *Victor David Hanson Private Papers* (September 4, 2018), https://www.realclearpolitics.com/2018/09/24/obama_won_454146.html.

[6] Steven Rosefielde, *Trump's Populist America* (Singapore: World Scientific Publishers, 2017).

[7] Peter Baker, "How Trump's Election Shook Obama: 'What if We Were Wrong?'," *New York Times* (May 30, 2018); Benjamin Rhodes, *The World as It Is: A Memoir of the Obama White House* (New York: Random House, 2018). "Benjamin Rhodes, a former White House staff member who served as the Deputy National Security Advisor for Strategic Communications for US President Barack Obama and as an adviser on the Joint Comprehensive Plan of Action (JCPOA) with Iran reported President Barack Obama's reaction to Donald Trump's victory shortly after the 2016 election. According to Rhodes, Obama "had read a column asserting that liberals had forgotten how important identity was to people and had promoted an empty cosmopolitan globalism that made many feel

The Biden–Harris Administration is Overreaching 5

Progressive and liberal media have beguiled the public into believing that America's domestic and foreign priorities today are the same as they were before the Bill Clinton and Barak Obama presidencies, and reflect the founding Enlightenment principles of 1776, when in fact they constitute a tectonic shift that has cast Biden's America adrift in uncharted waters.[8]

Therefore, a brief review of the tidal change that has occurred in the American Democratic Party should mitigate potential cognitive dissonance.[9] The pre-Clinton, post WWII American outlook was nationalist and competitive. The contemporary attitude is internationalist and anti-competitive, striving to subdue opposition everywhere in the name of social justice, regardless of economic and security consequences.

Biden–Harris progressives and liberals desire a worldwide American dominated global order that presses their agendas in the Third World and the authoritarian East.[10] They favor Washington-led transnational governance, militant environmentalism, entitlement, affirmative action, and

---

left behind." This prompted Obama "while riding in a motorcade in Lima" to muse: "What if we were wrong?" "Maybe we pushed too far," Mr. Obama said. "Maybe people just want to fall back into their tribe."

[8] Alvin Toeffler, *Power Shift: Knowledge, Wealth, and Power at the Edge of the 21st Century* (New York: Bantam Books, 1990).

[9] Sheila Fitzpatrick, "New Perspectives on Stalinism," *The Russian Review* 45, October 1986: 357–373; Marc A. Thiessen, "The New York Times Keeps Whitewashing Communism's Crimes," *The Washington Post* (November 2017), http://www.aei.org/publication/the-new-york-times-keeps-whitewashing-communisms-crimes/?mkt_tok=eyJpIjoiTWpCbFl6TXhOREZoTm1RMSIsInQiOiJWZ2p2U2lDZmNaRGNLcjVteWtpdkpEbGNEQ1JQTzJxUVJzVUtSMHpVNzB4MXZUUExHRGF2bE9OOXRoQnhpSTY0U1pDZWFDQ2Q1MTIyUlRwQ256M2U1RDBYUGRobkMxQWJPRGtRZVJNTUNwVFdsQ0IwZW9TV2WUNrak1IK3JJUyJ9. The term revisionist means different things. It is used here to call attention to the fact that left has long tried to rehabilitate discredited aspects of the Soviet's "social justice" program in order to restore their luster.

[10] Cf. Michael Sandel, *Justice: What's the Right Thing to Do?* (New York: Farrar, Straus and Giroux, 2009); John Rawls, *A Theory of Justice* (Cambridge: Belknap Press, 1971); Robert Nozick, *Anarchy, State, and Utopia* (Oxford: Blackwell Publishers, 1993). Just-cause activists hide behind the presumption that universal justice exists, is knowable, sublime and achieving it is the only right thing to do. Their claims are specious. Universal justice does not exist in any mundane sense, and the divine universal justice of events like the holocaust is incomprehensible to mortals. Universal justice is two little words. The corresponding concept has six meanings:

6 *Beleaguered Superpower: Biden's America Adrift*

restorative justice at home and abroad[11] and distain the Rights of Man, dissenting opinions,[12] and free speech for their critics. They dislike competitive wages, open society, libertarianism, *laissez faire*, the bourgeoisie, blue-collar workers, white males, humanism, Enlightenment,

---

(1) standard of justice presuming a standard of right conduct applied uniformly across the globe at any moment in time

(2) standard that applies across the ages

(3) standard (abstract principle) that everyone correctly or incorrectly considers right

(4) standard that everyone correctly or incorrectly considers right in all contexts (homicide, murder, war)

(5) standard that in practice is uniformly upheld

(6) standard that is transcendentally right (divine justice)

Universal justice in the first five senses does not to exist. Socrates agrees.

Divine justice by definition is beyond human understanding.

Implications: 1. Humans cannot be deemed guilty for transgressions against universal concepts of right and justice both profane and sacred that do not exist and in the divine case is beyond their comprehension.

People sometimes are accountable for transgression against mundane moral and legal constructs, but revolutionaries, activists, and rulers are wrong to claim that their laws and actions are universally just in any of the six senses listed above.

2. If humans choose to assume that universal justice exists in any or all of the six senses listed above as a guide to their personal conduct, they should avoid self-righteousness because their assumption is only a matter of convenience. The assumption itself is false.

3. Humans are inclined to assume that universal justice exists because acknowledging the truth is disorienting. Many people who accept that there are no universal right things to do lose their gyroscopes and cannot manage their personal and interpersonal relations effectively. The right solution here is the Buddhist solution. Do not fret about what is beyond your understanding and control. Concentrate instead on managing challenges as you encounter them with wisdom and compassion in the hope that as you proceed you will make your choices with higher transcendental understanding (enlightenment).

[11] Howard Zehr, *The Little Book of Restorative Justice* (Intercourse, PA: Good Books, 2002). Restorative justice is an international movement that seeks to assure that courts compel victimizers to pay reparations to victims.

Black Lives Matter is an international activist movement, originating in the African-American community, that campaigns against violence and systemic racism toward black people that often asserts demands for reparations as compensation for slavery and other past injustices.

[12] Katherine Mangan, "Michigan's Bias-Response Team Uses Indirect Threats to Chill Free Speech, Appeals Court Finds," *Chronicle of Higher Education* (September 25, 2019).

and modernism.[13] Biden–Harris progressives and liberals identify with victims of colonialist oppression. Many defend North Korea's statist socialism, Chinese market communism, Marxist–Leninist communism with a "human face" (Cuba), and Venezuelan socialism. They support progressive educational "training" and "guidance" to indoctrinate students and alter public attitudes.

The socialist aspects of their foreign policy lie in Saint Simonian-style advocacy of a supranational European Union,[14] and neo-Marxist–Leninist internationalism, although today's progressives differ from their predecessors by the emphasis placed on minorities, radical feminists, gender politics, iconoclastic consensual behavior, and environmental activism over working class welfare. Otherwise, the rhetoric, liberation philosophy, consciousness raising, internationalist orientation are much the same. It is impossible for us to say whether contemporary progressive-liberal foreign policy as practiced by the Biden–Harris administration is a romantic neo-Marxist domestic policy agenda projected onto the world stage, or a daffy foreign policy agenda projected onto domestic politics.[15] The intersection of progressive and romantic neo-Marxist sentiment is continuous, and they reinforce one another. Causal connections run both ways.

Strobe Talbott (12th United States Deputy Secretary of State, February 23, 1994–January 19, 2001), under President William Jefferson Clinton

---

[13] Modernism is a socially progressive anti-religious, secular trend of thought that affirms the power of human beings to create, improve and reshape their environment with the aid of practical experimentation, scientific knowledge, or technology. It has been replaced in New West circles by post-modernism.

[14] Claude Henri de Rouvroy, the Comte de Saint-Simon, *On the Reorganization of European Industry*, 1814.

Saint-Simon is considered as the father of the European Union.

[15] Socialism is a concept of government that allows the people to rule directly (participatory democracy) or indirectly (vanguard of the proletariat) by abolishing or managing markets for the benefit of the toiling masses. Socialists trade personal liberty for social programs. Optimal socialist constructs are utopian (Karl Marx and Frederick Engels, *Economic and Philosophical Manuscripts of 1844*). Satisficing constructs (bounded rationality) either fetter individual freedom and ration output to the proletariat (Marxist–Leninist–Stalinist "command economy") (Nikolai Bukharin and Evgeny Preobrazhensky, *ABC's of Communism*, 1919) or curtail individual economic liberty to provide the nation with universal free public education, and subsidized housing, health and transport services to those who cannot afford them (social democracy).

appears to have been the first prominent American progressive-liberal policy maker to provide a conceptual foundation for the reorientation of the Democratic Party's post-war bipartisan competitive nationalist platform to its current anti-competitive and anti-nationalist orientation in the post-Soviet era.[16] He published an influential article entitled "The Birth of the Global Nation" July 1992 in *Time Magazine*,[17] (shortly before Bill Clinton defeated George Bush) and *The Great Experiment: The Story of Ancient Empires, Modern States, and the Quest for a Global Nation*, more than a decade and a half later.[18] These works provide insight into the contemporary Democratic Party's new thinking because of Talbott's close personal ties to President William Jefferson Clinton. Talbott and Clinton were roommates and Rhodes scholars at Oxford University 1968–1969 during the Vietnam War,[19] and worked closely together in the Clinton White House. Talbott is not the acclaimed guru of internationalist progressive-liberalism, but his ideas clearly mirror its open immigration and transnational aspects.

Talbott advocated globalization that assigns Washington the task of ruling the planet through virtuous example,[20] smart diplomacy, soft power, and transnational institutions. He did not consider the "globalist" possibility that transnational institutions might exploit vulnerable countries.[21] His vision requires America to disown its founding nativist culture and

---

[16]Steven Rosefielde and Quinn Mills, *Democracy and its Elected Enemies: American Political Capture and Economic Decline* (New York: Cambridge University Press, 2013).

Strobe Talbott and Bill Clinton were fellow Rhodes Scholars and roommates at Oxford. Talbott was a senior editor at Foreign Affairs specializing in Russia before becoming Deputy Secretary of State. He holds a MA in Philosophy from Oxford and translated Khrushchev's memoirs.

[17]Strobe Talbott, "America Abroad: The Birth of the Global Nation," *Time* (July 1992), http://channelingreality.com/Documents/1992_Strobe_Talbot_Global_Nation.pdf.

[18]Strobe Talbott, *The Great Experiment: The Story of Ancient Empires, Modern States, and the Quest for a Global Nation* (New York: Simon and Schuster, 2008).

[19]Bill Clinton, *My Life* (New York: Knopf, 2004).

[20]Thomas *Wolfe, Radical Chic* (New York: Farrar, Straus and Giroux, 1970); Strobe Talbott, "America Abroad: The Birth of the Global Nation," *Time* (July 1992), http://channelingreality.com/Documents/1992_Strobe_Talbot_Global_Nation.pdf.

[21]Steven Rosefielde, Masaaki Kuboniwa, Kumiko Haba, and Satoshi Mizobata, eds., *The Unwinding of the Globalist Dream: EU, Russia, China* (Singapore: World Scientific Publishers, 2017).

The Biden–Harris Administration is Overreaching 9

adopt other values — said to be better values — by subordinating its 18th century Enlightenment heritage, and alleged modernist insensitivities to the special needs of scorned minorities.[22] He urged America to choose sides; to abridge its open society by transforming the country's racial, ethnic, and religious mix to match the global norm; to empower women, transgenders, and oppressed minorities; to fight inequality whatever its causes (including superior productivity), champion progressive justice, and fully embrace said-to be superlative universal rights for the world's untouchables.

Talbott's progressive-liberal paradigm is a globalist variant of James Meade's control-transfer open economy with Washington as Coryphaeus and sheriff.[23] It blends markets, affirmative action-driven open immigration, regulation, and transfers for the benefit of favored constituencies.[24]

---

[22] The claim here is that modernists' fixation with technological progress distracts attention from the cause of social justice.

[23] Peter Fabienne, "Political Legitimacy," *Stanford Encyclopedia of Philosophy*, 2017, https://plato.stanford.edu/entries/legitimacy/; David Held, *Democracy and the Global Order: From the Modern State to Cosmopolitan Governance* (Palo Alto: Stanford University Press, 1995); Daniele Archibugi, *The Global Commonwealth of Citizens: Toward Cosmopolitan Democracy* (Princeton: Princeton University Press, 2008).

Political cosmopolitanism "takes features of individuals — their interests or their rights — as basic for legitimacy. At present, the most comprehensive contemporary philosophical treatment of international legitimacy of this kind is probably Allen Buchanan's *Justice, Legitimacy, and Self-Determination* (Oxford: Oxford University Press, 2003). Buchanan advocates a moralized conception of legitimacy, according to which entities are legitimate if they are morally justified to wield political power. Specifically, political legitimacy requires that a minimal standard of justice is met."

[24] Steven Rosefielde, "Salvaging the European Union: The Inclusive Multi-Track Supranational Option," *Holistica* 8, no. 1, 2017: 7–18; James Meade, *The Controlled Economy: Principles of Political Economy*, Vol. 3 (Albany: State University of New York Press, 1972); James Meade, *Wage-Fixing* (London: Unwin Hyman, 1982). Supranationalism is a multi-level governance concept that enables a high body to control key aspects of national behavior on a universal basis, while allowing states control over some tradition spheres of activity. Supranational schemes can be one-track requiring members to operate on a unity system of rules, or multi-track allowing clusters to operate separately. For example, some EU nations are Eurozone members, while others have retained their own currencies. Supranationalism is one among many approaches to creating world governance to marginalize and/or supersede national government.

10   *Beleaguered Superpower: Biden's America Adrift*

The competitive alternative by contrast is a nationalist self-regulating transfer open economy, compatible with a welfare state that even handedly blends markets, public regulation, and prudent immigration for everyone's benefit.[25] It is moderate, anti-partisan, anti-true believer,[26] and anti-historicist,[27] relying on Herbert Simon bounded rational pragmatism,[28] free markets, democracy,[29] and "optimal" immigration.

Both approaches are ethical and assume that people choose rationally. Neither paradigm is autarkic, centrally planned, overtly authoritarian, proletarian, or racist. Both are compatible with globalization and endorse charity.

They differ only in two fundamental respects: "efficiency" (positive economic behavior) and "equity" (normative preference). Talbott's Global Nation is a protoype Biden–Harris transnational big government regime. It is over-regulated by design (and hence inefficient), privileges select identity groups and burdens the nation with huge "deadweight economic efficiency losses."[30]

Progressives and many liberals consistent with Talbott's vision favor non-whites, women, homosexuals, transgenders, consensual liberationists, non-Christians (especially Moslems), poor, and selected minorities — all

---

[25] Robert Skidelsky, "Inconvenient Truths About Migration," *Project Syndicate* (November 2017), https://www.project-syndicate.org/commentary/immigration-inconvenient-truths-by-robert-skidelsky-2017-11?utm_source=Project+Syndicate+Newsletter&utm_campaign=3cb5da1806-sunday_newsletter_26_11_2017&utm_medium=email&utm_term=0_73bad5b7d8-3cb5da1806-93559677.

"Standard economic theory says that net inward migration, like free trade, benefits the native population after a lag. But recent research has poked large holes in that argument, while the social and political consequences of open national borders similarly suggest the appropriateness of immigration limits."

[26] Eric Hofer, *The True Believer: Thoughts On The Nature Of Mass Movements* (New York: Harper and Brothers, 1951); Raymond Aron, *The Opium of the Intellectuals* (Paris: Calmann-Levy, 1955).

[27] Karl Popper, *The Poverty of Historicism* (London: Routledge, 1957).

[28] Steven Rosefielde and Ralph W. Pfouts, *Inclusive Economic Theory* (Singapore: World Scientific Publishers, 2014).

Herbert Simon, *Models of Man: Social and Rational — Mathematical Essays on Rational Human Behavior in a Social Setting* (New York: John Wiley and Sons, 1957).

[29] Steven Rosefielde and Quinn Mills, *Democracy and Its Elected Enemies: American Political Capture and Economic Decline* (New York: Cambridge University Press, 2013).

[30] Deadweight loss, also known as excess burden, is a measure of lost economic efficiency when the socially optimal quantity of a good or a service is not produced.

who benefit at the middle and working classes' expense. Their agenda is objectionable from the competitive perspective because it fosters dead-weight economic inefficiencies and discriminates against workers, white men and those who succeed by dint of their effort and talent.

The rival competitive outlook by contrast is pro-productive (hence efficient). It is meritorious insofar as it promotes equal opportunity, fosters prosperity and tolerance at home and abroad without burdening the nation with heavy deadweight economic efficiency losses.

Global Nation

Strobe Talbott's Global Nation manifesto paints a vivid picture of the progressive-liberal internationalist idea. It is a Washington led "anti-imperialist," cosmopolitan, pro-American big corporate business order, connecting the Biden–Harris administration's progressive domestic agenda with America's foreign and national security policies,[31] purged of white male nativists, just as the Bolsheviks liquidated capitalists "as a class."[32] The *New York Times* lauded this as a "revelation."[33]

Bill Clinton, Barak Obama, and Biden–Harris progressive-liberals bought into Talbott's concept and embellished it.[34] Their Global Nation outlook prioritizes consciousness raising and liberationist activism including unrestricted immigration aimed at adjusting America's racial, ethnic, and religious composition to the global norm, coupled with the pursuit of an anti-competitive, anti-meritocratic entitlement, affirmative action, restorative justice, and a bloated big government agenda.[35]

---

[31] Cf. David Sanger, "The Nation: Agony of Victory; America Finds It's Lonely At the Top," *New York Times* (July 18, 1999). Lawrence H. Summers, a champion of democratic free enterprises claimed that America is "the first outward-looking, non-imperialist, continental superpower." The unspoken comparisons are with the old Soviet Union, which was continental but expansionist and the continental but inward-looking China.

[32] Cf. Natan Sharanstky, *Defending Identity: Its Indispensable Role in Protecting Democracy* (New York: Public Affairs, 2008).

[33] Max Fisher and Amanda Taub, "National Identity Is Made Up," *The New York Times* (February 28, 2018), https://www.nytimes.com/2018/02/28/world/national-identity-myth.html.

[34] Talbott does not explain whether nations will continue to exist in his model, or are to be replaced by administrative units under Washington's control.

[35] Greg Sargent, "Biden is Already Signaling Big Moves on Immigration. That Bodes Well," *Washington Post* (November 12, 2020).

12 *Beleaguered Superpower: Biden's America Adrift*

The Biden–Harris administration congruent with Clinton and Obama precedents has declared its intention to redistribute income and wealth from the richest to the deserving at home and reduce global inequality, despite past failures (inegalitarianism sharply increased under the Obama–Biden watch).[36] It promises to manage civic relations, education, job, healthcare, social security, and political access through the rule of American law, judicial activism, executive orders, mandates, quotas, preferences, subsidies, tax credits, and public service programs across the globe progressively.[37] It will join forces with domestic and foreign progressive-liberal media, business, and intellectuals in managing deficit spending, money and credit, the environment and social policy for the same purposes.

It will strive to erect new transnational trade institutions similar to the North American Free Trade Agreement (NAFTA), and resuscitate the Trans-Pacific Partnership Agreement (TPP), claiming contrary to the adverse Council for Mutual Economic Assistance (CMEA) experience that adding layers of government administration over existing national units creates positive synergies including economies of planning and trust.[38]

Talbott's prototype cosmopolitan globalism together with the Biden–Harris administration's embellishments violates Adam Smith's principles of free enterprise, John Locke's social contract, equal opportunity, and equal treatment under the rule of law. They are consistent with the late 19th century consensus that governments have a duty to protect society from the

---

[36] Thomas Piketty, *Capital in the Twenty-First Century* (Cambridge: Belknap Press, 2014); Thomas Piketty, *Chronicles: On Our Troubled Times* (New York: Viking Press, 2016); Thomas Piketty, *Why Save the Bankers? And Other Essays on Our Economic and Political Crisis* (New York: Houghton Mifflin Harcourt, 2016); Thomas Piketty, *Top Incomes in France in the Twentieth Century: Inequality and Redistribution, 1901–1998* (Cambridge: Harvard University Press, 2018).

[37] Steven Rosefielde, "Salvaging the European Union: The Inclusive Multi-Track Transnational Option," *HOLISTICA — Journal of Business and Public Administration* 8, no. 3, 2018: 7–18; Steven Rosefielde, "EU Reform: Two speed or Inclusive Multi-Track?" *Contemporary Economics* (2018); Steven Rosefielde and Bruno Dallago, "The Strange Fate of Brexit and Grexit and the Eurozone Integration and Disintegration," *Contemporary Economics* (2018).

[38] Comecon (the Council for Mutual Economic Assistance), 1949–1991, an economic organization under the leadership of the Soviet Union that comprised the countries of the Eastern Bloc along with a number of socialist states elsewhere in the world. Steven Rosefielde, "International Trade Theory and Practice under Socialism," *Journal of Comparative Economics* 1, no. 1, March 1977: 99–104.

harmful effects of imperfect competition, and the 20th century Keynesian mandate to defend the public from market failure and provide basic services, insofar as these actions reflect majority democratic preferences and preserve constitutional minority (and majority) rights. They wink at anti-competitiveness (monopoly and oligopoly power in business and finance), subordinating equal opportunity to affirmative action, entitlement and restorative justice. They expand resident and foreign "stakeholder" rights (diluting shareholder rights),[39] and license iconoclastic social behavior. They treat public services as private businesses allowing government officials to outsource state administrative services for their personal benefit.[40]

Talbott's Global Nation priorities do not represent the will of America's citizens, just as Lenin's government in 1921 did not represent the will of the overwhelming majority of the Russian population who were peasants, merchants, artisans, clergy, and former aristocracy.[41] Talbott spoke for what he imagined would be tomorrow's cosmopolitan electoral majority after his pro-Latin American, Asian, Middle Eastern, African ethnicities, and pro-Islam immigration policies alter America's racial, ethnic, and religious composition.

The Biden–Harris administration incorporating Talbott's outlook asserts that it wants America to be efficient, productive, dynamic, and crisis resistant, but these goals are inconsistent with its anti-competitive, anti-meritocratic, and internationalist principles. Excess indebtedness, massive deficit spending, high levels of non-employment,[42] over-taxation, government waste, fraud and abuse, financial crises, and deteriorating life quality for large segments of society are hardwired into the Democratic Party's progressive-liberal agenda.

---

[39] Steven Rosefielde, "Stakeholder Capitalism: Progressive Dream or Nightmare?" *HOLISTICA — Journal of Business and Public Administration* (2021).

[40] Steven Rosefielde and Quinn Mills, *Democracy and Its Elected Enemies: American Political Capture and Economic Decline* (New York: Cambridge University Press, 2013).

[41] *Narodnoe Khoziaistvo SSSR za 70 Let, Finansy i Statistika, Moskva, 1987.*

[42] America officially is at full employment, but millions of discouraged workers have dropped out of the labor force. The term non-employment is used by economists describe this form of economic malfunction.

Chapter 2

Resulting Security Morass

National Insecurity

The Biden–Harris administration opposes stout national security. It inclines toward a utopian harmonist credo.[1] Just as the French Popular Front naively dismissed the Nazi threat, the progressive-liberal establishment believes that most international conflicts can be peacefully resolved through inspiring idealism and goodwill. The key to national security for them is remaking the world with the consciousness raising attraction of their ideals, rule of law, soft power, denuclearization, disarmament, smart diplomacy and strategic patience. They refuse to spend the funds needed for stout hard power deterrence, choosing to protect "entitlements." Many of Biden–Harris administration supporters assail the American Defense Department for being in the pockets of the "military industrial complex,"[2]

---

[1] Robert Owen, *A New View of Society: Or, Essays on the Formation of Human Character, and the Application of the Principle to Practice* (London: 1813). Karl Marx and Friedrich Engels, *Communist Manifesto* (London: Penguin Classics, 1848).

[2] Rachel Weber, "Military-Industrial Complex," *Encyclopedia Britannica*, https://www.britannica.com/topic/military-industrial-complex.

"Military–industrial complex, network of individuals and institutions involved in the production of weapons and military technologies. The military–industrial complex in a country typically attempts to marshal political support for continued or increased military spending by the national government. The term military–industrial complex was first used by US President Dwight D. Eisenhower in his Farewell Address on January 17, 1961."

16 *Beleaguered Superpower: Biden's America Adrift*

and "merchants of death."[3] They point out that America spends more on the military than the rest of the world combined,[4] and fret that war may lead to mass annihilation. They are willing to snarl at Eastern authoritarians, but prefer to temporize, a syndrome transparent to America's great power rivals.

Biden–Harris supporters also are double-minded. While they oppose maintaining an adequate defense against Eastern authoritarians, they are keen to militarily assist radical Third World insurrectionaries like Fidel Castro and Venezuela's socialist regime, and have been notably active promoting violent "color revolutions" and "regime-change" in Belarus,[5] Russia, China, North Korea, and some parts of the Islamic world.

Morass

The Biden–Harris administration's progressive-liberal mindset is drawing America into a global security morass. Its leaders delude themselves that Washington can manage authoritarian adversaries without maintaining robust hard power.[6] They narcissistically pretend that Eastern authoritarian

---

[3] H. C. Engelbrecht and F. C. Hanighen, *Merchants of Death* (New York: Dodd, Mead & Co., 1934).

[4] "Trends in World Military Expenditure, 2016," *Stockholm International Peace Research Institute*, April 2017; Steven Rosefielde, *False Science: Underestimating the Soviet Arms Buildup* (Rutgers: Transaction Press, 1987); Steven Rosefielde, "Russian Military Industry" in Steven Rosefielde, ed., *Putin's Russia: Economic, Political and Military Foundations* (Singapore: World Scientific Publishers, 2018). SIPRI reports that global defense spending in 2015 was 1,686 trillion dollars. America spent $611.2 billion. These figures are official data converted with misleading purchasing power parities and are misleading in myriad ways. China alone, spends more than America and SIPRI Russia estimate is silly. This is a very arcane subject, but readers can appreciate the essence by consulting Steven Rosefielde.

[5] "Lukashenka Accuses West of Trying To 'Destroy' Belarus With Another 'Color Revolution'," *Radio Free Europe*, September 16, 2020.

[6] Steven Rosefielde, Masaaki Kuboniwa, Kumiko Haba, and Satoshi Mizobata, eds., *The Unwinding of the Globalist Dream: EU, Russia, China* (Singapore: World Scientific Publishers, 2017).

There are many varieties of globalization and globalism. Globalization has three distinct meanings.

(1) For many advocates, it is the worldwide rule of democratic free enterprise that preserves the nation state as the fundamental unit of government. (2) For some advocates,

leaders know that the West's progressive order is best and understand that they cannot win a sustained competition. They believe that Washington's foes will roll back their spheres of influence, allowing the West to pick up the pieces as it did in the post-Soviet space after the USSR's collapse in the Baltics, Visegrad Group (Poland, Hungary, Czechia, and Slovakia), Eastern Europe, the Balkans and various former republics of the USSR. Success from their perspective is inevitable. There are no perils, only opportunities.

This whistling past the graveyard exacerbates the dangers. It embold-ens the Washington establishment to press ahead with an adventurist agenda, including fostering "color revolutions" and "regime-change" in

---

it means global free enterprise plus the welfare state. (3) For others, it means the creation of a progressive cosmopolitan world order governed transnationally with progressive val-ues like free migration, egalitarianism, women and transgender liberation, entitlement, affirmative action and restorative justice (Strobe Talbott's Global Nation) founded on transnational or World government rather than the nation state. Globalizationists of all three persuasions urge foreign nations to abandon their economic, social and cultural sys-tems in favor of this or that Western ideal. Anti-Globalizers contend that globalization is a euphemism for "globalism"; that is, American economic imperialism. They urge Asian nations to defend themselves against globalization (Western imperialism). Some want foreign nations to retain their diverse economic systems without assimilating Western values; others advocate embracing the welfare state and/or progressive values like cosmo-politanism, free migration, egalitarianism, women and transgender liberation, entitlement, affirmative action, and restorative justice.

Cf. Joseph Stiglitz, "The Globalization of Our Discontents," *Project Syndicate* (December 2017), https://www.project-syndicate.org/commentary/globalization-of-discontent-by-joseph-e--stiglitz-2017-12?utm_source=Project+Syndicate+Newsletter&utm_campaign=9ec68ad59b-sunday_newsletter_10_12_2017&utm_medium=email&utm_term=0_73bad5b7d8-9ec68ad59b-93559677.

"Globalization, which was supposed to benefit developed and developing countries alike, is now reviled almost everywhere, as the political backlash in Europe and the US in recent years has shown. The challenge is to minimize the risk that the backlash will inten-sify, and that starts by understanding — and avoiding — past mistakes." "To someone like me, who has watched trade negotiations closely for more than a quarter-century, it is clear that US trade negotiators got most of what they wanted. The problem was with what they wanted. Their agenda was set, behind closed doors, by corporations. It was an agenda written by and for large multinational companies, at the expense of workers and ordinary citizens everywhere."

18 *Beleaguered Superpower: Biden's America Adrift*

the East,[7] while ignoring three fundamental vulnerabilities. (1) Eastern authoritarians are becoming increasingly powerful, (2) Eastern authoritarians know that progressives and many liberal members of the Washington establishment are committed to paring American hard power, and (3) America's home front is in disarray. Western economies burdened by progressive and liberal anti-competitive programs are underperforming, and West polities are at each other's throats. This syndrome is endemic in the Biden–Harris administration home front agenda.

Today's Democratic Party continues to thwart expanded defense spending as they did during 2011–2017, despite the budget busting, deficit financed compromise 2018 authorizing a half trillion dollar increase in defense and civilian expenditures. The defense "sequester" rule in the Budget Control Act of 2011 defined the battle lines. It compelled the Department of Defense to reduce military expenditures from 4.3 percent of GDP in 2012 to just 2.8 percent of GDP in 2023,[8] a loss of

---

[7]Stephen Cohen, "Ukraine Revisited," *Nation* (February 2017), https://www.thenation.com/article/ukraine-revisited/.

"The orthodox US narrative that Putin alone is responsible for the new Cold War hangs largely on his alleged unprovoked 'aggression' against Ukraine in 2014 and ever since. (The narrative is sustained in part by the near-total absence of any American mainstream reporting of what is actually happening in Kiev-controlled or rebel-controlled territories.) In fact, Putin's actions both in Donbass, where an indigenous rebellion broke out against the overthrow of the legally elected president in Kiev three years ago, and in Crimea, which had been part of Russia for 300 years (longer than the existence of the United States), was a direct reaction to the longstanding campaign by Washington and Brussels to bring Ukraine into NATO's 'sphere of influence,' itself a form of political aggression. Cohen discusses the centuries of intimate relations between large segments of Ukrainian society and Russia, including family ties, concluding that it was reckless and immoral for Washington and Brussels to impose upon Kiev a choice between Russia and the West, thereby fostering, if not precipitating, civil war. And to flatly reject Putin's counter-proposal for a three-way Ukrainian–Russian–Western relationship. In this regard, Washington and Brussels bear considerable responsibility for the 10,000 who have died in the ensuing civil and proxy war, but they have yet to assume any responsibility at all."

[8]Todd Harrison, "What Has the Budget Control Act of 2011 Meant for Defense?" *Center for Strategic and International Studies (CSIS)* (August 2016), https://www.csis.org/analysis/what-has-budget-control-act-2011-meant-defense.

The Budget Control Act of 2011 (BCA) was signed into law five years ago on August 2, 2011. It is a resurrection of a much older law, known as Gramm–Rudman–Hollings, originally enacted in 1985. The BCA reinstates budget caps for a 10-year period ending in

$500 billion.[9] This is now a dead letter, but even restoring the 2012 defense-GDP ratio will be a futile uphill struggle under the Biden–Harris administration. The $2.2 trillion CARES deficit spending package gave the Department of Defense peanuts.[10]

Most important of all, progressives and many liberals underestimate China's threat potential. They refuse to believe that Xi Jinping's communist market system and armed forces might ever defeat the West, even though big business and American national security communities are becoming apprehensive. Ash Carter, former Secretary of Defense under the Obama administration reflects this attitude. He asserts that America should not "impose Cold War, NATO-inspired structures on the Asia-Pacific or on our relationship with China, but to invite China into a far different, but equally successful, multilateral security network," even though he acknowledges that the strategy has conspicuously failed since the turn of the new millennium.[11] His progressive-liberal mindset pulls the wool over his own eyes.[12] Instead of treating falsification as failure, he reiterates his unfounded faith that Xi Jinping's idea of Machiavellian

---

FY 2021 with separate caps for the defense and nondefense parts of the discretionary budget. For defense, the budget caps represent a reduction of roughly $1 trillion over 10 years compared to what the president had proposed in his FY 2012 budget request earlier in 2011.

[9]Ashley J. Tellis, "Covid-19 Knocks on American Hegemony," *National Bureau of Asian Research* (May 2020), https://www.nbr.org/publication/covid-19-knocks-on-american-hegemony/.

[10]Mackenzie Eaglen, "What's in the $2.2 Trillion Stimulus for Defense?," *RealClear Defense* (March 2020), https://www.realcleardefense.com/articles/2020/03/28/whats_in_the_2_trillion_stimulus_for_defense_115156.html?mkt_=eyJpIjoiWW1SaU9EWTNOb tokU0zWkRFeiIsInQiOiJoUm1XZlhrSkUyZXJLT1kxc1k3NTZHaW c3U1pIbFV5UEU5N0daaXlTWGhpOFRDSXo4MDN6aE9pOEo4VmM wdU02VjJBT2dhXC9XRmR3bDE0WW1SVGRrZGxpbXZ6b WU3S3pF NjVRTnVKd1FSejA2SUMwQlZIdDYzcFlJZWp1dnV2QjEifQ%3D%3D.

[11]Ash Carter, "Reflections on American Grand Strategy in Asia," *Belfer Center* (October 2018), https://www.belfercenter.org/publication/reflections-american-grand-strategy-asia?utm_source=SilverpopMailing&utm_medium=email&utm_campaign=Ash%20 Carter%20China%20Paper%20-%2010-18%20(1)&utm_content=&spMailingID=204066 37&spUserID=NTQ3ODk4MzgxNTgS1&spJobID=1361027524&spReportId=MTM2M TAyNzUyNAS2.

[12]Carter was born in 1954 and is a Boomer.

20   *Beleaguered Superpower: Biden's America Adrift*

geopolitics ultimately will coincide with our idealism, and that carrying a little stick and doubling down on persuasion will carry the day.

This is the essence of America's security morass. Progressive-liberal double-mindedness embroils Washington in quixotic adventures like the "Orange Revolution," but conflicted priorities prevent it from successfully coping with the repercussions.[13] Commitment to budget busting excessive social (mis) spending buttressed by pacifist attitudes toward Russia, China, North Korea, and the global jihadi crowds out funding a robust defense against Eastern authoritarianism. A hobbled economy and tattered national unity compound the dilemma, leaving America with no viable options other than accommodating Russian, Chinese, North Korean, and the global jihadi expansionism, and vainly trusting in "strategic patience." The prospect is for a replay of the "peace in our times" 1930s, with Eastern authoritarians slicing up their neighbors.

Some liberals are beginning to perceive the dilemma. However, most refuse to articulate the quandary to themselves and the public. They prefer to throw financial and security prudence to the winds, in the vain hope of avoiding the wisdom of rational choice.

There is no exit within Biden–Harris game plan, only golden parachutes for insiders. Progressives and liberals cannot square the circle. Washington cannot be the beacon on the hill that it was when America carried the flag for the inclusive open society, democracy, rule of law, and free enterprise (Washington Consensus) and simultaneously deter Eastern authoritarians under the progressive-liberal Global Nation banner.[14]

Putin, Xi, Kim, Ayatollah Khamenei, and the leaders of global jihadi know befuddled leaders and dysfunctional polities when they see them, and they see them in the Biden–Harris administration.

---

[13] Many members of the New West establishment are apologists for any aggressor that can be viewed as a victim of colonialism and imperialism. Some feel obligated to accept North Korea's nuclear and missile program because Kim Jong Un is "justifiably" afraid of the big bad wolf.

[14] John Williamson, "Development and the 'Washington Consensus'," *World Development* 21, 1993: 1329–1336.

The Washington Consensus is a set of 10 economic policy prescriptions considered to constitute the "standard" reform package promoted for crisis-wracked developing countries by Washington, D.C.–based institutions such as the International Monetary Fund (IMF), World Bank, and the US Treasury Department. The term was first used in 1989 by English economist John Williamson.

Resulting Security Morass 21

Authoritarian leaders across the globe are aware that the progressive-liberal muddle and partisan infighting are debilitating Western governments. They intend to capitalize on America and the European Union's distress. Russia, China, North Korea, Iran, and the global jihadi are sowing seeds of dissension among their adversaries and expanding their spheres of influence. Progressives and liberals want to eradicate insurgent Eastern authoritarianism, but can only deliver retreat, discord, and decline. The righteousness of the Biden–Harris administration's social ideals is neither here, nor there from a security perspective.[15] Whether one judges them sacred or profane, they constitute America's Achilles heel in the struggle against Eastern authoritarianism.

Threats — We Now Face

Five primary challengers threaten America and the West: Russia, China, North Korea, Iran, and the global jihadi.[16] All have long tested the United States. Progressives and liberals prefer to consider them fading relics of bygone times. They see Russia, China, North Korea, Iran, and the global jihadi as authoritarian actors in transition to virtuous cosmopolitans harmoniously integrated into an American led progressive-liberal global order. They depict China on the liberalization fast track, and Russia "returning to its common Western home" after the Russiagate fury subsides.[17] They could be right, but it is sensible to prepare for the

---

[15] Stephen Walt, "The Hell of Good Intentions," *Kirkus Reviews* (2018), https://www.kirkusreviews.com/book-reviews/stephen-m-walt/the-hell-of-good-intentions/

"Walt's arguments against 'liberal hegemony' — the adjective meaning not leftist in orientation but instead something that "seeks to use American power to defend and spread the traditional liberal principles of individual freedom, democratic governance, and a market based economy" — are coherent if sometimes strident, and his descriptions match what appears to be happening on the ground, such as the emergence of China as a foreign policy rival to the U.S."

[16] Samuel Huntington, "The Clash of Civilizations?" *Foreign Affairs* 72, no. 3, 1993: 22–49; Samuel Huntington, *Clash of Civilizations and the Remaking of the World Order* (New York: Simon & Schuster, 1996). Samuel Huntington, ed., *The Clash of Civilizations?: The Debate* (New York: Foreign Affairs, 1996).

[17] Stephen Cohen, "Unverified 'Russiagate' Allegations, Irresponsibly Promoted by Congress and the Media, Have Become a Grave Threat to American National Security," *The Nation* (August 2017), https://www.thenation.com/article/

22 *Beleaguered Superpower: Biden's America Adrift*

possibility that America's great power rivals will not soon fade quietly into the night.

There are many other challengers including communist Cuba,[18] Venezuela, and a host lesser threats,[19] but the big five are America's principal foes today because four of them possess or are on the cusp of possessing weapons of mass destruction. They all reject progressive-liberal values, and credibly seek to vigorously defend or expand their spheres of influence.

The Kremlin wants to restore its hegemony over parts of the former Soviet Union, the former Soviet bloc, and the Balkans, and refuses to return the Northern Islands captured from Japan after Tokyo agreed to surrender to the United States on August 15, 1945. China's sway over Tibet, the China Sea,[20] Ladakh, Pakistan, Southeast Asia, Central Asia, and Hong Kong is increasing, and it seeks inroads across the globe, including the Middle East and the West (One Belt, One Road (OBOR)).[21] Beijing supports North Korea, refuses to countenance Tibetan or Taiwanese independence, is skirmishing with India in Ladakh, dominates

---

unverified-russiagate-allegations-promoted-by-an-irresponsible-congress-and-media-have-become-a-grave-threat-to-american-national-security/; Mikhail Gorbachev, *Perestroika: New Thinking for Our Country and the World* (New York: Harper and Row, 1987).

[18]Communism's global ideological appeal has waned, but communist authoritarianism survives.

[19]Huntington speculated that cultural and religious identities would be the primary sources of conflict in the post-Cold War world rather than ideology, as was the case during the Cold War.

[20]Steven Rosefielde, "Rising Red Star," in Steven Rosefielde, Masaaki Kuboniwa, Kumiko Haba, and Satoshi Mizobata, eds., *The Unwinding of the Globalist Dream: EU, Russia, China* (Singapore: World Scientific Publishers, 2017): 237–244.

[21]OBOR (One Belt, One Road) is a development strategy and framework, proposed by Xi Jinping that focuses on connectivity and cooperation among countries primarily between the People's Republic of China and the rest of Eurasia, which consists of two main components, the land-based "Silk Road Economic Belt" (SREB) and oceangoing "Maritime Silk Road" (MSR). The strategy underlines China's push to take a bigger role in global affairs, and its need for priority capacity cooperation in areas such as steel manufacturing in 2016. The "belt" includes countries situated on the original Silk Road through Central Asia, West Asia, the Middle East, and Europe.

Pakistan,[22] and is on the cusp of becoming a major military and civilian technological competitor. North Korea threatens South Korea and Japan, and militant Islam is actively engaged in terrorism and armed combat with Israel, Syria, Iraq, Egypt, Turkey, Kurdistan, North and Sub-Saharan Africa, Iran, Afghanistan, Pakistan, Bangladesh, India, Indonesia, Thailand, Myanmar, China, Russia, Europe, and America.[23]

The threat posed by Russia, China, North Korea, Iran and global jihadism is not only territorial but also civilizational. All five adversaries are authoritarian and have deep-rooted anti-Western identities. They reject the West's open society, rule of law, democracy and free enterprise, civil liberties, entitlements, affirmative action, restorative justice, and oppose immigration into their domains. That is, they reject democratic free enterprise, progressive-liberalism, and Talbott's Global Nation. China and North Korea repress religion, Russia privileges Eastern Orthodox Christianity, and Iran global jihadi Islam. Radical Islam gives no quarter to infidels.[24] Each rival justifiably considers itself a civilization (including North Korea),[25] and finds empty cosmopolitan idealism repellent.

All abhor progressive-liberal doctrine on their own turf. Russia, China, North Korea, and Iran dislike its ideals and anti-patriotism.

---

[22]Michael Rubin, "The Unexpected Wrath of Imran Khan," *AEI* (December 15, 2020), https://www.aei.org/op-eds/the-unexpected-wrath-of-imran-khan/?mkt_tok= eyJpIjoiWkRFd05HUXhNMkUyWVRZMCIsInQiOiJKa2xWRlpObH FlT0g1VTl3SVFseHBaWHVVRWI3VXZlNlZiSzRhVWpXekRaYW91T3c5QWVI dnN6TVwvWUVORGJBaDRwRXE2ejVYNEpad0xINWxXTkVNYm1Qc3 hIdHRrMFk0MEN5UkJUekNNUHJNRlh0N2FBZDZQd1Y5SGRNVjVZ dUMifQ%3D%3D.

[23]This distinction recognizes that in Muslim-dominated countries it is unclear whether the population opposes militant Islam, although established state governments do.

[24]Jon Emont, "Jakarta's Christian Governor Sentenced to Prison in Blasphemy Case," *Washington Post* (May 9, 2017), https://www.washingtonpost.com/news/worldviews/ wp/2017/05/09/jakartas-christian-governor-sentenced-to-prison-in-blasphemy-case/?utm_ term=.4939ba44c93f. Even moderate Islam often is intolerant. Mubasher Bukhari, "Pakistani Court Sentences Christian Man to Death For Blasphemy," *Reuters* (September 15, 2017), http://www.reuters.com/article/us-pakistan-blasphemy/pakistani-court-sentences-christian-man-to-death-for-blasphemy-idUSKCN1BQ2LY?il=0 https://www.washington post.com/news/worldviews/wp/2017/05/09/jakartas-christian-governor-sentenced-to-prison-in-blasphemy-case/?utm_term=.35b3ee298ba0.

[25]Korean civilization usually is dated at least as far back at 37 AD, to the beginning of the Three Kingdom period under the rule of Goguryeo, Baekje, and Silla.

They consider progressive affirmative action on behalf of homosexuals, transgender people, ethnic minorities, and persecuted religious groups objectionable. Iran and the global jihadi oppose radical feminism and secularism. Both are appalled by apostasy,[26] and incensed by progressive campaigns aimed at secularizing Moslems.[27] These positions are not black and white and could change. Nonetheless, they capture today's reality.

The Biden–Harris administration's progressive-liberal politics constitute an inflammatory element in an already difficult national security environment. The challenge to America's national interests posed by Russia, China, North Korea, Iran, and the global jihadi would not evaporate by restoring pre Clinton–Talbott competitive policies, but threat management would improve.[28] The old adage "Peace through Strength" in all dimensions is a better choice than utopia now through weakness.[29] It is applicable to a wide spectrum of threats posed by frenemies, transnational organizations, rivals, and enemies, and will nurture prosperity.

---

[26]Sophia Saifi and Laura Smith-Spark, "Pakistan Strikes Deal To End Protests Over Asia Bibi Blasphemy Case," *CNN* (November 3, 2018), https://www.cnn.com/2018/11/03/asia/pakistan-asia-bibi-blasphemy-intl/index.html.

[27]Om Marathe, "Explained: What is in France's Draft Law against 'Islamism'?" *Indian Express* (December 11, 2020), https://indianexpress.com/article/explained/explained-whats-in-frances-draft-law-against-islamism-7100240/.

[28]Michael Gordon, "Russia Has Deployed Missile Barred by Treaty, U.S. General Tells Congress," *New York Times* (March 8, 2017), https://www.nytimes.com/2017/03/08/us/politics/russia-inf-missile-treaty.html?_r=0. The arms control community has begun urging Trump to oppose Russia's deployment of the SSC-8 nuclear capable cruise missile which it claims violates the INF Treaty, but has not acknowledge the success of Russia's military modernization.

[29]Morris Victor Rosenblum, Peace Through Strength: Bernard Baruch and a Blueprint for Security (New York: Farrar, Straus and Young, 1952); Bill Gertz, "Trump Administration: 'America First' and 'Peace Through Strength' National Security Policies," *Washington Times* (February 14, 2017), http://www.washingtontimes.com/news/2017/feb/14/trump-administration-america-first-and-peace-throu/.

The concept has been criticized for stressing military hard power but can be easily extended to include domestic economic prosperity, social harmony, and bipartisan political solidarity.

Part II

Authoritarian Regimes are Mounting Serious Challenges

Eastern authoritarians directly and obliquely threaten America. Part II details and documents the dangers posed by Russia, China, North Korea, Iran, and global jihadism to homeland security, America's allies, and global well-being.[1]

---

[1]"NATIONAL SECURITY: Long-Range Emerging Threats Facing the United States As Identified by Federal Agencies," cf. *GAO* (December 2018), https://www.gao.gov/assets/700/695981.pdf. "Global Trends: Paradoxes of Progress," *A Publication of the National Intelligence Council* (January 2017), www.dni.gov/nic/globaltrends.

Chapter 3

Russia

Russian civilization has continuously evolved for more than a millennium without shedding its authoritarian core.[2] Russia internalized aspects of the Enlightenment, socialism, communism, electoral governance, private property, markets and contract law, but remained true to its absolutist roots.

Russia has been a great military power for more than 500 years, economic backwardness notwithstanding. It has experienced spurts of economic growth over the centuries under Peter the Great, Catherine the Great, Alexander II, Alexander III, Joseph Stalin, Nikita Khrushchev, and Vladimir Putin, but its per capita GDP never rose to the Western mean. These continuities amid change suggest that although economically laggard, Russia is culturally, militarily, and materially resilient,[3] and that the state is durable enough to defend its heritage.

Russia's staying power makes Moscow unreceptive to Washington's blandishments. The Kremlin is allergic to the open society, democracy, the West's rule of law, and radical progressive agenda, professions to the contrary notwithstanding. Moreover, as Crimea's annexation suggests, Russia is inclined to expand its territories and spheres of influence when opportunity knocks, just as it has since the time of Ivan the Great (Ivan III

---

[2] Alexander Gerschenkron, *Economic Backwardness in Historical Perspective: A Book of Essays* (Cambridge: Belknap Press of Harvard University Press, 1962). Alexander Gerschenkron, *Europe in the Russian Mirror: Four Lectures in Economic History* (London: Cambridge University Press, 1970).

[3] Alexander Gerschenkron, *Continuity in History, and Other Essays* (Cambridge: Belknap Press of Harvard University Press, 1968).

28 *Beleaguered Superpower: Biden's America Adrift*

1440–1505 Grand Prince of Moscow and Grand Prince of all Rus). This means that there is an omnipresent danger that Russia will pose a major security threat whenever relations with the West sour. One prominent expert has already declared that Russia is already in a state of full spectrum war with the West.[4]

Shadow Boxing

Washington's national security community is conversant with Russian history. However, it is not prepared to take Moscow seriously enough today despite a great deal of belligerent rhetoric because it prefers to presume that Russia is no match for the United States. America must always prevail if Washington is strategically patient. This overconfidence predisposes American leaders to underestimate and inadequately respond to the Kremlin's threat, relying on "smart diplomacy" and soft power semaphore instead of stout hard power. The West's anemic response to Russia's annexation of Crimea and continued occupation of Donbass and Luhansk testifies to this false faith. Although, the Kremlin has not budged on the annexation dispute since 2014, liberals and progressives refuse to revise their unrealistic premises,[5] confident

---

[4] Stephen Blank, "Moscow's Competitive Strategy," *American Foreign Policy Council* (July 2018), http://www.lexingtoninstitute.org/wp-content/uploads/2018/07/7.25.18-Moscows-Competitive-Strategy.pdf.

"Since at least 2005, Russia's leadership has believed itself to be at war with the West. This war is not primarily one of kinetic combat though recent moves suggest that Moscow believes such a war is increasingly conceivable. Rather it should be described as a new form of political war fare that derives in many from Soviet precedents."

[5] James Sherr, "Russia's Strategy," *The Institute for Statecraft* (November 29, 2017).

"Over the past ten years, Russia has displayed an impressive degree of political-military integration in pursuit of its state objectives. Its pursuit of informatsionnaya voyna, straddles both domains. Since 2014, the Russian state leadership has openly characterised the post-Cold War order (which its predecessor co-authored) as illegitimate, inimical to its interests and intrinsically vulnerable. The belief that Russia is under geopolitical and 'civilisational' encroachment from the West has become unchallengeable. These premises are now firmly integrated into the threat assessments of the military establishment, which views NATO/EU enlargement, coloured revolutions, military intervention and regime change as staple ingredients of Western policy. Military policy now plays a key role during times of ostensible peace, whereas the social and political factors retain their classical preeminence in military conflict (which would aim to destroy the political West rather than the countries that comprise it). Infowar is seen both as a necessary component of military

Russia   29

that Putin will ultimately relent.[6] Progressives and big welfare state liberals are counting on Putin's awakening. Conservatives are awaiting his conversion to democratic free enterprise.

Foundations of Russian Power

The national security community's persistent mismanagement of US–Russian relations stems from its mindset.[7] It cannot bring itself to accept

---

strategy and as a form of confrontation [protivoborstvo] in its own right. From this holistic perspective, Russia believes that it is at war with the West, even if this conviction arouses disbelief amongst those who retain dated and stereotyped views of what war is and how it is fought."

[6]Nikolai Sokov, "Russia's New Conventional Capability: Implications for Eurasia and Beyond," *Ponars Eurasia* (April 2017).

"In late 2015 and early 2016, Russia demonstrated in Syria that it had acquired long range, precision-guided, conventional-strike capability, the use of which has implications far beyond military utility. Moscow's willingness to use this newly acquired class of military power in support of its foreign policy is a challenge both to the West's monopoly on global power projection, which it has held since the end of the Cold War, and to its state of denial about Russia's rearmament progress." Cf. Keir Giles, "Assessing Russia's Reorganized and Rearmed Military," *Carnegie Foundation for Peace* (May 2017), http://carnegieendowment.org/2017/05/03/assessing-russia-s-reorganized-and-rearmed-military-pub-69853?mkt_tok=eyJpIjoiT0dZMFlUWXpZal EzTWpKaSIsInQiOiJOdkVISXZcLzA4UkhwNEZGaFROd0ZWSlll RjNVazBkVXM5dU12S05QZFlSWlhMZHZFVFRHQWtHTDJrWXdKM3 FqaU5NYW9jcGVuZXVRT0tQUnZCMW1UemhyZXY1NXl2REdieXJF am1zSDdjMGtnN0lCRFI3ZWxnbVlvZ0tLMjhxRkUifQ%3D%3D.

"Russia's reorganized and rearmed Armed Forces are neither invincible nor still broken and incapable. Two points are beyond argument: First, in terms of equipment, experience, attitude, confidence, and more, the Russian military is a radically different force from the one that began the process of transformation in 2008. Second, change is still taking place. Snapshots of Russia's capability displayed in Ukraine and Syria tend to conceal ongoing developments; the true capability of the Russian military is not static but a rapidly developing phenomenon."

[7]Ludwig Wittgenstein, "Logisch-philosophiche Abhandlung," in *Annalen der Naturphilosophie* 14 (Leipzig: 1921): 185–262, reprinted in English translation as *Tractatus logico-philosophicus* (New York and London: 1922). "Idealist neoclassical theory essentially is a beguiling tautology in Ludwig Wittgenstein's demanding sense (given its premises, true under all circumstances; it cannot be negated). Pareto optimality assumes that everyone is comprehensively rational and omni-competent, and then gives its

30 Beleaguered Superpower: Biden's America Adrift

that contemporary Russia is a durable rival military superpower, but it is wrong.[8] Putin's has forged a sustainable competitive market and rent-granting economy that enables the Kremlin to field formidable firepower,

---

claims a scientific patina by analytically deducing from the construct's premises that outcomes are ideal (everyone maximizes his or her utility within the constraints of voluntary exchange). Idealist neoclassical theory is empirically testable, but results are mixed. The disconfirmation is widely disregarded while maintaining the fiction that Pareto analysis is behaviorally true. Idealist neoclassical theory should be more accurately called neoclassical 'tauto-nomics.'"

[8]Nikolai Sokov, "Russia's New Conventional Capability: Implications for Eurasia and Beyond," *Ponars Eurasia* (April 2017). "At the present technological level of Russia's new weapons, geography favors Russia more than it does the United States, particularly when it comes to today's 'hot spots,' most of which are located in Eurasia and are thus closer to Russia than to the United States. In particular, Moscow can bring the weapons to bear faster and cheaper than Washington for several reasons:

- The United States usually needs several weeks to move platforms with modern strike assets to an area; therefore, its capability is not truly stand-off. Russia, in contrast, is closer to potential target zones, as its missile strikes in Syria demonstrated. It can launch modern missiles from inside its own territory or from within its own territorial waters. Therefore, its weapons have the edge in stand-off capability. Moscow continues to build up the Caspian flotilla of small surface ships and diesel-powered submarines in the Black Sea, both equipped with long-range submarine-launched cruise missiles (SLCMs); it is also launching a large series of SLCM-carrying frigates, which will expand its reach to waters around most of Eurasia.
- To acquire a truly stand-off global capability, the United States has to pursue costly and time-consuming programs, which feature, among other elements, a hypersonic cruise missile with global reach. While Russia has been working on a similar program, in most contingencies it could limit itself to shorter-range assets, which could be developed quickly and at a lower cost (recent reports indicate that it has successfully tested the 400-km range Tsiklon hypersonic cruise missile).
- The United States had to abandon plans to equip strategic missiles with conventional warheads because almost any launch against targets in Eurasia would have these missiles flying toward or over Russia and China. The risk of misidentifying a target was rightly judged as unacceptable. In contrast, Russian strategic weapons armed with conventional warheads could be directed away from the United States. Such considerations led Moscow to undertake, for example, a program to create a dual-capable, liquid fuel, intercontinental ballistic missile (ICBM) using existing technologies and leveraging decades of experience with designing and building similar assets.
- Additionally, there are several important differences between Russia's emergent conventional arsenal and the capabilities and strategies of the United States, as follows:

Russia 31

supported with advanced cyber warfighting capabilities without impoverishing Russia's consumers. Russia's new system is not good enough to defeat American "free enterprise" in a full-throttle arms race, but could defeat a radical progressive USA.[9]

Russia is not as powerful as the Soviet Union was *vis-à-vis* the West in its heyday, even though the Kremlin maintains advantages over America in tanks, AFV/ APCs, Artillery/MRLs, combat aircraft, attack submarines, and strategic submarines.[10]

The Kremlin lost 24 percent of its territory in 1991 and its current population in 2020 is only 50 percent of the Soviet figure. The USSR's population was 16 percent greater than the US's 30 years ago. Now Russia's population is only 44 percent of the American benchmark.

- Following a long tradition, Russia continues to favor ground-launched missiles. In this category, they have the Iskandr with its declared 500-km range, which some estimate at 700 km or even more for the cruise missile version. They have plans to create a conventionally-capable ICBM (mentioned above). There are also reports about Russian tests of an intermediate-range ground-launched cruise missile, which led the United States to accuse Russia of violating the 1987 INF Treaty.
- Russia employs a greater variety of platforms. These include, for example, small surface ships and diesel-powered submarines. Russia even hints at launchers hidden inside standard shipping containers, which can conceal intermediate range SLCMs, the tracking of which would be almost impossible.
- Russia is enhancing the accuracy of its old, Soviet-era weapons, which demonstrates its propensity for quick and low-cost solutions. In Syria, for example, Russia was able to significantly increase the accuracy of 'dumb' bombs dropped from Su-24s fighter jets by more accurately positioning them and better calculating the moment the bomb is dropped.
- Perhaps the most tangible difference involves the relationship between nuclear and conventional capability. Since the early 1990s, the United States has shifted emphasis from the former to the latter because nuclear weapons seemed less relevant. In short, conventional capability partially replaced nuclear capability. While Moscow initially declared a desire to do the same, its approach seems to have changed and conventional capability appears to be an addition to nuclear capability. All of its new weapon delivery systems are dual-capable and can be used to carry either nuclear or conventional warheads depending on the mission."

[9] Steven Rosefielde, "New Millennial Economic Systems: Paradox of Power and Reason," *Foresight and STI Governance*, special issue: in "System Economics — Prospects of Development" (2020).

[10] Steven Rosefielde, *Russia in the 21st Century: The Prodigal Superpower* (Cambridge: Cambridge University Press, 2005): 65 (Table 4.2).

32 *Beleaguered Superpower: Biden's America Adrift*

Nonetheless, the Kremlin's threat potential is immense on its periphery with Europe (especially the Baltic States and Ukraine),[11] and in the Middle East where the possibility of persistent armed conflict is greatest.

Russia is rapidly modernizing its full spectrum military capabilities. More than half the new weapons procured during its arms buildup 2010–2015 were contemporary fifth-generation systems. The scope of the Kremlin's arms modernization program is vast. It includes information warfare, nuclear modernization, dual-use information systems, precision-guided munitions, advanced conventional weapons, anti-stealth radar, indigenously stealthy air-launched cruise missiles, the S-400 antiaircraft/antiballistic missile,[12] plasma coatings to make fifth-generation aircraft invisible to radar, chemical, and biogenetic weapons, and direct-energy weapons, lasers, microwave radiation emitters, particle-beam generators, subatomic particles to destroy targets at the speed of light. A new plasma weapon could ionize the atmosphere to destroy incoming missiles. Moscow is moving in the direction of high-tech combat aircraft, electronic control and information systems, weapons based on new physical principles, tactical nuclear weapons to be used in conventional conflicts to achieve strategic impact, and a reconnaissance fire (or strike) system that can make a strategic difference in large theater wars. Topol-M intercontinental ballistic missiles (ICBMs) and RS-24 Yars are replacing older land-based missiles for use as first-and second-strike weapons,[13] and

---

[11] Finland, Poland, Belarus, Azerbaijan, and Georgia also are at risk.

[12] "S-400 Triumph Missile Systems Put on Combat Duty in Siberia," *TASS* (March 1, 2016). The S-400 Triumf (Russian: С-400 Триумф) is an anti-aircraft weapon system developed in the 1990s by Russia's Almaz Central Design Bureau as an upgrade of the S-300 family. It has been in service with the Russian Armed Forces since 2007. The S-400 uses four missiles to fill its performance envelope: the very-long-range 40N6 (400 km), the long-range 48N6 (250 km), the medium-range 9M96E2 (120 km), and the short-range 9M96E (40 km). On March 1, 2016, acting commander of the 14th Air Force and Air Defense Army major-general Vladimir Korytkov said that six S-400 units had been activated pursuant to his order in the anti-aircraft missile regiment of the Novosibirsk air defense formation in Russia's Novosibirsk region. TASS also reported that as of the end of 2015, a total of 11 Russian missile regiments were armed with S-400, and by the end of 2016 their number was expected increase to 16.

[13] The RT-2PM2 «Topol-M» (Russian: РТ-2ПМ2) «Тополь-М») is one of the most recent intercontinental ballistic missiles to be deployed by Russia, and the first to be developed after the dissolution of the Soviet Union. It was developed from the RT-2PM Topol mobile intercontinental ballistic missile. By the end of 2010 the Russian Strategic Missile Troops operated 70 Topol-M missile systems including 52 silo-based and 18 mobile systems. A further 8 missiles were to join the Forces by 2011–2012.

Moscow has threatened to transform them into multiple independently targeted reentry vehicles (MIRVs) if the United States goes forward with its national missile defense program.[14] New smart conventional weapons coming on line include the Shkval torpedo missile;[15] the M-55 reconnaissance plane,[16] the Kh-31 supersonic anti-ship missile,[17] Kh55 strategic cruise missile,[18] Iskander anti-aircraft missile,[19] and unmanned aerial vehicles, all embodying large amounts of information, some upgradable

---

[14]A new missile loosely based on Topol-M and equipped with multiple re-entry vehicles (MIRV) is called RS-24 Yars. In January 2009, Russian sources hinted that the production of the mobile Topol-M missile would be shutting down in 2009 and that the new MIRVed RS-24 version would replace it.

[15]Kyle Mizokami, "Russia Has a Super Torpedo That Kills Submarines at 200 Miles Per Hour (And America Can't Match It)," *The National Interest* (January 2017), http://nationalinterest.org/blog/the-buzz/russia-has-super-torpedo-kills-submarines-200-miles-per-hour-18917.

The VA-111 Shkval (from Russian: шквал — squall) torpedo and its descendants are supercavitating torpedoes originally developed by the Soviet Union. They are capable of speeds in excess of 200 knots (370 km/h).

"Imagine the sudden revelation of a weapon that can suddenly go six times faster than its predecessors. The shock of such a breakthrough system would turn an entire field of warfare on its head, as potential adversaries scrambled to deploy countermeasures to a new weapon they are defenseless against. While a lull in great power competition delayed the impact of this new technology, the so-called 'supercavitating torpedo' may be about to take the world by storm."

[16]The Myasishchev M-55 (NATO reporting name: Mystic-B) is a high-altitude geophysical research aircraft developed by OKB Myasishchev in the Soviet Union, similar in mission to the Lockheed ER-2, but with a twin boom fuselage and tail surface design. It is a twin-engined development of the Myasishchev M-17 Stratosphera with a higher maximum take-off weight.

[17]Dave Majumdar, "The U.S. Navy's AEGIS Missile Defense vs. Russia's Supersonic Kh-31 Cruise Missile: Who Wins?" *The National Interest* (December 2016), http://nationalinterest.org/blog/the-buzz/the-us-navys-aegis-missile-defense-vs-russias-supersonic-kh-18662.

"The Russian Navy will be deploying Sukhoi Su-30SM Flanker-H fighters to its Baltic Fleet in 2017."

[18]The Kh-55 (Russian: X-55 is a Soviet/Russian subsonic air-launched cruise missile, designed by MKB Raduga. It has a range of up to 2,500 km (1,350 nmi) and can carry nuclear warheads. Kh-55 is launched exclusively from bomber aircraft and has spawned a number of conventionally armed variants mainly for tactical use, such as the Kh-65SE and Kh-SD, but only the Kh-101 and Kh-555 appear to have made it into service.

[19]Andrei Akulov, "Russian Iskander-M Missile System: Credible Deterrent," *Strategic Culture* (September 2016), http://www.strategic-culture.org/news/2016/09/19/russian-iskander-m-missile-system-credible-deterrent.html.

34 *Beleaguered Superpower: Biden's America Adrift*

to reconnaissance strike missions. The genstab (Russian General Staff) is promoting anti-satellite technologies for space wars.[20] Genstab analysts say that Russia will still have 3,000 "non-strategic" nuclear warheads,[21] and should be able to field 1,000 tactical nuclear weapons by 2020 (within the limits of the Strategic Offensive Arms Reduction Treaty and successor New START). Some even argue that Moscow has achieved nuclear superiority with its recent deployment of the hypersonic warhead "Object 4202."[22]

"The Iskander-M is a mobile short-range ballistic missile system designed to be used in theater level conflicts with an official range of up to 500 km (minimum-50 km) to comply with the limits of the INF Treaty. Highly mobile and stealth, it can hardly be detected even with the help of space reconnaissance assets."

[20]Weston Williams, "Russia Launches Anti-Satellite Weapon: A New Warfront in Space?" *Christian Science Monitor* (December 22, 2016), http://www.csmonitor.com/USA/Military/2016/1222/Russia-launches-anti-satellite-weapon-A-new-warfront-in-space.

"It was the fifth time the weapon, a PL-19 Nudol missile, had been tested. Some military analysts have expressed concern over the test, saying that it was a provocative demonstration of Moscow's might on a relatively new military frontier: outer space. But they suggest that it's more about Russian posturing than an imminent threat."

[21]Amy F. Woolf, "Nonstrategic Nuclear Weapons," *Congressional Research Service* (February 2017), https://fas.org/sgp/crs/nuke/RL32572.pdf.

"Estimates vary, but experts believe Russia still has between 1,000 and 6,000 warheads for nonstrategic nuclear weapons in its arsenal."

[22]Scott Ritter, "The U.S.–Russia Nuclear Arms Race is Over, and Russia has Won," *Newsweek* (April 2017), http://www.newsweek.com/us-russia-nuclear-arms-race-over-and-russia-has-won-581704.

"'Object 4202' was a new kind of weapon, a hypersonic warhead capable of speeds 15 times the speed of sound, and capable of evading any anti-missile system the United States has today, or may develop and deploy for decades to come. While the October 26 test used an older RS-26 intercontinental ballistic missile (ICBM) as the launch vehicle, 'Object 4202' will ultimately be carried on a newer ICBM, the RS-28. The RS-28 is itself a wonder of modern technology, capable of flying in excess of five times the speed of sound, altering its trajectory to confuse anti-missile radars, and delivering 15 independently targetable nuclear warheads (each one 10 times as powerful as the bombs the United States dropped on Japan at the end of World War II) or three 'Object 4202' hypersonic warheads, which destroy their targets through kinetic energy (i.e., through impact). A nuclear warhead-armed RS-28 would take about 30 minutes to reach the United States from a silo in central Russia; its warheads would be capable of destroying an area about the size of Texas."

Russia 35

Russia moreover is revamping its tank armies, replacing the fourth generation T-90 main battle tank with a far superior T-14 Armata scheduled for 2025.[23] In 2012, President Vladimir Putin announced a plan to build 51 modern ships and 24 submarines by 2020. Of the 24 submarines, 16 will be nuclear powered. On January 10, 2013, the Russian Navy accepted its first new Borei class SSBN (Yury Dolgorukiy) for service. A second Borei (Aleksandr Nevskiy) entered service on December 21, 2013, and the Kremlin commissioned a third Borei class boat (Vladimir Monomakh) in late 2014. It launched the more advanced Borei II in 2017.[24] On March 1, 2018, President Vladimir Putin announced six new Russian strategic weapons including the Sarmat ICBM. It is a liquid-fueled, MIRV-equipped, super-heavy thermonuclear armed intercontinental ballistic missile. Its large payload of about 10 tons accommodates 10 heavy MIRV warheads, or up to 24 Avangard hypersonic glide vehicles. The Samrat is equipped with countermeasures designed to defeat anti-missile systems and is billed as an invincible response to the US Prompt Global Strike.[25]

The US Defense department revealed in January 2018 that Russia tested an unmanned undersea vehicle capable of delivering a nuclear weapon. The Status-6 can be launched from at least two different classes of nuclear submarines. The Oscar-class can carry four Status-6 drones at a time. The drone has a range of 6,200 miles, a top speed in excess of 56 knots and can descend to depths of 3,280 feet below sea level.[26]

---

[23]Keir Giles, "Assessing Russia's Reorganized and Rearmed Military," *Carnegie Foundation for Peace* (May 2017), http://carnegieendowment.org/2017/05/03/assessing-russia-s-reorganized-and-rearmed-military-pub-69853?mkt_tok=eyJpIjoiT0dZMFlUWXpZalEzTWpKaSIsInQiOiJOdkVISXZcLzA4UkhwNEZGaFROd0ZWSlllRjNVazBkVXM5dU12S05QZFlSWlhMZHZFVFRHQWtHTDJrWXdKM3FqaU5NYW9jcGVuZXVRT0tQUnZCMW1UemhyZXNYNWX12REdieXJFam1zSDdjMGtnN0lCRFI3ZWxnbVVvZ0tLMjhxRkuUifQ%3D%3D. The T-14 Armata (Russian: T-14 «Армата») is a Russian main battle tank based on the Armata Universal Combat Platform. It is the first series-produced next generation tank.

[24]Franz-Stefan Gady, "Russia to Launch Its Most Powerful Ballistic Missile Sub in November," *The Diplomat* (October 2017), https://thediplomat.com/2017/10/russia-to-launch-its-most-powerful-ballistic-missile-sub-in-november/.

[25]"Putin: Russia Creates Advanced Weapons Responding to US Scrapping Missile Treaty," *Sputnik* (March 1, 2018).

[26]Valery Insinna, "Russia's Nuclear Underwater Drone Is Real And In the Nuclear Posture Review," *Defense News* (January 12, 2018), https://www.defensenews.com/

36 *Beleaguered Superpower: Biden's America Adrift*

Experts relying on unclassified official Western and Kremlin sources broadly acknowledge that Russia's full spectrum defense modernization has succeeded,[27] allowing it to challenge the North Atlantic Treaty Organization (NATO) along its eastern frontier and contested buffer states,[28] even though weapon and troop counts on both sides have diminished.[29] The Rand

---

space/2018/01/12/russias-nuclear-underwater-drone-is-real-and-in-the-nuclear-posture-review/?mkt_tok=eyJpIjoiT1RKaVptSmxabVZrWlRRNCIsInQiOiJCVnNTbnRQVGJPZ jk3THFjdVZ6QlZuMm9QeDhiVVZCY0xVb29mUVJkNmlTVnIwOWVJa1hVe-FlCTEV4UUFVOVBxWUJ5bkM5UTN2b2o0Y2ZPT2VQRTZ3bnM3cUdiNU5kMzM-1bllcL0M5SlhPbldtb3VnMWFWMUllQlwvUm9Sa1pHa0xpIn0%3D.

[27] Keir Giles, "Assessing Russia's Reorganized and Rearmed Military," *Carnegie Foundation for Peace* (May 2017), http://carnegieendowment.org/2017/05/03/assessing-russia-s-reorganized-and-rearmed-military-pub-69853?mkt_tok=eyJpIjoiT0dZMFlUWXpZa 1EzTWpKaSIsInQiOiJOdkVISXZcLzA4UkhwNEZGaFROd0ZWSl1 1RjNVazBkVXM5dU12S05QZFlSWlhMZHZFVFRHQWtHTDJrWXdK M3FqaU5NYW9jcGVuZXVRT0tQUnZCMW1UemhyZXY1NXl2REdieXJ Fam1zSDdjMGtnN0lCRFI3ZWxnbVlvZ0tLMjhxRkUifQ%3D%3D.

Cf. Valeriy Gerasimov, "The World on the Verge of War" [in Russian], *Voyenno-promyshlennyy kuryer* (March 15, 2017), http://vpk-news.ru/articles/35591. Cf. Aleksandr V. Rogovoy and Keir Giles, *A Russian View of Land Power* (Cambridge, UK: Conflict Studies Research Center, December 2014), http://amzn.to/2mJCS8l.

"For the time being, despite focus in the West on the 'hybrid' and 'nonlinear' aspects of state competition, the conclusion in Russia appears to be that the importance of high-intensity warfare remains undiminished, and that strategic deterrence with nuclear weapons and updated air and missile assets, supported by strong and capable land forces, will continue to play a fundamental role in securing state interests."

[28] Richard Sokolsky, "The New NATO-Russia Military Balance: Implications for European Security," *Carnegie Endowment for Peace* (March 2017), http://carnegieendowment. org/2017/03/13/new-nato-russia-military-balance-implications-for-european-security-pub-68222.

"Twenty-five years after the end of the Cold War, the military balance between NATO and Russia, after years of inattention, has again become the focus of intense concern and even alarm in some Western quarters."

[29] Nikolai Sokov, "Russia's New Conventional Capability: Implications for Eurasia and Beyond," *Ponars Eurasia* (April 2017). Igor Sutyagin, "The Russian Military Build-Up: Features, Limits, and Implications for International Security," *Royal United Services Institute (RUSI)*, forthcoming.Aleksandr Golts, "Rehearsals for War," *ECFR*, July 6, 2016, bit.ly/29ydCOY.

"A closer look at the new Russian capability suggests deficiencies in NATO planning (at least when it comes to publicly available information). NATO planning — for example,

Corporation concurs.[30] The real danger is probably far greater. CIA estimates during the Cold War seriously underestimated Soviet capabilities,[31] and Vitaly Shlykov former co-Chairman of the Russian Defense Council has insisted that little has changed.[32]

---

regarding the defence of the Baltic states (as with deployment of a few additional battalions and predeployment of heavy equipment) — seems to be predicated on the assumption that Russia will employ the same tactics that it used in Ukraine. NATO's other scenario is an invasion by Russian troops across Poland's Suwalki gap — in effect, a copy of the Cold War scenario of an invasion through Germany's Fulda gap. These scenarios appear to overlook Russia's capability to reach targets not only in the Baltic States or Poland, but literally across Europe, without Russian troops crossing borders, giving it a capability to disrupt NATO reinforcements, communications, and strike assets. These strikes can be launched from airborne platforms, from nuclear powered attack submarines, and even from SLCM-carrying diesel submarines in the Black Sea, whose range reaches to London."

[30] Scott Boston and Dara Massicot, "The Russian Way of Warfare a Primer," *Rand Corporation* (2017), https://www.rand.org/pubs/perspectives/PE231.html.

"Russia has recently carried out substantial reforms to its military forces, increasing capability in several key areas. Russia's military has improved to the extent that it is now a reliable instrument of national power that can be used in a limited context to achieve vital national interests. Russian strategists, concerned about the capability of an advanced military adversary to carry out a large-scale conventional aerospace campaign against the Russian heartland, focus on preserving Russian influence in buffer states along its borders and on reinforcing a series of defensive bulwarks. Russian operations will show a high degree of coordination across a wide range of military units, using deception and simultaneity to achieve objectives quickly and minimize periods of vulnerability to an adversary's most dangerous capabilities. Russian tactics will continue to heavily emphasize gaining and maintaining fire superiority over an adversary; leveraging improved ISR capabilities and a wide range of fires platforms; and using speed, surprise, and integrated combined arms in maneuver forces to disrupt and overwhelm enemies once encountered."

[31] Steven Rosefielde, *False Science: Underestimating the Soviet Arms Buildup* (New Brunswick: Transaction, 1987). Steven Rosefielde, *Russia in the 21st Century: The Prodigal Superpower* (Cambridge: Cambridge University Press, 2005). Steven Rosefielde, *The Kremlin Strikes Back: Russia and the West after Crimea's Annexation* (Cambridge: Cambridge University Press, 2017).

[32] Steven Rosefielde, *Russia in the 21st Century: The Prodigal Superpower* (Cambridge: Cambridge University Press, 2005): 52–53.

In a direct response to the proceedings of the conference entitled the CIA's Analysis of the Soviet Union 1947–1991, held a Princeton University on March 9 and 10, 2001, Shlykov declared that the entire American intelligence community, including Team B,

38 Beleaguered Superpower: Biden's America Adrift

Most Western analysts, however, take Russia's impressive military modernization surge 2010–2015 in stride, viewing it as insufficient. Some plausibly caution that gains are less than meets the eye.[33] They insist, without adequate theoretical and empirical support, that the Kremlin lacks the financial resources to continue its arms buildup, the economy is moribund, and the regime's days are numbered. They misjudge the sources of modern economic growth, forgetting that the Kremlin does not have to rely on the official budget to mobilize resources for defense. It has a concealed black budget and more than ample foreign currency reserves ($566 billion in May 2020). Soviet defense budgetary outlays barely covered a tenth of the Kremlin's officially published military expenditures. The CIA's budget is invisible in America's national budget. If the Soviets did, and Washington can hide portions of their defense activities in their official budgets, so can the Russians.

Putin provided partial confirmation that the Kremlin can and will continue its arms modernization program by announcing a new cruise missile aimed at US vulnerabilities.[34] His long-awaited State Armaments Program (GPV) 2018–27, signed February 28, 2018 and announced by Russian Deputy Prime Minister Dmitry Rogozin adds further credence to the possibility. In January 2018, the Russian Ministry of Defense (MoD) confirmed that a total of RUB20 trillion ($357 billion) would be allocated for implementation of the GPV-2027. Of that total, RUB19 trillion will be spent on the development, procurement, and repair of military equipment,

---

miscounted weapons, underestimated programs, under appraised costs, and misgauged the sustained mobilization capacity of the Soviet System. Data on Soviet weapons production remain secret, scattered, but declassified published statistics show that the United States more often underestimated, rather than overestimated the size of the Soviet Union's military arsenal. For example, the Americans believed that the Soviet Union deployed 30,000 nuclear weapons and had 500–600 tons of enriched uranium. But in reality, the figure was 45,000 weapons and 1,200 tons, according to Viktor Mikhailov, former Russian Minister of Atomic energy. The Americans were also mistaken about Soviet tank inventories. They thought that the USSR had a little more than 50,000 tanks, at a time when it had 64,000 or even 68,000 according to another source.

[33] Julian Cooper, "Russia's Invincible Weapons: Today, Tomorrow, Sometime, Never?" *CCW* (May 2018), http://www.ccw.ox.ac.uk/blog/2019/3/27/russias-invincible-weapons-an-update-by-julian-cooper.

[34] Neil MacFarquhar and David Sanger, "'Invincible' Missile is Aimed at U.S. Vulnerabilities," *New York Times* (March 1, 2018), https://www.nytimes.com/2018/03/01/world/europe/russia-putin-speech.html.

with the remaining RUB1 trillion used for the construction of related infrastructure.

The main emphasis of the new program is the development of nuclear systems, in addition to high-precision aerospace and ground-to-ground weapons. Also planned is the development of a vertical/short take-off aircraft in conjunction with a new generation aircraft carrier. Other programs include the Armata main battle tank and the Su-57 fighter. By 2021, 70 percent of Russian forces' weapons and equipment will be of the latest design. This target is broadly a restatement of the modernization goal initially established under the 2011–2020 GPV.[35]

Financial stringency thus does not appear severe enough to justify the presumption that Russia's impressive military modernization surge 2010–2015 and subsequent developments are a flash-in-the- pan, nor that it is prudent to suppose that the Kremlin's bark is worse than its bite because the regime is afflicted with a host of insoluble problems. It is premature to judge the sustained effects of COVID-19 on Russia economic potential 2020–2027.

The Soviet planned economy was far less efficient than Russia's contemporary mixed market and Muscovite rent granting system (see Appendix). The Bolsheviks criminalized entrepreneurship, stifled innovation, suppressed market-driven technological progress and quality change. The USSR thwarted the allocation of resources to best use, under-reward labor, and rationed consumer goods. Nonetheless, it managed to achieve substantial military industrial and civilian economic growth both before and after World War II.

Putin has built a better mousetrap. His economy is anti-competitive, rent seeking, and kleptocratic in various regards as critics allege. These deficiencies diminish military economic and civilian economic growth potential, but do not in and of themselves bar sustained military industrial growth or improved living standards. No scientific basis exists for claiming that Russia will underperform the Soviet benchmark; that the Kremlin's economic system prevents it from giving Biden's West a run for its money.

Likewise, while experts have grounds for taking a dim view of Russia's future,[36] similar misgivings in the past have not proven to be reliable predictors. Putin's regime is a "velvet" authoritarian martial police

---

[35] Bruce Jones and Craig Caffrey, "Putin Signs New State Armaments Programme," *Jane's Defense Weekly* (February 2018), http://janes.ihs.com/Janes/Display/FG_749810-JDW.

[36] Greg Butterfield, "Behind the Pension Crisis in Russia," *Workers World* (September 1, 2018), https://www.workers.org/2018/09/01/behind-the-pension-crisis-in-russia/.

40 *Beleaguered Superpower: Biden's America Adrift*

state. It is milder than the world Arthur Koestler portrayed in *Darkness at Noon*.[37] Its parliamentary democracy is more open than Stalin's so-called proletarian democracy. Dissent is permissible, citizens can travel easily at home and abroad, people have significant economic, cultural, and religious liberty. Police controls are relatively mild, penal incarceration is normal by past standards, and state terror is sparing. Velvet authoritarianism is vulnerable, but not enough to assume that the siloviki (power services),[38] or popular unrest will unseat Putin any time soon.

Furthermore, while some are predicting that changing demographics and Russian Orthodox religious populism imperil the federation's social and political stability, tectonic shifts need not be fatal.[39] Populations are shrinking, Moslem minorities are increasing, and populism is rising in many countries in Europe causing serious, but still manageable stresses. European Union leaders deny that declining populations and a burgeoning Moslem presence are harbingers of destruction. The assessment of Russia's future similarly deserve assessment with an open mind. The conviction that Russia's illiberal political and social order can neither long endure, nor pose a lasting threat to the West runs deep in Washington's psyche. However, this faith is insufficient to deter Russia's expansion, or prevent the outbreak of war.[40]

The Little Engine That Could

The Obama–Biden administration could not bring itself to take the Russian threat seriously.[41] It contended that Crimea's annexation was

---

[37] Arthur Koestler, *Darkness at Noon* (London: Macmillan, 1940).

[38] Peter Reddaway, *Russia's Domestic Security Wars: Putin's Use of Divide and Rule Against His Hardline Allies* (Cham: Palgrave Macmillan, 2018).

[39] Michael Zygar, *The Empire must die: Russia's Revolutionary Collapse, 1900–1917*, November 7, 2017. Nicholas Petro, "The Russian Orthodox Church," in Andrei P. Tsygankov, ed., *Routledge Handbook of Russian Foreign Policy* (London: Routledge, 2018): 217–232. Nicholas Petro, "The Russian Orthodox Church," in Andrei P. Tsygankov, ed., *Routledge Handbook of Russian Foreign Policy* (London: Routledge, 2018): 217–232.

[40] Stephen Blank, "Can Russia Sustain Its Defense Buildup?" in Steven Rosefielde, ed., *Putin's Russia: Economic, Political and Military Foundations* (Singapore: World Scientific Publishers, 2019).

[41] Joshua Keating, "Russia Resurgent," *Slate* (January 2017), http://www.slate.com/articles/news_and_politics/cover_story/2017/01/how_vladimir_putin_engineered_russia_s_return_to_global_power.html.

Russia 41

temporary, that Russia could not defeat America in Syria, modernize its armed forces enough to cause concern, and sustain any advantage if it did.[42]

These positions may seem plausible to casual observers. America's GDP in 2017 was 4.8 times larger than Russia's computed on a purchasing power parity basis,[43] and 13.2 times greater valued at the market exchange rate. Russia's per capita GDP in 2017 was 47 percent of America computed on a purchasing power parity basis, and a mere 17 percent valued at the market exchange rate.[44] American and Russian economic growth

---

"The Russians can't change us or significantly weaken us," Barack Obama said on December 16, during his final press conference as president. "They are a smaller country. They are a weaker country. Their economy doesn't produce anything that anybody wants to buy, except oil and gas and arms. They don't innovate. But they can impact us if we lose track of who we are. They can impact us if we abandon our values." "The theme of the second, as relations between Washington and Moscow deteriorated sharply following Vladimir Putin's return in 2012, has been dismissal bordering on mockery. The only thing we have to fear from Russia, the president seemed to argue, is the fear of Russia itself."

Cf. Julian Borger, "Barack Obama: Russia is a Regional Power Showing Weakness over Ukraine," *Guardian* (March 25, 2014), https://www.theguardian.com/world/2014/mar/25/barack-obama-russia-regional-power-ukraine-weakness.

"Speaking at the end of a summit on nuclear security in The Hague, Obama rejected the suggestion made by Mitt Romney — his Republican challenger in the last president election — that Russia was the United States' principal geopolitical foe. The president said he was considerably more concerned about the threat of a terrorist nuclear bomb attack on New York."

[42]Nikolai Sokov, "Russia's New Conventional Capability: Implications for Eurasia and Beyond," *Ponars Eurasia* (April 2017).

"Paradoxically, the greatest challenge to the interests of the United States and its allies is not the new Russian capability itself but rather Washington's state of denial regarding its strategic implications. Few in Washington seem prepared, psychologically and politically, to accept that Russia's demonstration of its newly acquired conventional capability amounts to: (1) the eventual loss of the West's monopoly on the proactive use of force in support of foreign policy; (2) changes in the nature of the global 'game'; and (3) the need to adjust global and regional strategies. Moscow's disruption of Washington's Syria strategy should be a tangible warning about the future."

[43]CIA, *The World Factbook: Russia.*

[44]CIA, *The World Factbook: Russia.*

42   *Beleaguered Superpower: Biden's America Adrift*

2008–2017, moreover, both were close to zero. America's growth has outpaced Russia's thereafter.

However, the Obama–Biden administration's supposition that Russia's military power could not keep pace with America's has proven erroneous. Russia has shown itself to be the "little engine that could."[45] It not only managed to increase weapons procurement at double-digit rates during 2010–2015 but the Kremlin also modernized its arsenal against the odds in the face of a catastrophic fall in natural resource prices and Western economic sanctions. The "little engine that could" disproved Doubting Thomas in 1917, 1941, 1949, 1951, 2000, and 2014, and there have been no new developments to suggest that the Kremlin has exhausted its bag of miracles.

An authoritative inventory of Russia's military industrial accomplishments compiled by Julian Cooper for FOI (Swedish Defense Research Agency) confirms this claim and serves as a baseline.[46] Cooper's appendix contains a complete line item inventory of Russia's weapons acquisitions 2010–2015 for those desiring full documentation.

---

[45] Watty Piper, *The Little Engine That Could* (New York: Grosset & Dunlap, 2001).

The Little Engine That Could is the story of a long train that must be pulled over a high mountain. Larger engines, treated anthropomorphically, are asked to pull the train; for various reasons they refuse. The request is sent to a small engine, who agrees to try. The engine succeeds in pulling the train over the mountain while repeating its motto: "I-think-I-can."

[46] Julian Cooper, "Russia's State Armament Programme to 2020: A Quantitative Assessment of Implementation 2011–2015," *FOI* (March 2016).

"This report provides an overview of the implementation of the Russian state armament programme to 2020 as the end of its first five year approaches. It is an empirical study designed to present data that is not readily accessible to analysts."

Cf. Eugene Kogan, "Russian Military Capabilities," *Georgian Foundation for Strategic and International Studies* (2016).Mikhail Barabanov, "Testing a 'New Look', The Ukrainian Conflict and Military Reform in Russia," *Centre for Analysis of Strategies and Technologies (CAST)* (December 2014), www.cast.ru/eng/?id=578.

Bettina Renz, "Russian Military Capabilities after 20 Years of Reform," *Survival* 56, no. 3, June–July 2014: 61–84. Julian Cooper, "Prospects For Military Spending In Russia in 2017 and Beyond," (April 2017), http://www.birmingham.ac.uk/Documents/college-social-sciences/government-society/crees/working-papers/prospects-for-military-spending-in-Russia-in-2017-and-beyond.pdf.

Armament Program for Russia for the years 2011–2020

The achievement Cooper documents was not serendipitous.[47] It was the consequence of well-conceived plans designed to restore Russia's great power status. These include the Reform and Development of the Defense Industrial Complex Program 2002–2006 signed by Prime Minister Mikhail Kasyanov in October 2001,[48] and the State Armament Programme (Gosudarstvennaia Programma Vooruzhenii) for Russia for the years 2011–2020 signed by President Dmitri Medvedev at the end of 2010.[49] The Russian State Armament Programme, 2011–2020 has two sources of support: (1) the FTSP Development of the defense–industrial complex, 2011–2020 [fderalnye tselevye progammy (Federal Targeted Programs)], and (2) the FTSP Development, restoration, and organization of the production of strategic scarce and import substituting materials and small-scale chemistry for armaments, military and special technology in 2009–2011 and the subsequent period to 2015 (inter-industrial supply). These programs underscore the fact that the Russian State Armament Program is more than a procurement policy. It entails the reform of the VPK and defense inter-industrial supply.

---

[47] Alexander Golts, *Military Reform and Militarism in Russia* (Washington: Jamestown Foundation, 2019).

[48] Cf. Vitaly Shlykov, "Russian Defense Industrial Complex after 9–11," *Russian Security Policy and the War on Terrorism* (June 2002).

The author possesses a signed copy of the unpublished program summary. The document reveal that the Kremlin intended to more toward reconsolidation of state authority, driven in part by the aging of the OPK's capital stock, underemployment, low pay, and poor enterprise finances.

For a discussion of earlier reforms, Alexei Izyumov, Leonid Kosals, and Rosalina Ryvkina, "Privatisation of the Russian Defense Industry: Ownership and Control Issues," *Post-Communist Economies* 12, no. 4, 2001: 485–496. Alexei Izyumov, Leonid Kosals, and Rosalina Ryvkina, "Defense Industrial Transformation in Russia: Evidence from a Longitudinal Survey," *Post-Communist Economies* 12, no. 2, 2001: 215–227.

[49] Julian Cooper, "Russia's State Armament Programme to 2020: A Quantitative Assessment of Implementation 2011–2015," *FOI* 13, March 2016: 28–31.

"It is a highly classified document in twelve sections. Ten are devoted to particular services of the MOD — ground forces, navy, air force, etc. — one to all other forces and one (the tenth) to R&D relating to the development of armaments — fundamental, exploratory and Applied." "Total funding is usually given as 20.7 trillion roubles."

44   *Beleaguered Superpower: Biden's America Adrift*

Cooper summarizes the program and its accomplishments through 2015 as follows:

> "This was a highly ambitious document setting out plans for the procurement of weapons and other military equipment, plus research and development for the creation of new systems, to a total value of over 20 trillion rubles, or US$680 billion at the exchange rate of the day. The aim of the program was to increase the share of modern armaments held by the armed forces from 15 per cent in 2010 to 30 percent in 2015 and 70 per cent in 2020. The annual state defense budget funded program, supplemented by state guaranteed credits. By 2014, the military output of the defense industrial sector was growing at an annual rate of over 20 percent, compared with 6 percent three years earlier. The volume of new weapons procured steadily increased, the rate of renewal being particularly strong in the strategic missile forces and the air force, but not as impressive in the navy and ground forces. In 2014, the Ukraine crisis slowed weapons production with a breakdown of military-related deliveries from Ukraine and the imposition of sanctions by NATO and European Union member countries. The performance of the economy began to deteriorate, putting pressure on state finances, and postponing the approval of the successor state armament programme, 2016–2025 by three years. Nevertheless, the programme to date has achieved meaningfully modernized the hardware of the Russian armed forces for the first time since the final years of the USSR."[50]

Insofar as Cooper is correct,[51] despite the petroleum price bust and adverse consequences of the global financial crisis of 2008, Russia not only succeeded in augmenting the size of its arsenal, but it significantly

---

[50] Cf. Richard Connolly and Cecilie Sendstad, "Russian Rearmament: An Assessment of Defense-Industrial Performance," *Problems of Post Communism* (October 2016), http://dx.doi.org/10.1080/10758216.2016.1236668.

[51] Steven Rosefielde, *Kremlin Strikes Back: Russia and the West after Crimea's Annexation* (Cambridge: Cambridge University Press, 2016); Michael Ellman, "Russia's Current Economic System: From Delusion to Glasnost," *Comparative Economic Studies* (2015): 1–18. cf. Gustav Gressel, "Russia's Quiet Military Revolution, and What It Means for Europe," *European Council on Foreign Relations (ECFR)* (December 2015), http://www.isn.ethz.ch/Digital-Library/Articles/Detail/?id=195415.

modernized its armed forces.[52] Masaaki Kuboniwa has independently confirmed Cooper's findings,[53] and Eugene Kogan concurs.[54] The quantitative improvement may be partly attributable to restarting existing weapon production lines with negligible systemic implications (economic recovery), but modernization is another story. It demonstrates that Russia's post-communist economy, like its Soviet predecessor is capable of manufacturing large quantities of technologically improved weapons systems.

Russia's New Market Fueled VPK

The latest success of the "little engine that could" is attributable in large part to a quantum improvement in Russia's military industrial system and economy achieved after the 2008 global financial crisis. The Kremlin embedded competitive markets inside the VPK (Military Industrial Complex; Voennyi Promyshlennyi Kompleks pri Pravitel'stve Rossiiskoi Federatsii). The literature provides a clear, if incomplete, picture of what has transpired. First, after Yeltsin's experiment with privatization, the VPK and closely associated "strategic enterprises" like Transneft, Gazprom, Rosneftegaz, Alrosa were renationalized in 2004. Initially, state ownership included some private shareholding

---

[52] Bryan Bender, "The Secret U.S. Army Study that Targets Moscow," *Politico* (April 2016), http://www.politico.com/magazine/story/2016/04/moscow-pentagon-us-secret-study-213811.

Lieutenant General H.R. McMaster told the Senate Armed Services committee last week that "in Ukraine, the combination of unmanned aerial systems and offensive cyber and advanced electronic warfare capabilities depict a high degree of technological sophistication."

Keir Giles, "Assessing Russia's Reorganized and Rearmed Military," *Carnegie Endowment of International Peace and Chicago Council* on Global Affairs (May 2017), http://carnegieendowment.org/specialprojects/taskforceonuspolicytowardrussiaukraine andeurasia/all/1546?lang=en&pageOn=1.

[53] Masaaki Kuboniwa, "Weapons Growth," in Steven Rosefielde, ed., *Putin's Russia: Economic, Political and Military Foundations* (Singapore: World Scientific Publishers, 2020).

[54] Eugene Kogan, "Russian Military Capabilities," *Georgian Foundation for Strategic and International Studies* (2016).

46 Beleaguered Superpower: Biden's America Adrift

participation, but now 100 percent state proprietorship is the norm.[55] However, unlike Soviet arrangements and as in Xi Jinping's market communist China, state ownership does not bar VPK enterprises or public–private partnerships (PPP) from competing among each other.[56] Military industrial firms (including holding companies) operate on a for-profit basis. They compete for state orders and foreign sales and can outsource. Shareholders and/or managers are incentivized to profit-seek and incompletely profit-maximize rather than comply with MOD commands and/or rent-seek. Although, they have fewer degrees of freedom than oligopolistic private Western defense corporations they are self-motivated to produce efficiently in accordance with Herbert Simon's bounded rationality and William Baumol's satisficing concepts.[57] This bolstered VPK initiative when the MOD stopped prioritizing military R&D after 2008. Weapon producers could have feigned production growth, continued rent seeking, and lived passively off state funds. This may have been the most likely outcome, but Putin beat the odds by imposing strict discipline and containing rent seeking, buttressed with competitive reforms and material incentives. No one denies that rent seeking persists, nor the latent threat that kleptocratic corruption poses to Russia's military industrial revival.[58] The system could relapse into indolence when Putin's fourth presidential term expires in 2024,[59] but Russia's new market powered VPK means that sustainable Russian military modernization is also a distinct possibility. Military spending is set to continue rising through 2020.[60]

---

[55]Carsten Sprenger, "State-Owned Enterprises in Russia Presentation at the OECD Roundtable on Corporate Governance of SOEs," Moscow (October 27), https://www.oecd.org/corporate/ca/corporategovernanceprinciples/42576825.pdf.

[56]Yiyi Liu and Steven Rosefielde, "Public Private Partnerships: Antidote for Secular Stagnation?" in Steven Rosefielde, Masaaki Kuboniwa, Satoshi Mizobata, and Kumiko Haba, eds., *The Unwinding of the Globalist Dream: EU, Russia, China* (Singapore: World Scientific Publishers, 2017).

[57]William Baumol, *Business Behavior, Value and Growth* (New York: Macmillan, 1959).

[58]Karen Dawisha, *Putin's Kleptocracy Who Owns Russia?* (New York: Simon & Schuster, 2014).

[59]Putin declared May 2018 that he would not seek a fifth presidential term in 2024. *Novosti RT*, March 25, 2018.

[60]Sergey Zhavoronkov, "Two Lean Years: Russia's Budget for 2018–2020," *Russia File* (December 8, 2017).

Russia's New Market Powered Civilian Economy

There is another justification for the national security community's conviction that the "little engine that could" is doomed to fail. Radical progressives, progressive, and centrist liberals contend that Russia's civilian economy cannot provide enough prosperity to support the Kremlin's great power agenda. Some assert that Russia is a "virtual economy" where requisitioning and rationing are in command, despite the rhetoric of market transition (*perekhod*).[61] Others contend that the dead hand of the Tsarist past continues to plague the federation's civilian sector; that Russian "capitalism" is a "neo-feudal" kleptocracy suffocating market forces.[62]

Both claims contain elements of truth. The first was valid in the 1990s before market institutions were firmly rooted,[63] but is now obsolete.

---

[61] Clifford G. Gaddy and Barry W. Ickes, "Russia's Virtual Economy," *Foreign Affairs* (September/October 1998): 53–67. Clifford G. Gaddy and Barry W. Ickes, *Russia's Virtual Economy* (Washington: Brookings Institution Press, 2002). Clifford G. Gaddy, "Russia's Virtual Economy," *Brookings* (February 2008). Daniel Treisman, "Inter-enterprise Arrears and Barter in the Russian Economy," *PostSoviet-Affairs* 16, no. 3, July–September 2000: 225–256.

[62] Anders Aslund, "Russia's Neo-Feudal Capitalism," *Project Syndicate* (April 2017), https://www.project-syndicate.org/commentary/russia-neofeudal-capitalism-putin-by-anders-aslund-2017-04. Anders Aslund, *How Russia Became a Market Economy* (Washington: Brookings Institution Press, 1995). Anders Aslund, *Building Capitalism: The Transformation of the Former Soviet Bloc* (New York: Cambridge University Press, 2001). Anders Aslund, *How Capitalism Was Built: The Transformation of Central and Eastern Europe, Russia, and Central Asia* (New York: Cambridge University Press, 2007). Anders Aslund, *Russia's Capitalist Revolution: Why Market Reform Succeeded and Democracy Failed* (Washington: Peterson Institute for International Economics, 2007). Andrei Shleifer and Robert Vishny, *The Grabbing Hand: Government Pathologies and Their Cures* (Cambridge: MIT Press, 2000).

"Vladimir Putin's Russia is looking more and more like the sclerotic and stagnant Soviet Union of the Leonid Brezhnev era. But in one area, Putin's regime remains an innovator: corruption. Indeed, in this, the 18th year of Putin's rule, a new form of crony capitalism has been taking hold."

[63] Steven Rosefielde, *Russian Economy From Lenin to Putin* (New York: Wiley, 2007). Steven Rosefielde and Stefan Hedlund, *Russia Since 1980: Wrestling With Westernization* (Cambridge: Cambridge University Press, 2008).

48 *Beleaguered Superpower: Biden's America Adrift*

The second is a plausible characterization. However, it mis-states the economic potential of Russia's neo-Muscovite (Ivan the Great) model.[64]

Russia today is a managed mixed market-rent granting economy. Putin has blended elements of the Tsarist and Soviet power vertical to create an authoritarian guided system commanded by a "vozhd" and his servitors at the top, and oligarchs below. The state owns the nation's natural resources, the military industrial means of production and supportive industries operated *de facto* on a leasehold basis. It owned 43.8 percent of the nation's assets in 2017, up from 31.2 percent in 2000.[65] Small and medium-sized enterprises are privately owned freeholds or leaseholds. Entrepreneurship is encouraged and small and medium-sized firms are workably competitive,[66] however, most large-scale production operates on a rent-granting basis by the regime's servitors in the Muscovite tradition. The *vozhd* (leader) grants "oligarchs" lucrative, semi-competitive state contracts and monopolies in return for services rendered. Unlike the United States, Russia's system directors view the "toiling masses" favorably, providing them with an adequate social safety net. The state manages its finances prudently, and the regime encourages economic growth and stability, displaying little sympathy for revolutionary progressive causes.[67]

State institutions provide public services and regulate, but mostly in the interest of Putin, the power services and oligarchs rather than the public good. These insiders run the government for their own benefit (authoritarian sovereignty rather than consumer sovereignty). They enrich

---

The transfer of state property to private hands was chaotic. Barter was ubiquitous. Wage arrears to workers were immense. There was no effective rule of law to support contracts and their enforcement. Workers and managers vied for enterprise control. Soviet era products were uncompetitive, but managers had no experience satisfying consumer demand. Credit was scarce and inflation ran in the triple and quadruple digits.

[64] Steven Rosefielde, "Russian Military, Political and Economic Reform: Can the Kremlin Placate Washington?" *U.S. Army War College, Carlisle Barracks* (May 2014).

[65] Michael Alexeev, paper presented at the ASEEES conference panel "Two Decades of Russia's Economic Policies: 2000–2020," (November 15, 2000). Alexeev did not define state assets.

[66] John Maurice Clark, "Toward a Concept of Workable Competition," *American Economic Review* 30, no. 2, 1940: 241–256. John Maurice Clark, *Competition as a Dynamic Process* (Washington: Brookings Institution, 1961).

[67] Steven Rosefielde, "Putin's Muscovite Economy" in Steven Rosefielde, ed., *Putin's Russia: Economic, Political and Military Foundations* (Singapore: World Scientific Publishers, 2020): Chapter 1.

Russia 49

themselves with unearned income that economists call rents and corrupt asset transfers (hence the term kleptocrats). The system is inherently unjust from a competitive economic perspective because income depends on connections and insider power rather than consumer sovereign value added.[68]

Nonetheless, the allocation of resources, choice of technologies, enterprise management, and finance can be efficient in unjust economic systems, given the prevailing distribution of income, wealth, and power.[69] It behooves Putin, the power services, and oligarchs to make Russia's managed mixed economy efficient and productive for their own benefit, a goal accomplished by encouraging competitive profit-seeking, labor mobility and full employment outside privileged circles to the extent that they are compatible with insider enrichment.

Putin, the power services and oligarchs do not have to act like the ruthless capitalists caricaturized by Karl Marx in *Das Kapital*. They need not drive wages to the subsistence level, and have chosen not to do so, leaving enough on the table to increase general well-being and promote regime loyalty.[70]

The improvement is visible to the naked eye and confirmed by World Bank assessments.[71] Living conditions today are manifestly better than they were during the Soviet era, and Yeltsin's *katakhod* (catastrophic

---

[68] Abram Bergson, "A Reformulation of Certain Aspects of Welfare Economics," *Quarterly Journal of Economics* 52, no. 1, February 1938: 310–334. Steven Rosefielde and Ralph W. Pfouts, *Inclusive Economic Theory* (Singapore: World Scientific Publishers, 2013).

[69] Abram Bergson, "The Concept of Social Welfare," *Quarterly Journal of Economics* 68, no. 2, May 1954: 233–252. Leonid Vitaliyevich Kantorovich, *The Best Use of Economic Resources* (Cambridge: Harvard University Press, 1965).

[70] Benis Aris, "Over 80% of Russians are still satisfied with Putin's work," *Intellines News* (April 28, 2017), http://www.intellinews.com/over-80-of-russians-are-still-satisfied-with-putin-s-work-120382/?source=russia.

[71] World Bank, "Country Partnership Strategy (CPS) for the Russian Federation," Report No. 65115-RU, November 2011. Cf. Torbjorn Becker, "Russia's Macroeconomy — A Closer Look at Growth, Investment, and Uncertainty," in Steven Rosefielde ed., *Putin's Russia: Economic, Political and Military Foundations*, (Singapore: World Scientific Publishers, 2020).

Another version of the same document is entitled: Russian Federation — Country Partnership Strategy for the period 2012–2016 (English).

"Russia is a middle income country (MIC) that strives to move to a high income status. In the period since 2005, the per capita GDP of Russia doubled to approximately US$10,500 in 2010, and the country moved to an upper MIC status."

50 *Beleaguered Superpower: Biden's America Adrift*

transition). Russia is no longer Igor Birman's "economy of shortage."[72] Private cars congest an expanding network of highways; retails stores brim with desirable consumer goods, and service standards have risen. Andrei Shleifer and Daniel Treisman contend that Russia has become a "normal" middle-income country,[73] and the World Bank considers the Federation to be a high tier member of the developing nations club.[74] The change partly reflects the squalor of the Soviet and Yeltsin era consumer sector, but Russia's evolving managed mixed market arrangements also deserve credit, even though the exact magnitude of the improvement is not precisely measurable.[75]

Figure 3.1 illustrates the institutional characteristics of Putin's mixed economy in Soviet perspective.[76] The cornerstone of the figure is the Soviet command system. The chart divides the planned economy into three basic parts. There is a regulatory apparatus on the left, a command-planning-*khozraschyot* (enterprise self-financing) mechanism in the center, and an information retrieval and plan formation process on the right. Soviet administrative command planning in its literal form was a requisition and rationing model that excluded the *khozraschyot* (self-regulating) panel in the central branch of Figure 3.1, as well as regulatory aspects of the left-hand branch. However, in practice, it was a dual directive and enterprise incentive top-down regulated regime.

Central planning authorities and the system directors computed and approved plans that were legally binding on enterprise red directors

---

[72] Igor Birman, *Ekonomika Nedostach* (The Shortage Economy) (New York: Chalidize Publishing, 1983); Steven Rosefielde, "The Soviet Economy in Crisis: Birman's Cumulative Disequilibrium Hypothesis," *Soviet Studies* 40, no. 2, April 1988: 222–244.

[73] Andrei Shleifer and Daniel Treisman, "A Normal Country," *Foreign Affairs* 83, no. 2, March/April 2004: 20–39. Cf. Steven Rosefielde, "An Abnormal Country," *The European Journal of Comparative Economics* 2, no. 1, 2005: 3–16.

[74] Andrei Shleifer and Daniel Treisman, "A Normal Country," *Foreign Affairs* 83, no. 2, March/April 2004: 20–39. Cf. Steven Rosefielde, "An Abnormal Country," *The European Journal of Comparative Economics* 2, no. 1, 2005: 3–16.

[75] Steven Rosefielde, "Tea Leaves and Productivity: Bergsonian Norms for Gauging the Soviet Future," *Comparative Economic Studies* 47, no. 2, June 2005: 259–273. Steven Rosefielde, "The Riddle of Postwar Russian Economic Growth: Statistics Lied and Were Misconstrued," *Europe-Asia Studies* 55, no. 3, 2003: 469–481. Steven Rosefielde, *The Kremlin Strikes Back: Russia and the West after Crimea's Annexation* (Cambridge: Cambridge University Press, 2017).

[76] Steven Rosefielde, *Russian Economy from Lenin to Putin* (New York: Wiley, 2007).

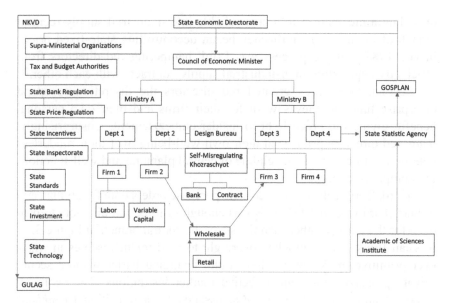

Figure 3.1   Soviet Institutional Foundations of Putin's Mixed Economy

(managers).[77] They served as a surrogate for Adam Smith's invisible hand. However, they could not direct resources to best use. Soviet systems directors knew this and sought to mitigate losses by requiring enterprises to cover their production costs (self-financing), and to harness manufacturing capacities by rewarding red directors for fulfilling and over-fulfilling plan directives. The regulatory apparatus on the left-hand side of Figure 3.1 set and enforced the rules governing *khozraschyot*-driven production.

The dual nature of the Soviet vertical control system made it easy to transition from a rudimentary mixed regulated-directive top-down economy into a managed mixed market and Muscovite rent-granting system. This occurred in five steps, obscured at the time by conflicting statements and patchy implementation. First, Mikhail Gorbachev abandoned coercive command planning in 1987 (right-hand branch of Figure 3.1), freeing red directors to disregard plan directives without

---

[77] Enterprise heads in the Soviet scheme were a mid-level link in the plan-implementation chain of command. The Soviet called them directors responsible for passing along plan assignments from the center to the enterprise staff. The word manager was reserved for "capitalist" CEOs.

52 Beleaguered Superpower: Biden's America Adrift

providing a mechanism to assure reliable inter-industrial supply (central branch of Figure 3.1). Gorbachev began decontrolling state-fixed prices in late 1987, but the process was fitful, hampering red directors from efficiently negotiating inter-industrial supply contracts with each other.[78]

Second, Gorbachev granted red directors the discretion to spend enterprise funds as they saw fit for their firms and their own personal benefit, giving the green light to insider embezzlement. Unsurprisingly, many red directors prioritized their own well-being over their rudderless enterprises, free from the discipline of central planning and well-functioning competitive markets.

Third, Boris Yeltsin canceled state purchase orders both for civilian and military hardware in 1992. This was enough to force red directors to produce for the market rather than the state (the central branch in Figure 3.1). Russian firms were compelled overnight to fend for themselves in whatever primitive market ways they could, including barter without secure private property rights and effective market institutions. The economy swooned into free fall 1990–1998, assailed by a transition (*perekhod*) induced hyper-depression, hyperinflation, financial crisis, and a massive ruble devaluation. Nearly 3.5 million Russians died prematurely.[79]

Fourth, it took the entire 1990s to put the administrative-regulatory, legal, and enterprise *khozraschyot* mechanisms on a workably competitive market basis with Muscovite characteristics (mixed state private ownership, rule of men, rent granting, kleptocracy, and corruption) viable enough for Russia to exit its "transitionary" hyper-depression. Fifth, Putin restored the "power vertical,"[80] and completed the process of regulatory institution building (the left-hand branch in Figure 3.1) in the early years of the new millennium. He created secure private and state property rights; improved contract enforcement under the rule of law, resuming large-scale state purchases with the revenue windfall occasioned by the 2001 oil price shock. Heeding the World Bank Group, Putin adopted sound structural reforms and macroeconomic management polices (the left-hand branch in Figure 3.1). These refinements were enough to tip the scales, allowing Russia to move

---

[78] CIA, "'Restructuring the Soviet Workplace': The New State Enterprise Law," *Directorate of Intelligence*, Washington, D.C. (May 1987), https://www.cia.gov/library/readingroom/docs/DOC_0000499785.pdf.

[79] Steven Rosefielde, "Premature Deaths: Russia's Radical Transition," *Europe-Asia Studies* 53, no. 8, December 2001: 1159–1176.

[80] Andrew Monaghan, "The Vertikal: Power and Authority in Russia," *International Affairs* 88, no. 1, January 1, 2012: 1–16, https://doi.org/10.1111/j.1468-2346.2012.01053.

beyond *katastroika* to a workably competitive, "neo-Muscovite,"[81] Kremlin "sovereign," mixed authoritarian, state-led, managed market system responsive to consumer demand warped by kleptocracy, and rent-granting. The Federation's impressive economic recovery spurt 2000–2008, turbo-charged by a huge inflow of foreign direct investment in the wake of 9/11, indicates the possibilities of Putin's managed market system. It, like Xi Jinping's market communism, is far from perfect, but other things equal appears capable of performing well enough to mollify popular discontent.

Sustainable Growth

The deficiencies of Russia's new market powered civilian sector and market assisted VPK do not preclude sustained economic growth because of improved possibilities for exogenous and endogenous technological progress, and technological transfers.[82] The only source of long-run economic growth in an otherwise steady state system is technological progress; that is, productivity improvements in capital and labor skills responsive to consumer demand.[83] These gains can be fostered by general advances in science (exogenous technological progress), government programs and policies (endogenous technological progress), and technology transfer.[84]

---

[81] Steven Rosefielde and Stefan Hedlund, *Russia Since 1980: Wrestling with Westernization* (New York: Cambridge University Press, 2009).

[82] Abram Bergson, *Planning and Productivity under Soviet Socialism* (New York: Columbia University Press, 1968); Abram Bergson, "Development Under Two Systems: Comparative Productivity Growth Since 1950," *World Politics* 23, no. 4, July 1971: 579–617. Abram Bergson, "Soviet Economic Perspectives: Toward a New Growth Model," *Problems of Communism* 32, no. 2, March–April 1973: 1–10. Abram Bergson, "The Soviet Economic Slowdown," *Challenge Magazine* 20, no. 6, January–February 1978: 22–33.

Abram Bergson believed that the technological potential of the Soviet command economy was deficient and inferred that growth would eventually become subpar. Russia's mixed economy qualifies this presumption.

[83] Robert Solow, "A Contribution to the Theory of Economic Growth," *Quarterly Journal of Economics* 70, February 1956: 65–94. Robert M. Solow, "Technical Change and the Aggregate Production Function," *Review of Economics and Statistics* 39, August 1957: 312–320. Trevor Swan, "Economic Growth and Capital Accumulation" *Economic Record* 32 (November 1956): 334–361.

[84] Peter Howitt, "Endogenous Growth and Cross-Country Income Differences," *American Economic Review* 90, September 2000: 829–846. Peter Howitt and Philippe Aghion, "Capital Accumulation and Innovation as Complementary Factors in Long-Run Growth,"

54 Beleaguered Superpower: Biden's America Adrift

Russia's new market powered civilian sector and market assisted VPK enhance growth prospects compared with the "structurally militarized" Soviet benchmark by making endogenous technological progress,[85] and technology transfer more response to consumer demand. Putin permits his top-down management regime to defer considerably to consumer preferences and Russia's workably competitive military industrial sector satisfies MOD demand more efficiently.[86] The combination of these

---

Journal of Economic Growth 3, June 1998: 111–130. Paul Romer, "Endogenous Technological Change." *Journal of Political Economy* 98, October 1990: S71–S102. Robert Lucas, "On the Mechanics of Economic Development," *Journal of Monetary Economics* 22, January 1988: 3–42. Vitaly Shlykov (former co-chair of Russia's Defense Council) coined the term structural militarization to suggest that excessive defense spending is an institutionalized aspect of the Soviet and Russian economic system. Insofar as his assessment remains valid, the Kremlin may be predisposed to invest inordinately large sums in VPK R&D which could augment the sustainable rate of Russia's armament and aggregate economic growth. This possibility is a form of the more general phenomenon of endogenous economic growth some Western macroeconomists contend can be achieved through government programs and policies. Vitaly Shlykov, "Chto Pogubilo Sovetskii Soiuz? Amerikanskaia Razvedka ili Sovetskiskh Voennykh Raskhodakh," (What Destroyed the Soviet Union? American Intelligence Estimates of Soviet Military Expenditures), *Voenny Vestnik*, no. 8, 2001.Vitaly Shlykov, "Russian Defence Industrial Complex after 9–11," *U.S. Naval Postgraduate School*, June 2003.Vitaly Shlykov, "Globalizatsiia voennoi promyshlennosti-imperativ XXI veka" (Globalization of Military Industry: The 21st Century Imperative), *Otechestvennye zapiski*, no. 5, 2005: 98–115. Vitaly Shlykov, "Nazad v budushchee, ili Ekonomicheskye uroki kholodnoi voiny" (Back to the Future, or Economic Lessons of the Cold War), *Rossiia v Global'noe Politike* 4, no. 2, 2006: 26–40. Shlykov "Nevidimaia Mobilizatsii Invisible Mobilization)," *Forbes*, no. 3, March 2006: 1–5. Vitaly Shlykov, "The Military Reform and Its Implications for the Modernization of the Russian Armed Forces," in Jan Leijonhielm and Fredrik Westerlund, eds., *Russian Power Structures, FOI* (Stockholm: Swedish Defence Research Agency): 50–60.

[85] Satoshi Mizobata, "State-Led Innovation and Uneven Adaptation in Russia," in Steven Rosefielde, ed., *Putin's Russia: Economic, Political and Military Foundations* (Singapore: World Scientific Publishers, 2020).

For a cautious assessment of Russia's technology prospects see Harley Balzer, "Can Russia Catch Up/Keep Up? Russian Science and Education in Putin's Fourth Term" in Steven Rosefielde, ed., *Putin's Russia: Economic, Political and Military Foundations* (Singapore: World Scientific Publishers, 2020), Chapter 6.

[86] Vitaly Shlykov (former co-chair of Russia's Defense Council) coined the term structural militarization to suggest that excessive defense spending is an institutionalized aspect of the Soviet and Russian economic system. Insofar as his assessment remains valid, the Kremlin

forces should allow the Kremlin to take better advantage of Russia's comparative economic backwardness, facilitating moderate economic growth for the next several decades, even though the economic system is relatively anti-competitive.[87]

---

may be predisposed to invest inordinately large sums in VPK R&D which could augment the sustainable rate of Russia's armament and aggregate economic growth. This possibility is a form of the more general phenomenon of endogenous economic growth some Western macroeconomists contend can be achieved through government programs and policies.

Vitaly Shlykov, "Chto Pogubilo Sovetskii Soiuz? Amerikanskaia Razvedka ili Sovetskiskkh Voennykh Raskhodakh, (What Destroyed the Soviet Union? American Intelligence Estimates of Soviet Military Expenditures)," *Voenny Vestnik*, no. 8 (2001). Vitaly Shlykov, "Russian Defence Industrial Complex after 9–11," *Russian Security Policy and the War on Terrorism conference* (June 2003). Vitaly Shlykov, "Globalizatsiia voennoi promyshlennosti-imperativ XXI veka (Globalization of Military Industry: The 21st Century Imperative)," *Otechestvennye Zapiski*, no. 5 (2005): 98–115. Vitaly Shlykov, "Nazad v budushchee, ili Ekonomicheskve uroki kholodnoi voiny (Back to the Future, or Economic Lessons of the Cold War)," *Rossiia v Global'noe Politike* 4, no. 2, 2006: 26–40. Shlykov "Nevidimaia Mobilizatsii (Invisible Mobilization)," *Forbes*, no. 3, March 2006: 1–5. Shlykov, "The Military Reform and Its Implications for the Modernization of the Russian Armed Forces," in Jan Leijonhielm and Fredrik Westerlund, eds., *Russian Power Structures, FOI* (Stockholm: Swedish Defense research Agency, Stockholm, January 2008): 50–60.

[87] Steven Rosefielde, "Russian Military, Political and Economic Reform: Can the Kremlin Placate Washington?" *U.S. Army War College, Carlisle Barracks* (May 2014). Steven Rosefielde, "The Impossibility of Russian Economic Reform: Waiting for Godot," *US Army War College, Carlisle Barracks* (2012). Steven Rosefielde, *Russia's Aborted Transition: 7000 Days and Counting*, (Institutional'naya ekonomika razvitie, 2010). Steven Rosefielde, "Postcrisis Russia: Counting on Miracles in Uncertain Times," in Carolina Vendil Pallin, and Bertil Nygren, eds., *Russian Defense Prospects* (New York: Routledge, 2012): 134–150. Steven Rosefielde and Stefan Hedlund, *Russia Since 1980: Wrestling with Westernization* (Cambridge: Cambridge University Press, 2008). Angus Maddison, *Development Centre Studies: The World Economy: A Millennial Perspective* (Paris: OECD, 2001). Steven Rosefielde, *Kremlin Strikes Back: Russia and the West after Crimea's Annexation* (Cambridge: Cambridge University Press, 2016). Moses Abramovitz, "Catching Up, Forging Ahead, and Falling Behind," *The Journal of Economic History* 46, no. 2, June 1986: 385–406.Cf. Karen Dawisha, *Putin's Kleptocracy* (New York: Simon and Schuster, 2014).

The statistical and econometric support for the proposition are inconclusive. On one hand, Russia has failed to catch up with and overtake Western living standards during the last 100 years. On the other hand, CIA data indicate that the postwar Soviet economy grew

Guns and Butter

The sum and substance of the foregoing overview is that Russia does not have an economic Achilles heel that prevents it from vigorously defending its spheres of influence. It has the industrial capacity and will to tilt the military correlation of forces favorably in contemporary zones of East–West conflict without impoverishing the nation, given prevailing and foreseeable levels of NATO defense spending.[88] Thirty years ago, the Soviet Union's economy of shortage could produce more than enough guns, but not enough butter. This is no longer true for Russia. Putin's insider managed market and Muscovite rent-granting system has changed the game.[89] The Kremlin can have both guns and butter.[90] It is not

---

faster than America's until the mid-1980s even after taking account of hidden inflation. Russian growth in the new millennium has outperformed the West too, just as it should have done ceteris paribus given its relative economic backwardness. On balance, the historical record does not support the often voiced claim that inferior long term GDP growth prospects pose a significant barrier to sustained Kremlin military competition with the West. Moscow's economy was inferior during the Soviet period when Russia was an impoverished superpower judged from the perspective of consumer sovereignty, but this did not prevent the Kremlin from achieving military superpower status. Angus Maddison, *The World Economy: A Millennial Perspective* (Paris: Development Centre Studies, OECD, 2001); Steven Rosefielde, *Kremlin Strikes Back: Russia and the West after Crimea's Annexation* (Cambridge: Cambridge University Press, 2016). Moses Abramovitz, "Catching Up, Forging Ahead, and Falling Behind," *The Journal of Economic History* 46, no. 2, June, 1986: 385–406.

[88] Steven Rosefielde, *Kremlin Strikes Back: Russia and the West after Crimea's Annexation* (Cambridge: Cambridge University Press, 2017).

[89] Michael Ellman, "Russia's Current Economic System: From Delusion to Glasnost," *Comparative Economic Studies* 57, 2015: 1–18.

[90] Paul Goble, "10 Percent Decline In Number Of Births In Russia Over Last Year Frightens Economists — OpEd," *Eurasia Review* (May 1, 2017), http://www. eurasiareview.com/30042017-10-percent-decline-in-number-of-births-in-russia-over-last-year-frightens-economists-oped/.

This does not mean that Russia like the West is economic and social problem free. For example, Russia is beset with demographic problems. Its population recently has declined, which means that labor force growth would not provide a fillip to economic growth.

seriously constrained by the budgetary restrictions implied by Stockholm International Peace Research Institute's (SIPRI) specious statistics,[91] or incapacitated by adverse health and demographic problems.[92] Russia can cross swords with America without condemning itself to impoverished superpower.[93] See Appendix for further clarification.

---

[91] Advocates of small Western defense spending have relied on budgetary data compiled by the Stockholm International Peace Research Institute to make it appear that the Soviet Union and now Russia cannot financial sustain a credible threat against the West. It confidence in the accuracy of Soviet defense budgetary statistics was destroyed in 1989 by Gorbachev's admission that the official data excluded weapons! Vitaly Shlykov insists that the published data have little bearing on the Kremlin's ability to procure and maintain its arsenal. Nonetheless, SIPRI persists with its disinformation. Purchasing power parities are massaged to understate the dollar value of Russia's arsenal. The subject is too tangled to elaborate here.

For insight into the problem see Steven Rosefielde, *False Science: Underestimating the Soviet Arms Buildup* (New Brunswick: Transaction Press, 1987).

For a contemporary assessment of Russia's military prospects using the budget data approach see Edward Hunter Christie, "Does Russia Have the Fiscal Capacity to Achieve Its Military Modernisation Goals?" *The RUSI Journal*, 2017: 4–15, https://doi.org/10.108 0/03071847.2017.1406697.

[92] Judyth Twigg, "Russian Health and Demographic Trends and Prospects" in Steven Rosefielde, ed., *Putin's Russia: Economic, Political and Military Foundations* (Singapore: World Scientific Publishers, 2020).

[93] Henry Rowen and Charles Wolf, Jr., *The Impoverished Superpower: Perestroika and the Soviet Military Burden* (Palo Alto: ICS Press, 1990).

Gertrude Schroeder (Greenslade) and Imogene Edwards insisted that Soviet consumer goods were growing rapidly throughout the post-war era. The dispute turns on plausible, but elusive claims about hidden inflation that are no longer germane.

Gertrude Schroeder and Imogene Edwards, *Consumption in the USSR: An International Comparison* (Washington, D.C.: *Joint Economic Committee of Congress*, 1981): 25, Table 14.

Schroeder's husband Rush Greenslade was the director of the CIA's SOVA shop.

Grigorii Khanin, "Ekonomicheskii Rost: Alternativnaia Otsenka," *Kommunist* 17, 1988: 83–90. Steven Rosefielde, "A Comment on David Howard's Estimate of Hidden Inflation in the Soviet Retail Sales Sector," *Soviet Studies* 32, no. 3, July 1980: 423–427. Steven Rosefielde, "The Illusion of Material Progress: The Analytics of Soviet Economic Growth Revisited," *Soviet Studies* 43, no. 4, 1991: 597–611.

Strategic Opportunism

Russia's arms buildup 2010–2015 and subsequent improvements surprised most analysts, raising the possibility that the Kremlin might be contemplating war sometime soon. Had the surge persisted unabated, these fears would have intensified. Instead, Moscow's actions blurred perceptions. It decided to stretch out the procurement goals of its state armaments program from 2025 to 2027. It has cut projected SU-57 fifth-generation stealth fighter acquisition from 60 to about 12 units, and delayed the Tupolev PAK-DA next generation long-range bomber program in favor of restarting production of the TU-160. The Kremlin is purchasing new armored vehicles and T-14 tanks in small batches. Russia is upgrading versions of systems like the SU-35s, TU-160s, and T-72 tanks lending credibility to those Western analysts who believe that Putin's endgame excludes war and his sphere of influence agenda is benign.

The tide seemed to be turning as oil prices rose partly in response to Russian–OPEC petroleum production curbs,[94] but petroleum prices turned bearish again after Saudi Arabia and Russia broke their production supply agreement in February 2020.[95] Apparently, volatile petroleum prices will continue being a wild card sometimes facilitating and other times impeding Russia's military modernization programs.

Russia traditionally has been strategically opportunistic. It tempers its geostrategic ambitions as the correlation of forces dictates, expanding them when economic and political opportunities knock.[96]

Economic Sanctions

This assessment should have a sobering effect on American policymakers. However, has not, because Washington in part believes rain or shine that

---

[94] Stephen Blank, "Can Russia Sustain its Defense Buildup?" Steven Rosefielde, ed., in *Putin's Russia: Economic, Political and Military Foundations* (Singapore: World Scientific Publishers, 2020).

[95] Timothy Puko and Rebecca Elliott, "U.S. Considers Intervention in Saudi-Russia Oil Standoff," *Wall Street Journal* (March 2020).

[96] Oren Liebermann, Frederik Pleitgen and Vasco Cotovio, "New Satellite Images Suggest Military Buildup in Russia's Strategic Baltic Enclave," *CNN* (October 17, 2018), https://edition.cnn.com/2018/10/17/europe/russia-kaliningrad-military-buildup-intl/index.html.

economic sanctions,[97] like those imposed by the Jackson–Vanik amendment (1974–2012), can tutor Russia to mend its ways.[98] The salubrious powers of economic sanctions have long been a placebo and face saving device in the West. They are a low-cost alternative to military force. Policymakers clung to the belief in the 1970s, even though some CIA experts contended that the Soviet military machine-building sector could support double-digit weapons growth indefinitely,[99] and continued to do

---

[97]Frances Cappola, "U.S. Sanctions on Russia Are Financial Warfare," *Forbes* (July 2014), http://www.forbes.com/sites/francescoppola/2014/07/18/u-s-sanctions-on-russia-are-financial-warfare/; Percy W. Bidwell, "Our Economic Warfare," *Foreign Affairs* (April 1942), https://www.foreignaffairs.com/articles/united-states/1942-04-01/our-economic-warfare.

The term economic sanctions refer to peacetime punitive measures, short of "economic war."

Policymakers impose economic sanctions to chasten adversaries by denying them access to factors of production, products, technology, and finance. Export subsidy stratagems (beggar-thy-neighbor policies) can be utilized to similar effect but are usually excluded from the concept because rivals can easily deflect them with quotas. High-intensity economic sanctions combatants employ during peace and wartime are commonly called economic warfare (blockades, blacklisting, preclusive purchases), even though the prohibitions have the same character as lower-intensity punitive measures. There is a large literature on economic warfare that stresses its reciprocal character and inconclusiveness.

The use of counter-value conventional and nuclear strikes against C3 (command, communications, and control), transport, and industrial targets is more effective than economic sanctions in compelling adversaries to yield, but hardly guarantees success.

[98]Vladimir N. Pregelj, "The Jackson–Vanik Amendment: A Survey," *CRS Report for Congress* (August 2005), https://fas.org/sgp/crs/row/98-545.pdf.

"The enactment of the so-called Jackson-Vanik amendment as part of the Trade Act of 1974 was directly a U.S. reaction to the severe restrictions the Soviet Union had placed in late 1972 on the emigration of its citizens, but was expanded in its scope to apply to all so-called 'nonmarket economy' (NME) countries. The amendment, in effect, requires compliance with its specific free-emigration criteria as a key condition for the restoration of certain benefits theretofore denied to NME countries in their economic relations with the United States. These benefits — access to nondiscriminatory (most-favored-nation; normal-trade-relations) treatment in trade; access to U.S. government financial facilities; ability to conclude a trade agreement with the United States) — may be extended to an NME country subject to the amendment only if the President determines that the country is not in violation of (i.e., is in full compliance with) the free-emigration criteria of the amendment, or if he waives, under specified conditions, the requirement of full compliance with the criteria. Such determinations or waivers must be renewed periodically."

[99]Steven Rosefielde, *False Science: Underestimating the Soviet Arms Buildup* (Brunswick: Transaction Press, 1987): 35, 38.

60   *Beleaguered Superpower: Biden's America Adrift*

so even when the World Bank Group reported that the sustainable rate of Russian GDP was 8 percent per annum, from 2002–2007.[100]

The scholarly literature indicates that economic sanctions are mostly ineffectual against great power adversaries like Russia,[101] and despite ever mounting punitive measures taken against Moscow in the wake of Crimea's annexation in 2014,[102] Putin has never retreated. He knows that Russia violated the Belovezha Accords that established the Commonwealth of Independent States in 1991, the Helsinki Accords, the Budapest Memorandum on Security Assurances of 1994 and the Treaty on friendship, cooperation and partnership between the Russian Federation and Ukraine, but has not budged. Economic sanctions have imposed significant economic costs on Russia. This is uncontestable. Inflicting

---

[100] Steven Rosefielde, *Kremlin Strikes Back: Russia and the West after Crimea's Annexation* (Cambridge: Cambridge University Press, 2017).

[101] Mark Kramer, "Exclusive: Sanctions and Regime Survival," *Ponars Eurasia* (March 2015), http://www.ponarseurasia.org/article/sanctions-and-regime-survival.

For a good summary of the literature on the effectiveness of sanctions see Susan Hannah Allen, "The Domestic Political Costs of Economic Sanctions," *Journal of Conflict Resolution* 52, no. 6, December 2008: 916–944, esp. 916–917. Nikolay Marinov, "Do Economic Sanctions Destabilize Country Leaders?" *American Journal of Political Science* 49, no. 3, July 2005: 564–576. Abel Escribà-Folch and Joseph Wright, "Dealing with Tyranny: International Sanctions and the Survival of Authoritarian Rulers," *International Studies Quarterly* 54, no. 2, June 2010: 334–359. which builds on David. Lektzian and Mark Souva, "An Institutional Theory of Sanctions Onset and Success," *Journal of Conflict Resolution* 51, no. 6, November 2007: 848–871. William Kaempfer, Anton Lowenberg, and William Mertens, "International Economic Sanctions against a Dictator," *Economics and Politics* 16, no. 1, March 2004: 29–51. William Kaempfer and Anton Lowenberg, "The Theory of International Economic Sanctions: A Public Choice Approach," *American Economic Review* 78, no. 4, December 1988: 786–793.

[102] Jen Psaki, "United States Expands Export Restrictions on Russia," *US State Department* (April 2014), www.state.gov/r/pa/prs/ps/2014/04/225241.htm. Susanne Oxenstierna and Per Olsson, "The Economic Sanctions against Russia: Impact and Prospects of Success," *FOI* (September 2015).

"The main conclusion of the report is that the targeted economic sanctions of the EU and the US have contributed to imposing a cost on the Russian economy in combination with other factors, but have so far not persuaded Russia to change its behaviour towards Ukraine." Oxenstierna and Olsson provide a complete listing of EU sanctions in their Appendix 2.

Viktor Gorshkov, "Sanctions" in Steven Rosefielde, Masaaki Kuboniwa, Satoshi Mizobata and Kumiko Haba, eds., *The Unwinding of the Globalist Dream: EU, Russia, China* (Singapore: World Scientific Publishers, 2017).

pain however is not the point. The purpose of sanctions is disciplining bad authoritarian behavior. Putin is unchasten. The belief that sanctions will eventually compel him to yield is the triumph of hope over experience, impervious to disproof.

National Security Framework

What do Washington and Moscow want from each other? As much as they can prudently get. If Washington has its druthers, it will transform Russia into an obedient vassal under its globalization banner. Putin would be compelled to replace insider governance, managed markets and rent granting with Biden's progressive-liberal agenda. The Kremlin would be forced to rescind Russia's annexation of Crimea, withdraw from the Donbas and Luhansk and renounce its unofficial claims on Novorossiya (most of Ukraine), and the Baltic States. Russia would denuclearize, disarm, keep only skeleton military forces and refrain from cyber meddling in foreign affairs. The Kremlin would help America fully exploit political and economic opportunities throughout the former Soviet Union and CMEA bloc, the Arctic, Middle East, Balkans, and Asia. It would cease meddling in Europe, Iran, Syria, Turkey, Egypt, Libya, and elsewhere across the globe. It would join the EU and NATO, sign a peace treaty with Japan concluding WWII, return the Northern Islands to Tokyo, badger Kim Jong-un into denuclearizing, shun mischief making in Latin America and Sub-Saharan Africa and praise Washington's wise counsel.

If Putin had his druthers,[103] he would restore Kremlin control over most of the post-Soviet space (Belarus, Estonia,[104] Latvia, Lithuania, Moldova, Ukraine, Armenia, Azerbaijan, Georgia, Kazakhstan, Kyrgyzstan, Tajikistan, Turkmenistan, Uzbekistan), the CMEA sphere of influence (Czechia, Slovakia, Hungary, Poland, Bulgaria, Romania), and other former zones of control including Finland, Balkans, Syria, Middle East,

---

[103] Lance Alred and Madina Rubly, "Russian International Relations: Russia's Great Power Revival and Engagement with the Global Community," in Steven Rosefielde, eds., *Putin's Russia: Economic, Political and Military Foundati*ons (Singapore: World Scientific Publishers, 2020).

[104] Keir Giles, Russia Hostile Action Against Estonia, *AEI* (December 2017), http://www.aei.org/wp-content/uploads/2017/12/Russian-Hostile-Action-Against-Estonia-Military-Options.pdf.

Stephen Blank, "Baltic Buildup," *Jane's Intelligence Review* (May 2017), 6–13.

62 *Beleaguered Superpower: Biden's America Adrift*

Cuba, Venezuela, North Korea, and Vietnam. This would mean rolling back NATO and EU membership to 1991. Putin said recently, "It would be nice for Russia if NATO were 'falling apart'."[105] Furthermore, if Putin had his way he would ally with China and other authoritarian nations to create an Eastern authoritarian bloc against the West.

Putin desires unilateral Western disarmament, and tolerance of the Kremlin's security "needs." These include Western recognition of Russia's great power status, a Yalta II agreement,[106] the annexation of the Kurile Islands,[107] the preservation of limited North Korean nuclear capabilities, control over the Sea of Azov,[108] accommodation of Kremlin

---

[105] Jacob Pramuk, "Putin: It Would Be Nice for Russia if NATO Were 'Falling Apart'," *CNBC* (June 2, 2017), http://www.cnbc.com/2017/06/02/putin-it-would-help-russia-if-nato-were-completely-falling-apart.html.

[106] Frida Ghitis, "Putin Wants Yalta 2.0 and Trump May Give It To Him," *CNN* (January 27, 2017), http://www.cnn.com/2017/01/25/opinions/putin-wants-yalta-2-0-and-trump-may-give-it-to-him-ghitis/; Steven Rosefielde, *The Kremlin Strikes Back: Russia and the West after Crimea's Annexation* (Cambridge: Cambridge University Press, 2017).

"It's clear what Putin wants. His vision of Yalta 2.0 is an agreement in which Russia regains an old-fashioned sphere of influence, keeping the former Soviet Republics (Russia's 'near abroad') on a short leash without US or NATO interference, and perhaps extending a version of that power over former Eastern European satellites. He wants NATO to stop expanding and become weaker; he wants the US and NATO and the US to relinquish their protective umbrella over Russia's sphere of influence. He wants the sanctions lifted. He wants the US to recognize Russia's illegal annexation of Crimea. In short, he wants the U.S. to turn a blind eye on many of its values, commitments, and international law."

[107] Denis Pinchuk and Andrew Osborn, "Putin Says U.S. Missile Systems in Alaska, South Korea Challenge Russia," *Reuters*, June 1, 2017, http://www.reuters.com/article/us-russia-economic-forum-putin-idUSKBN18S4NS.

Putin recently announced that he would unilaterally militarize Japan's Northern Islands occupied by Russia since September 1945 by deploying some of its newest missile defence systems and drones as a counter-measure to the deployment of the U.S. THAAD anti-missile system to South Korea and reported U.S. plans to beef up Fort Greely in Alaska, a launch site for anti-ballistic missiles.

[108] Stephen Blank, "Why Is the Sea of Azov So Important?" *Atlantic Council* (November 2018), http://www.atlanticcouncil.org/blogs/ukrainealert/why-is-the-sea-of-azov-so-important.

"Moscow has been busy building a bridge over the Kerch Strait and a railway upon that bridge. This bridge was deliberately built at a height that all but precludes Ukrainian commercial traffic from operating in the Sea of Azov, thus placing the port of Mariupol in economic

Russia 63

whims, financial assistance, revocation of the Magnitsky Act,[109] and Obama, Trump and Biden administration economic sanctions. These concessions in their entirety would be the death knell for Washington's global ambitions, and the subordination of the West to a Russian-Chinese authoritarian juggernaut.

Both sides know that their aspirations are pipedreams, and that the starting point of their engagement in normal circumstances should be defending the *status quo* and probing the other's vulnerabilities. "Normality" covers a range of cases short of full declarations of war, spanning peaceful coexistence (mutual tolerance) (opposed by those demanding global democratization),[110] Cold Peace (mutual tolerance plus reciprocal lobbying for the other side's conversion), and Cold War (reciprocal aggressive use of smart diplomacy, soft power and irregular violence to transform the opposition's system).[111]

Washington, on one side, and the Kremlin on the other must decide which engagement framework best serves each's purposes, taking account of national security, and the broader national (or globalist) interest. Neither has taken a firm position on the status of current relations, although for the moment the Kremlin perceives itself in the throes of a total war (that need not be an armed struggle) with the West. It is methodically striving to win, hoping to do so with a rational choice "satisficing" strategy that encompasses material production, political power, and cultural identity.[112]

---

jeopardy. And in another contravention of international law, it has declared that it will block any NATO attempt to send ships into the Sea of Azov, even if they are invited by Ukraine."

[109] The Magnitsky Act, formally known as the Russia and Moldova Jackson–Vanik Repeal and Sergei Magnitsky Rule of Law Accountability Act of 2012, is a bipartisan bill passed by the U.S. Congress and President Obama in November–December 2012, intending to punish Russian officials responsible for the death of Russian lawyer Sergei Magnitsky in a Moscow prison in 2009.

[110] Nikita Khrushchev, "On Peaceful Coexistence," *Foreign Affairs* 38, no. 1, October 1959: 1–18.

The Russia term for Peace Coexistence is "Mirnoye sosushchestvovaniye."

[111] For a fuller discussion of these concepts see Steven Rosefielde, *The Kremlin Strikes Back: Russia and the West after Crimea's Annexation* (Cambridge: Cambridge University Press, 2017).

[112] Steven Rosefielde and R.W. Pfouts, *Inclusive Economic Theory* (Singapore: World Scientific Publishers, 2014).

64   *Beleaguered Superpower: Biden's America Adrift*

Russia and the West both vacillate, sometimes favoring peaceful coexistence, other times Cold Peace, or even Cold War. Peaceful coexistence requires minimal engagement. It assumes that the *status quo* is stable allowing both sides to go about their business without trying to tilt the correlation of forces toward one or the other's advantage. Washington and Putin must prudently monitor bilateral relations. However, they need not alter their behavior as long as the *status quo* is preserved.[113]

Cold Peace is different. It permits both sides to employ a wide range of "smart diplomacy," soft power and low intensity, mostly non-lethal covert initiatives to alter the *status quo*. Putin and Biden can each tout the virtues of their social systems and institutions. They can counsel, misinform and give material assistance to fellow travelers abroad, but only up to the point where assistance morphs into insurrection, occupation or annexation, as Washington's sponsorship of "Orange Revolution" regime change did in Ukraine.

Russia and the West operated under the unwritten rules of Cold Peace from the moment Putin chastened by Kosovo War (1998–1999), abandoned Gorbachev's "transitionary" partnership framework of returning Russia to its "common European home" in 2000.[114] He embraced Cold Peace with the West until the Maidan events of February 2014 and Crimea's annexation,[115] drifting toward Cold War thereafter as the West struggled with the breach in the first Article of the Helsinki Accords prohibiting involuntary boundary changes in Europe.[116]

Cold War takes engagement to the next stage with one or both sides inciting social strife, regime change, fait accompli occupation, conquest,

---

[113]Peace coexistence is compatible with populism and economic globalization insofar as both parties see virtue in negotiated trade, investment, finance and migration.

[114]Fyodor Lukyanov, "Gorbachev's Abandoned 'European Home'," *Russia in Global Affairs* (March 2010), http://eng.globalaffairs.ru/redcol/n_14661.

[115]Russian back Ukrainian president Viktor Yanukovych was ousted from power following the February 2014 Euromaidan clashes in Kiev's "Maidan" Independence Square. Unlike the bloodless Orange Revolution, these protests resulted in more than 100 deaths, occurring mostly between 18 and 20 February.

[116]Thirty-five nations including America, Canada, and the Soviet Union signed the Helsinki Accords or Final Act in 1975. The agreement is called an accord because it did not have the official status of treaty. Article I stipulates: Sovereign equality, respect for the rights inherent in sovereignty.

or annexation. Russia and the West today are teeter tottering between patching up the Cold Peace and declaring outright Cold War.[117]

Putin appears committed to Cold War, at least with respect to the Donbas, Luhansk, Crimea, Belarus, Nagorno–Karabakh, and the Sea of Azov for the present, while lecturing the West on the virtues of Cold Peace, and chastising it for Russiagate-driven anti-Russophobia.[118] He does not intend to return any of these territories to Ukraine or grant Kiev assured access to the Sea of Azov in accordance with the Helsinki Final Act, despite his willingness to discuss the Donbas and Luhansk under the aegis of the Minsk II Protocols,[119] and his dismissal of Vladislav Surkov as his chief Crimea advisor.[120]

The Kremlin is continuing its arms modernization program, challenging the West outside Europe in the Middle East and provocatively

---

[117] Stephen Cohen, "Russia Is Not the 'No. 1 Threat'-or Even Among the Top 5," *The Nation* (November 2017), https://www.thenation.com/article/russia-is-not-the-no-1-threat-or-even-among-the-top-5/.

"By declaring Putin's Russia to be the greatest danger to America, the political-media establishment itself is endangering US national security. 'In the 1990s, the Clinton administration embraced post-Soviet Russia as America's 'strategic partner and friend.' Twenty years later, the US policy establishment, from liberals to conservatives, insists that Russia under Vladimir Putin is the number-one threat to American national security. The primary explanation for this transformed perception, which began under President George W. Bush, became more insistent during the Obama administration, and is now a virtual bipartisan axiom, lies in Washington, not in Moscow. But whatever the full explanation, it is gravely endangering US national security by diminishing real threats and preventing the partnership with Russia needed to cope with them."

[118] Denis Dyomkin, "Putin Says World Needs To Talk to North Korea Not Threaten It," *Reuters* (May 15, 2017), https://www.reuters.com/article/us-northkorea-missiles-putin/putin-says-world-needs-to-talk-to-north-korea-not-threaten-it-idUSKCN18B1AG.

[119] At a summit in Minsk on February 11, 2015, the leaders of Ukraine, Russia, France, and Germany agreed to a package of measures to alleviate the ongoing war in the Donbas region of Ukraine. The talks that led to the deal, overseen by the Organization for Security and Co-operation in Europe (OSCE), were organized in response to the collapse of the Minsk Protocol ceasefire in January–February 2015. The new package of measures is intended to revive the Protocol, which had been agreed to on September 5, 2014.

[120] Amy Mackinnon and Reid Standish, "Putin Fires His Puppet Master: Vladislav Surkov, Who Stage-Managed Russia's Involvement in Ukraine, is replaced," *Foreign Policy* (February 2020), https://foreignpolicy.com/2020/02/21/putin-fires-vladislav-surkov-puppet-master-russia-ukraine-rebels/

Beleaguered Superpower: Biden's America Adrift

testing NATO's readiness as it did during the Soviet era.[121] The West is ambivalent. Biden favors intensifying sanctions against Moscow now, and a reversion later to the soft power carrot and stick tactics employed during the Gorbachev phase of the waning Cold War without abandoning sponsorship of "color revolutions" and regime change in Russian's sphere.

State of the Debate

No impartial defense expert denies that Russia is once again a formidable nuclear and conventional military power. The debate today is between those who expect Russian military power to recede relative to the West in the not too distant future (sufficient deterrence school), and those who foresee the Kremlin trying to expand its territorial reach (the sphere of influence school). The possibility of a burgeoning "axis of evil" between Moscow and Beijing is a wildcard.[122]

The divergence of opinion reflects differing judgments about motives and capabilities. All experts concur that Putin's Kremlin sought to restore Russia's great military power and has successfully achieved this objective. The documentary evidence on this score is conclusive. Specialists also agree that Moscow desires to preserve its gains. However, they differ

---

[121] Matthew Bodner, "Russia Launches Much-Hyped Zapad Exercises in Belarus," *Defense News* (September 14, 2017), http://www.defensenews.com/smr/european-balance-of-power/2017/09/14/russia-launches-much-hyped-zapad-exercises-in-belarus/.

"In the lead-up to Zapad, that message seemed to be spectacularly received. The hype surrounding Zapad is likely exactly what the Kremlin wanted: a wave of hysteria hyping Russian military capabilities where they may or may not exist. In the words of Finnish Defence Minister Jussi Niinistö, Zapad is primarily a propaganda exercise. 'Western countries have taken the bait completely, they've plugged the exercises so much,' he told the Finnish Yle news agency on Monday."

[122] Stephen Blank, "Can Russia Sustain Its Defense Buildup?" in Steven Rosefielde, ed., *Putin's Russia: Economic, Political and Military Foundations* (Singapore: World Scientific Publishers, 2020).

Andrei Tsygankov, "Russia's Turn to the East, 2012–2018" in Steven Rosefielde, ed., *Putin's Russia: Economic, Political and Military Foundations* (Singapore: World Scientific Publishers, 2020): Chapter 15.

Russia 67

on whether Putin wants further increases in hard power and if so, whether he is willing to shoulder the burden.[123]

The sufficient deterrence school, exemplified by Julian Cooper and the Swedish International Peace Research Institute (SIPRI), takes the position that Russia has legitimate security concerns and no more. Neither foresaw Russia's arm modernization drive in 2010–2015, but after the fact concluded that recent accomplishments have allayed the Kremlin's fears and complexes. They do not see any justification for Putin building Russia's armed forces further. However, they believe that even if bureaucratic inertia sustained rapid weapons growth for a brief period, the momentum will ebb, and ultimately reverse due to the pressures of civilian priorities, and budgetary stringency. Both consider Russia a benign great nuclear power.

Their outlook is seconded by scholars who reject Cooper and SIPRI's assessments of Putin's motivation, but believe that the Kremlin lacks the economic and financial resources to realize its desires. These analysts surmise that Putin no longer feels a sense of urgency to protect Russia against western instigated color revolutions, and intensified allied pressure in Crimea, Luhansk, Donbas, Georgia, Belarus, Kyrgyzstan,[124] Syria, and elsewhere in the Middle East. They consider the emerging Sino-Russian entente unimportant, seeing no compelling reason why Moscow should neglect domestic concerns for incremental gains in national security.

The sphere of influence school including scholars like Stephen Blank looks at matters from the other end of the telescope. It believes that Putin wants to expand Russia's influence, citing official Russian military doctrine, the scope, and thoroughness of the Kremlin's military industrial modernization program, the priority placed on the modernization of the Aerospace Forces (VKS–Vozdushno–Kosmicheskiye Sily),[125] irredentist vendettas stemming from the dismemberment of the Soviet Union, and an

---

[123] Gudrun Perrson, "On War and Peace: Russian Security Policy and Military-Strategic Thinking," in Steven Rosefielde, ed., *Putin's Russia: Economic, Political and Military Foundations* (Singapore: World Scientific Publishers, 2020): Chapter 11.

[124] MK Bhadrakumar, "Kyrgyzstan The Dividing Line between Politics and Crime Will Be Thin If Not Non-Existent under Kyrgyzstan's New Strongman," *Asia Times* (October 16, 2020).

[125] Eugene Kogan, "Russian Aerospace Forces and the Syria Campaign: An Assessment," *The European Geopolitical Forum* (May 2018).

68 *Beleaguered Superpower: Biden's America Adrift*

objective reading of the shifting correlation of forces. They believe if Putin plays his cards right, he can conceal a continuous rapid arms buildup from Western public perceptions by drastically understating official military outlays just as the Kremlin did in the Soviet era. Putin understands that although Russia cannot compete with the West in an unrestrained arms race, he can enhance Russia's power in the theaters of military operations because the Biden–Harris administration has no stomach for cutting social services to bolster national security.

Some members of the sphere of influence school who believe that Putin will strive to gain the upper hand lean toward the view that he will fail for a laundry list of reasons. They appreciate that financial constraints are less stringent than the Cooper–SIPRI sufficient deterrence school contends, that Russia's military industrial sector is self-sufficiently capable of sustained rapid economic growth, and the Kremlin today can continuously increase supplies of both guns and butter. Nonetheless, they believe regime change is inevitable because Russians want to return to their "common European home" or will increasingly desire an alternative to Muscovite authoritarianism. Perhaps, they are right. Perhaps, the dissolution of Soviet communism was just a dress rehearsal for Putin's fall, but it is foolish to bet it that way.

Other members of the sphere of influence school including Blank take the opposite view. They expect Putin to grab the low hanging fruit that Washington places in his grasp.

Sources of Regime Change

A successful guns and butter authoritarian economy does not preclude pro or anti-democratic regime change.[126] Familiarity may breed contempt and new generations may find yesterday's leaders antique, even though Putin

---

"There is no doubt whatsoever that the lion's share of the Russian defence budget funds for the years 2011–20 was allocated to Aerospace Forces...." "President Putin's plan to increase the VKS inventory to 70 per cent of modern fleet by 2020 has already been fulfilled in 2017, and not as envisaged in 2020."

Susanna Oxenstierna, "Russian Defence Spending and the Economic Decline," *Journal of Eurasian Studies* 7, 2016.

[126] Cf., Richard Ellings and Robert Sutter, eds., *Axis of Authoritarians: Implications of China–Russia Cooperation* (New York: NBR Books, 2018).

can legally remain president until 2036. Factions within authoritarian ruling parties may undermine the "power vertical," usurp power from within, or launch their own insurgent anti-ruling party movements. The democratization of the Soviet Communist Party and the rise of alternative nationalist party insurgencies under Gorbachev's watch undermined the Kremlin's authority and abetted secession. Similar forces could subvert the authority of Putin and his *siloviki*, allowing rival authoritarians, nationalists or democrats to seize the reins of power even if living standards gradually rise, workers are fully employed, inflation tame, and Russian great power increases.

The key to Putin's and his *siloviki*'s survival is effective all-weather perceptions management. Kremlin authoritarians must convincingly tout their successes, camouflage their failures, and blame visible shortcomings on domestic and foreign enemies of the people (*vragy naroda*). Putin is adept at this and expects to prevail, while many Western analysts are confident that he will fail. It is difficult to gauge the probabilities because standard economic metrics have proven poor predictors of regime change, and even worse indicators of democratization. Material deprivation under Soviet rule created support for democratic regime change, but Yeltsin's hyper-depression turned out to be the harbinger of Putin, not a fast track transition to democratic free enterprise. It seems wisest to suppose that even if there is regime change in Russia's future, Kremlin great power authoritarianism may not vanish silently into the night.

Chapter 4

China

China's civilization has continuously evolved for more than two millennia without shedding its authoritarian core. Like Russia, it has internalized aspects of the Enlightenment, socialism, communism, balloting, private property, markets, and contract law but remains true to its "legalist" Qin Shi Huang tradition (221 BC–206 BC).[1]

China always has been an important military power. Its per capita GDP was on a par with the West's until 1500 when Europe's economic growth began outpacing the Middle Kingdom. China's per capita GDP fell to just 5 percent of the American level by 1950.[2] It modernized and recovered lost ground thereafter rising to 30 percent in 2018.[3] The CIA reports that China's GDP surpassed America's by 30 percent in 2018 computed on a purchasing power parity basis,[4] and its urban life style in major cities like Shanghai, Nanjing, and Beijing closely resembles Paris, London, and New York.

---

[1] Qin Shi Huang (18 February 259 BC–10 September 210 BC) was the founder of the Qin dynasty and first emperor of a unified China. Legalism (Fa-Jia) was an authoritarian governance philosophy that stressed obedience over morality.

[2] Angus Maddison, "The World Economy: Historical Statistics," *OECD* (2003): 643. For details, see Steven Rosefielde, *Asian Economic Systems* (Singapore: World Scientific Publishers, 2013).

[3] CIA, *World Factbook: China* (2017).

[4] CIA, *World Factbook: China* (2017).

72 *Beleaguered Superpower: Biden's America Adrift*

Precision is unimportant. The big picture is clear. China has one of the world's largest economies. Its living standard remains far below that of the developed West, but it has been recovering lost ground rapidly for more than 30 years, especially in its urban centers and the coastal zone ("Blue China").[5] China GDP growth is slowing. The forecast for 2020 is 5.6 percent per annum[6]; nonetheless, this rate is well above the Western norm (which is close to zero). China has become the industrial workshop of the world,[7] and is a significant technological competitor in both the civilian and military spheres.

These continuities amid change suggest that China is no longer an underdeveloped nation, although it has not yet fully modernized. It is culturally, militarily, and materially resilient, and the authoritarian state beneath the people's democratic republican veneer is durable enough for Beijing to defend its heritage and expand it spheres of influence.[8]

China's staying power makes its leaders impervious to Washington's soft power ploys and economic sanctions. The Forbidden City remains allergic to electoral democracy, the West's rule of law, freehold private

---

[5]Françoise Lemoine, Grégoire Mayo, Sandra Poncet, and Deniz Ünal, "The Geographic Pattern of China's Growth and Convergence within Industry," *CEPII* (February 2014), http://www.cepii.fr/PDF_PUB/wp/2014/wp2014-04.pdf.

"The coast includes here seven provinces Fujian, Guangdong, Hainan, Hebei, Jiangsu, Shandong, Zhejiang and three municipalities with provincial level (Beijing, Shanghai, Tianjin). It is home to 38% of the Chinese population on 10% of the territory, and creates about half China's GDP. The inland area includes all other provinces and can be subdivided into three regions: — The central region is the biggest one and includes 12 provinces (Anhui, Gansu, Guizhou, Henan, Hubei, Hunan, Jiangxi, Qinghai, Shaanxi, Shanxi, Sichuan, and Yunnan) and one municipality (Chongqing). It is home to 46% of the population on 37% of the territory. The northeast encompasses three provinces (Liaoning, Jilin, and Heilongjiang), with 8% of the population on 8% of the territory."

[6]"U.S.–China Trade War Dims Asia's 2019 Growth Outlook — ADB," *Reuters* (September 26, 2018). "IMF Downgrades China GDP Growth Outlook to 5.6%," *Nikkei Asian Review* (February 23, 2020), https://asia.nikkei.com/Spotlight/Coronavirus/IMF-downgrades-China-GDP-growth-outlook-to-5.6.

[7]Yuning Gao, *China as the Workshop of the World: An Analysis at the National and Industrial Level of China in the International Division of Labor* (London: Routledge, 2014).

[8]Steven Rosefielde and Jonathan Leightner, *China's Market Communism: Challenges, Dilemmas, Solutions* (London: Routledge, 2017).

property, and the Biden–Harris liberal agenda.[9] Xi Jinping does not intend to permit open immigration. Moreover, as Tibet's annexation, recent developments in the South China Sea,[10] the China–India border dispute in the Ladakh region, and the Hong Kong local autonomy dispute suggest,[11] China is inclined to expand its spheres of influence and territorial reach when opportunity knocks, just as it has since Qin Shi Huang's reign in the third century BC. Beijing is opposed to the West's economic, social, and political dominance, a point underscored by the Regional Comprehensive Economic Partnership (RCEP) accord covering 15 Asia-Pacific economies signed in Hanoi on November 15, 2020.[12] This means that China is apt to pose a greater security challenge to West as its economy converges closer to the global high frontier.

Shadow Boxing

Washington acknowledges the potential for Sino-American conflict, especially across the West Pacific, and is aware of Beijing's waxing power. Nonetheless, it is reluctant to treat the threat with sufficient prudence because it finds it convenient to believe that China is no match for the

---

[9] Sarah Cook, "China's Party Congress Hints at Media Strategy for a 'New Era'," *The Diplomat* (November 2017), https://thediplomat.com/2017/11/chinas-party-congress-hints-at-media-strategy-for-a-new-era/. Xi Jinping indicated that China will move forward in the future to a new strategy stressing socialist characteristics and global power at the 19th Party Congress, October 2017. It is unlikely that this strategy will be compatible with the Global Nation agenda.

[10] Steven Rosefielde, "Rising Red Star," in Steven Rosefielde, Masaaki Kuboniwa, Kumiko Haba, and Satoshi Mizobata, eds., *The Unwinding of the Globalist Dream: EU, Russia, China*, (Singapore: World Scientific Publishers, 2017): 237–244.

[11] Helen Davidson and Ben Doherty, "Explainer: What is the Deadly India-China Border Dispute About?" *Guardian* (June 16, 2020), https://www.theguardian.com/world/2020/jun/17/explainer-what-is-the-deadly-india-china-border-dispute-about.

[12] The RCEP is a free trade agreement in the Asia-Pacific region between the ten member states of ASEAN, namely Brunei, Cambodia, Indonesia, Laos, Malaysia, Myanmar, the Philippines, Singapore, Thailand, and Vietnam, and five of their FTA partners — Australia, China, Japan, New Zealand, and South Korea. The 15 negotiating countries account for about 30 percent of both the world's population and the global GDP, making it the largest trade bloc. It was signed at the Vietnam-hosted virtual ASEAN Summit on November 15, 2020. Charmaine Ng, "15 Countries, including Singapore, Sign RCEP, the World's Largest Trade Pact," *The Straits Times* (November 15, 2020).

74   *Beleaguered Superpower: Biden's America Adrift*

United States now or in the near future. It is confident that America's navy will prevail in the West Pacific. This attitude predisposes American leaders to underestimate and inadequately respond to the Chinese threat, relying on happy thoughts instead of stout hard power. Although, the Obama–Biden administration soft peddled the progressive agenda in China to avoid antagonizing Xi Jinping, its response to Beijing's challenge in the South China Sea under its watch testifies to its faith in strategic patience, Washington's "pivot to East Asia" notwithstanding.[13] The Biden–Harris administration appears more apprehensive about China's

---

[13] Hillary Clinton, "America's Pacific Century: The Future of Politics Will Be Decided in Asia, Not Afghanistan or Iraq, and the United States Will Be Right at the Center of the Action," *Foreign Policy* (October 2011), http://foreignpolicy.com/2011/10/11/americas-pacific-century/.

The centerpiece of America's national security policy toward China during the Obama era was his "pivot" to East Asia in 2012. Its goals were "strengthening bilateral security alliances; deepening our working relationships with emerging powers, including with China; engaging with regional multilateral institutions; expanding trade and investment; forging a broad-based military presence; and advancing democracy and human rights."

"One of the most important tasks of American statecraft over the next decade will therefore be to lock in a substantially increased investment — diplomatic, economic, strategic, and otherwise — in the Asia-Pacific region." "Our treaty alliances with Japan, South Korea, Australia, the Philippines, and Thailand are the fulcrum for our strategic turn to the Asia-Pacific. They have underwritten regional peace and security for more than half a century, shaping the environment for the region's remarkable economic ascent. They leverage our regional presence and enhance our regional leadership at a time of evolving security challenges."

"We all know that fears and misperceptions linger on both sides of the Pacific. Some in our country see China's progress as a threat to the United States; some in China worry that America seeks to constrain China's growth. We reject both those views. The fact is that a thriving America is good for China and a thriving China is good for America." "So the United States has moved to fully engage the region's multilateral institutions, such as the Association of Southeast Asian Nations (ASEAN) and the Asia-Pacific Economic Cooperation (APEC) forum, mindful that our work with regional institutions supplements and does not supplant our bilateral ties. There is a demand from the region that America play an active role in the agenda-setting of these institutions — and it is in our interests as well that they be effective and responsive."

The military component of the pivot has been ballyhooed, with little to show for the effort.

military assertiveness, but is inclined to temporize.[14] Progressives and liberals remain hopeful that Xi Jinping will not allow his ambitions to overwhelm his caution,[15] despite the festering South China Sea conflict,[16] and struggle over Taiwan.

Foundations of Chinese Power

The Biden–Harris administration cannot accept that China is poised to be more than a nascent superpower and implacable regional rival, but their

---

Prem Mahadeva, "Maritime Insecurity in East Asia" in *Strategic Trends 2013, Center for Security Studies (CSS)* (2013), http://www.css.ethz.ch/content/dam/ethz/special-interest/gess/cis/center-for-securities-studies/pdfs/Strategic-Trends-2013-EastAsia.pdf.

"Consequently, newly commissioned ships and fifth generation aircraft are being prioritized for the Pacific theater of U.S. military operations to maintain the balance of power."

"It is expected that when the 'rebalancing' or 'pivot' of forces from the Atlantic to the Pacific is complete, 60 percent of the U.S. Navy will be based in the Pacific — a 10 percent increase from current levels. In effect, the theater would gain one additional U.S. aircraft carrier, seven destroyers, ten littoral combat ships and two submarines, plus reconnaissance assets such as EP3 spy planes."

[14]Ana Swanson, "Biden's China Policy? A Balancing Act for a Toxic Relationship," *New York Times* (November 2020), https://news.yahoo.com/bidens-china-policy-balancing-act-130318173.html.

[15]Bethany Allen-Ebrahimian, "Democrats and Republicans Have Argued about China for 150 Years," *Axios* (April 29, 2020), https://www.axios.com/newsletters/axios-china.

[16]John Ford, "The Pivot to Asia Was Obama's Biggest Mistake," *The Diplomat* (January 2017), http://thediplomat.com/2017/01/the-pivot-to-asia-was-obamas-biggest-mistake/.

"Emblematic of this mistake was the roll-out of the Air-Sea Battle doctrine. First outlined in a then-classified memo in 2009, ASB became official doctrine in 2010. From the beginning, it was an effort to develop an operational doctrine for a possible military confrontation with China and then-Secretary of Defense Robert Gates openly discussed the need to counter China's growing military capabilities. The signal received in Beijing was the United States had hostile intentions toward China and was trying to contain it militarily. The result was that the entire pivot was seen by Beijing as part of a broader effort to encircle China."

attitude is unjustified.[17] China is no longer a Soviet-style socialist planned economy intrinsically inferior to the democratic free enterprise ideal. Chinese market communism today is a two-level authoritarian managed market system commanded by the Chinese Communist Party, which is the *de jure* freehold owner of the means of production. It is a top-down strategic indicative macroplanning regime governed by the Communist Party of China (CPC) from above, and party managed competitive leasehold enterprises below. Households purchase the goods they prefer in workably competitive markets, but the Communist Party regulates wages, terms of employment, and controls public expenditures (including defense). The system abridges personal freedom for the party's purposes, but claims to does so for the people's good. It has defects and vulnerabilities, nonetheless may well be superior to the American progressive-liberal model from an international security perspective.[18]

Beijing excels in regional hard power. It also exerts enormous influence across the entire Asia Pacific region economically through its manufacturing supply chains and foreign direct investment.[19] China has become

---

[17]Henry Kissinger, *On China* (New York: Penguin, 2011); Tilman Pradt, *China's New Foreign Policy: Military Modernisation, Multilateralism and the 'China Threat'* (London: Palgrave Macmillan, 2016).

[18]Steven Rosefielde, "New Millennial Economic Systems: Paradox of Power and Reason," *Foresight and STI Governance* (forthcoming 2021); Steven Rosefielde and Jonathan Leightner, *China's Market Communism: Challenges, Dilemmas, Solutions* (London: Routledge, 2017); Joseph Nye, Jr., *Bound to Lead: The Changing Nature of American Power* (New York: Basic Books, 1990).

Joseph Nye, the "father" of "soft power" is inexplicit about the classification of foreign trade, finance, and transnational institutions in his hard power/soft power dichotomy. He classifies "payments" like foreign aid as hard power, lumping other intangibles into the soft power category.

"When one country gets other countries to want what it wants-might be called co-optive or soft power in contrast with the hard or command power of ordering others to do what it wants."

Economists use the term "goodwill" to represent intangible value.

[19]Council on Foreign Relations, "The Future of Global Supply Chains," (June 29, 2016), file:///C:/Users/stevenr/Downloads/Workshop_Report_CSMD_Global_Supply_Chains_OR%20(1).pdf; Richard Baldwin and Javier Lopez-Gonzalez, "Supply-Chain Trade: A Portrait of Global Patterns and Several Testable Hypotheses," *The World Economy* 38, no. 11, November 2015: 1682–1721.

China 77

the industrial workshop of the world, accounting for a quarter of global manufacturing output.[20] Shrewd leaders like Xi Jinping can use hard military and soft economic power effectively for national advantage.

China's hard power today is not as great as the Soviet Union's was in its heyday *vis-à-vis* America, nor as Russia is today because Beijing's nuclear arsenal is relatively small (although far larger than the arms control community's 260 warhead estimate),[21] and communist ideology is no

---

[20] Council on Foreign Relations, "The Future of Global Supply Chains," (June 29, 2016), file:///C:/Users/stevenr/Downloads/Workshop_Report_CSMD_Global_Supply_Chains_OR%20(1).pdf.

[21] Steven Rosefielde, *False Science: Underestimating the Soviet Arms Buildup* (New Brunswick: Transaction, 1982). Melissa Hanham, "China's Happy to Sit Out the Nuclear Arms Race While Putin and Trump Push for Bigger Arsenals, Beijing Has All The Nukes It'll Ever Need," *Foreign Policy* (January 2017), http://foreignpolicy.com/2017/01/30/chinas-happy-to-sit-out-the-nuclear-arms-race/.

"While the number of nuclear weapons in the United States and the Soviet Union swelled to over 50,000 in the mid-1980s, and they produced warheads and delivery devices far deadlier than those used in Hiroshima and Nagasaki, China was content to stick with dozens, not thousands, of warheads. Even today, the United States and Russia believe nuclear deterrence requires thousands of warheads each, and at least three ways to deliver them. But the truth of the matter is that you can annihilate your adversary (or the planet) only so many times. In fact, some in the U.S. Air Force have argued that 311 warheads would provide nine-and-a-half times the destructive power needed to incapacitate the Soviet Union by former Defense Secretary Robert McNamara's count. For China, it's not the size of the arsenal that counts, it's how you use it. About 200 nuclear warheads are 'enough'." Jeffrey Lewis, *Paper Tigers: China's Nuclear Posture* (London: Routledge, 2015). Cf. "China 'Deploys Missiles' Amid Calls for More Nuclear Weapons to Deter Donald Trump," *Telegraph* (January 25, 2017), http://www.telegraph.co.uk/news/2017/01/25/china-deploys-missiles-amid-calls-nuclear-weapons-deter-donald/.

"Beijing is moving advanced ballistic missiles which are capable of hitting the US to its north-eastern frontier with Russia, according to media reports, amid suggestions that the weapons were revealed in response to Donald Trump's 'provocative remarks' towards China. The Chinese Internet has carried unverified pictures of the deployment of the nuclear capable Dongfeng-41 missiles to Heilongjiang province, which is also the closest point of China to the US. The weapon has a range of 8,700 miles (14,000 kilometres) and a payload of 10 to 12 nuclear warheads, reports said."

Jeffrey Lin and P.W. Singer, "The Nuclear Arsenals of China and the U.S.: Plans for a Future Armageddon: A Quick Run-Down of They Have Now, and What They'll Get in

78 *Beleaguered Superpower: Biden's America Adrift*

the Coming Decades," *Popular Science* (January 27, 2017), http://www.popsci.com/nuclear-arsenals-china-united-states.

"The 9,320-mile-range DF-41 ICBM is one of the world's most lethal missiles. Weighing about 80 tons, it is carried and launched by a 12X12 all-terrain truck, and can also be launched from rail. Its payload of 12 MIRV nuclear warheads can be augmented with decoys and jammers to confuse enemy sensors, letting the actual warheads slip past missile defenses. Currently, a Chinese Rocket Force brigade of 10–12 launchers is forming in northeastern China, near the Russian border. (Ironically, the DF-41 poses little threat to Russia there since its large minimum range makes it impossible to hit most Russian territory from its current position)."

Arms Control Association, "Nuclear Weapons: Who Has What at a Glance," (January 2017), https://www.armscontrol.org/factsheets/Nuclearweaponswhohaswhat.

The ACA estimates that China has 260 nuclear weapons. The US–China Military Scorecard: Forces, Geography and the Evolving Balance of Military Power, Rand (2015), http://www.rand.org/content/dam/rand/pubs/research_reports/RR300/RR392/RAND_RR392.pdf; Arms Control Association, "Nuclear Weapons: Who Has What at a Glance," (January 2017), https://www.armscontrol.org/factsheets/Nuclearweaponswhohaswhat.

"Historically, the People's Republic has adopted a policy of minimal deterrence, using the threat of intolerable damage to convince both Moscow and the United States that an attack was not in their interest. This has meant maintaining a deterrent nuclear arsenal distinctly, and intentionally, inferior to that of Russia and the United States. It has matched this arsenal with delivery systems generally inferior to those of the two superpowers. The second part of this is beginning to change, with the caveat that the boomer fleet remains substantially behind Russia or US standards. However, it's not yet certain that the first part is changing. For example, there's no indication that tactical nuclear warheads have become relevant to China's conventional warfighting plans, as remains the case with the Russian military. Indeed, China has concentrated on developing the conventional capabilities of systems often associated with nuclear weapons, such as ballistic and cruise missiles. The achievement of secure second strike, especially in context of the arsenal reduction by the two nuclear superpowers, does not require a massive expansion in the number of Chinese weapons. It simply requires making them more survivable. We probably aren't headed back to the reality of the 60s and 70s, when the US and the USSR faced off with thousands of tactical and strategic warheads apiece. But much depends on how China approaches the expansion, apart from the modernization, of its nuclear arsenal."

Hans M. Kristensen, "No, China Does Not Have 3,000 Nuclear Weapons," *Federation of Atomic Scientists* (December 3, 2011), https://fas.org/blogs/security/2011/12/chinanukes/.

"A recent example of how not to make an estimate is the study recently published by the Asia Arms Control Project at Georgetown University. The study (China's Underground Great Wall: Challenge for Nuclear Arms Control) suggests that China may have as many

China 79

longer a regional asset. China for the moment does not seek Third International style ideological global control[22]

Chinese Military Modernization

Nonetheless, Beijing's hard power makes it increasingly difficult for the United States to manage the Diaoyu (Senkaku) islands dispute, the North

---

as 3,000 nuclear weapons." "The most fundamental problem with the 3,000-warhead estimate is that there is no evidence — at least in the public — that China has produced enough fissile material to build that many warheads. Not even close. An arsenal of 3,000 two-stage thermonuclear warheads with yields of 300–500 kilotons would require 9–12 tons of weapon-grade plutonium and 45–75 tons of highly-enriched uranium (HEU)." Note that the CIA's estimate of Soviet fissile material was only one tenth the figure revealed after the USSR collapsed.

Anthony Cordesman and Steven Colley, "Chinese Strategy and Military Modernization," *Center for Strategic and International Studies* (*CSIS*) (December 2015), Rand, "An Interactive Look at the U.S.–China Military Scorecard," (2017), https://www.rand.org/paf/projects/us-china-scorecard.html; Office of the Secretary of Defense, "Annual Report to Congress: Military and Security Developments Involving the People's Republic of China 2016," (April 2016), http://www.defense.gov/Portals/1/Documents/pubs/2016%20China%20Military%20Power%20Report.pdf; Office of the Secretary of Defense, "Annual Report to Congress: Military and Security Developments Involving the People's Republic of China 2020,"(August 2020), https://media.defense.gov/2020/Sep/01/2002488689/-1/-1/1/2020-DOD-CHINA-MILITARY-POWER-REPORT-FINAL.PDF; Nadège Rolland, "China's National Power: A Colossus with Iron or Clay Feet?," in Ashley J. Tellis, Alison Szalwinski and Michael Wills, eds., *Strategic Asia 2015–16: Foundations of National Power in the Asia-Pacific* (November 2015), http://nbr.org/publications/element.aspx?id=836; "The US-China Military Scorecard: Forces, Geography and the Evolving Balance of Military Power," *Rand* (2015), http://www.rand.org/content/dam/rand/pubs/research_reports/RR300/RR392/RAND_RR392.pdf.

[22]The Communist International (Comintern) and also known as the Third International (1919–1943), was an international communist organization controlled by Moscow that advocated world communism. Stalin set up the Cominform, or Communist Information Bureau in September 1947 as an informal successor to Comintern. Its members included the Communist parties of Bulgaria, Czechoslovakia, France, Hungary, Italy, Poland, Romania, the Soviet Union, and Yugoslavia. The Cominform was dissolved in 1956. Communist parties of the world continued to maintain close relations with each other through a series of international forums.

80   *Beleaguered Superpower: Biden's America Adrift*

Korean imbroglio, Taiwan's independence, the militarization of the South China Sea, and China's challenge to freedom of navigation in the Asia Pacific.

China's official defense goals, as reported by the American Department of Defense are:

> "China is advancing a comprehensive military modernization program aimed at completing modernization by 2035 and making the PLA into a 'world-class' military by 2049."[23]

The critical aspect of the military balance centers on naval forces, missiles with conventional ordnance, and complementary air support, assuming as the evidence suggests that China maintains a credible first strike deterrent,[24] and that neither side relishes a ground war, a limited nuclear exchange within the Asia Pacific region, or global nuclear war.[25]

China has been concentrating its military investments precisely where they are most effective: in missiles with conventional ordnance,

---

[23] Office of the Secretary of Defense, "Annual Report to Congress: Military and Security Developments Involving the People's Republic of China 2019," (May 2019), https://fas.org/man/eprint/dod-china-2019.pdf.

Office of the Secretary of Defense, "Annual Report to Congress: Military and Security Developments Involving the People's Republic of China 2020," (August 2020), https://media.defense.gov/2020/Sep/01/2002488689/-1/-1/1/2020-DOD-CHINA-MILITARY-POWER-REPORT-FINAL.PDF.

[24] First strike capability is a country's ability to defeat another nuclear power by destroying its arsenal to the point where the attacking country can survive the weakened retaliation while the opposing side is left unable to continue war.

[25] Robert Farley, "Should America Fear China's Nuclear Weapons?," *The National Interest* (August 2014), http://nationalinterest.org/feature/should-america-fear-chinas-nuclear-weapons-11046.

"For example, there's no indication that tactical nuclear warheads have become relevant to China's conventional warfighting plans, as remains the case with the Russian military. Indeed, China has concentrated on developing the conventional capabilities of systems often associated with nuclear weapons, such as ballistic and cruise missiles."

Farley's statement is contradicted by the US Department of Defense.

Office of the Secretary of Defense, "Annual Report to Congress: Military and Security Developments Involving the People's Republic of China 2016," (April 2016).

China 81

naval forces, and complementary air support. According to the Office of the US Secretary of Defense 2019 assessment,[26] the People's Liberation Army (PLA) Rocket Force (PLARF) operates China's land-based nuclear and conventional missiles. It is developing and testing several new classes and variants of offensive missiles, including a hypersonic glide vehicle; forming additional missile units; upgrading older missile systems; and developing methods to counter ballistic missile defenses.

The force possesses approximately 1,200 short-range ballistic missiles (SRBM) in its inventory. China is increasing the lethality of its conventional missile force by fielding the CSS-11 (DF-16) ballistic missile with a range of 800–1,000 km (well within range of Taiwan and Tokyo). The CSS-11, coupled with the already deployed conventional land-attack and anti-ship variants of the CSS-5 (DF-21C/D) medium-range ballistic missile (MRBM), will improve China's ability to strike Taiwan, and other regional targets. The CJ-10 ground-launched cruise missile (GLCM) complements these ballistic missile systems. The CJ-10 has a range in excess of 1,500 km and offers flight profiles different from ballistic

---

"The official parade announcer also referenced a nuclear version of the DF-26, which, if it shares the same guidance capabilities, would give China its first nuclear precision strike capability against theater targets."

[26]Office of the Secretary of Defense, "Annual Report to Congress: Military and Security Developments Involving the People's Republic of China 2016," (April 2016).

"During 2015, the PLA continued to improve key capabilities that would be used in theater contingencies, including cruise missiles; short, medium, and intermediate-range ballistic missiles; high performance aircraft; integrated air defense networks; information operations capabilities; and amphibious and airborne assault units. The PLA is developing and testing new intermediate- and medium-range conventional ballistic missiles as well as long range, land-attack, and anti-ship cruise missiles, which once operational would extend the military's reach and push adversary forces further from potential regional conflicts. China is also focusing on counter space, offensive cyber operations, and electronic warfare (EW) capabilities meant to deny adversaries the advantages of modern, information technology-driven warfare" (p. ii).

Office of the Secretary of Defense, "Annual Report to Congress: Military and Security Developments Involving the People's Republic of China 2019," (May 2019), https://fas.org/man/eprint/dod-china-2019.pdf. Office of the Secretary of Defense, "Annual Report to Congress: Military and Security Developments Involving the People's Republic of China 2020," (August 2020), https://media.defense.gov/2020/Sep/01/2002488689/-1/-1/1/2020-DOD-CHINA-MILITARY-POWER-REPORT-FINAL.PDF.

missiles that can enhance targeting options. China is fielding a growing number of conventionally armed MRBMs, including the CSS-5 Mod 5 (DF-21D) anti-ship ballistic missile (ASBM). The CSS-5 Mod 5, with a range of 1,500 km and maneuverable warhead, gives the PLA the capability to attack ships, including aircraft carriers, in the western Pacific Ocean. It can also hit Manila. China unveiled the DF-26 intermediate-range ballistic missile (IRBM) during the September 2015 parade in Beijing. The DF- 26 is capable of conducting precision strikes against ground targets and contributes to strategic deterrence in the Asia-Pacific region. China has deployed 16 DF-26 launchers.[27]

Its official parade announcer also referenced a nuclear version of the DF-26, which will give China its first nuclear precision strike capability against theater targets. The PLARF continued to modernize its nuclear forces by enhancing its silo-based intercontinental ballistic missiles (ICBM) and adding more survivable, mobile delivery systems. China's ICBM arsenal to date consists of approximately 75–100 ICBMs, including the silo-based CSS-4 Mod 2 (DF-5) and multiple independently targetable reentry vehicle (MIRV)-equipped Mod 3 (DF-5B); the solid-fueled, road-mobile CSS-10 Mod 1 and 2 (DF-31 and DF-31A); and the shorter range CSS-3 (DF-4). The CSS-10 Mod 2, with a range in excess of 11,200 km, can reach most locations within the continental United States and Guam. China also is developing a new road-mobile ICBM, the CSS-X-20 (DF-41) capable of carrying MIRVs.

Over the past 18 years, China's ambitious naval modernization program has produced a more technologically advanced and flexible force. Beijing now possesses the world's second largest navy.[28] Its navy has the largest number of vessels in Asia, with more than 300 surface ships, submarines, amphibious ships, and patrol craft. China is rapidly retiring legacy combatants in favor of larger, multi-mission ships equipped with advanced anti-ship, anti-air, and anti-submarine weapons and sensors. China continues its gradual shift from "near sea" defense to "far seas" protection as espoused in its most recent Defense White Paper (DWP) 2018, with the PLAN conducting operational tasks outside the so-called "first island chain" with multi- mission, long-range, sustainable naval platforms that have robust self-defense capabilities. The PLAN places a

---

[27]DIA, Ballistic and Cruise Missile Threat (2017).

[28]The world's 10 largest navies in rank order those of the United States, China, Russia, Japan, the United Kingdom, France, India, and Italy.

high priority on the modernization of its submarine force and currently possesses five SSNs, four nuclear powered ballistic missile submarines (SSBN), and 53 diesel-powered attack submarines (SS/SSP). By 2020, this force will likely grow to between 69 and 78 submarines. In addition to the 12 KILO-class SS units acquired from Russia in the 1990s and 2000s, China has built 13 SONG-class SS (Type 039) and 13 YUAN-class SSP (Type 039A) with a total of 20 YUANs planned for production. China continues to improve its SSN force, and four additional SHANG-class SSN (Type 093) will eventually join the two already in service. These improved SHANG SSNs feature a vertical launch system (VLS) and may be able to fire the YJ-18 advanced anti-ship cruise missile (ASCM). Over the next decade, China may construct a new Type 095 nuclear-powered, guided missile attack submarine (SSGN), which not only would improve the PLAN's anti-surface warfare capability but might also provide it with a more clandestine land-attack option. Finally, China continues to produce the JIN-class SSBN (Type 094) with associated CSSN-14 (JL-2) submarine-launched ballistic missiles (SLBM) that has an estimated range of 7,200 km. This platform represents China's first credible, sea-based nuclear deterrent. China conducted its first SSBN nuclear deterrence patrol in 2016. Four JIN SSBNs are operational, and up to five may enter service before China begins developing and fielding its next-generation SSBN, the Type 096, over the coming decade. The Type 096 will be armed with the JL-3 SLBM. Since 2008, the PLAN has continued its robust surface combatant construction program, including guided missile destroyers (DDG) and guided-missile frigates (FFG). During 2015, the final LUYANG II-class DDG (Type 052C) entered service, bringing the total number of ships of this class to six. Additionally, a second LUYANG III-class DDG (Type 052D) entered service in 2015. It has a multipurpose VLS capable of launching ASCMs, land-attack cruise missiles (LACM), surface-to-air missiles (SAM), and antisubmarine missiles. China has also probably begun construction of a larger Type 055 "destroyer," a vessel better characterized as a guided-missile cruiser (CG) than a DDG. China has continued to produce the JIANGKAI II-class FFG (Type 054A), with 20 ships currently in the fleet and five in various stages of construction. These new DDGs and FFGs provide a significant upgrade to the PLAN's air defense capability, which will be critical as it expands operations into distant seas beyond the range of shore based air defense systems. Augmenting the PLAN's littoral warfare capabilities, especially in the South China Sea and East China Sea, is a new class of small

84 *Beleaguered Superpower: Biden's America Adrift*

combatant vessels. Twenty-five JIANGDAO-class corvettes (FFL) (Type 056) are in service and the latest ships have antisubmarine warfare (ASW) variants with a towed array sonar. China may build more than 60 of this class. China also has 60 HOUBEI-class wave-piercing catamaran guided-missile patrol boats (PTG) (Type 022) built for operations in China's "near seas." The PLAN continues to emphasize anti-surface warfare (ASUW) as its primary focus, including modernizing its advanced ASCMs and associated over-the-horizon targeting systems. Older surface combatants carry variants of the YJ-83 ASCM (65 nm, 120 km), while newer surface combatants such as the LUYANG II are fitted with the YJ-62 (120 nm, 222 km). The LUYANG III and Type 055 CG will be fitted with a variant of China's newest ASCM, the YJ-18 (290 nm, 537 km), which is a signifi-cant step forward in China's surface ASUW capability. Eight of China's 12 KILOs are equipped with the SS-N-27 ASCM (120 nm, 222 km), a system China acquired from Russia. Its newest indigenous submarine-launched ASCM, the YJ-18 and variants, represent an improvement over the SS-N-27. SONG, YUAN, and SHANG submarines will deploy them.

China's YJ-82 submarine-launched ASCM is a longer range version of the C-801. The PLAN recognizes that long-range ASCMs require a robust, over-the-horizon targeting capability to realize their full potential, and China is investing in reconnaissance, surveillance, command, control, and communications systems at the strategic, operational, and tactical levels to provide high-fidelity targeting information to surface and subsur-face launch platforms. Its investments in its amphibious ship force signal China's intent to develop an expeditionary and over-the-horizon amphibi-ous assault capability as well as HA/DR and counterpiracy capabilities. Since 2005, China has built three large YUZHAO class (Type 071) amphibious transport docks (LPD) with a fourth soon to enter service, providing considerably greater and more flexible capability for "far seas" operations than the older landing ships. The YUZHAO can carry up to four of the new YUYI-class air-cushion medium landing craft (LCMA) and four or more helicopters, as well as armored vehicles and marines for long distance deployments. Additional YUZHAO construction incorpo-rating a full flight deck for helicopters is expected. Two YUTING II-class tank landing ships (LST) are currently being built to support logistics operations, particularly in the South China Sea. In 2015, the PLAN's first aircraft carrier, LIAONING, certified its first cohort of domestically trained J-15 operational pilots. The air wing deployed on carrier in 2016. China also began construction of its first domestic aircraft carrier and could build multiple aircraft carriers over the next 15 years. LIAONING however, will not enable long-range power projection similar to US NIMITZ class carriers. LIAONING's smaller size limits the number of aircraft it can embark, while the ski-jump configuration limits aircraft fuel and ordnance loads. LIAONING is useful for air defense missions, extending air cover over a fleet operating far from land-based coverage. Although it possesses a full suite of weapons and combat systems, LIAONING will probably continue to play a significant role in training China's carrier pilots, deck crews, and developing tactics.

PLA Air Force (PLAAF) is the largest air force in Asia and the third largest in the world behind America and Russia, with more than 2,800 total aircraft (not including UAVs) and 2,100 combat aircraft (including fighters, bombers, fighter-attack, and attack aircraft). The PLAAF is rapidly closing the gap with western air forces across a broad spectrum of capabilities from aircraft and command-and-control (C2) to jammers, electronic warfare (EW), and datalinks. The PLAAF continues to field additional fourth generation aircraft (now about 600). It will probably become a majority fourth-generation force within the next several years. The PLAAF and PLAN may become more prominent within the PLA if China proceeds with the personnel reductions announced in September 2015. The personnel levels of the PLAAF and PLAN were reported to be just 398,000 and 235,000, respectively, in 2016,[29] accounting for 27.5 percent of the PLA overall.

China has developed the J-10B follow-on to its first indigenously designed fourth generation fighter. It will enter service in the near term. The PLA is also likely to acquire the Su-35 Flanker aircraft from Russia along with its advanced radar system. In November 2015, talks to purchase 24 Su-35 fighters reportedly concluded successfully. China has been pursuing fifth-generation fighter capabilities since at least 2009. It is the only country other than the United States to have two concurrent stealth fighter programs. China seeks to develop these advanced aircraft to improve its regional power projection capabilities and to strengthen its ability to strike regional airbases and facilities. PLAAF leaders believe stealth aircraft provide an offensive operational advantage that denies an adversary the time to mobilize and to conduct defensive operations. In 2015, China began flight-testing its fifth and sixth J-20 stealth fighter

---

[29] Soviet military manpower was six times larger than the official figure. China's military manpower should be viewed with suspicion.

prototypes. The prototype is similar in size to a US F-35 fighter and appears to incorporate design characteristics similar to the J-20. The FC-31 conducted its first flight on October 31, 2012, and debuted at China's 10th China International Aviation & Aerospace Exhibition in Zhuhai in November 2014. The Aviation Industry Corporation of China is actively marketing the FC-31 as an export fifth-generation multirole fighter to compete with the F-35 for foreign sales.

In addition to manned fighter aircraft, the PLAAF also views stealth technology as integral to unmanned aircraft, specifically those with an air-to-ground role, as this technology would improve that system's ability to penetrate heavily protected targets. China is also producing bomber-class aircraft. China continues to upgrade its H-6 bomber fleet to increase operational effectiveness and lethality by integrating new standoff weapons. The PLAAF operates three different H-6 bomber variants. The H-6H and the more capable H-6M have been in service since the last decade. The PLAAF also employs the new, fully redesigned H-6K variant with new turbofan engines for extended range and the capability to carry six LACMs. Converting the H-6 into a cruise missile carrier gives the PLA a long-range standoff offensive air capability with precision-guided munitions capable of striking Guam. In 2015, China flew H-6Ks into the western Pacific Ocean in a demonstration of the airframe's long-range capability. PLA Navy Aviation utilizes a nearly identical version of the earlier H-6, known as the H-6G equipped with systems and four weapons pylons for ASCMs to support maritime missions. China is also receiving receive IL-78s from Ukraine, which are outfitted as air-refueling tankers. China Ukraine negotiations for additional tankers will likely continue.

China is improving its airfields in the South China Sea with the availability of Woody Island Airfield in the Paracel Islands and construction of up to three new airfields in the Spratly Islands. All of these airfields could have runways long enough to support any aircraft in China's inventory. During late October 2015, the PLAN deployed four of its most capable air superiority fighters, the J-11B, to Woody Island. The PLAAF possesses one of the largest forces of advanced long-range SAM systems in the world, consisting of a combination of Russian-sourced SA-20 (S-300PMU1/2) battalions and domestically produced CSA-9 (HQ-9) battalions. In an effort to improve its strategic air defense systems even further, China plans to import Russia's S-400/Triumf SAM system and may simultaneously develop its indigenous CSA-X-19 (HQ-19) to provide the basis for a ballistic missile defense capability. China's aviation industry continues to test its Y-20 large transport aircraft for introduction into the PLA's operational inventory to supplement and eventually replace China's small fleet of strategic airlift assets, which currently consist of a limited number of Russian-made IL-76 aircraft. The large transports are intended to support airborne C2, logistics, para drop, aerial refueling, and strategic reconnaissance operations, as well as HA/DR missions.[30]

Chinese National Military Strategic Guidelines[31]

The Cold War ended in 1991. The ensuing three decades brought a "peace dividend" of sorts in Europe and the Asia Pacific. The United States and NATO reduced American troop levels and arms procurement.[32] Beijing's perception of America's threat should have diminished during this period, especially after China joined the World Trade Organization (WTO) in 2001, but it relentlessly modernized its armed forces at double-digit rates, expanding its force projection capabilities.[33] Why?

---

[30] Office of the Secretary of Defense, "Annual Report to Congress: Military and Security Developments Involving the People's Republic of China 2016," (April 2016): 22–37, 43–44.

Office of the Secretary of Defense, "Annual Report to Congress: Military and Security Developments Involving the People's Republic of China 2019," (May 2019), https://fas.org/man/eprint/dod-china-2019.pdf. Office of the Secretary of Defense, "Annual Report to Congress: Military and Security Developments Involving the People's Republic of China 2020," (August 2020). https://media.defense.gov/2020/Sep/01/2002488689/-1/-1/1/2020-DOD-CHINA-MILITARY-POWER-REPORT-FINAL.PDF.

[31] US Department of Defense, "Asia-Pacific Maritime Security Strategy: Achieving U.S. National Security Objectives in a Changing Environment Maritime Security Strategy," (2015).

[32] Michael Intriligator, "The Concept of a Peace Dividend," in James K. Galbraith, Jurgen Brauer, and Lucy Law Webster, eds., *Economics of Peace and Security* (Paris: EOLSS Publications, 2009), http://www.eolss.net/sample-chapters/c13/E6-28A-02-04.pdf.

"The 'peace dividend' is a concept that has been used to refer to the benefits derived from lower defense spending and the conversion of military production into civilian production."

[33] US Department of Defense, "Asia-Pacific Maritime Security Strategy: Achieving U.S. National Security Objectives in a Changing Environment Maritime Security Strategy," (2015).

88   *Beleaguered Superpower: Biden's America Adrift*

Lawrence Korb, former director of national security studies at the Council on Foreign Relations suggests that "the PLA aims to develop a robust 'anti-access and area denial' (A2/AD) capability *vis-à-vis* technologically superior opponents." The purpose of A2/AD operations is to deny the US, Japan, and UK unfettered access to the Western Pacific where Chinese core national interests are at stake, including Taiwan and territorial claims in the South China Sea.

To develop this capability, the PLA has invested heavily in anti-satellite weapons, ballistic missiles, cyber warfare, a growing fleet of submarines and the development of its J-20 stealth fighter. Through these weapon systems, PLA strategists hope to have the ability to degrade superior US C4ISR (command, control, communications, computer, intelligence, surveillance, and reconnaissance), ideally rendering the US military "deaf, dumb and blind" while simultaneously disrupting or shutting down US bases in the region, including aircraft carriers."[34] The United States Department of Defense concurs.[35]

Should Beijing succeed in denying American forces "unfettered" access to the Western Pacific, Taiwan's security together with the security of ASEAN would depend on their indigenous military power; that is, China would become the *de facto* arbiter of the West Pacific's fate. Beijing would become Southeast Asia's hegemon, impose direct rule over Taipei, control naval access to Pacific Rim markets and isolate Japan without ever having to fire a shot. All Xi Jinping would need to do is nullify America's naval deterrent, and he will become emperor of the Western Pacific.

Andrew Marshall,[36] Director of Net Assessment, Office of the Secretary of the Secretary of Defense 1973–2015 devised the Pacific Air Sea Battle plan (Joint Concept for Access and Maneuver in the Global Commons (JAM-GC)) strategy in 2009 to keep America one step ahead of China by continuously introducing new advanced

---

[34]Lawrence Korb (co-written with Bill French), "A Prudent Response to Chinese Military Modernization," *Huffington* Post (December 19, 2011), http://www.huffingtonpost.com/lawrence-korb/defense-spending_b_1158413.html.

[35]US Department of Defense, "Asia-Pacific Maritime Security Strategy: Achieving U.S. National Security Objectives in a Changing Environment Maritime Security Strategy," (2015).

[36]Greg Jaffe, "U.S. Model for a Future War Fan Tensions with China and Inside Pentagon," *The Washington Post* (August 1, 2012).

China 89

technologies and strategies.[37] The answer to Beijing's "anti-access and area denial" initiative is to keep the PLA technologically and strategically behind the power curve. If China cannot overcome America's military technological superiority, the Pentagon will always thwart Beijing's aspirations no matter how many weapons it deploys in its order of battle.[38]

The Pacific Air Sea Battle plan,[39] a corollary of the Revolution in Military Affairs (RMA),[40] requires America to perpetually best China in a military technology and strategy race to sustain the *status quo*, or outlast the Middle Kingdom in the West Pacific. Washington must enhance electronic and cyber warfare capabilities, backup communication systems, submersible drones, ballistic missile defenses, develop new long-range strike systems, and train the US military to operate in C4ISR.

---

[37]David Goldfein, "Document: Air Sea Battle Name Change Memo," (January 8, 2015), news.usni.org; Andrew Krepinevich, "CSBA: Why AirSea Battle? Center for Strategic and Budgetary Assessments (CSBA) — Scenarios," *CSBA* (2010), http://csbaonline.org/uploads/documents/2010.02.19-Why-AirSea-Battle.pdf.

[38]In modern use, the order of battle of an armed force participating in a military operation or campaign shows the hierarchical organization, command structure, strength, disposition of personnel, and equipment of units and formations of the armed force.

[39]AirSea Battle is an integrated battle doctrine that formed a key component of the military strategy of the United States. See CSBA "AirSea Battle: A Point-of-Departure Operational Concept," outlining the US military's growing operational difficulties in the Western Pacific Theater of Operations (WPTO). The report recommends that the United States to diversify its military strategy away from "the demands of modern irregular warfare" to one that highlights the Chinese PLA's quick ability to field anti-access/area-denial (A2/AD) technologies. A 2013 study showed how the AirSea Battle program was adopted by the Pentagon without either significant input from civilian authorities or public debate, despite the significant foreign policy implications of the AirSea Battle doctrine. The 2014 Exercise Valiant Shield tested Air-Sea concepts.

[40]Donald Rumsfeld, "Transforming the Military," *Foreign Affairs* 81, no. 3, May/June 2002: 20–32; Thomas Barnett, *The Pentagon's New Map: War and Peace in the Twenty-First Century* (New York and London: Penguin, 2004); Colin Gray, *Strategy for Chaos: Revolutions in Military Affairs and The Evidence of History* (London: Frank Cass, 2004); Mary FitzGerald, "Marshal Ogarkov and the New Revolution in Soviet Military Affairs," *Center for Naval Analysis*, 1987, http://dtic.mil/dtic/tr/fulltext/u2/a187009.pdf. Stephen Biddle, *Military Power: Explaining Victory and Defeat in Modern Battle* (Princeton: Princeton University Press, 2006).

90 *Beleaguered Superpower: Biden's America Adrift*

Military technological hard power; not adroit soft power is the security key. To the extent that Marshall is correct, the radical progressive-liberal mindset is wrong. Strategic patience and confidence building are not enough. It would be unwise to suppose that Xi Jinping will relent of his own accord.[41] America must bear the economic burden entailed by the Pacific Air Sea Battle plan, even though Washington to date refuses to pay the price.[42]

---

[41] Office of the Secretary of Defense, "Annual Report to Congress: Military and Security Developments Involving the People's Republic of China 2016," (April 2016): 44–45. Office of the Secretary of Defense, "Annual Report to Congress: Military and Security Developments Involving the People's Republic of China 2019," (May 2019), https://fas.org/man/eprint/dod-china-2019.pdf.

[42] Lawrence Korb (co-written with Bill French), "A Prudent Response to Chinese Military Modernization," *Huffington Post* (February 18, 2012), http://www.huffingtonpost.com/lawrence-korb/defense-spending_b_1158413.html.

"There is no question that the growing capabilities of the Chinese military require a response. However, given that the US-Chinese military spending gap has widened in favor of the United States and there are major factors constraining the size of future PLA budgetary increases, the conservative calls to raise US military spending are misguided. This is especially true because as Admiral Mullen, former Chairman of the Joint Chiefs of Staff, has pointed out: our burgeoning Federal deficit is the greatest threat to national security." "Second, implementing a serious version of AirSea Battle, whether that outlined by the CSBA or otherwise, must be done affordably. To be sure, this will require smart choices and compromising on some other defense concerns, at least for now. An appropriate starting place is to reassess the need for some of the Pentagon's currently planned procurements. For instance, even the CSBA has noted that in addressing PLA gains, purchases of the F-35 Joint Strike Fighter — the most expensive weapons program in history with a total projected cost exceeding $1 trillion, according to GAO — can be reduced and procurement of a new generation of aircraft carriers — the Ford Class — can be slowed. The F-35, of which the military plans to buy nearly 2,500 units, has too short of a range to be useful in the expansive Western Pacific. Its limited range cannot be extended without using external fuel tanks that sacrifice the stealth of the aircraft, and hence a major portion of its expensive advantage, or by relying on a vulnerable mid-air refueling tanker fleet. Regarding the Ford Class carriers, such multi-billion dollar vessels are vulnerable to PLA anti-shipping capabilities, especially the DF-21 anti-shipping ballistic missile designed specifically to destroy US carriers from a distance of 1,800 kilometers with conventional warheads. Investing heavily in the Ford Class would not only play into strengths of the PLA but would be redundant for a Navy that already possesses 11 aircraft carriers. Instead, the United States can upgrade and

Chinese authorities contest this assessment. Beijing characterizes its military strategy as one of "active defense," a concept it describes as strategically defensive but operationally proactive. It is rooted in a commitment not to attack, but to respond aggressively once an adversary decides to attack — a defense that counterattacks in order to disrupt an adversary's preparations or offensive rather than a defense that reacts passively. The PLA interprets active defense to include mandates for both de-escalation and seizing the initiative. Active defense is set in China's National Security Law (2015) and is included in the PLA's major strategy documents. Beijing may believe this, but its defensive doctrine does not change the reality of A2/AD as a vehicle for dominating the West Pacific.[43] In other words, an active defense is indistinguishable in practice from a concerted offense.[44]

The Industrial Powerhouse that Can

Neither the Obama–Biden nor the Trump administrations, despite the evidence inventoried above, could bring itself to take the Chinese threat seriously enough to fund the Pacific Air Sea Battle plan adequately. The progressive and liberal Washington security "establishment" continues to believe that the South China joust at the end of the day is ritualistic saber rattling, that Beijing cannot win the A2/AD contest, or even if it did, that

---

redeploy its current systems. For example, upon learning that the Chinese J-20 stealth fighter was ahead of its development schedule, the Air Force responded by upgrading the radars on some of its F-15 fleet — aircraft which have a combat record of over 100-to-0 — as an effective countermeasure. Similar frugal but smart upgrades on other weapon systems should be explored as AirSea Battle is developed. In response to the growing PLA ballistic missiles that threaten US ships and bases, advanced PATRIOT PAC-3 and AEGIS Standard-3 anti-ballistic missiles systems can be deployed to the region in greater numbers and further supplied to our allies there."

[43] Office of the Secretary of Defense, *Annual Report to Congress: Military and Security Developments Involving the People's Republic of China 2016* (April 2016): 44–45. Office of the Secretary of Defense, Annual Report to Congress: Military and Security Developments Involving the People's Republic of China 2019 (May 2019), https://fas.org/man/eprint/dod-china-2019.pdf.

[44] Daniel Blumenthal, *The China Nightmare: The Grand Ambitions of a Decaying State* (Washington DC: AEI Press, 2020).

92 Beleaguered Superpower: Biden's America Adrift

it does not matter because the Xi Jinping prioritizes commerce and amity over hegemonic power.[45]

Their position seems reassuringly plausible. America's per capita GDP in 2018 was almost quadruple China's on a purchasing power parity basis,[46] and seven times greater valued at the market exchange rate. Moreover, there are solid grounds for believing that Beijing's GDP statistics may exaggerate real consumption.[47]

American wealth is more than treble the PRC.[48] Credit Suisse puts the stock of American private wealth as $85.9 trillion and Chinese private wealth (owned on a freehold basis by the state) at $22.8 trillion circa 2015. Moreover, China's growth rate is diminishing as the advantages of economic backwardness wane. It might not be able to catch up as quickly

---

[45]Nadège Rolland, "China's National Power: A Colossus with Iron or Clay Feet?" in Ashley J. Tellis, Alison Szalwinski, and Michael Wills, eds., *Strategic Asia 2015–16: Foundations of National Power in the Asia-Pacific*, http://nbr.org/publications/element. aspx?id=836. Rand, "The US-China Military Scorecard: Forces, Geography and the Evolving Balance of Military Power," (2015), http://www.rand.org/content/dam/rand/pubs/research_reports/RR300/RR392/RAND_RR392.pdf.

[46]CIA, *The World Factbook: China.*

America's per capita GDP in 2016 was $57,300. China's 2016 GDP was $15,400 computed on a purchasing power parity basis and valued in 2016 prices (ranked 104th below the Dominican Republic and above Palau). The figure valued through the market exchange rate is $8,247.

[47]Derek Scissors, "America's Inconvenient Trillions," *AEI* (November 2017).

"Even less relevant is GDP adjusted by purchasing power parity (PPP). PPP requires computing a price level for all of China and comparing it to all of America, itself slightly absurd. It relies on 'the law of one price' — arbitrage across open markets causing prices for the same product to equalize. Chinese market barriers mean arbitrage often fails. Related, PPP is meant to apply to consumer buying power, while consumption is less than 50 percent of Chinese GDP. GDP adjusted by purchasing power is a poor measurement for many countries, including China."

[48]Derek Scissors, "45 Trillion Reasons Why China Can't Challenge America's Economic Might," *AEI* (October 2015). Derek Scissors, "America's Inconvenient Trillions," *AEI* (November 2017).

"From the end of 2012 to the middle of 2017, Chinese net private wealth has climbed $7.3 trillion, annual growth never touching 9 percent. American net private wealth jumped $26 trillion. The American base was much bigger and American growth also became a bit faster. The result: mid-2017 Chinese net private wealth was $29 trillion and American net private wealth was over $93 trillion. The Federal Reserve supports the Credit Suisse number, putting American household net worth at $96 trillion."

to America as it has done for the past decade, and there are legitimate concerns about the sustainability of China's local and regional debt. A major debt crisis could decimate the economy.[49]

Nonetheless, China like Russia has shown that it can modernize and expand military capabilities despite economic and political limitations.[50] It not only managed to increase defense spending at double-digit rates 1990–2019,[51] but it has mastered advanced weapons technologies faster than predicted and should be able to continue doing so in a less robust environment. American progressives and liberals no longer challenge China's military growth potential, but contend contrary to the evidence that it is irrelevant because China is more interested in commerce and getting along with the West than in geo-political expansion. China's relentless military modernization and aggressiveness in the South China Sea belies their summary judgment.

China's Market Economy

The national security community's conviction that China cannot succeed rests further on the progressive-liberal contention that China's civilian economy cannot provide sufficient prosperity and technological prowess to win the A2/AD competition because its communist market economy is flawed. They claim that authoritarianism is China's Achilles heel. Authoritarian states they insist cannot defeat American progressive-liberal version of democratic free enterprise.

---

[49]Keith Bradsher, "Why China's Growing Debt Load Worries the World," *New York Times* (May 24, 2017), https://www.nytimes.com/2017/05/24/business/china-downgrade-explained.html.

[50]*The Little Engine That Could* is the story of a long train that must be pulled over a high mountain. Larger engines, treated anthropomorphically, are asked to pull the train; for various reasons they refuse. The request is sent to a small engine, who agrees to try. The engine succeeds in pulling the train over the mountain while repeating its motto: "I-think-I-can."

Watty Piper, *The Little Engine That Could* (New York, NY: Grosset & Dunlap, 2001); Steven Rosefielde, "China's Rising Red Star," in Steven Rosefielde, Masaaki Kuboniwa, Satoshi Mizobata and Kumiko Haba, eds., *The Unwinding of the Globalist Dream — EU, Russia and China* (Singapore: World Scientific Publishers, 2017): Chapter 13.

[51]Richard Bitzinger, "China's Defence Spending: Settling in for Slow Growth?" *RSIS Commentary*, no. 042/2017 (March 2017), https://chinapower.csis.org/military-spending/.

94   *Beleaguered Superpower: Biden's America Adrift*

This viewpoint is misleading.[52] America's economy today is not competitively ideal, and Chinese market communism is indisputably superior to Mao's command economic system. China's economic mechanism is imperfect, but the defects are not fatal and are not enough to thwart is military ambitions. Although, the Chinese economy is anti-competitive in many respects, the leadership can succeed in its quest for anti-access and area denial (A2/AD) by deftly transferring technology from abroad and devoting sufficient domestic science resources to the task. It can license foreign technologies, buy international technology companies, train cadre abroad, participate in joint ventures, and employ covert methods.

Many have argued that Beijing must fail, but the evidence is against them. The findings of the 2013 and 2017 independent Commission on the Theft of American Intellectual Property show that China has "stolen" hundreds of billions of dollars-worth of American intellectual property,[53] including technologies used in the F-35 Lightning, the Aegis Combat System and the Patriot missile system.[54] Moreover, the DOD itself acknowledges that the PLA is making headway. This is the rationale for America's Pacific Air Sea Battle strategy.

Similar pragmatic considerations affect prospects for China's prosperity. The productivity and growth potential of Xi's economy are impaired by two factors. First freehold property is illegal.[55] Individuals and corporations cannot own productive assets in perpetuity and use them at their discretion. They can only lease the means of production from the state for

---

[52] Steven Rosefielde and Jonathan Leightner, *China's Market Communism: Challenges, Dilemmas, Solutions* (London: Routledge, 2017).

[53] IP Commission Report, "The Theft of American Intellectual Property: Reassessments of the Challenge and United States Policy," *National Bureau of Asian Research* (February 2017), http://ipcommission.org/report/IP_Commission_Report_Update_2017.pdf.

[54] Claude Barfield, "Renewed Chinese Cyberespionage: Time for the US to Act," *AEI* (April 2018), http://www.aei.org/publication/renewed-chinese-cyberespionage-time-for-the-us-to-act/?mkt_tok=eyJpIjoiT1RZeVlqWm1aVEptWmpSaSIsInQiOiJzY0ZmRkl yNEg5Tm9SM2lWOFZ6ZE1ES3huaWhPSUNZMDNcL1FTeGQweXlFN2FoZ0ZIM0 k1cW8xTXJcL3FcLzlBUFlWWkNvVFpjVVhxK0prNitYeVwvaHNBblY5REpaZGg0b2 NaZ0VvZDBUQkJrWjFRc1U1dEtLZFNybCtYc2Z3eHZzWmYifQ%3D%3D.

[55] The ban is ideologically motivated. It allows the CCP to justly claim that the people are the sole owners of China's productive assets. For-profit businesspersons are not "capitalists"; they are lessees.

China 95

fixed periods. This increases investment risk, diminishes inter-temporal economic efficiency and fosters corruption.[56]

Second, the Chinese Communist Party (CCP) as custodian of the "people's freehold property" and governor of the public sector has immense extra-market power. It can lease and re-assign leased property, set leasing terms, contract with lessees, subsidize and tax them, regulate them and their would-be competitors. These regulatory levers make high CCP members more powerful, and anti-competitive than their American counterparts. China's leaders not only anti-competitively manipulate factors, institutions, finance and production for their own advantage, but they operate above the "rule of law." They can acquire assets at will discretely by canceling leases and reassigning them without any danger of judicial censure.[57]

China's communist authoritarian market system consequently cannot be as productive or just as an open society, democratic, competitive market economy.[58] The regime's extraordinarily high income and wealth inequality confirms the potential for injustice.[59] It also follows that the mainland's sustainable long-term per capita GDP growth should become subpar in the not too distant future because enterprises choose technologies anti-competitively.

---

[56]Lessees do not have rights to the incomes generated by their investments beyond the lease's time horizon. This constrains investors' opportunity sets and degrades investment potential. See Irving Fisher, *The Theory of Interest* (New York: The Macmillan, 1930). The practical significance of proscribing freehold property depends on how the CCP manages its leasing regime. The Commonwealth of Massachusetts enshrines the same principle.

[57]Chinese courts are an instrument of the CCP, not impartial independent entities.

[58]Steven Rosefielde and Ralph W. Pfouts, *Inclusive Economic Theory* (Singapore: World Scientific Publishers, 2014); Amartya Sen, *The Idea of Justice* (London: Penguin, 2010).

The West's ideal is called Pareto optimal. It promises "consumer sovereignty" in the private sector and democratic sovereignty over consumer goods. Kenneth Arrow, *Social Choice and Individual Values*, 2nd edn. (New York: Wiley, 1963). There are other valid concepts of justice.

[59]Steven Rosefielde and Jonathan Leightner, *China's Market Communism: Challenges, Dilemmas, Solutions* (London: Routledge, 2017); Thomas Piketty, Li Yang, and Gabriel Zucman, "Capital Accumulation, Private Property and Rising Inequality in China, 1978–2015," *IZA Institute of Labor Economics* (April 2017), http://d.repec.org/n?u=RePEc:nbr:nberwo:23368&r=tra. Belton Fleisher, William McGuire, Xiaojun Wang, and Min Quiang Zhao, "Wages, Innovation, and Employment in China," *IZA Institute of Labor Economics* (April 2017), http://d.repec.org/n?u=RePEc:iza:izadps:dp10749&r=tra.

96 Beleaguered Superpower: Biden's America Adrift

Nonetheless, China's authoritarian market performs well enough, assisted in part by predatory foreign trade practices, flagrant copyright violations, counterfeiting, and technology pirating.[60] It provides its people with a higher living standard than Mao's command communist alternative, and is good enough to mollify ordinary citizens for decades to come. Xi's system, like Putin's provides China with both guns and butter. It is suboptimal from the democratic consumer sovereign standpoint, but sufficient to allow the CPC to press its A2/AD initiatives as long as it desires.

Economic Sanctions

The progressive and liberal mindsets encourage policymakers to believe that if worse comes to worst in the West Pacific, America can force Xi Jinping to stand down by threatening China with economic sanctions. This is a non-starter. If China achieves "anti-access and area denial" (A2/AD), economic sanctions will not deter Beijing. China can withstand the punishment.

National Security Framework

What do Washington and Xi Jinping want from each other? As in the Russia case, each wants as much as it can prudently get. If the establishment has its druthers, it would transform China into an obedient vassal under the banner of American hegemonic supranational globalism. Xi Jinping would be compelled to replace Communist Party governance and authoritarian markets with a radical progressive or a progressive-liberal welfare state under the rule of law and adopt entitlement, affirmative action and restorative justice programs. He would disband the RCEP covering 15 Asia-Pacific economies signed in Hanoi on November 15, 2020.[61] Beijing would rescind its annexation of Tibet, renounce most of

---

[60] AEI, "China Global Investment Tracker."

[61] The RCEP is a free trade agreement in the Asia-Pacific region between the 10 member states of ASEAN, namely Brunei, Cambodia, Indonesia, Laos, Malaysia, Myanmar, the Philippines, Singapore, Thailand, and Vietnam, and five of their FTA partners — Australia, China, Japan, New Zealand, and South Korea. The 15 negotiating countries account for about 30 percent of both the world's population and the global GDP, making it the largest

China 97

its claims to the South China Sea and the Senkaku (Diaoyu) islands, accept Taiwanese independence, cease trying to dominate ASEAN and would discipline North Korea. China would denuclearize, disarm, keep only skeleton military forces, and refrain from cyber meddling in foreign affairs.[62] Beijing would help America fully exploit political and economic opportunities throughout East, Southeast, South, and Central Asia. It would cease scheming in the Middle East, Africa, and Latin America, and praise America's sage counsel.

If Xi's dreams materialized, he would impose Chinese control over the West Pacific, the Diaoyu (Senkaku) islands, and ASEAN, Central Asia as well as disputed territories with India and Pakistan. China would push America out of South Korea, and supplant it as the world's "globalizer," using One Belt One Road (OBOR) as a lever. Beijing would become a major player in the Middle East, Africa, Latin America, and per-haps Europe.[63] Xi Jinping would ally with Russia and other authoritarian nations to create a potent bloc against the West.

Xi Jinping moreover would welcome unilateral Western disarmament, tolerance of the Beijing's security "needs," Western recognition of China's great power status, and unfettered access to America's military technology. These concessions in their entirety would be the death knell for Washington-led supranational globalization, and subordinate the West to a Beijing-led authoritarian world order.

Again, as in the Russian case, both sides know that their aspirations are fanciful, and that the starting point of their engagement should be defending the *status quo* and probing the other side's vulnerabilities. For the moment, neither Washington nor Beijing is especially concerned about Cold War-style ideological rivalry. They are prepared to coexist peace-fully without venturing into Cold Peace (mutual tolerance plus reciprocal lobbying for the other side's transformation) or Cold War (reciprocal

---

trade bloc. It was signed at the Vietnam-hosted virtual ASEAN Summit on November 15, 2020. Charmaine Ng, "15 Countries, Including Singapore, Sign RCEP, the World's Largest Trade Pact," *The Straits Times* (November 15, 2020).

[62] Elizabeth Van Wie Davis, "China's Cyberwarfare Finds New Targets," *Fair Observer* (October 27, 2017), https://www.fairobserver.com/region/asia_pacific/china-cyberwarfare-cybersecurity-asia-pacific-news-analysis-04253/.

[63] Anders Fogh Rasmussen, "China's Investment in Europe Offers Opportunities — and Threats," *Financial Times* (November 20, 2017), https://www.ft.com/content/9e7428cc-c963-11e7-8536-d321d0d897a3.

98 *Beleaguered Superpower: Biden's America Adrift*

aggressive use of soft power and irregular violence to promote systemic transformation).[64]

This relatively benign relationship is unlikely to last. Washington is already contesting Beijing over its illegal state trading practices under WTO rules, and bullying in the South China Sea. Cold War is looming on the horizon, driven by Xi's A2/AD initiative, the South China Sea dispute, the PLA's continuing its arms modernization program, and other challenges across Asia and beyond in the Middle East, Africa, Latin America, and even the Arctic. Cold War is looming too because Xi Jinping aspires to become *primus inter pares* among world leaders through trade, development aid, economic achievement, cyber-engagement, transnational organizational sparring, and smart diplomacy. The Washington establishment is ambivalent. The dovish faction is inclined to permit China to control the South China Sea gradually, and even abandon sponsorship of "color revolutions" and regime change in China, with one significant exception. Recently, Richard Haass endorsed ending America's policy of "strategic ambiguity" toward Taiwan, defying Beijing's warning.[65]

Some Republicans are more hawkish, and stumbling into a hot war with China is always possible. The West should not expect better prospects until it puts its house in order.[66]

---

[64]For a fuller discussion of these concepts, see Steven Rosefielde, *The Kremlin Strikes Back: Russia and the West after Crimea's Annexation* (Cambridge: Cambridge University Press, 2017).

[65]Richard Haass and David Sacks, "American Support for Taiwan Must Be Unambiguous," Foreign Affairs (September 2020); https://www.foreignaffairs.com/articles/united-states/american-support-taiwan-must-be-unambiguous; Gary Schmitt and Michael Mazza, "The End of 'Strategic Ambiguity' Regarding Taiwan: Here are the Steps the U.S. Can Take, and Why We Should Take Them," *Dispatch* (September 2020), https://thedispatch.com/p/the-end-of-strategic-ambiguity-regarding?mkt_tok=eyJpIjoiWkRoak56azVNMkZqTURRMiIsInQiOiI4dmVVM0RhWFQ0eVVOejhGZFFzWU54ek02Nlwvb1hOWXZETDdaY056aHBHQWtlbkNnQVJpSjQwa3JXUHBSaHRnQzJlZHBodHZaXC82YVdGS2x3eHNpUndVUTQ4ZDNLUm9vSW1WbXNFcHAyaDJ1M29hXC82cUNycllXc1RFMkJ0a2JuUyJ9Sep%2016.

[66]Daniel Blumenthal, "U.S. Policy in Asia: A Strategy for China's Imperial Overstretch," *American Interest* (March 2017), http://www.the-american-interest.com/2017/03/01/a-strategy-for-chinas-imperial-overstretch/.

"In trying to defend an enormous empire with dwindling resources, Beijing has overstretched itself. Here's how Washington can take advantage.

Notwithstanding the facile talk of China's 'gains' from Donald Trump's imagined withdrawal from the world, Beijing is no position to lead the world. Instead it is very close to imperial overstretch. A new U.S. strategic approach should hasten a Chinese reckoning with its geopolitical troubles.

Contrary to the recent, post-Davos 'wisdom' about a new era of Chinese global leadership, things do not look good for Beijing. The Chinese economy continues to struggle and Chinese Communist Party (CCP) Secretary-General Xi Jinping believes that China faces a deteriorating security environment. Even so, China continues to expand its grandiose foreign policy ambitions, slowly extending its control over the South China Sea while also planning to create a 'New Silk Road' linking Asia with Europe. But China is biting off more than it can chew.

The CCP was founded on an anti-imperialist doctrine and is offended by the suggestion that it rules an empire. Nevertheless, it does. Indeed, China is the world's last standing multi-ethnic empire. Its physical borders today mirror those of China's last imperial dynasty, the Qing Dynasty, whose emperors conducted the greatest imperial expansion in China's history. From the 17th to 19th centuries, they succeeded in conquering Xinjiang, Tibet, Mongolia, and Taiwan. By virtue of these achievements, the Qing expanded the empire to a truly continental scale.

With the exception of Mongolia and Taiwan, all of the Qing's imperial conquests, including Xinjiang and Tibet, are again under Chinese control today. And Beijing has regained *de facto* suzerainty over Hong Kong as it exerts close to total control over the city-state's politics.

Finally, the international community long ago accepted the CCP's position that Taiwan is part of China, never mind that this 'claim' is mostly based on the Qing imperial conquest of the island more than a century ago. Beijing's continued hold over its empire is unique in global affairs. For some context, imagine if Turkey still controlled the Ottoman lands of the Levant and the Middle East. Or for another comparative image, what if the Austo-Hungarian empire still controlled much of Europe?

Today the CCP's desire for more territory does not stop with the old Qing maps. Though the Qing Empire was not a maritime power, the CCP has 'discovered' new imperial territories in its surrounding seas. Chinese commentators frequently refer to China's 'three million square kilometers of blue territory,' which would incorporate 'nearly 90% of the area within the major bodies of water within the First Island Chain, including the Bo Hai, the Yellow Sea, the East China Sea, and the South China Sea.'

China has claimed everything within the 'nine-dash line' as its 'indisputable territory' — this arbitrary series of dashes on Chinese maps encompasses the South China Sea. To advance this claim, Beijing has built over 3,000 acres of new 'island' bases and deployed military forces to help control the surrounding waters. It has set up a provincial administration to govern these maritime 'territories,' which directs its fleets of maritime militias and law enforcement agencies to harass foreign vessels.

All told, China's territorial claims now extend from the westernmost reaches of Xinjiang, bordering Afghanistan, to the easternmost point in the East China Sea. The sheer expanse of Beijing's claims might explain why Xi is so pessimistic about China's security. The PLA must defend an overwhelming amount of land and maritime territory from 'enemies' foreign and domestic.

Nonetheless, Xi Jinping is pressing ahead with a key component of his national development strategy, called 'One Belt One Road' (OBOR) — a network of economic infrastructure projects linking China with more than sixty Central Asian, Middle Eastern, and European countries. This plan is intended to proceed along two distinct routes. First, the Silk Road Economic Belt, consisting of rail routes and oil and natural gas pipelines, will stretch overland from China, through Central Asia to Eastern Europe.

Second, the 21st Century Maritime Silk Road, made up of a series of port projects, will extend through the Indian Ocean and into the Suez Canal to reach the Mediterranean Sea. The underlying promise of OBOR is that Chinese infrastructure investment can link together China's maritime and continental interests. Xi wants this program to be his stamp on China's future, just as Deng Xiaoping was known for the policy of 'reform and opening.' In practice, China will have even more territory and assets to protect.

Where Are the Resources?"

Chapter 5

North Korea

North Korean civilization has evolved from the Goguryeo state in 57 AD (the northern component of the Three Kingdoms after the inclusion of Silla) without shedding its authoritarian core. It was a vassal of China before the Treaty of Shimonoseki in 1895, and then Japan until 1945. Soviet and American post-war occupation led to the peninsula's partition into the Republic of Korea (ROK) and the Democratic People's Republic of Korea (DPRK) in 1947.[1] Thereafter, South Korea gradually embraced

---

[1] Korea is derived from the ancient state of Goryeo. North Korean calls itself Chosen. The name designates the state, not the family or clan. It does not constitute a family dynasty. The principle Korean states were Silla (57–668), Unified Silla (669–918), Goryeo (935–1392), and Chosen (Joseon) (1392–1910). Slavery (the Nobi system) was wide spread (average 30 percent) until 1808 when it was banned in the government sector. Slavery persisted thereafter but was gradually replaced by agrarian wage labor. North Korea was agricultural and scorned commerce, but slowly industrialized after Japan annexed Korea in 1910. Kim Il-Sung and his communist successors prioritized heavy industry after assuming power in 1947. North Korea was capable of high technological feats even under Silla (huge bells, architecture, fine jewelry, etc.). Korea before Japanese annexation was called the hermit kingdom, not because it failed to absorb foreign influences (mostly Chinese), but because it restricted international commerce.

This combination of factors limited and skewed the systems potential. There were large cities like Unified Silla, contemporary with Anchang (modern day Xian). The nobility were highly stratified and affluent. The vast majority however were poor. Modernization in these conditions depended on the evolution of social forces (education, equal opportunity, etc.), and this essentially was delayed until Japanese annexation, and then warped along colonial lines until 1960 when a state-led industrialization drive radically altered the landscape.

102   Beleaguered Superpower: Biden's America Adrift

democratic rule under American tutelage,[2] while North Korea remained true to its authoritarian heritage in a 20th century Stalinist guise.

Korea before 1947 had been a predominantly defensive Asian military power after 57 AD.[3] Its per capita GDP was on a par with the West's until 1500 when European economic growth began outpacing the Hermit Kingdom. Korea's per capita GDP fell to just 20 percent of the West European level by 1950.[4] South Korea modernized and recovered lost ground thereafter rising to 66 percent of the United States standard in 2019.[5] The CIA reports by contrast that North Korea failed to converge, sinking instead to just 3 percent of the US level in 2015.[6] The Agency bases its estimates on South Korean sources.[7] They may be downward biased. Nonetheless, there are no grounds for doubting that North Korea's living

---

[2] South Korean democratization was a slow process. Syngman Rhee launched a democratic government with strong American support run in an authoritarian manner 1948–1960. Despite constitutional formalities, electoral democracy was not firmly established in the south run 1988 when President Roh Tae-Woo replaced Chun Doo-Hwan. Lee Myng-bak's inauguration February 25, 2008 made only the second time that power was peacefully transferred from one party to political opponents.

[3] Jinwung Kim, *A History of Korea: From "Land of the Morning Calm" to States in Conflict* (Bloomington: Indiana University Press, 2012).

[4] Steven Rosefielde, *Asian Economic Systems* (Singapore: World Scientific Publishers, 2013): 74.

[5] CIA, *World Factbook: North Korea* (2017).

South Korea's estimated per capita GDP in 2016 is $37,900 (PPP). American per capita GDP is $57,300.

[6] CIA, *World Factbook: North Korea,* Washington, D.C. (2017).

"North Korea, one of the world's most centrally directed and least open economies, faces chronic economic problems. Industrial capital stock is nearly beyond repair as a result of years of underinvestment, shortages of spare parts, and poor maintenance. Large-scale military spending and development of its ballistic missile and nuclear program severely draws off resources needed for investment and civilian consumption. Industrial and power outputs have stagnated for years at a fraction of pre-1990 levels. Frequent weather-related crop failures aggravated chronic food shortages caused by on-going systemic problems, including a lack of arable land, collective farming practices, poor soil quality, insufficient fertilization, and persistent shortages of tractors and fuel."

[7] "How to Measure North Korea's Economy: In the Absence of Reliable Numbers, Scholars Try New Forms of Guesswork," *Economist* (February 9, 2017), http://www. economist.com/news/finance-and-economics/21716615-absence-reliable-numbers-scholars-try-new-forms-guesswork-how.

North Korea 103

standard deteriorated sharply after the Soviet Union collapsed from a very low level, stagnating thereafter. The USSR had been Pyongyang's principal trade partner and source of foreign assistance. When Russia swooned into hyper-depression, North Korea's economy plummeted with it.

Per capita GDP today lies well below its 1950 global ranking. North Korea, as the CIA assesses its per capita income is one of the world's least developed countries with a rank of 215.[8] The CIA moreover contends that Chinese import and export sanctions mandated by the UN have hobbled North Korea's economy.[9] The Bank of Korea (South) reports that North

---

"FACTS about the North Korean economy are not so much alternative as non-existent. The country has never published a statistical yearbook. If it did, no one would believe it. Nicholas Eberstadt of the American Enterprise Institute, a think-tank, calls analysis of its economy 'essentially pre-quantitative.'

The most-cited estimate of the size of the economy comes from South Korea's central bank. Its methodology is opaque but is based, at least in part, on the South Korean intelligence agency's estimates of the North's physical output, which is then translated to South Korean prices. But it is hard to estimate market valuations for goods that are not traded on the market, and physical goods make up only a fraction of overall economic output. Another technique is to 'mirror' statistics from the country's trading partners. But most North Korean trade is with China, where statistics are unreliable.

A recent paper by Suk Lee of the Korea Development Institute, a South Korean government think tank, puts a new spin on this approach. It estimates North Korea's national income by comparing the share of its households that use solid fuels for cooking with that in other lower-income countries. The data, as reported by the North Korean census of 2008, show that nearly 93 percent of households lack access to gas or electricity and rely on firewood or coal. Assuming the numbers bear some relation to reality, they put North Korea in line with countries such Uganda and Haiti, and suggest that North Korea's purchasing-power-adjusted income per person was somewhere between $948 and $1,361 in 2008.

North Korea's economy has made great strides since the country's famine in the 1990s. The government has tacitly allowed the market economy to grow. Although the rest of the country is still indisputably poor, visitors to Pyongyang, at least, cannot help but note the rise of shops and taxis. The paradox is that as the North Korean economy modernises, the data may actually be deteriorating. The size of the country's apparently burgeoning service sector is a complete mystery. Many scholars believe that the South Korean numbers are too low."

[8] CIA, *World Factbook: North Korea* (2017).
[9] *Ibid.*

"Throughout 2017, North Korea's continued nuclear and missile tests led to a tightening of UN sanctions, resulting in full sectoral bans on DPRK exports and drastically

104   *Beleaguered Superpower: Biden's America Adrift*

Korea's GDP fell 3.5 percent in 2017.[10] The World Bank using official North Korean data reports positive 3.4 percent GDP growth for the same year.[11]

The negatives however do not accurately convey North Korea's economic capabilities. The country like its Soviet predecessor is not uniformly backward. North Korea has a predominantly industrialized dual economy distinguished by a feeble, but improving consumer goods sector,[12] and an advanced military machine-building sector, especially in the subcategories of ballistic missiles and nuclear technology.[13] Like the former Soviet Union, it is an impoverished nuclear power,[14] perhaps in glacial transition to a "guns and butter" regime.[15]

These continuities amid change suggest that although economically laggard and beleaguered by economic sanctions, North Korea is

---

limited key imports. Over the last decade, China has been North Korea's primary trading partner."

[10] Colin Dwyer, "North Korean Economy Suffered Sharpest Drop In 2 Decades, South Says," *NPR* (July 20, 2018), https://www.npr.org/2018/07/20/630781976/north-korean-economy-suffered-sharpest-drop-in-2-decades-south-says.

"Mining production in North Korea, which relies on coal as its No. 1 export, dropped 11 percent in 2017 — a breakneck reversal from the 8.4 percent growth it had seen the year before. Production in heavy and chemical industry also dropped more than 10 percent."

[11] https://tradingeconomics.com/north-korea/gdp.

[12] Nicholas Eberstadt, "The Method in North Korea's Madness," *Commentary* (January 16, 2018), https://www.commentarymagazine.com/articles/method-north-koreas-madness/.

[13] Steven Rosefielde, "Communist Asia," in Paul Hare and Gerard Turley, eds., *The Economics and Political Economy of Transition: Handbook* (London: Routledge, 2012): 445–455.

[14] Hans Kristensen and Robert Norris, "North Korean Nuclear Capabilities, 2018," *Bulletin of Atomic Scientists* (January 2, 2018), https://thebulletin.org/2018/january/north-korean-nuclear-capabilities-201811409.

"The authors cautiously estimate that North Korea may have produced enough fissile material to build between 30 and 60 nuclear weapons, and that it might possibly have assembled 10 to 20. Although North Korea is thought to have the capability to develop an operationally functioning re-entry vehicle to deliver an operational nuclear warhead, there is some uncertainty about whether it has demonstrated that it has succeeded in doing so. Nonetheless, North Korea's nuclear weapons program has made considerable progress over the years, including a wide variety of ballistic and powerful nuclear tests. Presumably, if it hasn't happened already, it is only a matter of time before Pyongyang's nuclear arsenal can be considered fully functioning."

[15] Nicholas Eberstadt, "The Method in North Korea's Madness," *Commentary* (January 16, 2018), https://www.commentarymagazine.com/articles/method-north-koreas-madness/.

militarily resilient, and its authoritarian state is durable enough for Pyongyang to defend its heritage, if Supreme Leader and Marshal of the DPRK Kim Jong-un chooses to avoid provoking an annihilating American strike.[16] Pyongyang is allergic to liberal democracy, the West's rule of law, and progressive agendas. Kim intends to prevail, not just survive. He is committed to preserving a Korean Workers' Party (KWP) controlled state and his personal survival while striving to unify the Korean peninsula on his own terms to the extent political conditions in the South permit,[17] and fending off Chinese suzerainty as best he can.

North Korea's staying power steels Kim's resistance to Washington's threats, sanctions, and soft power, even though he hints periodically about mending fences. His acquisition of nuclear weapons and ballistic missile delivery systems decreases the risk both of unprovoked or retaliatory American conventional attacks, and fortifies his faith that the Korean Peninsula can be unified under Pyongyang's control if America eventually withdraws in response to his wiles, or South Korea signs a peace treaty to the same effect without ironclad assurances.[18] Kim Jong-un cannot successfully invade, conquer, and annex Chinese, Russian, Japanese, South Korean, or American territory at the present juncture without risking

---

[16] In nuclear strategy, a first strike is a preemptive surprise attack employing overwhelming force. First strike capability is a country's ability to defeat another nuclear power by destroying its arsenal to the point where the attacking country can survive the weakened retaliation while the opposing side is unable to continue war.

[17] Kyung-Hwa Lee, "김정은 정권의 통일전략 (Kim Jong Un's Unification Strategy)," Ministry of Unification (2016): 4.

[18] Nicholas Eberstadt, "From 'Engagement' to Threat Reduction: Moving Toward a North Korea Policy that Works," *AEI* (January 2017), (p. 118) "striving to unify the Korean peninsula on his own terms."

"Like all other states, the North Korean regime relies at times upon diplomacy to pursue its official aims — thus, for example, the abiding call for a 'peace treaty' with the US to bring a formal end to the Korean War (since 1953 only an armistice, or cease-fire, has been in place). Yet strangely few foreign policy specialists seem to understand why Pyongyang is so fixated on this particular document. If the US agreed to a peace treaty, Pyongyang insists, it would then also have to agree to a withdrawal of its forces from South Korea and to a dissolution of its military alliance with Seoul — for the danger of 'external armed attack' upon which the Seoul-Washington Mutual Defense Treaty is predicated would by definition no longer exist. If all this could come to pass, North Korea would win a huge victory without firing a shot."

106　*Beleaguered Superpower: Biden's America Adrift*

catastrophic conventional or nuclear casualties. Nor can he create a sphere of influence in Asia. Survival and unifying the Korean Peninsula must be his primary objectives.[19] South Korea, America, China, Russia, and Japan

---

[19]Christopher Hill, "North Korea's Real Strategy" *Project Syndicate* (June 2017), https://www.project-syndicate.org/commentary/north-korea-nuclear-program-invasion-by-christopher-r-hill-2017-06?utm_source=Project+Syndicate+Newsletter&utm_campaign=2200ecc304-sunday_newsletter_25_6_2017&utm_medium=email&utm_term=0_73bad5b7d8-2200ecc304-93559677; Sue Mi Terry, "North Korea's Strategic Goals and Policy towards the United States and South Korea," *International Journal of Korean Studies* 17, no. 2 (Fall 2013): 63–92, http://www.icks.org/data/ijks/1482461379_add_file_3.pdf. "Pyongyang under the Kim dynasty has pursued three broad and consistent strategic goals: (1) pursuing a nuclear weapons program in order to gain international acceptance of the North as a bona fide nuclear weapons state; (2) securing a peace treaty in an effort to remove US forces from the Korean Peninsula; and, (3) reunifying with South Korea on its own terms — the ultimate if increasingly unrealistic objective" (p. 67).

Nicholas Eberstadt, "From 'Engagement' to Threat Reduction: Moving Toward a North Korea Policy that Works," *AEI* (January 2017), http://www.aei.org/publication/from-engagement-to-threat-reduction-moving-toward-a-north-korea-policy-that-works/.

"The DPRK is a project pulled by tides and shaped by sensibilities all but forgotten to the contemporary West. North Korea is a hereditary Asian dynasty (currently on its third Kim) — but one maintained by Marxist–Leninist police state powers unimaginable to earlier epochs of Asian despots and supported by a recently invented and quasi-religious ideology. And exactly what is that ideology? Along with its notorious variant of emperor worship, 'Juche thought' also extols an essentially messianic — and unapologetically racialist — vision of history: one in which the long-abused Korean people finally assume their rightful place in the universe by standing up against the foreign races that have long oppressed them, at last reuniting the entire Korean peninsula under an independent social-ist state (i.e., the DPRK). Although highly redacted in broadcasts aimed at foreign ears, this call for reunification of the mijnok (race), and for retribution against the enemy races or powers (starting with America and Japan), constantly reverberates within North Korea, sounded by the regime's highest authorities. This is where its nuclear weapons program fits into North Korea's designs. In Pyongyang's thinking, the indispensable instrument for achieving the DPRK's grand historical ambitions must be a supremely powerful military: more specifically, one possessed of a nuclear arsenal that can imperil and break the foreign enemies who protect and prop up what Pyongyang regards as the vile puppet state in the South, so that the DPRK may consummate its unconditional unification and give birth to its envisioned earthly Korean-race utopia. In earlier decades, Pyongyang might have seen multiple paths to this Elysium, but with the collapse of the Soviet empire, the long-term decline of the DPRK's industrial infrastructure, and the gradually accumulating evidence that South Korea was not going to succumb on its own to the revolutionary upheaval

are not imminent threats to Pyongyang as some Western experts speculate.[20] Kim doubtlessly prefers to survive and unify the Korean Peninsula with guile. However, he may be willing to risk the use of force if expected costs including Chinese coercion are not prohibitive.[21]

This means that North Korea poses a major security challenge that is sure to intensify as its nuclear arsenal and ballistic missile capabilities grow.[22] Kim is assiduously building forces perhaps including

---

Pyongyang so dearly wished of it, the nuclear option increasingly looks to be the one and only trail by which to reach the Promised Kingdom." For penetrating discussions of North Korea's ideology, see B. R. Myers, *The Cleanest Race* (New York: Melville House, 2010) and B. R. Myers, *North Korea's Juche Myth* (Busan: Sthele Publishers, 2015).

[20] David Kang, "Trump's Team is Floating an Attack on North Korea. Americans Would Die," *Washington Post* (February 27, 2018), https://www.washingtonpost.com/opinions/trumps-team-is-floating-an-attack-on-north-korea-americans-would-die/2018/02/27/8e6cdf66-1826-11e8-92c9-376b4fe57ff7_story.html?utm_term=.028e8eb0814e.

[21] Economist, "North Korea Blows Up the South's *De Facto* Embassy: And With it, Detente on the Korean Peninsula," (June 2020), https://www.economist.com/asia/2020/06/18/north-korea-blows-up-the-souths-de-facto-embassy.

[22] Nicholas Eberstadt, "From 'Engagement' to Threat Reduction: Moving Toward a North Korea Policy that Works," *AEI* (January 2017).

"But with apologies to Clausewitz, diplomacy is merely war by other means for Pyongyang. And for the dynasty the onetime anti-Japanese guerrilla fighter Kim Il Sung established, policy and war are inseparable — this is why the DPRK is the most highly militarized society on the planet. This is also why the answer to the unification question that so preoccupies North Korean leadership appears to entail meticulous and incessant preparations, already underway for decades, to fight and win a limited nuclear war against the United States."

Uri Friedman, "North Korea Says It Has 'Completed' Its Nuclear Program. What Does That Mean?" *The Atlantic* (November 2017), https://www.theatlantic.com/international/archive/2017/11/north-korea-nuclear/547019/?mkt_tok=eyJpIjoiTlRKbVlUQTBNRGMwTUdOaiIsInQiOiJXU0RaMnZnTmJwSjFvXC9hV2Z1NGsrb1NZY0pGV3BZTndzYm5Vd3R1ZE8wQzRzaGhwU1hcLzdiTkpsWVhZeFIzMUVPTFFMdEtPbzd0aVVnaUhCCR29KbWd2QkRnNXdkeDdHaW9EVytQRUxrV0lzNE5zVXRuNW96bnR0ekZBVUhqNHFFaln0%3D.

"On Wednesday, after conducting its longest-range missile test yet, North Korea declared itself a globe-spanning nuclear-weapons power and insisted the United States deal with it on those terms. Kim Jong Un's government claimed that it had launched a new type of intercontinental ballistic missile (ICBM) — a 'Hwasong-15' — capable of 'carrying [a] super-heavy [nuclear] warhead and hitting the whole mainland of the U.S.'"

108   *Beleaguered Superpower: Biden's America Adrift*

thermonuclear weapons,[23] he believes can nudge America into acquiescing to a North Korean dominated reunification, promises to the contrary notwithstanding. It is even thinkable that he could wreak havoc on his neighbors in a suicidal conventional attack and/or nuclear Götterdämmerung.[24]

Reunifying the Korean Peninsula

The national security community acknowledges the potential for North Korean–American conflict. The United States and South Korea have never agreed on terms for concluding the Korean War (June 25, 1950–July 27, 1953), which claimed 2.5 million lives, and the ROK never signed the armistice.[25] There is an armistice suspending combat, but also concern

---

It quoted the Dear Leader, who announced that his nation had 'finally realized the great historic cause of completing the state nuclear force.'

[23] Chris Buckley, "North Korea Says It Has a Hydrogen Bomb. Here's What That Means," *New York Times* (September 3, 2017), https://www.nytimes.com/2017/09/03/world/asia/north-korea-hydrogen-bomb.html?mcubz=0.

[24] Nicholas Eberstadt, "From 'Engagement' to Threat Reduction: Moving Toward a North Korea Policy That Works," *AEI* (January 2017), http://www.aei.org/publication/from-engagement-to-threat-reduction-moving-toward-a-north-korea-policy-that-works/.

"To almost any Western reader, the notion that North Korea might actually be planning to stare down the USA in some future nuclear face-off will sound preposterous, if not outright insane. And indeed it does — to us. Yet remember: as we already know from press reports, North Korea has been diligently working on everything that would actually be required for such a confrontation: miniaturization of nuclear warheads, intercontinental ballistic missiles, and even cyberwarfare (per the Sony hacking episode). Note further that while North Korean leadership may be highly tolerant of casualties (on the part of others, that is) it most assuredly is not suicidal itself. Quite the contrary: its acute interest in self-preservation is demonstrated prima facie by the fact of its very survival, over 25 years after the demise of the USSR and Eastern European socialism. It would be unwise of us to presume that only one of the two forces arrayed along the DMZ is capable of thinking about what it would take to deter the other in a time of crisis on the Peninsula." Cf. Nicholas Eberstadt, *The End of North Korea* (Washington D.C.: AEI Press, 1999).

[25] Allan R. Millett, "Korean War 1950–1953," *Encyclopedia Britannica*, https://www.britannica.com/event/Korean-War.

Korean War, conflict between the Democratic People's Republic of Korea (North Korea) and the Republic of Korea (South Korea) in which at least 2.5 million persons lost their lives. The war reached international proportions in June 1950 when North Korea,

North Korea 109

that this "frozen conflict" could erupt into renewed civil war or even a wider conflagration.[26] Christopher Hill, former US Assistant Secretary of State for East Asia, and many others contend that Kim intends to unify the two Koreas under Pyongyang's authority,[27] and that a nuclear option is a

---

supplied and advised by the Soviet Union, invaded the South. The United Nations, with the United States as the principal participant, joined the war on the side of the South Koreans, and the People's Republic of China came to North Korea's aid. After more than a million combat casualties had been suffered on both sides (see the table of casualties), the fighting ended in July 1953 with Korea still divided into two hostile states. Negotiations in 1954 produced no further agreement, and the front line has been accepted ever since as the *de facto* boundary between North and South Korea.

Korea was ruled by Japan from 1910 until the closing days of World War II. In August 1945, the Soviet Union declared war on Japan, as a result of an agreement with the United States, and liberated Korea north of the 38th parallel. US forces subsequently moved into the south. By 1948, as a product of the Cold War between the Soviet Union and the United States, Korea was split into two regions, with separate governments. Both governments claimed to be the legitimate government of all of Korea, and neither side accepted the border as permanent.

On July 27, 1953, when an armistice was signed. The agreement created the Korean Demilitarized Zone to separate North and South Korea, and allowed the return of prisoners. However, no peace treaty has been signed, and the two Koreas are technically still at war. Periodic clashes, many of which are deadly, continue to the present.

[26] Jacob Argue, "Frozen Conflicts: The Long View," *Diplomatic Courier* (July 27, 2016), http://www.diplomaticourier.com/frozen-conflicts-long-view/.

In international relations, a frozen conflict is a situation in which active armed conflict has been brought to an end, but no peace treaty or other political framework resolves the conflict to the satisfaction of the combatants. Therefore, legally the conflict can start again at any moment, creating an environment of insecurity and instability.

[27] Christopher Hill, "North Korea's Real Strategy," *Project Syndicate* (June 2017), https://www.project-syndicate.org/commentary/north-korea-nuclear-program-invasion-by-christopher-r-hill-2017-06?utm_source=Project+Syndicate+Newsletter&utm_campaign=2200ecc304-sunday_newsletter_25_6_2017&utm_medium=email&utm_term=0_73bad5b7d8-2200ecc304-93559677. Christopher R. Hill, former US Assistant Secretary of State for East Asia, was US Ambassador to Iraq, South Korea, Macedonia, and Poland, a US special envoy for Kosovo, a negotiator of the Dayton Peace Accords, and the chief US negotiator with North Korea from 2005–2009.

North Korea's quest for nuclear weapons is often depicted as a "rational" response to its strategic imperatives of national security and regime survival. After all, the country is surrounded by larger, supposedly hostile states, and it has no allies on which it can rely to come to its defense. It is only logical, on this view, that Kim Jong-un wants to avoid the

110   *Beleaguered Superpower: Biden's America Adrift*

critical component of North Korea's strategy because it "makes the world (Korean peninsula) free for conventional war."[28]

---

mistake made by Iraq's Saddam Hussein and Libya's Muammar el-Qaddafi, both of whom would still be alive and in power had they acquired deliverable nuclear weapons.

In fact, North Korea's appetite for nuclear weapons is rooted more in aggression than pragmatism. North Korea seeks nothing less than to decouple the United States from its South Korean partner — a split that would enable the reunification of the Korean Peninsula on Kim's terms. In other words, North Korea does not want only to defend itself; it wants to set the stage for an invasion of its own.

Of course, such a scenario is, in many ways, the stuff of fancy. But to be a North Korean today is not necessarily to accept the world as it is. And North Korean propaganda continues to reiterate the view that the Korean Peninsula consists of one people, sharing one language and one culture, indivisible — except by outsiders like the US. By this logic, the North needs to find a way to discourage those outsiders from intervening in the peninsula's affairs.

As it stands, the US–South Korea relationship operates on the basis of something like the North Atlantic Treaty's collective-defense clause, Article 5: any North Korean aggression against South Korea will, it is assured, be met by the combined forces of South Korea and the US. Such a counterattack would be decisive, ensuring the total destruction of the North Korean regime.

If North Korea had long-range nuclear weapons, however, it might be able to change the strategic calculus, by threatening to launch a nuclear attack on the US mainland in response to US intervention on the Korean Peninsula. The US might intervene anyway, launching its own devastating attack on North Korea. But it might also choose not to risk casualties on its own soil.

If the US did shirk its collective-defense responsibilities, South Korea would still have plenty of recourse against its northern neighbor. After all, South Korea's conventional forces are far better trained, equipped, and motivated than their North Korean counterparts. The idea that North Korea will abandon its weapons programs in exchange for the promise of security and regime survival has been tested has failed whenever it has been tested. In September 2005, five world powers, including the US, offered North Korea an unimpeded civilian nuclear program, energy assistance, economic aid, and diplomatic recognition, as well as a promise to establish a regional mechanism for maintaining peace and security in Northeast Asia. A US commitment not to attack North Korea with conventional or nuclear weapons was also included in the deal.

The North was not willing to allow for a credible verification protocol. Instead, it attempted to limit verification to that which was already known. In the end, it walked away from the agreement, rather than work to find an acceptable way forward.

[28] Robert Lekachman, "Making the World Safe for Conventional War," *New York Times* (July 31, 1988); Steven Pifer, "A Realist's Rationale For a World Without Nuclear

North Korea's nuclear buildup is not primarily an insurance policy to assure regime survival as often claimed,[29] it is an attempt to unfreeze an otherwise frozen conflict that kills two birds with one stone.[30]

Progressives and liberals avert their eyes from this truth. They refuse to accept that Pyongyang could reunite the peninsula on its own terms, with or without China's complicity, or may not even mind if Kim wins, preferring to protect America's domestic programs. They restrict themselves to discussing "tried and failed" solutions for preventing the North's conventional and nuclear modernization like economic sanctions,[31] and

---

Weapons," *Brookings*, (2016), https://www.brookings.edu/wp-content/uploads/2016/06/A-Realists-Rationale-for-a-World-without-Nuclear-Weapons.pdf; Christine Leah and Adam B. Lowther, "Conventional Arms and Nuclear Peace," *Joint Air & Space Power Conference 2017*; George H. Quester, *Deterrence Before Hiroshima: The Airpower Background of Modern Strategy* (New York: John Wiley & Sons, 1966): 62–64.

"The main role of nuclear weapons has always been to deter conventional war among the world's 'big powers' (the USA, the USSR, the UK, France, West Germany, China, and Japan) by posing a clear risk that such a war would escalate to nuclear war. If ballistic missiles were abolished, raising again the prime strategic question of the 1950s — could a conventional war be fought without going nuclear, and if it went nuclear, could it be won? — it would diminish nuclear deterrence of conventional war."

[29]Anthony H. Cordesman and Charles Ayers, "The Military Balance in the Koreas and Northeast Asia: Final Review Edition," *Center for Strategic and International Studies (CSIS)* (November 2016).

[30]Nicholas Eberstadt, "North Korea: Why Do They Want Nukes?" *AEI* (August 2017), http://www.aei.org/multimedia/north-korea-why-do-they-want-nukes-in-60-seconds/?aei.org?utm_source=paramount&utm_medium=email&utm_campaign=Eberstadt-DPRK-in60seconds-mailing-082817.

[31]Sophia Lotto Persio, "North Korea and the U.S. Are on 'Brink of Large-Scale Conflict,' Putin Warns," *Newsweek* (September 2017), http://www.newsweek.com/north-korea-and-us-are-brink-large-scale-conflict-putin-warns-658580.

"Moscow has already told Washington that additional sanctions on North Korea could prove 'counterproductive and dangerous.' In his statement, Putin invited all parties to reject belligerent rhetoric and instead engage in dialogue."

"The Latest: EU calls on U.N. to adopt further NK sanctions," *ABC News* (September 3, 2017).

"Donald Tusk said the European Union stands ready to sharpen its policy of sanctions and invites North Korea to restart dialogue on its nuclear and missile programs without condition."

112 *Beleaguered Superpower: Biden's America Adrift*

"strategic patience."[32] Economic sanctions, which were part of the Trump administration's policy package too, did not compel leaders of North Korea's command regime to capitulate, and strategic patience is just a euphemism for hope.[33]

Biden cannot persuade Kim to denuclearize irreversibly by resuming the six power nuclear weapons talks with China's assistance if Xi demurs,[34] and the establishment's confidence that Kim Jong-un will not

---

[32] Eli Lake, "Trump Is Right. Nuclear Talks With North Korea Are Pointless. But That Doesn't Mean War is the Only Option," *Bloomberg* (August 31, 2017), https://www.bloomberg.com/view/articles/2017-08-31/trump-is-right-nuclear-talks-with-north-korea-are-pointless?mkt_tok=eyJpIjoiTWpOalptWTRPREUyTWpRMiIsInQiOiJq YjIyNWFNdEZrcmRhamVhYjljZWRpUk1QMHRqdEZwNjBPdUx0Y1Y0OHB1Vlltbk 0yVXhiZkVjakNHNUprczRqK2YrTUcrQndUOE5PeTJ2OFM5SnQ0M05hd3Nu citaREhYalBvQzV4d0dHcENwYXU2QjFJZ2JweEpKZVFQNTRWMyJ9.

[33] Henry Kissinger, *On China* (New York, NY: Penguin, 2011); Tilman Pradt, *China's New Foreign Policy: Military Modernisation, Multilateralism and the 'China Threat'* (London: Palgrave Macmillan, 2016). For an alternative view see Nicholas Eberstadt, "The Method in North Korea's Madness," *Commentary* (January 2018), https://www.commentarymagazine. com/articles/method-north-koreas-madness/.

[34] Christian Shepherd, "After High-Level Diplomatic Talks, US and China Agree on Goal of 'Complete, Irreversible' Denuclearization of North Korea," *Business Insider* (June 24, 2017), http://www.businessinsider.com/r-china-us-agree-aim-of-complete-irreversible-korean-denuclearization-2017-6; Nicholas Eberstadt, "From 'Engagement' to Threat Reduction: Moving Toward a North Korea Policy that Works," *AEI* (January 2017).

'At this juncture, as so often in the past, serious people around the world are calling to 'bring North Korea back to the table' to try to settle the DPRK nuclear issue. However, seeing the DPRK for what it is, rather than what we would like it to be, should oblige us to recognize two highly unpleasant truths. Cf. Chuck Downs, *Over The Line: North Korea's: Negotiating Strategy* (Washington, D.C.: AEI Press, 1999).

"First, the real existing North Korean leadership (as opposed to the imaginary version some Westerners would like to negotiate with) will never willingly give up their nuclear option. Never. Acquiescing in denuclearization would be tantamount to abandoning the sacred mission of Korean unification: which is to say, disavowing the DPRK's *raison d'etre*. Thus submitting to foreign demands to denuclearize could well mean more than humiliation and disgrace for North Korean leadership: it could mean delegitimization and destabilization for the regime as well. Second, international entreaties — summitry, conferencing, bargaining, and all the rest — can never succeed in convincing the DPRK to relinquish its nuclear program. Sovereign governments simply do not trade away their vital national interests."

Cf. White House Press Release, "Mattis and Tillerson: 'We're Holding Pyongyang to Account'," (August 14, 2017), https://www.whitehouse.gov/the-press-office/2017/08/14/mattis-and-tillerson-were-holding-pyongyang-account.

"In response, the Trump administration, with the support of the international community, is applying diplomatic and economic pressure on North Korea to achieve the complete, verifiable and irreversible denuclearization of the Korean Peninsula and a dismantling of the regime's ballistic-missile programs. We are replacing the failed policy of 'strategic patience,' which expedited the North Korean threat, with a new policy of strategic accountability. The object of our peaceful pressure campaign is the denuclearization of the Korean Peninsula. The U.S. has no interest in regime change or accelerated reunification of Korea. We do not seek an excuse to garrison U.S. troops north of the Demilitarized Zone. We have no desire to inflict harm on the long-suffering North Korean people, who are distinct from the hostile regime in Pyongyang."

Michael Swaine, "Time to Accept Reality and Manage a Nuclear-Armed North Korea," *Carnegie Endowment for International Peace* (September 2017), http://carnegieendowment.org/2017/09/11/time-to-accept-reality-and-manage-nuclear-armed-north-korea-pub-73065?mkt_tok=eyJpIjoiTUdVNE9EWTBPRGRoT0dRMiIsInQiOiJCNDVSZmF1MzVuYmR0VWJlU1VOWW8xK25HXC9ldVVmQlVFTG95NllcL0t3T0pFV0pkWFQ3RW00d3hLM1prTWMwbTZJb2JnNWxmdmFHWElBVVZQT1BHSURjaGhKUDhaOXF2KzNVTTNEVUQxWm16eWlaajY3OUNmY3g5UnVHaTlCM2JGIn0%3D.

"Anyone following the growing crisis on the Korean Peninsula in recent weeks has been treated to an endless parade of op-eds on what to do about it, written from almost every conceivable angle. Despite the variation among these perspectives, most such proposals remain focused on how to get Pyongyang to give up its nuclear weapons. Unfortunately, this objective appears less and less viable with every new North Korean (DPRK) missile and nuclear test. This suggests the need for policymakers in the United States, China, South Korea, and Japan to adopt a more realistic approach focused on deterrence, containment, and an array of crisis management measures." Swaine recommends the old placebos: "Shifting Gears: Deterrence, Crisis Management, and Confidence Building."

Kim Jong-un's attitude toward resolving the impasse between the Trump administration and North Korea over Pyongyang's denuclearization appears to have been affected by his first visit to China in April 2018 after which he agreed to halt nuclear testing and seek a negotiated settlement, and his second visit on May 8, 2018 when he reverted to bellicose rhetoric. These twists allow for various interpretation, but it seems that Xi Jinping has considerable influence of Kim Jong-un.

Steven Jiang, Ben Westcott and Sol Han, "Kim Jong Un holds second meeting with Xi Jinping in China," *CNN* (May 8, 2018), https://www.cnn.com/2018/05/08/asia/kim-jong-un-xi-jinping-china-intl/index.html.

114   *Beleaguered Superpower: Biden's America Adrift*

allow his bombast to cross the nuclear threshold may be misplaced.[35] Fifty years of futile negotiation including the delisting of the DPRK from the State Sponsors of Terrorism in 2008 by President George Bush[36] and

---

[35] John Bolton, "FDR's 'Rattlesnake' Rule and the North Korean Threat," *AEI* (September 2017), http://www.aei.org/publication/fdrs-rattlesnake-rule-and-the-north-korean-threat/?mkt_tok=eyJpIjoiWTJRNVpXWTNZVGM0TnpZMCIsInQiOiJOWTdFbzRMZnNnZzRGRUVcL05WN05vaTN6YXN2ZUhubEx6ZUxhRVpjb3VoWXRNZnExNzdRWE9CMmFnNmlOSjdPRkVCdUhueURtNkZXRG5XTUR2T215YmVhbm8zS1NBMGZLRnFhN3NLRnlNMUptXC8yalY4S3Z6SUl6TFJoMFpEMlJmIn0%3D; Louisa Lim, "While U.S. and South Korea Militaries Drill, 'Bombast Continues' From The North," *WUNC* (March 11, 2013), http://wunc.org/post/while-us-and-south-korea-militaries-drill-bombast-continues-north#stream/0; Cf. Joshua Rhett Miller, "Why the Killing of Kim Jong Un's Brother is a Terrifying Sign," *New York Post* (February 15, 2017), http://nypost.com/2017/02/15/why-the-killing-of-kim-jong-uns-brother-is-a-terrifying-sign/.

"'When you see a rattlesnake poised to strike, you do not wait until he has struck before you crush him.' By these words in a Sept. 11, 1941, fireside chat, Franklin Roosevelt authorized US warships to fire first against Nazi naval vessels, which he called 'the rattlesnakes of the Atlantic.' Nonetheless, we hear echoes from Roosevelt's day that 'there is no acceptable military option' when it comes to Pyongyang. This means, as Susan Rice said recently, 'we can, if we must, tolerate nuclear weapons in North Korea,' as we did with the Soviets in Cold War days. The US should not accept such counsels of despair, based on dangerously facile and wildly inaccurate historical analogies. We're moving rapidly to the point where Roosevelt said squarely, It is the time for prevention of attack.' George W. Bush spoke equally directly in 2002: 'Our security will require all Americans to be ... ready for preemptive action when necessary to defend our liberty and to defend our lives.' The alternative is potentially global proliferation of nuclear weapons, with the attendant risks lasting beyond our power to calculate."

[36] Marc Thiessen, "The Warmbiers are Right: North Korea Should be Back on the State Sponsors of Terror List Asia," *AEI* (September 2017), http://www.aei.org/publication/the-warmbiers-are-right-north-korea-should-be-back-on-the-state-sponsors-of-terror-list/?mkt_tok=eyJpIjoiWVRJeU1EWmxOREJqTnpaayIsInQiOiI4dXFvUk9qRXY2dVRoNUR6eTVpRUF3RVEzYW4rRW4wWXFZdEs5YW5nVEdPZFFFKbkZEQ2RpcjJuNXRPYkN1dWZjSDNVQzFPc1hpSkFMZGxTOVwvQzc0Y1liRG0wRW1FSlJiNkErc3ZvZTBlM3U2YitZNlpGaGNSUFQ2aUhKWTFmM1cifQ%3D%3D.

"Two decades later, the Bush administration removed North Korea from list in 2008 — not because the North Koreans had given up their support for terror, but because they promised to give up their nuclear weapons. The designation was rescinded as part of a terrible deal negotiated by Secretary of State Condi Rice and Ambassador Chris Hill in exchange for a promise by North Korea to dismantle a plutonium facility and allow inspections of its Yongbyon nuclear facility. North Korea obviously did not keep up its end of

America's unilateral removal of tactical nuclear weapons from the ROK,[37] show that Kim Jong-un will not content himself with the *status quo* solely under American pressure.[38]

South Korean attempts to woo North Korea with its "sunshine policy" likewise have failed.[39] These efforts include the 1992 Agreement on Reconciliation, Nonaggression and Exchanges and Cooperation between the South and the North, and the Joint Declaration of the Denuclearization of the Korean Peninsula. The South–North 2000 summit Joint Declaration was a bust, making a mockery of South Korean President Kim Dae-jung post-summit boast that: "There is no longer going to be any war.

---

the bargain. So the Trump administration should put North Korea back on the list. They more than qualify."

[37] David Rosenbaum, "U.S. to Pull A-Bombs From South Korea," *New York Times* (October 20, 1991), http://www.nytimes.com/1991/10/20/world/us-to-pull-a-bombs-from-south-korea.html.

[38] Robin Emmott and Philip Blenkinsop, "China 'Fully Committed' to Stopping North Korean Missile Programme," *Reuters* (June 2, 2017), http://in.reuters.com/article/northkorea-missiles-china-idINKBN18T26I.

"China, North Korea's only significant diplomatically, is opposed to Pyongyang's missile launches and will support any new United Nations sanctions against the country, China's Premier Li Keqiang said on Friday.

'We are firmly committed to the denuclearisaton of the peninsular and opposed to nuclear tests and missile launches by North Korea,' he told a news conference following a meeting with European Union leaders.

'China has always vigorously implemented (U.N.) Security Council resolutions. Sanctions lists issued by the Security Council have been strictly complied with by China. Should the Security Council ask for new actions, we will act accordingly.'"

[39] Kyung-Hwa Lee, "김정은 정권의 통일전략 (Kim Jong Un's Unification Strategy)," Ministry of Unification (2016): 4.

Currently, the South Korean government is using a two-track strategy that combines sunshine policy with existing hard-line measures but is struggling to overcome the structural limitations inherent in South Korea's policy toward North Korea. As long as China continues to assist North Korea, South Korea will not exert a strong influence on North Korea. China is not willing to participate in active economic sanctions against North Korea because of concerns over side effects associated with the collapse of North Korea and vested interests in maintaining the North Korean regime. Using such a dilemma of China, North Korea will expand its political autonomy by conducting nuclear tests in the presence of China and amplifying the instability of the East Asian situation.

116 *Beleaguered Superpower: Biden's America Adrift*

The North will no longer attempt unification by force, and at the same time we will not do any harm to the North."[40]

The joint "peace declaration" in the eight-point agreement signed by Kim Jong-il and President Roh Moo-hyun October 2007 fared no better. "The South and the North both recognize the need to end the current armistice regime and build a permanent peace regime."[41]

Following the election of Moon Jae-in in 2017, South Korea began reconciling with North Korea once more. Moon Jae-in's effort in improving inter-Korean relationship resulted in three inter-Korean summits, including two held in Panmunjom (April 2018 and May 2018), and one in Pyongyang (September 2018). In recognition of Moon's endeavors as the first president to hold multiple summits in a year, his version of Sunshine Policy created a new epithet called "Moonshine Policy." Moon remains optimistic,[42] but Kim continues to send mixed signals.[43] Moon's concept is to press for a peace treaty by reassuring the North of the ROK's peaceful intentions, building down South Korea's military, and developing a roadmap for disarmament before his Presidential term ends in 2022.[44]

Neither bluster, nor idealist appeals at the end of the day are apt to deter Kim's ambitions. Nor is it prudent to count on China and Russia to pull America's chestnuts out of the fire as Washington sometimes hopes.

---

[40]Nicholas Eberstadt, "North Korea's Phony Peace Ploy," *AEI* (April 2018), http://www. aei.org/publication/north-koreas-phony-peace-ploy/?mkt_tok=eyJpIjoiWlRBeVpqazNP RGd6WkdVMiIsInQiOiJBc2dxOFpBMHFKREJKU0tKZTBSK1Jnc1V4dGl6bCtWd00r d09hbXoxNEIwa1ZZU0RUalQwMVV6VTZPM1FjTFErNUZPRFZ5OXVtNFgwan NRK3U0SDRXdzZNZ2pCeUVBKzluNGpDbWdRMUUrQkxOaWl1TTlxQVlqak9YO HVqUTlGdCJ9.

[41]*Ibid.*

[42]Saeme Kim, "Moon Jae-in Is Serious About Inter-Korean Cooperation: Moon is Intent on Pushing Ahead with North–South Cooperation, But He Needs to Remain Cognizant of the Risks," *The Diplomat* (January 2020), https://thediplomat.com/2020/01/moon-jae-in-is-serious-about-inter-korean-cooperation/.

[43]"North Korea Warns of Return to Nuclear Policy: Pyongyang Expresses Frustration Over the Slow Progress of the Lifting of Sanctions While US Insists on Denuclearization," *Aljazeera* (November 4, 2018), https://www.aljazeera.com/news/2018/11/north-korea-warns-return-nuclear-policy-181104091327163.html.

[44]Lee Chung Min, "The Case of Moon Jae-in," *ASAN Forum* (January 20, 2020), http://www.theasanforum.org/the-case-of-moon-jae-in/.

North Korea   117

Kim is unlikely to attack his fellow authoritarians,[45] and both benefit from the West's tribulations. Like North Korea, Beijing and Moscow oppose Pax Americana and want the United States to vacate the Korean peninsula.[46] They both have an interest in restricting North Korea's nuclear arsenal, but beyond this are content to shed crocodile tears while the United States twists in the wind, unless Kim Jong-un recklessly threatens to attack them.[47]

Thwarting Kim's Endgame

Nonetheless, there are plausible grounds for believing that Kim's reinvigorated, on-and-off, Korean reunification campaign can be thwarted with stout hard power without provoking a nuclear exchange. It is hard power, not Washington's soft power that is the key. Hard power can ensure that Kim someday accepts North Korea's dilemma to the extent that rationality and Beijing can hold the "Supreme Leader" in check.[48] Pyongyang

---

[45] China poses a greater threat to North Korea's independence than South Korea, America and Japan in the long run. Pyongyong knows this and undoubtedly is pleased to have killed two birds with one stone by nuclear weapons that give pause to all his overt and latent adversaries.

[46] This leads to some revealing paradoxes. The United States restricts South Korean and Japanese defense capabilities to placate China's "fears and complexes" and retain in regional supremacy, but in doing so invites North Korean aggression. China for its part want America out of the peninsula, but risks South Korea and Japan vastly increasing their firepower as America withdraws. Neither side can have its cake and eat it.

[47] Vipin Narang, "Why Kim Jong-Un Wouldn't Be Irrational to Use a Nuclear Bomb First," *Washington Post* (September 9, 2017), https://www.washingtonpost.com/outlook/why-kim-jong-un-wouldnt-be-irrational-to-use-a-nuclear-bomb-first/2017/09/08/a9d36ca4-934f-11e7-aace-04b862b2b3f3_story.html?utm_term=.4cc8da7c1d80.

China, but not Russia could find itself in the anomalous position of having fewer nuclear weapons in 2027 than North Korea. Some who perceive America as the aggressor on the peninsula argue that it would be rational for Kim Jong-Un to initiate a tactical nuclear first strike. This might be so, but is also irrelevant because the ROK is not planning to invade the DPRK.

[48] Reihan Salam, "Is Kim Jong-Un a Rational Actor?," *National Review* (September 2017), http://www.nationalreview.com/corner/451578/north-koreas-kim-jong-un-rational-actor-or-madman.

Some speculate that Kim is not a rational actor. If they are right, the situation requires psychological management to the extent that is possible.

118 *Beleaguered Superpower: Biden's America Adrift*

cannot defeat America on the ground, in the air and at sea or expand North Korea's sphere of influence if Washington is determined to fight, even if the North temporarily achieves tactical victories.[49] Kim can only prevail, if America and South Korea flinch, succumbing to his and Xi's wiles.[50] His only choices are saber rattling, nuclear suicide, and contenting himself with half-a-loaf (nation building on whatever terms suit him). Kim can bluster to his heart's content, but eventually Pyongyang will have to face the fact that its bellicosity will never pay dividends if America and South Korea stand firm.[51] Even adept bluffers have to recognize that the costs of bluster vastly exceed the gains, when there are no neighbors to conquer or subjugate.

Some speculate that Kim is not a rational actor. If they are right, the situation requires psychological management to the extent that is possible.

[49] Anthony Cordesman, "Keeping the North Korean Threat in Proportion," *Center for Strategic and International Studies* (*CSIS*) (August 2017), https://www.csis.org/analysis/keeping-north-korean-threat-proportion.

"North Korea has enough ground power to pose a serious threat and the initial phase of any serious war would cost South Korea a great deal. Once again, however, much of the North Korea force is far less capable in terms of advanced ground weapons systems. Unless China came to its aid, it could not come close to the initial advances it made in the Korean War. It would take massive losses in any intense fighting, and it would lose over time."

[50] Robert McNamara, and Brian VanDeMark, *In Retrospect: The Tragedy and Lessons of Vietnam* (New York: Times Books, 1995).

It should be assumed that Kim Jong-un has and will continue to have sufficient military strength to wage a protracted land war against South Korea with ambiguous rules of engagement. South Korea and America should be able to control the skies on both sides of the 38th parallel, but the danger of nuclear escalation is likely to restrain air and missile targeting against the North as it did during the Vietnam War.

[51] Joseph Nye, "Understanding the North Korea Threat," *Project Syndicate* (December 2017), https://www.project-syndicate.org/commentary/understanding-north-korea-threat-by-joseph-s--nye-2017-12?utm_source=Project+Syndicate+Newsletter&utm_campaign=9ec68ad59b-sunday_newsletter_10_12_2017&utm_medium=email&utm_term=0_73bad5b7d8-9ec68ad59b-93559677.

Joseph Nye believes that America does not have to stand firm to benefit from North Korea's inability to expand its territorial reach. He thinks that nuclear deterrence and soft power are enough.

"The US has talked itself into Kim Jong-un's trap of exaggerating how much power his rocketry gives him. If the US could deter a much stronger Soviet Union from taking an isolated West Berlin for three decades, it can deter North Korea."

The United States does not have to accept North Korean nuclear power if Kim reneges on his promises to Washington, but if cool heads prevail Biden can achieve a satisfactory outcome nonetheless by perpetually maintaining superior conventional forces on the peninsula. America can use advanced technologies,[52] buttressed by non-conventional threats to power grids and other critical infrastructure as supplements to economic sanctions.[53] President Trump's and President Moon's decision "in principle" to revise a bilateral American–South Korean treaty that limits the weight and range of the South's ballistic missiles is a sound first step.[54] It not only augments ROK counterforce capabilities, it signals that

---

[52] Jason Sherman, "Senate Panel Would Boost Pentagon's Eleventh-Hour Gambit to Accelerate RKV Development," *The Insider Digest* (November 28, 2017), https://insidedefense.com/insider/insider-daily-digest-nov-28-2017.

"The Senate Appropriations Committee has endorsed a Pentagon plan to accelerate development of the new Ground-based Midcourse Defense warhead — which aims to improve defenses against a potential North Korean or Iranian intercontinental ballistic missile — lifting proposed spending even beyond the Trump administration's requested increase."

[53] John Yoo and Jeremy A. Rabkin, "Taming North Korea — Without Firing a Shot," *New York Post* (August 2017), http://www.aei.org/publication/taming-north-korea-without-firing-a-shot/?mkt_tok=eyJpIjoiWm1JNE1USXdPR1k1T0RneiIsInQiOiJSYmt6VHpQV3NBYWFGUWJsbHBZcmkwSk11SUhpMTZVYjY0MXpLVDlxVVIzVUQyOCtqZFMxZ1JrYTk5dEpGZUFtZlhoYWJ1Qm51VGtOcGFSYnJU"a0ZhNlhJT3diSm9kSjhBTGZHaEFVU3dJTWM2UThpS3lvRTk0SlU1WFdEWUtNWSJ9.

Yoo and Rabkin argue that cyber war and other new technologies can be used to diminish the probability of successful nuclear strikes, and serve as surrogates to economic sanctions in tutoring Kim Jong-un to keep the peace. "Advances in robotics may allow drones to disable electricity grids or arms factories without physical destruction. Undersea devices could enforce blockades more precisely than minefields. Satellites can disrupt an opponent's communication networks. New technologies will allow us to impose harm equivalent to economic sanctions, but without waiting for the rest of the world to join us in restricting trade."

Sofia Lotto Persio, "South Korea 'Blackout Bombs' Can Take Down Pyongyang Without Firing a Shot," *Newsweek* (October 2017), http://www.newsweek.com/south-korea-builds-blackout-bombs-take-down-pyongyang-without-firing-shot-680465; Nicholas Eberstadt, "The Method in North Korea's Madness," *Commentary* (January 16, 2018), https://www.commentarymagazine.com/articles/method-north-koreas-madness/.

[54] Laura Smith-Spark, Taehoon Lee, and Catherine Treyz, "US, South Korea Set to Revise Bilateral Missile Treaty," *CNN* (September 2, 2017), http://www.cnn.com/2017/09/02/asia/south-korea-us-missile-treaty/index.html.

120   *Beleaguered Superpower: Biden's America Adrift*

America can eliminate velvet restraints on South Korean and Japanese military capabilities.[55] The reintroduction of sea launched Tomahawk missiles carrying tactical nuclear warheads would also demonstrate Washington's resolve, and grab Kim's attention because both initiatives adversely alter the correlation of forces from Pyongyang's perspective.[56]

North Korea's epiphany is not predestined.[57] America, South Korea, and Japan must make it clear to Kim that their conventional forces are

---

"Under the bilateral pact last revised in 2012, South Korea is allowed to develop ballistic missiles with a range of up to 800 kilometers (500 miles) and a payload weight of up to 500 kilograms (1,100 pounds).

The White House said Trump gave Moon his "conceptual approval" for the planned purchase by the South of billions of dollars of US military equipment."

Monique M. Maldonado, "As North Korea Rattles Saber, The F-35 Jet Fighter Is Now Combat-Ready," *Homeland Security* (September 1, 2017), http://inhomelandsecurity.com/f-35a-combat-north-korea/.

"Although there are no projected timetables for deploying the latest F-35s in theater, there have been discussions about establishing a security system to deploy F-35As in the Asia-Pacific region on semi-annual rotations."

[55]"The Latest: Trump OKs More Military Sales to SKorea," *Washington Post* (September 5, 2017).

"U.S. President Donald Trump says he has given the go-ahead for Japan and South Korea to buy a 'substantially increased amount' of sophisticated military equipment from the United States. The move comes amid tensions over North Korea's latest nuclear test. The U.S. is weighing a number of military, economic and diplomatic responses. The White House said that in a phone call with South Korean's president on Monday, Trump gave approval 'in principle' to lifting previous restrictions on South Korean missile payloads and to approving 'many billions' in weapons sales to South Korea."

Bruce Klinger, "South Korea: Taking the Right Steps to Defense Reform," Heritage Foundation (October 2011), http://www.heritage.org/asia/report/south-korea-taking-the-right-steps-defense-reform.

[56]Akio Kawato, "Will Japan Go Nuclear?" *Blog* (September 25, 2017), http://www.japan-world-trends.com/en/japan_diary/will_japan_go_nuclear.php.

[57]Yeo Jun-suk, "Concern Rises Over Alleged Leak of Allies' Wartime Operational Plan," *Korean Herald* (October 10, 2017), http://www.koreaherald.com/view.php?ud=20171010000828.

"Suspicions that South Korea's classified wartime operational plan may now be in the hands of the North Korean army continued to roil South Korea on Tuesday after a lawmaker revealed more disturbing details about the alleged North Korean hacking of South Korea's military network system last year." "Among the secrets stolen were the OPLAN

North Korea   121

robust,[58] and their ABM systems can degrade a Pyongyong nuclear offensive.[59] The most promising endgame is a draw that does not defeat Kim, but defangs the "Supreme Leader," allowing him to decide whether gradual liberalization, perhaps along the lines pioneered by Deng Xiaoping and Xi Jinping is better than war.[60]

Kim Jong-un is hoping for a higher return on his nuclear investment. He does not want the peninsula to be an eternally frozen conflict and may win his wager.[61] He may rightly grasp that South Korea's President Moon Jae-in cannot resist pressing his "moonshine" policy that gives North

---

5015, which includes the so-called decapitation plan of the regime's leader Kim Jong-un, and the OPLAN 3100, which deals with the North's small-scale provocations such as its artillery attack on a South Korean island of Yeongpyong in 2010, Rhee said."

[58] Kingston Reif, "Missile Defense Can't Save Us From North Korea," *War on the Rocks* (May 29, 2017), https://warontherocks.com/2017/05/missile-defense-cant-save-us-from-north-korea/?mkt_tok=eyJpIjoiWlRJeU9EWXpNamhpTTJabCIsInQiOiJSZEpJdjI4T2Rt U2dMc00wM1phcUJ5YktUMlFYQkFiREQxV2RoQVwvR2xqUHJkVzFDUlNXS1ZW eCtDMGNzRHNHNlBUNllROE83ZUxkWlR2MThIQm9nQ0lkZE1ib3o0MEltNmNBW FNEdGxCM0xVQVBzdzM2SkZ1YklwUTN3SDExelcifQ%3D%3D.

America's antiballistic missile capability is not a powerful as public officials pretend. BMD can only increase the uncertainty of an adversary's attack. It is not an impenetrate shield.

[59] Patrick Tucker, "Newly Revealed Experiment Shows How F-35 Could Help Intercept ICBMs," *Defense One* (December 6, 2017), http://www.defenseone.com/technology/ 2017/12/newly-revealed-experiment-shows-how-f-35-could-help-intercept-icbms/144365/?mkt_tok=eyJpIjoiWkRBeFlXUTROR0ZpTnpaaiIsInQiOiJvcHljcE4raEp UaXJXTWtXaG5wUUVkb3gxMm9xVVFoYXFsXC9idW1KTzBoS0xmRkF0 eW9jeVlPN295T3dqWkphQm5TbkNGVlRhT0VoTm1pdjBTVUZKWlRNMUVHREw 4WHByc1N1OVRnSmhUOGUrVHJlVFZBN2l5THJ5amtZMzBuRHcifQ%3D%3D.

[60] Stalemate is a situation in the game of chess where the player whose turn it is to move is not in check but has no legal move. The rules of chess provide that when stalemate occurs, the game ends as a draw (i.e. having no winner). In the North Korea case a stalemate would mean that Kim remains in power but has no viable conventional or nuclear option to defeat his adversaries. The conflict will remain frozen, or Kim can abandon the game; that is, try to survive with a new non-belligerent strategy.

[61] Nicholas Eberstadt, "From 'Engagement' to Threat Reduction: Moving toward a North Korea Policy that Works," *AEI* (January 2017), http://www.aei.org/publication/from-engagement-to-threat-reduction-moving-toward-a-north-korea-policy-that-works/?mkt_ tok=eyJpIjoiTTJRMllqTTBOMlZqTURObSIsInQiOiIrNTFEbUdjNksrQlJ2cTBOWGN3 dGUwM2NLalNxbktLWHVVTUV1MlwvMGwwOGNUUXNRV2xjdUhOT2x

122 *Beleaguered Superpower: Biden's America Adrift*

Korea something for nothing,[62] and that Biden prizes his domestic agenda more than a prudent settlement of the Korean imbroglio. Kim is not blind. He recognizes that America's commitment to South Korea is more pliable than Washington proclaims.

South Korea also might play into Kim's hands because Moon may prefer a disadvantageous reunion of the Peninsula to the two Koreas solution that a draw implies. Fishing in troubled waters for the moment appears to be the best option for Pyongyang, given prevailing constraints.

Hard Power

North Korea's desire to become a formidable nuclear power with reliable ballistic missile capabilities is hardly news.[63] Its nuclear weapons program dates back to the 1980s when it began operating facilities for uranium fabrication and conversion, and conducting high-explosive detonation

---

wVUZmeDc4SnZFU1llMDFrV2FRZHYyR2pwOHZtMWNDeWljbjBMdTczdjdcL0FT
VTIzanptSkwwNnJreVlFRU5pQVRFcW1nZ3hrIn0%3D.

[62]Nicholas Eberstadt, "Can South Korea Avoid Getting Played by the North?" *AEI* (January 2018), http://www.aei.org/publication/can-south-korea-avoid-getting-played-by-the-north/?mkt_tok=eyJpIjoiWkRnd01qQTVPVFF3TjJKbSIsInQiOiJWUE1YT1wvQ3 lGOXZrQnZwQ0hKZnRvSkdaelNmRkNtdXU0SFJ4aG1TcGpMTlE4R1pEMEw0RzRX eXpZaytyUEpFRU5kbGhDYm9WQVZPcStMQ0FkQ2tTQjI3NUFiVVc1ajFpUnpWVH doeEdkWUMwVDNwZTdjQ0xFMU5ieWdlaWFZTmcifQ%3D%3D.

"So how can the Moon administration avoid getting played? First, by recognizing the North's ulterior goals in these talks, and the other traps it may be readying. Then, by insisting ruthlessly on a quid pro quo at every step — requiring, for example, that if Seoul postpones military exercises, then Pyongyang should too. And finally, by tucking a few tricks up its own sleeves. Mr. Kim says he wants more contact between the North and the South? Insist on it, including by requiring that news from South Korea be allowed to reach the North. Don't shy away from raising unpleasant topics, like North Korea's appalling human rights situation, and calling for it to cooperate with the existing United Nations commission of inquiry. And why not confidentially mention that a large majority of South Koreans now seem to favor hosting United States tactical nuclear weapons to counter the North's new threats? South Korean negotiators are not used to turning the tables on their North Korean interlocutors, but they should start."

[63]Office of the Secretary of Defense, "Military and Security Developments Involving the Democratic People's Republic of Korea 2015," (January 2016).

tests. Pyongyang ratified the Treaty on the Non-Proliferation of Nuclear Weapons (NPT) in 1985, but withdrew in 2003. It began conducting nuclear tests in 2006.

The crucial point of North Korea's nuclear program is that it has succeeded despite Washington's repeated insistence that the DPRK's feeble economy could not support the development of nuclear weapons and ballistic missiles.[64] Soviet and Maoist precedent went unheeded.[65] North Korea is the third communist nation with an anorexic consumer sector coexisting side by side with a formidable military industrial complex to nuclearize. It now has a demonstrated capability for producing a lethal array of weapons that compels adversaries to compete or cede the field.

The North–South Korean military balance has long been precarious. South Korea's capabilities buttressed with American reinforcements are strong on quality and weak on quantity.[66] South Korea has air and naval superiority, North Korea has larger ground forces. The mix has been potent enough to deter a full-scale resumption of hostilities for more than 60 years, but the situation could change quickly if North Korea follows up its nuclear and missile successes with a surge in conventional force modernization, while the West dithers. Progressives and liberals deny that North Korea will try, but their assurances are worthless, and are dangerous because they

---

[64]Anthony H. Cordesman and Charles Ayers, "The Military Balance in the Koreas and Northeast Asia: Final Review Edition," *Center for Strategic and International Studies (CSIS)* (November 2016).

[65]The People's Republic of China has developed and possesses weapons of mass destruction, including chemical and nuclear weapons. The first of China's nuclear weapons tests took place in 1964, and its first hydrogen bomb test occurred in 1967. The Soviet atomic bomb project was authorized by Joseph Stalin during World War II. The Soviet scientific community discussed the possibility of an atomic bomb throughout 1930s. David Holloway, *Stalin and the Bomb: The Soviet Union and Atomic Energy 1939–1956* (London: Yale University Press, 1994); Richard Rhodes, *The Making of the Atomic Bomb* (New York: Simon and Schuster, 1987); Jim Baggott, *The First War of Physics: The Secret History of the Atom Bomb, 1939–1949* (New York: Pegasus Books, 2010).

[66]Expert assessments vary greatly and depend partly on the possibilities of limited nuclear war. For an complete analysis, see Anthony H. Cordesman and Charles Ayers, The Military Balance in the Koreas and Northeast Asia: Final Review Edition, *Center for Strategic and International Studies* (November 2016).

124　*Beleaguered Superpower: Biden's America Adrift*

needlessly encourage Kim Jong-un to push the envelope without incurring unacceptable risk. There is a better way. Let the Kim regime keep the illusion of a nuclear option, but use conventional hard power to deter the use of whatever systems may be openly or covertly deployed, and simultaneously guarantee South Korea's territorial integrity. Diplomatic hysteria, sanctions, UN resolutions, and Chinese pressure make colorful headlines, but are superfluous. Just tell Kim tirelessly that unifying the peninsula on his terms is delusional. Back the declaration with conventional hard power, and leave him twisting in the wind until reality sinks in.

The evidence suggests that this is what the Trump administration tried to accomplish,[67] but sustained progress beyond the halt in nuclear weapons testing remained elusive.[68] Kim Jong-un for the moment seems marginally less reckless than his old bluster suggested. Trump's persistent, hard power backed negotiation strategy has slowed North Korea's nuclear and missile programs, without exacerbating the conflict as progressives and liberals predicted. The risks of nuclear war in East Asia for the moment have diminished,[69] and should continue declining if Biden relentlessly parries Kim's gambits.[70]

---

[67] Josh Smith, "Buying A Big Stick: South Korea's Military Spending Has North Korea Worried," *Reuters* (September 19, 2019), https://www.reuters.com/article/us-southkorea-military-analysis/buying-a-big-stick-south-koreas-military-spending-has-north-korea-worried-idUSKCN1VW03C.

[68] Ken Dilanian and Andrea Mitchell, "North Korea Still Operating, Improving Major Nuclear Fuel Plant, Experts Say: Joseph Bermudez Jr. And Victor Cha Say Images from March Show Activity at the Pyongsan Uranium Concentrate Plant, Believed to Produce Yellowcake Uranium," *NBC News* (May 20, 2020), https://www.nbcnews.com/politics/national-security/north-korea-still-operating-improving-major-nuclear-fuel-plant-experts-n1216606.

[69] Chung Min Lee and Kathryn Botto, "Korea Net Assessment: Politicized Security and Unchanging Strategic Realities," *Carnegie Endowment* (March 2020), https://carnegieendowment.org/2020/03/18/korea-net-assessment-2020-politicized-security-and-unchanging-strategic-realities-pub-81230?utm_source=carnegieemail&utm_medium=email&utm_campaign=announcement&mkt_tok=eyJpIjoiWTJZeFlqZzJaR1F5TURoaCIsInQiOiJmdk ZHMTNQcmhnN3VibzVjVUNKeE5EcHBXYTFVRWVRU1BQaFQ5OWYzR2Zw cjZvQkRkbnJyQTJLdVNocHE1R3c4VmJVRWMwMUg3c01WNm1wam50Vyt KZFJMZmdaenRNSVdyaHhTamRtMDJYWFFjVk1EMERBbjBqUDFiMm1Ga0JSYiJ9.

[70] Frank Miles, "North Korea Executes 5 Officials Over Failed Kim–Trump Summit," *Fox News* (May 31, 2019), https://www.foxnews.com/world/north-korea-executes-5-officials-over-failed-kim-trump-summit-south-korean-media.

Chapter 6

Iran[1]

Iranian civilization never successfully democratized from its foundation 2,500 years ago to the present.[2] Iran became an Islamic republic in 1979 (theocratic counterpart to a people's republic) after Shah Mohammad Reza Pahlavi was overthrown and exiled. Today, Iran is an Islamic theocracy led by conservative clerical forces under the religious scholar Ayatollah Ali Khamenei. Only Islamic scholars may serve as Supreme Leader, accountable to a popularly elected 86-member clerical body (the Assembly of Experts). Iranian culture has internalized aspects of the

---

[1] Reza Aslan, *Global Jihadism: A Transnational Social Movement* (Saarbrücken: VDM (Verlag Dr. Müller), 2010).

Jihadism (also jihadist movement, jihadi movement and variants) is a 21st-century neologism found in the Western languages to describe Islamist militant movements perceived as military movements "rooted in Islam" and "existentially threatening" to the West.

[2] Iran was known as Persia until 1935. The country has always been a complex mix of ethnicities. Its peoples were predominantly Zoroastrian until the 7th century when Islam became ascendant. Persia was ruled by a series of imperial regimes: Achaemenid Empire (550–330 BC), Sasanian Empire (224–651), Safavid dynasty (1501–1736), Afsharid dynasty (1736–1796), Zand dynasty (1751–1794), Qajar dynasty (1785–1925), and Pahlavi dynasty (1925–1979). Iran became an Islamic republic in 1979 after the ruling monarchy was overthrown and Shah Mohammad Reza Pahlavi was forced into exile.

126　*Beleaguered Superpower: Biden's America Adrift*

Enlightenment, socialism,[3] communism,[4] electoral governance,[5] rule of law, private property, markets and contract law, but is primarily an Islamic theocracy.

Iran periodically has been an expansionist empire, spreading it domains north, south, east, and west. It has no formal irredentist claims as North Korea does against South Korea, but mullahs toy with the idea of Pan-Iranianism and speak of "greater Iran."[6]

Iran's per capita GDP is 34 percent of the US level, a figure well below Russia, but above China.[7] Its military industrial capabilities do not rival Russia or China and lag North Korea, but CIA data indicate that Iran's living standard is higher than the DPRK.

---

[3] Iranian socialism traces its beginnings to the 20th century and encompasses various political parties. Iran experienced a short Third World Socialism period at the zenith of the Tudeh Party after the abdication of Reza Shah and his replacement by his son, Mohammad Reza Pahlavi (though the party never rose to power).

[4] The Communist Party of Iran was an Iranian communist party founded by former Social Democratic Party's members who supported Baku-based Bolsheviks. It was named the Communist Party of Iran in 1920.

[5] Iran has a popularly elected president, but he is subordinated to the theocratic leader. The system is theocrat, not democratic.

[6] Pan-Iranism is an ideology that advocates solidarity and reunification of Iranian peoples living in the Iranian plateau and other regions that have significant Iranian cultural influence, including the Persians, Azerbaijanis, Ossetians, Kurds, Zazas, Tajiks of Tajikistan and Afghanistan, the Pashtuns and the Baloch of Pakistan. Pan-Iranism is linked with the idea of forming a Greater Iran, including informal claims to parts of the Caucasus, West Asia, Central Asia, and South Asia.

[7] CIA, *World Factbook: Iran* (2017), https://www.cia.gov/library/publications/the-world-factbook/geos/ir.html.

"Iran's economy is marked by statist policies, inefficiencies, and reliance on oil and gas exports, but Iran also possesses significant agricultural, industrial, and service sectors. The Iranian government directly owns and operates hundreds of state-owned enterprises and indirectly controls many companies affiliated with the country's security forces. Distortions — including inflation, price controls, subsidies, and a banking system holding billions of dollars of non-performing loans — weigh down the economy, undermining the potential for private-sector-led growth.

Private sector activity includes small-scale workshops, farming, some manufacturing, and services, in addition to medium-scale construction, cement production, mining, and metalworking. Significant informal market activity flourishes and corruption is widespread."

Iran   127

Iran is not uniformly backward. Like other authoritarian nations, it has a potent military machine-building sector, especially in the subcategories of ballistic missiles and nuclear technology.[8] Iran is militarily resilient, and the theocracy is durable enough for Tehran to defend itself against most adversaries. Iran's theocracy is allergic to the open society, civil liberties, democracy, the West's rule of law, and radical progressive values. Unlike Shah Mohammad Reza Pahlavi, Khamenei intends to prevail by challenging American interests.

Shah Mohammad Reza Pahlavi, (1919–1980), shared many of the United States' international security goals. He maintained a pro-Western foreign policy, and fostered a White Revolution economic development program that included construction of expanded road, rail, and air networks, dam and irrigation projects, the eradication of diseases such as malaria, the encouragement of land reform, and industrial growth.

The Shah opposed Soviet communism, Pan Arab socialism in Iraq and Syria, had amicable relations with Israel and viewed America as a friend. This era of cordiality abruptly ended in 1979 when Iranian Islamic revolution deposed the Shah. On November 4, 1979, the revolutionary group Muslim Student Followers of the Imam's Line occupied the American embassy in Tehran and took American diplomats hostage. It held 52 American diplomats hostage for 444 days, and an abortive rescue operation to free them (Operation Eagle Claw) on April 24, 1980 claimed the lives of eight American soldiers. These events ruptured Iranian–American relations,[9] causing lasting economic and diplomatic damage. The United States severed relations on April 7, 1980, prompting

---

[8] J. Matthew McInnis, "Understanding Tehran's Defense Acquisition and Research and Development Decision-Making," *AEI* (April 2017), http://www.aei.org/wp-content/uploads/2017/04/Building-the-Iranian-Military.pdf.

"With the possible exception of North Korea, no other medium-sized power is as focused on deepening the indigenization of its military production as the IRI. This is a near-impossible challenge without the resources of a world power such as the United States, China, or Russia. Iran chose this path partly out of an ideological desire to be independent from foreign influence. IRI's drive toward self-sufficiency by way of procurement, research, and development is mostly a matter of necessity."

[9] The shah's rule was said to be oppressive and provide some justification for Khomeini behavior.

128   *Beleaguered Superpower: Biden's America Adrift*

Khomeini to denounce America as the "Great Satan."[10] Tehran cut diplomatic ties with Israel. It denies the legitimacy of the Israeli state. It adopted a hostile attitude to Saudi Arabia and the Gulf States. Iran promotes Islamic fundamentalism everywhere, proxy wars in Iraq, Afghanistan, Lebanon, and Syria, and maintains cordial relations with Russia and China.

These policies threaten American security in diverse ways. The United States has responded with diplomatic, soft and hard power countermeasures. It imposed economic sanctions and used hard power to deter conventional Iranian military threats and those posed by Tehran's militant Islamic fundamentalist surrogates and allies. The Obama–Biden and Biden–Harris administrations and the EU leadership advocate diplomacy to prevent Tehran from acquiring nuclear weapons. Trump preferred tough sanctions and military countermeasures.

Washington's soft power, Nuclear Non-Proliferation Treaty (NPR) control and confidence building policies in force from 1956 until 2017 had limited success. Iran did not annex new territories or attack American

---

[10]Ruhollah Khomeini, "American Plots Against Iran," *Imam's Sahifeh* (November 5, 1979).

"In this revolution, the Great Satan is America that gathers around other devils blatantly ... If we see the US, this great Satan, raising chain and bringing the devils together around him, it is because the US grip over our country and our resources curtailed."

"The post-revolution government of Iran has regarded the United States and the United Kingdom as Imperialist states, who have a long history of interfering in Iran's internal affairs. In 1907, an Anglo-Russian agreement between Russia and Britain divided Iran into spheres of influence, calling into question [clarification needed], although not terminating, Iran's sovereignty. In 1953, during the Cold War, British intelligence officials and the administration of the US President Dwight D. Eisenhower planned a joint Anglo-American operation to overthrow the elected prime minister, Mohammad Mossadeq. The Eisenhower administration was concerned that Mossadeq's national socialist aspirations could lead to an eventual communist takeover of Iran. The operation was code-named Operation Ajax. At first, the military coup seemed to fail, and Shah Mohammed Reza Pahlavi fled the country. After widespread rioting and with help from the CIA and British intelligence services, Mossadeq was defeated and the Shah returned to power, ensuring support for Western (chiefly British) oil interests and ending the perceived threat of communist expansion. General Fazlollah Zahedi, who led the military coup, became prime minister."

Iran 129

assets in neighboring countries, but this did not stop the mullahs from gaining footholds across the region including Yemen.[11] The Obama–Biden administration and the Trump's policies did not enable Washington to roll back the tide of militant Islamic fundamentalism or stop Iran's nuclear weapon acquisition program.[12] Imminent large-scale Iranian-American armed hostilities seem improbable under the Biden–Harris administration; nonetheless, the threat requires serious attention.[13]

Biden has two broad options. He can "sleep with the enemy,"[14] or persevere with efforts by former president Trump to stem Iran's

---

[11] Maher Farrukh and Katherine Zimmerman "President Saleh is Dead. What's Next for Yemen?," *Critical Threats* (December 6, 2017), https://www.criticalthreats.org/analysis/president-saleh-is-dead-whats-next-for-yemen?mkt_tok=eyJpIjoiTmpJellUUmhaREU0WmpKaSIsInQiOiJjTUd4akZNQ251UjF2RXBiTVpCc3BHcWlzc1lpMjMzSEVub1U3UDRIRHNHdFpBbXhwYTVLWEtQUms1XC91WEZDS0RwSnVyYm5kbjJmbXd0VDF0alZCN0N1bkcrMnVPMEFhdEF2WHNNTlNGZ0c4c1huMUNtTjZ3amhOdWhXN3BHaGoifQ%3D%3D.

[12] "Iran's Nuclear Timeline," *NTI* (Updated June 2020), https://www.nti.org/learn/countries/iran/nuclear/.

"Iran reduced its compliance with the JCPOA in five phases: on 1 July 2019, Iran exceeded 300 kilograms of uranium hexafluoride; on 8 July 2019, Iran enriched uranium past 3.67% up to 4.5%; and on 8 September, Iran announced that its commitments for research and development under the JCPOA would be completely removed. Iran proceeded to invest in research and development of centrifuge technology that is not compliant with IAEA monitoring and safeguards, and on 16 November, Iran notified the Agency that its stock of heavy water had exceeded 130 metric tons. On 5 January, Iran proceeded with the planned fifth and final rollback to its commitments, forgoing all agreed-to limits on centrifuges. Iran did not declare any intent to pursue a nuclear weapon and pledged to continue cooperation with the IAEA."

[13] Lucas Tomlinson, "Navy Destroyer Has Close Encounter with Iran Vessel In Persian Gulf," *Fox* (April 25, 2017), http://www.foxnews.com/world/2017/04/25/navy-destroyer-has-close-encounter-with-iran-vessel-in-persian-gulf.html. Iran's military has repeatedly harassed US Navy ships in the Persian Gulf, including the seizure of two naval vessels and 10 US sailors in January 2016. Iranian ships have taken a range of provocative actions within international waters, including charging American ships at close range.

[14] Michael Rubin, "The Iran Nuclear Deal Weakness that Even Republicans Ignore," *AEI* (November 2017), http://www.aei.org/publication/the-iran-nuclear-deal-weakness-that-even-republicans-ignore/?mkt_tok=eyJpIjoiWTJJM05HSTFOamc1WmpKaiIsInQiOiJyRGF2SGRLNEZuZlo0RXpzemZyNWx0dE9lekZcL1RMclJVVEdwcFJSQzgxcFI

130　*Beleaguered Superpower: Biden's America Adrift*

militant Islamic fundamentalist tide. The first strategy advocated by Obama–Biden progressives and liberals hopeful of eventually secularizing Iranian society, requires America to normalize relations with Tehran on the assumption that the benefits of strengthening Iran's economy and military outweigh the risks.[15]

The second option adopted by the Republicans assumes the reverse; that, America is better off trying to contain Tehran's ambitions with economic sanctions, hard and soft power insisting that Iran honor its NPR commitments, because the mullahs will not relent, and indulgence will reward perfidy.

Both positions are plausible, but their comparative merit is moot because the preponderance of the evidence lies in the eye of the beholder. Those who have faith that Iran must inevitably secularize, modernize, and embrace America's good example, prefer curbing economic sanctions and deterrent hard power, allowing nature to take its course, even if Iran

---

wT2E5RWlnZ2hTNGd2V0NldFwvcHVYQ05NZmVlVDVVWFM3ZlFnMEsxaUdjYU Nwc3crT09FWCtJWnpBMnBPZGZ1NmljYm1KbjVXTHBCWE1zRzVzRjVBIn0%3D. "Senator Tom Cotton, R-Ark., has put together a fact sheet highlighting some of the problems the JCPOA did not address and identified three major flaws:

Sunsets: At year eight of the deal, restrictions on Iran's nuclear program begin to 'sunset,' allowing Iran to steadily industrialize its uranium enrichment program. By year 15, all restrictions expire, bringing Iran to the brink of nuclear breakout.

Verification: The JCPOA fails to provide the International Atomic Energy Agency (IAEA) necessary authority to verify Iran's compliance with the agreement.

Research and Development: The JCPOA allows Iran to develop advanced centrifuges which dramatically reduces the time needed to produce a nuclear weapon."

[15]Michael Ruben, "6 Things You Need To Know About the Iran Protests," *AEI* (January 2018).

"While many Americans imagine falsely that Iran's population is overwhelmingly youthful (it's not) or pro-American (sorry, no), the concerns of ordinary Iranians are more mundane: They want back wages paid, living wages, and safe working conditions. The speed at which working-class Iranians turned on the regime is because the IRGC controls many of the factories and industries in which they work and uses its influence and military force to avoid adherence to the law. Ordinary Iranians feel they have no other recourse. The IRGC has such a stranglehold on the economy, it's impossible to improve the livelihoods of ordinary Iranians while the security forces remain parasitic to Iran's economy."

Iran 131

becomes a nuclear power with potent ballistic missile delivery systems.[16] Those who take the mullahs at their word, counsel the reverse — robust containment.

Biden supports "sleeping with the enemy" because he believes either that the mullahs days are numbered, or the theocrats will discover the virtues of peaceful coexistence before inflicting catastrophic damage on the West. Neither supposition is compelling, but Democrats prefer to pave the way for Western business penetration of Iran's market and blink rather than divert domestic funds from domestic social programs.

Trump by contrast believed that the enmity of Khomeini's successor, Sayyid Ali Hosseini Khamenei current Supreme Leader of Iran, in office since 1989 required firm counter-measures to temper Tehran's ambitions.[17] There is a middle ground, but it is elusive because Biden does not believe that ending sanctions and ignoring treaty violations

---

[16] John Bolton, "16 Years Later: Lessons Put into Practice?" *AEI* (September 2017), https://www.aei.org/publication/16-years-later-lessons-put-into-practice/?mkt_tok=eyJpIjoiTVRJell6Qm1ZVGcwTURreiIsInQiOiJmMXorN1hsRjZvRXU0WG EzY3pSZFJJVG5sWFA3VTZQdWR5T1ZVRFFsZHp0REFWVThiVWdxTDFQbWZW Tm1uYkFWSnE5SFFHejRMcVNiZ2plY1RHN11xZ3FrXC9IRjRITEFvS3U 1czY5U0p0V1d6dWV0SFdXbFp3b1JHQk13Ritka2IifQ%3D%3D. "And, in a dangerous unforced error that could be considered perfidious if it weren't so foolish, Obama entered the 2015 Vienna nuclear and missile deal that has legitimized Tehran's terrorist government, released well over a hundred billion dollars of frozen assets, and dissolved international economic sanctions. Iran has responded by extending its presence in the Middle East as ISIS had receded, to the point where it now has tens of thousands of troops in Syria and is building missile factories there and in Lebanon.

[17] *Ibid.* "Tomorrow marks the 16th anniversary of al-Qaida's 9/11 attacks. We learned much that tragic day, at enormous human and material cost. Perilously, however, America has already forgotten many of Sept. 11's lessons.

The radical Islamicist ideology manifested that day has neither receded nor 'moderated' as many naive Westerners predicted. Neither has the ideology's hatred for America or its inclination to conduct terrorist attacks. Iran's 1979 Islamic Revolution brought radical Islam to the contemporary world's attention, and it is no less malevolent today than when it seized our Tehran embassy, holding U.S. diplomats hostage for 444 days."

132   *Beleaguered Superpower: Biden's America Adrift*

entail significant risks,[18] and does not think the domestic opportunity costs of Iranian containment are worth the national security benefit.[19] Biden progressive-liberals in short counsel appeasement and trade that are apt to allow theocratic Iran to become a nuclear threat in the not too distant future. Republicans favor holding the line with sanctions and stout hard power.

Global Jihadism

The "Iranian Islamic revolution" was a Shiite *coup d'etat* that allowed the mullahs to seize the reins of state power. Its success soon spawned

---

[18]*Ibid.* "Nor can we shelter behind a robust national missile-defense capability, hoping simply to shoot down missiles from the likes of North Korea and Iran before they hit their targets. We do not have a robust national missile defense capability, thanks yet again to Barack Obama's drastic budget cuts." John Bolton, "Iran Deal Devotees Try in Vain to Save a Sinking Ship," *AEI* (September 2017), http://www.aei.org/publication/iran-deal-devotees-try-in-vain-to-save-a-sinking-ship/?mkt_tok=eyJpIjoiWm1NMlpXWXlabVJoWTJOayIsInQiOiJmS01EWUtsUkptMjMrakR5Mnl0ZmVaYlYrNHA0R1JGSVdnY2JJNTNHdzZmM3g1YVJRa1BWV3E5U3pQakhPTWJ0cU5HXC90eFp5YjB4SXZzTEQ3cTVNYVBEUFJtRU1xVHhXQ2M5dkZRamdMbWWVsZTBuYlA5XC9vVXpxa1pvUUZ5bmFIIn0%3D. "At the most basic level, the agreement's adherents ignore how ambiguous and badly worded it is, allowing Iran enormous latitude to continue advancing its nuclear-weapons and ballistic-missile programs without being even 'technically' in violation. The adherents ignore Iran's actual violations (exceeding limits on uranium enrichment, heavy-water production and advanced-centrifuge capacity, among others). Having first argued strenuously there were no violations, they now plead that the violations are 'not significant.'" "The adherents ignore Iran's ongoing belligerent behavior in the Middle East, including constructing an Iranian "arc of control" once ISIS is defeated in Iraq and Syria, giving Tehran's military forces a strategic highway from Iran through Shia-dominated Iraq, into Assad's Syria and then Hezbollah-dominated Lebanon. Israel and our Arab friends clearly see this danger.

[19]*Ibid.*

"During Barack Obama's presidency, he ignored these growing threats and disparaged those who warned against them. His legacy is terrorist attacks throughout Europe and America, and a blindness to the threat that encouraged Europe to accept a huge influx of economic migrants from the MENA region, whose numbers included potentially thousands of already-committed terrorists."

Iran 133

Sunni copycats. Al-Qaeda, a militant Sunni Islamist multi-national organization founded in 1988 by Osama bin Laden, joined the fray with the goal of restoring an Islamic caliphate.[20] The Islamic State (IS), the Islamic State of Iraq and the Levant (ISIL), Hamas,[21] and an alphabet soup of other militant Islamic fundamentalist groups threw their hats into the ring seeking to create states as springboards to a jihadist caliphate.

---

[20]Cole Bunzel, "From Paper State to Caliphate: The Ideology of the Islamic State," *Brookings*, no. 19 (March 2015), https://www.brookings.edu/wp-content/uploads/2016/06/The-ideology-of-the-Islamic-State.pdf.

"The Islamic State, like al-Qaeda, identifies with a movement in Islamic political thought known as Jihadi-Salafism, or jihadism for short. Two streams of Islamic thought contributed to the emergence of the jihadi school in the later 20th century. The first is associated with the Muslim Brotherhood in Egypt. Founded in 1928 by Hasan al-Banna as a political movement bent on winning power and influence in society and capturing the state, the Muslim Brotherhood has never been as doctrinally rigorous as present-day jihadis. The Brotherhood is an exclusively Sunni movement, but it is not implacably hostile to other Islamic sects, such as Shi'ism, or orientations, such as Sufi mysticism. The movement emerged in response to the rise of Western imperialism and the associated decline of Islam in public life, trends it sought to reverse via grassroots Islamic activism. The Muslim Brotherhood championed the restoration of the caliphate as the ideal system of government for the Islamic world, a popular theme in the earlier 20th century. With the dissolution of the Ottoman Caliphate in 1924, various Muslim leaders and groups across the world, from North Africa to Arabia to Southeast Asia, called for the reestablishment of the caliphate." "Al-Qaeda shared a similar ideology but advocated a different strategy, focusing on attacking the United States as the first step to creating an Islamic state in the Middle East. Al-Qaeda's leader, Osama Bin Laden, spoke frequently of restoring the caliphate." "In the last 20 years jihadism has thus been increasingly dominated by its Salafi dimension."

[21]Hamas is a Palestinian militant movement that also serves as one of the territories' two major political parties. A nationalist-Islamist spinoff of Egypt's Muslim Brotherhood, Hamas was founded in 1987, during the first intifada, and later emerged at the forefront of armed resistance to Israel. The United States and the European Union consider Hamas a terrorist organization. Its rival party, Fatah, which dominates the Palestine Liberation Organization (PLO), has renounced violence.

134 *Beleaguered Superpower: Biden's America Adrift*

Iran chose to join forces with some jihadists like Al-Qaeda[22] and Hamas,[23] and oppose others transforming a state-to-state conflict between Tehran and Washington into a battle between America, Iran, and a host of non-state actors. The United States found itself mired in a clash of civilizations between "infidels" and "jihadists" for a pan-Islamic Caliphate and/or other local Islamic objectives, exacerbated by Russian sphere of influence seeking. The conflict is an intense engagement with non-state-terrorist actors including Iranian "revolutionary guards,"[24] embroiled in an

---

[22]Michael Rubin, "The Real Scandal of the Declassified Osama Bin Laden Trove Implicates Obama and the CIA," *AEI* (November 2017), http://www.aei.org/publication/the-real-scandal-of-the-declassified-osama-bin-laden-trove-implicates-obama-and-the-cia/?mkt_tok=eyJpIjoiTkRCa1pHTXhOamt5TWpoayIsInQiOiIyM3NkV3JEUFMwa3Z1M3JqY0dTbGtKTzBTNlJyMVRZczVKUTM2Y1VQY2twSHhEU1hIOVRVSEYzZTV0QkFNVWJ2b0VuQlcrYTZRdGxDVXc0MG82dlNhTDdpdk54R2FCWVFwQ3hseEN6ZXgyb01hYXd2WlczXC9cL0d3MXJKdVZ6QjZoIn0%3D. "Documents newly released by the Central Intelligence Agency reveal just how deep Iran-al Qaeda links are. The close operational relationship between the Islamic Republic of Iran and al Qaeda is well known. The 9/11 Commission, for example, detailed tight relations between the two on several occasions. After the 2003 invasion of Iraq, Iranian officials acknowledged sheltering senior al Qaeda operatives when they sought to use their presence to compel the United States to turn over all Mujahedin al-Khalq members at the time present in Iraq. The real scandal now seems to be how Obama and his CIA heads Leon Panetta, David Petraeus, John Brennan, and acting head Mike Morell released only what upheld and affirmed Obama's tenuous theories about Iran. Had the US public known about the Iranian leadership's outreach and association with al Qaeda, even Democratic congressmen might have been far less willing to tolerate the trust which Obama and Secretary of State John Kerry placed in their Iranian counterparts. After all, Iranian President Hassan Rouhani was secretary of the Supreme National Security Council, the coordinating body for Iran's security and defense policy, at a time when Iran was developing its al Qaeda outreach. Indeed, the refusal to declassify documents not out of fear that sources and methods might be exposed but rather to enable the White House and State Department to avoid calibrating their own policy goals with reality and in pursuit of Obama and Kerry's goals appear to be both an abuse of classification and textbook intelligence politicization."

[23]In July 2015, a senior Hamas official reported that the organization was no longer receiving aid from Iran, possibly due to Hamas's support for the rebels in the Syrian Civil War, as well as its improving relations with Saudi Arabia.

[24]The Islamic Revolutionary Guard Corps (IRGC), "Army of the Guardians of the Islamic Revolution" is a branch of Iran's Armed Forces founded after the Iranian Revolution on 5May, 1979. The Revolutionary Guards have roughly 125,000 military personnel including ground, aerospace and naval forces. During the Lebanese Civil War, the IRGC

Iran 135

intra-Islamic fundamentalist civil war and a struggle with Russia. Kurdish separatists and Turkish regional aspirations muddy the waters further. This witch's brew called for an integrated solution that maximized American security and well-being using surgically targeted economic sanctions, hard power and soft power, and "smart" diplomacy built on the concept of peaceful coexistence that was beyond Foggy Bottom's ken.

The Obama–Biden and the Trump administrations meandered, sometimes combating non-state-Islamic fundamentalists, and sometimes supporting them. They have opposed Russia, but also cooperated with the Kremlin. They have aided and alienated allied monarchies and sheikhdoms, launched a campaign to depose Alawite and Baathist socialist Syrian President Bashar al-Assad,[25] without a coherent anti-jihadist

---

allegedly sent troops to train fighters in response to the 1982 Israeli invasion of Lebanon. Prior to the Syrian war, Iran had between 2,000 and 3,000 IRGC officers stationed in Syria, helping to train local troops and managing supply routes of arms and money to neighboring Lebanon. Iranian Revolutionary Guard soldiers, along with fellow Shi'ite forces from Hezbollah and members of Iran's Basij militia participated in the capture of Qusair from rebel forces on June 9, 2013. Two battalions of Revolutionary Guards were reported to operating in Iraq trying to combat the 2014 Northern Iraq offensive.

[25]Bashar al-Assad (a secularist non-Muslim) is Hafez al-Assad's son. The father (an Alawite non-Muslim) was a leader of Syria's Arab Socialist Ba'ath Party, and military strongman who assumed power in a successful *coup d'etat* and became Syria's president in 1970 until his death in 2000. Bashar al-Assad's election inspired the "Damascus Spring" and hopes of reform, but by autumn 2001, the authorities had suppressed the movement, imprisoning some of its leading intellectuals. The "Damascus Spring" morphed into a Syrian civil war among numerous factions: the Syrian government and its allies, a loose alliance of Sunni Arab rebel groups (including the Free Syrian Army), the majority-Kurdish Syrian Democratic Forces (SDF), Salafi jihadist groups (including al-Nusra Front) and the Islamic State of Iraq and the Levant (ISIL), with a number of countries in the region and beyond being either directly involved, or rendering support to one or another faction.

Syrian opposition groups formed the Free Syrian Army (FSA) and seized control of the area surrounding Aleppo and parts of southern Syria. Over time, some factions of the Syrian opposition split from their original moderate position to pursue an Islamist vision for Syria, joining groups such as al-Nusra Front and ISIL. In 2015, the People's Protection Units (YPG) joined forces with Arab, Assyrian, Armenian and some Turkmen groups, to form the Syrian Democratic Forces, while most Turkmen groups remained with the FSA. Russia and Hezbollah support the Syrian government militarily, while beginning in 2014, a coalition of NATO countries began launching airstrikes against ISIL.

136 *Beleaguered Superpower: Biden's America Adrift*

national security endgame, or viable scheme for promoting peaceful coexistence.

The rationales for weakening Saudi Arabia during the Obama–Biden years, deposing Bashar al-Assad, taking sides in the Syrian civil war and allying with or opposing Moscow are murky, and these policies contributed little to containing Iran and defeating global jihadism. The establishment has given them a constructive gloss by suggesting that solving each issue separately creates stepping stones for settling the entire Middle East conundrum, but this is disingenuous. The Iranian and the global jihadist threats do not hinge on the resolution of other regional subconflicts.[26] They are free standing, and are likely to endure unless one accepts the radical progressive premise that Middle Eastern Islamic fundamentalist militants will abandon their faith for the Global Nation's secular credo.[27]

The Iranian and the global jihadist threats are high regional priorities requiring complex solutions that take adequate account of spillovers on Iraq, Syria, and Israel.[28] Iraq and united Syria should not be Iranian vassals.

The Trump administration just prior to Biden electoral victory showed how to counter Iran and the global jihadi masterly without compromising

---

[26] Michael Doran and Peter Rough, "What America Should Do Next in the Middle East," *Mosaic* (September 2017), https://mosaicmagazine.com/essay/2017/09/what-america-should-do-next-in-the-middle-east/.

"Obama dreamed of an entirely new Middle Eastern order. In place of American primacy, which had led to thankless military interventions, he would substitute a concert system, a club of powers."

[27] Michael O'Hanlon, "America Is Not in a Zero-Sum Contest with Iran," *Mosaic* (September 2017), https://mosaicmagazine.com/essay/2017/09/what-america-should-do-next-in-the-middle-east/.

[28] Joschka Fischer, "The New Fulcrum of the Middle East," *Project Syndicate* (December 2017), https://www.project-syndicate.org/commentary/israel-saudi-arabia-alliance-by-joschka-fischer-2017-12?utm_source=Project+Syndicate+Newsletter&utm_campaign=fee9988f36-sunday_newsletter_24_12_2017&utm_medium=email&utm_term=0_73bad5b7d8-fee9988f36-93559677.

"In 1947, a two-state solution was not viable, because Arab states responded to Israel's founding by waging war against it. When the Palestinians finally recognized the existence of Israel in 1993, that decision alone was seen as a big step forward. Although diplomats still speak of a Middle East peace process, there has been no process to achieve peace for many years. A two-state solution remains the only conceivable option for satisfying both sides, but it is becoming less credible with time, and with the continued expansion of Israeli settlements in the West Bank. And now America's recognition of Jerusalem as Israel's capital could mean the end of the two-state solution once and for all."

Israel by orchestrating a strategic realignment in the Middle East. It coaxed the United Arab Emirates and Bahrain to normalize relations with Israel, formalizing a *détente* that has been years in the making. Saudi Arabia could be next. The realignment is a major setback for Iran, which has to contend with the prospect that Israeli may provide military support for the Gulf States and Saudi Arabia.[29] America now should intensify its economic sanctions, and take whatever actions are required to prevent Tehran from acquiring nuclear weapons,[30] building advance ballistic

---

[29] Michael Rubin, "The Middle East Strategic Realignment Reverberates Through South Asia," *AEI* (September 2020); https://www.aei.org/op-eds/the-middle-east-strategic-realignment-reverberates-through-south-asia/?mkt_tok=eyJpIjoiTkRSaFltWTNNemcyT 0dKbSIsInQiOiJjbTFwaE9Bb2lFdkhMWkxhZm5tc21CdU1paUIrNG5DR2UzNlc3cUM zM29CZWU5YlhWRzB5aTdkdVhnT01INGpmWnowa1RsRHhZeWJ1RW1X MGRzeERBd0V5eUtRWDJrNHhuTlgwUDJqclpcL1ZrUXRFU01idVBMR05oa2drMX JoVjYifQ%3D%3D.

[30] Jordan Fabian, "Trump Makes His Move on Iran Nuke Deal," *The Hill* (October 13, 2017), http://thehill.com/homenews/administration/355316-trump-makes-his-move-on-iran-nuke-deal. "Trump did not call on Congress to impose sanctions on Iran for its nuclear activities, something that would effectively remove the United States from the deal. Instead he asked Congress to pass new benchmarks Iran would need to meet in order to stave off nuclear-related sanctions in the future. That includes revisiting sunset provisions that allow Iran to ramp up uranium enrichment activity after 10 years." "Trump also ordered the Treasury Department to impose new penalties on the Islamic Revolutionary Guard Corps (IRGC), which is an overseer of Iran's nuclear and ballistic-missile program."

Frederick Kagan, "The Future of the Iran Deal, Explained," *AEI* (October 2017), http://www.aei.org/publication/confusion-over-the-iran-deal/?mkt_tok=eyJpIjoi TVRNNU1tUTNNamxpTjJVNSIsInQiOiIxVm9QWTRZRDNQSXBaK2FhbGJ4 cGpMTFZUaU0xbTdTMUt5cWtEUVdoZW9sWDh6aXdJaTVMMXBhZVwv TnJaVFZPWmJMZXd2eG1JXC9pQnpZSXBuakdpZ3lrb2IrSnZQN21aNHNMV 1RxR2hTZEF2OFNDMjBzTkJ0UUV2OWtLZVZEXC91MyJ9.

"It is not a treaty, and Congress chose not to vote on whether or not to approve it after it had been signed.

Presidential certification under the law does not turn only on Iran's compliance with the deal. The president must also certify, independent of the question of compliance, that 'suspension of sanctions related to Iran pursuant to the agreement is (I) appropriate and proportionate to the specific and verifiable measures taken by Iran with respect to terminating its illicit nuclear program; and (II) vital to the national security interests of the United States.

Here are some key points:

The deal itself says nothing whatsoever about the Iranian missile program. That program appears only in the United Nations Security Council Resolution approving the deal

138 *Beleaguered Superpower: Biden's America Adrift*

missiles,[31] and promoting global jihadism.[32] The Biden–Harris administration is apt to do just the reverse without publically disclosing that the

(UNSCR 2231). But even there, the UN only 'calls on' Iran to refrain from advancing its missile program in certain ways — it does not require Iran to do so, and specifies no penalties if Iran continues its missile program.

The deal imposes no restrictions on Iranian malign activities in the region — supporting proxies such as Lebanese Hezbollah, Iraqi Shi'a militias, or the (sanctioned) Assad regime. UNSCR 2231 does not mention those activities at all.

The deal does, however, facilitate all of those activities, including advancing Iran's missile program, by lifting all restrictions on providing advanced and offensive weaponry to Iran in about three years. It also helps Iran build its military, support its proxies, and continue its activities against the US and its allies in the region by providing financial relief without even nominally constraining what that relief could be used for.

The deal does not in any way constrain America's ability to impose sanctions or take other actions against the Iranian missile program or regional activities. It requires the US only to lift nuclear-related sanctions, not all sanctions as the Iranians periodically suggest. Imposing sanctions on Iranian entities for the missile program, for proxy activity, terrorism, cyber activity, or human rights violations is not a violation of nor withdrawal from the deal."

[31] Marie Donovan, "America Needs a New Strategy to Deter Iran's Destabilizing Behavior," *AEI* (October 2017), http://www.aei.org/publication/america-needs-a-new-strategy-to-deter-irans-destabilizing-behavior/?mkt_tok=eyJpIjoiT0Raa1ptTmh Zemc1WVdaayIsInQiOiJTbjVQT1JyM0JLT2xYdjBOTHJYdkR3SEFYaW 1hSXNjWVNaRzVSTlN5U1AxYnZYV3E0ZkZtVzlzV1dac3F0dFJYRWJkS 0ZocXJpV3h1VFZzRTJ5d0Y2WE1oYWZ3M25hMVpOQnZQSXBHeE9SW W1tV29oUkJTWGFtVVd5TldHaUlCWiJ9.

"The Axis of Resistance and the ballistic missile program form the basis of Iran's national security doctrine. The Islamic Republic has long considered the U.S. its number one enemy but recognizes that it does not have the capacity to match American conventional power. Iran thus directs its proxy groups at — and threatens to use its ballistic missiles against — U.S. positions, allies and partners in the region in order to deter the U.S. from initiating military action against the Iranian homeland. This also allows Iran to expand its influence in the area. The preservation and expansion of the Axis of Resistance is also at the core of the regime's political ideology. The Islamic Republic uses the network to project its ideas, especially its revolutionary form of governance, well beyond its borders. Iran's nuclear program, while important, has never been as significant in Iran's security doctrine. From Tehran's standpoint, the limited constraints on Iran's nuclear program under the nuclear deal were more than worth the price of sanctions relief and other benefits."

[32] Michael Doran and Peter Rough, "What America Should Do Next in the Middle East," *Mosaic* (September 2017), https://mosaicmagazine.com/essay/2017/09/what-america-should-do-next-in-the-middle-east/.

Iran   139

Joint Comprehensive Plan of Action (JCPOA) does not contain controls over Iran's development of advanced ballistic missiles.[33]

The Obama–Biden administration opposed including advanced ballistic missile controls in JCPOA because it was willing to accept a half loaf that did not burden domestic programs. It had no backup plan other than pursuing fluid foreign policy objectives amid a prolonged internecine regional power struggle among multiple stakeholders until as hoped regional rivals embrace American tutelage.[34] A rational, integrated policy for the Middle

---

"Misrepresenting the deal to the American people, Obama dressed it up as a successful application of coercive diplomacy; in fact, it represented a collapse of American power. Iran's two goals in the negotiations had been to end any legal restrictions on the country's nuclear program within a defined time horizon and to secure international recognition of Tehran's right to enrich uranium. Obama offered both as an unreciprocated gift before the negotiations ever began. This preemptive American cringe set the tone for all subsequent stages of the negotiations, which were propelled forward by further concessions." "Over the span of two years, Obama dismantled the architecture, built up brick by brick over the previous decade, designed to contain Iran's nuclear ambitions. Thus, he ended all covert American efforts to sabotage the Iranian program and pressured Israel to end its efforts as well. He shut down investigations of Iranian networks dedicated to the illegal procurement of nuclear technology. He delivered to the Iranian government many tens of billions of dollars in cash at a moment when Tehran was starved of funds. Worst of all, he dismantled the international sanctions regime: the single best tool, short of military action, for punishing Iranian violations of any prospective agreement."

[33]Frederick Kagan, "The Future of the Iran Deal, Explained," *AEI* (October 2017), http://www.aei.org/publication/confusion-over-the-iran-deal/?mkt_tok=eyJpIjoi TVRNNU1tUTNNamxpTjJVNSIsInQiOiIxVm9QWTRZRDNQSXBaK2FhbGJ4 cGpMTFZUaU0xbTdTMUt5cWtEUVdoZW9sWDh6aXdJaTVMMXBhZV wvTnJaVFZPWmJMZXd2eG1JXC9pQnpZSXBuakdpZ3lrb2IrSnZQN21aNHN MV1RxR2hTZEF2OFNDMjBzTkJ0UUV2OWtLZVZEXC91MyJ9.

[34]Kenneth Pollack, "Iraq: Finding Calm after the Storm," *AEI* (September 2017), http://www.aei.org/publication/iraq-finding-calm-after-the-storm/?mkt_tok=eyJpIjoiTlRjeFpqU m1PRGc0TVRKaylsInQiOiI5STFZZ2ZFdXhJT1diZUh4amU5YzV2VV YzUWh5Y3EzQXVsRkZnRWhDSHphQUJ0ZVg2MWxCWUZVcnBkekc0TERDWE tkQ3JVaEp0MmFUc0pFbkpxWEVzTUVrM0NMWHV0OHhObG1haXc4eTFia0xjWHB 6UUwxNHErc1lrVHUwOHRcL1YifQ%3D%3D.

"First, even the military side is not without its problems. Of greatest importance is the question of the Shi'a militias. Some of these merely answered the call when Iraq's greatest Shi'a religious figure, Grand Ayatollah 'Ali Sistani, called them to defend Baghdad from Da'ish. But others predated the fall of Mosul and have extensive ties to Iran. These militias represent alternative sources of military power and it would be tragic for Iraq if they

140 *Beleaguered Superpower: Biden's America Adrift*

East and other parts of the Islamic world is conceivable, but there is no progressive, liberal, or Republican political consensus for doing it.[35]

Syria

The defeat of ISIS forces in Raqqa in late October 2017, led Donald Trump to declare that America had destroyed its arch foe.[36] The US troops

---

evolved into an Iraqi version of Hizballah or the Iranian Revolutionary Guard, with all of the problems they created for their countries." "Politically, Iraq remains badly divided — both in organization and perspective. Its minority Sunni community desperately needs help rebuilding its key towns and cities after their destruction under Da'ish. Moreover, they need to see real political reconciliation if they are going to trust Baghdad not oppress them as the Maliki government did in 2009–2013 (which paved the way for Da'ish in the first place). In stark contrast, Iraq's majority Shi'a population is fixated on the need for political, bureaucratic, and economic reform so that they can live the better lives they have been promised since 2003. For their part, Iraq's Kurds are focused on the longer term goal of independence from Iraq and the near-term need to extract more resources from Baghdad to address their own (even-more-severe) economic problems."

[35]Nikolas K. Gvosdev, "Russia's Hand is Visible Everywhere in the Middle East, Moscow Has Used Its New-Found Influence in the Middle East to Thwart the U.S. Effort to Use Saudi Arabia as a Pressure Point Against the Russian Economy," *The National Interest* (September 2017).

"The Russian hand is visible everywhere in the Middle East. Moscow is presiding over the effort to tap down the Syrian civil war and establish the deconfliction zones between the various factions and their outside patrons. Russia has inserted itself into the volatile Kurdish issue-both with regards to any Kurdish zone in Syria *vis-a-vis* Turkey and the efforts to clarify a final status between Iraqi Kurdistan and the government in Baghdad. Russia has played a major role in sustaining the Iran-Iraq-Syria 'Shi'a Crescent' but also is involved in direct talks with Saudi Arabia and the Gulf emirates on how to maintain a fragile balance of power in the region. Egypt and Israel both now have their own lines of communication with the Kremlin and see Vladimir Putin as a more reliable statesman who does what he says and follows through on his commitments. This assessment is also apparently shared by Turkish president Recep Tayyip Erdogan, who seems prepared to forge a new strategic axis with Russia on energy, Eurasian security and the future alignment of the Middle East. Moscow has hosted meetings of the various Libyan factions, Palestinian political parties, Kurdish representatives and members of the Syrian opposition, and Middle Eastern leaders regularly make the journey to Moscow to confer with the Kremlin."

[36]Hilary Clarke, Nick Paton Walsh, Eliza Mackintosh, and Ghazi Balkiz, "ISIS Defeated in Raqqa as 'Major Military Declared Over'," *CNN* (October 18, 2017), https://www.cnn.com/2017/10/17/middleeast/raqqa-isis-syria/index.html.

remained for mop up operations, which if successful raise the question of what is next? The answer at first seemed to be that the United States would withdraw its troops, and await the results of the 2021 Syrian presidential election before considering its next move.[37] This might have been the wisest course. Syria has been embroiled in a tangled civil war since March 2011, without any easy solutions. The Trump administration; nonetheless, chose instead to continue the battle against ISIL and has allowed Turkey to join the fray despite pledges of support for the Kurds.[38]

This battle is simultaneously a struggle with Russia for influence in Syria. If the United States and Turkey control North Syria, it prevents Russia's client Assad from consolidating his control across the nation, making the Kremlin a more powerful foreign force in the Middle East.

Dmitri Trenin called attention to this paradigm shift.[39] He contends that, "Taking on Russia, for many in the West has become a continuation of the war on terror, with Putin cast in the role of Saddam Hussein." Where Russia and America until April 4, 2017 were both interlopers in Syria's civil war, Russia is likely to be type-cast as a "rogue state" that cannot be allowed to prevail. This is a recipe for armed engagement between two nuclear superpower in the same theater of military operations. It needs judicious management.[40]

---

[37] Robin Wright, "Trump to Let Assad Stay Until 2021, as Putin Declares Victory in Syria," *New Yorker* (December 11, 2017), https://www.newyorker.com/sections/news/trump-to-let-assad-stay-until-2021-as-putin-declares-victory-in-syria.

[38] "Trump Makes Way for Turkey Operation Against Kurds in Syria," *BBC* (October 7, 2019).

[39] Dmitri Trenin, "The New Cold War is Boiling Over in Syria," *Foreign Policy* (April 2018), https://carnegie.ru/2018/04/14/new-cold-war-is-boiling-over-in-syria-pub-76081? utm_source=ctw&utm_medium=email&utm_campaign=20180418&mkt_tok=eyJpIjo iWXpReE9EaGxaV0V3WmpWbCIsInQiOiJ3ajRxNXZHTUt1eVBvQVdJR TRiaW9vOURSNkl6ZWFcL0ZXQ3dqU2s5S0p6YlwvdnR4MlQwSG9KV mlGVTF0NmNYVTlwRjF3ZUJ3TzNZRnFyYlFzVnRVcFd0SFNkVVpZYm1 lYXErVjZFXC91dTZiZjc5Y1RDOFwvVEU4UnNOZm5hWkw4QmhpT0NsOSt0 bzNMc2IyRlwvUm9nWHpOZz09In0%3D.

[40] Harvey Solomon-Brady, "DANGER ZONE Russia Sends its Biggest Ever Warship Force to Syria after US Threat to Launch New Airstrikes against Assad: Ten Warships and Two Submarines, Equipped with Kalibr Cruise Missiles, Have Been Sent to the Mediterranean Sea," *Sun* (August 28, 2018), https://www.thesun.co.uk/news/7116023/ russia-warships-syria-us-threaten-airstrike-assad/.

Chapter 7

Power of Their Collusion

Authoritarian Coalitions

The Eastern authoritarian threat is greater than the sum of its parts. Russia, China, North Korea, Iran, and global jihadi threaten America separately, and collectively. They have not formed an "axis of evil" akin to the Cold War era "communist bloc,"[1] nor have they forged Comintern (Communist International) style ideological alliances with Third World countries like Venezuela and Cuba,[2] but the Eastern authoritarians tend to support or shield each other in the international arena. The giant gold "best friend" necklace given to Vladimir Putin by Xi Jinping symbolizes the potential synergy.[3]

Eastern authoritarians are learning techniques of regime control from each other. Xi Jinping's move to become the president of China and secretary of the Chinese Communist Party (CCP) for as long as he desires is

---

[1] George Bush, "State of the Union Address" (January 29, 2002). "States like these and their terrorist allies constitute an axis of evil, arming to threaten the peace of the world."

[2] Kurt Weyland, "Latin America's Authoritarian Drift: The Threat from the Populist Left," *Journal of Democracy* 4, no. 3, July 2013: 18–32.

[3] Adam Pasick, "Xi Jinping Gave Vladimir Putin a Giant Gold 'Best Friend' Necklace," *Quartz* (June 8, 2018), https://qz.com/1300974/chinas-xi-jinping-gave-russian-president-vladimir-putin-a-best-friend-necklace/.

144 *Beleaguered Superpower: Biden's America Adrift*

a ploy taken directly from Vladimir Putin's playbook.[4] Russia's decision to bar the North Atlantic Treaty Organization (NATO) from the Sea of Azov mimics Xi's efforts to control access to the South China Sea.[5]

Both are cultivating fellow travelers in the Third World who harbor anti-Western sentiments and desire to shield their regimes for diverse reasons from American globalism.[6] These regimes do not pose a serious military threat to the American homeland today, but they complicate containment of Russia,[7] China, North Korea, Iran, and global jihadism, and

---

[4]David Blumenthal, "Xi's 'Putinization' of China is a Massive Wake-Up for America," *AEI* (March 2, 2018), http://www.aei.org/publication/xis-putinization-of-china-is-a-massive-wake-up-for-america/?mkt_tok=eyJpIjoiTTJGbU9HRmpZMlk0TUdZeCIsIn QiOiJ4TjB2T3ZSY01KVlZuQ0o2d0NaU1VUNTI1THRjZnZnVmFaRExLS zN0dGtzcEhGWWN3WFUxVExcL0xHS2Z2QlAyQUszZHpNcUpcL2l2RG w0UGdYV3Yzc2dQdHdMUURCdHZBTU9cLzF2cVM0ZTBFWnBVQTZaUzR0T mdvakwxMFViZkJJaCJ9.

"Russia's Highest Court Opens the Way for Putin to Rule until 2036," *New York Times* (March 16, 2020), https://www.nytimes.com/2020/03/16/world/europe/russia-putin-president-for-life.html.

[5]Stephen Blank, "Why is the Sea of Azov So Important?" *Atlantic Council* (November 2018), http://www.atlanticcouncil.org/blogs/ukrainealert/why-is-the-sea-of-azov-so-important.

"Russian officials are also boarding Ukrainian ships illegally, enforcing a blockade of the Sea of Azov and of Ukraine's coastline while also reinforcing its fleet in the area. Additionally, they are threatening to launch a variety of potential military operations against Ukraine: naval shelling of land targets, an amphibious operation against Mariupol or the coastline, and another ground force invasion, all supported by naval artillery."

"Moreover, even a casual examination of Russian actions reveals the deep and continuing parallels with China's equally illegitimate actions in the South and East China Sea. In the Asian case, the United States has mounted and continues to stage numerous Freedom of Navigation Operations to demonstrate to China that it will uphold the time-honored principle of the freedom of the seas."

[6]Paul Hollander, *The End of Commitment: Intellectuals, Revolutionaries, and Political Morality in the Twentieth Century* (Chicago: Ivan R. Dee, 2006).

[7]Chris Cheang, "Russia's Interest in North Korea Crisis," *RSIS* (December 12, 2017). The Kremlin is offering its good offices to resolve the standoff between America and North Korea, but on terms that are beneficial to Pyongyang.

reduce the economic and political benefits America derives from globalization[8] and globalism.[9]

Hard Power Collaboration

The dangers posed by Eastern authoritarian coalitions are already substantial. Russia and China joined forces in 2015 to ensnare America into a flawed agreement that exchanged empty promises by Iran's mullahs to stop nuclearizing in exchange for lifting US economic sanctions.[10] They

---

[8] Orley Ashenfelter, Robert F. Engle, Daniel L. McFadden, and Klaus Schmidt-Hebbel, "Globalization: Contents and Discontents," *Contemporary Economic Policy* 36, no. 1 (January 2018): 29–43, http://onlinelibrary.wiley.com/doi/10.1111/coep.12237/full. Globalization has three distinct meanings. (1) For many advocates, it is the worldwide rule of democratic free enterprise that preserves the nation state as the fundamental unit of government. (2) For some advocates, it means global free enterprise plus the welfare state. (3) For others, it means the creation of a progressive cosmopolitan world order governed transnationally with progressive values like free migration, egalitarianism, women and transgender liberation, entitlement, affirmative action and restorative justice founded on transnational or World government rather than the nation state. For a discussion of the pros and cons of globalization in the first sense.

[9] Steven Rosefielde, Masaaki Kuboniwa, Kumiko Haba, and Satoshi Mizobata, eds., *The Unwinding of the Globalist Dream: EU, Russia, China* (Singapore: World Scientific Publishers, 2017).

Anti-Globalizers contend that globalization is a euphemism for "globalism"; that is, American economic imperialism that allows Western multinational companies to penetrate and exploit less developed nations. They urge developing nations to defend themselves against globalization (Western imperialism). Some want developing to retain their diverse economic systems without assimilating Western values; others advocate embracing the welfare state and/or progressive values like cosmopolitanism, free migration, egalitarianism, women and transgender liberation, entitlement, affirmative action, and restorative justice outside the Global Nation framework.

[10] John Miller, "Europe Will Do Everything To Preserve Iran Nuclear Deal — EU Diplomat," *Reuters* (October 4, 2017), https://in.reuters.com/article/iran-nuclear-eu/europe-will-do-everything-to-preserve-iran-nuclear-deal-eu-diplomat-idINKCN1C911Y. "European countries will do their utmost to preserve a deal limiting Iran's nuclear programme despite misgivings by U.S. President Donald Trump, a senior European Union diplomat said on Wednesday. 'This is not a bilateral agreement, it is a multilateral agreement. As Europeans, we will do everything to make sure it stays,' Helga Schmid, secretary

146   *Beleaguered Superpower: Biden's America Adrift*

are deterring a conventional attack on North Korea's nuclear assets and ballistic missiles by threatening to intervene on Pyongyang's behalf, claiming that an American pre-emptive strike close to their borders constitutes a *casus belli*. If the armistice is broken and South Korea conquers parts of the DPRK, China and Russia may well limit the South's advance by sending troops, weapons, and supplies to North Korea as they did in 1951.[11]

Russia is aiding Iran and Shiite jihadists across the Middle East, strengthening the Kremlin's regional presence, and providing a diversion for Russia's hybrid warfare in Novorossiya. Both Russia and China are allying with Venezuela and Cuba to weaken America's global reach by destabilizing Latin America, sowing divisions between the United States and the European Union.

They also may be scheming to join forces against Japan to strengthen China's territorial claims in the East China Sea (Diaoyu),[12] and Russia's stance on the Sea of Japan (Kuril) islands.[13]

Some Western security analysts tend to believe that Russia and China are congenital rivals. The 1956 Sino-Soviet split supports this surmise,[14]

---

general of the EU's foreign policy service, told an Iranian investment conference in Switzerland's financial capital. The deal was brokered in 2015 by the bloc between Iran, the United States, France, Germany, Britain, Russia and China. Trump is weighing whether the pact serves U.S. security interests as he faces an Oct. 15 deadline for certifying that Iran is complying, a decision that could sink an agreement strongly supported by the other world powers that negotiated it."

[11]Lyle J. Goldstein, "What Russia's Vostok-18 Exercise with China Means Moscow Knows What It is Doing and Washington Should Take Note," *National Interest* (September 2018), https://nationalinterest.org/feature/what-russias-vostok-18-exercise-china-means-30577.

[12]The Japanese call the Diaoyu islands the Senkaku islands. They are a group of uninhabited islands controlled by Japan in the East China Sea. They are located roughly due east of Mainland China, northeast of Taiwan, west of Okinawa Island, and north of the southwestern end of the Ryukyu Islands.

[13]The Japanese call these disputed islands "Northern Territories" (Kunashiri, Etorofu, Shikotan, and the Habomai islands). Akihiro Iwashita, "Bested by Russia: Abe's Failed Northern Territories Negotiations," *Wilson Center* (2020), https://www.wilsoncenter.org/publication/kennan-cable-no-60-bested-russia-abes-failed-northern-territories-negotiations.

[14]Lorenz Lüthi, *The Sino-Soviet Split: Cold War in the Communist World* (Princeton, NJ: Princeton University Press, 2008).

but the joint Sino-Russian "Vostok-18" military exercises suggest that Moscow and Beijing may beat the odds.[15] These exercises held in September 2018 were on a scale not seen since the early 1980s. They involved more than 1,000 aircraft, almost 300,000 soldiers, and nearly all Russian military installations in the Central and Eastern military regions, including also the Northern and Pacific fleets. The exercises entailed the coordinated mobilization of 36,000 pieces of equipment including tanks and armored personnel carriers. About 3,200 Chinese soldiers accompanied by 30 fixed wing aircraft and helicopters participated.

This unprecedented military cooperation does not constitute a formal alliance, but Stephen Blank believes that a formal alliance is already in the cards.[16] It seems reasonable to suppose that a formidable Sino-Russian united front extending from Southeast Asia to the Arctic will complicate America's management of Asia-Pacific relations. Beijing explicitly supports the Kremlin's new concept of a "Polar Silk Road" — as a critical part of the larger Belt and Road initiative. China's announcement that it will build a nuclear icebreaker (with likely Russian assistance) suggests a commitment to revitalizing Northern Sea Route (NSR), facilitating Russia's long-held dream of a vibrant Arctic maritime corridor.[17]

---

[15]Lyle J. Goldstein, "What Russia's Vostok-18 Exercise with China Means Moscow Knows What It is Doing and Washington Should Take Note," *National Interest* (September 2018), https://nationalinterest.org/feature/what-russias-vostok-18-exercise-china-means-30577.

[16]Stephen Blank, "Whither the Russian-Chinese Alliance?" *European Security and Defense*, no. 4 (2018): 6–7; Robert Sutter, "China–Russia Relations: Strategic Implications and U.S. Policy Options," *NBR* (September 2018), http://nbr.org/publications/element. aspx?id=1000. "The Russian-Chinese relationship has grown closer and more intimate, and Russian dependence on China has increased. Slowly but surely, the relationship is developing into an alliance," Robert Sutter concurs.

[17]For a more ominous assessment of Vostok-18's significance see Stephen Blank, "Russia's Vostok-2018: A Rehearsal for Global War?" *RealClear Defense* (September 2018), https://www.realcleardefense.com/articles/2018/09/04/russias_vostok-2018_a_ rehearsal_for_global_war_113764.html. "Clearly Russia is rehearsing a large-scale war. But since Russia is not demobilising in the West against NATO and the Ukraine, Vostok-2018 will likely stress and thus test Russia's steadily developing capability for mobilising the entire panoply of reservists and multiple militaries at its disposal, along with the civil administration."

148   *Beleaguered Superpower: Biden's America Adrift*

Soft Power Collaboration

Eastern authoritarians are thwarting Washington's soft power in three ways. First, they are orchestrating opposition to Western values (both Huntington's idea of the West, and AOC's progressive values) domestically and abroad creating nationalist and religious barriers to globalism. They are debunking Western precepts to accelerate Washington's retreat. Iran and the global jihadism are rallying their troops around the flag of fundamentalist Islam. Russia and China are further dampening the West's appeal by intensifying their domestic patriotism and national pride campaigns (indoctrination).[18] Fellow travelers like Venezuela and Cuba are redoubling their opposition to globalism by preaching socialism and anti-Yankee imperialism. Palestinians are colluding with the EU against the United States.[19]

Second, Eastern authoritarians are working together to mitigate economic and political sanctions. Russia is providing an Internet platform and other assistance to North Korea.[20] Russia and China are striving to capture globalist institutions like the International Monetary Fund (IMF), World Bank, World Trade Organization, United Nations, and World Health Organization for their own nationalist purposes.[21]

---

[18] Ilya Rozhdestvensky, "The Russian Patriotic Groups Teaching Children How to Defend Their Country," *Guardian* (August 10, 2015), https://www.theguardian.com/world/2015/aug/09/russia-patriotic-education-rise-ukraine-military.

[19] "After Israel and Egypt's Secret Military Partnership is Revealed, Palestinian Hopes Lay in Europe," *Albawaba* (February 5, 2018), https://www.albawaba.com/news/ororiginal-after-israel-and-egypt%E2%80%99s-secret-military-partnership-is-revealed%2C-palestinian-hopes-lay-in-europe-1084672.

[20] Andrew Osborn, "Russia Throws North Korea Lifeline To Stymie Regime Change," *Reuters* (October 4, 2017), https://www.reuters.com/article/us-northkorea-missiles-russia-analysis/russia-throws-north-korea-lifeline-to-stymie-regime-change-idUSKBN1C91X2. "A Russian company began routing North Korean internet traffic this month, giving Pyongyang a second connection with the outside world besides China. Bilateral trade more than doubled to $31.4 million in the first quarter of 2017, due mainly to what Moscow said was higher oil product exports." At least eight North Korean ships that left Russia with fuel cargoes this year have returned home despite officially declaring other destinations, a ploy US officials say is often used to undermine sanctions against Pyongyang.

[21] Pavel Baev, "Russia Seeks to Rebuild Its International Respectability," *Eurasia Daily Monitor* 14, no. 117 (September 25, 2017), https://jamestown.org/program/russia-seeks-to-rebuild-its-international-respectability/.

Power of Their Collusion   149

Third, Eastern authoritarians are countering the attraction of Western globalist institutions by building competing economic alliances and blocs like the Shanghai Cooperation Organization (SCO) that includes China, Kazakhstan, Kyrgyzstan, Russia, Tajikistan, India, Pakistan, and Kazakhstan.[22] Iran is knocking at the SCO door.[23] Russia also is the leading force behind the Eurasian Economic Union (EEU). Belarus, Kazakhstan and Russia, Armenia, and Kyrgyzstan are all members.[24] The Regional Comprehensive Economic Partnership (RCEP) covering 15 Asia-Pacific economies was launched in November 2020, which serves as a partial alternative to abortive Trans-Pacific Trade agreement provides another example of Beijing's resourcefulness.[25]

---

[22] Stephen Blank, "Making Sense of the Shanghai Cooperation Organisation," *European Security and Defense* 34, no. 1, 2017: 17–21. "The evidence of the last few years repeatedly points to Moscow abandoning Western initiatives in favour of alignment with China and not only in Central Asia. The current Korean crisis has strengthened Sino-Russian ties, and China has supported Moscow's Afghan policy of including the Taliban in any future Afghan government by endorsing this so-called shadow if not the substance of Chinese support for the sustainment of its position. In Europe there is now an increasing number of reports of Sino-Russian cooperation in 'active measures' and economic policies in Eastern Europe, such as joint activities connected to Chinese investment in the Greek port of Piraeus. Similarly the joint naval manoeuvres of 2015 in the Mediterranean and of 2017 in the Baltic show Russia invoking Chinese power as a crutch in its efforts to demonstrate its great power presence and capability in those two theatres. In the Arctic and in energy affairs too we see China gaining equity in Russian firms to an extent that five years ago would have been unimaginable. For example, China is now the third largest investor in Rosneft and is present in other critical Arctic and Moscow poses as the gendarme of Central Asia, China is its banker. And there are signs of thought in Beijing that at some future date it might have to act in the region to protect its investments. Recent political and military gambits point to the expansion of Chinese strategic perspectives."

[23] Eugene Kogan, "Russian–Iranian Relations: A Mixed Bag," *European Security and Defense* (December 2017): 12–15.

[24] Jaloliddin Usmanov, "The Shanghai Cooperation Organization: Harmony or Discord?," *The Diplomat* (June 2018), https://thediplomat.com/2018/06/the-shanghai-cooperation-organization-harmony-or-discord/.

[25] "The Regional Comprehensive Economic Partnership (RCEP) is a free trade agreement in the Asia-Pacific region between the ten member states of ASEAN, namely Brunei, Cambodia, Indonesia, Laos, Malaysia, Myanmar, the Philippines, Singapore, Thailand, and Vietnam, and five of their FTA partners — Australia, China, Japan, New Zealand, and South Korea. The 15 negotiating countries account for about 30% of both the world's population and the global GDP, making it the largest trade bloc. It was signed at the

150 *Beleaguered Superpower: Biden's America Adrift*

Smart Diplomacy

Eastern authoritarians often outsmart Western "smart diplomacy."[26] Russia, China, North Korea, and Iran outfoxed Western diplomats bilaterally and multilaterally in the Ukraine, Syria, WTO trade agreements, and the control of weapons of mass destruction. They will continue to do so until the Washington prioritizes national security.

Correlation of Forces

The magnitude of the threat posed by Eastern authoritarians individually and synergistically to American national security depends on the "correlation of forces,"[27] a term coined by the Soviets to calibrate comparative

---

Vietnam-hosted virtual ASEAN Summit on 15 November 2020." Charmaine Ng, "15 Countries, including Singapore, Sign RCEP, the World's Largest Trade Pact," *The Straits Times* (November 15, 2020).

"Shunning the Trans-Pacific Partnership Was a Costly Mistake," *YahooNews* (November 2020), https://news.yahoo.com/shunning-trans-pacific-partnership-costly-190715078.html.

[26] Alexander Gabuev, "China and Russia's Dangerous Entente," *Carnegie Russia* (October 2017), http://carnegie.ru/2017/10/04/china-and-russia-s-dangerous-entente-pub-73310? mkt_tok=eyJpIjoiWXpoaVpEbGxNbUZoTlRreSIsInQiOiJDcXd1REZhRWthSzFoMnZ3 dWpVek90aW0yZFQwZnlEVXdWd2UyMkVBTW9meUl4UVZteHRWRUg5cDdOX C9rWjNqemJlNjY5XC8wWHpPdGYrdjJCbnpqXC9TbzdpMmF5SnViT3dQWm ZMeEVldFI3ek1lVFNtbXVlYTlrbVBQOURvcnJTaSJ9.

"In reality, Mr. Xi has worked out a good-cop/bad-cop routine with Russian President Vladimir Putin, and the two countries are working together to torpedo some of the most important U.S. proposals on North Korea. While China looks like a constructive partner, Russian diplomats at the U.N. were able to water down language in Security Council Resolution 2375 that would have restricted oil shipments to North Korea and totally banned the use of North Korean labor abroad." "In reality, Mr. Xi has worked out a good-cop/bad-cop routine with Russian President Vladimir Putin, and the two countries are working together to torpedo some of the most important U.S. proposals on North Korea. While China looks like a constructive partner, Russian diplomats at the U.N. were able to water down language in Security Council Resolution 2375 that would have restricted oil shipments to North Korea and totally banned the use of North Korean labor abroad."

[27] Julian Lider, "The Correlation of World Forces: The Soviet Concept," *Journal of Peace Research* 17, no. 2, June 1980: 151–171, http://jpr.sagepub.com/content/17/2/151.abstract; Allen Lynch, *The Soviet Study of International Relations* (Cambridge: Cambridge University Press, 1989). The term correlation of forces, borrowed from physics, is a

power.[28] The concept is akin to the Western term "balance of power," but stresses the importance of military might, economic prowess, and leadership instead of national coalitions and blocs. America is militarily and economically stronger than its foes. The NATO alliance and advanced US cyber capabilities leverage this advantage.[29] America holds a military technological edge over Russia and China, and its armed forces are superior to North Korea, Iran, and global jihadism.[30] Per capita income and most other economic power metrics likewise favor the United States and NATO.

These advantages are real and important, but they are not decisive as the armistice in Korea (1951), defeats in Eastern Europe (1945–1947), Cuba (1959), Vietnam (1975), Iran (1979), Ukraine (2014), Syria (2017), and Afghanistan (2018) attest. American national security is vulnerable to Eastern authoritarianism despite its various advantages for the following 12 reasons:

(1) The United States and NATO face multiple, geographically dispersed threats that prevent them from concentrating military assets against a single adversary.[31]

---

multi-factor version of the balance of power concept widely employed by Soviet and Russian security analysts.

[28] N.V. Ogarkov, *Vsegda v Golovnosti k Zashchite Otechestva* (Moskva, 1982): 31; N. V. Ogarkov, *Istoriya Uchit vditel'nosti* (Moskva, 1985): 41;

[29] Greg Austin, "The US Will Win the Cyber War With China in 2017," *The Diplomat* (November 2016), http://thediplomat.com/2016/11/the-us-will-win-the-cyber-war-with-china-in-2017/; The Department of Defense, "The DoD Cyber Strategy," (April 2015), https://thediplomat.com/2016/11/the-us-will-win-the-cyber-war-with-china-in-2017/.

[30] America's military technological advantage is widely attributed to the "revolution in military affairs." The doctrine has been variously interpreted, but the core idea stresses the decisive role of advanced weapons technology, information technology, military organization, and military doctrine in dominating the modern battlefield through intelligence, surveillance and reconnaissance, command, control, communications, intelligence processing, and precision force. Steven Metz and James Kievit, "Strategy and the Revolution in Military Affairs: From Theory to Policy," *US Army War College* (June 27, 1995), Stephen Biddle, *Military Power: Explaining Victory and Defeat in Modern Battle* (Princeton: Princeton University Press, 2006); Donald Rumsfeld, "Transforming the Military," *Foreign Affairs* 81, no. 3, May/June 2002: 20–32.

[31] Mackenzie Eaglen, "Repair and Rebuild: Balancing New Military Spending for a Three-Theater Strategy," *AEI* (October 2017), http://www.aei.org/publication/repair-and-rebuild-balancing-new-military-spending-for-a-three-theater-strategy/?mkt_tok=eyJpIjo

152 *Beleaguered Superpower: Biden's America Adrift*

(2) China, Russia, North Korea, Iran, global jihadism, and other authoritarian regimes do not have to confront America one-on-one. They can forge diverse coalitions against the West.

(3) America and NATO are politically constrained from fighting large-scale land wars against Russia, China, North Korea and Iran, and depend on ROK armies to fight North Korea.

(4) The Pentagon's and EU naval forces are declining and over-extended.

(5) The US and EU economic growth are subpar, especially compared with China. It is a cliché that Russia, North Korea, Iran, and the global jihadi are economically vulnerable, but this is no longer self-evident for China, which seems capable of economically and technologically outperforming a moribund West committed to over-regulation and punishing the productive to advance social progressive programs.

(6) Russia, China, North Korea, and Iran have huge military industrial capabilities, and devote disproportionately large shares of national resources to defense.[32] Russia, North Korea, and especially China are closing the military technology gap.[33]

(7) Russia, China, North Korea, and Iran can impose and sustain larger defense burdens on their people because they have the instruments

---

iT0Raak5EWTVNalJpTkRBMyIsInQiOiJ1bGRCM3Uwenh1T2xhdnpDNjEyTCs0djhxb VdJYW9jQUVMM0ZLb0hDQ2tuNWIrbHRaRldacjZaTndQNmVmcmkySWphbWpZal ZVYlQ0UTZoS3Vlb3hiT01sd241S3gyK2ZxaFpBbXJ1Wm1UbnpydGx3M2p6 MDAwOVZuYXl2SDlGZyJ9.

"The Pentagon must resolve near-term readiness issues, expand its force structure, and invest in technological breakthroughs to sustain simultaneous operations across three theaters. The Army must be large enough to support stability operations in the Middle East and lethal enough to win decisively in any conventional conflicts in Europe and Asia. Over the next five years, AEI's plan would spend $672 billion above the Budget Control Act caps."

[32] Steven Rosefielde, *False Science: Underestimating the Soviet Arms Buildup* (Transaction, 1982) (Expanded Second Edition, 1987).

[33] Bing West, "Deter the Cyber Weapon from Being Employed," *Hoover* (September 26, 2017), http://www.hoover.org/research/deter-cyber-weapon-being-employed. Secretary of Defense Jim Mattis recently testified, "For decades the United States enjoyed uncontested or dominant superiority in every operating domain or realm. ... Today every operating domain is contested."

to control private spending and the power to curb private consumption and repress dissent.

(8) Russia, China, North Korea, and Iran sometimes have strong leaders who are able to act more decisively than factious Western statespersons.[34] Contemporary American leadership is deficient.

(9) Russian, Chinese, North Korean, and Iranian polities are less divisive than America society to the extent that authoritarians are able to repress dissent and mobilize their publics against foreign enemies. Their populations are more patriotic than the cosmopolitan Global Nation, which prioritizes planetary over national citizenship.

(10) America's "smart diplomacy" short changes hard power and national security. It conflates national security with radical progressive objectives like open migration, refugee sanctuary (euphemism for disregarding legal quotas), radical environmentalism, fourth wave radical feminism, and sundry other causes.

(11) Eastern authoritarians disdain Washington's soft power credo. Their leaders and populace are repelled in varying degrees as Obama phased it by empty cosmopolitan idealism.[35]

(12) progressive-liberal pro-dependency, anti-middle class (bourgeoisie), and anti-defense policies, together with the radical progressive "cancel culture" assault on the open society democracy have tutored Eastern authoritarians that the American Goliath will appease them. The Trump administration tilted against this tide with very limited success, and the Biden–Harris administration is going with the flow. Although America and the EU have successfully forged a powerful alliance, their security is eroding. The correlation of forces are turning against America and the EU,[36] a trend that will persist until the Washington discards empty cosmopolitan idealism.

---

[34] In America and the EU hard power decision making authority is dispersed across the executive, legislative and judicial branches of government. NATO as a transnational organization also has a voice in determining hard power decisions.

[35] "Four out of Five Russians Find Gay Sex 'Reprehensible' — Poll," *Moscow Times* (January 11, 2018). See 2018-#8-*Johnson's Russia List.*

[36] Dmitri Trenin, "Russia and the United States: A Temporary Break or a New Cold War?," *Carnegie Moscow Center* (January 2015), http://carnegie.ru/2014/12/08/russia-and-united-states-temporary-break-or-new-cold-war/hxw4?mkt_tok=3RkMMJWWfF9wsRol uaXPZKXonjHpfsX56OsvXqGg38431UFwdcjKPmjr1YACTsV0aPyQAgobGp5I 5FEIQ7XYTLB2t60MWA%3D%3D. Trenin in his testimony to the Duma characterizes

154   *Beleaguered Superpower: Biden's America Adrift*

Defense, Economy, and Leadership

The correlation of forces shaping national security, including the ability to deter foes from expanding spheres of influence are case specific. The relative importance of the 12 elements of the correlation of forces enumerated earlier and other omitted factors differ conflict by conflict. The details may be significant in some instances, but three mega factors suffice to sketch the big picture: defense, economy, and leadership.

Defense (deterrence and compulsion when necessary)[37] is the ability to deter foreign aggression against the homeland and spheres of influence with hard power (including weapons, arms control, cyber countermeasures, hybrid war, combat readiness, competence, and willingness to defend), soft power (ideals, enticements and punitive sanctions), and "smart diplomacy" (astute hard and soft power blended negotiation).

The West's defense component of the correlation of forces has significantly deteriorated over the last decade for two reasons. First, Eastern authoritarian hard power capabilities (weapons, cyber and hybrid war, combat readiness, competence, and willingness to defend) have rapidly improved (see Chapters 3–6). Second, changes in American and NATO hard power have failed to keep pace. American weapons procurement and investment spending have not risen appreciably in real terms since the start of Russia's arms modernization drive in 2010. Defense spending by European members of NATO has declined in real terms, and American naval deployments have sharply fallen in the face of burgeoning Chinese naval capabilities. The emergence of coalitions among America's main rivals including Russia, China, North Korea, Iran, global jihadism, Cuba, and Venezuela compounds the danger of these asymmetries. Even more important, Eastern authoritarians have made substantial headway closing the technology gap. The Pentagon has always relied on the technology

---

Russia's strategic vision and the correlation of forces as follows: "a. Strategic vision means understanding that: a. Russian-American relations now are different than during the Cold War; they do not determine world development by themselves, though they fully conform to its logic. b. The new competition is not 'a life and death struggle,' but a struggle to set the terms of future interaction, in other words, tough competition. c. The outcome of Russian-American confrontation will be determined not in Ukraine or Syria but mainly in the areas of economics, science, and technology, social development, and, more broadly, the internal state of Russia."

[37]Defense can be passive or active. Active defense includes pre-emptive strikes and war winning.

Power of Their Collusion 155

edge to overcome numerical disadvantages, but America's counterweight has grown razor thin.[38]

The practical effects of these inverse movements are conspicuous. NATO has not, and cannot compel Moscow to rescind Crimea's annexation and Russia's bridgeheads in Donetsk and Luhansk. NATO faces serious military threats in the Baltics and the Kremlin is gradually expanding its sphere of influence in the Balkans and Eastern Europe. Russia is using cyber measures to sow the seeds of dissension in the European Union.

The situation in Asia and the Middle East is worse. The ascent of Chinese hard power is making the defense of Taiwan, and America's position in the South China Sea precarious. North Korea's acquisition of nuclear weapons and intercontinental ballistic missiles is curtailing Washington's room for maneuver in the Asia Pacific and testing America's relationship with Japan. The likely acquisition of nuclear weapons and long-range ballistic missiles by Iran has the United States on the defensive in the Middle East. It permits the mullahs to intensify their support for Shiite jihadists.

Many progressives and liberals are conversant with these realities; however, they use misleading statistics to reassure themselves that America remains invincible. The CIA concocts defense purchasing power parities that drastically understate the value of Russian and Chinese weapons and give the false impression that high "pay and benefits" for American forces and contractors translate into superior warfighting capabilities. The Russians, Chinese, Iranians, North Koreans, and global jihadism leverage the combat effectiveness of their defense spending by keeping pay and benefits to soldiers and contractors comparatively low. American intelligence myopia is a replay of CIA's Cold War "false science" cost-underestimating tactics.[39] American "defense activities" also misleadingly include expenditures for the "war on drugs," environmental "defense" and military social welfare programs, which whatever

---

[38] Bing West, "Deter the Cyber Weapon from Being Employed," *Hoover* (September 26, 2017), http://www.hoover.org/research/deter-cyber-weapon-being-employed. Secretary of Defense Jim Mattis recently testified, "For decades the United States enjoyed uncontested or dominant superiority in every operating domain or realm.... Today every operating domain is contested."

[39] Steven Rosefielde, False Science: *Underestimating the Soviet Arms Buildup* (Brunswick: Transaction, revised edition, 1987); Steven Rosefielde, *Russia in the 21st Century: The Prodigal Superpower* (Cambridge: Cambridge University Press, 2005).

156 *Beleaguered Superpower: Biden's America Adrift*

their merits, do not deter Eastern authoritarians. Spending more on pay and benefits, and other defense inessentials like affirmative action masks the ongoing deterioration in the correlation of military forces. It does not address the threat.

The Western soft power component of the correlation of forces (ideals, enticements, and punitive sanctions) also is deteriorating, but for different reasons. The quality of Russian and Chinese life today has vastly improved compared with the Soviet and Maoist epochs, and living standards in Russia and China continue rising, while the West has slipped into secular stagnation.[40] Russians, Chinese, and Iranians perhaps are still attracted to the classic American dream (democracy, liberty, rule of law, and free enterprise with secure freehold property rights), however material gains, pride in their traditional values, and nationalism have blunted the appeal of America's traditional virtues. Russian and Chinese economic development also has reduced the effectiveness of American economic enticements and sanctions. Potential gains from free trade, and losses from sanctions affect the attitudes of Russia, China, North Korea, and Iran's people and leaders, but the impact of enticements and sanctions diminish as their economies become more prosperous.

On the other side of the ledger, soft power ideals (entitlements, affirmative action, restorative justice, open migration, fourth wave radical feminism, and consensual iconoclastic morality) have proven to be less attractive than the traditional American dream. Fewer Russians, Chinese, North Koreans, Iranians, and global jihadi want to be radical progressives than were previously attracted to democratic free enterprise. Anti-globalizers do not want to be absorbed in a Washington dominated Global Nation, and prefer to strengthen their own spheres of influence, turning the soft power component of the correlation of forces against the United States.

The leadership component of the correlation of forces (hard and soft power management) completes the picture. Vladimir Putin, Xi Jinping, Kim Jong-un, and Ali Khamenei are hard headed, competent, effective, and committed to improving their nations' military power. They have modernized their armed forces and successfully indoctrinated their people, instilling them with patriotic pride and duty.[41] Eastern authoritar-

---

[40]CIA, *CIA World Factbooks* (2017).

[41]Ekaterina Khodzhaeva, Irina Meyer (Olimpieva), Svetlana Barsukova, and Iskender Yasaveev, "Mobilizing Patriotism in Russia," *Center for Security Studies (CSS)*, ETH

Power of Their Collusion 157

ian leaders also have successfully organized programs to foster nationalism as an antidote to Washington's soft power, and Xi Jinping has striven to export China's version of soft power abroad through state-financed Confucian institutes.[42]

American progressives and liberals, together with EU social democrats by contrast are rudderless when it comes to national security, and it is difficult for Republicans to right the ship of state. Washington and Brussels cannot bring themselves to confront the adverse turn in the correlation of forces, refusing both to adequately rebuild defense capabilities, and modify the globalist soft power credo so that it is more appealing to Eastern authoritarians. Once again, improvements abroad and deterioration at home combine to diminish Western security. There are no pluses. American and EU power are withering without any sign of renewal.

This full spectrum adverse turn in the correlation of forces does not imply that Eastern authoritarians will soon be in a position to conquer the American homeland. Geography is still on America's side, and Americans broadly find foreign forms of authoritarianism unattractive. There are "fifth column" Russian, Chinese, and Islamic foreign-sponsored forces in play on the home front, just as there were Nazi and Japanese agents of influence prior to WWII, but their threat for the moment does not seem ominous, Russiagate hysteria notwithstanding.[43]

The hard power danger lies across the Atlantic and Pacific. It is to America's allies, spheres of influence, and the pre-Obama post-war order. The Eastern authoritarian threat affects a broad set of vulnerable states and territories. Russia may annex Novorossiya and the Baltic states. China

---

Zurich, Switzerland, 2017. "During his third presidential term, Vladimir Putin formulated a new version of Russia's national idea. He replaced the idea of making the country competitive in all spheres with a new militarized patriotism."

[42] Syed Hasanat Shah, Hafsa Hasnat, Steven Rosefielde, and Li Jun Jiang, "Comparative analysis of Chinese and Indian Soft Power Strategy," *Asian Politics & Policy* 9, no. 2 (April 2017): 268–288.

[43] Shahram Akbarzadeh and Joshua Roose, "Muslims, Multiculturalism and the Question of the Silent Majority," *Journal of Muslim Minority Affairs* 31, no. 3 (September 2011): 309–325. A fifth column is any group of people who undermine a larger group from within, usually in favor of an enemy group or nation. The activities of a fifth column can be overt or clandestine. Counter-jihad literature has sought to portray Western Muslims as a "fifth column," collectively seeking to destabilize Western nations' identity and values for the benefit of an international Islamic movement intent on the establishment of a caliphate in Western countries.

158   *Beleaguered Superpower: Biden's America Adrift*

may conquer Taiwan and seize control over navigation in the South China Sea. North Korea may control the peninsula. Iran and the global jihadism may dominate Levant and the entire Middle East. All may become hegemons of their respective regions, and beyond, except North Korea. Their gains will be our losses with potentially severe negative impacts on US wealth, income and global security. It would be wise to resist, but difficult to see how an American house divided against itself can withstand the rise of formidable and determined foes. Progressives and liberals will trot out placebos like "arms control and disarmament,"[44] global denuclearization,[45] or discover the "realism" of negotiating with nuclearized North Korea.[46] They will continue conflating empty cosmopolitan globalism with national and global security because they remain unwilling to face up to the repercussions of empty cosmopolitan idealism.

---

[44]Ulrich Kuhn, "With Zapad Over, Is It Time for Conventional Arms Control in Europe?" *Carnegie Endowment for Peace* (September 27, 2017), http://carnegieendowment. org/2017/09/27/with-zapad-over-is-it-time-for-conventional-arms-control-in-europe-pub-73242?mkt_tok=eyJpIjoiTkRJeE1qTTNOamt6TmpaayIsInQiOiI4V3ZMVFRTczdPWV UyNHpNSDBzblNBYWJnak5KTTF2SHZmZ2F6SnlSVVwvSm9EVUlDZnY5cnZPN 1dRWm83RGtMTDNkVkgrd1NpckJ2NWlxcll4T1JEd1gwY3ZGUk83Tm92em5ldWpk c0tVbCtkQjdBcTJiY2RsaUJaQkZSSGs0QkYifQ%3D%3D.

[45]Edith M. Lederer, "Countries Band Together to Sign Treaty Banning Nuclear Weapons," *AP* (September 20, 2017), https://globalnews.ca/news/3758556/united-nations-nuclear-weapons-treaty/.

[46]Dan Blumenthal, "It's Time to Reckon with What It Would Really Take to Deter North Korea," *AEI* (September 2017), http://www.aei.org/publication/its-time-to-reckon-with-what-it-would-really-take-to-deter-north-korea/?mkt_tok=eyJpIjoiT1dVMVpHTmhNVF 15TmpneCIsInQiOiIxa2wzK1BTS2E3bnJUVmpCakhFaFhvdHdvYk9ndGdVOXExUkV wSXB6d2lBXC96WHl0VzlyQ3hITE9XdWtJUlYwbWRraXhoSEJtYUI4UE9vazFNaD dObGh5UmJjSUVCR1wvU1wvUFRMQlZoWEhydXR4MWFETXAwcXF5WmlyM 3JiYjdWYSJ9. "There is a new piece of conventional wisdom on North Korea in Washington: The idea that the United States should 'recognize' North Korea as a nuclear state and move toward a policy of containment and deterrence. To be sure, this may be the only option left, but many who are advocating the policy don't seem to be thinking through its military requirements and possible regional consequences.

A meeting of DPRK of the central committee is held as they vow a sacred war against the U.S. during an anti-U.S. rally, in this undated photo released by North Korea's Korean Central News Agency (KCNA) in Pyongyang September 22, 2017. KCNA via REUTERS

It is indeed an astonishing turn that some of the people most deeply involved in the failed engagement or strategic patience policies of the past have been born again as tough-minded deterrers."

Institutional Paralysis

American transnational entanglements and EU's supranationalism aggravate this sober assessment. The West needs a well-functioning alliance to keep Eastern authoritarians at bay, but shared sovereignty among nations and other self-proclaimed "stakeholders" too often infringe the will of the people (nation),[47] and tie Washington and the EU's hands. The stated intent of transnationalism and supranationalism is to facilitate conflict resolution. The reality more and more appears to be institutional paralysis, just as America's founding fathers cautioned.

George Washington in his Farewell Address asserted — "It is our true policy to steer clear of permanent alliance with any portion of the foreign world." The inaugural pledge of Thomas Jefferson was no less clear: "Peace, commerce, and honest friendship with all nations-entangling alliances with none."[48]

The Obama administration rejected this advice. Progressives and liberals avidly promoted entangling military alliances, economic partnerships, political treaties, social pacts, and aspire more ambitiously to create a supranational "Global Nation" that reflects its sentiment and power-seeking agenda. The assumption is that contradictions between globalist idealism and Washington pragmatism are too small to matter, that entanglements are sure to advance their cause.

Progressives and liberals never doubt that they will succeed, and that national security will remain strong enough to serve its purposes, if they fail. They do not fear that Bad Samaritans[49] and frenemies[50] could impair America's homeland defense, hamper rational choice policymaking,[51]

---

[47] Stephen Krasner, "Sharing Sovereignty: New Institutions for Collapsed and Failing States," *International Security* 29, no. 2, 2004: 85–120.

[48] David Fromkin, "Entangling Alliances," *Foreign Affairs* 48, no. 4, July 1970: 688; Michael Beckley, "The Myth of Entangling Alliances: Reassessing the Security Risks of U.S. Defense Pacts," *International Security* 39, no. 4, Spring 2015: 7–48, https://www.belfercenter.org/sites/default/files/legacy/files/IS3904_pp007-048.pdf.

[49] Ha-Joon Chang, *Bad Samaritans: The Myth of Free Trade and the Secret History of Capitalism* (London: Bloomsbury Press, 2007).

[50] Walter Winchell, "Howz about Calling the Russians our Frienemies?" *Nevada State Journal* (May 1953).

[51] "Politico investigation: Obama Protected Hezbollah in Order to Preserve Iranian Nuclear Deal," *The Blaze* (December 2017).

foment civil strife, assist Russia, China, North Korea, Iran and the global jihadist's empire building.

Brexit, however, provides an instructive counter-example. It demonstrates that supranational idealism and stakeholder activism may become institutionalized barriers to effective national management that cause internal strife and divert attention from mounting authoritarian global security threats.

The United Kingdom joined the European Community in 1973 seeking benefits that required modest dilution of its national sovereignty. Its leaders did not anticipate ensnarement in intra-union conflicts, or the specter of secession. At first things seemed to go well enough, but net benefits began diminishing as the UK surrendered more and more of its sovereignty for smaller and smaller incremental gains. The Schengen Agreement (1985), opened intra-union borders, eroding domestic worker protections. The Single Market Act (1986), mandated unimpeded labor and refugee migration. The Maastricht Treaty (1993) expanded the scope of the European Community beyond free trade and labor mobility to cover a host of other activities and morphed into the European Union (EU). The Lisbon Treaty (2009) created a single legal entity, with a permanent President of the European Council, and a strong High Representative of the Union for Foreign Affairs and Security Policy. Each revision of the contract euphemistically called "more Europe" shifted power from the British electorate to bureaucrats in Brussels and policymakers in Berlin to the UK's detriment.

Many Britons discovered to their dismay that they were victims of a "democratic deficit."[52] Non-partisan analyses concluded that Brussels and EU diplomats had pre-decided approximately 60 percent of all legislation enacted by Britain's Parliament.[53] They also learned the unhappy lesson, as former Soviet Republics did in the 1990s that the costs of regaining their freedom of action were enormous, and that supranational rigidities

---

Michael Wilner, "Trump Announces US Moving Embassy to Jerusalem," *Jerusalem Post* (December 6, 2017), http://www.jpost.com/Middle-East/WATCH-LIVE-Trump-delivers-much-anticipated-announcement-about-Jerusalem-517201.

[52] Simona Piattoni, "Institutional Innovations and EU Legitimacy after the Crisis," in Bruno Dallago and John McGowan, eds., *Crises in Europe in the Transatlantic Context: Economic and Political Appraisals* (London: Routledge, 2016): 119–136.

[53] John Bolton, "Brexit Victory is a True Populist Revolt," *AEI* (June 2016), http://www.aei.org/publication/brexit-victory-is-a-true-populist.

are apt to ensnare members in destructive internecine struggles that impair Europe's ability to cope effectively with external threats.[54]

The lesson for American national and global security is clear. The enemy within supranational governing bodies may compound the external authoritarian threat.

There is always hope. For those who enjoy grasping at straws, Russia and China have problems with their rapidly rising Muslim populations that may divert them from adventures abroad.[55] Coronavirus 19 might shift the correlation of forces in America's direction. Hope however is not a strategy.

---

[54] Steven Rosefielde and Bruno Dallago, "New Principles for a Better EU" in Kumiko Haba and Satoshi Mizobata, eds., *100 Year of World Wars and Postwar Regional Collaboration and Governance in the EU and Asia* (Berlin: Springer, 2020).

[55] Stephen Blank, "Imperial Strategies: Russia's Exploitation of Ethnic Issues and Policy in the Middle East," *Jamestown Foundation* (December 2017), https://jamestown.org/program/imperial-strategies-russias-exploitation-ethnic-issues-policy-middle-east/.

Part III

Civic Discord on the Home Front is Crippling Us

Progressive and liberal attitudes toward the home front aggravate the present danger to global security posed by Eastern authoritarians. They retard economic growth, sow the seeds of national disunity and underfund national security. Part III explains how excessive state economic management and social expenditures undertaken to achieve immoderate progressive-liberal goals divide the nation and straitjacket America's ability to defend by overburdening the middle and working classes, engendering chronic economic underperformance, fostering black swan financial crisis risks, skimping on hard power, and fanning the flames of civic strife. Most Western security analysts disregard these vulnerabilities, presuming that they are transitory growing pains of healthy democracies. They should not. Home front shortcomings as Ashley Tellis now appreciates negatively affect the correlation of forces, jeopardize global security and may not be transitory.[1]

---

[1]Ashley J. Tellis, "Covid-19 Knocks on American Hegemony," *National Bureau of Asian Research* (May 2020), https://www.nbr.org/publication/covid-19-knocks-on-american-hegemony/.

Chapter 8

Non-Partisanship and Bi-Partisanship are Both Disappearing

Progressives and liberals inflame social discord by privileging themselves and pressing anti-competitive programs like guaranteed incomes, equal pay for equal work (wage fixing), and cancel culture. They diminish America's economic power and unity, essential for strong national and global security. "Witch-hunting" university kangaroo courts presume the guilt of professors and students anonymously accused of "heresy," and deny legal recourse to those falsely accused.[2] Nancy Pelosi insisted that

---

[2]Alan Deshowitz, *Guilt by Accusation: The Challenge of Proving Innocence in the Age of #MeToo* (New York: Hot, 2019). Frederick Hess, "DeVos Gets Title IX Right," *AEI*, https://www.aei.org/education/devos-gets-title-ix-right/.

"On Wednesday, Education Secretary Betsy DeVos issued final Title IX regulations, overturning the Obama administration's rules on how colleges must handle sexual assault. Under Obama's edicts, students accused of sexual assault were expelled after university-run show trials with no right to an attorney, no right to have someone question their accuser, and no right to see all the evidence presented against them. In a bizarre twist on double jeopardy protections, the Obama administration even allowed the accuser to appeal the verdict while affording no such right to the accused.

Deprived of due process and without other recourse, expelled students started filing lawsuits against universities for violating their due process rights. Out of roughly 300 lawsuits filed since Obama's 2011 edict, US federal and state courts ruled against universities over half the time.

The new regulations give the accused the right to an attorney, to see evidence against them, and to have a representative question the accuser. DeVos also adds a right of appeal, allows the parties to opt for informal remediation (if those parties agree), and allows the

166   *Beleaguered Superpower: Biden's America Adrift*

Tara Reade's sexual assault accusation against Joe Biden was unproven, but switched legal ground when condemning Brett Kavanaugh.[3] Progressives portray themselves as champions of equal opportunity, while demanding quotas and sets asides for their constituents. They argue for preferential female undergraduate admissions and scholarships without any qualms about fairness. Sixty percent of undergraduates at the University of North Carolina, Chapel Hill are women.[4] Much of polarizing Vietnam War era agenda aimed at legalizing and subsidizing counter-culture lifestyles (recreational marijuana, feckless sexual unions) is now legal, and dependency no longer stigmatized. Progressive-liberals view dependency and decadence as virtues, and castigate detractors.

Staunchly anti-competitive quotas and rationing degrade American economic efficiency, productivity, equity, free choice, fairness, stability, and growth. They increase moral hazard, waste, fraud, and abuse. They aggravate domestic fragmentation, impede assimilation, miss educate, spawn alienation, and foment political strife, while ironically failing to curb inequities of income and wealth.[5] They diminish patriotism, and desensitize the nation to the Eastern authoritarian threat.

These maladies hobble the economy, subvert solidarity, and weaken the nation's will to defend. They starve defense, and cause adverse spill-overs across the globe, making the United States a lucrative target for authoritarian aggression.

Dependency, free-riding, degeneracy, moral hazard, straitjacketed markets, hiring quotas and contract set asides, underinvestment, and

---

institution to raise the level of evidence required from the *de minimis* standard "preponderance of evidence."

Remarkably, these sensible modifications were met by furious denunciations from some prominent voices on the left. Presumptive Democratic presidential nominee Joe Biden slammed the new regulations for giving "colleges a green light to ignore sexual violence." Senator Patty Murray, the top Democrat on the Senate education committee, thundered that the rules were all about "silencing survivors." House Speaker Nancy Pelosi decried DeVos's "attacks" on "the civil rights of students."

[3] Frederick Hess, "DeVos Gets Title IX Right," *AEI*, https://www.aei.org/education/devos-gets-title-ix-right/.

[4] Sarah Salinas, "The Road to a 60 Percent Female Campus," *Daily Tarheel*, April 12, 2016. https://www.dailytarheel.com/article/2016/04/the-road-to-a-60-percent-female-campus.

[5] For a nuanced view see James Pethokoukis, "Maybe Wealth Inequality Isn't As Dramatic As We Think," *AEI*, April 30, 2020, https://www.aei.org/economics/maybe-wealth-inequality-isnt-as-dramatic-as-we-think/.

Non-Partisanship and Bi-Partisanship are Both Disappearing   167

repressed entrepreneurship impair technological progress and diffusion, and diminish American economic growth. They reduce America's foreign competitiveness, jeopardizing US supply chains, and diminish synergies from globalization. The world's democracies not only have to accommodate authoritarian political pressures but they also face the prospect of flagging global economic vitality and societal strife.

Irresponsible debt accumulation raises the risk of a Black Swan global catastrophe. Covid-19 deficit spending has ballooned America's and the European Union's (EU) national debts.

The political and social consequences of progressive-liberalism, including immoderate environmentalism, do not need belaboring. They are headline news. Progressive-liberals use the mass media that they control to throttle opposition and instigate cancel culture street protests. Conservatives and populists fight back through the Internet, counter demonstrations and the ballot box.[6] It is obvious that America has become a house divided against itself, reminiscent of conditions on the eve of the Civil War,[7] and the Vietnam War era, undercutting the country's ability to defend itself from external threats and preserve global security.

The economic consequences of progressive-liberal economic policies often fly under the radar,[8] obscured by clever rhetoric and finger pointing.

---

[6] Steven Rosefielde and Quinn Mills, *Populists and Progressives* (Singapore: World Scientific Publishers, 2020).

[7] Abraham Lincoln, "House Divided" speech, June 16, 1858, https://www.battlefields.org/learn/primary-sources/house-divided.

[8] Nicholas Eberstadt, "Big Government's Overlooked Americans: A Dearth of Data Has Kept Suffering Hidden," *AEI* (December 2020), https://www.aei.org/articles/big-governments-overlooked-americans/?mkt_tok=eyJpIjoiWXpKbFkyVXlNR1ZpWVRneC IsInQiOiJvQnRST2psemtjWCtEXC9KU1IwMjdXSHJvMG9PaUhwZVRE SmFhWnFzQXNYeXBFR3VsUTdHMmNIeFVsUDB5cUc5UDhtb1o3NXRyOE 5pa1VheXlpc1U1Z010RHk5XC9KdjV6MkhqVWo0eVBIWGdhT 3ZMR3o2ZXIwOG5r M1hmZGFyN3NyIn0%3D.

"Consider the saga of 'deaths of despair' in modern America. In the late 1990s, America's white working class was suddenly seized by a terrible health crisis. Among non-Hispanic white men and women of working age with no more than a high-school education, death rates commenced a gruesome rise. Between 1999 and 2015, mortality rates for these less educated Anglos jumped in every age group between 25 and 64 — and the spikes were practically Soviet in magnitude and nature." "Whatever else may be said about this signal U.S. failure in disease prevention and control, it occasioned remarkably little reflection, self-criticism, and course correction on the part of America's public-health

168 *Beleaguered Superpower: Biden's America Adrift*

Progressives and liberals extol the micro and macroeconomic virtues of their programs and blame neo-liberalism for their failures. On the micro-economic side of the ledger, they claim that their imprudent environmental, entitlement, affirmative action, and restorative justice policies are competently designed for everyone's benefit (we together), that they enrich human capital (and hence productivity), and that preferential treatment for the underproductive enhances the quality of societal existence. Hence, they are the right things to do.

They deny that government is bloated, over-regulated and mis-regulated; that preferences and transfers may be unwarranted on numerous grounds, or that growth is retarded. They do not accept responsibility for anemic economic growth (although some now claim that this is a badge of success), inordinate income and wealth inequality, stagnant real wages, boondoggling, featherbedding, overtaxation of the middle class, worker alienation, welfare dependency, addiction, mental disorder, dogmatic education (progressive indoctrination), and financial crises. These problems will be remedied they insist by doubling down on immoderate policies, despite the ineffectiveness of tens of trillions of dollars of past social expenditures (war on drugs, war on crime, subprime loans, etc.).

In the interim, they call for greater environmental, entitlement, affirmative action and restorative justice spending, larger budgetary deficits and expansionary monetary policy (New Monetary Policy) to bolster aggregate effective demand, employment, wages, and growth, deferring tax hikes on the working and middle classes and shifting the burden to future generations. They blame fiscal conservatism for killing jobs, causing underproduction and chilling economic vitality. When large deficits and reckless monetary expansion do not suffice for their purposes, they blame economic underperformance on "austerity"; contending that

---

apparatus. The 'dying whites,' for their part, doubtless have drawn their own conclusions about why a highly educated elite that often publicly holds them in disdain might also have been so inattentive to the suffering and unnatural demise among their ranks." "In 2017, a team of university demographers estimated that as many as 19 million Americans had a felony in their background as of 2010. According to that study, as of 2010, one in eight adult American men had been convicted of a felony. Among black American men, the ratio was one in three nationwide and even higher in some states. By this reckoning, for example, in 2010 some 40 percent of California's black adults — men plus women — were convicts or ex-cons."

Non-Partisanship and Bi-Partisanship are Both Disappearing 169

budgetary deficits are too small, and monetary easing too timid, heedless of America and the globe's monumental national debts.

Progressive-liberalism is a one-way street. There is no concept of economic scarcity and limits, only manna from heaven, free riding,[9] and "free lunches." Progressives and liberals always want to spend more, resolving the resulting macroeconomic distortions by sticking workers with wage erosion, non-employment and underemployment, retirees with shriveled pensions, consumers with inflation and low interest on their savings, bondholders with the debt baby, and the nation with an inadequate defense.

Entitlements — Social Security plus Medicaid and Medicare plus unemployment insurance and Obamacare — already absorb 70 percent of all federal spending. These budget items grow automatically faster than other federal expenditures. Twenty years ago, entitlements accounted for 43 percent of the budget. The Office of Management and the Budget predicts that they will reach 75 percent in the early 2020s; a gain of about 1.3 percentage points a year.[10]

This puts national security in the cross hairs. If Washington decides merely to balance the budget (without reducing the national debt), it will have to suspend defense activities entirely because almost all other spending categories are protected as entitlements.[11] If Congress chooses to stay the course, the national debt will swell precipitating a multitude

---

[9]In the social sciences, the free-rider problem is a type of market failure that occurs when those who benefit from resources, public goods (such as public roads or hospitals), or services of a communal nature do not pay for them or underpay. Free riders are a problem because while not paying for the good (either directly through fees or tolls or indirectly through taxes), they may continue to access or use it. Thus, the good may be underproduced, overused, or degraded. William Baumol, *Welfare Economics and the Theory of the State* (Cambridge: Harvard University Press, 1952).

[10]Milton Ezrati, "Entitlements Threaten the Entire Federal Budget," *Forbes* (February 2018), https://www.forbes.com/sites/miltonezrati/2018/02/09/entitlements-threaten-the-entire-federal-budget/#f311a4258923.

[11]Kimberly Amadeo, "Current U.S. Federal Budget Deficit," *The Balance* (September 2018), https://www.thebalance.com/current-u-s-federal-budget-deficit-3305783.

"The Trump administration will set new records of defense spending. It is estimated to reach $874.4 billion in FY 2018 and $886 billion in FY 2019. Trump wants the additional funding to fight ISIS. Congress also granted a two-year reprieve from sequestration for military spending," https://www.thebalance.com/current-u-s-federal-budget-deficit-3305783.

170   *Beleaguered Superpower: Biden's America Adrift*

of adverse economic consequences that will prevent America from adequately responding to present dangers. The nation loses either way, and the problem is not resolved by asserting that modern wars will be short.

Deterrence requires a will to defend and a sound economy is essential for America keeping pace with its foes.

Chronic Underperformance

There are solutions to the dilemma. Democrats and Republicans on a bipartisan basis can reduce environmentalist excesses, abusive "entitlements," affirmative action and restorative justice outlays, redirecting revenues to fund a robust national defense and pare the national debt. They can revitalize the economy from a supply side perspective by curtailing boondoggles, eliminating anti-productive regulations,[12] and reallocating resources to legitimate value-adding activities, including technological innovation and investment that are the foundation stones of sustainable economic growth. Faster and durable growth will raise all boats. It will provide new revenues for defense and non-defense programs alike, and permit accelerated national debt reduction. The result will be win–win–win–win: higher efficiency, faster growth, superior social welfare and enhance national security.

When asked, progressives and liberals claim that win–win–win–win is their intention and that they will surely succeed if their programs come to fruition. Their optimism is unfounded and their denial disingenuous. Win–win–win–win is incompatible with the progressive anti-defense, anti-productive, free lunch, dependency agenda that erodes real wages and the after tax income of middle and working class workers, encourages parasitism, and fans the flames of financial speculation (negative interest rates). Nor is it consistent with misgivings about America and the EU's dyspeptic post-2008 economic recovery voiced by prominent economic theorists who openly fret about the danger of chronic underperformance, or in their jargon "secular stagnation." Some on the continent call the

---

[12]The supply side logic here is microeconomic and independent of the macroeconomic debate on Arthur Laffer's supply side economic theory. Victor Canto, Douglas Joines, and Arthur Laffer, *Foundations of Supply-Side Economics* (New York: Academic Press, 1983).

same phenomenon "Eurosclerosis."[13] Alvin Hansen coined the term secular stagnation in the late 1930s to highlight the danger of permanent hard times.[14] Although many economists are comfortable with the term "secular stagnation," we substitute "chronic underperformance" here for the sake of clarity. Chronic underperformance and secular stagnation are identical in Hansen's sense. They are an aspect of "deadweight efficiency losses."[15]

Larry Summers, Paul Krugman, and Joseph Stiglitz revived the concept a decade ago to describe America and the West's subpar economic recovery and anemic economic growth prospects following the global financial crisis of 2008.[16] No one disputes the fact that the

---

[13]Eurosclerosis is a term coined by German economist Herbert Giersch in the 1970s to describe a pattern of economic stagnation in Europe that may have resulted from government over-regulation and overly generous social benefits policies.

[14]Alvin H. Hansen, "Economic Progress and Declining Population Growth," *American Economic Review* 29, no. 1, March 1939: 1–15.

[15]Deadweight loss, also known as excess burden, is a measure of lost economic efficiency when the socially optimal quantity of a good or a service is not produced.

[16]Paul Krugman, *The Return of Depression Economics and the Crisis of 2008* (New York: W.W. Norton Company, 2009). Lawrence Summers, "Washington Must Not Settle for Secular Stagnation," *Financial Times*, December 5, 2013, http://www.ft.com/cms/s/2/ba0f1386-7169-11e3-8f92-00144feabdc0.html#ixzz2pi6xfiEe; Joseph Stiglitz, "Stagnation by Design," *Project Syndicate* (February 2014), https://www.project-syndicate.org/commentary/joseph-e--stiglitz-argues-that-bad-policies-in-rich-countries--not-economic-inevitability--have-caused-most-people-s-standard-of-living-to-decline?barrier=accessreg; James Pethokoukis, "The Slump That Never Ends: Does the US Face 'Secular Stagnation'?" *AEI* (November 2013). Henry Blodget, "Has the US Entered a 'Permanent Slump'?" *Daily Ticker*, November 18, 2013, http://finance.yahoo.com/blogs/daily-ticker/ueconomy-entered-permanent-slump-165120719.html.

John Taylore (2014), "Economic Hokum of 'Secular Stagnation': Blaming the Market for the Failure of Bad Government policies Is No More Persuasive Now Than it Was in the 1930s," *Wall Street Journal*, January 1, 2014.

"Summers speculates that the natural interest rate 'consistent with full employment'" fell "to negative 2% or negative 3% sometime in the middle of the last decade." But conventional monetary policy cannot push rates that low. The dreaded Zero Lower Bound. Thus, Summers concludes, "We may well need, in the years ahead, to think about how we manage an economy in which the zero nominal interest rate is a chronic and systemic inhibitor of economic activity, holding our economies back, below their potential." John Taylor has dismissed the Summers–Krugman secular stagnation crisis as Hokum because he believes that free markets assure a robust American economic recovery.

172   *Beleaguered Superpower: Biden's America Adrift*

post-crisis recoveries in America and the EU have been anemic, and few predict a return to the long-term historical GDP growth rate anytime soon. Some are now contending that stagnation is a badge of economic success.[17]

The pre-COVID-19 consensus expectation for American economic growth was 2 percent before the current hyper-stimulation of monetary expansion and burgeoning deficit spending; a rate well below the 3.4 percent historical norm.[18] It is expected to revert to 2 percent after 2021. Prospects for the EU are worse, around 1 percent per annum.[19] COVID-19 has not altered the Organisation for Economic Co-operation and Development's (OECD) forecasts for 2020 and 2021.[20]

This is the "good news." There are sound reasons for believing that the real rate of growth is lower than officially reported. America's national income accounting procedures disguise some price increases by treating them as "value added" (growth) instead of inflation. The phenomenon, called "hidden inflation" conceals the true inflation rate, and overstates America's growth rate. For example, the quality of America higher education understood as the acquisition of knowledge, comprehension and critical analytic ability over the past decade has declined. Politically correct brainwashing akin to Marxist–Leninist–Stalinist indoctrination

---

However, while he is justified in challenging Krugman's liquidity trap framework, his own critique of abusive American government points to a plausible alternative explanation for the United States' economic dyspepsia.

[17]Dietrich Vollrath, *Fully Grown: Why a Stagnant Economy is a Sign of Success* (Chicago: University of Chicago Press, 2020).

[18]Phil Gramm and Mike Solon, "Don't Be Fooled By 'Secular Stagnation'," *Wall Street Journal* (December 2017), https://www.wsj.com/articles/dont-be-fooled-by-secular-stagnation-1512171654.

[19]Carmen Reinhart, "Recovery is Not Resolution," *Project Syndicate*, August 1, 2017, https://www.project-syndicate.org/commentary/advanced-economy-recovery-vulnerable-by-carmen-reinhart-2017-08?utm_source=Economics%20readers%20from%20Mather&utm_campaign=ba317fda52-lehman_10_year_anniversary_mailing&utm_medium=email&utm_term=0_991b581537-ba317fda52-106454839&barrier=accesspaylog.

[20]OECD Interim Economic Assessment, "Coronavirus: The World Economy at Risk," *OECD Library* 2019, no. 2 (March 2020), https://www.oecd-ilibrary.org/economics/oecd-economic-outlook/volume-2019/issue-2_7969896b-en.

now passes for education, at the same time that government mandated "consciousness raising" programs ("active and inclusive learning") cause tuition to spiral upward. These forced substitution costs count as growth (increased demand responsive value added) in national income accounting even though they reduce most students' utility (an element of their quality of existence). They give the illusion of growth, but are merely a form of "hidden inflation" where higher tuition fees are mis-ascribed to better education (quality improvement) for all students and entered into GDP as value added.

Much of the growth in the value added of American healthcare services, given government price-setting rules, is similarly spurious. The government fixes medical product and service prices using Soviet methods,[21] allowing pharmaceutical companies to charge higher prices for nominally improved medicines.[22] Similarly, they reclassify supplements as medicine sold at 10 times the generic price. Corporate profits increase with negligible consumer benefit, but the government reports this price gouging as value added. These accounting sleights of hand and rising superfluous medical insurance paperwork costs have helped drive healthcare spending as a share of GDP from 5 percent in 1960 to 18.2 percent today,[23] providing the semblance, but not the substance of material progress.[24]

---

[21] Steven Rosefielde, *Russian Economy From Lenin to Putin* (New York, NY: Wiley, 2007).

[22] Danny Lewis, "Why a Single Vial of Antivenom Can Cost $14,000, It's Not Because All Antivenom is Expensive to Make," *Smithsonian Magazine*, September 11, 2015, https://www.smithsonianmag.com/smart-news/why-single-vial-antivenom-can-cost-14000-180956564/.

[23] "U.S. National Health Expenditure as Percent of GDP from 1960 to 2018," *Statista*, https://www.statista.com/statistics/184968/us-health-expenditure-as-percent-of-gdp-since-1960/; https://data.oecd.org/healthres/health-spending.htm.

The OECD average health spending GDP share is 8.9 percent.

[24] Disregard for skyrocketing administrative costs, likewise treated as value added is another way in which American GDP statistics provide only the illusion of success. Administration of healthcare constitutes 30 percent of the US healthcare costs.

Jeffrey Pfeffer, "The Reason Health Care is So Expensive: Insurance Companies," *Bloomberg*, April 10, 2013. https://www.bloomberg.com/news/articles/2013-04-10/the-reason-health-care-is-so-expensive-insurance-companies.

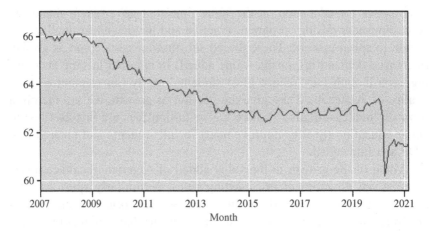

Figure 8.1   Labor Force Participation Rate
Source: *Bureau of Labor Statistics*, April 3, 2021; https://data.bls.gov/timeseries/LNS11300000SS.

The government's headline unemployment statistics likewise show American economic performance in an unduly favorable light.[25] Figure 8.1 reveals a substantial increase in "non-employment" (discouraged workers dropping out of the labor force), despite what the government purports to be a solid economic recovery.[26] The headline unemployment rate (U-3) November 2017 was 4.1 percent, but the labor underutilization rate (U-6) was 8 percent.[27]

---

[25] James Galbraith, "What Trump's Tax Cut Really Means for the US Economy," *Project Syndicate* (January 2018), https://www.project-syndicate.org/onpoint/what-trump-s-tax-cut-really-means-for-the-us-economy-by-james-k-galbraith-2018-01?utm_source=Project%20Syndicate%20Newsletter&utm_campaign=dc2ccb3349-op_newsletter_2018_1_19&utm_medium=email&utm_term=0_73bad5b7d8-dc2ccb3349-93559677&mc_cid=dc2ccb3349&mc_eid=a749d91574&barrier=accesspaylog.

"Despite low headline unemployment — 4.1% as of December — the US economy is neither at full employment nor constrained by labor supply, as some have argued. The employment-to-population ratio has risen from its post-crisis low of around 58% to just over 60%, but it is still three percentage points below the 2007 level, and five points below its peak in 2000."

[26] Labor Force Statistics from the Current Population Survey, *Bureau of Labor Statistics*, December 7, 2017, https://data.bls.gov/timeseries/LNS11300000.

[27] Aparna Mathur, "Monthly Jobs Report: Beyond the Headlines," *AEI* (December 2017), http://www.aei.org/multimedia/monthly-jobs-report-beyond-the-headlines/?mkt_tok=eyJ

The preponderance of these "should be" workers are native-born male victims of the new work place.[28] Moreover, the combined effects of reduced labor protection,[29] flimflam speculative financial practices,[30] diminished fringe benefits (particularly pensions), stagnant real wages,[31] poor job quality,[32] rising monopsony power, government manipulated sub-competitive interest savings rates, hidden inflation,

---

pIjoiTm1ZMk1tTmlOREZrT1dNeiIsInQiOiIrajRBVzNWYm05cXc1a1wv cUgrd0dZRHJCVmp3Q2xSTTNaQmVlNk1qcXcyRHAxdHpVYmludit0cTlmWU JadEdieFhTNUxKeGRHcEpnR1RCZnRPemlORHR2MVJcL2tYQXlxYXhSWDFnZ DA2TURrRlkwTW4yNlpIRWZFbWxwZTQzNHlpIn0%3D.

[28] Nicholas Eberstadt, "Men Without Work," *AEI* (January 2018), http://www.aei.org/ publication/men-without-work-2/?mkt_tok=eyJpIjoiTm1aall6UXlaVFpoWXpNdyIsInQ iOiJsS3hlMmpNM09tNVJCQ2pXZkpiSXc3bUNoZTl2Yjl4OE12Nzh1ek05 WXdsQ2pSOElzanhGQzVXV1IzRFVyZ1wvODF1SE1GRkNpeUZiamFMZ1paMTh FMmtwU2M0aEt3K1E0K3MxMWVzVnBMVTZnTXFZU2E1czM4WExwSTc1QmZq XC9xIn0%3D.

"How big is our 'men without work' problem today? Consider a single fact: In 2015, the work rate (or employment to population ratio) for American males aged 25–54 was slightly lower than it had been in 1940, at the tail end of the Great Depression. And according to the latest official monthly 'jobs report' data available at this writing, the work rate for prime-age men in November 2017 was still below the 1940 level.

The general decline of work for grown men, and the dramatic, continuing expansion of a class of nonworking males constitutes a fundamentally new and unfamiliar sort of crisis for America."

[29] John Komlos, "The Real U.S. Unemployment Rate is Twice the Official Rate, and the Phillips Curve," unpublished manuscript, September 9, 2019.

[30] Adam Pasick, "Two US Grocery Chains Are on the Verge of Bankruptcy as Amazon Moves in," *Quartz*, February 18, 2018, https://qz.com/1210253/two-us-grocery-chains-are-on-the-verge-of-bankruptcy-as-amazon-moves-in/.

The classic PE playbook is to buy a company with borrowed money, take out enormous loans, and pocket the proceeds. According to S&P Global Market Intelligence, from 2013 to 2017 PE firms received $100 billion in debt-funded payouts, while PE-owned companies defaulted on $49.2 billion worth of loans.

[31] Steven Rosefielde and Quinn Mills, *Global Economic Turmoil and the Public Good* (Singapore: World Scientific Publishers, 2015).

Real inflation adjusted wages of the bottom 70% of American workers have been flat or falling since 2002, despite rising productivity, corporate profits, and executive compensation.

[32] David Graeber, *Bullshit Jobs: A Theory* (New York, NY: Simon & Schuster, 2018).

176 *Beleaguered Superpower: Biden's America Adrift*

open inflation, burgeoning inequality,[33] and increasing taxation is eroding real, after tax worker compensation and wealth.[34] Adding insult to injury, half the savings that should be going to retirement now is being spent supporting young adults who cannot find employment at a living wage.[35]

The middle and working classes were the big losers in the 2008 financial crisis and its aftermath.[36] The "Great Recession" pummeled them with income losses and the housing market collapse. Economic policies intended to restart job creation and income growth took four years to ameliorate their plight. The Recovery Act protected the most vulnerable, but it left the middle and working classes behind. They feel the pain and

---

[33] Piketty, Thomas, *Capital in the Twenty-First Century* (Cambridge: Harvard University Press, 2014). Cf. Aparna Mathur, "Income Inequality Isn't as Bad as You May Think," *AEI* (January 2018), https://www.aei.org/publication/income-inequality-isnt-as-bad-as-you-may-think/?mkt_tok=eyJpIjoiTVRJeU56TmlORFl5T0RsayIsInQiOiI4TkNuUlF sb3R4VFBsamVFUkV4N3IyQVhUVU9EQ05SM1NjZFY0UUV0ZVlhTk9kejF ENTlaK1dFWEI4YnJjZFQrUFVLSXdyWk1GckdRTEtFV25UXC9vcDA2bGJPNW VNa2FyZW5TdDRWV240ZzVqR3dzaGZcL05Ib0paRkJKTHJEK0gxIn0%3D.

The data used by Piketty suffer from serious under-reporting biases.

[34] James Galbraith, "What Trump's Tax Cut Really Means for the US Economy," *Project Syndicate* (January 2018), https://www.project-syndicate.org/onpoint/what-trump-s-tax-cut-really-means-for-the-us-economy-by-james-k-galbraith-2018-01?utm_source= Project%20Syndicate%20Newsletter&utm_campaign=dc2ccb3349-op_newsletter_2018_ 1_19&utm_medium=email&utm_term=0_73bad5b7d8-dc2ccb3349-93559677&mc_cid= dc2ccb3349&mc_eid=a749d91574&barrier=accesspaylog.

"The cost will be borne by middle-class Americans with mortgages and homes that they might now want to sell; and, as always, by the poor, who will suffer from higher sales taxes, social-spending cuts, and unemployment."

[35] Lorie Konish, "Parents Spend Twice as Much on Adult Children Than They Save for Retirement," *CNBC*, October 2, 2018, https://www.cnbc.com/2018/10/02/parents-spend-twice-as-much-on-adult-children-than-saving-for-retirement.html.

[36] Robert Doar, "Whose Recovery?" *AEI* (September 2018), http://www.aei.org/publication/ whose-recovery/?mkt_tok=eyJpIjoiTURSaE9XVmpabU01TXpjMSIsInQiOiJ3V0g0T0 hmSnIxeXNteXpqeHJmcGh5ZDcrRkVkMU1tSWprZno3WUF1ZzJVdWpjMXhcL3 hJWTBhR1l0K29DUDVmbTdPR0lRYlwvUEFjZEMzaW83bTYxMlNwblwvVEpw Wjd2MlJYK040QXpWdDNReWtGYWFyM1NRelJvcitROUtGVU1JUyJ9.

retaliate by reserving their effort.[37] COVID-19 has not improved their prospects.[38]

National Debt

Dangerously high government debt exacerbated by Covid-19 compounds the problem. The gross debt to GDP ratio as of November 2020 is 132 percent,[39] and the net debt to GDP ratio excluding debt like social security owed by the government to itself is 98.4 percent.[40] The same problem is besetting the EU.[41] The United States has the largest external debt in the world. As of June 2020, the total of US Treasury bonds held by foreign countries was $7.04 trillion, up from $6.63 trillion in June 2019.[42] Taxpayers must ultimately repay a substantial portion of these debts

---

[37] Cf. Brink Lindsey and Steven Teles, *The Captured Economy: How the Powerful Become Richer, Slow Down Growth, and Increase Inequality* (London: Oxford University Press, 2017).

Lindsey and Teles argue that it is not just that technology and offshoring have wiped away middle-income jobs, but that high-income individuals and big-profit businesses have rewritten the rules of the economy, "capturing" the regulatory system and using it to squeeze out their competition. The result is both greater inequality, and a more sclerotic economy. Lindsey and Teles do not discuss the establishment or the Global Nation. They suggest a libertarian solution arguing for restructuring policy processes in the legislature, the courts, and the executive branch — and at the federal, state, and local levels — to promote competition, reduce rent-seeking, and thus help new businesses and the middle class. Their recommendations are economically sound, but do not confront the larger political reality.

[38] Sean Collins, "Why the Covid-19 Economy is Particularly Devastating to Millennials, in 14 Charts," *Vox*, May 5, 2020, https://www.vox.com/2020/5/5/21222759/covid-19-recession-millennials-coronavirus-economic-impact-charts.

[39] http://www.usdebtclock.org/.

[40] https://www.newsweek.com/national-debt-could-surpass-25-trillion-amid-spending-combat-coronavirus-1493758.

[41] European Central Bank, September 11, 2020. https://www.ecb.europa.eu/press/key/date/2020/html/ecb.sp200911_slides~d99f3020a8.en.pdf?f0e6377d091c1f1d633bb727cd429eee.

[42] "MAJOR FOREIGN HOLDERS OF TREASURY SECURITIES (in billions of dollars)." ticdata.treasury.gov. United States Department of the Treasury. Archived from the original on October 18, 2020.

178　*Beleaguered Superpower: Biden's America Adrift*

including the funds that government owes to itself to cover corresponding obligations, or face the consequence of *de facto* or *de jure* default. There are no free lunches, progressive and liberal suggestions to the contrary notwithstanding. This makes it difficult for Washington to finance America's national security needs through increased borrowing without implicitly defaulting, threatening a replay of the 2008 financial crisis.[43] The credit bubble is even worse abroad, but progressives, liberals who failed to foresee the 2008 and 2020 financial crises and fix the systems vulnerabilities remain in denial.[44]

---

[43] Desmond Lachman, "Bubbles Pervade World Economy," *AEI* (January 2018), http://www.aei.org/publication/bubbles-pervade-world-economy/?mkt_tok=eyJpIjoiWkRnd0 1qQTVPVFF3TjJKbSIsInQiOiJWUE1YT1wvQ3lGOXZrQnZwQ0hKZnRvSkdae lNmRkNtdXU0SFJ4aG1TcGpMTlE4R1pEMEw0RzRXeXpZaytyUEpFRU5kbGhDY m9WQVZPcStMQ0FkQ2tTQjI3NUFiVVc1ajFpUnpWVHdoeEdkWUMwVDNwZTd jQ0xFMU5ieWdlaWFZTmcifQ%3D%3DIn.

"Bubbles are much more pervasive today than in the run-up to the 2008 financial crisis, when they were contained to the US housing and credit markets." "If one had any doubt that global credit markets have lost touch with reality, all one need do is to consider some recent international bond issues. Argentina, which has distinguished itself by defaulting no less than five times in the past century, managed to issue a 100-year bond. War-torn Iraq or little-known Mongolia not only placed bonds in the market, but had them massively oversubscribed."

[44] Desmond Lachman, "Bubbles Pervade World Economy," *AEI* (January 2018), http://www.aei.org/publication/bubbles-pervade-world-economy/?mkt_tok=eyJpIjoiWkRnd 01qQTVPVFF3TjJKbSIsInQiOiJWUE1YT1wvQ3lGOXZrQnZwQ0hKZnRvSkdae lNmRkNtdXU0SFJ4aG1TcGpMTlE4R1pEMEw0RzRXeXpZaytyUEpFRU5kbGhDY m9WQVZPcStMQ0FkQ2tTQjI3NUFiVVc1ajFpUnpWVHdoeEdkWUMwVDNwZTdjQ 0xFMU5ieWdlaWFZTmcifQ%3D%3DIn.

"A more serious risk yet for global financial stability has to be the surge in lending to the emerging market corporate sector by more than US$1 trillion a year over the past few years on very favorable terms. Investors seem to be unfazed by the fact the emerging market corporate sector has issued much of its debt in US dollar denominated terms. That would seem to be setting them up for real trouble if their countries' currencies were to depreciate against the dollar.

An even more serious risk to the global financial system has to be the serious mispricing of government bonds in the Eurozone. Investors are blithely lending the Italian government money at lower interest rates than they would charge the US government. Never mind that Italy has a very high public debt, a rickety banking system, an economy that is unable to grow, and a dysfunctional political system. Never mind too that Italy is the

The culprit during the Clinton and Bush administrations was the "affirmative action" motivated imposition of reckless affordable housing goals on Fannie Mae and Freddie Mac.[45] The Department of Housing and Urban Development gradually raised the quota during the new millennium, so that by 2008, 56 percent of all loans Fannie and Freddie acquired went to borrowers with below median incomes. To meet this quota, Fannie and Freddie reduced their underwriting standards by permitting underqualified buyers to purchase homes without any down payment. Because Fannie and Freddie dominated the market, when they lowered their down payment standards, lenders followed suit, overstimulating demand, and sending housing prices through the roof.

By 2008, housing prices had reached levels that no amount of concessionary lending could make affordable. Buyers dropped out of the market and home prices fell. Refinancing a mortgage became impossible and buyers who could not meet their obligations began to default. This reduced home values even for families who were meeting their mortgage obligations; it also dried up market liquidity, forced layoffs, sharply reduced consumer spending, weakened banks and other financial firms, created a great recession, and threw Fannie and Freddie into bankruptcy at cost to taxpayers of $186 billion. This was the root cause of the 2008 financial crisis. The story is well known and accepted as a, if not the fundamental cause of Wall Street's crash.[46]

What has escaped public notice is that the Obama and Trump administrations failed to reform the housing finance system. It is functioning

---

world's third largest government bond market with more than US$2½ trillion in outstanding debt.

Topping all of this folly has to be the case of China, the world's second largest economy which is experiencing a credit market bubble that makes that in Japan in the 1980s and that in the United States in the run up to the 2008 bust pale. Like the Japanese bubble before it, this one too will at some stage burst and usher in a prolonged period of very slow Chinese economic growth that will cast a long shadow over the global economy."

[45] Steven Rosefielde and Quinn Mills, *Democracy and its Elected Enemies: American Political Capture and Economic Decline* (Cambridge: Cambridge University Press, 2013).
[46] Peter J. Wallison, "Government Ignorance is No Excuse for Another Dreadful Financial Crisis," *AEI* (September 2018).

180   *Beleaguered Superpower: Biden's America Adrift*

today in substantially the way it did before the crisis for the same affirmative action reasons.[47] Housing prices are again rising as quickly as they did then.[48] Indeed, the highest rate of increase is occurring for the lowest price homes, exactly the opposite of what a sensible housing policy would produce. Another financial crisis is brewing,[49] unless Washington drastically pares affirmative action-driven concessionary lending.[50] The 1.5 trillion student loan debt and the 2.3 trillion CARES spending deficit compound the danger.[51] The issue is not on the media radar screen.

Chronic economic underperformance, periodic financial crises, and related economic dysfunctions are key home front causes of the global security quagmire.[52] They foreclose the West's security options.

---

[47]Carmen Reinhart and Vincent R. Reinhart, "The Crisis Next Time: What We Should Have Learned from 2008," *AEI* (September 2018), http://www.aei.org/publication/the-crisis-next-time/?mkt_tok=eyJpIjoiWlRkbFltSXpOR014T0RCaiIsInQiOiJjN1wv TndzUWVEZE5scGNNUU5wc1lqSnpTT0VLSndvTlVtZUhVVmxXSndRUmZKcm FLOWlndVI0ZElPRlwveWlHdlVLUm9UaGFPZm5hQzVUWDR5SXlEYUUrY2lvTVh SUzJcL3k3ajBMdWRvU2trOFdObHFGeXRIT1IPWkUxYk9UQUc4diJ9.

[48]http://www.in2013dollars.com/Housing/price-inflation.

[49]Nouriel Roubini and Brunello Rosa, "The Makings of a 2020 Recession and Financial Crisis," *Project Syndicate* (September 2018), https://www.project-syndicate.org/commentary/financial-crisis-in-2020-worse-than-2008-by-nouriel-roubini-and-brunello-rosa-2018-09?utm_source=Project+Syndicate+Newsletter&utm_campaign=cb8165502d-sunday_newsletter_16_9_2018&utm_medium=email&utm_term=0_73bad5b7d8-cb8165502d-93559677.

"Although the global economy has been undergoing a sustained period of synchronized growth, it will inevitably lose steam as unsustainable fiscal policies in the US start to phase out. Come 2020, the stage will be set for another downturn — and, unlike in 2008, governments will lack the policy tools to manage it."

[50]Adam Tooze, *Crashed: How a Decade of Financial Crises Changed the World* (London: Penguin Random House, 2018). The New West begs to differ. It blames the severity and duration of the 2008 financial crisis on "austerity"; that is, the slow post-crash growth of national deficits and debts.

[51]Katie Lobosco, "Student Loan Debt Just Hit $1.5 Trillion. Women Hold Most Of It," *CNN*, June 5, 2018, https://money.cnn.com/2018/06/05/pf/college/student-loan-stats/index.html. Twenty percent of student loan debtors are behind in their payments.

[52]Annie Lowrey, "Millennials Are the New Lost Generation: They're facing a second once-in-a-lifetime downturn at a critical moment," *Atlantic*, April 13, 2020, https://www.theatlantic.com/ideas/archive/2020/04/millennials-are-new-lost-generation/609832/.

Washington cannot credibly fund America's national security needs if it refuses to purge distortions hobbling the economy, including affirmative action lending risks and excessive CARES crisis deficit spending. Progressive and liberal Democrats oppose spending cuts on their social programs including affirmative action, restorative justice, education, Medicare and Medicaid,[53] welfare, social security, unemployment benefits, and the environment. They are willing to raise taxes on the middle class (including most workers), but are reluctant because they hope to attract voters from the Republican populist constituency. They cannot tax the poor (except through sales taxes, fees, and inflation) and both the Democratic and Republican parties are in league with wealthy political contributors.

As long as the progressive-liberal spending tide keeps rising, funds for entitlements, affirmative action, and restorative justice programs will persistently increase at the expense of defense, the national debt, and the middle and working classes.[54] Taxes, eroding fringe benefits, disguised inflation, open inflation, sub-competitive interest rates (indirect taxes on savers), foreign competition, excessive immigration,[55] falling real wages,

---

[53] Joseph Antos and James C. Capretta, "National Health Expenditure Report Shows We Have Not Solved the Cost Problem," *AEI* (December 2017), http://www.aei.org/publication/national-health-expenditure-report-shows-we-have-not-solved-the-cost-problem/?mkt_tok=eyJpIjoiWlRBNVpqYzFNemxrT0RJeCIsInQiOiJKcGRxZEdjXC9PRUQ0Mm1ST0hqNlFPaGtodDRnZmw1cVFhU2xDb0MrSStyK0dGTzhGVGNGczVr eDZIckJHWEdIM3lrS1JcL05OUStPUXpBcXdiVUs2VlloeWg2YitEMWI3Qm VxSWpUM2RVbmtjRDRiSklGY1wvRjZYMWFDSGI3WHhjOCJ9.

"The latest update from the Centers for Medicare and Medicaid Services (CMS) finds that national health expenditures (NHE) rose 4.3 percent in 2016, 1.5 percentage points faster than growth in gross domestic product (GDP)."

[54] Steven Rosefielde, *Trump's Populist America* (Singapore: World Scientific Publishers, 2017).

[55] John Yoo, "Executive Non-Enforcement in the Era of the Trump Presidency," AEI (July 2020). https://www.aei.org/op-eds/executive-non-enforcement-in-the-era-of-the-trump-presidency/?mkt_tok=eyJpIjoiTXpnM1l6ZzFNVGcyWlRZNSIsInQiOiIzdzk5VUtcL2F wSGRKYWJyZ2RYU2JLN0l4K2w5bmJKU1VielBNZWVKRkdxblU5Z1VtRkdUN FYzcVwvT1BuUlFqV2d2WWpsb05BZDBEVnJicOFZRGVUTlo5QnNmczRZV2 xza2pxbVUzU3pheVNEa2tjRmNtMjgwbHdjR0V1d1VtQ3cxIn0%3D.

"In 2012, the Obama administration announced the Deferred Action for Childhood Arrivals (DACA) program, a non-enforcement policy that halted the deportation of those who were illegally brought to the United States as children. In 2014, the administration

182 *Beleaguered Superpower: Biden's America Adrift*

and loss of worker pensions will beleaguer ordinary citizens without adequate non-partisan and bi-partisan constraint. The gap between the rich and the middle will widen, with more and more of the middle class pushed down into the ranks of poor by hidden inflation, open inflation, and negligible returns on savings.[56] National debt will mount well beyond the pre-COVID-19 projected 150 percent of GDP,[57] culminating alternatively in a "black swan" financial crisis,[58] rampant inflation, or "haircuts" for private investors, foreign and domestic alike.[59] Whatever the precise outcome, national security will be on the chopping block.[60]

---

followed up with the Deferred Action for Parents of Americans (DAPA) program, which blocked the removal of those here illegally whose children were either U.S. citizens or green card holders. These two policies combined allowed at least five million aliens — about half of the entire undocumented population — to remain in the United States in violation of federal immigration laws. In creating DACA and DAPA, the Obama administration created exceptions that swallowed the rule."

[56]Thomas Piketty and Emmanuel Saez, "Inequality in the Long Run," *Science* 344, no. 6186 (May 2014): 838–843.

[57]Michael Strain, "Next Task for GOP: Spend Less and Help the Poor," *AEI* (December 2017), http://www.aei.org/publication/next-task-for-gop-spend-less-and-help-the-poor/?mkt_tok=eyJpIjoiTldNM1pHUXhPVEV6WWpreSIsInQiOiJ3S0NhQnl0bjM4bHdOQktmNWZJMWljalIwblR6dHpBTUZsazJxNEt1Q3hiQ0xkcVRBK21oS0tvRUN0M VJQM3oxRmVOeW4zZTMzTkJIeVpoXC9SdG9OWkdDYklOOUVxUDkyRHV0Y3hx VkhhV24wY2lVS0daaHpFQ0J5bWVTV1wvRkxXIn0%3D. The debt to GDP ratio here excludes debt that the government owes to its. The gross debt to GDP including debt the government owes to itself is 105 percent (December 20, 2017).

"The national debt is projected to more than double over the next 30 years, rising from 77 percent of annual economic output in 2017 to 150 percent in 2047. This is driven in large part by spending on Medicare, which is projected to double over those three decades, rising from 3.1 percent of annual gross domestic product in 2017 to 6.1 percent in 2047. Spending on Social Security is projected to increase by 1.4 percentage points to 6.3 percent of GDP in 2047. Interest payments on the debt will grow significantly, from 1.4 percent of GDP today to a whopping 6.2 percent three decades from now."

[58]Nassim Taleb, *The Black Swan: The Impact of the Highly Improbable*, 2nd ed. (London: Penguin, 2010).

[59]Haircut is a term used in the debt literature to describe a state improved write down on the face value of a sovereign debt instrument.

[60]Desmond Lachman, "Congress' Deficit Hawks Seem to Have Gone Missing in Action," *AEI* (December 2017), http://www.aei.org/publication/congress-deficit-hawks-seem-to-have-gone-missing-in-action/?mkt_tok=eyJpIjoiTkRGa01ETTVNR1ZppT0RrMSIsIn

Non-Partisanship and Bi-Partisanship are Both Disappearing 183

There is at least one sensible "exit."[61] Moderates in the Democratic and Republican parties can prevail upon Washington to find common ground for the public good. This is difficult to accomplish because contemporary political attitudes are polarized. Issues resolvable on their merit go unresolved because politicians treat them as matters of principle and faith.[62] Progressives and liberals refuse to downsize the federal bureaucracy, deregulate,[63] fine-tune essential regulatory activities curb affirmative action driven concessionary lending in the housing and student loan markets. They are unwilling to pare legislative mandates and executive orders, curtail excessive environmental restrictions, rein abusive outsourcing,

---

QiOiJHYzBJR3VNd0U2MGdIYUVtVkczZHNJUkFYMmk0aDZxY05YZE9xU mdyV2tnVWVNWTBuTXgzbHB4UTZGMUpneHNrd3NHXC9tS0dWU0VGNUw2b mthaGx3Y095aU9xZDFyZXZVOGx1QmRvQVBPc3NPc2lqVDc3SHRcL3U2dH FjWVdNRWpqIn0%3D.

[61] Steven Rosefielde and Quinn Mills, *Democracy and its Elected Enemies: American Political Capture and Economic Decline* (Cambridge: Cambridge University Press, 2013). Steven Rosefielde and Quinn Mills, *Global Economic Turmoil and the Public Good* (Singapore: World Scientific Publishers, 2015).

[62] Dani Rodrik, "In Defense of Economic Populism," *Project Syndicate* (January 2018), https://www.project-syndicate.org/commentary/defense-of-economic-populism-by-dani-rodrik-2018-01?utm_source=Project+Syndicate+Newsletter&utm_campaign=bf05d082c0-sunday_newsletter_14_1_2018&utm_medium=email&utm_term=0_73bad5b7d8-bf05d082c0-93559677. Dani Rodrik is an exception.

[63] Paul H. Kupiec, "Democrats Lamenting Trump Policies Now See Dodd-Frank's Problems," *AEI* (December 2017), http://www.aei.org/publication/democrats-lamenting-trump-policies-now-see-dodd-franks-problems/?mkt_tok=eyJpIjoiWW1JNU1HTTVZ elExTTJFMSIsInQiOiJZVURSVllMbWR1OXc0WWNObFBablF5YnE4UkdEN 1ZjSjFqV29HN0tDZ0JNYmhQcnJiWkpcL1wvZDZOVjNxNTk0QmhlaHFSSUZJR3p FaUpmQUtxejVxOExoV3JnajUrQVwvNEJEZmlnbnNPNDEwUGtGV3BaYUlGbmZLc lwvZFF1NHplZGYifQ%3D%3D.

"The main impact of the Fed's 'enhanced transparency' disclosure is likely to be additional bank expenditures to ensure that bank models reproduce loss rates that mirror those reported by the Fed, regardless of the bank's actual business history of losses. The situation is even more egregious when one realizes that there is no requirement in Dodd-Frank that the Fed's own stress test models produce accurate predictions of covered institutions' losses under adverse and severely adverse economic conditions. There are no blind scales of justice — the Fed alone decides a bank's guilt or innocence."

184 *Beleaguered Superpower: Biden's America Adrift*

restrain judicial activism, lower immigration quotas, foster competition,[64] cut back entitlements, and other excessive social expenditures because they view compromise as apostasy.[65]

There have been bipartisan agreements, but they typically reflect electoral concerns, rather than the public good. The agreements between Democrats and Republicans to increase federal budgetary deficits and the national debt without any time limits, supplemented with CARES

---

[64] Derek Thompson, "Craft Beer Is the Strangest, Happiest Economic Story in America: Corporate Goliaths are Taking Over the U.S. Economy. Yet Small Breweries Are Thriving. Why?," *Atlantic*, January 19, 2018. https://www.theatlantic.com/business/archive/2018/01/craft-beer-industry/550850/.

[65] David Leonhardt and Yaryna Serkez, "America Will Struggle After Coronavirus. These Charts Show Why," *New York Times*, April 10, 2020, https://www.nytimes.com/interactive/2020/04/10/opinion/coronavirus-us-economy-inequality.html. David Leonhardt and and Yaryna Serkez are journalists. Their charts are inaccurate, given the inaccurate data that they use. The inaccuracy of the data is very deep and goes far beyond the choice of indicators selected to support this or that point. Most economists cannot cope with deep data issues, and pretend that official data are accurate. Even if one disregards, the dubious nature of all national income statistics, indicators selected can be very misleading. For example, income inequality is partly corrected (insofar as correction is theoretically justified) by transfers. The United States spends roughly $5 trillion annually on transfers. These transfers are excluded from the Leonhardt and Serkez charts which highlight per capita income before transfers, and healthcare insurance data, which ignore the fact that the uninsured are covered free by American hospitals.

The article also tells the socialist romance that the villain of the piece is the top 1 percent. Disregarding the issue of the relevance of pre-tax data, highlighting the top 1 percent miss suggests that the anti-competitive actions of the top 1 percent are responsible for the negative trends in Leonhardt and Serkez's other charts. This cannot be true in two important senses. First, much of the reported income of the top 1 percent is gains from passive asset ownership, not direct "capitalist" exploitation. Second, the top 1 percent's control over employment and wages is surely negligible in the big picture. Industrial workers comprise only 7 percent of the labor force. This means that what Leonhardt and Serkez fail to consider is that Washington, not the 1 top percent is primarily responsible for the persistent adverse behavior of America's "welfare state" economic system. Washington over-regulates, mis-regulates, and miss controls the economy with broadly adverse consequences claiming to be the sword and shield of the needy. Leonhardt and Serkez's solution is "more Washington," even though the "more Washington" crowd has been in charge during all the years covered by their statistics. They apparently believe that "next time will be different."

emergency spending, is not a solution. It is a blind commitment to kicking the can down the road and steadfastly ignoring the consequences.[66]

Few professional national security analysts grasp that chronic economic dyspepsia, middle-class alienation, and progressive agitation pose a present danger. Fewer still adequately appreciate that implacable political polarization impedes the dilemma's swift resolution, and grasp the global and security ramifications. They have little understanding of competitive economic theory, and rely on naïve (often Marxist) political economic nostrums to navigate in perilous waters.[67] Some place their faith in tooth fairies, others presume market competition will eventually resolve all problems,[68] that technology will save the day,[69] or that we will muddle through. Blithe optimism sometimes holds politicians in good stead, but is misplaced now because polarization is destroying bi-partisanship.

Some might be tempted to counter-argue that the EU manages well enough despite its progressive, liberal, and social democratic politics, but this exception proves the rule. Most Europeans may be reconciled and

---

[66]Lucrezia Reichlin, "Avoiding the Japanification of Europe," *Project Syndicate*, August 5, 2020, https://www.project-syndicate.org/commentary/eu-fiscal-monetary-coordination-institutional-reform-by-lucrezia-reichlin-2020-08; Yanis Varoufakis, "Solidarity with the Germans," *Project Syndicate*, August 3, 2020, https://www.project-syndicate.org/commentary/next-generation-eu-recipe-for-divisiveness-paralysis-by-yanis-varoufakis-2020-08.

[67]Romano Harré and Paul Secord, *The Explanation of Social Behaviour* (Oxford: Blackwell, 1973).

[68]James Pethokoukis, "December Jobs Report: Maybe America's 'Great Stagnation' Isn't So Bad," *AEI*, January 5, 2018, http://www.aei.org/publication/december-jobs-report-maybe-americas-great-stagnation-isnt-so-bad/?mkt_tok=eyJpIjoiTUdaak9HUTJNVFE0T URKaCIsInQiOiJYZWRMMkp0T3lLa0U1QVByT2RoeVlBMkJWSzRhcm9PdC tLeG5lXC9ha25rNUthQmMzbVkzU1p0QVwvSUJZSDdNK3RGSVRkRkw5U 3JOb1VtbFN3Z0hSQkNiZ3pJdm91QzNoejFDOU01NGFZMTl5UXYzSnlsbmYwdnVx d2wxalRJUjdGIn0%3D.

JPMorgan notes, "'The gap between white and African American unemployment rates narrowed to 3.1%, the lowest on record going back to the early 1970s.' So if this is 'stagnation,' perhaps more of it wouldn't be so unwelcome."

[69]Joseph Stiglitz, "The Myth of Secular Stagnation," *Project Syndicate* (August 2018), https://www.project-syndicate.org/commentary/secular-stagnation-excuse-for-flawed-policies-by-joseph-e-stiglitz-2018-08?utm_source=Project+Syndicate+Newsletter&utm_campaign=58788e9f11-sunday_newsletter_2_9_2018&utm_medium=email&utm_term=0_73bad5b7d8-58788e9f11-93559677.

even satisfied with their eroding quality of their existence; however, the EU is not a superpower. It is a free rider, enjoying a free security lunch. The EU cannot defend itself and the world's democracies against Eastern authoritarians without America. If it had to serve as the bulwark against contemporary authoritarianism, the game already would be over.

Part IV

Trying to Manage the Threats

Most experts acknowledge the foreign threats described in Part II and many of the domestic problems elaborated in Part III. The Biden–Harris administration however is not perturbed because it is convinced that these threats are illusory or are surmountable. Wise conflict management is possible, but America is not doing it. Progressive-liberals are loath to curtail their cosmopolitan idealist agenda one iota, let alone enough to deter the Russian, Chinese, North Korean, Iranian, and global jihadi challenges. They count on slim reeds like economic sanctions, assistance, and soft power to offset the Eastern authoritarian challenge.

Part IV

Trying to Manage the Threats

Chapter 9

Sanctions Are of Limited Use

Economic Sanctions

Economic sanctions are peacetime punitive measures less bellicose than martial combat and economic war (the destruction of productive assets and naval blockades).[1] They punish specific misdeeds to tutor rather than vanquish opponents. Policymakers use economic sanctions to deny rogue actors access to natural resources, productive facilities, labor, goods, technology, and finance. Tariffs, subsidies, quotas, export and import bans, financial restrictions, asset sequestration, blacklisting, preclusive purchases of strategic goods, embargoes, and peacetime blockades are all standard tools of the repertoire.[2]

Economic sanctions are cudgels for penalizing political, social, and ethical misconduct, when reasoning, pleadings, economic enticements, and soft power fail. They complement diplomacy and are substitutes for armed force. Their purpose is to persuade offenders to mend their ways, not to seek economic advantage, or conquer them. Policymakers can

---

[1] Frances Cappola, "U.S. Sanctions on Russia Are Financial Warfare," *Forbes* (July 2014). http://www.forbes.com/sites/francescoppola/2014/07/18/u-s-sanctions-on-russia-are-financial-warfare/.Percy W. Bidwell, "Our Economic Warfare," *Foreign Affairs* (April 1942), https://www.foreignaffairs.com/articles/united-states/1942-04-01/our-economic-warfare. There is a large literature on economic warfare. It stresses the reciprocal character and inconclusiveness of economic war.

[2] Beggar-thy-neighbor policies fixing import quotas and subsidizing exports are protectionist measures, not sanctions because they are intended to help domestic constituencies rather than punish foreign governments to their perceived misconduct.

combine economic sanctions and economic war, but seldom do because economic sanctions in contemporary parlance are synonymous with defending the free trade order favored by moderates, liberals, some progressives and conservatives, while economic war is anti-competitive and punitive. American economic sanctions are righteous in Washington's eyes; economic war benighted because reprisals that seek to vanquish opponents evoke the specter of the Hawley–Smoot tariffs and the "beggar-thy-neighbor" policies alleged to have been the principal cause of the Great Depression.

Economic sanctions are an attractive foreign policy tool for policy-makers because they allow them to seize the moral high ground eschewing material self-interest and avoiding violence, while holding out hope that economic pain will discipline foes at tolerable domestic cost. They work best when weak rivals believe that expected asymmetric losses make resistance futile.

Most progressives, liberals, and conservatives suppose that they can subdue Russia, China, North Korea, Iran, and the global jihadi with economic sanctions because the West is stronger than the authoritarian East. They expect to prevail believing that America and the European Union can dish out more pain than Eastern authoritarians can endure.

This judgment is plausible, given prevailing economic asymmetries, but things are not as simple as they seem.[3] Vladimir Putin, Xi Jinping, Kim Jong-un, the ayatollahs, and global jihadi are not playing a utilitarian quality of existence game where their personal pain is decisive. Putin, Xi, Kim, and the ayatollahs are affluent.[4] Their living standards are secure. Economic sanctions cannot reduce their consumption enough to make them wince.[5]

---

[3] Steven Rosefielde, ed., *Putin's Russia: Economic, Political and Military Foundations* (Singapore: World Scientific Publishers, 2020). For a complete theoretical discussion of interactive effects, see Susanne Oxenstierna, "The Western Sanctions against Russia. How Do They Work?" in Steven Rosefielde, ed., *Putin's Russia: Economic, Political and Military Foundations* (Singapore: World Scientific Publishers, 2020).

[4] Mary Hanbury and Aine Cain, "No One Knows Putin's Exact Net Worth, but Many Speculate He's the Wealthiest Person on the Planet — His $1 Billion Palace and $500 Million Yacht Explain Why," *Business Insider* (July 16, 2018), https://www.businessin sider.nl/how-putin-spends-his-mysterious-fortune-2017-6/?jwsource=cl.

[5] Cf. Anders Aslund, "Want to Hit Putin Where It Hurts? Target His Friends!" *The Hill* (September 2, 2018), thehill.com/opinion/international/404524-want-to-hit-putin-where-it-hurts-target-his-friends.

Sanctions Are of Limited Use 191

Putin, Xi, Kim, the ayatollahs, and global jihadi only pay attention to economic sanctions insofar as punitive measures affect their power and ambitions. Economic sanctions could constrain their room for maneuver by jeopardizing their legitimacy and national goals. If economic sanctions reduce national living standards, or anger key regime supporters, Putin's, Xi's, Kim's, the ayatollahs', and global jihadi grip on power might crumble. If economic sanctions thwart investment, flagging GDP growth might de-legitimize their regimes. If Eastern authoritarians cannot acquire advanced technologies, their economic competitiveness might be impaired. If economic sanctions thwart military modernization and increase the risks of defeat in armed conflicts, Putin, Xi, Kim, the ayatollahs, and global jihadi may temporarily relent to advance their ambitions later.

Punitive threats that jeopardize imperial aspirations and power may strike Eastern authoritarians as burdensome, but are not decisive because they allow them to shift blame by claiming that their nations are under attack; that external enemies are to blame for hardships, transforming a political negative into a plus. Instead of capitulating, Russia, China, North Korea, the ayatollahs, and global jihadi may become more defiant and dangerous.

The effectiveness of strategic technology embargoes and credit restrictions on living standards also is easily exaggerated. Eastern authoritarians can cut their losses by importing close substitutes from friendly sources,[6] and circumventing restrictions with various ruses. If Putin perceives advantage in retaining Crimea, Kim links North Korea's nuclear

---

[6]Michael Corbin, "Kennan Cable No. 33: A Russian Pivot to Asia? Russian Trade with Asia from 2006 to 2016," *Kennan Institute* (May 18, 2018), https://www.wilsoncenter.org/publication/kennan-cable-no-33-russian-pivot-to-asia-russian-trade-asia-2006-to-2016?mkt_tok=eyJpIjoiT0dZd1lqWTVZakJpTURJMyIsInQiOiJhcllkXC9MM3RnZ0RN aW4wOWwxN2I0dFZVSzIwbzhaV2NcLzM3UlwvTWJ0YUJrRUx4S0VCd HJhZGV4WCtOZm44N25GOXFYeUlQYzR5bTJLMkw0UXNIaEVUcFpxOVlCWm VCWFdwUUczend3cjJmNWJ5XC9UZXo5bmhFNXNUeTljODhhcXoifQ%3D%3D.

"Although First Deputy Prime Minister Shuvalov's prediction remains unrealized, Russian trade is moving in an eastward direction and Russia could quite possibly see trade with Asia on par with the EU by 2022. If so, Russia will have made impressive steps towards balancing trade relations between East and West and undergone a clear change in trade flows in under 20 years. Most importantly, the change in direction cannot be viewed solely as a knee-jerk reaction to Russia's geopolitical tensions with the West during the last five years. Rather, it is the fruition of a policy effort to improve relationships in order to significantly increase trade with Asia over the last decade and a half."

192 *Beleaguered Superpower: Biden's America Adrift*

arsenal to his regime's eventual triumph over Seoul, and Xi prioritizes controlling the South China Sea, economic sanctions alone will not deter them.

Moreover, insofar as these reservations apply to the most favorable scenario where the West is strong and the East weak, economic sanctions are even less potent in unfavorable circumstances. The Russian, North Korean, Iranian, and global jihadi economies are relatively weak, but China's international trade sector is immense, its balance of trade with America is more than $300 billion in surplus,[7] and it holds more than $3 trillion in foreign reserves.[8] The direct and indirect costs to the West from the economic sanctions that America might impose on China could easily turn out to be intolerable. A sharp contraction in the West's access to China's market might have extremely negative repercussions at home. The sudden withdrawal of trillions of dollars and euros parked by China in Western government bonds could precipitate a massive financial crisis, aggravating economic pain beyond the point that Western politicians can withstand.

Thus, while there is a place for economic sanctions as a tool for getting the attention of Russia, China, North Korea, the ayatollahs, and global jihadi, Washington and Brussel's faith in the potency of sanctions against Eastern authoritarians is exaggerated.

Policy

The United States currently imposes economic sanctions against all the Eastern authoritarians. Advanced weapons and strategic technologies are embargoed and selected imports are prohibited, especially those dumped on Western markets. Assets are sequestered, firms blacklisted, and credit is restricted.

These sanctions have teeth and could grow harsher if current conflicts remain unresolved. The only outlier is China. America and the European Union have been largely victims of Chinese subsidized state trading

---

[7]US Department of the Census, "US Trade in Goods with China," (September 2018), https://www.census.gov/foreign-trade/balance/c5700.html.

[8]"China's Foreign Reserves Hold Steady in June as Trade War Loomed," *Bloomberg* (July 8, 2018), https://www.bloomberg.com/news/articles/2018-07-09/china-s-foreign-reserves-increased-in-june-as-trade-war-loomed.

(judged from the fair-trade standard),[9] not foreign policy disciplinarians. Washington and Brussels refrained from using economic sanctions as a tool for discouraging Chinese predatory state trading practices including the requirement that Western firms transfer their advanced civilian technologies as a *quid pro quo* for doing business in the Middle Kingdom until 2017 when Trump imposed heavy tariffs on Beijing's exports.[10] Economic sanctions against China before Trump were limited to embargoes on advanced weapons and related technologies. Pundits expect Biden to toughen sanctions on Russia,[11] and reverse Trump's retaliatory duties on China's exports.[12]

Efficacy

Economic sanctions together with a host of other measures have not persuaded Putin to rescind Crimea's annexation, checked Xi's expansion into the South China Sea, compelled Kim to denuclearize, the ayatollahs to curb their missile threat, or convinced the global jihadi to throw in the towel. Eastern authoritarians have neither curtailed their hostile behavior nor been enticed by the siren song of soft power to integrate themselves into America's transnational global order. These failures occurred even though the stringency of economic sanctions against Russia and North Korea steadily and significantly increased after 2014. This does not prove that economic sanctions were useless, or that they will never work, but

---

[9] Steven Rosefielde, "China's Perplexing Foreign Trade Policy: Causes, Consequences and a Tit for Tat Solution," *American Foreign Policy Interests* 33, no. 1, January–February 2011: 10–16.

Steven Rosefielde, "Export-led Development and Dollar Reserve Hoarding," in Steven Rosefielde, Masaaki Kuboniwa, and Satoshi Mizobata, eds., *Two Asias: The Emerging Postcrisis Divide*, (Singapore: World Scientific, 2012): 251–266.

[10] Nicholas Lardy, "China: Forced Technology Transfer and Theft?" *PIIE* (April 20, 2018), https://piie.com/blogs/china-economic-watch/china-forced-technology-transfer-and-theft.

[11] Steven Pifer, "Managing US Sanctions toward Russia," *Brookings* (December 11, 2020), https://www.brookings.edu/blog/order-from-chaos/2020/12/11/managing-us-sanctions-toward-russia/.

[12] Jamie Dettmer, "Diplomats: Biden Administration Likely to 'Sharpen Bite' of Russia Sanctions," *Voice of America* (November 19, 2020), https://www.voanews.com/europe/diplomats-biden-administration-likely-sharpen-bite-russia-sanctions.

194 *Beleaguered Superpower: Biden's America Adrift*

does demonstrate as Judy Twigg contends for Russia that they are not magic bullets.[13] The Russian case is illustrative.

Russia

American and European leaders in the aftermath of the Kremlin's annexation of Crimea on March 21, 2014 imposed economic sanctions on Russia,[14] some of which replicated Jackson–Vanik controls rescinded by

---

[13] Judy Twigg, "Russia is Winning the Sanctions Game," *National Interest* (March 2019), https://nationalinterest.org/blog/skeptics/russia-winning-sanctions-game-47517.

"These sanctions were supposed to punish Moscow's elite, but instead they've spurred economic development and patriotism."

"In at least one sector, though, the sanctions are a textbook case of unintended consequences: they've put Russian farmers in the best shape they've ever been. Countersanctions aimed at imported Western food products-put into effect just days after the initial sanctions in the summer of 2014-initially sent Russian consumers into a tailspin, hungry from a lack of immediate alternatives to tasty European cheeses and processed foods. But palates adjusted quickly, and the import substitution effects boosted Russia, by 2016, to the position of top wheat exporter in the world. As the United States hemorrhages global agro-market share courtesy of Trump-era tariffs and trade wars, Russia is actively and aggressively filling the gap."

[14] Frances Cappola, "U.S. Sanctions On Russia Are Financial Warfare," *Forbes* (July 2014), http://www.forbes.com/sites/francescoppola/2014/07/18/u-s-sanctions-on-russia-are-financial-warfare/. Percy W. Bidwell, "Our Economic Warfare," *Foreign Affairs* (April 1942), https://www.foreignaffairs.com/articles/united-states/1942-04-01/our-economic-warfare.

The term economic sanctions refers to peacetime punitive measures, short of "economic war." Policymakers impose economic sanctions to chasten adversaries by denying them access to factors of production, products, technology, and finance. Export subsidy stratagems (beggar-thy-neighbor policies) can be utilized to similar effect but are usually excluded from the concept because rivals can easily deflect them with quotas. High intensity economic sanctions employed by combatants during peace and wartime are commonly called economic warfare (blockades, blacklisting, preclusive purchases), even though the prohibitions have the same character as lower intensity punitive measures. There is a large literature on economic warfare which stresses its reciprocal character and inconclusiveness.

The use of counter-value conventional and nuclear strikes against C^3 (command, communications, and control), transport, and industrial targets is more effective than economic sanctions in compelling adversaries to yield, but hardly guarantees success.

Sanctions Are of Limited Use 195

the Obama–Biden administration as a soft power reward to Moscow less than two years earlier on December 20, 2012.[15]

Neither scolding nor narrowly targeted sanctions induced the Kremlin to relent.[16] The economic sanctions covered the export of technologies and services regulated under the US Munitions List. This blocked property of 14 defense companies and individuals in Putin's inner circle.[17] Financial restrictions were placed on six of Russia's largest banks and four energy companies, prohibiting the supply, export, re-export of goods, services, or technology in support of exploration or production for deep water, Arctic offshore, or shale projects.

---

[15]"New Era in Russia–US Trade Relations: Obama Scraps Jackson–Vanik Amendment," *RT* (December 20, 2012).

[16]Jen Psaki, "United States Expands Export Restrictions on Russia," *US State Department* (April 28, 2014), www.state.gov/r/pa/prs/ps/2014/04/225241.htm.

"Today, in response to Russia's continued actions in southern and eastern Ukraine, the United States is implementing additional restrictive measures on defense exports to Russia. Accordingly, the Department of State is expanding its export restrictions on technologies and services regulated under the U.S. Munitions List (USML). Effective immediately, the Department's Directorate of Defense Trade Controls (DDTC) will deny pending applications for export or re-export of any high technology defense articles or services regulated under the U.S. Munitions List to Russia or occupied Crimea that contribute to Russia's military capabilities. In addition, the Department is taking actions to revoke any existing export licenses which meet these conditions. All other pending applications and existing licenses will receive a case-by-case evaluation to determine their contribution to Russia's military capabilities. The United States will continue to adjust its export licensing policies toward Russia, as warranted by Russia's actions in Ukraine. We urge Russia to honor the commitments it made in Geneva on April 17 to deescalate the situation in Ukraine." Susanne Oxenstierna and Per Olsson, *The Economic Sanctions against Russia: Impact and Prospects of Success*, FOI-R--4097—SE, September, 2015. "The main conclusion of the report is that the targeted economic sanctions of the EU and the US have contributed to imposing a cost on the Russian economy in combination with other factors, but have so far not persuaded Russia to change its behaviour towards Ukraine." Oxenstierna and Olsson provide a complete listing of EU sanctions in their Appendix 2.

[17]"U.S. Sanctions Russia's State-Owned Arms Exporter Rosoboronexport," *Reuters* (September 3, 2015), http://news.yahoo.com/u-sanctions-russias-state-owned-arms-exporter-rosoboronexport-165633514--business.html.

"The United States has imposed sanctions on Russian and Chinese companies, including Russian state-owned arms exporter Rosoboronexport, for violating a U.S. law restricting weapons trade with Iran, North Korea and Syria." These sanctions apparently were imposed for violating U.S. law, unconnected with Crimea's annexation.

196   *Beleaguered Superpower: Biden's America Adrift*

Plummeting petroleum prices, the voluntary withdrawal of Western business from Russia's market,[18] and a 31 percent export drop in the first quarter of 2015 made it more difficult for Putin to absorb Crimea and Sevastopol,[19] but he persevered,[20] buoyed by the knowledge that Crimean voters themselves favored their annexation by Russia.[21] The West also had difficulties forging a consensus in favor of military intervention,

---

[18] Maria Kiselyova and Gleb Stolyarov, "Russia's GAZ in Talks with Foreign Car Makers to Replace GM," *Reuters* (June 20, 2015), http://news.yahoo.com/russias-gaz-talks-foreign-car-makers-replace-gm-175823896--finance.html.

"Russian businessman Oleg Deripaska's GAZ Group is in talks with at least six foreign car producers to let them use its idle capacity after General Motors Co pulled out of the market, GAZ Chairman Siegfried Wolf said."

[19] Mark Adomanis, "Russia's Foreign Trade is Collapsing," *Forbes* (March 2015), http://www.forbes.com/sites/markadomanis/2015/03/25/russias-foreign-trade-is-collapsing/.

The decline is mostly attributable to the collapse of petroleum prices.

[20] David Herszenhorn, "A Diplomatic Victory, and Affirmation, for Putin," *New York Times* (May 15, 2015), http://www.nytimes.com/2015/05/16/world/europe/a-diplomatic-victory-and-affirmation-for-putin.html?_r=0.

Adrian Croft, "EU Extends Trade and Investment Ban on Crimea," *Reuters* (June 19, 2015). Anjli Raval, "Saudi claims oil price strategy success," *Financial Times* (May 13, 2015), http://www.ft.com/intl/cms/s/2/69350a3e-f970-11e4-be7b-00144feab7de.html#axzz3a7307zHU.

Mr. Obama led the charge by the West to punish Mr. Putin for his intervention in Ukraine, booting Russia from the Group of 8 economic powers, imposing harsh sanctions on some of Mr. Putin's closest confidants and delivering financial and military assistance to the new Ukrainian government .... In recent months, however, Russia has not only weathered those attacks and levied painful countersanctions on America's European allies, but has also proved stubbornly important on the world stage. That has been true especially in regard to Syria, where its proposal to confiscate chemical weapons has kept President Bashar al-Assad, a Kremlin ally, in power, and in the negotiations that secured a tentative deal on Iran's nuclear program.

"EU governments extended for a year a ban on trade and investment with Crimea on Friday, meaning European help for Russian Black Sea oil and gas exploration and visits by European cruise ships will remain outlawed."

This judgment holds even if as some suspect the West conspired to drive petroleum prices down to cripple Russia's economy. The West may even encourage this sort of speculation to persuade Putin that it is the arbiter of Russia's economic well-being.

[21] Gerard Toal, John O'Loughlin, and Kristin M. Bakke, *Near Abroad: Putin, the West and the Contest for Ukraine and the Caucasus* (London: Oxford University Press, 2019).

diplomatic retaliation, or summit level Yalta II negotiations. Instead, leaders gradually escalated their rhetoric and added fresh economic sanctions without compelling Moscow to yield.[22]

Six years and $20 billion in Russian investment later, Crimeans are happy with Russian annexation. They show high levels of trust in Putin — though lower than in 2014.

[22] Department of the Treasury, "Ukraine and Russia Sanctions".

On March 6, 2014, President Obama signed Executive Order 13660 that authorizes sanctions on individuals and entities responsible for violating the sovereignty and territorial integrity of Ukraine, or for stealing the assets of the Ukrainian people. These sanctions put in place restrictions on the travel of certain individuals and officials and showed our continued efforts to impose a cost on Russia and those responsible for the situation in Crimea.

On March 17, 2014, President Obama issued Executive Order 13661 under the national emergency with respect to Ukraine that find that the actions and policies of the Russian government with respect to Ukraine — including through the deployment of Russian military forces in the Crimea region of Ukraine — undermine democratic processes and institutions in Ukraine; threaten its peace, security, stability, sovereignty, and territorial integrity; and contribute to the misappropriation of its assets.

On March 20, 2014, the President issued a new Executive Order, "Blocking Property of Additional Persons Contributing to the Situation in Ukraine" expanding the scope of the national emergency declared in Executive Order 13660 of March 6, 2014, and expanded by Executive Order 13661 of March 16, 2014, finding that the actions and policies of the Government of the Russian Federation, including its purported annexation of Crimea and its use of force in Ukraine, continue to undermine democratic processes and institutions in Ukraine; threaten its peace, security, stability, sovereignty, and territorial integrity; and contribute to the misappropriation of its assets, and thereby constitute an unusual and extraordinary threat to the national security and foreign policy of the United States.

Utilizing these Executive Orders, the United States has steadily increased the diplomatic and financial costs of Russia's aggressive actions towards Ukraine. We have designated a number of Russian and Ukrainian entities, including 14 defense companies and individuals in Putin's inner circle, as well as imposed targeted sanctions limiting certain financing to six of Russia's largest banks and four energy companies. We have also suspended credit finance that encourages exports to Russia and financing for economic development projects in Russia, and are now prohibiting the provision, exportation, or reexportation of goods, services (not including financial services), or technology in support of exploration or production for deepwater, Arctic offshore, or shale projects that have the potential to produce oil in the Russian Federation, or in maritime area claimed by the Russian Federation and extending from its territory, and that involve five major Russian energy companies.

198 *Beleaguered Superpower: Biden's America Adrift*

Russia's imperviousness to economic sanctions mirrors the Soviet record. During the Cold War era, 1947–1987 the USSR managed to grow, develop, and modernize despite stringent Western economic sanctions (Jackson–Vanik amendment[23] and CoCom[24]).[25]

These actions, in close coordination with our EU and international partners, send a strong message to the Russian government that there are consequences for their actions that threaten the sovereignty and territorial integrity of Ukraine. The United States, together with international partners, will continue to stand by the Ukrainian government until Russia abides by its international obligations. The United States is prepared to take additional steps to impose further political and economic costs. A secure Ukraine, integrated with Europe and enjoying good relations with all its neighbors, is in the interests of the United States, Europe, and Russia.

Executive Orders:

12/19/14 EO 13685; Blocking Property of Certain Persons and Prohibiting Certain Transactions With Respect to the Crimea Region of Ukraine

03/20/14 EO; Blocking Property of Additional Persons Contributing to the Situation in Ukraine

03/17/14 EO 13661; Blocking Property of Additional Persons Contributing to the Situation in Ukraine

03/06/14 EO 13660; Blocking Property of Certain Persons Contributing to the Situation in Ukraine.

[23] The Jackson–Vanik amendment is a 1974 provision in United States federal law, intended to affect U.S. trade relations with countries with non-market economies (originally, countries of the Communist bloc) that restrict freedom of emigration and other human rights. It is believed that it was a response to the Soviet Union's "diploma taxes" levied on Jews attempting to emigrate. The law which made the Soviet Union and later Russia ineligible for normal trade relations, programs of credits, credit guarantees, or investment guarantees, or commercial agreements was repealed together with the adoption of the Magnitsky bill by President Obama on December 14, 2012. The Magnitsky Act prohibits Russian officials thought to be responsible for the death of Sergei Magnitsky from entering the United States and using its banking system.

[24] CoCom (Coordinating Committee for Multilateral Export Controls) was established by Western bloc powers in the first five years after the end of World War II, during the Cold War, to put an arms embargo on COMECON countries. It was rescinded on March 31, 1994.

[25] For a good summary of the literature on the effectiveness of sanctions see Mark Kramer, "Exclusive: Sanctions and Regime Survival," *Ponars Eurasia* (March 2015), http://www.ponarseurasia.org/article/sanctions-and-regime-survival; Susan Hannah Allen, "The Domestic Political Costs of Economic Sanctions," *Journal of Conflict Resolution* 52, no. 6, December 2008: 916–944, esp. 916–917. Nikolay Marinov, "Do Economic Sanctions Destabilize Country Leaders?" *American Journal of Political Science* 49, no. 3, July 2005:

564–576. Abel Escribà-Folch and Joseph Wright, "Dealing with Tyranny: International Sanctions and the Survival of Authoritarian Rulers," *International Studies Quarterly* 54, no. 2, June 2010: 334–359.which builds on David Lektzian and Mark Souva, "An Institutional Theory of Sanctions Onset and Success," *Journal of Conflict Resolution* 51, no. 6, November 2007: 848–871. William Kaempfer, Anton Lowenberg, and William Mertens, "International Economic Sanctions against a Dictator," *Economics and Politics* 16, no. 1, March 2004: 29–51. William Kaempfer and Anton Lowenberg, "The Theory of International Economic Sanctions: A Public Choice Approach," *American Economic Review* 78, no. 4, December 1988: 786–793.

"In a study of 136 countries from 1947 to 1999, Nikolay Marinov sought to determine whether 'economic sanctions hurt the survival of government leaders in office.' [2] After comparing the longevity of leaders in countries that were targeted by sanctions with the longevity of leaders in countries that were not targeted, he concluded that sanctions do in fact 'destabilize the leaders they target.' 'Escribà-Folch and Wright find that although economic sanctions do, on average, contribute to the destabilization and removal of personalistic dictators, sanctions do not have any appreciable effect on the longevity of single-party regimes and military juntas.' 'A different take on this question comes in a study coauthored by William Kaempfer, Anton Lowenberg, and William Mertenis that relies on a model derived from public-choice theory. [4] The three authors claim that 'damaging economic sanctions can have the counterproductive effect of encouraging the ruling regime and its supporters while at the same time undermining the political influence of the opposition.' 'One of the implications of this approach is that sanctions cannot be effective in precipitating the downfall of the regime unless 'there exists within the target country a reasonably well-organized opposition group whose political effectiveness potentially could be enhanced as a consequence of sanctions.' Even in this case, however, the sanctions might still have debilitating effects on the opposition.' 'In the case of the Soviet regime and the sanctions imposed by the Carter administration in 1980 after the Soviet invasion of Afghanistan, we know for sure from declassified CPSU Politburo transcripts that Soviet leaders hated the sanctions and resented their effects. The sanctions did not, however, produce any near-term change in Soviet policy in Afghanistan.' 'Hence, assessing the longer-term effects of the 1980 sanctions is inherently difficult. The sanctions may have had a small deterrent effect on subsequent Soviet foreign policy decisions (e.g. during the crisis in Poland), but they did not change fundamental Soviet goals. Gorbachev's adoption of a vastly different approach to foreign policy is not directly traceable to the impact of past sanctions (though indirectly they may have played a small role).

In the case of the Russian Federation today, the U.S. and EU sanctions have not produced any discernible change in Russian policy vis-à-vis Crimea and eastern Ukraine, and Putin's regime has given no indication that it will back down even if the sanctions are tightened. Will the sanctions help to bring about a change of regime? With Putin's popularity ratings at 85 percent and few if any signs of a debilitating split in the ruling elite, this goal, too seems elusive, at least for now. Although one cannot fully rule out a longer-term impact on the stability of the regime,that seems a distant prospect at best."

200   *Beleaguered Superpower: Biden's America Adrift*

The legal basis for the West's economic sanctions imposed against Russia in 2014 rests on the United Nations General Assembly Resolution 68/262 on Ukraine's territorial integrity,[26] condemning the legislature of the Autonomous Republic of Crimea and the local government of Sevastopol (both subdivisions of Ukraine) for declaring their independence from Ukraine and their subsequent referenda on annexation. The UN ruled that Crimea and Sevastopol's secessions and referenda and Russia's subsequent annexation of these territories illegal because Ukraine did not consent. It ordered Russia to rescind these annexations, returning the territories to Ukraine's sovereign control. The West began imposing economic sanctions to coerce Putin into de-annexing Crimea and Sevastopol because Russia refused to comply. Economic sanctions were enacted immediately thereafter in fits and starts.[27]

EU Sanctions against Russia

The European Union imposed three different sanctions regimes against individuals, businesses, and the Russian government.

(a) A list of individuals and businesses whose actions undermined or threatened the territorial integrity, sovereignty, and independence of Ukraine was created and their assets frozen.
(b) Imports originating in Crimea or Sevastopol were restricted and later banned.
(c) Russia's use of EU financial markets was restricted and the export of armaments, dual-use goods, and petroleum equipment and services embargoed.

EU sanctions started in March 2014 directed against individuals and businesses undermining Ukraine's sovereignty. The EU imposed

---

[26]UN Res. 68/262, Territorial integrity of Ukraine (2014), http://www.un.org/en/ga/search/view_doc.asp?symbol=A/RES/68/262.

[27]Susanne Oxenstierna, "The Western Sanctions against Russia. How Do They Work?" in Steven Rosefielde, ed., *Putin's Russia: Economic, Political and Military Foundations* (Singapore: World Scientific Publishers, 2020).

"Treasury Designates Russian Oligarchs, Officials, and Entities in Response to Worldwide Malign Activity," *U.S. Department of Treasury* (April 6, 2018).

Sanctions Are of Limited Use 201

sanctions on imports from Crimea and Sevastopol in June.[28] Sanctions banning sectoral investments and exports followed in July.[29] Restrictions on Russian use of EU financial markets and the embargoing of armaments, dual-use goods, and petroleum equipment and services commenced only after escalation of military action in eastern Ukraine and the downing of Malaysia Airlines flight MH-17 on July 17, 2014 over separatist-controlled territory.[30] Investment or trade in Russian state securities with a state share of over 50 percent and a maturity of over 90 days was proscribed for dealing with five state-owned Russian banks — Sberbank, VTB, VEB, Vneshekonombank, and Rosselkhozbank — and financial institutions and their subsidiaries. The EU prohibited the export and import of arms from Russia. The export embargo includes dual-use products and advanced technologies used by the oil industry, particularly for exploration on the Arctic shelf. The arms embargo and the other trade restrictions only applied to new contracts.

The EU strengthened and broadened these economic sanctions in September 2014.[31] The duration of credits was cut to 30 days for Russian state-owned banks, and the rule was extended to three state-owned defense companies — Oboronprom, United Aircraft Corporation, and Uralvagonzavod) and three state energy companies — Rosneft, Transneft, and Gazprom Neft. These restrictions exclude trade credits.

---

[28] Council Regulation (EU) 692/2014 of June 23, 2014, "Council Decision (CFSP) 2017/1087 of June 19, 2017, Amending Decision 2014/386/CFSP Concerning Restrictive Measures in Response to the Illegal Annexation of Crimea and Sevastopol," *Council Regulation* (June 2014), http://eur-lex.europa.eu/legal-content/EN/TXT/PDF/?uri=CELE X:32014R0692&from=SV.

[29] Council Regulation (EU) 825/2014 of July 30, 2014, "Amending Regulation (EU) No 692/2014 Concerning Restrictions on the Import into the Union of Goods Originating in Crimea or Sevastopol, in Response to the Illegal Annexation of Crimea and Sevastopol," *Council Regulation* (July 2014), http://eur-lex.europa.eu/legal-content/EN/TXT/PDF/?uri =CELEX:32014R0825&from=SV.

[30] Council Regulation (EU) 833/2014 of July 31, 2014, "Concerning Restrictive Measures in View of Russia's Actions Destabilising the Situation in Ukraine," *Council Regulation* (July 2014), http://eur-lex.europa.eu/legal-content/EN/TXT/PDF/?uri=CELEX:32014R08 33&from=EN.

[31] Council Regulation (EU) 960/2014 of September 8, 2014, "Amending Regulation (EU) No 833/2014 Concerning Restrictive Measures in View of Russia's Actions Destabilising the Situation in Ukraine," *Council Regulation* (September 2014), http://eur-lex.europa.eu/ legal-content/EN/TXT/PDF/?uri=CELEX:32014R0960&from=EN.

202 *Beleaguered Superpower: Biden's America Adrift*

Sector specific economic sanctions expired on August 1, 2018,[32] the remainder on 16 September 2018.[33] Restrictive measures against individuals and legal entities expired on 31 July 2020,[34] but have been renewed.

US Sanctions against Russia

The foundation stones for America's economic sanctions against Russia are four Presidential Executive Orders. President Barack Obama signed Executive Order 13660 on March 6, 2014, followed by Executive Orders 13661 and 13662 in March 2014, and Executive Order 13665 on December 9. Each successive executive order upped the ante, granting the President the discretion to sanction any company involved in the construction of Russia's hydrocarbon export pipelines. President Trump extended all these executive orders for one year on March 2, 2018.[35]

---

[32] Council Decision (CFSP) 2017/2426 of December 21, 2017, "Amending Decision 2014/512/CFSP concerning restrictive measures in view of Russia's actions destabilising the situation in Ukraine" (December 21, 2017), http://eur-lex.europa.eu/legal-content/EN/TXT/?uri=CELEX:32017D2426.

[33] Council Decision (CFSP) 2017/1087 of June 19, 2017, "Amending Decision 2014/386/CFSP concerning restrictive measures in response to the illegal annexation of Crimea and Sevastopol" (June 19, 2017), https://eur-lex.europa.eu/legal-content/EN/TXT/?uri=CELEX%3A32017D1087.

[34] "EU & US Extend Russia–Ukraine Sanctions by 1 Year," *European Sanctions* (March 5), https://europeansanctions.com/category/latest-eu-measures/. "Russia: EU Prolongs Economic Sanctions by Six Months," *European Council* (December 2019).

[35] "Executive Order (2018) of March 2, 2018 on the President's Continuation of the National Emergency with Respect to Ukraine," *Code of Federal Regulations*. Andrew Movchan, "Sanctions and Retaliation: Where Russia-U.S. Relations Are Headed," *Carnegie Moscow Center* (April 2018), https://carnegie.ru/commentary/76120?mkt_tok=eyJpIjoiWmpVM09HWXpNelJtTldNNSIsInQiOiJhd2VzaCs2N2NIZHlEa2p6T0wwbWJoOUhkVndRXC9IU29Sam5pYjNFWm8xNTFwXC9uMmZKcVpNMlhDZDRtRWVoT0RxTXo1b09VUlJLQnAzQ2FlS1BDaUVtd0EwRkp6WWxaaUh3dnE5dmRcL3FYbkNYQ3NOQis2VWNZaEZiRGFldDRIeCJ9.

"The expansion of U.S. sanctions to 24 individuals and 14 companies linked closely to Russia should not have come as a surprise to anyone: the United States had warned many times that oligarchs close to the Kremlin might be added. Andrei Skoch and Suleiman Kerimov, two of the businessmen who were added, have long been politicians, and have restructured their property accordingly, and therefore won't fall under the

Sanctions Are of Limited Use 203

US sanctions include:

- Asset freezes against selected individuals, particularly, close associates of Vladimir Putin. Americans cannot legally engage in financial transactions with them.
- Asset freezes against selected businesses, particularly state-owned banks, and energy companies, and arms producers.
- Restrictions on financial transactions with Russian firms in finance, energy, and defense.
- Restrictions on exports of oil-related technology.
- Restrictions on exports of dual-use technology.

These sanctions apply to six banks: Gazprombank VEB, Bank of Moscow, Rosselkhozbank, VTB Bank, and Sberbank; seven energy firms Novatek, Rosneft, Gazprom Neft, Transneft, Lukoil, Surgutneftegas, and Rosneft, and 17 arms firms. The latter are Almaz-Antey, Federal State Unitary Enterprise State Research, and Production Enterprise Bazalt, JSC Concern Sozvezdie, JSC MIC NPO Mashinostroeniya, Kalashnikov Concern, KBP Instrument Design Bureau, Radio-Electronic Technologies, Uralvagonzavod, United Shipbuilding Corporation, Dolgoprudny Research Production Enterprise, Mytishchinski Mashinostroitelny Zavod, Kalinin Machine Plant JSC, Almaz-Antey GSKB, and JSC NIIP. The assets of these banks, energy companies and weapons manufactures in the US are frozen, and transactions with them prohibited.

---

purview of the sanctions. Vladimir Bogdanov, the head of Surgutneftegaz oil company, who was also included on the latest list, had only been left off previous lists by a fluke: Surgutneftegaz itself has long been under sanctions. Only two names add a new dimension to the list: Oleg Deripaska and Viktor Vekselberg.

The choice of two major Kremlin-controlled businessmen who had been working productively with the United States and with Americans would seem random if not for one thing that unites them: aluminum. Deripaska's En+, together with SUAL, co-owned by Vekselberg, are the two main owners of Rusal, the Russian aluminum giant.

The United States consumes 16 percent of the world's aluminum, but due to economic inefficiency in recent years, American production has dropped fivefold to less than 1 million tons a year. The Trump administration has announced the beginning of a fight to revive domestic aluminum production. That's why the 10 percent import tax on aluminum was conceived, and it's also the reason for the sanctions against Rusal and En+: as a result, there will be 700,000 tons less aluminum on the U.S. market."

Key Features of EU and American Sanctions

EU and American economic sanctions imposed against Russia are broadly similar and do not provide loopholes that permit the Kremlin to play one side against the other. EU members applied the sanctions uniformly even though some countries were reluctant to comply. Problems with intra-EU discipline and trans-Atlantic coordination, including Norway and Canada do not explain Putin's unwillingness to rescind Crimea's annexation.

Moreover, the scope of EU and American economic sanctions did not provide grounds for Putin digging in his heels. EU and American economic sanctions were not tantamount to a declaration of economic war. They do not prohibit EU and American business with Russia or impose tariffs and quotas on most goods and services. They are narrow cast to achieve the single purpose of returning Crimea and Sevastopol to Ukraine by threatening to turn the correlation of forces in the West's favor. The idea is to frighten Russia with the specter of diminished long-term economic growth and military potential by constraining foreign financed investment and the stream of expected future petroleum revenues, restricting Kremlin access to advanced military and dual-purpose technologies and annoying Putin's cronies. The pain implied stems from thwarting Kremlin ambitions, not immediately pressuring the living standard of the Russian people or fostering prompt regime change.[36]

The hope was that Putin would return Crimea and Sevastopol to Ukraine to further his other ambitions. Policymakers wagered that the benefits of gaining reliable access to foreign financed investment, an expanded stream of expected future petroleum revenues, and access to advanced military and dual-purpose technologies would sway Putin resolve. The West's economic sanctions package was designed in this way to capitalize on Putin's time preference (winning big later as opposed to retaining Crimea and Sevastopol now), leaving open the larger problem of containment. Apparently, EU and American leaders decided that from their perspective a bird in hand (de-annexation of Crimea and Sevastopol) was worth two in the bush (achieving permanent containment). The wisdom of the strategy is moot, but this does not matter in the larger picture

---

[36] Susanne Oxenstierna, "The Western Sanctions against Russia. How Do They Work?" in Steven Rosefielde, ed., *Putin's Russia: Economic, Political and Military Foundations* (Singapore: World Scientific Publishers, 2019).

Sanctions Are of Limited Use   205

because regardless of the rationale, Putin has not budged.[37] Russia remains in firm control of Crimea and Sevastopol seven years after their annexation, and has extended his reach by dominating the Sea of Azov.[38]

Effects on the Russian Economy

EU and American economic sanctions hit Russia when its economy was swooning. The global financial crisis of 2008 reduced Russia's GDP by nearly 8 percent before the imposition of economic sanctions, and recovery up to 2014 was sluggish. Plummeting petroleum prices in 2015 took a heavy toll because national income and the state budget are dependent on oil revenues. Capital flight aggravated matters. It more than doubled in 2014 to $152 billion from $61 billion in 2013.[39] The ruble depreciated by more than 50 percent against the dollar. The combined impact of these shocks culminated in a sharp 3.7 percent contraction in Russia's GDP in 2015.

Plummeting petroleum prices inflicted immense macroeconomic hardship dwarfing any additional pain attributable to the financial component of America's and the European Union's economic sanctions. Embargoes on petroleum equipment, restrictions on advanced military and dual-purpose technologies and annoying Putin's cronies are primarily microeconomic penalties with negligible short-term macroeconomic ramifications.

---

[37] Also, it is worth noting that the strategy chosen may have been the European Union and America's only viable option because various EU member states were averse to stronger punitive measures.

[38] Gwendolyn Sasse, "Crimea Annexation 2.0," *Carnegie Europe* (November 2018), https://carnegieeurope.eu/strategiceurope/77828?utm_source=ctw&utm_medium=email&utm_content=buttonlink&mkt_tok=eyJpIjoiWTJNNE5qQTJNamt6TlR CaSIsInQiOiJKdVwvdndwVFlPTjUzRThEaDZMUVY2ZXNJMlU1Mm0rZW 93UnBKSVluYlZDVVJmenNQcDVVM2hoTFhaSzJSZDZVNnVFamFqY3BB dVJMODJKS2dvTUxHS09vVjJFOXJOWTZuTmQ3dE8rYmM1akM2ejdVbWZC cVN0QnM0cmFGMXhzV1UifQ%3D%3D.

"Similar to Russia's annexation of Crimea in 2014, Western powers have been confined to watching events from the sidelines without finding an effective response — so far."

[39] World Economic Outlook Reports, *IMF*, http://www.imf.org/external/ns/cs.aspx?id=29.

206　*Beleaguered Superpower: Biden's America Adrift*

The West's financial sanctions hit Russia's banking sector hardest. Gazprombank VEB, Bank of Moscow, Rosselkhozbank, VTB Bank, and Sberbank found it difficult to substitute foreign funding for state projects postponed due to falling petroleum revenues.[40] The resulting decline in aggregate effective demand via the multiplier effect in all likelihood exacerbated the decline in GDP triggered by plunging petroleum prices and capital flight.

Putin tried to mitigate these negatives by announcing an amnesty to entice Russians holding assets abroad to repatriate them.[41] He has supported massive money laundering operations to circumvent sanction,[42]

---

[40]Victor Gorshkov, "Finance," in Steven Rosefielde, Masaaki Kuboniwa, Satoshi Mizobata, and Kumiko Haba, eds., *The Unwinding of the Globalist Dream: EU, Russia and China* (Singapore: World Scientific Publishers, 2017): 193–212.

[41]Poslanie (2014) Poslanie Prezidenta RF ot 04.12.2014 (O polozhenii v strane i osnovnykh napravleniyakh vnutrennei i vneshnei politi gosudarstva), 4 December, http://kremlin.ru/acts/bank/39443 (accessed 4 April 2018).

[42]Gabriella Gricius, "The Danske Bank Scandal is the Tip of the Iceberg," *Foreign Policy* (October 2018), https://foreignpolicy.com/2018/10/08/the-danske-bank-scandal-is-the-tip-of-the-iceberg-money-laundering-estonia-denmark-regulation-financial-crime/.

"On Sept. 19, Bruun & Hjejle, general practice attorneys hired by Danske Bank, released a chilling report revealing how over 200 billion euros, about $230 billion, were illegally laundered through its branch in Estonia over a nine-year period. Despite this negligence, the report cleared Borgen and the board of directors of any kind of legal responsibility." "What makes matters more interesting is that 42 employees and eight former employees may have been colluding with criminals to maintain this money laundering activity. According to the report, two of the main perpetrators were the Russian and Azerbaijani "Laundromat" operations." "The Laundromats were criminal financial vehicles that helped to launder money worldwide through shell companies by using fraud, the rigging of state contracts, and customs and tax evasion. The Russian Laundromat worked between 2011 and 2014 by creating 21 "core" companies in the United Kingdom, Cyprus, and New Zealand.

These companies generated fake debt, then obtained a Moldovan court order that required 19 Russian companies pay these debts to Moldova-based Moldindconbank and Latvia-based Trasta Komercbanka. Once out of Russia, the money was transferred all around the world, accounting for 26,746 payments totaling $20.8 billion to 5,140 companies with accounts at 732 banks in 96 countries. At Danske Bank, 177 customers received payments from these core companies." "Then, in 2013, the first whistleblower came forward to disclose that the Estonian branch was knowingly dealing with funds from the family of Russian President Vladimir Putin and the Russian security service, the FSB. However, these claims were not properly investigated and faded into the woodwork."

expanded economic relations with other nations, and established an import substitution program necessitated by declining state reserves and Russia's retaliatory restrictions on EU, American, and Ukrainian consumer goods.[43]

It is econometrically difficult to disentangle the effects of EU and American financial sanctions reliably from other negative factors for 2014–2020. Some have tried, even though Western authorities contend tongue-in-check that financial sanctions are not supposed to harm Russian living standards.

The IMF estimated in 2015 that US and EU Ukraine-related sanctions together with Russia's retaliatory ban on agricultural imports reduced GDP by 1–1.5 percent in the short term. It predicted the loss to be 9 percent in the medium term.[44] Gurvich and Prilepskiy estimated that the effect would be 2.4 percent for 2014–2017.[45] They look at both direct effects, restrictions on the foreign borrowings, and indirect effects.

Both estimates exaggerate the long-term effect of EU and American financial sanctions because with rising petroleum prices up until 2020 the Kremlin acquired the state revenues it needed to fund its programs without recourse to foreign borrowing.[46]

---

[43] Anders Aslund, "Making Sense of Russia's New Draconian Sanctions on Ukraine," *Atlantic Council* (November 2018), http://www.atlanticcouncil.org/blogs/ukrainealert/making-sense-of-russia-s-new-draconian-sanctions-on-ukraine.

On November 1, the Russian government imposed severe economic sanctions on 322 Ukrainian individuals and 68 Ukrainian companies. These are the most extensive sanctions imposed by any country in the tit-for-tat confrontation between Russia and Western countries over Ukraine.

[44] Nelson, Rebecca, "U.S. Sanctions and Russia's Economy," *Congressional Research Service* (February 2017).

[45] Evsey Gurvich and Ilya Prilepskiy, "The Impact of Financial Sanctions on the Russian Economy," *Russian Journal of Economics* 1, no. 4, 2016: 1–27. Evsey Gurvich and Ilya Prilepskiy, "Western Sanctions and Russian Responses: Effects After Three Years" in *Perspectives on the Russian economy under Putin*, eds. Torbjörn Becker and Susanne Oxenstierna (eds.) (London: Routledge, forthcoming).

[46] Gunter Deuber, "Five Years of Financial Market and Banking Sector Sanctions — A 'New Equilibrium' Locally and Internationally," *Russian Analytical Digest*, no. 236 (June 2019), https://css.ethz.ch/content/dam/ethz/special-interest/gess/cis/center-for-securities-studies/pdfs/RAD236.pdf.

"After adjustments following their introduction in 2014, the Western financial market and banking sector sanctions against Russia have produced hardly any lasting negative

208   *Beleaguered Superpower: Biden's America Adrift*

Putin's economic advisors are aware of these and other estimates of the penalty Russia is paying for refusing to rescind the Kremlin's annexation of Crimea and Sevastopol, and he understands the strategic significance of petroleum prices. He also doubtlessly is aware that the West's economic sanctions must reduce Russia's long-term economic and military potential. He may care, but obviously not enough to alter course. Nor is he apt to change his mind soon for economic reasons even if America bans investors purchasing Russia's sovereign debt,[47] because Russian GDP growth resumed its upward trajectory in 2017. The IMF consistently predicted better times thereafter, until Covid-19 wreaked havoc on the global economy. It now estimates the Russia's GDP will decline 5.5 percent in 2020, before resuming its upward course.[48] Much will depend on petroleum prices, which rose to $83 per barrel in 2018 before plummeting to $9 after the supply control agreement Moscow negotiated with Saudi Arabia in 2016 collapsed in March 2020.[49] A new supply control deal

---

market effects in the last 12–24 months. This outcome has to do with some win-win constellations between international investors and the Russian state. These deals work as long as the US does not seek harsh escalations in economic and financial mar-ket sanctions. In addition, Western sanctions even support some of Russia's national economic policy goals indirectly, including consolidation of the banking sector."

[47]Laura Litvan, "Senators Propose Boosting Sanctions on Russia, Including Debt," *Bloomberg* (July 24, 2018), https://www.bloomberg.com/news/articles/2018-07-24/senators-propose-boosting-sanctions-on-russia-including-debt.Marc Jones and Daniel Bases, "For Investors In Russia, U.S. Sanctions Will Not Pack the Same Punch as Before," *Reuters* (August 3, 2018), https://www.reuters.com/article/us-russia-markets-sanctions-analysis/for-investors-in-russia-us-sanctions-will-not-pack-the-same-punch-as-before-idUSKBN1KO0LV.Rebecca Nelson, "Proposals to Impose Sanctions on Russian Sovereign Debt," *Congressional Research Service (CRS)* (August 6, 2018), https://fas.org/sgp/crs/row/IN10946.pdf.

"… it is a move to ban purchases of any new Russian sovereign debt going forward that has raised the most eyebrows. It is considered one of Washington's most potent tools because it would effectively freeze the Russian government out of international borrowing markets, creating a similar scenario to that faced by Argentina for a decade until 2015, following a default and a U.S. court ruling against it. The measure may create fewer problems for Russia though than were faced by Argentina, given Russia has one of the lowest debt levels in the world and nearly half a trillion U.S. dollars in reserves thanks to huge oil and gas export revenues."

[48]https://www.imf.org/external/datamapper/profile/RUS/WEO.

[49]Ruby Lian, Josephine Mason, Rania El Gamal, "Saudi Arabia, Russia Sign Oil Pact, May Limit Output in Future," *Reuters* (September 5, 2016), https://www.reuters.com/

reached the next month pushed the Brent crude price back into the $63 per barrel range by April 2021.[50]

Effects on the Russian Defense

Putin is cognizant that economic sanctions are apt to hamper the Kremlin's military aspirations. Although, Russia's defense industry does not rely heavily on imports from the West; nonetheless, it is dependent on foreign electronic components. Tomas Malmlöf, an FOI expert, reports that as much as 90 percent of electronic components in Russian armaments are of Western origin and that it would take at least six years for Russia to manufacture domestic substitutes.[51] The dependency is particularly high for rocket, unmanned vehicle, civilian aircraft, and space equipment components.[52]

Sanctions moreover played a pivotal role in the cancellation of the delivery of French Mistral-class amphibious assault ships in August 2015, impairing Russia's naval development program. The Kremlin had hoped to benefit considerably from the transfer of Mistral technologies. These losses were painful, but not decisive in Putin's rational choice calculus.

Restraining Effects of Economic Sanctions

Nothing, including economic sanctions has persuaded Putin to rescind Russia's annexation of Crimea and Sevastopol. He is strengthening Russian naval power in the Sea of Azov.[53] Western leaders however are not disheartened. They had to do something, and can always claim that

---

article/us-g20-china-saudi-russia-oil-idUSKCN11B0UF. Javier Blas, Salma El Wardany, and Grant Smith, "Saudi Arabia and Russia End their Oil-Price War with Output Cut Agreement," (April 9, 2020), https://www.worldoil.com/news/2020/4/9/saudi-arabia-and-russia-end-their-oil-price-war-with-output-cut-agreement.

[50] https://markets.businessinsider.com/commodities/oil-price.

[51] Tomas Malmlöf, "A Case Study of Russo-Ukrainian Defense Industrial Cooperation: Russian Dilemmas," *Journal of Slavic Military Studies* 29, 2016: 1–22.

[52] Vladimir Faltsman, "Importozameshchenie v TEK i OPK," *Voprosy Ekonomik*, 1, 2015: 116–124.

[53] Bruce Jones, "Russia pressures Ukraine with naval build-up in Sea of Azov," *Jane's Defense Weekly* (June 2018), https://janes.ihs.com/Janes/Display/FG_952221-JDW. Stephen Blank, "Russia's Attack on Ukraine is an Act of War," *The Hill* (December 3,

210   *Beleaguered Superpower: Biden's America Adrift*

success awaits them just around the corner, and that economic sanctions deterred Putin from taking other offensive actions.

These sorts of consolations may be comforting, but have little merit. The fact that Putin could have conquered and annexed all of Novorossiya, but did not attempt it does not prove that Western economic sanctions deterred him.[54] He may have been prudently biding his time.

There always are excuses; nonetheless, the record is clear. There is no compelling basis for believing that Western economic sanctions are a reliable tool for disciplining authoritarian misbehavior of powerful states in the short term and deterring the expansion of spheres of influence over the longer haul. Economic sanctions will not stop Moscow from meddling in Western politics. Responsible policymaker must prepare for

---

2018), https://thehill.com/opinion/international/419534-russias-attack-on-ukraine-is-an-act-of-war.

"By any standard, Russia's attack upon Ukrainian vessels in the Black Sea is an act of war.

The pretext for this step is to strengthen the security of the newly-constructed Kerch bridge, linking occupied Crimea with southern Russia, defence responsibility for which was recently devolved to Russia's National Guard internal military force." "The build-up, which as part of a plan may continue, provides Russia with a wide new range of capabilities in the shallow Sea of Azov. With Moscow's control of the Kerch Strait, Ukraine has little or no opportunity to reinforce, or even fully maintain, its maritime presence in the enclosed waters. The developments make Ukraine's 375 km southern coastline between Mariupol and annexed Crimea and its coastal shipping increasingly vulnerable."

Russian President Vladimir Putin ordered the Nov. 25 incident that occurred in the Black Sea (not in the Russian-held Kerch Strait, as Moscow claims). This operation also climaxed a long series of Russian abuses: seizure of Crimea and energy facilities of its coast, claiming that Crimea, the Sea of Azov and the Kerch Strait are exclusively Russian waters, building a bridge over the strait deliberately to impede Ukrainian commerce in the Sea of Azov, forcibly inspecting and boarding Ukrainian ships, blockading the Ukrainian coast — and now ramming, firing upon and taking prisoners off of Ukrainian ships in international waters." "Ukraine could lease ports on the Black Sea and even in the Sea of Azov to the U.S. while we lend them military equipment they need for air, naval, and ground warfare. The U.S. or NATO naval vessels could then stay at those ports for as long as necessary without bringing Ukraine formally into NATO. It would greatly diminish the chance of Russian attack if those forces patrolled the Black Sea and the Sea of Azov."

[54] Stanislav Secrieru, "Have Sanctions Changed Russia's Behaviour in Ukraine," in Iana Dreyer and Jose Leugno-Cabrera, ed., *On Target? EU Sanctions as Security Policy Tools* (Paris: ISS, 2015): 39–47. Edward H. Christie, "The Design and Impact of Western Economic Sanctions," *The RUSI Journal* 161, no. 3, June/July 2016: 52–64.

Sanctions Are of Limited Use 211

the contingency that retaliatory measures of any plausible scope and harshness will be insufficient to discipline Eastern authoritarians.[55]

Fair Trade, Economic Warfare, and Security

America began imposing economic sanctions on China from March 22, 2018 with a double purpose.[56] The Trump administration said that it sought to restore the fairness of the trade relationship and enhance US national security. It wanted to protect America's military technological edge in the Asia Pacific, by forcing Beijing to cease strong-arming Western firms into transferring their technologies as a *quid pro quo* for doing business in China, and to halt cyber-espionage and military provocations in the South China Sea. Trump also insisted that Beijing honor liberalization and democratization commitments made in 2001 when China joined the World Trade Organization (WTO) requiring the phased elimination of anti-competitive state trading practices. The storm had been brewing for more than a decade.[57]

Xi Jinping for obvious reasons preferred the *status quo*. It allowed Beijing to continue reaping gains from technology transfer and protectionism without a *quid pro quo*. If Washington failed to act, China's misbehavior wound persist. This left the West with two options. It could grin and bear China's unfair state trading, coerced technology transfers and cyber-security provocations, or it could retaliate.

The progressive and liberal mindsets encouraged patience, presuming that consciousness raising eventually would lead Beijing to do the right thing. Some Obama-style progressives even felt that China's unequal benefits are righteous compensation for centuries of Western imperialism (restorative justice).

---

[55] Cf. *Overextending and Unbalancing Russia*, *RAND* (May 2019).

[56] Benjamin Haas, Ben Jacobs, and Edward Helmore, "US Imposes Sanctions On China, Stoking Fears of Trade War," *Guardian* (March 22, 2018), https://www.theguardian.com/world/2018/mar/22/china-us-sanctions-trade-war.

[57] Derek Scissors, "Sino-American Trade: We Know Where This Is Headed," *AEI* (April 2018), http://www.aei.org/publication/sino-american-trade-we-know-where-this-is-headed/?mkt_tok=eyJpIjoiWVdJeVpETXlOV1U0WmpRNSIsInQiOiJCNGs0Szl3bk U3Y Vk3bzA5bjR4QXd3TW9iMnAxV3JLcjU5bXliYmFCYzdrODNvdDRDeXBrN2dw U3BPd2E0UStxZ1hKOUI0WIl0RGd1TlM0RVZKUDRNd09RSnpycmxqc0RLSFB4c3 I5Wkt4VlpjZ1J5VWIxWnRRTUdBSDJaTzB2diJ9.

212 *Beleaguered Superpower: Biden's America Adrift*

They opposed sanctions against China, characterizing them as instruments of "economic war," even though Beijing's exertion of state trading power is analogous to domestic violence against wives willing to bear abuse. They criticized tariffs, quotas, and financial restrictions that the Trump administration imposed on Beijing as belligerent, irrational and counter-productive. Many multinational corporations concerned solely with their commercial profits, concurred.[58]

No one denied that China receives unfair benefits from managed anti-competitive state trading, but progressives, liberals, and conservatives considered disciplinary sanctions as a greater evil because they would prevent Western businesses from maximizing profits under existing WTO and Chinese rules. Wall Street, *laissez-faire* Republicans, and Democratic Party progressive-liberals concurred that America was better off accepting an unequal trade regime to avoid losing the gains from trade that the West already enjoyed because the losses are born by American workers.

Trump however counter-contended that if disciplinary sanctions persuaded Beijing to honor its WTO liberalization pledge, China and America would both be better off. The volume of mutually profitable trade would increase. American workers would gain, and coerced technology transfers and cyber piracy would cease. Trump's populist approach was Pareto superior because it assured that competition occurs on a level playing field. His critics preferred a Pareto inferior strategy, even though they concealed this behind a fog of pro-competitive rhetoric. Progressives and some liberals wanted to aid China. Other liberals and conservatives

---

[58]MacKenzie Eaglen, "What If the Pentagon Skipped 5G?," *Defense One* (May 2020), https://www.defenseone.com/ideas/2020/05/what-if-pentagon-skipped-5g/165277/?oref=d-river&mkt_tok=eyJpIjoiTURNM09EY3lNek5oTkRGaiIsInQiOiJGUTZzU0NzS3dHMmQrWEJ0SjR4ZVpSbWowWE4yZXJJcFBudVhTN3NUcGw5aE44cytxSUNjOW5NSzJyQld4Wlc5dFVyTlpFV3BBQUNkSzNHY0UrRGFsMlVQYWZaNHZVaUhpd0JRUnIxM0RhTHozeXdGeG9GdFVmY0ViTWVcL0FmNVMifQ%3D%3D.

"Against DoD objections, the FCC approved a license modification for Ligado Networks to establish a new 5G communications service last month. And while some Trump administration senior officials hailed this as a boon to U.S. firms vying to build the world's 5G networks, others rightly argue that it imperils national security."

This may come as some surprise. After all, the White House and Pentagon have loudly warned allies in recent years that information passing through 5G networking gear made by Huawei, the Chinese telecom giant, might be forwarded to Beijing's intelligence agencies.

Sanctions Are of Limited Use   213

on behalf of some American businesses wanted to avoid a confrontation that might curb Chinese discriminatory trade practices at their expense.

The merit of these conflicting positions depends on the expected benefit-cost ratio of the WTO compliance battle, and Washington's attitude toward tolerating abuse. There is ample room for honorable disagreement about the expected benefit-cost ratio of tolerating trade discrimination or resisting it on pragmatic grounds, which makes it difficult to form a consensus about judicious disciplinary sanctions, but just as in the case of domestic violence, the right decision more often than not is to resist abuse, especially when it endangers security.

Trump's allegations against Chinese state trading, military industrial cyber-espionage, and security provocations were supported in multiple sources (including reports by the Japanese government), but relied heavily on the March 2018 Section 301 Report,[59] and the findings of the 2013 and 2017 independent Commission on the Theft of American Intellectual Property.[60] The later estimated that China had "stolen" hundreds of billions of dollars-worth of American intellectual property.[61] Furthermore, the Commission's authors contended, "Chinese agents have gone after the United States' most significant weapons, such as the F-35 Lightning, the Aegis Combat System and the Patriot missile system; illegally exported unmanned underwater vehicles and thermal-imaging cameras; and stolen documents related to the B-52 bomber, the Delta IV rocket, the F-15 fighter and even the Space Shuttle."[62]

---

[59] "Section 301 Report into China's Acts, Policies, and Practices Related to Technology Transfer, Intellectual Property, and Innovation," *Office of the United States Trade Representative*, https://ustr.gov/about-us/policy-offices/press-office/press-releases/2018/march/section-301-report-chinas-acts.

[60] "IP Commission Report, The Theft of American Intellectual Property: Reassessments of the Challenge and United States Policy, Update," *National Bureau of Asian Research* (February 2017), http://ipcommission.org/report/IP_Commission_Report_Update_2017.pdf.

[61] Claude Barfield, "Renewed Chinese Cyberespionage: Time for the US to Act," *AEI* (April 2018), http://www.aei.org/publication/renewed-chinese-cyberespionage-time-for-the-us-to-act/?mkt_tok=eyJpIjoiT1RZeVlqWm1aVEptWmpSaSIsInQiOiJzY0ZmRklyN Eg5Tm9SM2lWOFZ6ZE1ES3huaWhPSUNZMDNcL1FTeGQweXlFN2FoZ0ZIM0k1c W8xTXJcL3FcLzlBUFlWWkNvVFpjVVhxK0prNitYeVwvaHNBblY5REpaZGg0b 2NaZ0VvZDBUQkJrWjFRc1U1dEtLZFNybCtYc2Z3eHZzWmYifQ%3D%3D.

[62] Dennis C. Blair and Keith Alexander, "China's Intellectual Property Theft Must Stop," *Wall Street Journal*, Op-ed (August 2017), https://www.nytimes.com/2017/08/15/opinion/china-us-intellectual-property-trump.html.

214　*Beleaguered Superpower: Biden's America Adrift*

The Department of Justice moreover has indicted Jinhua for conspiring to steal vital core intellectual property from Micron, with an estimated worth of almost $9 billion. It asserts that the Chinese participated in a five-year campaign (2010–2015) against US aerospace, and turbine manufacturers. In pursuit of their espionage goals, they "conducted sustained computer intrusions into 13 companies to find technical information that would allow a state-owned Chinese aerospace firm to design its own jetliner and an accompanying turbofan engine."[63]

The Trump administration decided to begin redressing these diverse grievances in March 2018 invoking section 301 of the US Trade Act of 1974 and levying restrictions on investment and tariffs on $60 billion worth of products.[64] It imposed tariffs of 25 percent on steel and 10 percent on aluminum aimed primarily at China.

Beijing swiftly retaliated levying a 25 percent tariff on $16 billion of goods including passenger cars and motorcycles.[65] On September 24, 2018, the US applied 10 percent tariffs to $200 billion more imports from China. The rate rose to 25 percent on January 1, 2019.[66] This tit-for-tat response and counter-response imposed significant material (deadweight inefficiency) losses on both nations. The phenomenon of escalating reciprocal sanctions resembles "war" because winning the WTO compliance

---

[63]Claude Barfield, "The Dual Goals of the Trump Administration's New Attack on Chinese Intellectual Property Theft," *AEI* (November 2018), www.aei.org/publication/the-dual-goals-of-the-trump-administrations-new-attack-on-chinese-intellectual-property-theft/?mkt_tok=eyJpIjoiTVRrek9EVTJaR1JtWldJMiIsInQiOiJuV0JDNGFsSEh0aHVpa ENNZmtpODkxWTVNZnZZeHgyZ0M1enJPRWw1Y2dPaDh4YVpZWjE5Y 1BUY3ZnTHFJWSsrNTNrbkxmYjFwU2lkRjRneGlJc0ZDS3p2ZTcxd1pMcnJu clJKR2laVm8yT3pWQlZ2T3dpeHkwUnpOcGJGTkxIWSJ9.

[64]Benjamin Haas, Ben Jacobs, and Edward Helmore, "US Imposes Sanctions on China, Stoking Fears of Trade War," *Guardian* (March 22, 2018), https://www.theguardian.com/world/2018/mar/22/china-us-sanctions-trade-war.

[65]Fred Imbret, "China Slaps 25% Tariffs on $16 Billion Worth of US Goods," *CNBC* (August 8, 2018), https://www.cnbc.com/2018/08/08/china-announces-25percent-tariffs-on-16-billion-worth-of-us-goods-including.html.

[66]Derek Scissors, "China Tariffs: Wrong Weapons, Right Result?" *AEI* (September 2018), http://www.aei.org/publication/china-tariffs-wrong-weapons-right-result/?mkt_tok=eyJpIjoiTWpVd1p qQmpPR0l6T0RZMSIsInQiOiJPbDE3VTZUcm1LMEdhYk5VWndSTFMxcHFiYm hndWYzWVwvWHFoKzhtZFNEc29wOUNaNERkMWtzRGF6dFhSUWgzMVlVSk k4TmNKOGhnN3NYTE1hYmJWcTlsb1VtdDlXVW9LREJiNHpuOGxMd3ZOa1FhTFRpYmt 3OEtPdkhMYkZOXC9rIn0%3D.

Sanctions Are of Limited Use 215

battle depends on both sides ability to bear losses (value subtracted), but the term "war" is misleading. Washington and Beijing did not try to beggar or vanquish each other. Both only want to improve their economic and security positions by controlling the rules of engagement.

The Trump administration sought to fix fair terms of trade including the elimination of Chinese business subsidies (China's "Made in China 2025" plan),[67] reduce coerced technology transfer, restrain cyber theft, and improve national security in accordance with the terms of China 2001 admission to the WTO. It did not seek conquest, tribute, or reparations. These purposes are sound, and although hardly failsafe, the wisest course for America was experimenting with punitive sanctions. It tried, but the Department of Commerce's export control regime has been dismal.[68]

---

[67]Claude Barfield, "The Dual Goals of the Trump Administration's New Attack on Chinese Intellectual Property Theft," *AEI* (November 2018), www.aei.org/publication/the-dual-goals-of-the-trump-administrations-new-attack-on-chinese-intellectual-property-theft/?mkt_tok=eyJpIjoiTVRrek9EVTJaR1JtWldJMiIsInQiOiJuV0JDNGFsSEh0aHVpaENNZmtpODkxWTVNZnZZeHgyZ0M1enJPRWw1Y2dPaDh4YVpZWjE5Y1BUY3ZnTHFJWSsrNTNrbkxmYjFwU2lkRjRneGlJc0ZDS3p2ZTcxd1pMcnJuclJKR2laVm8yT3pWQlZ2T3dpeHkwUnpOcGJGTkxIWSJ9.

[68]Derek Scissors, "The Department of Commerce Ignores Congress," *AEI* (August 2020), https://www.aei.org/foreign-and-defense-policy/the-department-of-commerce-ignores-congress/?mkt_tok=eyJpIjoiTW1ReVpqQmxPVFppWkRaaSIsInQiOiJvZGRmUUFsS1wvR2hmWXZcL0hpUlE5YTNjU1FXT25hWmF2SEJBclVcL1JDdm83Y3FncExpemJNMGF3Sjl3QmNlT3BpdVh5UmtBS3NnT3Npdm1pb0hYR2hXU29HMUFUUEtpZFpzNzFBTUlqaHI3UEhmSllXbmRuQlZrZ1p3a0U4XC8yYkQifQ%3D%3D.

"This week, Commerce finally remarked on an important element of export control implementation. There's no action. It's a notice for future action and solicitation of public comment in 60 days, when industry has already lobbied Commerce for two years. Then Commerce will take more time to formulate a rule and to implement it, finally reaching its ultimate goal: a new administration and Congress in 2021 and possible export control reset."

When this endless process started, I was a naïve, fresh-faced China analyst expecting actual regulations. The scope of export control coverage would be given, allowing calculation of how much money would be affected (versus industry hysterics). Would there be obvious flaws, as with other Commerce actions? China's likely response could be evaluated. But Commerce has still published almost nothing to assess, not even definitions of the technology involved.

216　*Beleaguered Superpower: Biden's America Adrift*

The United States was compelled to deal with the WTO compliance, coerced technology transfer, and cyber theft issues in the final analysis because the progressive and liberal faith in the curative economic and security powers of globalization did not pan out despite Xi Jinping's promises to Barack Obama in 2015 to end China's abusive trading practices.[69] China has refused to subordinate itself to America's supranational order, seizing the day instead to become a formidable authoritarian economic and military rival.[70]

Hedging

America can fend off foreign aggression by refurbishing Huntington's ideal of the West. An attractive, vibrant, prosperous, well-functioning, open, just, democratic society that serves as a beacon on the hill will increase the solidarity of allies and hinder the machinations of Eastern authoritarians. This requires a progressive and liberal epiphany unachievable any time soon; however, America can still enhance its and the planet's security by persuading allies to hedge; that is, to limit participation in entangling projects.

Nord Stream 1 and 2 illustrate the principle. Nord Stream 1 is an offshore natural gas pipeline from Vyborg in the Russian Federation to Greifswald in Germany owned and operated by Nord Stream AG

---

[69]Claude Barfield, "The Dual Goals of the Trump Administration's New Attack on Chinese Intellectual Property Theft," *AEI* (November 2018), www.aei.org/publication/the-dual-goals-of-the-trump-administrations-new-attack-on-chinese-intellectual-property-theft/?mkt_tok=eyJpIjoiTVRrek9EVTJaR1JtWldJMiIsInQiOiJuV0JDNGFsSEh0aHVpa ENNZmtpODkxWTVNZnZZeHgyZ0M1enJPRWw1Y2dPaDh4YVpZWjE5Y 1BUY3ZnTH FJWSsrNTNrbkxmYjFwU2lkRjRneGlJc0ZDS3p2ZTcxd1pMcnJuclJKR2l aVm8yT3pWQlZ2T3dpeHkwUnpOcGJGTkxIWSJ9.

"Chinese President Xi Jinping promised President Barack Obama that, henceforth, the Chinese government would not conduct economic espionage to pass IP and trade secrets along to Chinese companies. Although Chinese economic espionage decreased in the following months, over the past two years it has picked up again, at a rapid pace (as stated by Sessions) — with government or government-directed groups using increasingly sophisticated cyberespionage techniques."

[70]For a Chinese perspective on the trade issue see "China Economic Transition," *Higher Education Press* 1, no. 2 (September 2018), http://journal.hep.com.cn/cet/EN/volumn/volumn_3317.shtml.

Sanctions Are of Limited Use   217

(50 percent owned by Gazprom, Russia's state-owned energy company). The project includes two parallel lines. The first line commenced operation November 2011; the second line October 2012. The two lines together traverse 1,222 kilometers, making Nord Stream 1 the longest sub-sea pipeline in the world, with an annual capacity of 55 billion cubic meters. Nord Stream 2 is a supplementary venture of Gazprom, half financed by five European companies: Engie (France), OMV (Austria), Shell (Netherlands/UK), Uniper (Germany), and Wintershall (Germany). It is currently under construction. Nord Stream 2 will double the capacity of the Nord Stream system to 110 billion cubic meters of natural gas.

Europe's dependency on Russian natural gas is sure to increase when Nord Stream 2 is completed, but the precise amount is contingent on the reduction of Russia natural gas deliveries from other existing transmission channels. Russia supplied 37 percent of Europe's natural gas imports in 2017, up 5 percent from the previous year. The figure for 2020 could be much higher, barring a significant Covid-19 disruption.[71]

Natural gas is not Europe's sole source of energy. It has abundant supplies of coal, nuclear energy, petroleum, liquefied natural gas, and renewables. Russia moreover is not Europe's only natural gas supplier. In 2012, Norway accounted for about 31 percent of all the EU's natural gas imports. Europe is eyeing the possibilities of obtaining natural gas from Azerbaijan via a South Stream pipeline.

Nonetheless, the Oxford Institute for Energy Studies forecasts that natural gas will soon be "king" in Europe because of environmentalist opposition to coal and nuclear energy.[72] It therefore is reasonable to suppose that Nord Stream 2 will make Europe more susceptible to Kremlin political pressure.

The Trump administration, European Commission and President of the European Council, Poland, the Baltic States, Ukraine, and many members of Congress argued that Nord Stream 2 would enable Russia to leverage its influence over Germany and others. Critics also contended that Nord Stream 2 could leave some countries more vulnerable to supply

---

[71] Paul Belkin, Michael Ratner, and Cory Welt, "Nord Stream 2: A Geopolitical Lightning Rod," *Congressional Research Service* (August 2018), https://fas.org/sgp/crs/row/IF10943.pdf.

[72] Dave Keating, "In Europe, Gas is King," *Forbes* (April 2018), https://www.forbes.com/sites/davekeating/2018/04/30/in-europe-gas-is-king/#6dbdaaf367ad.

218 *Beleaguered Superpower: Biden's America Adrift*

cutoffs or Russian price manipulation. They added that by reducing the transit of Russian gas through Ukraine, Nord Stream 2 could deprive Ukraine of revenue and reduce its importance to Russia as a transit state. It is also ironic that while America and the EU impose sanctions on Russian energy producers to discipline Kremlin misbehavior in Ukraine, momentum favors making Russian gas king of the European mountain despite its adverse impact on Kiev.

Should the West hedge its national security bets by torpedoing Nord Stream 2, changing Europe's energy mix in favor of coal, nuclear energy, LNG, and renewables, or develop contingency plans mitigating the force of the Kremlin's natural gas card?[73] The answer depends on the threat. If it seems likely that hot war is imminent, the West should try to deter Moscow by canceling the project. If the threat is real, but not pressing, the European Union should hedge by tilting the policy balance away from environmentalism and toward European security. Emergency contingency plans should always be at the ready.

Hedging is a rational choice option, but less useful than it should be because American and EU societies undervalue national and global security. In the Nord Stream 2 case, environmentalists abhor coal and nuclear energy and prefer not to substitute American shale oil based LNG for Nord Stream 2 natural gas supplies. They find it comfortable to suppose that Kremlin machinations are much to do about nothing, an attitude that

---

[73]Tim Daiss, "Russia Just Won Big In The European Gas War," *Oilprice.com*, May 28, 2018.

The European were able to obtain fair pricing concessions of Eastern Europe from Gazprom as a quid pro quo for moving forward with Nord Stream 2.

"Last week, Gazprom, the world's largest gas producer, and the European Commission resolved a seven-year anti-trust dispute after the Russian state-controlled energy giant agreed to change its operations in central and Eastern Europe. Per terms of the deal that was reached on Thursday, Gazprom will be banned from imposing restrictions on how its customers in central and Eastern Europe use gas. Meanwhile, Bulgaria, the Czech Republic, Estonia, Hungary, Latvia, Lithuania, Poland and Slovakia will no longer be banned from exporting gas to another country. These countries originally sought to remedy over pricing problems for Russian gas. Going forward, customers in Bulgaria, Estonia, Latvia, Lithuania and Poland have the right to demand a price in line with those in Germany and the Netherlands. The deal has teeth since these customers can take their complaints to an EU arbitration body if Gazprom fails to live up to terms of the new settlement."

Sanctions Are of Limited Use 219

takes hedging for practical purposes off the table, even if they are wrong. Hedging may seem like an effective tool, but it is unlikely to work because progressive environmentalists are loath to amend their environmental priorities.

The Obama–Biden administration strongly supported Nord Stream 2. Biden publicly stated that he now strongly opposed it and would impose sanctions on insurance and certification authorities in late November 2020,[74] but Germany approved the project's completion on December 10, 2020 presumably believing that Biden had reversed himself.[75]

Intimidation

Leaders from time to time supplement economic sanctions and hedging with military intimidation. Vladimir Putin and Kim Jong-un are not bashful about raising the specter of nuclear war to chasten their adversaries. Western politicians in the post-war era have been more self-restrained, but the Trump administration was inclined to threaten China aggressively with the possibility of grievous economic harm, and Russia with a preemptive strike on its cruise missiles.[76]

---

[74]"Joe Biden Stands Against Construction of Nord Stream 2," *112 Ukraine* (November 19, 2020). https://112.international/politics/joe-biden-stands-against-construction-of-nord-stream-2-56623.html

[75]"Gazprom Restarts Construction on Controversial Nord Stream 2 Pipeline U.S. Sanctions had Frozen Work on the Underwater Pipe Linking Russia and Germany or Almost a Year," AFP (December 11, 2020), https://www.themoscowtimes.com/2020/12/11/gazprom-restarts-construction-on-controversial-nord-stream-2-pipeline-a72336.

[76]Robin Emmott, "U.S. Would Destroy Banned Russian Warheads if Necessary: NATO Envoy," *Reuters* (October 2, 2018), https://www.reuters.com/article/us-usa-nuclear-russia/us-would-destroy-banned-russian-warheads-if-necessary-nato-envoy-idUSKCN1M C1J6?mkt_tok=eyJpIjoiWVRnMFpqYzVPR1kxT1RObCIsInQiOiJWMzFsO E9cL2d6b0c2YnF3M01xWkpiY1hcL2ZRQlJYYjg5Qm1zcnBkbEZrd0p ZWFwvQ2xXQjlWRk1NeTVodllDNXNUOWZmRmhlODZUdE9lV1kwYW5lV VRHMU1CeitNdXZiRnBIRXcwNlpoQ2dKdk02dXpXUEloRHBBLOUN4dTJ ROXJTZCJ9.

"Russia: U.S. Comments on Possible Destruction of Russian Warheads are Dangerous," *TASS* (October 2, 2018), https://www.reuters.com/article/us-usa-nuclear-russia-ministry/russia-u-s-comments-on-possible-destruction-of-russian-warheads-are-dangerous-tass-idUSKCN1MC29J.

220 *Beleaguered Superpower: Biden's America Adrift*

There sometimes is a place for intimidation tactics in disciplining rogue actors,[77] but both the gains and costs too often are nebulous.

"The United States believes Russia is developing a ground-launched system in breach of a Cold War treaty that could allow Russia to launch a nuclear strike on Europe at short notice, but Moscow has consistently denied any such violation. U.S. ambassador to NATO Kay Bailey Hutchison said Washington remained committed to a diplomatic solution but was prepared to consider a military strike if development of the medium-range system continued."

[77]Donald Trump and Tony Schwartz, *The Art of the Deal* (New York: Random House, 1987).

Chapter 10

Assistance Can Be Too Costly

Economic enticements offer policymakers an alternative to disciplinary economic sanctions. Sanctions are sticks. Economic enticements are carrots. Economic enticements may influence unruly behavior alone, or together with sticks. Not all economic enticements are alike. They run the gamut from cordial entertainment to lavish bribes. If sanctions fail to persuade Russia to rescind its annexation of Crimea and Sevastopol, China to halt its South China Sea arms buildup, North Korea to denuclearize, Iran to become good neighbors, perhaps economic assistance can tip the scales.

American and EU policymakers have tried. Russia was the beneficiary of a high profile "Grand Bargain" overseen by Vice President Al Gore that held out the lure of Marshall Plan scale economic assistance in return for Boris Yeltsin's pledge to transform the post-Soviet space into a bastion of democratic free enterprise.[1] Jiang Zemin's China gained membership to the World Trade Organization (WTO) on generous terms. William Jefferson Clinton gave North Korea 500,000 tons of oil a year and $4 billion toward the construction of a light-water reactor capable of producing nuclear energy (but no nuclear weapons) in exchange for Pyongyang false promise to abandon its the nuclear development

---

[1] Graham Allison and Robert Blackwill, "America's Stake in the Soviet Future," *Foreign Affairs* (Summer 1991): 77–97. Steven Rosefielde, "What is Wrong with Plans to Aid the CIS," *Orbis* 37, no. 3, Summer 1993: 353–363. Steven Rosefielde, "The Grand Bargain: Underwriting Catastroika," *Global Affairs* (Winter 1992): 15–35. The Soviet Union refused to accept the strings that came attached to Marshall Plan aid in 1947.

222   Beleaguered Superpower: Biden's America Adrift

program.[2] He also gave more than $3 million to Iran for similar reasons.[3]

Russia, China, North Korea, and Iran all took the money, but remained unruly actors. They did not succumb to the West's blandishments, and did not honor their pledges. The compliance mechanisms installed to prevent this failed too. Russia and China did not transition to democratic free enterprise; North Korea and Iran did not forsake their nuclear ambitions.

Aid recipients often do not want to change their behavior and economic enticements seldom seem to be enough to bind them to their word. Nations like Estonia, Latvia, and Lithuania that wanted to rejoin the West after forced annexation by the Soviet Union in 1940 gladly accepted Western assistance, and fulfilled their commitments, but these exceptions proved the rule. The Baltic States wanted to align with the West and would have done so without enticements. Rogue actors more often than not choose a different path. They accept the largesse, but ignore what they consider pro-forma conditionality. As one high Soviet official put it, "We are not cheating you. You are compelled to offer bribes for domestic political reasons, and we are just accommodating you by accepting the gifts!"[4]

Russia provides a classic example of the difficulties entailed in trying to entice recalcitrant great powers to integrate with the West. Boris Yeltsin's Russia was ripe for radical transition and the "Grand Bargain" sought to assist him.

Yeltsin loathed the Soviet Communist Party because it exiled him to the hinterland under humiliating circumstances from the position of First Party Secretary of Moscow in November 1987, and he was justifiably chary of the Kremlin power services (*siloviki*). When he subsequently assumed the presidency of post-Soviet Russia, Yeltsin quickly stripped the Russian Communist Party of its privileged status, cut military spending

---

[2] Sofia Lotto Persio, "Did the U.S. Really Pay North Korea 'Extortion Money' for 25 Years? Fact-Checking Trump's Tweet," *Newsweek* (August 2017), http://www.news week.com/did-us-really-pay-north-korea-extortion-money-25-years-fact-checking-trumps-657177. According to a 2014 report from the Congressional Research Service, between 1995 and 2008, the United States provided North Korea with more than $1.3 billion in aid: slightly more than 50 percent for food and about 40 percent for energy assistance.
[3] https://borgenproject.org/u-s-benefits-from-foreign-aid-to-iran/.
[4] Vitaly Shykov, private conversation.

Assistance Can Be Too Costly 223

by ninety percent, and tamed the secret police (KGB rechristened FSB). He endorsed the sovereignty of the post-Soviet newly independent states, embraced democratization, radical market economic transition (*perek-hod*), and sought deep integration into the global community. Yeltsin for a time even considered membership in the European Union.

Many of his economic and political actions matched his words. He denationalized most the means of production, transforming state assets into both freehold and leasehold property. He abandoned price controls, floated the ruble in the foreign exchange market, encouraged competition among small and medium size enterprises, welcomed direct foreign investment, and free labor mobility at home and abroad. Neoclassical microeconomic and macroeconomic theory displaced Marxist economics in Russia's academia. Yeltsin's chief economic advisor, Prime Minister Yegor Gaidar energetically oversaw transition in close collaboration with the World Bank, International Monetary Fund (IMF), the European Bank for Reconstruction and Development, and the G-8.[5]

Yeltsin did all these things of his own accord,[6] cheered on and assisted by Western carrots. America, the European Union, and G-7 gave Russia billions of dollars in foreign assistance, generous technical advice, and encouraged direct Western corporate investment. Ron Childress hand delivered $50 million to Yeltsin to improve the organization of Russia White House.[7] President Clinton tasked Vice President Al Gore to oversee America's assistance effort to Russia (the "Gore–Chernomyrdin Commission").[8] It is difficult to imagine a more propitious scenario for

---

[5]Steven Rosefielde and Stefan Hedlund, *Russia Since 1980* (Cambridge: Cambridge University Press, 2009); Yegor Gaidar and Karl Otto Pohl, *Russian Reform* (Cambridge: MIT Press, 1995). Sergei Vasiliev and Yegor Gaidar, *Ten Years of Russian Economic Reform* (London: Centre for Research into Post-Communist Economies, 1999). Yegor Gaidar, *The Economics of Russian Transition* (Cambridge: MIT Press, 2003).

[6]Grigori Yavlinski, Boris Fedorov, Stanislav Shatalin, Nikolai Petrakov, and Sergei Aleksashenko, *500 Days: Transition to the Market* (London: St. Martin's Press, 1991).

[7]Ron Childress, "'The Children's Crusade' — Namely the Needless American 'Humanitarian' Assistance to Post-Soviet Russia," *American Association for the Advancement of Slavic Studies* (September 1998).

[8]The Gore–Chernomyrdin Commission, or U.S.–Russian Joint Commission on Economic and Technological Cooperation, was a United States and Russian Joint Commission developed to increase cooperation between the two countries in several different areas. The Commission was developed by the United States' President Bill Clinton and Russian President Boris Yeltsin at a summit in Vancouver in April 1993.

224 *Beleaguered Superpower: Biden's America Adrift*

permanently winning a former adversary to the West's side. There were great expectations. Anders Aslund declared as early as 1995 that Russia had become a market economy.[9] Pundits were enthusiastic about Russian democratization, the eradication of structural militarization, the taming of the FSB, and Moscow's return to its "common European home," until Crimea's annexation punctured the balloon in March 2014. What went wrong?

The "Grand Bargain" fizzled for two broad reasons. It went against the grain of Russia's Muscovite culture, and the Clinton administration including Strobe Talbott botched the transition process by betting on "shock therapy."

Russia has been an authoritarian patrimonial society for more than a millennium, starting in Kievan Rus under Princess Olga (925–969). It took on its canonical form under Ivan the Great (1440–1505) and Ivan the Terrible (1530–1584). The key features of the Muscovite paradigm are absolutism and rent granting. The tsar is the law. His authority transcends constitutions, administrative law, and morality (Russian Orthodox Church). He is *de facto* owner of all he surveys and his people are obedient to his authority. Those in his inner circle are "servitors." They derive their wealth and power from grants of income generating assets (patrimonialism) revocable at the tsar's sufferance in return for taxes and political support. This dependency and foreknowledge that those who lose the tsar's favor swiftly become outcasts solidifies the dependency. Muscovite society ostracizes deposed servitors making it difficult to retaliate against the throne. The secret police (Okhrana, Cheka, NKVD, KGB, and FSB) and military repress and terrorize those suspected of disloyalty.

Muscovite rent-granting systems both of the tsarist and post-tsarist types may not be as harsh as they were under Peter the Great and Stalin (authoritarian, martial, police states), or as mild as Putin's regime is today. They are compatible with markets and plans. Their key features are the supreme leader's (*vozhd*) absolute authority behind the veil of representative institutions, the subordination of servitors and markets, the privileged position of the secret police and the military, nationalism and a penchant for imperial power.

The Muscovite tradition allowed Boris Yeltsin to pose as a democrat, a proponent of a competitive market economy, and champion of an open

---

[9]Anders Aslund, *How Russia Became a Market Economy* (Washington: Brookings Institution Press, 1995).

civil society founded on the rule of law, while acting like a Catherine the Great style "liberal" Muscovite ruler. However, when push came to shove, Yeltsin shuttered parliament, and imposed an authoritarian constitution in 1993. He granted benefices to his servitors, "oligarchs" who ran the economic commanding heights in return for political support and financial favors. He held the *siloviki* at bay, but also preserved the entire Soviet military industrial complex intact. Yeltsin chose Vladimir Putin, head of the FSB to be his successor.

Clinton Administration "Grand Bargainers" were aware of these Muscovite tendencies,[10] but did not take them to heart. They refused to appreciate that Muscovy would reinvent itself, and failed to take timely preventative action, preferring to construe Yeltsin's misbehaviors as misdemeanors, bumps on the road to democratic free enterprise and globalization under American tutelage.

Neoliberal shock therapy supported both by the progressive Clinton White House and conservative Republicans made this myopia fatal. The technical advice given to Russia by the World Bank, IMF, and the European Bank for Reconstruction and Development was catastrophic. These institutions insisted that Russia foreswear Deng Xiaoping's successful gradualist strategy of "crossing rivers one stone at a time," claiming that prudence was too politically risky. They asserted that cautiously building democratic free enterprise and a competitive society step-by-step in tandem with the development of the rule of law was sure to backfire because obstructionists would fight tooth and nail to preserve the *status quo*. China's successful gradualism in their eyes was a high risk/low reward transition strategy, even if adroitly guided by Washington.

G-7 leaders relying on the World Bank and IMF's advice urged Yeltsin to cut the Gordian knot by commanding the state to abruptly

---

[10]Anders Aslund, "Why Has Russia's Economic Transformation Been So Arduous?" *Annual World Bank Conference on Development Economics* (April 1999), worldbank.org/INTABCDEWASHINGTON1999/Resources/aslund.pdf. Anders Aslund, *How Russia Became a Market Economy* (Washington: Brookings, 1995). Newsweek Staff, "A Grand Bargain: Aid For Arms Control," *Newsweek* (September 1991), https://www.newsweek.com/grand-bargain-aid-arms-control-203408.

Aslund is quoted as saying "It seems obvious to me that we have to help the Soviet Union avoid this catastrophe. It is in our national interest. I would propose a Grand Bargain: give the Soviets aid on the strict condition that they dismantle all or most of the nuclear forces that now threaten them as much as us."

226 *Beleaguered Superpower: Biden's America Adrift*

severe all links with the national economy. He complied, urged on by Gaidar. Yeltsin denationalized state property through "voucher privatization." State contracts were comprehensively canceled (Gorbachev abolished mandatory central planning in 1987). Enterprises, left to fend for themselves, had to create market-friendly products, and managers compelled to master the dark art of marketing. New financial institutions were supposed to emerge from the woodwork to meet expected market demand, and Russians were supposed to transform themselves into entrepreneurs overnight (necessity is the mother of invention).

The West cheered Yeltsin on in these risky waters. It urged him to let the economy go "cold turkey" (sudden withdrawal of most state contracts) on the premise that profit-seekers would seize the day, replacing outmoded institutions with state-of-the-arts substitutes. The World Bank Group acknowledged that shock therapy might initially cause a sharp economic contraction, but predicted that the pain would be brief, compensated by a swift recovery and rapid sustainable prosperity. The prognosis was for a "j-curve" transition characterized by a short downward thrust followed by sharp economic ascent allowing Russian per capita GDP to overtake the Portuguese standard.[11] Thumbing its nose at commonsense, the G-7 insisted that shock therapy rather than Deng Xiaoping's gradualism was the low risk/high reward strategy. Yeltsin drank the "Kool-Aid."

The result was catastrophic. Russia swooned into a coma, a hyper-depression perhaps twice as severe as the Great Depression in the United States at its nadir.[12] The collapse caused 3.4 million excess deaths 1990–1998.[13] The West did provide Russia with carrots to ease the post-Soviet transition, but the shock therapy it recommended was lethal. Instead of paving the way for Russia's transition and integration into the global system, it opened the door to Putin. There may only have been less than a 50–50 chance that an astute gradualist transition strategy would have fully Westernized Yeltsin's Russia in line with the Huntington (or Strobe

---

[11] Josef Brada and Arthur King, "Is There a J-Curve for the Economic Transition from Socialism to Capitalism?" in Kazimierz Z. Poznanski, ed., *Stabilization and Privatization in Poland An Economic Evaluation of the Shock Therapy Program*, (Boston: Kluwer Academic Publishers, 1993): 251–269.

[12] Steven Rosefielde and Stefan Hedlund, *Russia Since 1980* (Cambridge: Cambridge University Press, 2009).

[13] Steven Rosefielde, "Premature Deaths: Russia's Radical Economic Transition in Soviet Perspective," *Europe-Asia Studies* 53, no. 8, 2001: 1159–1176.

Talbott's "Global Nation") paradigm, and integrated it into a Washington dominated global order, but shock therapy as the World Bank and IMF applied it virtually assured Muscovy's great power resurrection.

The mishandling of Russia's post-Soviet transition project was partly a matter of bad luck. The World Bank and IMF's experience coping with the Latin American debt crisis in the 1980s had created the presumption that "austerity" (now a progressive dirty word) was better than financial accommodation.[14] If the Latin American debt crisis had been successfully resolved with gradualist reforms, Western leaders might have counseled Yeltsin more judiciously. Another piece of bad luck was Bill Clinton's distaste for Soviet experts (other than his Oxford roommate Strobe Talbott). He might have assigned responsibility for overseeing Russia's transition to old Soviet hands like Abram Bergson (Head of the Russia Analytic Division of the OSS during WWII) and ruling American dean of the discipline, but the World Bank and IMF won the intra-bureaucratic battle.

Moreover, the economic devastation caused by shock therapy was not ubiquitously lamented. Some Clinton era insiders like Andrei Shleifer profited from it,[15] and many old hands in the security community felt that shock therapy would forestall any possibility of communism's revival. It can safely be inferred, therefore that even when opportunity knocks,[16] Washington may be apt to use economic enticements maladroitly.

---

[14]Jeffrey Sachs, "New Approaches to the Latin American Debt Crisis," *Essays in International Finance*, no. 174 (July 1989).

[15]Nicholas M. Ciarelli and Anton S. Troianovski, "Tawdry Shleifer Affair' Stokes Faculty Anger toward Summers," *Harvard Crimson* (February 10, 2006), https://www.thecrimson.com/article/2006/2/10/tawdry-shleifer-affair-stokes-faculty-anger/.

[16]Steven Rosefielde, *Kremlin Strikes Back: Russia and the West after Crimea's Annexation* (Cambridge: Cambridge University Press, 2017). Kirk Bennett, "What Gorbachev Did Not Hear," *American Interest* (March 2018), https://www.the-american-interest.com/2018/03/12/gorbachev-not-hear/.Mark Kramer, "The Myth of a No-NATO-Enlargement Pledge to Russia," *The Washington Quarterly* 32, no. 2, April 2009: 39–61.

The West's decision to press for and incorporate Central Europe and other states of the former Soviet Union into the EU and NATO is a subject of continuing debate. Had Russia successfully transitioned to democratic free enterprise, the subject would be a minor historical footnote, but it remains alive because the *siloviki* believe that Washington stabbed Russia in the back.

228 *Beleaguered Superpower: Biden's America Adrift*

China offers another good case in point. Deng Xiaoping decided in 1992 that China must redouble its efforts to create a communist market economy and open its doors to foreign commerce. The West welcomed his initiative construing it as a waystation on the road to democratic free enterprise. It provided economic carrots to expedite the process, but had to devise a different package of enticements than the one given to Yeltsin because Deng Xiaoping opposed shock therapy and was content with authoritarian communist power. Beijing listened politely to President Ronald Reagan's democratic free enterprise advocacy, but democratization and freehold capitalism themselves were off the table.

The Clinton Administration decided to start the process of economic engagement by permitting China's entry into the WTO on favorable terms hoping that market expansion and international economic participation would inevitably spur democratization and the peaceful inclusion of China in the West's global order. Zhu Rongji took full advantage of the opportunity consummating China's WTO accession in 2001 under George W Bush's presidential watch.[17] WTO accession greatly facilitated Beijing's successful creation of a powerful communist managed market economic mechanism based exclusively on leasehold property.[18]

The country thereafter modernized and developed rapidly. Living standards rose and China is now a major player in global finance and commerce. However, contrary to Washington establishment's hopes this has not stopped Beijing from being an unruly authoritarian actor. Xi Jinping refuses to abide by the global fair trade rules of commerce, WTO prohibitions against business subsidies,[19] and illegal technology pirating. The Communist Party maintains its monopoly grip on government power.

---

[17]Nicholas Lardy, "Issues in China's WTO Accession," *Brookings* (May 2001), https://www.brookings.edu/testimonies/issues-in-chinas-wto-accession/.

[18]The Chinese Communist Party contends that China's markets are communist become the people, not individuals or corporations are the sole freehold owner of the means of production.

[19]Claude Barfield, "The Dual Goals of the Trump Administration's New Attack on Chinese Intellectual Property Theft," *AEI* (November 2018), www.aei.org/publication/the-dual-goals-of-the-trump-administrations-new-attack-on-chinese-intellectual-property-theft/?mkt_tok=eyJpIjoiTVRrek9EVTJaR1JtWldJMiIsInQiOiJuV0JDNGFsSEh0aHVpaENNZmtpODkxWTVNZnZZeHgyZ0M1enJPRWw1Y2dPaDh4YVpZWjE5Y1BUY3ZnTHFJWSsrNTNrbkxmYjFwU2lkRjRneGlJc0ZDS3p2ZTcxd1pMcnJuclJKR2laVm8yT3pWQlZ2T3dpeHkwUnpOcGJGTkxIWSJ9.

Civil liberties are restricted. China has become a major military rival in the South China Sea. It is well on the way toward the domination of Southeast Asia, seeking to create a rival "global" economic order under its control. Events might have played out this way with a lag anyway had China been barred from the WTO, conditioned on its meeting the organization's requirements, but carrots by themselves clearly did not make Beijing a benign global partner.

The experience with "nation building" outside the communist and post-communist frameworks offer further insight into the unreliability of economic enticements. Afghanistan before the December 1979 Soviet invasion was a pre-modern Islamic nation, with an unpopular communist government that had forcibly seized power in April 1978. The United States backed an anti-communist Mujahideen resistance, which depopulated and decimated the countryside until the Soviets withdrew in February 1989. The Peshawar Accords established an Islamic State among rival Afghan parties in 1992, but factional militia discord led to civil war. NATO invaded Afghanistan under Operation Enduring Freedom in 2001 following Al Qaeda's 9/11 attack on the United States to suppress terrorism with no resolution yet in sight. The West finds itself mired in an intractable struggle for power with the Taliban Islamic Emirate.

The battle has been military, but Washington also has endeavored to win the hearts and minds of Afghanis with a "nation building" economic enticement program. NATO has tried to instill a unitary national Afghan identity into a majority formed across a multitude of regional tribes by developing a national community with government provided infrastructure, economic, educational, and propaganda programs. NATO believed that a stable and prosperous Afghan nation would defeat the Taliban.

This goal required a sound economic development and modernization plan, attuned to realities on the ground, rather than inapplicable off-the-shelf generic programs. Parochial bureaucratic interests must be subdued and inter-bureaucratic harmony achieved to minimize waste, fraud, and abuse. Interactions with locals must be culturally sensitive not only for positive results, but to avoid making enemies of today's allies. These tasks are not rocket science. Government professionals should have been conversant with the technologies for infrastructure building and alert to the

---

"Beijing has outed itself by publicly announcing plans to provide $50 billion to domestic semiconductor companies — A clear violation of World Trade Organization subsidy rules (as is the specific subsidy for Jinhua)."

230 Beleaguered Superpower: Biden's America Adrift

pitfalls of program miss management. Knowing and doing however are not the same thing. Clinton, Bush, and Obama–Biden by default approached national building in Afghanistan as they did in Iraq with mixed motives. They wanted to achieve official goals, but only on a business as usual basis that coddled outsourcers and prioritized bureaucratic concerns. The results reported by the Special Inspector General Report for Afghanistan Reconstruction (SIGAR) confirm that nation building economic enticements were unreliable instruments of sound national security policy.[20]

The United States has spent nearly $48 billion on non-security assistance to private sector development since 2001 trying to entice unruly actors with little tangible benefit and scant hope for victory. The US Agency for International Development with additional significant roles played by the Departments of State, Defense, Commerce, and Treasury led the Afghan nation building initiative. SIGAR reports that Afghanistan's early economic gains after NATO intervention in 2001 were mostly due to foreign spending, and were not sustainable. Optimistic predictions of future progress did not reflect the reality of Afghanistan's economic and security environment, the capacity of institutions, the country's relations with its neighbors, or the impact of corruption. The US government and other stakeholders inadequately grasped the relationships between corrupt strongmen and the speed at which Afghanistan could transition to a liberal democratic market economy, in part because they did not try.[21]

Customs and tax sector reforms focused on generating revenue instead of supporting nation building. The US government and other

---

[20] SIGAR, "Private Sector Development and Economic Growth: Lessons from the U.S. Experience in Afghanistan," *Special Inspector General for Afghanistan Reconstruction* (April 2018), https://www.sigar.mil/interactive-reports/private-sector-development-and-economic-growth/index.html.

[21] SIGAR, "Private Sector Development and Economic Growth: Lessons from the U.S. Experience in Afghanistan," *Special Inspector General for Afghanistan Reconstruction* (April 2018), https://www.sigar.mil/interactive-reports/private-sector-development-and-economic-growth/index.html.

"The U.S. government did not engage, anywhere in any of its various departments and agencies, in extensive planning for a post-Taliban Afghanistan. There was no time, and not much incentive, to do so ... The assumption was that the international community would pick up the pieces after the Taliban regime was displaced.' Dov Zakheim, former DOD Comptroller."

stakeholders failed to provide the business sector with the required transparency. The revisions to the tax laws in 2005, 2009, and 2015 complicated matters further. The changes confused businesses and often increased their tax burden, encouraging non-compliance.

A new legal framework was a *sine quo non* for sound monetary policy, but the one forged was defective. It adapted laws from other countries and drew too heavily from international experience, rather than tailoring the framework to local needs. These laws reflected a wide range of legal ideas and concepts. Many conflicted with local precedent and tradition and were superfluous because supporting institutions were not established. Afghanistan's weak judicial system left even the best-crafted laws vulnerable to manipulation.

Low cost finance posed another problem. The US failed to foster private commercial banks and non-banks, and sector-specific financial institutions essential for making low cost loans available to micro and small enterprises. The institutions that did emerge continue to rely on external assistance, and face ownership, management, and operational sustainability challenges. Some investment was stimulated, but it was limited for a variety of reasons, primarily uncertainty, insecurity, and poor economic governance.

High staff turnover, insecurity, poor maintenance of facilities, and corruption contributed to Afghanistan's trade imbalance, which has grown since 2002, with imports tripling by 2015, while exports remained stagnant and low.

The United States began emphasizing direct support to individual enterprises in 2006, based on the belief that local companies needed direct financial and technical assistance to compete in the formal economy, access external markets, and mitigate risk. However, shortcomings in design, implementation, and oversight hampered direct support to enterprise programs. While some companies used financial support and technical assistance to expand their access to markets, other companies that received direct grants became dependent on these sources of "free money," without which they could not sustain profitable operations.

The US financial aid practices not infrequently encouraged corruption, complicating the challenges of coordination within and between US agencies, and kept unprofitable Afghan enterprises afloat. These negatives hobbled economic growth.

Entrenched political interests were another minus. Many of the business elites who dominated the Afghan market only thrived because of

232 *Beleaguered Superpower: Biden's America Adrift*

their privileged access to contracts, tax exemptions, security, and money-laundering channels.

All these various failures soured public attitudes toward the goal of competitive *laissez-faire*. Locals came to conflate the market economy with unfair competition, monopolization by politically well-connected firms, unfair trade practices by regional neighbors, and administrative corruption.

Institutional and cultural differences complicated civil-military coordination. Personnel often had very different views of their own roles and missions, and lacked understanding of or confidence in the other's expertise and capabilities. The US military forces were unaccustomed to the distinct culture and priorities of the civilian development agencies responsible for private sector development.

Capacity and organizational constraints within US military institutions were often at odds with civilian-centric programs and overall objectives. The major human resource constraint was short tours of civilian administrative duty and the resulting staff turnover rates — which led to increasingly limited pools of qualified applicants, delayed activities, and a lack of continuity and institutional memory. There was also low institutional tolerance for risk that precluded allowing development personnel to leave their offices and bases to monitor projects and assess general conditions.

In large part due to contracting and management incentives, the US and other economic programs focused on inputs rather than outcomes, measuring success in the number of jobs created, regardless of their stability. There was no overarching mechanism for targeting endemic poverty.

Washington policymakers appreciate the potential usefulness of economic enticements, but they failed to transform theory into sound practice in Afghanistan. They have yet to devise a viable economic development and modernization plan despite nearly 20 years of battle-hardened experience. They have not quelled inter-bureaucratic conflicts of interest to minimize waste, fraud and abuse. Interactions with locals have been insensitive turning allies into enemies. The Washington establishment has been unable to wean itself from a business as usual mindset that coddles outsourcers and prioritizes parochial bureaucratic concerns. The Special Inspector General Report for Afghanistan Reconstruction condemns this ineptitude.

Chapter 11

Arms Control is Problematic

Arms control is an aspect of smart diplomacy. It employs soft power techniques (artful persuasion) to achieve hard power ends (improvement in the correlation of forces). This makes it an attractive tool for managing relations with Eastern authoritarian regimes. The concept covers a wide spectrum of possibilities from specific weapons, and small changes in deployments to universal disarming. Universal disarmament for the moment appears to be off the table, but arms control and arms reduction remain options with Russia, China, Iran, and North Korea. Attention recently has focused on strategic nuclear forces. Eastern authoritarians also might agree to controlling conventional weapons. America could conceivably improve its national security, not by strengthening its armed forces, but reducing them advantageously *vis-à-vis* rivals. Is arms control today a promising Pareto superior win–win threat reduction strategy that allows America to expand its domestic programs by reallocating funds from defense to civilian projects?

The answer is no because Russia, China, North Korea and Iran's imperial ambitions take priority over prospective peace dividends in their leaders' eyes, and the military cost savings to America are too small to justify the risks of being hoodwinked. The United States faces growing nuclear and conventional military threats from Eastern authoritarians and a wide array of other rogue nations likely to act in bad faith.

There is no harm in exploring arms control and reduction possibilities if Russia, China, North Korea, Iran, and the global jihadi are willing to cooperate, but expectations should be low. Nuclear non-proliferation treaties have

234 Beleaguered Superpower: Biden's America Adrift

not stopped nuclear proliferation,[1] and cost savings for America cannot be great compared to the risks of deception. For example, if Washington agreed to cut nuclear force replacement and modernization expenditures by half in return for sundry Russian, Chinese, North Korean, and Iranian *quid pro quos*, the "peace dividend" would be miniscule compared to the security risks.

The Congressional Budget Office (CBO) reported in October 2017 that taxpayers are obligated to pay $1.2 trillion for nuclear force maintenance and modernization between fiscal years 2017 and 2047, or $41 billion annually over the next 29 years to deter its adversaries. Washington could decrease or increase these planned outlays in response to changing nuclear threat perceptions, but cuts cannot be substantial unless Russia, China, North Korea, and Iran fully reciprocate because most of the intended expenditures are for replacing or modernizing aging and obsolete systems. The maximum annual cost saving realized from under-maintaining America's nuclear deterrent cannot plausibly exceed two-tenths of 1 percent of 2017 GDP.[2]

Prospects for negotiating meaningful cost savings from balanced conventional arms controls and reductions are even dimmer because this would require agreement among multiple parties on a wide range of non-nuclear systems.[3] Russia withdrew from the Treaty on Conventional

---

[1] India, Pakistan, and Israel are not signatories to the Treaty on the Non-Proliferation of Nuclear Weapons (NPT), first signed in 1968. India and Pakistan became nuclear states, and Israel is widely believed to possess nuclear weapons. Japan has the capability of building and deploying nuclear weapons in six months (virtual nuclear power). South Sudan created later is a non-signatory. North Korea nuclearized despite the treaty. Iran is following in Pyongyang's footsteps. Iran is a signatory, but is building the capacity to become a nuclear state.

[2] Arms Control Association, "U.S. Nuclear Modernization Programs," *Arms Control Association* (March 2018), https://www.armscontrol.org/factsheets/USNuclearModernization.

[3] Johan Engvall, Gudrun Persson, Robert Dalsjö, Mike Winnerstig, and Carolina Vendil Pallin, "Conventional Arms Control — A Way Forward or Wishful Thinking?" *FOI* (May 2018), https://www.foi.se/rapportsammanfattning?reportNo=FOI-R--4586--SE.

"Russia perceives the comprehensive and cooperative security order as rigged in favour of Euro-Atlantic organisations. It is actively seeking to establish an alternative order that would grant Moscow a sphere of privileged interests in its 'near abroad'. In practice, this implies a Russian veto on further NATO enlargement. The US wants to uphold existing rules and agreements, and identifies Russia's aggressive behaviour as the root cause of the European security problem. Arms control is, thus, only meaningful as long as it is embedded in a rules-based security order. — There is an underlying tension between the diplomatic interest of dialogue and negotiation on the one hand and the hard military security interests of states on the other hand. — One Western line of thought perceives the unresolved

Armed Forces in Europe (CFE) in 2015,[4] and there are no global conventional arms control initiatives of any sort currently on the table. The world has had some encouraging success limiting chemical and biological weapons.[5] However, prospects for other weapons systems are dim.[6]

---

territorial conflicts in Russia's neighbourhood as the source of the current European security crisis. — Another Western line believes that tensions between Russia and the West can be reduced if discussions on CAC and CSBMs are disentangled from the unresolved conflicts. — The Baltic Sea region has emerged as a geopolitical focal point in the stand-off between Russia and the West. The region has become the subject of conflicting interests wishing to see either a military build-up or a special arms control regime as the way to address current security concerns. — Russia has two military-strategic priorities in the Baltic Sea region: to constrain NATO deployment of additional military forces to the region, and to preclude the non-NATO members in the region joining NATO. — For the major Western powers, the Baltic Sea region is crucial for the credibility of NATO. — The Baltic countries and Poland, as well as non-NATO member Finland, share a common interest in ensuring that the security arrangements for the Baltic Sea region remain firmly attached to the overall European security order. — At present, the prospects for negotiations on a new CAC regime are slim. No changes are to be expected as long as the two major players — Russia and the US — remain on the fringes of the dialogue. The incentives in contemporary Europe are not the same as they were when existing agreements were negotiated and adopted."

[4]In 2007, Russia "suspended" its participation in the treaty, and on March 10, 2015, citing NATO's *de facto* breach of the Treaty, Russia formally announced it was "completely" halting its participation in it as of the next day.

[5]Arms Control Association, "The Chemical Weapons Convention (CWC) at a Glance," (March 2018), https://www.armscontrol.org/factsheets/cwcglance. Klaus Wiegrefe, "The Fraught Cold War History of Novichok," *Yerepouni News* (April 26, 2018).

The Chemical Weapons Convention prohibits: developing, producing, acquiring, stockpiling, or retaining chemical weapons. The direct or indirect transfer of chemical weapons. Chemical weapons use or military preparation for use. Assisting, encouraging, or inducing other states to engage in CWC-prohibited activity.

The use of riot control agents "as a method of warfare."

The limits however have been evaded.

"The Russians have repeatedly lied to us about the Novichok program," says Weber. For many years, diplomats, intelligence officials and politicians in Berlin, Washington and London largely accepted Moscow's inscrutable approach without too much complaint. They hoped that, as McDonald's spread across Russia and democracy took root, problems like Novichok would disappear, says British Rear Admiral John Gower, who is an expert on chemical weapons."

[6]"A farewell to arms control — Old Deals to Limit Nuclear Weapons are Fraying: They May Not Be Repaired — Politics and Technology Make Arms Control Harder Than

236 *Beleaguered Superpower: Biden's America Adrift*

The Fog of Arms Control

The reality of arms control agreements seldom corresponds with official texts. The Strategic Arms Limitation Treaty (SALT) between the United States and the Soviet Union was not about strict numerical controls as publicly proclaimed.[7] Its purpose was to justify the strategic arsenal that Washington considered appropriate, guided by the concept of mutual assured destruction (MAD),[8] while allowing the USSR to maintain a larger arsenal than the US through various ruses, despite the hocus pocus of verification.

The SALT agreement pertained only to "deployed" weapons. This allowed the Kremlin the wiggle room it needed. The concept of deployed systems permitted ballistic missile spares and reloads on the assumption that silos could only support the launch of a single missile in a timely

---

Ever," *Economist* (May 2018), https://www.economist.com/news/briefing/21741537-politics-and-technology-make-arms-control-harder-ever-old-deals-limit-nuclear-weapons?mkt_tok=eyJpIjoiWmpKallqUTNaR0UxWWpJeCIsInQiOiJYa3VGRkFaWitzWlVadkVFZUNWQkhUOHJmalY2THdDXC95SXYwNEVmZkVzaWNGWENzTlUrRjhFMWJtTit0eGh5Rm0yTFJrZzJXNGU0MFI0WVh3ZWhPOTFjT0RtV0xXZ3B6QktEbkJHMmFQdDlTSHVNeGU0N2pRSFRIMmhKUFd1Sm4ifQ%3D%3D.

Eugene Rumer, "A Farewell to ... Arms Control," *Carnegie Endowment for Peace* (April 2018), https://carnegieendowment.org/2018/04/17/farewell-to-arms-.-.-.-control-pub-76088.

[7]Robert Jervis, "The Dustbin of History: Mutual Assured Destruction," *Foreign Policy* (November 2009), http://foreignpolicy.com/2009/11/09/the-dustbin-of-history-mutual-assured-destruction/.

The first agreements, known as SALT I and SALT II, were signed by the United States and the Union of Soviet Socialist Republics in 1972 and 1979, respectively, and were intended to restrain the arms race in strategic (long-range or intercontinental) ballistic missiles armed with nuclear weapons. First suggested by U.S. President Lyndon B. Johnson in 1967, strategic arms limitation talks were agreed on by the two superpowers in the summer of 1968, and full-scale negotiations began in November 1969.

[8]Mutually assured destruction (MAD) was the doctrine that America and the Soviet Union's nuclear arsenals were sufficient to make nuclear war unthinkable. Secretary Defense Robert McNamara declared MAD to be America's nuclear defense strategy in the early 1960. The logic of MAD led to the Single Integrated Operational Plan (SIOP) for nuclear war aimed about obliterating the Soviet Union should it launch a nuclear attack. President James Carter found the SIOP approach too inflexible and introduced the possibility of limited nuclear salvos in executive order PD-59. For a recent assessment of the concepts merit.

manner. The Soviets circumvented the problem by using hard pads that allowed them to launch spares alongside expended silos.[9] Warheads could be "decommissioned" and held legally in reserve by temporarily removing nuclear triggers, and ballistic missiles stockpiled applying the same reasoning. Viktor Mikhailov acknowledged in a private conversation that the Soviets had 52,000 nuclear warheads (some non-strategic),[10] a figure incompatible with the public perception created by the limits set in SALT agreements. The illusion of nuclear arms control apparently was far more important than the reality of strategic parity.

Arms control from the White House's perspective meant accepting that the Soviets would act mostly as they pleased because we could not prevent them from doing otherwise,[11] while reducing pressure within the VPK and MOD for unrestrained structural militarization. SALT provided cover for America disengaging from the strategic nuclear arms race in order to build enough confidence to coax the Kremlin into following America's lead.[12]

---

[9] Steven Rosefielde, *False Science: Underestimating the Soviet Arms Buildup* (Piscataway: Transaction, 1982, Expanded Second Edition, 1987).

[10] Hans Kristensen, "Non-Strategic Nuclear Weapons," *Federation of American Scientists* (May 2012), https://fas.org/_docs/Non_Strategic_Nuclear_Weapons.pdf.Cf. Hans Kristensen and Robert Norris, "Status of World Nuclear Forces," *Federation of Atomic Scientists*, https://fas.org/issues/nuclear-weapons/status-world-nuclear-forces/.

Neither the Soviet Union (Russia) nor America publish official non-strategic nuclear weapons counts.

Hans Kristensen estimates circa 2012 at the beginning of the START II nuclear weapons reduction era that Russia has 2,760 non-strategic nuclear weapons, and that 2,000–3,000 have been decommissioned. Mikhailov's figure has been verified by Vitaly Shlykov. It refers to the mid-1990s, and in Shlykov's view declined to about 40,000 warheads by 2000.

[11] Confirmed to the author by Paul Nitze. He was member of the US delegation to the Strategic Arms Limitation Talks (SALT) (1969–1973). Later, fearing Soviet rearmament, he opposed the ratification of SALT II (1979).

[12] *Modern History Sourcebook: The Molotov-Ribbentrop Pact, 1939* (New York: Fordham University), https://sourcebooks.fordham.edu/mod/1939pact.asp.

Hidden understandings are frequently more important than the official text of sovereign treaties. The official text of the Nazi-Soviet Nonaggression Pact signed in August 1939, revealed only after Germany's defeat also concealed hidden motives. The open text provided for consultation, arbitration if either party disagreed, neutrality if either went to

238 *Beleaguered Superpower: Biden's America Adrift*

The Washington establishment's gambit may or may not have been wise, depending on one's judgment about MAD's validity, but it reveals how little power the West actually had in negotiating mutual arms reductions with Eastern authoritarians unwilling to abandon their ambitions. Arms control is more about legitimizing controversial procurement decisions governed by concepts like MAD (repackaged in 2013 as mutually assured stability MAS),[13] and capitalizing on illusory idealist hopes,[14] than the dry-eyed calculus of cost savings and tactical advantage.

---

war against a third power, no membership of a group "which is directly or indirectly aimed at the other."

The secret protocol to the pact divided Romania, Poland, Lithuania, Latvia, Estonia, and Finland into German and Soviet spheres of influence. Finland, Estonia, and Latvia were assigned to the Soviet sphere. Poland was to be partitioned in the event of its political rearrangement. Pisa, Narev, Vistula, and San rivers would go to the Soviet Union, while Germany would occupy the west. Lithuania, adjacent to East Prussia, would be in the German sphere of influence, although a second secret protocol agreed to in September 1939 reassigned the majority of Lithuania to the USSR. According to the protocol, Lithuania would be granted its historical capital Vilnius, which was under Polish control during the inter-war period. Another clause of the treaty stipulated that Germany would not interfere with the Soviet Union's actions towards Bessarabia, then part of Romania; as a result, not only Bessarabia, but Northern Bukovina and Hertza regions were occupied by the Soviets and integrated into the Soviet Union.

[13]"From Mutual Assured Destruction to Mutual Assured Stability Exploring a New Comprehensive Framework for U.S. and Russian Nuclear Arms Reductions," *NRDC* (March 2013), https://www.nrdc.org/sites/default/files/NRDC-ISKRAN-Nuclear-Security-Report-March2013.pdf.

On American strategic nuclear doctrine see Katarzyna Zysk, "Escalation and Nuclear Weapons in Russia's Military Strategy," *The RUSI Journal* (2018), DOI: 10.1080/03071847.2018.1469267.

[14]White House, "FACT SHEET: The Prague Nuclear Agenda," (January 11, 2017), https://obamawhitehouse.archives.gov/the-press-office/2017/01/11/fact-sheet-prague-nuclear-agenda.

"President Obama's historic speech in Prague in 2009 outlined his vision of a world without nuclear weapons and outlined work for achieving this goal in four pillars: (1) preventing nuclear terrorism and promoting nuclear security; (2) strengthening the non-proliferation regime; (3) supporting the peaceful use of nuclear energy; and (4) reducing the role of nuclear weapons. This administration has worked diligently since 2009 to develop enduring institutions and strengthen existing frameworks that will continue, under their own momentum, to produce a safer world when it comes to the threat of nuclear weapons."

Anti-Ballistic Missile (ABM) Treaty

The cogency of mutually assured destruction as a guide to nuclear strategy depended on the belief that America had and would retain the capability of annihilating the Soviet Union in any series of nuclear volleys. The Kremlin did not have to believe anything because it intended to use its own pragmatic judgment on the matter.

Anti-ballistic missiles capable of significantly degrading offensive nuclear ballistic missile strikes threatened to undermine the credibility of the doctrine. The ABM Treaty or ABMT (1972–2002) was devised to preserve Washington's faith in MAD. American strategists in the early 1970s did not fret about Soviet ballistic missile defense technologies; nonetheless, they were concerned that if the Kremlin built a thick ballistic missile defense network it would undermine public confidence in MAD. The Soviets feared American technological prowess,[15] and wanted to prevent Washington from gaining the upper hand.

Both sides therefore decided to negotiate an amicable agreement of no practical importance. It allowed America and the Soviet Union two ABM defense sites, one for the capitol and one for ICBM silos. The 1974 Protocol reduced the number of sites to one per party, each with 100 anti-ballistic missiles. The USSR chose Moscow, America the North Dakota Safeguard Complex.

President Ronald Reagan's Strategic Defense Initiative (SDI) was announced on March 23, 1983, which committed America to building a formidable anti-ballistic missile shield, shook the *status quo* because it raised the possibility that America might someday achieve strategic nuclear superiority, even though it did not immediately violate the letter of the ABM Treaty. The Soviets acquiesced, but President George Bush nonetheless judged that domestic politics made the ABM Treaty an obstacle to developing the comprehensive ballistic missile shield needed to protect America from attack from third parties. He gave Moscow notice and withdrew the United States from the ABM Treaty on December 13, 2001 with little consequence. America continued developing its ballistic missile defense capabilities as it could have done legally under the ABM Treaty, and proponents of MAD (and now MAS) have successfully prevented the deployment of a comprehensive ABM shield without any Russian assistance. The ABM Treaty had some positive benefit in

---

[15] Vitaly Shlykov, "Nevidimaia Mobilizatsii," *Forbes* no. 3 (March 2006): 1–5.

240   *Beleaguered Superpower: Biden's America Adrift*

establishing the initial parameters of anti-ballistic missile deployments, but beyond this failed to compel the Soviet Union and Russia to do anything they preferred not to do.

From Arms Control to Arms Reduction

Mikhail Gorbachev's Luddite economic and governmental reforms (*perestroika* [radical economic reform] and *novoe myshlenie* [new thinking]) launched in 1987 wrecked the economy, dismembered the Soviet Union and crippled its armed forces. On Christmas day 1991, the Russian remnant of the USSR was in a state of catastrophic shock. It ceased being a threat to any nation other than itself. Arms control between Washington and Moscow became superfluous as a tool for disciplining yesterday's unruly actor. Suddenly what had seemed to be indispensable nuclear assets, no longer served any useful purpose. The United States had no reason to annihilate Russia, and the Kremlin had every reason to encourage Washington to downsize its nuclear arsenal.

This new confluence of interest led to a sequence of nuclear arms reduction agreements. Strategic Arms Reduction Treaty (START I) (1991–2009), De-MIRV-ing Treaty (START II) (never came into effect because US withdrew from the ABM Treaty), NEW START (2011–2021) (Treaty of Prague; replaced SORT), and SORT (Strategic Offensive Reduction Treaty) (Treaty of Moscow 2003–2011). The arms control community claims that this has brought about a huge decrease in America and Russia's deployed nuclear assets and reserves.[16] Although, the official figures for Russian nuclear reserves are suspect, Washington and Moscow preserved the concept of strategic nuclear parity at significantly lower levels of lethality.

American leaders wisely seized the opportunity provided by the USSR's collapse to reduce redundant nuclear forces on both sides. There will be fewer casualties if the United States and Russia decide to fight a nuclear war, and this benefit may survive in the new Biden–Harris age of revived Russo-American enmity. Nonetheless, the accomplishment does not change two important facts. First, American perceptions of nuclear war have not changed since the early 1960s. Pentagon insiders today do

---

[16] Hans M. Kristensen and Robert S. Norris, "Russian Nuclear Forces, 2018," *Bulletin of the Atomic Scientists* 74, no. 3 (2018): 185–195.

Arms Control is Problematic 241

not find nuclear war any more thinkable than yesterday during the heyday of MAD.[17] Nuclear war was MAD then and remains so today. Second, America and Russia are back to square one. They have resumed their rivalry. The Kremlin will maximize its military advantage within SORT paying little heed to its formal treaty obligations, and America will have to grin and bear it to the extent that the Washington establishment remains enthralled by MAD (MAS). Arms controls are likely to constrain America under SORT, and unlikely to discipline unruly Russian behavior any time in the immediate future under the Biden–Harris administration.[18]

Joint Comprehensive Plan of Action

Iran and the United States have been in a Cold War since November 1979. Iranian Revolutionary Guards are embroiled in armed conflicts across the Middle East, and the mullahs actively support the global jihadi. America has tried to tame Iranian aggression with military operations and sanctions without success. Could arms control tip the scale in Washington's favor?

The Joint Comprehensive Plan of Action (JCPOA) political agreement (it is not a treaty) devised to keep Iran from developing nuclear weapons inadvertently tested the possibility with illuminating results.[19] JCPOA was a tripartite political agreement negotiated between America and key European nations about lifting American economic sanctions restricting European investments in Iran and incentivizing Iran to comply with its Nuclear Non-proliferation Treaty (NPT) obligations on the one hand, and on the other hand getting Iran to accept the deal. The JCPOA

---

[17] Tom Collina and William Perry, *The New Nuclear Arms Race and Presidential Power from Truman to Trump* (New York: BenBella Books, Inc. 2020).

[18] Cf. Sarah Hummel and Andrey Baklitskiy, "Nuclear Arms Control and U.S.–Russia Relations," *US–Russia Future* (May 2018), https://us-russiafuture.org/2018/05/10/nuclear-arms-control-and-u-s-russia-relations/.

[19] Jarret Blanc, "Trump's Iran Deal Decision: What Comes Next," *Carnegie Endowment for International Peace* (May 2018), https://carnegieendowment.org/2018/05/07/trump-s-iran-deal-decision-what-comes-next-pub-76272?utm_source=ctw&utm_medium=email&mkt_tok=eyJpIjoiT0dabE4yRTBZVGswTnpBdyIsInQiOiJyYzRaYmFn dGVxbW9qMjBBUXJkKzh4QzRJWGJoNFZpSWVVd3hvWjdCcWZoVXQ5XC9 xeE11QllTaHRNMmVRSDhDc0hBc1JvdkZaW1c3K1BkNlpBNlJ0clo0dXp pQ1RxZ0N1SGJKWmtXMm01QTJqVm9CaURlUURKT0wxRHg1S2YwalM4S DA5UkdrWkhiMkFycDJIb1B3OVwvUT09In0%3D.

242 *Beleaguered Superpower: Biden's America Adrift*

agreement that went into force in 2016 stressed NPT compliance with little regard for controlling other aspects of Iran's rogue behavior. The deal demonstrated that Teheran's agreement to adhere to some aspects of its NPT commitment in exchange for America ending its sanctions, did not stop the mullahs from developing nuclear capable ballistic missiles for future use should Iran go nuclear at a time of its choosing,[20] or curtail the Iran's aggression in the Middle East. Arms control provided a carrot and eliminated a sanctions stick, but did nothing whatsoever to limit Iran's nuclear and imperial aspirations.

The essentials are as follows. Mohamed Reza Shah initiated Iran's nuclear program during the 1950s with assistance from the US Atoms for Peace Program. Iran has been a non-nuclear weapon state party to the NPT since 1970. In 1979 after the Iranian Revolution deposed the Shah, Ayatollah Khomeini deemed the nuclear program "un-Islamic" and ordered it terminated. In 1984, Khomeini reversed course on the issue of nuclear power and sought international partners to continue building the Bushehr reactors. Currently, Iran has complete nuclear fuel cycle capabilities including uranium mining, milling, conversion, and enrichment facilities.[21] Iran's extensive enrichment program, capable of producing highly enriched uranium for a nuclear weapon, has been particularly controversial. At its 2015 peak, the program comprised nearly 20,000 gas centrifuges at three major facilities.[22]

The International Atomic Energy Agency (IAEA) Board of Governors found Iran in non-compliance with its Comprehensive Safeguards Agreement in 2005, and the UN Security Council passed seven resolutions demanding that Iran halt its enrichment and reprocessing activities. Beginning in 2002, Iran, the IAEA, and various groupings of powers — first with France, Germany, and the United Kingdom (the EU-3), and later accompanied by China, Russia, and the United States (the P5+1) tried

---

[20] Iran is not a member of the Missile Technology Control Regime (MTCR), and is actively working to acquire, develop, and deploy a broad range of ballistic missiles and space launch capabilities.

[21] "Iran's Nuclear Fuel Cycle," *Institute for Science and International Security (ISIS)*, www.isisnucleariran.org.

[22] David Sanger and William Broad, "U.S. and Allies Warn Iran Over Nuclear 'Deception'," *The New York Times* (September 25, 2009), www.nytimes.com. The International Atomic Energy Agency, "Implementation of the NPT Safeguards Agreement and Relevant Provisions of Security Council Resolutions in the Islamic Republic of Iran," (November 2011), www.iaea.org.

Arms Control is Problematic 243

several times to negotiate a settlement to the dispute.[23] Negotiations between the P5+1 and Iran culminated in the Joint Comprehensive Plan of Action (JCPOA) in July 2015, a comprehensive 25-year nuclear agreement limiting Iran's nuclear capacity in exchange for sanctions relief including cash payments concealed from Congress running several billion dollars.[24] On January 16, 2016, America and the Europeans lifted all nuclear-related sanctions on Iran in response to Teheran's progress meeting key metrics of the deal.[25]

The deal had loopholes.[26] The JCPOA allowed Iran to keep its base nuclear infrastructure intact and sidestep ratification of the

---

[23]IAEA, "IAEA, Iran Sign Joint Statement on Framework for Cooperation," (November 2013), www.iaea.org.

[24]Marc Thiessen, "Obama Took Lying to New Heights with the Iran Deal," *AEI* (June 2018), http://www.aei.org/publication/obama-took-lying-to-new-heights-with-the-iran-deal/?mkt_tok=eyJpIjoiWVRVM01EazFNRFJtTjJWaiIsInQiOiJHZ2dMQmVFemdXaVc 5cHhPYTdxa2RFQUdFeEs5aHFKcGsweU5KeHlYSG53bWthT2JpWGt LUkNQY1B1OUxtakRzK3p5UjE1VHV4R1gwNDdPRFM2VnVncm1ZUXpTSUl VQURrVUFTeEVLNUhPOW1BOTZcL1pmaWZla2tGdGxzaVZwZGcifQ%3D%3D.

Washington Examiner, "Ben Rhodes Can't Answer Questions About Obama Secretly Granting Iran Access to US Financial System," (June 8, 2018), https://www.washington examiner.com/news/ben-rhodes-cant-answer-questions-about-obama-secretly-granting-iran-access-to-u-s-financial-system.

"… the Obama administration had secretly sent a plane to Tehran loaded with $400 million in Swiss francs, euros and other currencies on the same day Iran released four American hostages, which was followed by two more secret flights carrying another $1.3 billion in cash. Now, in a bombshell revelation, Republicans on the Senate Permanent Subcommittee on Investigations, led by Sen. Rob Portman (R-Ohio), have revealed in a new report that the Obama administration secretly tried to help Iran use US banks to convert $5.7 billion in Iranian assets, after promising Congress that Iran would not get access to the US financial system — and then lied to Congress about what it had done." "Investigators also found internal State Department emails, in which officials admitted that the Obama administration had "exceeded our JCPOA commitments" by authorizing Iranian access to US banks." Cf. Christian Datoc, "Trump Signs Executive Order Reinstating Pre-Nuke Deal Iran Sanctions Despite UN Objections — Adds 27 New Targeted Bodies To Sanctions List," Daily Caller, September 21, 2020. https://dailycaller.com/2020/09/21/trump-signs-executive-order-pre-nuclear-deal-jcpoa-iran-sanctions/.

[25]IAEA, "Iran Sign Joint Statement on Framework for Cooperation," (November 2013), www.iaea.org.

[26]Michael Rubin, "Statement before the Committee on Oversight and Government Reform, Subcommittee on Nation Security On 'Protecting America from a Bad Deal: Ending U.S. Participation in the Nuclear Agreement with Iran', Putting American Security

244   *Beleaguered Superpower: Biden's America Adrift*

"Additional Protocol," requiring greater verification of states' compliance with safeguard agreements. Likewise, Iran retains the capability of working on nuclear warhead designs,[27] and building missiles capable of delivering nuclear ordnance.[28]

Media attention focused on compliance and the possibility that Iran was merely bidding its time before going nuclear, without linking JCPOA to Iran's misbehavior in the Middle East. This omission gave the mullahs a pass, allowing them to intensify their aggression and openly prepare an attack on Israel without triggering sanctions because Teheran remained formally in JCPOA compliance.[29] America did not reap any confidence building peace dividend in return for the termination of sanctions. This was not an explicit *quid pro quo*, but the failure of Iran to modify its hostile behavior confirms clearly that adding arms control to Washington's disciplinary kit is not fail-safe. It also reveals the degree to which Obama–Biden era "empty cosmopolitan idealism" inclined Washington toward indulging Eastern authoritarians.

President Trump announced that the United States would withdraw from the agreement on May 8, 2018 based on compelling evidence of Iran's intention to go nuclear,[30] and failure to obtain agreement with the

---

First in the Post-JCPOA Order," *AEI* (June 2018), http://www.aei.org/wp-content/uploads/2018/06/2018-06-Rubin-Testimony.pdf.

[27] *Ibid.* "The Iranian nuclear archives exposed publicly by Israeli Prime Minister Benjamin Netanyahu make clear that Iranian work on warheads is well advanced, and, even if it has since been shelved, Iranian authorities have taken steps to preserve the knowledge."

[28] *Ibid.* "UN Security Council Resolution 2231 'called upon [Iran] not to undertake any activity related to ballistic missiles designed to be capable of delivering nuclear weapons.' Iranian authorities have subsequently tested more than two dozen ballistic missiles, but they argue that they are designed for other purposes and that, even if they are capable of carrying nuclear warheads, they are allowed."

[29] Kenneth Timmerman, "Israel Strikes Back at Iranian Aggression, While Iran Lies and Pretends It Won a Victory," *Fox News* (May 10, 2018), http://www.foxnews.com/opinion/2018/05/10/israel-strikes-back-at-iranian-aggression-while-iran-lies-and-pretends-it-won-victory.html.

[30] Jarret Blanc, "Trump's Iran Deal Decision: What Comes Next," *Carnegie Endowment for International Peace* (May 2018), https://carnegieendowment.org/2018/05/07/trump-s-iran-deal-decision-what-comes-next-pub-76272?utm_source=ctw&utm_medium=email&mkt_tok=eyJpIjoiT0dabE4yRTBZVGswTnpBdyIsInQiOiJyYzRaYmFndGVxbW9qMjBBUXJkkKzh4QzRJWGJoNFZpSWVVd3hvWjdCcWZoVXQ5XC9xeE11QllTaHRNMmVRSDhDc0hBc1JvdkZaW1c3K1BkNlpBN1J0clo0dXpppQ1RxZ0N1SGJKWmtXMm01QTJqVm9CaURlUURKKT0wxRHg1S2YwaIM4S

Europeans about toughening Iran's obligation to rein its misbehavior in the Middle East.[31] The Europeans have pledged to try upholding the agreement by investing in Iran's development to the fullest extent possible within American re-imposed economic sanctions regime,[32] while Iran

---

DA5UkdrWkhiMkFycDJIb1B3OVwvUT09In0%3D. Michael Rubin, "How Did the US Get It So Wrong on Iran's Nuclear Program?" *AEI* (May 2018), http://www.aei.org/publication/how-did-the-us-get-it-so-wrong-on-irans-nuclear-program/?mkt_tok=eyJpIjoiTVdFNFkySXdNemRqWWpnMyIsInQiOiJVY1lBSDFWVEZEVWIwamh1ek FzTWpoSSsxalNsZWc3eHlid1grYVR2VVltaDFaTnA0MENrTzZpUWxyT2FHUXI0bG w1a2k4eXlRMmJPNnFmV01HbFZRZVFWOFNJWncyVVRPY2dPWnRBV3V5UzB hY0ZCU0pSN05vclp0TFdHRDNhKyJ9.

"One waiver is due for renewal on May 12 — a threat to sanction third countries if they do not reduce purchases of Iranian oil. The U.S. secretary of state formally issues this waiver."

[31] Jarret Blanc, "Trump's Iran Deal Decision: What Comes Next," *Carnegie Endowment for International Peace* (May 2018), https://carnegieendowment.org/2018/05/07/trump-s-iran-deal-decision-what-comes-next-pub-76272?utm_source=ctw&utm_medium=email&mkt_tok=eyJpIjoiT0dabE4yRTBZVGswTnpBdyIsInQiOiJyYzRaYmFndGVxbW 9qMjBBUXJkKzh4QzRJWGJoNFZpSWVVd3hvWjdCcWZoVXQ5XC9xeE11 Ql1TaHRNMmVRSDhDc0hBc1JvdkZaWlc3K1BkNlpBNlJ0c1o0dXp pQ1RxZ0N1SGJKWmtXMm01QTJqVm9CaURlUURKT0wxRHg1S2YwalM4S DA5UkdrWkhiMkFycDJIb1B3OVwvUT09In0%3D.

"The administration is demanding that Europe agree in advance that there will be a forceful and coordinated reaction, including powerful new sanctions, if Iran crosses one of three hypothetical lines. Reportedly, the United States and Europe have largely reached agreement on how to respond if Iran develops intercontinental ballistic missiles (ICBMs) or if it denies access to the International Atomic Energy Agency (IAEA)."

More work remains on the issue of "sunsets" in the JCPOA. Some of Iran's commitments under the JCPOA are in perpetuity, while other restrictions begin to loosen in about eight years. The administration wants Europe to threaten the reimposition of JCPOA sanctions if Iran takes advantage of any loosened restriction; the Europeans correctly consider the U.S. stance to be a violation of the JCPOA and poor policy, since it would fail to prioritize different aspects of Iran's potential future nuclear activity. Nonetheless, Europe and the United States have always shared a common perspective that if Iran again takes steps that do not fit into its civil nuclear program, it would require a strong and coordinated response. There is a clear middle ground between these two positions, and progress has been made in negotiations to reach it.

[32] James McAuley, "After Trump Says U.S. Will Withdraw From Iran Deal, Allies Say They'll Try to Save It," *Washington Post* (May 8, 2018), https://www.washingtonpost.com/world/backers-of-iran-nuclear-deal-wage-last-ditch-blitz-seeking-to-

246　*Beleaguered Superpower: Biden's America Adrift*

flagrantly continues to nuclearize.[33] Other things equal, the Biden–Harris administration is likely to reinstate JCPOA, but Brexit and Macon's battle with "Islamists" in France may prompt reconsideration of an arms control agreement that tacitly flouts nuclear non-proliferation.[34]

Olive Branch

Arms control and arms reduction are feeble tools in Western hands for disciplining Eastern authoritarians. Nonetheless, they can play a useful role in facilitating reconciliation when hostile parties contemplate mending fences. If Kim Jong-un is serious about his recent peace overtures, an arms control olive branch provides an excellent device for sustaining momentum. It is unlikely to usher in an era of eternal peace as some arms control advocates never tire promising,[35] but it can help keep the wolf at bay.

---

sway-trump/2018/05/08/9b15e3f0-523e-11e8-a6d4-ca1d035642ce_story.html? noredirect=on&utm_term=.0118ed4c7a01.

Jarret Blanc, "Trump's Iran Deal Decision: What Comes Next," *Carnegie Endowment for International Peace* (May 2018), https://carnegieendowment.org/2018/05/07/trump-s-iran-deal-decision-what-comes-next-pub-76272?utm_source=ctw&utm_medium=email&mkt_tok=eyJpIjoiT0dabE4yRTBZVGswTnpBdyIsInQiOiJyYzRaYmFndGVxbW9qMjBBUXJkKzh4QzRJWGJoNFZpSWVVd3hvWjdCcWZoVXQ5XC9xeE11QllTaHRNMmVRSDhDc0hBc1JvdkZaWlc3K1BkNlpBNlJ0clo0dXpppQ1RxZ0N1SGJKWmtXMm01QTJqVm9CaUWlUURKT0wxRHg1S2YwaIM4SDA5Ukdr WkhiMkFycDJIb1B3OVwvUT09In0%3D. Ellie Geranmayeh, "The Coming Clash: Why Iran Will Divide Europe from the United States," *European Council on Foreign Relations* (October 2017), http://www.ecfr.eu/publications/summary/why_iran_will_divide_europe_from_the_united_states_7230.

The European and American Middle East agendas have always been ajar, driven by colonial and post-colonial entanglements, and foreign investment priorities.

[33] "Nuclear," *NTI*, Updated June 2020, https://www.nti.org/learn/countries/iran/nuclear/.

[34] Kim Willsher, "Macron Outlines New Law to Prevent 'Islamist Separatism' in France," *Guardian* (October 2020), https://www.theguardian.com/world/2020/oct/02/emmanuel-macron-outlines-law-islamic-separatism-france. Alec Ward, "The US and Iran have their first real chance to revive the nuclear deal: Washington and Tehran will meet indirectly in Austria next week as part of a gathering to keep the Iran nuclear deal alive," VOX, April 2, 2021. https://www.vox.com/2021/4/2/22363847/iran-nuclear-deal-biden-vienna-austria-jcpoa.

[35] "Prague Nuclear Agenda," *The White House President Barack Obama*, https://obama whitehouse.archives.gov/the-press-office/2017/01/11/fact-sheet-prague-nuclear-agenda.

Jeffrey Sachs, "Denuclearization Means the US, Too," *Project Syndicate* (May 2018), https://www.project-syndicate.org/commentary/denuclearization-also-for-united-

Farewell to Arms Control and Arms Reduction?

Arms control and arms reduction diplomacy are established tools of international relations. The American Arms Control and Disarmament Agency (ACDA) is no longer an independent entity,[36] but it survives inside the State Department as an institutional voice for arms control and arms reduction. The nostalgic note voiced by Eugene Rumer that arms control is fading quietly into the night is wrong.[37] Nonetheless, repeated failure and tectonic shifts in global power alignments in the last decade are dampening political ardor for arms controls, even in Europe. China, for example, has been developing intermediate and short-range missiles outside the framework of the Intermediate-Range Nuclear Forces (INF) Treaty.

The discovery by the United States that Russian tested and subsequently deployed a ground-launched cruise missile (a decision made by Putin himself at a meeting National Security Council meeting that he chaired April 29, 1999),[38] appears to have been a bad omen.[39] It prompted

---

states-by-jeffrey-d-sachs-2018-05?utm_source=Project+Syndicate+Newsletter&utm_campaign=33a09b0d78-sunday_newsletter_13_5_2018&utm_medium=email&utm_term=0_73bad5b7d8-33a09b0d78-93559677.

"By all means, let us urge a rapid and successful denuclearization of North Korea; but let us also, with equal urgency, address the nuclear arsenal of the US and others. The world is not living under a Pax Americana. It is living in dread, with millions pushed into the vortex of war by an unrestrained and unhinged US military machine, and with billions living in the shadow of nuclear annihilation."

[36] The U.S. Arms Control and Disarmament Agency (ACDA) was established as an independent agency of the United States government by the Arms Control and Disarmament Act, September 26, 1961. As of April, 1999, ACDA was merged into the Department of State. ACDA's four Bureaus were merged with the Bureau of Political-Military Affairs to form three new Bureaus, for Political-Military Affairs (PM), Arms Control (AC), and Nonproliferation (NP). In 2000, a fourth Bureau for Verification and Compliance (VC) was added by statute. All four Bureaus reported to the Secretary and Deputy Secretary of State through the Under Secretary of State for Arms Control and International Security Affairs. Rose Gottemoeller has served as Under Secretary for Arms Control and International Security since February 7, 2012, when Ellen Tauscher was named Special Envoy for Strategic Stability and Missile Defense.

[37] Eugene Rumer, "A Farewell to ... Arms Control," *Carnegie Endowment for Peace* (April 2018), https://carnegieendowment.org/2018/04/17/farewell-to-arms-.-.-.-control-pub-76088.

[38] Milto Leitenberg, email, April 25, 2019.

[39] Kevin Ryan, "After the INF Treaty: An Objective Look at US and Russian Compliance, Plus a New Arms Control Regime," *Russia Matters* (December 7, 2017), https://www.

248 *Beleaguered Superpower: Biden's America Adrift*

the Trump administration to start the process of withdrawing from the INF treaty on February 2, 2019.[40] Under Article XV of the treaty, withdrawal can happen after six months' notice. The United States formally withdrew for the INF Treaty on August 2, 2019.[41]

The 2018 National Defense Authorization Act provided funds to the US Department of Defense for research and development of an INF missile, which enables the United States to field a missile to counter the alleged Russian deployment of the Iskandar-K cruise missile setting off tit-for-tat retaliation.[42]

The toxic political climate that surrounds bilateral ties in both Washington and Moscow shows no sign of abating. The New START, negotiated in 2010 and ratified in 2011 is likely to be the last arms control treaty between Russia and the United States for a long time to come,

---

russiamatters.org/analysis/after-inf-treaty-objective-look-us-and-russian-compliance-plus-new-arms-control-regime. Steve Pifer and Oliver Meier, "Are We Nearing the End of the INF Treaty?" *Arms Control Today* 48 (January/February 2018), https://www.armscontrol.org/act/2018-01/features/we-nearing-end-inf-treaty.

[40] David Reid, "Russia Threatens Military Response to Any NATO Citing Russian Aggression as a Serious Threat Action Over Nuclear-Ready Missile," *CNBC* (June 26, 2019), https://www.cnbc.com/2019/06/26/russia-threatens-response-to-nato-over-nuclear-ready-ssc-8-missile.html.

"The same day, Russian President Vladimir Putin announced that Russia had also suspended the INF Treaty in a 'mirror response' to President Donald Trump's decision to suspend the treaty, effective that day. The next day, Russia started work on new intermediate range (ballistic) hypersonic missiles along with land based (club kalibr — biryuza) systems (both nuclear armed) in response to the USA announcing it would start to conduct research and development of weapons prohibited under the treaty."

On March 8, 2019, the foreign ministry of Ukraine announced that since the United States and Russian Federation have both pulled out of the INF treaty, it now has the right to develop intermediate-range missiles, Ukraine had about 40 percent of Soviet space industry, but never developed a missile with the range to strike Moscow (only having both longer and shorter-range missiles). Ukrainian president Petro Poroshenko said, "We need high-precision missiles and we are not going to repeat the mistakes of the Budapest Memorandum." Ukraine remains a party to the Nuclear Non-Proliferation Treaty.

[41] Dan Smith, "The Crumbling Architecture of Arms Control," *SIPRI* (October 23, 2018), https://www.sipri.org/commentary/essay/2018/crumbling-architecture-arms-control.

[42] Hans Kristensen, "Russia Declared In Violation of INF Treaty: New Cruise Missile May Be Deploying," *Federation of American Scientists* (July 30, 2014).

The Iskandar K cruise missile range exceeds 500 kilometers, making it an intermediate range missile under the INF treaty.

should the enmity persist. It will lapse in 2021 unless the Biden–Harris administration negotiates a last minute extension.

Politics is only one aspect of the problem. Technological change poses a raft of fresh challenges. Missile defense, new capabilities, and activities in the cyber domain, and an array of new and emerging nuclear and conventional systems threaten the relevance of surviving treaties, and China has become a wild card.[43]

Thus, arms control is at risk of becoming a casualty of more than just the political vagaries in Russia and the United States. It could be losing its relevance to both countries as more pressing issues arise from new geopolitical and technological challenges.

Arms control was never much more than what adversaries considered mutually advantageous behind the purple prose, and is unlikely to serve as an effective tool for restraining the behavior of Eastern authoritarians in the future.[44] The problem was not merely a matter of mutual distrust, resolvable with confidence building measures. The deeper issue is the unpredictability of authoritarian intentions.[45]

Transnational Sheriffs

Arms control treaties are contractual tools that empower principals to bring legal pressure on each other to comply with mutually agreed restrictions on research, development, testing, deployment, and stockpiling weapons. Monitoring authority is subject to negotiation. Contracting parties can monitor and enforce treaty terms independently, or assign the task to an autonomous body as sheriff.

---

[43] Guy Norris, "China Takes Wraps Off National Hypersonic Plan," *Aviation Week and Space Technology* (April 10, 2017). Guy Norris, "Classified Report on Hypersonics Says U.S. Lacking Urgency," *Aviation Week and Space Technology* February 20, 2017.Guy Norris, "U.S. Air Force Plans Road Map to Operational Hypersonics," *Aviation Week and Space Technology*, July 27, 2017.

[44] Rose Gottemoeller, "Russia is Updating Their Nuclear Weapons: What Does that Mean for the Rest of Us?" *Carnegie Endowment for International Peace* (January 2020), https://carnegieendowment.org/2020/01/29/russia-is-updating-their-nuclear-weapons-what-does-that-mean-for-rest-of-us-pub-80895.

[45] Pavel Felgenhauer, "Moscow Clarifies Its Nuclear Deterrence Policy," *Jamestown Commentaries* (June 4, 2020), 17, Issue 80, https://jamestown.org/program/moscow-clarifies-its-nuclear-deterrence-policy/.

250 *Beleaguered Superpower: Biden's America Adrift*

The IAEA, under the jurisdiction of the United Nations Office of Disarmament Affairs serves as the transnational monitor and sheriff for the NPT. The IAEA has 169 member states, and reports to higher bodies within the United Nations organization, including the Security Council.[46]

The concept of trans-national sheriff is general and can serve national security purposes whenever it is possible to persuade sovereigns to relinquish some of their national authority. Iran did not enter into a nuclear non-proliferation agreement with America, and Washington is not its sheriff. Nonetheless, America has a degree of influence on Tehran as a UN National Security Council member. Washington is in a position to speak on behalf of all NPT members in response to an IAEA finding of non-compliance against Iran.

The United States has been trying to capture the potential benefits of trans-national sheriff-ship for national security, economic and political purposes throughout the postwar period. North Atlantic Treaty Organization (NATO) is a prime example. It is a voluntary alliance among sovereign equals, but America is formally and informally the primary force in the organization. NATO's supranational dimension greatly enhances Washington's ability to project power, while also providing members with more security than might otherwise be feasible.

The United States has tried to draw the European Union into analogous non-security transnational organizations. The Transatlantic Trade and Investment Partnership (TTIP) is not only an effort to capture economic synergies but also implicitly can be employed for national security purposes. America already utilizes its special relationship with the European Union to coordinate its economic sanctions against Russia, North Korea, and Iran. It would be able to do so even more effectively if the Transatlantic Trade and Investment Partnership and the Trans-Pacific Partnership become realities.

The World Bank and International Monetary Fund, unlike the United States Agency for International Development are also transnational organizations.[47] They allow America to use the financial resources of

---

[46]Treaty on the Non-Proliferation of Nuclear Weapons (NPT), *United Nations*, https://www.un.org/disarmament/wmd/nuclear/npt/.

[47]The United States Agency for International Development (USAID) is an independent agency of the United States federal government that is primarily responsible for administering civilian foreign aid and development assistance. With a budget of over $27 billion, USAID is one of the largest official aid agencies in the world, and accounts for more than

189 member states when required for Washington's national security purposes. The International Monetary Fund has been especially active in trying to bolster Ukraine's independence *vis-à-vis* Russia by stabilizing and jump-starting its economy.[48]

Clash of Trans-national Sheriffs

What is good for the goose is good for the gander. The Soviet Union tried to counter the transnational security benefits of NATO and the Brussels Treaty (1948) with its own rival organizations: the Council for Mutual Economic Assistance CMEA (1949) and the Warsaw Pact (1955). Russia followed suit with the Commonwealth of Independent States (CIS), Collective Security Treaty Organization (1992),[49] and the Eurasian Economic Union (2014).[50]

China created its own regional transnational organization in 2003, the Shanghai Cooperation Organization (SCO) to buttress its national security interests through military cooperation,[51] intelligence sharing, counterterrorism activities, and economic persuasion. It added the Asian Infrastructure Investment Bank (AIIB) in 2015, a multilateral development bank that supports building infrastructure in the Asia-Pacific region. Xi Jinping has made it clear that the AIIB's mission is to provide Beijing with transnational economic and security influence by promoting the deep integration of China's economy into the global system through multiple channels. The AIIB will fund "connectivity"; that is, the Belt and Road Initiative (BRI) or (OBOR), an immense regional development project that will inevitably make its neighbors financially and economically

---

half of all U.S. foreign assistance (which in absolute dollar terms is the highest in the world).

[48] Steven Rosefielde and Bruno Dallago, *Transformation and Crisis in Central and Eastern Europe: Challenges and Prospects* (London: Routledge, 2016).

On March 11, 2015, IMF approved a four-year extended funding facility worth $17.5 billion for Ukraine. Financing for Ukraine was suspending after the spring of 2017 because Kiev failed to launch large-scale privatization, set up an anti-corruption court, and reduce gas subsidies.

[49] Russia, Armenia, Kazakhstan, Kyrgyzstan, and Tajikistan.

[50] Russia, Belarus, Armenia, Kazakhstan, and Kyrgyzstan.

[51] China, Kazakhstan, Kyrgyzstan, Russia, Tajikistan, and Uzbekistan.

252 *Beleaguered Superpower: Biden's America Adrift*

dependent.[52] Xi Jinping just launched the Regional Comprehensive Economic Partnership (RCEP) covering 15 Asia-Pacific economies to promote economic globalization and regional integration. There has been a great deal of speculation concerning the feasibility of BRI's goals, but there can be no doubt that the project will succeed enough to confer enormous security benefits on China.[53] For the moment, it seems that Beijing will gain more from its transnational sheriff-ship than America.

The national security benefits of trans-nationalization are precarious. Transnational institutions are fair weather national security, political, and economic instruments. Most nations are content with delegating sovereign rights to supranational bodies when trans-nationality provides synergies sufficient to offset sacrifices, but holding members together and negotiating compromises become harder in stormy weather.[54] The European Union, which is a supranational governance body in its own right was buoyant and content during the salad days following the launch of the euro on January 1, 1999, but has lost much of its cohesion in the aftermath of the 2008 financial and 2015 refugee immigration crises.[55] COVID-19 has sparked a momentary surge in cooperation.[56]

Trans-nationalization also may turn from a bonanza into an albatross. Supranational potentates are vulnerable to counter pressures and intrigues.

---

[52] "The Silk Road Economic Belt and the 21st-century Maritime Silk Road or The Belt and Road Initiative (BRI) is a development strategy proposed by the Chinese government that focuses on connectivity and cooperation between Eurasian countries, primarily the People's Republic of China (PRC), the land-based Silk Road Economic Belt (SREB) and the ocean-going Maritime Silk Road (MSR). he initial focus has been infrastructure investment, education, construction materials, railway and highway, automobile, real estate, power grid, and iron and steel.[8] Already, some estimates list the Belt and Road Initiative as one of the largest infrastructure and investment projects in history, covering more than 68 countries, including 65% of the world's population and 40% of the global GDP as of 2017."

[53] Zhikai Wang, "Belt and Road Strategy" in Masaaki Kuboniwa, Kumiko Haba, and Satoshi Mizobata, eds., *The Unwinding of the Globalist Dream: EU, Russia, China* (Singapore: World Scientific Publishers, 2017): 249–262.

[54] Steven Rosefielde and Yiyi Liu, "Sovereign Debt Crises: Solidarity and Power," *The Journal of Comparative Economic Studies* 12 (2017): 101–112.

[55] Steven Rosefielde, "EU Reform: Two Speed or Inclusive Multi-Track?" *Contemporary Economics* (2018).

[56] "EU Global Response to COVID-19," https://ec.europa.eu/international-partnerships/topics/eu-global-response-covid-19_en.

Weak members can forge coalitions and outmaneuver their masters (Biden, Merkel, Xi, and Putin). This can cause dissension, paralyze institutions, and lead to traumatic ruptures. Brexit provides a vivid example.[57] Moribund institutions moreover are difficult to revive and harder to discard. The post-war experience to date with trans-nationalization as a vehicle for bolstering American security is not encouraging. Insiders vigorously press supranational gambits of all sorts for diverse reasons, but the proliferation of Western supranational institutions does not appear to hold much promise for disciplining Russia, China, North Korea, Iran and the global jihadi. Likewise, the hope that the Association of Southeast Asian Nations (ASEAN) will restrain China's ambitions in the South China Sea is probably misplaced. It is naïve to suppose that ASEAN declaring the South China Sea a Zone of Peace will restrain China from using the threat potential of its fortified artificial islands for Beijing's advantage. Xi might pay lip service to the idea, but a scrap of paper will not deter him.[58]

---

[57] Steven Rosefielde and Bruno Dallago, "New Principles for a Better EU" in Kumiko Haba and Satoshi Mizobata, eds., *100 Year of World Wars and Postwar Regional Collaboration and Governance in the EU and Asia* (Tokyo: Aoyama Gakuin, 2020). Steven Rosefielde and Bruno Dallago, "Post Brexit European Integration" (Berlin: Springer, 2020).

[58] Steven Rosefielde and Bruno Dallago, "New Principles for a Better EU" in Kumiko Haba and Satoshi Mizobata, eds., *100 Year of World Wars and Postwar Regional Collaboration and Governance in the EU and Asia*, (Tokyo: Aoyama Gakuin, 2020).

Chapter 12

Technology is Crucial

Many analysts contend that technology is America's trump card in matters of national and global security. They claim that superior technological prowess will always make the United States richer and mightier than its foes. Eastern authoritarians consequently sooner rather than later will mind their manners to share prosperity and avoid fruitless military competition. If this epiphany eludes them, American can bar their access to crucial technologies, a sanction already examined in Chapter 9.

The United States has technologically outshined Russia, China, North Korea, and Iran for two centuries. Should these foes accept the inevitable and throw in the towel? This would have been the rational choice until China demonstrated in the new millennium that it had viable alternatives. Russia is learning the lessons of Chinese technology reform.

Five reforms transformed the mainland's economic and military technological potential: (1) relaxing the Chinese Academy of Sciences monopoly on technology research, development, testing and evaluation, (2) linking the Chinese Academy of Sciences to for-profit entrepreneurial intermediaries, (3) encouraging business RDT&E, (4) fostering technology transfer (via China's role in Western outsourcing), and (5) takeovers of Western corporations.

After the establishment of the People's Republic in 1949, China reorganized its science establishment along Soviet lines. Mao Zedong created the Chinese Academy of Sciences by amalgamating research institutes under the former Academia Sinica and Beijing Research Academy (the former Beijing Research Laboratory). Sergei Vavilov, Stalin's director of

256 *Beleaguered Superpower: Biden's America Adrift*

the Soviet Academy of Sciences, helped remodel China's traditional research establishment along Soviet lines.

The main task of the Chinese Academy of Sciences was to provide a scientific foundation for central planning and the development of the national economy,[1] relying on bureaucratic principles of organization. Civilian and military research were restricted to institutes and prohibited in enterprises. The Chinese Academy of Science concentrated on applied science, engineering and technology, although senior academicians preferred to pursue pure science when they could.

The Soviet Academy of Sciences evolved from the Russian Academy of Sciences founded by Peter the Great in 1724. The institution from the outset maintained high standards of academic training and accomplishment. It was thoroughly professional in these regards, and the Chinese Academy of Sciences followed the Soviet Union's good example.

While both institutions competently served the national economy as their political masters desired, they were vulnerable to scientific parochialism, and disinterested in commerce and consumer welfare. Scientists and mathematicians pursuing their pet projects often outfoxed political overseers,[2] and the Academy of Sciences did not have to pass the competitive test. Enterprise managers were indifferent to quality improving technological modernization because they received bonuses for whatever they produced, not whether buyers were pleased. The Ministry of Defense alone had the power to hold the Academy of Sciences accountable for quality improving innovations. It received special care, and did well enough for the Soviets to defeat Nazi Germany in WWII, but was unable to keep pace with the Western R&D establishment in the post-war years, especially in microelectronics.

Deng Xiaoping's experiment with market communism paved the way for constructive change, and the Russian Academy of Sciences under Putin has followed China's example. Both institutions restructured to serve their clients better. They still must be attentive to the military industrial complex, but also do contract work for market-based firms. In the

---

[1]The Common Program of the Chinese People's Political Consultative Conference stated in 1949 that "Efforts should be made to develop the natural sciences in order to serve the construction of industry, agriculture, and the national defense."

[2]David Joravsky, *The Lysenko Affair* (Chicago: University of Chicago Press, 2010). Loren Graham, *What Have We Learned About Science and Technology from the Russian Experience?* (Palo Alto: Stanford University Press, 1998).

Technology is Crucial 257

Chinese case, the Academy of Sciences owns hundreds of commercial companies including Lenovo, the world's largest personal computer vendor by unit sales.[3] This makes them responsive directly to for-profit enterprises and derivatively to final purchasers. The Chinese and Russian Academies of Sciences remain bureaucratic, but have added entrepreneurial components and are more attentive to market demand.

During the heyday of command communism, central state authorities planned and funded investment (new capital formation). Enterprises could not construct new firms and managers had limited authority to modernize their facilities. This is no longer true in either country. For-profit companies undertake the lion's share of new capital formation and enterprise modernization. They are able to borrow funds at home and abroad mimicking the Western model.

Contemporary China and to a lesser extent Russia both benefit from direct foreign investment and outsource-driven technology transfer.[4] Foreign companies build plant, supply equipment, and train personnel using these facilities as low cost intermediate input suppliers in global

---

[3] Lenovo was founded in Beijing in November 1984 as Legend and was incorporated in Hong Kong in 1988. It became a wholly state-owned company established on April 12, 2002, part of Chinese Academy of Sciences Holdings Co., Ltd. ("CAS HOLDINGS" for short). CAS HOLDINGS exercises, on behalf of the Chinese Academy of Sciences, the investors' rights for the state-owned operative assets. Lenovo acquired IBM's personal computer business in 2005 and agreed to acquire its Intel-based server business in 2014. Lenovo entered the smartphone market in 2012 and as of 2014 was the largest vendor of smartphones in Mainland China. In 2014, Lenovo acquired the mobile phone handset maker Motorola Mobility from Google. Lenovo is listed on the Hong Kong Stock Exchange and is a constituent of the Hang Seng China-Affiliated Corporations Index, often referred to as "Red Chips."

All Chinese productive assets are the freehold property of the Chinese people, administered by China's communist party. The party leases its 100 percent freehold-owned stake in Lenovo to the Chinese Academy of Sciences, which in turn has the right to sell leasehold shares on the Shanghai stock exchange. As freehold owner, the Chinese people (meaning the communist party) has the right to do anything it wants with its leased property. The number of savvy Western businessmen who understand this must be close to zero, but the Chinese understand the matter clearly.

[4] Steven Rosefielde, "The Illusion of Westernization in Russia and China," *Comparative Economic Studies* 49, 2007: 495–513.

value-added chains.[5] The strategy has enabled Chinese and Russian firms to climb the value-added ladder. Skills and technologies transferred to foreign joint venture firms are fungible. This allows domestic entrepreneurs to start their own ventures at high technological levels, super-charging rapid economic growth.

Finally, Chinese and Russian multinational firms acquire advanced technologies by purchasing bankrupt firms (the Russians do this with oil drilling companies),[6] and by buying established Western businesses like Volvo. The magnitude of their success is a subject of professional debate, but the potential is apparent. American technological superiority is no longer certain. One way or another, China and Russia both can plausibly hope to continue closing both the civilian and military technology gaps with the West. China may even be able to surpass America's high technology frontier.

Hybrid Warfare

Moreover, cyber technologies as key elements of the "Fourth Industrial Revolution" (FIR) underpinning hybrid warfare are becoming as important as traditional civilian and military technological prowess.[7] The world today is neither at peace, nor in a state of large-scale military engagement

---

[5]Derek Scissors, "Sino-American Trade: We Know Where This is Headed," *AEI* (April 2018), http://www.aei.org/publication/sino-american-trade-we-know-where-this-is-headed/.

"It was thought China would respect intellectual property more as it climbed the technology ladder. Instead, it has refined tools to coerce technology transfer or steal it outright." "But fast or slow, clear or chaotic, the United States will not accept another decade of a much-larger China warping competition in its home market while demanding open markets overseas. It will not tolerate another decade of China mining the relationship for resources to seize technological leadership."

[6]Vitaly Shlykov personally oversaw the purchase of defunct American petroleum drilling companies in Houston after the 2008 financial crisis. Private conversation.

[7]Derek Scissors, "Sino-American Trade: We Know Where This is Headed," *AEI* (April 2018), http://www.aei.org/publication/sino-american-trade-we-know-where-this-is-headed/.

The Fourth Industrial Revolution is the convergence of technologies blurring the lines between the physical, digital, and biological worlds. It is interchangeable with the term "Industry 4.0" coined by the German government in 2011.

Technology is Crucial   259

among powers like America, Russia, China, North Korea, and Iran. The main battleground is the twilight zone between peace and high intensity armed conflict where the West and Eastern authoritarian regimes both try to harm foes and defend themselves using low intensity military means, proxies, ransomware,[8] espionage, sabotage, disinformation, virtual reality deception,[9] propaganda, and sowing the seeds of political strife, rebellion, social disintegration, and regime change. The combination of low intensity combat, proxies, sabotage, and regime change strategies is "hybrid warfare,"[10] distinguished in the modern context from historical predecessors by the core role assigned to cyber technologies.

The term cyber refers to computers and the networks connecting them, collectively known as the domain of cyberspace. Western states depend on cyberspace for the everyday functioning of nearly all aspects of modern society. Everything modern society needs to function from critical infrastructures and financial institutions to modes of commerce and tools for national security depends to some extent upon cyberspace. Therefore, if America has the cyber edge over its adversaries, and foes

---

[8] Alan Blinder and Nicole Perlroth, "A Cyberattack Hobbles Atlanta, and Security Experts Shudder," *New York Times* (March 17, 2018), https://www.nytimes.com/2018/03/27/us/cyberattack-atlanta-ransomware.html.

[9] "A former FSB agent is teaching students at Moscow State University how Britain defeated Russia in the 'infowar' over Sergey Skripal," *Meduza* (November 7, 2018), https://meduza.io/en/feature/2018/11/08/a-former-fsb-agent-is-teaching-students-at-moscow-state-university-how-britain-defeated-russia-in-the-infowar-over-sergey-skripal.

The computer-generated simulation of a three-dimensional image or environment that can be interacted with in a seemingly real or physical way.

[10] "Military Balance," *International Institute for Strategic Studies* 115, no. 12015 (February 2017).

Hybrid warfare is a military strategy that blends conventional warfare, irregular warfare (guerrilla warfare), and cyberwarfare. This is a Western Definition. The Russians only use "gibridnaia voina" when they refer to the Western debate.

For a discussion of the nature of Russian military strategy in Ukraine and against NATO more generally see Samuel Charap, "The Ghost of Hybrid War," *Survival* (December 2015–January 2016). Frank Hoffman, *Conflict in the 21st Century: The Rise of Hybrid War* (Arlington: Potomac Institute for Policy Studies, 2007). Brian Fleming, "Hybrid Threat Concept: Contemporary War, Military Planning and the Advent of Unrestricted Operational Art," *United States Army Command and General Staff College* (May 19, 2011).

260 Beleaguered Superpower: Biden's America Adrift

have no realistic expectation of capturing the lead, then the West might be able to rein Eastern authoritarian misbehavior.

The weight of the evidence is not encouraging.[11] Russia has shown itself to be adept at hybrid warfare against America,[12] and in Ukraine,[13] and is rapidly improving its capabilities.[14] The Chinese,[15] North Koreans,[16]

---

[11]USCYBERCOM, "Achieve and Maintain Cyberspace Superiority Command Vision for US Cyber Command," (March 2018), https://assets.documentcloud.org/documents/4419681/Command-Vision-for-USCYBERCOM-23-Mar-18.pdf. Ralph Langner, "Defending Cyber Dominance," *Brookings* (March 2014), https://www.brookings.edu/on-the-record/defending-cyber-dominance/. Richard Harknett and Michael Fischerkeller, "Deterrence is Not a Credible Strategy for Cyberspace," *Orbis* (Summer 2017), https://www.fpri.org/article/2017/06/deterrence-not-credible-strategy-cyberspace/. Richard Harknett, "United States Cyber Command's New Vision: What It Entails and Why It Matters, *Lawfare Blog* (March 23, 2018), https://www.lawfareblog.com/united-states-cyber-commands-new-vision-what-it-entails-and-why-it-matters.

[12]"Report on Russian Active Measures," *House Permanent Select Committee on Intelligence* (March 22, 2018).

[13]Thomas Ricks, "Hybrid War's Sword Arm: The Russians Have Found Good Tactical Innovations," *Foreign Policy* (June 2017), http://foreignpolicy.com/2017/06/14/hybrid-wars-sword-arm-the-russians-have-found-good-tactical-innovations/. Samuel Charap, "The Ghost of Hybrid War," *Survival* (December 2015–January 2016). Jacob Kipp, "Putin's Ukrainian Gambit," *Conference on Challenges to the European Union, University of North Carolina, Chapel Hill* (September 2014).

[14]Daniel Terdiman, "Senator: On Cyberwarfare, Russia Has the U.S. 'Behind The Eight Ball'," *Fast Company* (March 2018), https://www.fastcompany.com/40542710/senator-on-cyberwarfare-russia-has-the-u-s-behind-the-eight-ball.

[15]Zi Yang, "China is Massively Expanding Its Cyber Capabilities," *National Interest* (October 2017). http://nationalinterest.org/blog/the-buzz/china-massively-expanding-its-cyber-capabilities-22577.

"In 10 years' time, the plan seeks to establish four to six world-class cybersecurity schools in Chinese universities as training grounds for cyber-warriors. All resources at these institutions — from teaching staff to incentive structures — will be dedicated solely to fostering top-notch cyber-warriors."

[16]Roger McDermott, "Russia's Electronic Warfare Capabilities to 2025: Challenging NATO in the Electromagnetic Spectrum," *International Centre for Defense and Security* (September 18, 2017).

Tara Seals, "Russia, China's Cyber-Capabilities Are Catastrophic," *Infosecurity* (January 2018), https://www.infosecurity-magazine.com/news/russia-chinas-cybercapabilities/.

"The report finds that Moscow is stepping up its efforts to renew and modernise the EW inventory, and this effort is complemented by changes to organisation, doctrine,

and Iranians[17] all have formidable cyber warfare capabilities. For example, Beijing has incorporated AI in autonomous unmanned aerial systems that could utilize neural networks to deny the US the freedom of navigation in the South China Sea.[18]

Once upon a time, it was reasonable to deduce from the institutional characteristics and documented under-achievement of Chinese and Russian investment, research, design, testing, and evaluation that Beijing and Moscow could not keep up with Western technological innovation in both civilian and military sectors. Many analysts inferred that China and Russia should accept the inevitable and embrace democratic free enterprise. China and increasingly so Russia have shown that they can use state-led market incentives inside their Academies of Science, in for-profit corporations and joint ventures, and via technology transfer to sustain their rivalries with the West. There no longer are compelling grounds for supposing that Beijing and Moscow will restrain themselves because their systems are technologically uncompetitive.

---

command structure, training and tactics, as well as techniques and procedures. The effect of those changes is evident in Russia's aggression against Ukraine, where EW forms an organic part of Russia's kinetic and non-kinetic operations — both in support of proxy forces and conducted independently. Further EW capability development will pose a serious challenge to the proper planning and execution of NATO's defence of the Baltic states, and NATO's entire Eastern Flank, in the event of a Russian assault. This capability is an integral part of Russia's anti-access/area denial (A2/AD) approach and is clearly tailored to target NATO's C4ISR."

[17] Collin Anderson and Karim Sadjadpour, "Iran's Cyber Threat: Espionage, Sabotage, and Revenge," *Carnegie Endowment for International Peace* (January 2018), https://carnegieendowment.org/2018/01/04/iran-s-cyber-threat-espionage-sabotage-and-revenge-pub-75134.

"Incidents involving Iran have been among the most sophisticated, costly, and consequential attacks in the history of the internet. The four-decade-long U.S.–Iran cold war has increasingly moved into cyberspace, and Tehran has been among the leading targets of uniquely invasive and destructive cyber operations by the United States and its allies."
"Iran's cyber capabilities appear to be indigenously developed, arising from local universities and hacking communities. This ecosystem is unique, involving diverse state-aligned operators with differing capabilities and affiliations."

[18] Cung Vu, "The Fourth Industrial Revolution: Its Security Implications," *RSIS* (May 2018).

Part V

Rescuing a Beleaguered Superpower

The evidence from the Cold War and ensuing post-Soviet decades demonstrates that stout hard power is indispensable for deterring and containing Eastern authoritarians because soft power is not a reliable surrogate. A strong, competitive, pro-meritocratic, and pro-growth economy is essential for sustaining stout hard power. Part V explains how America can restore its national security and advance the cause of global security by discarding social progressive pipedreams and applying competitive principles in its economy, society, and security.

Chapter 13

Rejecting Denial and Drift

America has been a superpower throughout the post-war era. Its nuclear arsenal, power projection, and economic might assure that the United States will remain a superpower well into the future. The utility of America's superpower, however, is an entirely different matter. Much depends on the correlation of forces and prospects for the virtuous application of America's influence. If American democracy withers, its economy rots and its military shrivels, then Washington's sphere of influence will shrink. If the United States is vibrant, then it should be able to contain the present danger.

America provided its citizens and assisted its allies to enjoy a much higher standard of living and quality of existence during the Cold War than the Soviet Union and communist China. It was able to preserve and augment a critical military technological edge, and an open society, democratic life style that induced Gorbachev and the East Europeans to blink. America was not always able to contain Soviet and Chinese spheres of influence, but the cumulative effects of the open society, democratic free enterprise, and superior quality of existence ultimately carried the day.

Obama–Biden era progressives and liberals chose a different course, downsizing American military power, tolerating slow economic growth, and closing society to expand the welfare state and assist those considered oppressed or hapless victims.

Their policies have improved the lot of some variously deserving and undeserving, and backfired for the nation, workers and much of the middle class. During the Obama–Biden years, the correlation of forces turned favorably for Eastern authoritarians. Russia, China, North Korea, Iran,

266 *Beleaguered Superpower: Biden's America Adrift*

and the global jihadi expanded their spheres of influence, American economic growth waned, and bi-partisanship withered, with no prospect for reversal in sight.

There have been benefits, but the costs hidden in plain sight have been greater, and keep mounting. They will continue outweighing future benefits unless the body politic accepts the truism that there are no free lunches and re-enthrones competition in the economy, politics, society, and national security. Competitiveness does not preclude cooperation and compassion. It only requires treating them as elements of a Pareto social welfare maximizing processes rather than as substitutes for efficiency, productivity, and growth. If pressed further Russia, China, North Korea, Iran, and the global jihadi will expand their spheres of influence, American economic growth will lag, and society will become increasingly rowdy.

Donald Trump confronted progressive and liberal denial, tried to right the ship, rebalancing and/or reversing Obama–Biden domestic and national security policies. Trump's US National Security Strategy (NSS), unveiled on December 18, 2017 was a thoroughly realist document that placed premium on effective deterrence,[1] and rejected the "lead from behind" approach at least in outer space.[2] He discarded Obama's promise

---

[1]Nikolai Sokov, "The Russification of U.S. Deterrence Policy: After a Quarter-Century Monopoly on Such Capabilities, the United States Finds Itself Essentially in the Same Predicament That the Russians or Chinese Have Faced Since the End of the Cold War," *The National Interest* (December 2017), http://nationalinterest.org/feature/the-russification-us-deterrence-policy-23785. Colin Dueck, "Trump's National Security Strategy: 10 Big Priorities," *National Interest* (January 2018), http://nationalinterest.org/feature/trumps-national-security-strategy-10-big-priorities-23994?page=2.

[2]John Yoo, "Military Use of Space is Coming, Trump Can Help America Prepare," *AEI* (December 2017), http://www.aei.org/publication/military-use-of-space-is-coming-trump-can-help-america-prepare/?mkt_tok=eyJpIjoiT1RnME16QXpOREF5TWpJei IsInQiOiJUcEtkNFpFZng0VWtyYlYzXC9cL29wNzVIeHlOTitxWk9Wc FJQM0VPQ2U4endFczVYd1VcL1pVME1uSEZUVWxmU2dLWFk3RDRyUW NvdVpPNldGZ1BwVVYrMm9kZDg0OGlJRzQ0Sndvb0JkUkxlY0ZuTXJmdU 5SMTNrM1NORHZNUStvRCJ9.

"As American military and civilian networks have increased their dependence on satellite networks, the Obama White House deferred to European efforts to develop a 'Code of Conduct' that would reduce the chances of armed conflict in space.

Rejecting these treaties and vague international norms, the Trump administration instead relies on unilateralism: "any harmful interference with or an attack upon critical

Rejecting Denial and Drift 267

to denuclearize America.[3] ISIS was declared defeated under his watch on December 9, 2017, but American troops remain in Syria.[4] Trump engaged Russia, China, North Korea, Iran, and global jihadism on an "America First" basis, without obstructive transnational entanglements.[5] He exerted

components of our space architecture that directly affects this vital U.S. interest will be met with a deliberate response at a time, place, manner, and domain of our choosing. Trump has the central issue right: control of space underlies the United States's predominant position in world affairs. Communications satellites provide the high-speed data transfer that stitches the U.S. Armed Forces together, from generals issuing commands to pilots controlling drones. Other satellites monitor rival nations for missile launches, strategic deployments, or troop movements. America's nuclear deterrent itself uses space: land- or sea-based ballistic missiles leave and then reenter the atmosphere, giving them a global reach that is difficult to defend against."

[3] "In Shift from Obama Policy, Trump Plans Flexible Use of Nuclear Weapons, Including Low-Yield Arm," *Japan Times* (January 8, 2018), https://www.japantimes.co.jp/news/2018/01/08/world/politics-diplomacy-world/shift-obama-policy-trump-plans-flexible-use-nuclear-weapons-including-low-yield-arms/?mkt_tok=eyJpIjoiTUdFNU1HV TVaRGN6TkdGaiIsInQiOiJST2xhdnJ4ZnNmT003R0ppVk5YeW92UVJ3S3F kUnFzZTFRQ2NCeHUzTFdmb1BTakcrMUlDdGFcLzJNb2RBM3oxM1M2eGdNbXE0 WlJES3RNeGdQdEYxOVd5Z1V2SEtzeURYSXhGUGk4OWNJbThcL2xJenl3VUU3N 1k4UlIrYmcrcnFCIn0%3D#.WlVKmExFx1Y.

"Such a shift would mark a major departure from the nuclear policy advocated by Trump's predecessor, Barack Obama, who pledged in 2009 to pursue a 'world without nuclear weapons'."

[4] Ramesh Ponnuru, "Trump's Strong Start on Policy," *National Review* (December 2017), http://www.nationalreview.com/article/454927/donald-trump-strong-first-year-report-card. Carol E. Lee, Courtney Kube, and Adam Edelman, "Trump Agrees to Keep U.S. Troops in Syria for Undetermined Period of Time to Defeat ISIS," *NBC News* (April 4, 2018), https://www.nbcnews.com/politics/politics-news/trump-agrees-keep-u-s-troops-syria-undetermined-time-defeat-n862691.

[5] "President Donald J. Trump's First Year of Foreign Policy Accomplishments," *Foreign Policy* (December 2017). Dan Blumenthal, "Trump Sets the Tone on China: America Will Not be Challenged," *AEI* (December 19, 2017), http://www.aei.org/publication/trump-sets-the-tone-on-china-america-will-not-be-challenged/?mkt_tok=e yJpIjoiTldNM1pHUXhPVEV6WWpreSIsInQiOiJ3S0NhQnl0bj M4bHdOQktmNWZJMWlja1IwblR6dHpBTUZsazJxNEt1Q3hiQ0xkcVRBK21oS 0tvRUN0MVJQM3oxRmVOeW4zZTMzTkJIeVpoXC9SdG9OWkdDDYklOOUVxU DkyRHV0Y3hxVkhhV24wY2lVS0daaHpFQ0J5bWVTV1wvRkxXIn0%3D.

"The Trump administration has crafted a strong and comprehensive new National Security Strategy (NSS). Most importantly, it recognizes that the fundamental driver of

268   *Beleaguered Superpower: Biden's America Adrift*

pressure on NATO allies to increase their defense spending,[6] and added billions of dollars to the European Reassurance Initiative (now European Deterrence Initiative, EDI).[7] He forward deployed troops in the Baltics, providing anti-tank weapons to Ukraine,[8] and parried the Kremlin in the Middle East. He re-imposed economic sanctions on Iran,[9] challenged China by sending American warships to Taiwanese ports and disputed

---

contemporary geopolitics is a Sino-American rivalry and that Washington must compete more vigorously with Beijing."

"The Trump administration believes (correctly) that the driver of China's strategic behavior is to undermine US influence in Asia, and increasingly, in other critical parts of the world. The strategy also recognized that under the rule of the Chinese Communist Party (CCP), China will never be a 'responsible stakeholder' in a US-created liberal world order — it would rather be the sole owner of a China-led world order." "The administration began to highlight this approach with a trade action to investigate Chinese Intellectual Property theft." "It further developed key themes of its Asia strategy during Trump's trip to Asia where Trump spoke of a 'free and open Indo-Pacific.' It reaffirmed India as a Major Defense Partner and offered it advanced military weaponry. And it joined the 'quad-meeting' of the big Indo-Pacific democracies of Australia, India, and Japan."

[6] Michael Birnbaum and Thomas Gibbons-Neff, "NATO Allies Boost Defense Spending in the Wake of Trump Criticism," *Washington Post* (June 28, 2017), https://www.washington post.com/world/nato-allies-boost-defense-spending-in-the-wake-of-trump-criticism/2017/06/28/153584de-5a8c-11e7-aa69-3964a7d55207_story.html?utm_term=. d63d461627d9.

[7] "The European Deterrence Initiative: A Budgetary Overview," *Congressional Research Service* (August 2018), https://fas.org/sgp/crs/natsec/IF10946.pdf.

[8] Allen Cone, "U.S. to Send Anti-Tank Missiles to Ukraine," *UPI* (December 23, 2017), https://www.upi.com/Top_News/World-News/2017/12/23/Reports-US-to-send-anti-tank-missiles-to-Ukraine/1371514042106/. James Sherr, "Ukraine and the Black Sea Region: The Russian Military Perspective," in Stephen Blank, ed., *The Russian Military in Contemporary Perspective* (Carlisle: Strategic Studies Institute, US Army War College: September 23, 2016).

[9] "Trump Administration to Reinstate All Iran Sanctions," *BBC* (November 2, 2018), https://www.bbc.com/news/world-us-canada-46071747.

President Donald Trump confirmed August 2018 that he would reinstate sanctions on Tehran that had been waived as part of the 2015 Iran nuclear deal from which he withdrew the US in May. On November 2, 2018 Trump announced that all previously waived sanctions would be reinstated.

"The US sanctions will cover shipping, shipbuilding, finance and energy. More than 700 individuals, entities, vessels and aircraft will be put on the sanctions list, including major banks, oil exporters and shipping companies. US Treasury Secretary Steven

Rejecting Denial and Drift 269

islands in the South China Sea,[10] coordinating with Japan, Australia, and India to bolster free shipping in the China Sea and Indo-Pacific, and matched Kim Jong-un's threats tit-for-tat. Trump imposed tariffs against China partly in retaliation for Beijing's compelling American companies to transfer their technology as a *quid pro quo* for doing business on the

---

Mnuchin also said that the Brussels-based Swift network for making international payments was expected to cut off links with targeted Iranian institutions.

Being disconnected from Swift would almost completely isolate Iran from the international financial system.

They are the second lot of sanctions re-imposed by Mr Trump since May. US Secretary of State Mike Pompeo set out 12 demands that Iran must meet if sanctions are to be lifted — including ending support for militants and completely ballistic missile development."

[10]Emanuele Simia, "Possible Port Visits to Taiwan by US Warships Angers Beijing," *Asia Times* (December 17, 2017), http://www.atimes.com/possible-port-visits-taiwan-us-warships-angers-beijing/. Gary J. Schmitt, "Trump, Taiwan: Calling China's Bluff," *AEI* (December 2017), http://www.aei.org/publication/trump-taiwan-calling-chinas-bluff/? mkt_tok=eyJpIjoiWkRaaE9HRTRZVEZtTkRjeSIsInQiOiJBZWJvRVF1MVwvRG gwUDRvT3d6dE1CdDlYdEFGaWZPMFVmMHVlWkNYVzNrOGpDWURNUE hQUXlkV29wRHQ3V3BZNmN6RkZqVmFoWlN0eVwvNHRreDhtWHd3ckhn M1U0QXphbThNTmc1NGZpTFhiT0Q2QmROT0NjbmszczFCU1drNDlVIn0%3D. Gordon Lubold and Jeremy Page, "American Warship Sails Near Disputed Islands, Challenging China USS Decatur Conducts 10-hour Patrol in the South China Sea, Sailing Within 12 Nautical Miles of Chinese-held Outposts in Spratly Island Chain," *Wall Street Journal* (September 2018), https://www.wsj.com/articles/american-warship-sails-near-spratly-islands-challenging-china-1538290867.

"The United States may re-establish port-of-call exchanges in Taiwan for warships of both countries, a move that has brought a strong protest from the Chinese government. The controversial idea is contained in the National Defense Authorization Act for 2018, which President Donald Trump signed into law last Tuesday. Congressmen on Capitol Hill called on the commander-in-chief to consider resuming regular port-of-call exchanges between the United States Navy and its Taiwanese counterpart. Beijing immediately lodged a formal protest with Washington. Now it is up to Trump to decide whether US naval vessels will dock at Taiwan ports in the future. Taiwanese leaders likely would gladly barter port visits by US warships for the possibility of buying US-made submarines. But in military terms, mutual port calls and subsurface combat assets are of equal importance to the security of the island." The Trump administration has crafted a strong and comprehensive new National Security Strategy (NSS). Most importantly, it recognizes that the fundamental driver of contemporary geopolitics is a Sino-American rivalry and that Washington must compete more vigorously with Beijing."

270   *Beleaguered Superpower: Biden's America Adrift*

mainland, and for its failure to honor its World Trade Organization (WTO) commitment to abolish state trading. He withdrew from the Obama–Biden Iran nuclear deal (JCPOA),[11] the 1955 Treaty Normalizing Relations with Iran,[12] publically protested Russian violations of the Intermediate-range Nuclear Forces (INF) agreement threatening a pre-emptive strike,[13]

---

[11] James Conca, "The Iran Nuclear Deal Without the United States," *Forbes* (October 2017). Lawrence Harley, "Supreme Court Lets Trump's Latest Travel Ban Go Into Full Effect," *Reuters* (December 4, 2017), https://www.reuters.com/article/us-usa-court-immigration/supreme-court-lets-trumps-latest-travel-ban-go-into-full-effect-idUSKBN1DY2NY.

"Three months ago, on the two-year anniversary of the Iran Nuclear Deal, President Trump reluctantly certified that Iran is complying with the international nuclear agreement that prevents Iran from attaining an atomic weapon. But not anymore. Trump told the world last Friday that Iran is not in compliance with the Deal, even though they are, and that the Deal needs to be renegotiated, even though our allies, and even our enemies, do not agree."

[12] Edward Wong and David Sanger, "U.S. Withdraws From 1955 Treaty Normalizing Relations With Iran," *New York Times* (October 3, 2018), https://www.nytimes.com/2018/10/03/world/middleeast/us-withdraws-treaty-iran.html?rref=collection%2Fsectioncollection%2Fworld&action=click&contentCollection=world&region=stream&module=stream_unit&version=latest&contentPlacement=2&pgtype=sectionfront&mkt_tok=eyJpIjoiTWpWbE1EVTBabVkyWXpjeiIsInQiOiJvc0tIK3BRRTR6Q2ZSVW1mWEc1cGtcL2F3RysycU1yekRlYnZkQVNHUFY5ZzU0dVRsVThmbUNVTmw1Z1RzWFA4Z1NYbVJiQisycTM4N3JCVlVGd3JJTmMxazlzYVA2aW1pa0dNWVlDQ2l1WGZneGFMT29wVHpodHdxWFBzQmprMllifQ%3D%3D.

"Secretary of State Mike Pompeo announced on Wednesday that the United States was pulling out of a six-decade-old treaty with Iran that had provided a basis for normalizing relations between the two countries, including diplomatic and economic exchanges.

The largely symbolic move came hours after the International Court of Justice ordered the United States to ensure that a new round of American sanctions imposed against Tehran this year did not prevent food, medicine and aircraft parts from reaching Iran."

[13] Ryan Browne, "US says Russia Intentionally Violating Syria Military Agreement," *CNN* (December 22, 2017), http://www.cnn.com/2017/12/21/politics/us-says-russia-violating-syria-agreement/index.html.

"US NATO Envoy's Threat to Russia: Stop Developing Missile Or We'll 'Take It Out'," *Guardian* (October 2, 2018), https://www.theguardian.com/world/2018/oct/02/us-ambassador-nato-russia-kay-bailey-hutchison.

Rejecting Denial and Drift 271

and resisted the temptation to pretend that arms control deals provide sufficient hope to postpone rebuilding American hard power.[14] He strengthened Saudi armed forces against the global jihadism,[15] curtailed Islamic immigration,[16] and challenged the stalled peace process in the Middle East by moving America's embassy to Jerusalem,[17] defunding the Palestinian

---

"The US ambassador to NATO has warned Russia that if it does not halt the development of a new cruise missile in violation of a treaty between the countries, the US will 'take out' the missile."

[14] Stephen Blank, "Mission Impossible: Pursuing Arms Control with Putin's Russia," *Euroatlantic Policy Security Brief* (January 2018), https://www.europeanleadershipnetwork.org/policy-brief/mission-impossible-pursuing-arms-control-with-putins-russia/.

Blank puts the blame for the crisis of European arms control firmly on Russia. According to his analysis, the current Russian approach to security makes an increase of Moscow's military potential, coercion and threat of the use of force inherent parts of Russian policy toward the West. Taken together with the war with Ukraine, that makes meaningful and productive engagement on arms control impossible. He questions the rationale for formulating new arms control proposals toward Moscow, noting the poor state of implementation of the existing instruments and mechanisms such as the CFE Treaty, Open Skies and Vienna Document.

[15] Joschka Fischer, "The New Fulcrum of the Middle East," *Project Syndicate* (December 2017), https://www.project-syndicate.org/commentary/israel-saudi-arabia-alliance-by-joschka-fischer-2017-12?utm_source=Project+Syndicate+Newsletter&utm_campaign=fee9988f36-sunday_newsletter_24_12_2017&utm_medium=email&utm_term=0_73bad5b7d8-fee9988f36-93559677.

"The postwar international order is undergoing a substantial realignment, and so, too, is the Middle East. Whereas the Israel-Palestinian conflict once determined most other geopolitical developments in the region, it is now largely crowded out by other disputes, not least the hegemonic struggle between Saudi Arabia and Iran."

[16] Lawrence Hurley, "Supreme Court Lets Trump's Latest Travel Ban Go Into Full Effect," *Reuters* (December 5, 2017). Deborah Amos, "The Year The U.S. Refugee Resettlement Program Unraveled," *NPR* (January 1, 2018), https://www.npr.org/sections/parallels/2018/01/01/574658008/the-year-the-u-s-refugee-resettlement-program-unraveled.

"The final tally for refugee admissions in fiscal year 2018 is likely to be closer to 20,000 rather than the cap of 45,000, based on the recent pace of resettlements."

[17] Jeremy Diamond and Nicole Gaouette, "White House: Jerusalem Embassy Move a 'Recognition of Reality'," *CNN* (December 6, 2017), http://www.cnn.com/2017/12/05/politics/trump-abbas-us-embassy-jerusalem/index.html.Joschka Fischer, "The New Fulcrum of the Middle East," *Project Syndicate* (December 2017), https://www.

272 *Beleaguered Superpower: Biden's America Adrift*

authority,[18] denying the existence of a Palestinian state,[19] and proposed a "Deal of the Century" to resolve the Israeli–Palestinian conflict.[20] Trump increased economic sanctions against Russia and successfully pressured

---

project-syndicate.org/commentary/israel-saudi-arabia-alliance-by-joschka-fischer-2017-12?utm_source=Project+Syndicate+Newsletter&utm_campaign=fee9988f36-sunday_newsletter_24_12_2017&utm_medium=email&utm_term=0_73bad5b7d8-fee9988f36-93559677.

In 1947, a two-state solution was not viable, because Arab states responded to Israel's founding by waging war against it. When the Palestinians finally recognized the existence of Israel in 1993, that decision alone was seen as a big step forward.

"Although diplomats still speak of a Middle East peace process, there has been no process to achieve peace for many years. A two-state solution remains the only conceivable option for satisfying both sides, but it is becoming less credible with time, and with the continued expansion of Israeli settlements in the West Bank. And now America's recognition of Jerusalem as Israel's capital could mean the end of the two-state solution once and for all."

[18]"Trump Administration Cuts More Than $200 Million in Aid to Palestinians," *CBS* (August 24, 2018), https://www.cbsnews.com/news/trump-administration-cuts-more-than-200-million-in-aid-to-palestinians/.

[19]Jason Lemon, "Trump's National Security Adviser, John Bolton, Says 'So-Called State of Palestine,' Uses Air Quotes," *Newsweek* (October 2018), https://www.newsweek.com/trump-national-security-advisor-john-bolton-says-so-called-state-palestine-1151344.

"Unlike the U.S. and 56 other nations, 137 member states of the United Nations officially recognize the Palestinian territories as a sovereign state."

[20]Clifford D. May, "Two Palestinian Dreams: Exterminate Israel and a Real Nation-State," *Washington Times* (February 4, 2020), https://www.washingtontimes.com/news/2020/feb/4/two-palestinian-dreams-exterminate-israel-and-a-re/.

The Trump plan offers Palestinians a recognized nation-state with twice as much land as they currently occupy, a capital with a U.S. embassy in East Jerusalem, more than $50 billion in investments and other benefits. But, Palestinian must accept the Jewish state.

Palestinian leaders were handed a great and unexpected victory in late 2016 when President Obama facilitated the passage of U.N. Security Council Resolution 2334. It asserts that there is "no legal basis" for Israeli claims to the West Bank — for centuries known as Judea and Samaria — including even the 2,000-year-old Jewish Quarter of the Old City of Jerusalem, and the ancient Jewish holy sites of the Temple Mount.

If that were true, on what basis would Israelis have a right to anything — even a right to exist?

By putting forward a plan that licenses Israelis, should they face continued Palestinian rejectionism, to alter facts on the ground through annexations, President Trump has changed the dynamic — at least for now.

the European Union to follow America's lead.[21] He withdrew from the entangling transnational Paris Climate and Transpacific Partnership Agreements with no apparent losses despite apocalyptic claims of tipping point global warming,[22] and Congress passed a major pro-productivity tax reform bill.[23] He tried to prune Obamacare, and rein social progressive education,[24] trimmed the regulatory state,[25] and combated the transnational

---

[21]Yasmeen Serhan, "Why Europe Opposes America's New Russia Sanctions: Moscow Isn't the Only One That Could Be Negatively Impacted," *Atlantic* (August 2017), https://www.theatlantic.com/international/archive/2017/08/why-europe-opposes-the-uss-new-russia-sanctions/535722/.

[22]Ramesh Ponnuru, "Trump's Strong Start on Policy," *National Review* (December 2017), http://www.nationalreview.com/article/454927/donald-trump-strong-first-year-report-card.

"The Environmental Protection Agency, now run by Trump appointee Scott Pruitt, has also taken steps to end the practice of 'sue and settle,' in which activist groups get the agency to adopt new policies through lawsuits. Trump killed President Obama's Clean Power Plan, which would have imposed significant economic costs while doing little to reduce the risks of global warming."

[23]James Pethokoukis, "Americans Might Really Like the Trump Tax Cuts. What Will Democrats Do Then?" *AEI* (December 2017), http://www.aei.org/publication/americans-might-really-like-the-trump-tax-cuts-what-will-democrats-do-then/.

[24]Chris Enloe, "White House Bans Seven Politically Correct Terms from CDC Budget Items — Here's What They Are," *Blaze* (December 12, 2017), http://www.theblaze.com/news/2017/12/16/white-house-bans-seven-politically-correct-terms-from-cdc-budget-items-heres-what-they-are; Ramesh Ponnuru, "Trump's Strong Start on Policy," *National Review* (December 2017), http://www.nationalreview.com/article/454927/donald-trump-strong-first-year-report-card.

"Trump's education secretary, Betsy DeVos, has withdrawn Obama-era regulations that led colleges to lower the burden of proof for sexual-misconduct allegations and to monitor professors' speech."

Read more at: http://www.nationalreview.com/article/454927/donald-trump-strong-first-year-report-card.

[25]Marc Thiessen, "Trump's Little-Noticed War on Hidden Taxes," *AEI* (December 2017), https://www.aei.org/publication/trumps-little-noticed-war-on-hidden-taxes/?mkt_tok=eyJpIjoiWVRJeVpXSTVOV1poTXpSaCIsInQiOiJrZ0tlemxyend6SllzSXF1Q1dcL0FkSmtHOXVwaE5wcWZJdDRqRzRLTHB5Z0tlU0QwSmg4MzhWYkJ0blZoalRyd3BYbnZreWlsT29zdmtwK1gzckpJRXR4S3ZzSEJlcFA2cUtGWUxSeEhWN1NabjVza GlxVjh0eWpYS2s3bmxLTXMifQ%3D%3D.Cf., John Dawson and John Seater, "Federal Regulation and Aggregate Economic Growth," unpublished manuscript (2013).

274   *Beleaguered Superpower: Biden's America Adrift*

assault on America's sovereignty,[26] including the International Criminal Court, which claims jurisdiction over Americans in Afghanistan.[27] He slowed the progressive campaign for open immigration, and began

---

"When Trump came into office, he immediately began reversing this trend. He worked with Congress to repeal 14 major regulations implemented under Obama, and withdrew or delayed more than 1,500 others by executive action. Most importantly, he issued Executive Order 13771, which directed government agencies to eliminate two existing regulations for each new one issued, and to ensure that the net costs of any new regulations are zero. Last Thursday, Trump announced the first results of this effort: His administration achieved $8.1 billion in lifetime regulatory savings — and is on track to achieve an additional $9.8 billion in savings in fiscal 2018. Since excessive regulations are a hidden tax on American workers and businesses, that amounts to an $18 billion tax cut. These actions have helped unleash the growth we are experiencing today. It is no mere coincidence that under Obama, the most regulation-happy president in modern times, GDP growth averaged less than 2 percent."

They estimate that the past 50 years of federal regulations have reduced real GDP by roughly two percentage points a year, or nearly $40 trillion.

[26] John Bolton, "Expect America's Tensions with China and Russia to Rise in 2018," *AEI* (December 2017), http://www.aei.org/publication/expect-americas-tensions-with-china-and-russia-to-rise-in-2018/?mkt_tok=eyJpIjoiT0RjM01UY3dZV1U1TXpGayIsInQ iOiJsU3NBQWh0bmYxczB5aFU1eEo3Q3VzWXVvXC9tQWlGZUNwNHVJXC 94dCtqNXpIUWFKd1N4cFdQVitqclZUc1dzb0dtODNxbzhBMFZMT21PR XNrV0VRV25RNlRTeHA2cGRUV202WmlXY2IxMTFhdmV2UkpWYzJyYUZW cGpmeGJlNjdxIn0%3D.

"Finally, the pure folly of both the U.N. Security Council and the General Assembly crossing the United States on the Jerusalem embassy decision was a mistake of potentially devastating consequences for the United Nations. Combined with the International Criminal Court's November decision to move toward investigating alleged U.S. war crimes in Afghanistan, there is now ample space for the White House to expand on the president's focus on protecting American sovereignty. Trump's first insight into the rage for 'global governance' among the high minded came on trade issues, and his concern for the World Trade Organization's adjudication mechanism. These are substantial and legitimate, but the broader issues of 'who governs' and the challenges to constitutional, representative government from international bodies and treaties that expressly seek to advance global governing institutions are real and growing. America has long been an obstacle to these efforts, due to our quaint attachment to our Constitution and the exceptionalist notion that we don't need international treaties to 'improve' it."

[27] Billy Perrigo, "'Already Dead to Us': Why the Trump Administration Has a Problem with the International Criminal Court," *Time* (September 2018), http://time.com/5393624/john-bolton-international-criminal-court/.

Trump's policies were more than old wine in new bottles.[28] They were contrarian efforts in the right direction that slowed the deteriorating trend in the correlation of forces between the United States and its Eastern authoritarian rivals, and the growth of radical progressive anti-meritocratic, anti-productive, anti-competitive and anti-open society initiatives.[29] Trump's pushback marked an effort to restore robust

---

[28]Trump has not taken clear stands yet on the CMEA sphere of influence (Bulgaria, Czechia, Slovakia, Hungary, Poland, Romania), Turkey, Cuba, frozen conflicts in Transdnistria and the Kurile Islands, Trump and the establishment oppose Russian cyber meddling in global politics, but do not have an effective strategy to combat it. On the offensive side of the ledger, the Trump administration has been silent about sponsoring color revolutions, regime change, global rule of law as a vehicle for opening up Russia to Western market penetration, replacing Kremlin insider governance; managed markets and rent-granting with democratic free enterprise and adopting western social justice programs. Nor has he taken a clear stand on forcing Russia's de-annexation of Crimea, withdrawal from the Donbas and Luhansk and the status of Russia's claims on Novorossiya, the Baltic States and the Arctic, and deterring meddling in Europe. He has said nothing about influencing Russia's role in Iran, much of the Middle East North Korea, and Latin America. Trump has been mute on Russia's exclusion from NATO, on denuclearization, and on disarmament. In short, while Trump says that he desires to return to fundamentals, placing US–Russian relations on a sound professional basis unencumbered by politics and outdated legacies, he appears to have devised neither a public nor secret plan to cost effectively manage the defensive and offensive aspects of the challenge.

[29]Marc Thiessen, "Chaos or Not, Trump is Racking Up a Record of Foreign Policy Success," *AEI* (September 19, 2018), http://www.aei.org/publication/chaos-or-not-trump-is-racking-up-a-record-of-foreign-policy-success/?mkt_tok=eyJpIjoiWXpaaE5tWTNNR0Z qTnpNeiIsInQiOiJoY2Yxb2ppY0JBd2pUUEVwK2NjNlMwWjh1ZFV2dmg2Wm5 HWkhuVEF2NnRZTTlmWWtheTBaWUQyck9SZ3IzWVkyZXc2UUxaeENpUk00b3E rVzJPNFV4bzNiQTExN0lpR2Q5MEZKTlh3K084b1ZIdFFzakhWQXJkMU4yZ HRjZm16OCJ9.

"When Trump was elected in 2016, many worried that he would usher in a new age of American isolationism and withdrawal. That hasn't happened. Trump has pursued a foreign policy that is not only not isolationist but also a significant improvement over his predecessor's.

In Syria, while Trump did not eliminate Assad, he did enforce President Barack Obama's red line against the use of chemical weapons, punishing violations not once but twice — and restoring America's credibility on the world stage. Last week, Trump launched the U.S.-led coalition's assault on the Islamic State's last stronghold on the

276   *Beleaguered Superpower: Biden's America Adrift*

Syrian-Iraqi border, which will eliminate its physical caliphate. And unlike Obama, Trump is not taking America's boot off the terrorists' necks. The Post reports that the president has approved a new strategy that 'indefinitely extends the military effort' in Syria until a government acceptable to all Syrians is established and all Iranian military and proxy forces are driven out. Conservative columnist Patrick Buchanan, a die-hard isolationist, recently asked: 'Is Trump Going Neocon in Syria?'

In Israel, Trump moved the U.S. Embassy to Jerusalem, which he recognized as the country's capital — something three of his predecessors promised, but failed, to do. He also withdrew from the Iran nuclear deal and refocused U.S. efforts in the Middle East on shoring up relations with allies such as Israel and Saudi Arabia instead of courting Iran.

In Afghanistan, after a careful deliberative process in which Trump (correctly) pressed his generals for answers to tough questions, the president reversed his campaign position favoring a troop pullout and sent additional forces, with no timetable for withdrawal.

In Turkey, Trump is taking a hard line with President Recep Tayyip Erdogan's regime, imposing tariffs as the Turkish lira has gone into free fall. Trump's move was intended to punish Erdogan for his continued detention of an American pastor, Andrew Brunson, and followed his threats against U.S. forces in Syria and his plans to buy an S-400 advanced air-defense system from Moscow.

Trump has also taken a surprisingly tough line with Russia. He approved a massive arms and aid package for Ukraine, expelled 60 Russian diplomats and authorized new sanctions against Moscow at least four times for: (1) interfering in U.S. elections, (2) violating the Intermediate-Range Nuclear Forces Treaty, (3) launching a chemical-weapon attack against a Russian national in Britain and (4) violating North Korea sanctions. And the Trump administration recently warned Russia that it would face 'total economic isolation' if Moscow backed the Assad regime's assault in Idlib. Trump's policies more than make up for his disastrous Helsinki news conference with Russian President Vladimir Putin in July.

On North Korea, Trump issued credible threats of military action, which brought Kim Jong Un to the negotiating table. The chances of successful denuclearization are slim, but every other approach by Trump's predecessors has failed. And there is reason for hope that Trump will not sign a bad deal, because he set a very high bar for a good deal when he withdrew from Obama's nuclear agreement with Iran.

The list of good foreign-policy moves goes on. Trump has taken a strong stand against the narco-dictatorship in Venezuela, and his administration even considered supporting coup plotters seeking to remove the Maduro regime. He strengthened NATO by getting allies to kick in billions more toward the alliance's collective security. He declared war on the International Criminal Court, which purports to have jurisdiction over U.S. soldiers and citizens even though America is not a signatory to the treaty creating the ICC.

Liberals might not like any of these developments, but long-standing policy goals of conservative internationalists are being achieved. There may be chaos in the Trump White House, but so far at least the chaos is producing pretty good results."

American hard power, competitiveness, and open society. It was consistent with populism and conservative Republican Party sentiment, and was not authoritarian nativist as progressives allege.[30]

Trump was rejecting denial and trying to combat drift, but progressives and liberals stopped him from saving the day. A great deal more is required to keep Eastern authoritarians permanently deterred and contained by restoring America's economic, social, and national security competitiveness. The Biden–Harris administration may preserve some of these gains but is also poised to resume building an anti-meritocratic Global Nation at the expense of economic vitality, social amity, and American national security.

---

[30] Steven Rosefielde, *Trump's Populist America* (Singapore: World Scientific Publishers, 2017). Steven Rosefielde and Quinn Mills, *The Trump Phenomenon* (Singapore: World Scientific Publisher, 2017).

Chapter 14

Shifting Power in America to Create Strength

Headwinds

Neither Trump nor the Republican Party were up to the task of restoring America's competitive mindset. No one may be. Progressivism and liberalism appeal to people's hearts, their yearnings, frustrations, guilt, and desire to cut the Gordian knot of scarce economic resources. They have found a gullible mana-from-heaven seeking audience.

The progressive-liberal media does its utmost to mobilize support for expanding the welfare state, and assisting those it portrays as oppressed, needy, and scorned, while ignoring the middle class and national security. Most of the media downplays the deteriorating correlation of forces, acknowledging authoritarian misdeeds only to express outrage that enhances Democrats electoral prospects. The media rarely report Russia and China's arms buildups. North Korean and Iranian nuclear advances and arms control violations receive scant attention. When these threats occasionally are noted, progressive-liberal journalists and think tanks invariably assure readers that soft power, sanctions, foreign assistance, confidence building, and superior American technological prowess provide sufficient protection and that cutting hard power further is the only sane thing to do.

An educational campaign informing the public of the facts, heightening appreciation of dangers and awareness of the competitive options is essential, but cannot carry the day until the progressive- liberal tide loses momentum. In the interim, the beleaguered American superpower will

Beleaguered Superpower: Biden's America Adrift

take a pummeling because Biden–Harris administration cannot accept that there are no free lunches.

Specific Remedies

The pummeling is avertable, if the electorate has an epiphany. America can quickly improve the correlation of forces, strengthen deterrence and containment, prosper, enhance worker and middle-class quality of existence, reduce social victimization, and improve the lot of the needy by restoring the competitive paradigm. It can deter small local wars, win if regional wars erupt, and in the process minimize the risks of World War III by adopting the following policies[1]:

First, recognizing that the West is in the midst of an undeclared new Cold War, America should modernize its nuclear forces (warheads and missiles) to reduce their vulnerability and increase their effectiveness.

Second, it should accelerate funding for anti-ballistic missile defense systems and eliminate arms-control restrictions that impair systems potency. National Missile Defense (NMD) spending has continuously fallen over the past nine years. A high-reliability anti-ballistic missile network would be a particularly powerful deterrent to North Korean and Iranian nuclear threats because both lack the industrial capacity to overcome America's technology advantage. This will require permanently rescinding the defense "sequester" rule in the Budget Control Act of 2011.

Third, the United States should expedite its technological development for the land-sea battle in the South China Sea.

Fourth, Washington should substantially increase naval forces in the South China Sea and the Asia Pacific to counter Beijing and Pyongyang's aspirations. A reinvigorated shipbuilding program will take a decade, and should start as soon as possible.

Fifth, NATO should adequately fund all programs required to reduce the risk of Russian aggression against the Baltic States and Novorossiya.

---

[1]Cf. Robert Blackwill and Philip Gordon, "Containing Russia How to Respond to Moscow's Intervention in U.S. Democracy and Growing Geopolitical Challenge," *Council on Foreign Relations*, no. 80 (January 2018), https://cfrd8-files.cfr.org/sites/default/files/report_pdf/CSR80_BlackwillGordon_ContainingRussia.pdf.

Shifting Power in America to Create Strength 281

Sixth, America should junk its patch-as-patch-can Middle East national security strategy, refocusing on rolling back and defeating the global jihadism and Iranian expansion. It will still have to improvise protecting Israel from Shiite attack, however should keep its priorities straight deploying the hard power required to accomplish these missions as circumstances dictate.[2]

Seventh, Washington should stick to Trump's decision to settle the Palestinian quagmire based on existing settlements and Israel's right to assure its national identity.[3] This commitment is applicable in either a one, or two state solution.

Eighth, the United States should declare that a solution to the Korean conflict that cedes control over the peninsula to Pyongyang, and/or Chinese hegemony is unacceptable.

Ninth, America should sharply reduce immigration quotas, harden its borders, and expel illegal immigrants to mitigate social turmoil and facilitate assimilation.

Tenth, Washington should dedicate the resources needed to improve American defensive and offensive hard power cyber capabilities.

Eleventh, America should take whatever prudent measures it can to weaken coalitions among Russia, China, North Korea, Iran, Cuba, Venezuela, global jihadi, and other rivals.

Twelve, America should get out of the color revolution and regime change businesses on the home turf of Russia and China, and in their historical spheres of influence. These policies have curb appeal for some, but too often are counterproductive and excessively dangerous.

There is also a simple remedy for the United States' waning soft power. It should replace progressivism and extravagant welfare state liberalism with the competitive paradigm essential for the achievement of the classical American dream. This is not nostalgia for paradise lost.

---

[2] Michael Doran and Peter Rough, "What America Should Do Next in the Middle East," *Mosaic* (September 2017), https://mosaicmagazine.com/essay/2017/09/what-america-should-do-next-in-the-middle-east/.

[3] David Brennan, "Trump Won't Consider Palestinian 'Right of Return' in Peace Deal: Haley," *Newsweek* (August 2018), https://www.newsweek.com/trump-wont-consider-palestinian-right-return-peace-deal-haley-1094318.Kaled Elgindy, "How the Peace Process Killed the Two-State Solution," *Brookings* (April 2018), https://www.brookings.edu/research/how-the-peace-process-killed-the-two-state-solution/.

282 Beleaguered Superpower: Biden's America Adrift

Competitiveness in the economic, social, and defense spheres is a rational imperative, not an ideological placebo. Enthroning competitiveness prioritizes reason over political opportunism.

Washington should manage its relations with Russia and China more judiciously by applying punitive sanctions only when there is a realistic prospect for success,[4] not as an empty political gesture falsely suggesting that soft power is a sufficient substitute for stout defense. It is better to speak softly and carry a big stick (hard power), than pretend that Russia and China can be jawboned into compliance with increasingly harsh punitive economic sanctions.

Emphasizing democracy, liberty, tolerance, free speech, free enterprise, and the rule of law as the touchstones of soft power has other benefits. It will bolster national security by revitalizing the economy and promoting unity. America requires a pro-productive, pro-labor, pro-middle class and pro-entrepreneurial ethic to provide a solid economic foundation for the nation's security. It needs self-disciplined, scrupulous, empathetic democracy, tolerance, liberty, free speech, the rule of law, free enterprise, merit-based education, and compassionate social transfers to dampen social strife and the restoration of national unity. Progressive programs and revolutionary incitement tactics thwart these objectives. They degrade the economy's potential, foment discord, and deter funding for an adequate defense.[5] America will be stronger without these

---

[4] If issues are important to Russia and China, they won't capitulate to economic pressure, unless their leaders find it convenient to use sanctions as a cover mollifying domestic opposition.

[5] Luke Strange, "A Troubling Outlook for Future Defense Spending," *AEI* (November 2018), http://www.aei.org/publication/a-troubling-outlook-for-future-defense-spending/? mkt_tok=eyJpIjoiTURobE1HWmhObU5oT1daaSIsInQiOiJhNnZyUkJ4SjVrN UNLSmlCUk8xUkhnSUU3Q2s1U1p2dUZJcnY3MVZSZDR5blpSSEFVSXl3NVVXS jAxbW5mUytmSGxwRjJhV0g5WUJVdkxvc0JHNE4wS2FxQ2ZjVXJ3OVdHSF wvSExzdlwvRm56OWViZnNLOWdkSTJ3dkpXTVwvYjh3NiJ9.

"At the end of the current fiscal year in September, absent Congressional action, spending will revert to levels set a decade ago — slashing tens of billions of dollars just as the rebuild gets underway. If past patterns hold, after what many expect will be a short-term continuing resolution to start the fiscal year, Congress will eventually come to an agreement on budget numbers for FY20-21 that are not much higher than the current levels, but also not as low as those prescribed by the Budget Control Act." "What it all means: after 2021, there is both motive and opportunity for a political reaction to rising

Shifting Power in America to Create Strength   283

obstacles. There is a place for some progressive programs, but they are not substitutes for a pro-competitive society.

Finally, progressive-liberal "smart diplomacy" is not smart enough.[6] "Smart diplomacy" as Biden's Democratic Party practices it serves America's authoritarian rivals, not the United States. The purpose of "smart diplomacy" should be maximizing national security, not taking unacceptable risks like sleeping with the enemy on the supposition that Eastern authoritarians may someday convert,[7] transforming themselves into Talbott's Global Nation super-persons.[8] The problem is easily rectified. "Smart diplomacy" should serve the countries of the competitive free world, not empty cosmopolitan romanticism.

---

deficits at a massively inopportune time for the Department of Defense. The motive is renewed interest in deficit reduction, spurred by the very real threat of rising deficits."
[6] William Perry, "North Korea Called Me a 'War Maniac.' I Ignored Them, and Trump Should Too:

Smart Diplomacy Backed by the Threat of Force, Not Twitter Bluster, is the Way to Deal with Kim Jong Un," *Politico Magazine* (October 2017), http://www.politico.com/magazine/story/2017/10/03/north-korea-war-maniac-donald-trump-215672?mkt_tok=eyJpIjoiWVRjd09EbGlNVGc1TWpOaCIsInQiOiJ1MllqTmdKMG1vNUx0VERFR216ZXJpWjkzRDBjSk1XS1NtR1R2RG1rTE1rRWxuekdOeCtYaTBIUmJWdFwvR2c4ZzNHQkI0ZHFCTUpPZnFYQm9jUlorWnR6K3Z6c3lyYlwvQnBZRUlPbmtJckQrQXdzczdyT0VnYU1wTUtuOENDWnV6In0%3D.

"For the past 16 years, the United States has had a history of talking tough with North Korea without actually being tough, and the results have been spectacularly unsuccessful. It may have felt satisfying for President George W. Bush to denounce North Korea as part of the 'axis of evil,' but it accomplished nothing beyond giving time for Pyongyang to make dramatic strides in its nuclear capability. A policy of confrontation that sounded strong masked consequences that left us weaker. For the past 16 years, the United States has had a history of talking tough with North Korea without actually being tough, and the results have been spectacularly unsuccessful. It may have felt satisfying for President George W. Bush to denounce North Korea as part of the 'axis of evil,' but it accomplished nothing beyond giving time for Pyongyang to make dramatic strides in its nuclear capability. A policy of confrontation that sounded strong masked consequences that left us weaker."
[7] "Corruption in Conflict: Lessons from the U.S. Experience in Afghanistan," *Special Inspector General for Afghanistan Reconstruction* (September 2016).
[8] The notion of a new superior Global person is reminiscent of the Soviet "new man." The New Soviet man or New Soviet person was a selfless, learned, healthy, muscular, and enthusiastic in spreading the socialist Revolution. Evgeny Steiner, *Stories for Little Comrades* (Seattle & London: University of Washington Press, 1999).

Chapter 15

Security Lessons of COVID-19

Art of War

The COVID-19 epidemic provides a vivid example of how tunnel vision and politicking degrade stout security.[1] American government officials, both Republicans and Democrats characterized efforts to combat COVID-19 as a war against a virus of unknown virulence, lethality, and duration, requiring sound management.[2] Washington should have gathered intelligence, and devised a prudent strategy to contain the assault, and win the war at minimum cost to the people's quality of existence. Casualties were inevitable, regardless of the strategy adopted. COVID-19 was waging war, not peace for America's hearts and minds. Some people would die and others suffer whether the war ended in victory, Pyrrhic victory, defeat or annihilation — though there was little chance of annihilation. Strategy and tactics would involve both hard power and soft power, and determine the outcome.

Battle managers had to solve a sophisticated social utility optimization problem.[3] Washington did not competently meet the challenge.

---

[1] Wenhong Zhang, ed., *Prevention and Control of COVID-19* (Singapore: World Scientific Publishers, 2020).

[2] Eric Levenson, "Officials Keep Calling the Coronavirus Pandemic a 'War.' Here's Why," *CNN* (April 2, 2020), https://www.cnn.com/2020/04/01/us/war-on-coronavirus-attack/index.html.

[3] Herbert Simon, "A Behavioral Model of Rational Choice," in Herbert Simon, ed., *Models of Man: Social and Rational-Mathematical Essays on Rational Human Behavior in a Social Setting* (New York, NY: Wiley, 1957).

286   *Beleaguered Superpower: Biden's America Adrift*

Politicians ignored Sun Tzu's classic *Art of War*,[4] pandering to incipient panic and sparing for partisan Brownie points, rather than winning wisely. Washington failed to harness forces efficiently for a protracted campaign,[5] avoiding needless catastrophic self-inflicted suffering, averting a Pyrrhic victory, or defeat.

The data needed for sober assessment were on hand. The world had been through several smaller scale epidemics in recent years and had experienced the "Spanish flue," 1918 Pandemic (H1N1 virus) which claimed 675,000 in America and at least 50 million worldwide.[6]

The American Center for Disease Control (CDC) publishes comprehensive historical data on influenza.[7] Influenza and Covid-19 are viral

---

The sophisticated problem that had to be solve formally is a Herbert Simon intertemporal bounded rational satisficing "quality of existence" problem taking full account of output, employment, consumption, and macroeconomic stability in the household (H) and public (P) production and distribution GDP spaces, and the other utilities (X) space [casualties, Gini coefficients and sundry unpaid self-services and community services]. See Appendix, Figures 1–3 and 5.

[4] Sun-tzu, *The Art of War: The Oldest Military Treatise in the World*, translated by Lionel Giles (London: Luzac, 1910).

Sun-tzu was a 6th century BC Chinese military tactician.

[5] "Washington did make some indirect provision to protect productive assets by providing small businesses with forgivable loans to remain operating. This only applied if businesses were not shuttered by government decree and locked down employees continued working. The Paycheck Protection Program (PPP), established as part of the CARES Act, offers 'forgivable loans' (essentially, government grants) to small businesses with the goal of helping these businesses avoid closure and avoid laying off their workers." "Borrowers are eligible for loan forgiveness equal to the amount spent on payroll costs, mortgage interest, rent, and utilities for an eight-week period beginning with the origination of the loan, provided they do not lay off workers or make large reductions in their pay. Business that have already laid off workers due to concerns about the coronavirus can rehire them and receive loan forgiveness."

Michael Strain, "The Paycheck Protection Program: An Introduction," *AEI* (April 2020), https://www.aei.org/research-products/report/the-paycheck-protection-program-an-introduction/?mkt_tok=eyJpIjoiTXpJelptVXhPREl3WldabSIsInQiOiJ6ZXpyS2VQa0VhM1RnK0duQ3htUkRrOTdsOHF3eDNMeWhWNnFjU01kcG1PUlV0Nkhh dTZXUVV3YUlOQzFmamFEVWNOK2V6Yk02SXpoblA2Q1wvTjZzM1ByWGx1d EVUa3pCY0FwZ2J3Rlp0VTNGT3VqK0lOcmR5NmhLNDBZamY5UnMifQ%3D%3D.

[6] CDC, "1918 Pandemic (H1N1 virus)," https://www.cdc.gov/flu/pandemic-resources/1918-pandemic-h1n1.html.

[7] CDC, "Estimated Influenza Illnesses, Medical Visits, Hospitalizations, and Deaths in the United States — 2018–2019 Influenza Season," https://www.cdc.gov/flu/about/burden/2018-2019.html.

infections that attack the respiratory system.[8] CDC estimates that 35.5 million America contracted influenza during the 2018–2019 season. Healthcare providers treated 16.5 million of them, and 34,200 died. The cohort 50–65 experienced 5,676 death (17 percent). The elderly (65+) accounted for 25,555 fatalities or 75 percent of the total. This means that influenza had only a small impact on the able-bodied labor force's mortality rate. A stay-at-home order on the elderly, combined with essential social distancing might have significantly reduced fatalities, without imposing a heavy national economic burden. This nuanced approach for improved management of routine influenza however did not appear on Washington's radar screen in 2019. Several tens of thousands of influenza deaths were not a political problem during the 2018–2019 season, but were in 2020 when American progressives and liberals found it expedient to exploit catastrophic fears for partisan benefit.

The CDC reports that as of November 19, 2020 America experienced 11,465,722 Covid-19 cases (32 percent of influenza cases 2018–2019), which caused 249,670 deaths.[9] The figure includes pneumonia fatalities.[10] The age distribution of Covid-19 fatalities closely resembles the influenza incidence in 2018–2019. The primary difference between the two phenomena is the small number of American COVID-19 cases in 2019–2020 (11.5 million) compared to the 35.5 million influenza infections in 2018–2019, and their relatively high lethality. People infected with COVID-19 are much more likely to die from the disease. Although, there are far fewer cases of COVID-19 than influenza, body counts are seven times greater.

---

[8] Webmd, "Coronavirus and COVID-19: What You Should Know," https://www.webmd.com/lung/coronavirus#1-2.

"COVID-19 is a disease that can cause what doctors call a respiratory tract infection. It can affect your upper respiratory tract (sinuses, nose, and throat) or lower respiratory tract (windpipe and lungs). It's caused by a coronavirus named SARS-CoV-2. SARS-CoV-2 is one of seven types of coronavirus, including the ones that cause severe diseases like Middle East respiratory syndrome (MERS) and sudden acute respiratory syndrome (SARS). The other coronaviruses cause most of the colds that affect us during the year but aren't a serious threat for otherwise healthy people."

[9] CDC, "Cases in the U.S." https://covid.cdc.gov/covid-data-tracker/?CDC_AA_refVal=https%3A%2F%2Fwww.cdc.gov%2Fcoronavirus%2F2019-ncov%2Fcases-updates%2Fcases-in-us.html#cases_casesper100klast7days.

[10] https://www.cdc.gov/nchs/nvss/vsrr/covid19/index.htm.

288 *Beleaguered Superpower: Biden's America Adrift*

The high incidence of elderly death in both the influenza and COVID-19 statistics clearly suggests that Washington might have significantly reduced COVID-19 deaths merely by imposing a stay-at-home order on the elderly with negligible economic and social impact, supplemented with smart social distancing for other cohorts. Simple arithmetic shows that if only the elderly had been required to stay home in 2020 (assuming that staying home sufficed to avoid infection), the death toll from COVID-19 would have been 62,418 a figure 80 percent greater than the total influenza deaths in 2018–2019.

Economic and social harm might have been further limited by curtailing social activities, and by paying high-risk employees not to work. COVID-19 threatened to harm and kill some workers and employers. The government could have paid them to save themselves for future productive service, financed out of the tax eventually levied on their expected future incomes.

The government might also have mitigated the economic costs by permitting some people to work where COVID-19 risks were low. These industries and locations could have been determined on a learning by doing basis.

The government might have let new service contracts for workers and employers in low risk COVID-19 localities.

The government might have let new teleworking contracts for workers and employers idled in locked down communities.

The government could have targeted new contracts for all types of bio-medical research to expedite the discovery of a COVID-19 cure and vaccine. It might also have contracted for the construction of medical facilities and manufacturing and distribution of medical supplies, as of course it did.

The government might have targeted miscellaneous new contracts to ameliorate the suffering of COVID-19 victims of all descriptions.

The government might by all these measures have avoided policies that shut down much of the economy, tactics that squandered resources, and needlessly increased the risks of a ruinous financial crisis in the post-COVID-19 future.

Progressives and liberals pressed instead for draconian action, with some conservative and populist support. They chose to campaign for a comprehensive stay-at-home shutdown, coupled with politically targeted deficit spending. They fought for a $2.2 trillion CARES deficit spending package (with an additional $4 trillion package pending) that lavishly funded pet projects in a bizarre attempt to stimulate aggregate effective demand for production frozen in place by the lockdown.[11] The absurdity of combating COVID-19 by locking down productive facilities and futilely enticing workers and employers to violate the lock down with deficit spending was entirely lost on "house arrest" advocates. They refused to accept that it was counterproductive to squander a fortune on "pork barreling," and wise to avoid the needless danger of excessive national indebtedness.[12] Relief for COVID-19 victims was fully justified.

Donald Trump and the Republican Party's response to COVID-19 was better, but hardly up to Sun Tzu's high standard, and as should be expected the national security share of the $2.2 trillion CARES deficit spending package was miniscule.[13]

The injudiciousness of the progressive and liberal approach to COVID-19 management is rooted in its "take no prisoners" mindset, and political expediency.[14] Pandering to fear outweighed national well-being,

---

[11]CDC, "Daily Updates of Totals by Week and State, Provisional Death Counts for Coronavirus Disease 2019 (COVID-19)," https://www.cdc.gov/nchs/nvss/vsrr/covid19/index.htm. Emily Jacobs, "Biden to announce up to $4 trillion infrastructure plan with massive tax hikes," New York Post, March 30, 2021. https://nypost.com/2021/03/30/biden-to-announce-up-to-4-trillion-infrastructure-plan-with-tax-hike/.

[12]Robert Barro, "Cutting GDP to Counter the Coronavirus Pandemic," *National Review* (March 2020), https://www.nationalreview.com/2020/03/coronavirus-response-will-curbing-economic-activity-to-slow-virus-work/#slide-1.

[13]Mackenzie Eaglen, "What's in the $2.2 Trillion Stimulus for Defense?" *RealClear Defense* (March 2020), https://www.realcleardefense.com/articles/2020/03/28/whats_in_the_2_trillion_stimulus_for_defense_115156.html?mkt_tok=eyJpIjoi WW1SaU9EWTNObU0zWkRFeiIsInQiOiJoUm1XZlhrSkUyZXJLT1kxc1k3NTZHa Wc3U1pIbFV5UEU5N0daaXlTWGhpOFRDSXo4MDN6aE9pOEo4VmMwdU02Vj JBT2dhXC9XRmR3bDE0WW1SVGRrZGxpbXZ6bWU3S3pFNjVRTnVKd1FSejA2 SUMwQlZIdDYzcFlJZWp1dnV2QjEifQ%3D%3D.

"Defense spending in the stimulus totals $10.5 billion, with likely more to come later. Of this, $1 billion is allocated to the Defense Production Act (DPA), and the bill waives several restrictions to supercharge it for pandemic recovery. Other priorities include $1.5 billion for working capital funds, $1.2 billion for uniformed personnel, $2 billion for Operations and Maintenance, nearly $5 billion for the Defense Health Program, and $2.8 million for the Armed Forces Retirement Home."

[14]Sally Satel, "The Public-Health Establishment Has Diminished Its Credibility," *AEI* (June 2020), https://www.aei.org/articles/the-public-health-establishment-has-diminished-its-credibility/. "Mere weeks ago, public-health experts worried about transmission of

290 *Beleaguered Superpower: Biden's America Adrift*

as did currying favor among minorities at the expense of workers and the middle class. Progressives and liberals perceived COVID-19 as a once in a decade opportunity (like the 2008 subprime mortgage lending crisis) to waste a substantial portion of $2.2 trillion CARES package on boondoggles, financed by debt they do not expect themselves to ever pay, and believe that they can fool the public by labeling opponents "pandemic deniers." Progressives and liberals did not fret about future productivity and growth because they prioritized entitlement, affirmative action and restorative justice. The public health establishment benefits from the same attitude and gives credence to the notion that saving lives (without a full accounting of indirect health and direct economic consequences) takes precedence over all other considerations.

Although bandwagon progressives and liberals should have looked more closely at influenza statistics, and evidence from the 1919 pandemic showing that quarantines and surgical masks were useless,[15] many people

---

coronavirus sternly warned against large, crowded gatherings. That was before the protests sparked by the killing of George Floyd, a 46-year-old black man, by a white police officer in Minneapolis on May 25.

From that moment on, many epidemiologists and public-health officials have justified people congregating to demonstrate against police brutality. On June 2, for example, Dr. Tom Frieden, former head of the Centers for Disease Control and former health commissioner of New York City, tweeted, 'People can protest peacefully AND work together to stop covid.' That same day, a senior epidemiologist at Johns Hopkins tweeted, In this moment the public health risks of not protesting to demand an end to systemic racism greatly exceed the harms of the virus."

[15] John M. Barry, *The Great Influenza: The Story of the Deadliest Plague in History* (New York: Viking, 2004): 456–461. Barry makes the following points in his concluding chapter:

* "One tool of no use is widespread quarantine."
* "Closing borders would be of no benefit either."
* "washing one's hands … in a disciplined way … matters."
* "Surgical masks are next to useless …"

He recommends: keeping sick children home from school… and having sick adults stay home from work … cough etiquette … telecommuting … closing theaters, bars and even banning sports events."

* "those who occupy positions of authority must lessen the panic that can alienate all within a society."
* "Those in authority must retain the public's trust. The way to do that is to distort nothing, to put the best face on nothing, try to manipulate no one … A leader must make whatever horror exists concrete."

Security Lessons of COVID-19 291

feel nonetheless that being safe is better than sorry. If the number of COVID-19 infections matched those of the 1918–1919 Spanish flu (H1N1 virus), American deaths might have risen from 249,670 (November 19, 2020) to 2,137,721 (adjusted for population growth). The possibility is undeniable, but worst-case thinking does not justify rash action.

Sweden offers an instructive example, corroborated by Taiwan's experience.[16] The Swedes did not comprehensively lockdown the country because worker protection and prosperity are their highest priorities, not progressivism (Sweden is a corporatist, not a progressive society). They could have easily followed Washington's lead, but resisted because their version of the "Nordic model" strongly protects the working class and the people's material welfare.[17] They rejected calls for a nationwide lockdown to save lives above all other considerations, striving instead to balance worker well-being and COVID-19 death prevention through voluntary social distancing supplemented with mild restrictions on large public gatherings.[18] Schools remained open and domestic travel was unimpeded.

---

[16] Mark Thiessen, "Thiessen: As Taiwan Shows, the Antidote to the Virus is Freedom, Taiwan Has Had Six Deaths Out of a Total of Just 393 Confirmed Cases," *Mercury News* (April 19, 2020).

"What is most impressive is that Taiwan has done all this without ordering its population to shelter in place or shutting down schools, restaurants, stores and other businesses. As a result, Taiwan's economy is not experiencing the same economic damage as countries under lockdown."

[17] The Nordic model is the combination of social welfare and economic systems adopted by Nordic countries. It combines features of capitalism, such as a market economy and economic efficiency, with social benefits, such as state pensions and income distribution.

[18] Government Offices of Sweden, "The Government's work in response to the virus responsible for COVID-19," https://www.government.se/government-policy/the-governments-work-in-response-to-the-virus-responsible-for-covid-19/. Gary Schmitt and Craig Kennedy, "Swedish Model on Crisis Response Will Be Tested Over Next Few Weeks," *The Hill* (April 20, 2020), https://thehill.com/opinion/international/493761-swedish-model-on-crisis-response-will-be-tested-over-next-few-weeks.

"The Swedish Government has presented a range of different measures to limit the spread of the COVID-19 virus and to mitigate the economic impact of it. The Government's policy and decisions aim to:

- Limit the spread of infection in the country
- Ensure health care resources are available

The results speak for themselves. As of November 19, 2020 Sweden's health authorities report that there were 208,295 confirmed cases and 6,406 COVID-19 deaths.[19] The comparable per capita COVID-19 death rate for America is approximately 15 percent higher. This means that Sweden protected the nation's economic well-being,[20] and saved lives! It won–won. Thanks to the progressive and liberal politically driven hysteria, America lost–lost!

The same rational analytics apply to global security and economic prosperity. It is foolish to maximize progressive and liberal social programs at the expense of national security and affluence.

• Limit the impact on critical services
• Alleviate the impact on people and companies
• Ease concern, for example by providing information
• Ensure that the right measures are taken at the right time."

"Unlike most of the developed world, including neighboring Norway or Denmark, Sweden has kept its elementary schools running and allowed most its businesses, including restaurants and bars, to remain open. Travel in and out of the country remains possible for E.U. nationals. And social distancing remains, for the most part, voluntary, provided the group in question has fewer than 50 people. In short, Sweden has refused to join the rest of us in a lockdown" Gary Schmitt and Craig Kennedy.

[19] ARCGIS, "Public Health Agency of Sweden — Official Statistics," https://experience. arcgis.com/experience/09f821667ce64bf7be6f9f87457ed9aa.

[20] Sweden's decision to continue work as usual is associated with a 12 percent increase in per capita COVID-19 mortality. *Ceteris paribus*, if it had followed the American paradigm, Sweden would have incurred 4,945 deaths. This is a savings of 674 lives, or 169 fewer death in the cohort 0–65.

Chapter 16

Prospects 2021–2030

American progressive and liberal politicians are becoming increasingly foolhardy. Their influence peddling, loot, and squander mentality is eroding the country's superpower, retarding economic growth, and spawning social discontent.

Although, many applaud stout national security, prosperity, and social tranquility, American political sentiment has been moving against economic and national security competitiveness in a liberal rules-based order. Just as in the case of COVID-19, Democratic Party politicians want it all, and refuse to optimize social utility (the quality of existence). The more Washington sacrifices competitive efficiency for other ends, the more it degrades America's capacity to contain authoritarianism and foster global democracy. The adverse turn in correlation of forces that gained momentum during the Obama–Biden era is reversible, but not without a commitment to preserve national economic, political, and social competitiveness, including personal freedom.[1] Our allies are in no position to pull America's chestnuts out of the fire.[2]

---

[1] Natan Sharanstky, *Defending Identity: Its Indispensable Role in Protecting Democracy* (New York: Public Affairs, 2008).

[2] Gary Schmitt, *A Hard Look at Hard Power: Assessing the Defense Capabilities of Key US Allies and Security Partners — Second Edition* (Carlisle, PA: US Army War College Press, 2020), https://press.armywarcollege.edu/monographs/921. Spencer Kimball, "German Army Falls below European Standards," *Deutsche Welle* (July 3, 2011), https://www.dw.com/en/german-army-falls-below-european-standards/a-15207035.

America can maintain sufficient military hard power now and in the future, if the Biden–Harris administration chooses to counter the Eastern authoritarian threat. This is its wisest option. Achieving sufficient hard power merely obligates Washington to provide and competently employ the necessary funding today for potent warfighting programs out of current resources, and tomorrow's growth driven revenues.

Will Washington meet the challenge?

Biden's progressive-liberal coalition is intent on underfunding defense and debasing warfighting capabilities consonant with pacifist misgivings. Establishment pundits refuse to confront the post-Soviet authoritarian present danger resolutely, confident that they can beguile Russia, China, North Korea, and Iran into behaving as Washington thinks they ought.[3] If this mood persists, American deterrence will diminish and East authoritarianism will grow more pugnacious.

---

[3] Rose Gottemoeller, Thomas Graham, Fiona Hill, Jon Huntsman Jr., Robert Legvold, and Thomas R. Picering, "It's Time to Rethink Our Russia Policy America's Current Mix of Sanctions and Diplomacy Isn't Working. An Open Letter on How to Reconsider Our Approach to Putin-and Whoever Comes Next," *Politico* (August 2020); https://www.politico.com/news/magazine/2020/08/05/open-letter-russia-policy-391434.

"The following open letter was signed by 103 foreign-policy experts, whose names and affiliations appear below.

U.S.–Russia relations are at a dangerous dead end that threatens the U.S. national interest. The risk of a military confrontation that could go nuclear is again real. We are drifting toward a fraught nuclear arms race, with our foreign-policy arsenal reduced mainly to reactions, sanctions, public shaming and congressional resolutions. The global Covid-19 pandemic and the resulting serious worldwide economic decline, rather than fostering cooperation, have only reinforced the current downward trajectory.

Meanwhile, the great challenges to peace and our well-being that demand U.S.–Russia cooperation, including the existential threats of nuclear war and climate change, go unattended. Because the stakes are so high, both in the dangers they entail and the costs they contain, we believe that a careful, dispassionate analysis and change of our current course are imperative.

We go into this open-eyed. Russia complicates, even thwarts, our actions, especially along its extended periphery in Europe and Asia. It has seized territory in Ukraine and Georgia. It challenges our role as a global leader and the world order we helped build. It interferes in our domestic politics to exacerbate divisions and tarnish our democratic reputation. At best, our relations will remain a mix of competition and cooperation. The policy

Prospects 2021–2030 295

The divide between the Democratic Party progressives-liberal coalition on the one hand and the public on the other has widened

---

challenge will be to strike the most beneficial and safest balance between the two. To this end, we offer six broad prescriptions for U.S. policy.

* We must first find a way to deal effectively with Russian interference in U.S. elections and, most important, block any effort to corrupt the voting process. Hardening our electoral infrastructure, sanctioning Russians who weaponize stolen information and countering Russia's capacity to hack our systems are all necessary measures. So is exposing Russian disinformation. We must, however, also engage Russia through negotiations out of the public glare, focused on each side's capabilities to do great damage to the other side's critical infrastructure.

* It makes no sense for two countries with the power to destroy each other and, in 30 minutes, to end civilization as we know it to lack fully functioning diplomatic relations. In the wake of the Ukrainian crisis, key governmental contacts were severed, consulates shuttered and embassy staff drastically reduced. Too often we wrongly consider diplomatic contacts as a reward for good behavior, but they are about promoting our interests and delivering tough messages. We need them as a matter of essential security to minimize the misperceptions and miscalculations that can lead to unwanted war. Restoring normal diplomatic contacts should be a top priority for the White House and supported by the Congress.

* Our strategic posture should be that which served us well during the Cold War: a balanced commitment to deterrence and détente. Thus, while maintaining our defense, we should also engage Russia in a serious and sustained strategic dialogue that addresses the deeper sources of mistrust and hostility and at the same time focuses on the large and urgent security challenges facing both countries:

* The imperative to restore U.S.–Russian leadership in managing a nuclear world made more dangerous by destabilizing technologies, shifting attitudes toward the use of nuclear weapons, discarded nuclear agreements and new tension-filled nuclear relationships. That means extending the New START Treaty and swiftly moving to a next phase of arms control to strengthen nuclear stability, carefully adjusted to a world of multiple nuclear actors.

* The imperative to make safer and more stable the military standoff that cuts across Europe's most unstable regions, from the Baltic to the Black Sea, working vigorously to preserve existing constraints, such as the Open Skies Treaty-now under challenge-and the Vienna Document 2011, and creating new confidence-building measures.

* The success of U.S.–China policy will in no small measure depend on whether the state of U.S.–Russia relations permits three-way cooperation on critical issues. Our current policies reinforce Russia's readiness to align with the least constructive aspects of China's U.S. policy. Moving the needle in the opposite direction will not be easy, but should be our objective.

296   *Beleaguered Superpower: Biden's America Adrift*

dramatically since 2016. Progressives have become increasingly influential in the Democratic Party coalition, and if the trend persists, hard power defense appropriations will decline at a faster rate.

A more progressive Global Nation inspired Washington establishment with strong pacifist sensibilities will more vigorously oppose nuclear testing and seek deeper cuts in several vital military programs.

A few key indicators reflect the Democratic Party's bottom-line attitude toward defense. American defense spending trended downward during 2010–2019, falling from 850 to 719 billion in constant 2018

---

* On salient issues where U.S. and Russian interests are in genuine conflict, such as Ukraine and Syria, the U.S. should remain firm on principles shared with our allies and critical to a fair outcome. More attention, however, should be paid to the cumulative effect that measured and phased steps forward can have on the overall relationship, and in turn the opportunity an improving relationship creates for further steps forward.

* While sanctions should be a part of our Russia policy, they should be judiciously targeted and used in conjunction with other elements of national power, especially diplomacy. The steady accumulation of congressionally mandated sanctions as punishment for Russian actions in Crimea and eastern Ukraine, the poisoning in Salisbury, violations of the INF treaty and election meddling reduces any incentive Moscow might have to change course since it considers those sanctions permanent. We need to restore flexibility to our sanctions regime, focusing on targeted sanctions that can be eased quickly in exchange for Russian steps that advance negotiations toward acceptable resolutions of outstanding conflicts, including a demonstrable Russian effort to cease interference in our electoral process. Doing so will require political will on the part of both the White House and the Congress.

Ultimately, the reality is that Russia, under Vladimir Putin, operates within a strategic framework deeply rooted in nationalist traditions that resonate with elites and the public alike. An eventual successor, even one more democratically inclined, will likely operate within this same framework. Premising U.S. policy on the assumption that we can and must change that framework is misguided. Likewise, we would be unwise to think that we have no choice but to stick with current policy. We must deal with Russia as it is, not as we wish it to be, fully utilizing our strengths but open to diplomacy. So focused, we can both cope with the challenge that Russia poses and strive to put the relationship on a more constructive path. Failure to do so carries too high a price.

Rose Gottemoeller, Under Secretary of State for Arms Control and International Security, 2014–2016; Thomas Graham, Senior Director for Russia, National Security Council staff, 2004–2007; Fiona Hill, Senior Director for European and Russian Affairs, National Security Council staff, 2017–2019; Jon Huntsman Jr., Ambassador to Russia, 2017–2019; Robert Legvold, Columbia University; Thomas R. Pickering, Ambassador to Russia, 1993–1996."

Prospects 2021–2030 297

dollars.[4] It was 4.6 percent of GDP in 2010, and declined to 3.1 percent in 2019.[5] The personnel and maintenance share of defense spending increased over this interval, with weapons procurement, military construction, and research and development falling reciprocally.[6] The hard power of America's allies displayed the same negative trends.[7] The United Kingdom is the only exception.[8]

What are America's defense spending prospects for 2021–2030 likely to be, given the 2020 benchmark?

Two scenarios are worth pondering, one is bad, the other worse. The bad option extrapolates the experience of the last decade into the next. Defense spending on this supposition will continue falling about 1.5 percent annually, with the brunt of the cuts being borne by weapons procurement, military construction, and research and development. China and Russia by contrast will continue modernizing their forces shifting from fourth to fifth generation weapons systems. The correlation of forces consequently will move eastward, and the influence of Eastern authoritarians will expand *ceteris paribus*. The risks of war between nuclear powers will increase.

The alternative would make matters worse. Zealous progressives would push the Biden–Harris administration to build down America's nuclear forces faster, terminate the national missile defense program

---

[4] Erin Duffin, "U.S. Military Spending from 2000 to 2019," *Statista* (June 2, 2020), https://www.statista.com/statistics/272473/us-military-spending-from-2000-to-2012/.

[5] Erin Duffin, "U.S. Defense Outlays and Forecast 2000–2029 (As a Percentage of the GDP)," *Statista* (January 29, 2020), https://www.statista.com/statistics/217581/outlays-for-defense-and-forecast-in-the-us-as-a-percentage-of-the-gdp/.

[6] David E. Mosher, "Prospects for DoD's Acquisition Budget Over the Next Decade," Congressional Budget Office (October 29, 2019), https://www.cbo.gov/system/files/2019-10/55772-CBO-presentation.pdf.

[7] Gary Schmitt, *A Hard Look at Hard Power: Assessing the Defense Capabilities of Key US Allies and Security Partners — Second Edition* (Carlisle, PA: US Army War College Press, 2020), https://press.armywarcollege.edu/monographs/921.

[8] Gary Schmitt, "Good (defense) news from London," *AEI* (November 2020). https://www.aei.org/foreign-and-defense-policy/good-defense-news-from-london/?mkt_tok=eyJpIjoiTm1WaVl6WTVabU15TldFMyIsInQiOiJ1dkxSRDRMNlZwcEhXUDZUbFBHVkRRZSt3YVlSMDhrN2FrUEhyVUtqYlRlQThES3R0YnZCa1hCbU1SVTVFTEcyQWwybmJwUXM5d3hKcmVVQ0pUQ3l5NzcxblwvUHhCT2Y4NGx1OE5pamFqdXhJTFBHMXJtWDh6Z0w3MHVnSUdSUGYifQ%3D%3D.

(NMD),[9] deliberately degrade the nation's military technological edge, and strive to eliminate nuclear weapons following Barack Obama's lead.[10] It would restore the Joint Comprehensive Plan of Action (JCPOA) and terminate economic sanctions, allowing Iran to nuclearize despite continued violations of the Treaty on the Nonproliferation of Nuclear Weapons.[11] A progressive dominated establishment is likely to acquiesce to North Korean nuclear deployments, compel South Korea to cope as best it can and ensnare America in the one-sided, high-cost Paris climate accord.

Pacifist-inclined progressives will demand cutting conventional forces, including the navy stationed in the South China Sea, and provide military aid to Cuba, Venezuela, and other left regimes and insurgencies. Although these policies aim to serve progressive purposes including a peaceful global order, they will make the world free for a tidal shift in geopolitical power from America to Russia, China, North Korea, Iran, and other authoritarian potentates. Russia will consolidate its hold on the Crimea and expand its reach in Novorossiya, the Baltics, Nagorno-Karabakh,[12] Belarus, and Kyrgyzstan. China will control the Asia-Pacific region curbing freedom of navigation in the South China Sea,[13] and pirating seabed resources in violation of international maritime law. North Korea will gradually destabilize South Korea. Iran and the global jihadi will become more combative, and Israeli–Palestinian relations will be

---

[9]"Current U.S. Missile Defense Programs at a Glance," Arms Control Association (August 2019), https://www.armscontrol.org/factsheets/usmissiledefense.

[10]Steven Pifer, "Order from Chaos: 10 Years After Obama's Nuclear-Free Vision, The US and Russia Head in the Opposite Direction," *Brookings* (April 2019), https://www.brookings.edu/blog/order-from-chaos/2019/04/04/10-years-after-obamas-nuclear-free-vision-the-us-and-russia-head-in-the-opposite-direction/.

[11]Meira Svirsky, "Iran Moving Advanced Centrifuges Underground in Violation of Nuclear Deal," Clarion Project (November 22, 2020).

[12]FOI, "The End of the Second Karabakh War: New realities in the South Caucasus," *The FOI Russia and Eurasia Studies Programme* (December 2020).

[13]Zack Cooper and Bonnie S. Glaser, "What Options are on the Table in the South China Sea?" War on the Rocks (July 22, 2020), https://warontherocks.com/2020/07/what-options-are-on-the-table-in-the-south-china-sea/?mkt_tok=eyJpIjoiWWpnd1pHVT JPR1ZsTkdWbCIsInQiOiJUaGk0THVGeG5WUklIVkRUY2NPUzUyV0V5WTFoQj RiUGVlbzQzTXZUNDc5d0Z0OHdrcU1SYkhkMko2aDZZTHIzTjNlZitMOHdWSm ZYd29RVmtxN3E3OGRtZFBNZEQyUmIrelpSQ1BRMFZSbUY3R0FWYXNJWEF1b0 RHc0VLak93RiJ9.

inflamed. Strategic nuclear stability will be undermined,[14] and Eastern authoritarians will obtain a free hand in initiating conventional wars.

The Biden–Harris administration as Hillary Clinton recently urged is apt to use soft power, dewy-eyed "détente" and lofty appeals to progressive-liberal idealism with China, North Korea, and Iran to offset the hard power deficit[15]; however, these pleas will fall on deaf Eastern authoritarian ears. Biden's treatment of Russia is apt to be less indulgent than Hillary Clinton advises because hostility and distain in the Democratic Party toward Putin and Russia are intense. American restraints on both China and Russia therefore will likely wane in tandem with deteriorating US military power and economic malaise regardless of whether Biden chooses to "reset" with the East.[16] The West cannot hope to charm its adversaries as long as it remains wedded to instigating color revolutions in Russia, China, North Korea, and Iran.

Progressives eventually will rue their policies. Eastern authoritarians will march across the globe imposing regimes progressives, liberals, conservatives, and populists abhor, and the risks of both conventional and nuclear war will increase.

---

[14]"UK and US Say Russia Fired A Satellite Weapon in Space," *BBC* (July 23, 2020), https://www.bbc.com/news/world-europe-53518238.

"The US and UK have accused Russia of testing a weapon-like projectile in space that could be used to target satellites in orbit." Tom Collina and William Perry, "How the Biden Administration Could Create a Win–Win Situation For Nuclear Policy," *Washington Post* (November 18, 2020), https://www.washingtonpost.com/opinions/2020/11/17/how-biden-administration-could-create-win-win-situation-nuclear-policy/.

"The Biden–Harris administration can make a sole-purpose policy more credible and further reduce the risk of accidental launch by retiring the ICBMs. ICBMs are most likely to be used first in response to a false alarm. They are highly unlikely to ever be used in retaliation, as most would be destroyed in any (highly unlikely) Russian nuclear attack against the United States. Thus, ICBMs have no logical role in a U.S. sole-purpose, deterrence-only policy."

Tom Collina and William Perry, *The New Nuclear Arms Race and Presidential Power from Truman to Trump* (New York: BenBella Books, Inc. 2020).

[15]Hillary Clinton, "A National Security Reckoning How Washington Should Think About Power," *Foreign Affairs* (November/December 2020).

[16]David Kramer, "Biden Has a Clear-Eyed View of the Threat Posed by Russia — But a Lot of Bad Advice to Ignore," *Foreign Policy* (November 2020), https://foreignpolicy.com/2020/11/13/biden-putin-russia/.

300 *Beleaguered Superpower: Biden's America Adrift*

The wheel does not turn in one direction. A myriad of other scenarios are conceivable.[17] For the moment, however it seems that the Biden–Harris administration is intent on playing into Moscow, Beijing, Teheran, Pyongyang, and the global jihads' hands by fecklessly retarding domestic economic growth, while pursuing its hegemonic global order, instigating color revolutions, and stoking a mega financial crisis gutting America's military hard power and striving to deter Eastern authoritarians with economic sanctions.

---

[17]Tom Wyler and Ashley J. Tellis, "Sustaining America's Role in the World Demands Renewal at Home," *Carnegie Endowment for International Peace* (October 2020), https://carnegieendowment.org/2020/10/21/sustaining-america-s-role-in-world-demands-renewal-at-home-pub-83017?utm_source=carnegieemail&utm_medium=email&utm_campaign=announcement&mkt_tok=eyJpIjoiWkdNeFpEVXhOVGxsTkRCbCIsInQiOiJhQmJLXC9uRDU0UFFHK3loMEFndEdrdnVobHZQVVZhUjdRZm9HQSt1XC9OeHp1K0lCeThKY3U5VkdvbU12VzlIeDY4TUlUK0FqN1BYSzhCcit5ekRDbTZlbUNYSzRCd29UQ1ZQRnNkbXlwU3FRY01jODJBVEZ0amZhT1RURHBcL0R0OCJ9.

Conclusion

America is on the cusp of seizing defeat from the jaws of Cold War victory by unilaterally reducing its hard power one baby step at a time. The Washington establishment today, under the thrall of progressive and liberal idealism, opposes maintaining a robust military deterrence against Russia, China, North Korea, Iran, and the global jihadi on a solid competitive foundation, and is intent on expanding America's stultifying mega-welfare state.[1] It champions excessive entitlements, affirmative action, restorative justice, environmental radicalism, and venal establishment boondoggles at the expense of financial prudence, rapid economic growth,[2] full employment, technological modernization, and social

---

[1] Equal opportunity was the touchstone of Lyndon Johnson's Great Society, a set of domestic American programs launched by President Lyndon B. Johnson in 1964–1965. He coined the term in a speech delivered at the University of Michigan in 1964. It came to represent his domestic agenda. The main goal was the total elimination of poverty and racial injustice. New major spending programs that addressed education, medical care, urban problems, rural poverty, and transportation were launched. The Great Society in scope and sweep resembled the New Deal domestic agenda of Franklin D. Roosevelt.

On anti-meritocracy see Daniel Markovits, *The Meritocracy Trap: How America's Foundational Myth Feeds Inequality, Dismantles the Middle Class, and Devours the Elite* (New York: Penguin, 2019).

[2] William Nordhaus, "Projections and Uncertainties about Climate Change in an Era of Minimal Climate Policies," *American Economic Journal: Economic Policy* 10, no. 3 (2018): 333–360. Bjorn Lomborg, *False Alarm: How Climate Change Panic Costs Us Trillions, Hurts the Poor, and Fails to Fix the Planet* (New York: Basic Books, 2020); Cf. Benjamin Zycher, "Joe Stiglitz Reviews Bjorn Lomborg's New Book," *AEI* (August

302　Beleaguered Superpower: Biden's America Adrift

harmony. It is playing a perverse double-think, double game abroad using transnationalism, and economic globalization to project political and business power, while espousing incompatible progressive causes.[3]

Washington acknowledges the emergence of a host of formidable Eastern authoritarian military, security, and economic threats,[4] including a Chinese nuclear buildup,[5] but avoids responsibly confronting them insisting that they are manageable with bluster, bluff, consciousness raising, radical social change, soft power, superior technology, arms control, and strategic patience.[6] Progressives likewise recognize that anti-meritocratic

---

2020), https://www.aei.org/articles/joe-stiglitz-reviews-bjorn-lomborgs-new-book/
?mkt_tok=eyJpIjoiTmpkaE1qUXpNbVJrTWprMiIsInQiOiJCWWFsQzR
1YzllRXdWUzNQcFVSanJxZkc1Y2hLdm1VNDNZTEVmTmxKb1Bze
EhCOGRxdTJ5SH1SXC9cL2xqazVXV0ZtNm9PQ3oyeF1XY313TGF
peEdFQmw3TUdnNHRFSnJ0QmM1ZHowb0o5cFFvc3lQbVwvY2V5VGdTMlppT
0NRZmlnSiJ9.

[3] Samuel Huntington, "The Lonely Superpower," *Foreign Affairs* 78, no. 2, March–April 1999: 35–49.Cf. Sebastian Mallaby, "The Reluctant Imperialist: Terrorism, Failed States, and the Case for American Empire," *Foreign Affairs* 81, no. 2, March/April 2002.

Lawrence Summers called the United States the "first non-imperialist superpower."

[4] Anne Applebaum, "A KGB Man to the End," *Atlantic* (September 2020). https://www.theatlantic.com/magazine/archive/2020/09/catherine-belton-putins-people/614212/.

It is incredible, but a group of cynical, corrupt ex-KGB officers with access to vast quantities of illegal money — operating in a country with religious discrimination, extremely low church attendance, and a large Muslim minority — have somehow made themselves into the world's biggest promoters of "Christian values," opposing feminism, gay rights, and laws against domestic violence, and supporting "white" identity politics. This is an old geopolitical struggle disguised as a new culture war. Yakunin himself told Belton, frankly, that "this battle is used by Russia to restore its global position."

Catherine Belton, *Putin's People: How the KGB Took Back Russia and Then Took On the West* (New York: Farrar, Straus and Giroux, 2020).

[5] Hal Brands, "China's Nuclear Buildup Changes Balance of Power," *AEI* (September 2020). https://www.aei.org/op-eds/chinas-nuclear-buildup-changes-balance-of-power/?
mkt_tok=eyJpIjoiTWpNNE1EUX1NR1V4TWpjdyIsInQiOiJ1Wmhhb0FxRloy
XC8wRHdEZ2l6MjRjV1YwXC9YZitYODMrUWJZa3E0ME52OCtUbzNwQVpWajJJ
OVg3MjhibnFUV1VhT2FPdW5sanBhOUdwY1wvRkRJbGRhSWZIRGdpWVZPWlh
5bXhzZmQ3MmNqNVd2WFZUbVFHanpFMTBKdStuVFlUdiJ9.

[6] Paul Wolfowitz, "Is China Pivoting to the Middle East?" *AEI* (September 2020). https://www.aei.org/articles/is-china-pivoting-to-the-middle-east/?mkt_tok=eyJpIjoiWVdNNFp
tVmxNbVptTnpOOaSIsInQiOiJrWG04XC9LaDdETnNlUkprWGg0SWhcL0tIQWN6S1w
vQlVvZXVkV29CQVNoRjVDQzRWUjRsUDltc2E0YUNrbU1yTHRmYm1xakh

Conclusion 303

(productivity degrading) policies will retard American economic growth further exacerbating the problem of keeping Eastern authoritarians at bay, but do not care and characteristically are silent about the security ramifications.[7]

Progressives and liberals are prepared to horse-trade with Republican conservatives and populists to enhance the Democratic Party's prospects for continued electoral success, but not enough to stoutly counter Russia's, China's, North Korea's, Iran's, and global jihadi ambitions.[8] The National Defense Authorization Act for Fiscal Year 2021 passed by a veto-proof majority of the House and Senate on July 21, 2020 confirms the attitude. It makes no substantive response to the mounting Eastern authoritarian threat, beyond allowing soldiers to use cannabis derivatives like CBD![9] Hillary Clinton's "smart more with less defense strategy" is more old wine in new bottles prioritizing the diversion of funds within the defense budget to progressive social causes.[10] It is as meaningless as the Biden–Harris "unity" slogan.

SeUFTNzdHazIrQXZPdlorMXdkNTIzYlB6SXV5Y2xYUE53OUN4Z2JROUQ3aXFI aE1MdlREYXNXdVE3dCJ9.

[7] Michael Sandel, *The Tyranny of Merit: What's Become of the Common Good?* (New York: Macmillan, 2020).

[8] Mackenzie Eaglen, "Defense Strategy and Priorities: Topline or Transformation?" *AEI* (March 2020), https://www.aei.org/articles/defense-strategy-and-priorities-topline-or-transformation/?mkt_tok=eyJpIjoiWVddZMVpqYzNNMkV6WW1ZMCIsInQiOiJldkJCU 1ZoaHdTZ3JrbEM4emt6MnZqY2p4UFBLMzlnNFZlVlwvOU5UeG1PUnlqYV hraVBMdFo0dzBaYmVkZDRKSk85akgxVFN2OCs5WVhWYW9GUGZzK3kzTmVt MnJHZXdwSzdaWHFEeHhJQkpaaHJRVVBoXC9iT2R0ZWExM3VESHlvIn0%3D.

"While the 2018 National Defense Strategy charts a more honest and realistic priority set of threats and challenges for the U.S. military, it is still purely additive. Like every post-Cold War strategy before it, the document simply piles on newer and harder missions without meaningfully reducing or shedding others deemed less important."

[9] The National Defense Authorization Act for Fiscal Year 2021 (H.R. 6395 S. 4049) is an act which specifies the budget, expenditures and policies of the U.S. Department of Defense (DOD) for fiscal year 2021. The House of Representatives passed the bill with a veto-proof 295–125 vote on July 21, 2020.The bill approved by the House, as amended, included a provision to require the executive to consult with the Congress before invoking the Insurrection Act, and blocked appropriations from being used for nuclear testing. It also included an amendment introduced by Rep. Tulsi Gabbard and passed by the House 336–71 which "would let soldiers use cannabis derivatives like CBD" and "would countermand the Department of Defense policy" if the bill becomes law.

[10] Hillary Clinton, "A National Security Reckoning How Washington Should Think About Power," *Foreign Affairs* (November/December 2020).

304 *Beleaguered Superpower: Biden's America Adrift*

Washington's stance on improving America's economic prowess is the same. The Obama–Harris administration is unwilling to curb octopus big government and anti-meritocratic programs to restore American and worldwide economic vitality, forestall another global debt crisis and protect the supply chains of the planet's democracies. It prefers to accommodate global economic secular stagnation rather than soften the Democratic Party's anti-meritocratic policies.

Conservatives and populists do not and are unlikely to soon have enough political power to forge a bipartisan United Front to deter authoritarian gains abroad, restore merit-based economic competition and responsibly reduce the national debt.[11] For many willing to wager on the power of consciousness raising,[12] or who tacitly support Chinese and North Korean "socialism" this is welcome news.

For those who still remember Neville Chamberlain's appeasement of Nazi Germany and Fascist Italy 1935–1939, and the economic antics of the French Popular Front in 1937, the establishment's nonchalant attitude to international economic and military security is *déjà vu*. It seems that from time to time Western politicians cannot stop fiddling even when the lion is roaring at the gate.

Perhaps, they are encouraged by the positive conclusion of the First Cold War. Although, socialists, progressives, and most welfare state liberals chose to discount, disregard, or deny the Soviet arms buildup 1960–1989, the West triumphed because the USSR self-destructed contrary to Washington and Brussels' expectations that it would democratically self-transform. Socialists, progressives, and most welfare state liberals had been doubly wrong. They failed to comprehend that the Soviet Union was structurally militarized and that an internecine struggle within the Communist Party would undermine the viability of the Soviet Marxist–Leninist system.

Fortune, however, this time around is likely to be fickle. Neither economic deficiencies nor internecine power struggles are apt to save the day. There are no grounds for supposing that Chinese market communism is economically inferior to American government-warped "free enterprise" or the EU's anti-meritocratic market system, or that Kremlin mixed

---

[11] Steven Rosefielde and Quinn Mills, *Progressive and Populists* (Singapore: World Scientific Publishers, 2020).

[12] Cf., Ivan Turgenev, *Fathers and Children* (*Отцы и дети*) (Leipsig: Wolfgang Gerhard, 1880).

Conclusion 305

economy powered military industrial prowess cannot imperil the North Atlantic Treaty Organization (NATO).[13]

The West is embroiled once again in a Cold War between rival superpowers with imperial aspirations, even though some in Russia,[14] China, America, and the EU prefer Cold Peace. America, the EU, Russia, and China all have made themselves over. They have modified their ideologies, personas, and strategies, but not their imperial penchants. Washington still uses the rhetoric of harmonious liberal democracy and free enterprise in projecting America's image abroad, but no longer practices them. It prattles about assured deterrence and nuclear non-proliferation, but is committed to neither. Establishment pacifists still believe that America can prudently abolish its nuclear arsenal in return for Putin's "ironclad" assurances.[15] Progressive and liberal Democrats never tire of imagining happy-endings and pretending that make believe is enough to assure that dreams come true.

---

[13] Anders Åslund, "Putin's Karabakh Victory Sparks Alarm in Ukraine," *Atlantic Council* (November 11, 2020). https://www.atlanticcouncil.org/blogs/ukrainealert/putins-karabakh-victory-sparks-alarm-in-ukraine/.

"The big lesson of the Azerbaijan-Armenia peace settlement is that military power rules. In a matter of weeks, the use of force has achieved what decades of diplomacy failed to deliver. The only two relevant international players in the South Caucasus region are Russia and Turkey. The United States has taken leave, while the European Union is a paper tiger without troops."

[14] Andrei Tsygankov, "The Revisionist Moment: Russia, Trump, and Global Transition," *Problems of Post-Communism* (August 2020), https://doi.org/10.1080/10758216.2020.1788397; Stephen Blank, "Dealing with Russia: Bringing the Outlaw State to Justice," *The Hill* (September 2020). https://thehill.com/opinion/international/515251-dealing-with-russia-bringing-the-outlaw-state-to-justice?rnd=1599311254. "Over the summer, the Kremlin has poisoned Alexei Navalny, beaten up and incarcerated other dissidents, stonewalled any progress on negotiations over its invasion of Ukraine, made nuclear threats and probed NATO allies within their air spaces and territorial waters and stepped up its cyber war against the U.S. and Europe. This last action can be seen in its intensified efforts to intervene in the U.S. presidential election. Indeed, Russia is so heavily invested in President Trump's victory that Russian English language media is running articles using tropes and memes coming out of the Trump campaign. Yet Moscow has committed all of these acts with remarkable impunity."

[15] David Kramer, "Biden Has a Clear-Eyed View of the Threat Posed by Russia — But a Lot of Bad Advice to Ignore," *Foreign Policy* (November 2020), https://foreignpolicy.com/2020/11/13/biden-putin-russia/.

306 *Beleaguered Superpower: Biden's America Adrift*

Russian and Chinese leaders by contrast perceive themselves as the people's defenders against perfidious Western imperialism. Both want to expand spheres of influence and annex territories when opportunity knocks (Ukraine, Baltics, Taiwan, and the South China Sea). Russia has ditched Marxist-Leninism, but China has not. They are both staunchly nationalist and patriotic, and bristle at the West's efforts to dominate them with soft power and transnational entanglements. Their authoritarian leaders are benighted, but not bemused. Their wariness of Washington's "resets" is fully justified.

Although, today's Cold War is not about communism versus capitalism, nor the "evil empire" versus the "free world,"[16] it is still essentially a replay of post-WWII imperial East–West superpower rivalries. Round two is especially dangerous because of Washington's fecklessness,[17] nuclear proliferation,

---

[16] The "Evil Empire" speech was delivered by US President Ronald Reagan to the National Association of Evangelicals in 1983 during the Cold War. In that speech, Reagan referred to the Soviet Union as an "evil empire" and as "the focus of evil in the modern world." He asserted that the Cold War was a battle between good and evil.

[17] Andrei Tsgankov, "Gulliver at the Crossroads: America's Strategy During the Global Transition," *Journal of International Analytics* 11, no. 2, 2020: 28–44 (in Russian), https://doi.org/10.46272/2587-8476-2020-11-2-28-44.

"The article discusses the modern stage of international relations as a transition from the US-centric to another, polycentric world order. America has many opportunities to influence the formation of the future world order, which it uses for maintaining a dominant role in the world. However, America also has severe weaknesses for making the global transition; the main one considers the psychological unpreparedness of the country's establishment for a change in the global role of the United States. The country's transitional situation gives rise to an identity crisis, accompanied by the most heated debates in the political class regarding the development of foreign policy and strategy. In the variety of positions and narratives of the American strategy, one can distinguish (1) proponents of the liberal globalization and maintaining America's dominant position, (2) advocates of superpower status and resource dominance by coercion and (3) realists or those who call for building a new global balance of power and coordinating the US interests with other powers. This identity crisis is associated with the globally changing position of the country that has been at the center of the international system for the past 75 years. The American political class was never monolithic before and even during the Cold War, representing a range of different foreign policy ideas and positions. However, foreign policy disagreements previously did not question the national identity and fundamental value of the country. For America, these values were associated with a global role in promoting the ideals of freedom and liberal democracy, previously underpinned by confrontation with the USSR. The disappearance of the Soviet power strengthened the position of liberal

Conclusion 307

Russian and Chinese market successes, and Moscow and Beijing's determination.[18] It seems as Soviet wags used to say, there is going to be a "bloody battle for peace and friendship" during the Biden presidency thanks mostly to the folly of America's progressives and liberals.[19]

Once upon a time, in the aftermath of the Soviet Union's demise, it seemed that American unipolar superpower would culminate in a golden age of global peace and prosperity, but this is no longer plausible. If progressive and liberal priorities prevent America from stemming the Eastern authoritarian tide, the United States risks becoming a fratricidal polity, an anemic zero-sum society at home,[20] a failed democratic free enterprise model abroad, and "paper tiger" in global affairs.[21] American influence abroad will wane. The domestic living standard may improve glacially, or even decline, alienating a large segment of the middle class. Liberalization and competitiveness in Asia, Europe, and much of the Third World will be in retreat, the global economy will atrophy, and Eastern authoritarians will triumph.

The Democratic Party's progressive-liberal agenda makes better outcomes improbable. Biden's America is dazed, straitjacketed, and adrift with little prospect for safely weathering the storms looming on the dark horizon.

---

globalists and enhanced the strategic narrative of the global promotion of American values. The difference of the contemporary period is that nationalists and realists no longer accept the arguments of liberal globalists, resulting in a deepening of ideological polarization in the political class and society. The domestic ideational and political crisis splits the elites, delays the transition to a new world order, and makes it impossible to pursue a sound international strategy. Such a strategy will be the result of both an internal political struggle and a response of the country's leadership to the processes of pluralization and polycentrism developing in the world."

[18] Nadège Rolland, ed., *An Emerging China-centric Order: China's Vision for a New World Order in Practice*, The National Bureau of Asian Research (August 2020), https://www.nbr.org/publication/an-emerging-china-centric-order-chinas-vision-for-a-new-world-order-in-practice/.

[19] Office of the Secretary of Defense, "Annual Report to Congress: Military and Security Developments Involving the People's Republic of China 2020," (August 2020). https://media.defense.gov/2020/Sep/01/2002488689/-1/-1/1/2020-DOD-CHINA-MILITARY-POWER-REPORT-FINAL.PDF.

[20] Lester Thurow, *The Zero-Sum Society* (Lexington: Basic Books, 1980).

[21] Mao Zedong, "U.S. Imperialism is a Paper Tiger," *Selected Works of Mao Zedong*, (July 1956), https://www.marxists.org/reference/archive/mao/selected-works/volume-5/mswv5_52.htm.

Appendix

"Guns and Butter" Superpower

Washington during the Obama years belittled post-Soviet Russia as a "regional power" that could be "contained,"[1] and rolled back (via color revolutions and regime change) because Putin's consumer economy was too fragile to survive a protracted arms competition with the West. The

---

[1] George Kennan ("X"), "The Sources of Soviet Conduct," *Foreign Affairs* 25, no. 4, July 1947: 566–582; Office of the Historian, "Kennan and Containment, 1947," https://history. state.gov/milestones/1945-1952/kennan. George F. Kennan, a career Foreign Service Officer, formulated the policy of "containment," the basic United States strategy for fighting the cold war (1947–1989) with the Soviet Union. His ideas, which became the basis of the Truman administration's foreign policy, first came to public attention in 1947 in the form of an anonymous contribution to the journal Foreign Affairs, the so-called "X-Article." "The main element of any United States policy toward the Soviet Union," Kennan wrote, "must be that of a long-term, patient but firm and vigilant containment of Russian expansive tendencies." To that end, he called for countering "Soviet pressure against the free institutions of the Western world" through the "adroit and vigilant application of counter-force at a series of constantly shifting geographical and political points, corresponding to the shifts and maneuvers of Soviet policy." Such a policy, Kennan predicted, would "promote tendencies which must eventually find their outlet in either the break-up or the gradual mellowing of Soviet power."

Despite all the criticisms and the various policy defeats that Kennan suffered in the early 1950's, containment in the more general sense of blocking the expansion of Soviet influence remained the basic strategy of the United States throughout the cold war. On the one hand, the United States did not withdraw into isolationism; on the other, it did not move to "roll back" Soviet power, as John Foster Dulles briefly advocated. It is possible to say that each succeeding administration after Truman's, until the collapse of communism in 1989, adopted a variation of Kennan's containment policy and made it their own.

310 *Beleaguered Superpower: Biden's America Adrift*

attitude persists. Washington today portrays Russia as an "impoverished superpower,"[2] with a low living standard, anemic growth prospects, festering social and political discontents, often on the cusp of a "black swan" economic catastrophe.[3] This faith has not always been steadfast,[4] but dominates contemporary Biden establishment thinking. It is the cornerstone of Washington and Berlin's "strategic patience" doctrine.[5]

The faith harks back to the time when the establishment felt "iron curtain" top-down command-planned economies were comprehensively inferior to their "free-world" horizontal competitive market rivals. The deep state believed that the Soviet economy was defective because it criminalized freehold private property, for-profit entrepreneurial business, competitive wage and price setting, and democracy (The Soviet Union by law was a one party communist monopoly serving the working class). The Soviet military industrial complex (VPK) was the exception that proved the rule. It performed well, but the CIA believed this was only because the VPK had priority access to the nation's best resources, labor, skills, and technology. This explained the paradox of the USSR military superpower.

Washington was right in these regards.[6] Times however have changed. Russia is not the Soviet Union. The old benchmark is obsolete. It no longer adequately reflects today's complex economic potentials. The Soviets abolished central planning more than 34 years ago. The Kremlin has ceased being Russia's sole freehold and leasehold owner of the means

---

[2] Charles Wolf, Jr. and Henry Rowen, *The Impoverished Superpower: Perestroika and the Soviet Military* (Palo Alto: ICS Press, 1990).

[3] Nassim Taleb, *The Black Swan: The Impact of the Highly Improbable* (New York: Random House, 2007).

[4] Abram Bergson, "The Great Economic Race," *Challenge* 11, no. 6, March 1963: 4–6; Steven Rosefielde, "Tea Leaves and Productivity: Bergsonian Norms for Gauging the Soviet Future," *Comparative Economic Studies* 47, no. 2, June 2005: 259–273.

[5] Gopal Ratnam, "White House Unveils Call for 'Strategic Patience'," *Foreign Policy* (February 2015), http://foreignpolicy.com/2015/02/05/white-house-to-unveil-call-for-strategic-patience-russia-ukraine-syria-iraq-china-asia/. Mark Salter, "Putin, Merkel and Cold War Lessons," *RealClear Politics* (February 2015), https://www.realclearpolitics.com/articles/2015/02/24/putin_merkel_and_cold_war_lessons.html.

[6] Steven Rosefielde, *The Kremlin Strikes Back: Russia and the West after Crimea's Annexation* (Cambridge: Cambridge University Press, 2016); Steven Rosefielde, *Russian Economy from Lenin to Putin* (New York: Wiley, 2007).

of production. Enterprise managers are no longer state employees (red directors). Wages and prices today are set by the market, not the state. The state does not assign or tie workers to their enterprises. Rationing has ended. Entrepreneurship is legal. Business is for-profit. Citizens can freely engage in international businesses and travel abroad. Foreigners are encouraged to invest, transfer technology, and trade in Russia. There are residues. Nonetheless, but Putin's mixed market-rent granting economic system is substantially more flexible.[7]

The establishment knows this, but still cannot accept the strategic significance of the post-Soviet transformation, in part because Russia's liberalization is incomplete, the stability of the macro-economy is fragile, natural resources prices are subject to violent fluctuations, the labor force is shrinking, property rights and the rule of law are insecure, and market entry rules are opaque.[8] These caveats are valid, but not decisive. Russia's markets do not have to be perfectly competitive for the Kremlin to escape the "impoverished superpower" syndrome. Moscow can give Washington a run for its geopolitical money merely by establishing a mixed workably competitive market and rent granting consumer sector that provides an adequate and rising living standard,[9] while turbocharging the state-owned VPK by introducing competitive for-profit, competitive business principles. Theory clearly teaches that the introduction of workably competitive markets should allow Russia's consumer sector and VPK to outperform their Soviet predecessors.[10] The Kremlin like the Forbidden City has become an authoritarian "guns and butter" superpower capable of the sustained civilian and military growth needed to compete with Washington in theaters of its choosing.

---

[7] Julian Cooper, "The Russian Economy Twenty Years after the End of the Socialist Economic System," *Journal of Eurasian Studies* 4, 2013: 55–64.

[8] Gerard Turley and Peter Luke, *Transition Economics: Two Decades On* (London: Routledge, 2010).

[9] World Bank, "Russian Economy Returns to Modest Growth in 2017, Says World Bank," November 29, 2017, http://www.worldbank.org/en/news/press-release/2017/11/29/rer-38.

"These shoots have allowed consumer demand and consumption to rise, as the business environment improved, and underpin projections that Russia's economy will grow 1.7% in both 2017 and 2018, and 1.8% in 2019."

[10] John Clark, "Toward a Concept of Workable Competition," *The American Economic Review* 30, no. 2, June 1940: 241–256.

312   *Beleaguered Superpower: Biden's America Adrift*

Inclusive economic theory illuminates the details.[11] It pinpoints how Russia's micro and macro-economies have become more efficient, and how non-pecuniary utilities have enhanced the quality of existence. The quality of life in Russia today has improved partly because supply is more responsive to consumer demand (pecuniary utilities), and partly because government is more responsive to the people's will (allowing voter preferences to better influence public goods). The Kremlin is less repressive, allowing citizens more personal, civic, political, and religious liberties (benefits provided by the regime not counted in GDP statistics).

The demonstration requires the analysis of five spaces: factor, production, distribution, transfer and quality of existence). Efficiency gains including technological progress are attributable to a more dexterous "invisible hand" (Walrasian price and Marshallian output adjustment mechanisms replacing rationing). Gains in other quality of existence benefits stem from improvements in civil rights and liberties, and democratic participation.

The analysis for all five spaces is "comparative static," not instantaneous (snap shot).[12] All spaces contrast Russian economic performance in 2020 with the Soviet experience circa 1985 before Mikhail Gorbachev dismantled communist command central planning in 1987 with his radical economic reforms (perestroika).

Factor Space

Figure A1 is a comparative static version of the Edgeworth–Bowley factor/production box. It illustrates the allocation of variable capital and labor to the civilian sector and the VPK in 1985 and 2020. The ordinate represents variable capital (not the capital stock captured by the isoquants), and the abscissa labor for both activities. The supply of both factors is the equilibrium general competitive volume for the benchmark years in the 1985 and 2020 segments of the factor space. The origin for

---

[11] Steven Rosefielde and Ralph W. Pfouts, *Inclusive Economic Theory* (Singapore: World Scientific Publishers, 2014).

[12] Steven Rosefielde and Jonathan Leightner, *China's Market Communism: Challenges, Dilemma and Solutions*, London (Abingdon: Routledge, 2017). For a full geometric illustration of the process of achieving an instantaneous general competitive equilibrium.

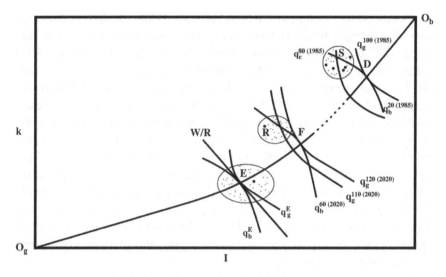

Figure A1   Factor Space

the VPK (guns) is located at the southwest corner of the Edgeworth–Bowley box; the consumer sector (butter) production begins at the northeast corner. The space between the origins contains isoquants for the two goods. The isoquants are elements of production functions that link varying amounts of capital and labor to unit levels of output. There are two nested sets of isoquants generated by two production functions. One set is for guns, the other for butter. The production functions containing these two nested sets of isoquants are:

$q_g = F(k, l)$ and $q_b = G(k, l)$, where q_g represents guns and q_b butter; k is variable capital and l is labor. The price of variable capital is r; the wage rate is w.

The superscripts on the isoquants represent output volumes; that is, the number of guns or units of butter produced. The amounts produced increase the further isoquants lie from their respective origins (the greater the volume of capital and labor utilized), given the prevailing embodied technologies. The more productive the technology, the higher the superscript. Isoquants are convex to their respective origins and "nested" (they do not intersect). They fill the entire production space and illustrate the possibilities for efficient factor substitution between the two activities. The supplies of variable capital and labor on the ordinate and abscissa are the equilibrium volumes.

314 *Beleaguered Superpower: Biden's America Adrift*

Under perfect competition (general equilibrium),[13] there exists one and only one equilibrium (E) (or a fuzzy set of possible E points in accordance with "bounded rationality" theory (the circular sets in Figure A1)) that reflects perfectly competitive consumer demand. Fuzzy sets do not alter basic conclusions, given sensible assumptions about information sufficiency and people's ability to choose rationally.[14] If consumer preferences change (demand) in a perfectly competitive world, point E must adjust accordingly. Conjectured changes in consumer preferences are counterfactual. The set of all equilibria, real and conjectured are illustrated by the contract curve connecting the two origins (given perfectly competitive technology, labor and variable capital supplies), which serves as a useful referent for grasping how Russia's economic performance has changed between 1985 and 2020. The contract curve here has two discontinuous segments, one reflecting Soviet supply and demand conditions, the other post-Soviet realities.

Russia's economy in 1985 operated inefficiently at point S. Capital and labor under top-down command-planned communism were misrationed. The Bolshevik's criminalization of private property, markets, and entrepreneurship precluded competitive factor allocation, forcing planners to ration capital and labor to alternative use without knowledge of consumer demand (required for a general competitive consumer

---

[13] Kenneth Arrow and Gerard Debreu, "The Existence of an Equilibrium for a Competitive Economy," *Econometrica* 22, no. 3, 1954: 265–290; William Novshek and Hugo Sonnenschein, "General Equilibrium with Free Entry: A Synthetic Approach to the Theory of Perfect Competition," *Journal of Economic Literature* 25, no. 3, September 1987: 1281–306.

[14] Herbert Simon, "A Behavioral Model of Rational Choice," in Herbert Simon, ed., *Models of Man: Social and Rational-Mathematical Essays on Rational Human Behavior in a Social Setting* (New York: Wiley, 1957); Herbert Simon, "A Mechanism for Social Selection and Successful Altruism," *Science* 250, no. 4988, 1990: 1665–1668; Herbert Simon, "Bounded Rationality and Organizational Learning," *Organization Science* 2, no. 1, 1991: 125–134; Gerd Gigerenzer and Reinhard Selten, *Bounded Rationality* (Cambridge: MIT Press, 2002); Ariel Rubinstein, *Modeling Bounded Rationality* (Cambridge: MIT Press, 1998); Clem Tisdell, *Bounded Rationality and Economic Evolution: A Contribution to Decision Making, Economics, and Management* (Cheltenham: Brookfield, 1998); Daniel Kahneman, "Maps of Bounded Rationality: Psychology for Behavioral Economics," *The American Economic Review* 93, no. 5, 2003: 1449–1475.

sovereign solution). The Politburo had a strong preference for guns (structural militarization) and took a Spartan attitude toward worker consumption. Russia produced 80 guns and 20 sticks of butter at point S, but Figure A1 shows that it could have done better merely by sliding along the butter isoquant from S to D, where the production of guns increases to 100, without any reduction in butter. This "Pareto superior" outcome, illustrates the general case where one participant gains without the other losing. Point D in Figure A1 however overstates Russian performance because Kremlin technologies were not perfectly competitive. Unit production is lower than the competitive ideal whenever reference is to the actual productivity of fixed Russian capital. We will illustrate the importance of this distinction later in the production space (Figure A2).

Washington was right. Soviet top-down command planning was inherently defective. It could not allocate resources efficiently subject to Bolshevik preferences and planners chose inferior technologies. Moreover, Figure A1 shows that the Kremlin was producing too many guns from a consumer sovereign perspective with the technologies at its

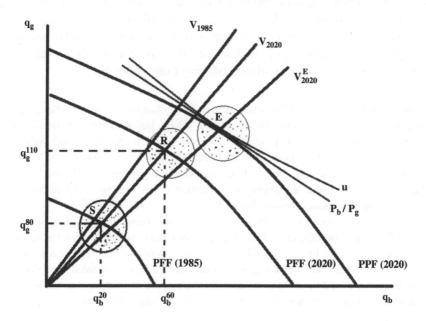

Figure A2 Production Space

316 *Beleaguered Superpower: Biden's America Adrift*

disposal.[15] Consumers wanted more butter, but the Communist Party overruled them. Russians wanted the assortment of guns and butter illustrated by point E (symbolized here by 2020 preferences), but the Party chose point S. Communism's flawed factor allocation mechanism, backward consumer good technologies, and the leadership's addiction to structural militarization explain why the Soviet Union was an "impoverished superpower."

Fast forward to 2020. "Sovereign democracy" has replaced communism,[16] and workably competitive markets hampered by rent-granting prevail in both the guns and butter sectors. Foreign direct investment and technology transfer have increased factor productivity economy wide, with production now occurring at point R. The superscripts on the isoquants at point R indicate that post-Soviet Russia is producing more butter and more guns (quality adjusted) than in it did in 1985.[17] Factor allocation at point R remains inefficient, but less so than before. R is closer to the economy's Pareto contract curve (production possibility frontier) than the corresponding Soviet era point S. If Russia's market were perfectly competitive, the wage/rental ratio would increase, shifting production from R to F via the Walrasian excess-demand wage adjustment mechanism (Adam Smith's invisible hand) illustrated in Figure A6. Excess labor demand in the guns sector shifts labor out of butter production to weapons (the supply of labor itself arrayed along the abscissa is invariant by assumption) without reducing butter output.

---

[15] Vitaly Shlykov, "Chto Pogubilo Sovetskii Soiuz? Amerikanskaia Razvedka o Sovetskiskh Voennykh Raskhodakh (What Destroyed the Soviet Union? American Intelligence Estimates of Soviet Military Expenditures)," *Voenny Vestnik*, no. 8 (2001); Vitaly Shlykov, "Nevidimaia Mobilizatsii," *Forbes*, no. 3, March 2006: 1–5; Vitaly Shlykov, "The Military Reform and Its Implications for the Modernization of the Russian Armed Forces," in Jan Leijonhielm and Fredrik Westerlund, eds., *Russian Power Structures* (Kista: Swedish Defense Research Agency, January 2008): 50–60.

[16] Sovereign democracy is a term describing modern Russian politics first used by Vladislav Surkov on February 22, 2006 in a speech before a gathering of the Russian political party United Russia. According to Surkov, sovereign democracy is: A society's political life where the political powers, their authorities and decisions are decided and controlled by a diverse Russian nation for the purpose of reaching material welfare, freedom and fairness by all citizens, social groups and nationalities, by the people that formed it.

[17] The VPK is now producing fifth generation weapons. The Soviets only produced less sophisticated fourth generation military hardware.

Figure A1 also shows that the Kremlin is still producing too many guns from the people's point of view. Consumers want more butter, but Putin driven by his military priorities has over-ruled them. Point E illustrates the assortment of guns and butter that Russians desire. The Kremlin cannot do better than point R due to the imperfections of Russia's workably competitive Walrasian wage adjustment mechanism (invisible hand), even though it would prefer to be at point F on Russia's counterfactual contract curve.

Soviet Russia was unable to reach point R in 1985 because it lacked the technology and Marshallian excess-price adjustment mechanism (competitive profit seeking) to do so (see Figure A7). Improvements in technology and competitiveness in the intervening years have made it possible for the Kremlin to have more butter and more guns at R. The people prefer point E, but Putin's priorities are in political command. If Russia's economy grows beyond 2020 as the International Monetary Fund (IMF) and World Bank forecast, it will be a more affluent guns and butter economy.

The sum and substance of all these changes has transformed Russia from an impoverished superpower to a "guns and butter" superpower that allows consumer preferences to curb Putin's otherwise insatiable appetite for weapons. Advances in technology, factor allocative efficiency, and supply responsive demand have enabled the Kremlin to escape the impoverished superpower dilemma. Putin can and is contesting America's military superiority without undermining his legitimacy in the eyes of frustrated consumers.

Production Space

Remapping the contract curve in Figure A1 in the production space (Figure A2), underscores this judgment.[18] Guns are arrayed on the ordinate and butter on the abscissa. The highest concave curve to the origin is the 2020 production possibilities frontier (PPF). It is analogous to the Pareto contract curve in Figure A1, which assumes generally competitive technologies (not a contract curve derived from Russia's inferior

---

[18] Figure A1 is a comparative static represent of the relevant parts of two separate contract curves, one for 1985, the other 2018. The remapping in Figure A2 is from the full contract curves not fully displayed in Figure A1.

318   *Beleaguered Superpower: Biden's America Adrift*

isoquants), and represents the menu of guns and butter supplies Russia could generate, given its inferior technology, defective factor allocative mechanism, and the spectrum of the Kremlin's sovereign demands. The community indifference curve U (the nation's, not the Kremlin's demand function) is tangent to the PPF (the aggregate perfectly competitive supply curve) at point E. The double tangency at the price ratio p_b/p_g indicates a complete equilibrium of Russian demand and supply in 2020. It is Pareto optimal.

Russian production is suboptimal. It occurs at point R on the 2020 production feasibility frontier, where Russia's inferior technologies and allocative inefficiencies generate a Pareto dis-preferred assortment and volume of guns and butter (The people's iso-utility curve intersects the PFF). Nonetheless, point R is superior to point S because Russia's post-Soviet economy produces more guns and more butter in a better mix than 1985, from both Putin's and the people's points of view.[19] The Soviet Union could have produced more guns and butter too, but the Politburo could not have done so as efficiently as Putin with his mixed workably competitive-rent granting system, assisted with international standard transferred consumer good technologies. Russia today is not only producing more due to improved production possibilities. It provides consumers and Putin alike with a more desirable supply of superior goods and services.

Distribution Space

Guns and butter moreover are more efficiently distributed to final purchasers in 2020 than they were in the "bad old USSR" when goods were rationed. Money meant little then because retail shelves were nearly bare. Workers purchased what they could in factory stores. Shopping was tantamount to scavenging in 1985. The Soviet Union was an "economy of shortage,"[20] a sellers' market where consumer options for the most part were "take it, or leave it." This meant not only that goods and services produced at point S in Figures A1 and A2 were inadequate. It also meant that short supplies were mal-distributed.

---

[19] Figures A2 omits Putin's iso-utility curves.

[20] Igor Birman, *Ekonomika Nedostach* (*Economy of Shortage*) (New York: Chalidze Publications, 1983).

"Guns and Butter" Superpower 319

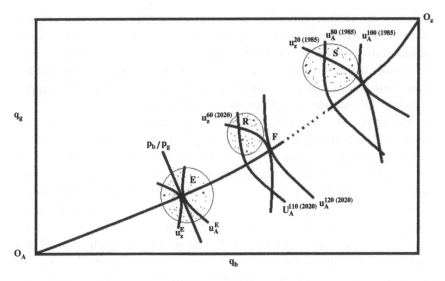

Figure A3 Distribution Space

Figure A3 illustrates how Putin has improved the situation. It is a comparative static version of the Edgeworth–Bowley retail distribution box. Figure A3 depicts the allocation of guns and butter to two purchasers, A and Z in 1985 and 2020. The ordinate represents guns, and the abscissa butter. The supply of both products is determined in Figures A1 and A2 at points S in 1985 and R in 2020. The origin for individual A is located at the southwest corner of the Edgeworth–Bowley box; Z's purchases begin at the northeast corner. The space has two zones, one for 1985, the other 2020. The hatched line discontinuity in the contract curve connecting the A and Z origins separates the two periods.

The interior of the Edgeworth–Bowley retail distribution box contains A and Z's iso-utility (indifference) curves for the two goods q_g and q_b. The iso-utility curves are components of utility functions that link varying amounts of guns and butter consumption to utility. There are two nested sets of iso-utility curves, one for A, the other for Z.

$u_A = F(q_g, q_b)$ and $u_Z = G(q_g, q_b)$, where U represents utility, q_g guns and q_b butter. The price of guns is p_g; the price of butter p_b.

The superscripts on the iso-utility curves represent ordinal (degrees) of utility; that is, the ordinal magnitude of utility subjectively experienced in the consumption of guns and butter by individuals A and Z. Utilities are subjective, non-comparable, and non-additive. The degree of utility

320 *Beleaguered Superpower: Biden's America Adrift*

increases the further iso-utility curves lie from their respective origins, given each individual's psychological scale of sensibilities.[21] The greater the sensibility, the higher the superscript.[22] Iso-utility curves are convex to their respective origins and "nested" (they do not intersect). They fill the entire distribution space and illustrate the possibilities for efficient barter ("product substitution") between individuals A and Z.

Under perfect competition (general equilibrium),[23] there exists one and only one equilibrium (E) (or a fuzzy set of a possible E points in accordance with "bounded rationality" theory (the circular sets in Figure A3)) that reflects prevailing consumer demand. Fuzzy sets do not alter basic conclusions, given credible assumptions about sufficient information and people's ability to choose rationally. If consumer preferences change, point E must adjust accordingly. Conjectured changes in consumer preferences are counterfactual. The set of all equilibria, real and conjectured are illustrated by the contract curve connecting the two origins, which serves as a useful referent for grasping how Russia's distributive performance has changed between 1985 and 2020. The contract curve here has two discontinuous segments, one reflecting 1985 Soviet Russian supply and demand conditions, the other 2020 post-Soviet Russian realities.

Russia's retail distribution in 1985 operated inefficiently at point S. Guns and butter under command-planned communism were mis-rationed by Gossnabsbyt (the state wholesale distribution system). The Bolshevik's criminalization of private property, markets, and entrepreneurship precluded competitive retail distribution, forcing planners to ration guns and butter to recipients without knowledge of consumer demand (required for a general competitive consumer sovereign solution). Russia distributed too much to individual A (Stalin), and too little to individual Z (a proletarian), and did so inefficiently at point S. Figure A3 shows that the Kremlin

---

[21] A and Z are assumed to have difference "sensibilities," that is, appreciative capacities.

[22] Individual sensibilities may increase or diminish between 1985 and 2018. If they increase, then this can be validly reflected in the 2018 superscript with reference to the 1985 ordinal ranking.

[23] Kenneth Arrow and Gerard Debreu, "The Existence of an Equilibrium for a Competitive Economy," *Econometrica* 22, no. 3, 1954: 265–290; William Novshek and Hugo Sonnenschein, "General Equilibrium with Free Entry: A Synthetic Approach to the Theory of Perfect Competition," *Journal of Economic Literature* 25, no. 3, September 1987: 1281–1306.

"Guns and Butter" Superpower 321

could have done better merely by forcing Z to slide along its iso-utility curve at S to D, where individual A's utility increases from 80 to 100, without reducing individual Z's utility. This "Pareto superior" outcome, illustrates the general case where one party is able to gain, without the other losing.

Western advocates of strategic patience during the Cold War were right about the shortcomings of the communist economic system. Soviet command planning was comprehensively defective. It could neither allocate resources nor distribute retail supplies efficiently. Moreover, Figure A3 shows that rationing was inequitable. The Kremlin favored A over Z. Russians by assumption in a counterfactual competitive consumer sovereign universe, would have desired a retail distribution that moved consumption from point D in 1985 toward point E in 2020, but the Party chose point S. Had Gorbachev recognized this, he should have transferred income from A to Z in 1985.

Communism's flawed retail distribution mechanism compounded the underproduction of consumer goods and Soviet anti-competitive factor price setting (hence earned purchasing power). Soviet "impoverished superpower" was comprehensive.

Fast forward to 2020 in Figure A3. "Sovereign democracy" and workably competitive markets have replaced communism and central planning. There are more guns and butter produced in the 2020 than in 1985,[24] (not shown in Figure A3)[25] and distributive efficiency has improved too. People's demand based on competitively determined income and purchasing power governs retail distribution more than rationing. Supplies of guns and butter are greater, characteristics are better and consumer's utility sensibilities may be higher (people have become more discerning),[26] with consumption now occurring at point R. The superscripts on the iso-utility curves at point R indicate that Z is experiencing utility levels closer

---

[24]The sides of the Edgeworth–Bowley box for 2018 (not drawn) are larger than the Edgeworth–Bowley box for 1985.

[25]The greater availability of guns and butter in 2020 can be depicted by increasing the sides of the Edgeworth–Bowley box in the 2020 region when discussing the Russian period.

[26]The assertion here is that superscripts on A's and Z's iso-utility curves in 2018 could be higher than 1985, not just because supplies and qualities have been improved but also because there could be an external benefit of a freer society where people appreciate the things they consume more than before.

322 *Beleaguered Superpower: Biden's America Adrift*

to the "normal" level achievable in competitive economies and that A also could be better off, given the increased supply of guns and butter, even though A's share of national purchasing power has diminished. Retail distribution at point R remains inefficient, but less so than at S. R is closer to the contract curve (utility possibilities frontier) than the corresponding Soviet era point S.[27]

If Russia's market were perfectly competitive, the price ratio p_b/p_g in Figure A3 could increase, shifting distribution from R to F via the Walrasian excess-demand price adjustment mechanism illustrated in Figure A6. F is Pareto superior to R.

Figure A3 also shows that the Kremlin in 2020 is still privileging A's consumption over Z's from the consumer sovereign perspective (point E). Z deserves a larger share of national consumption on competitive grounds, but Putin has ruled otherwise. Point E illustrates the retail distribution that Russians desire. The Kremlin however cannot even reach point F because its Walrasian price adjustment mechanism is imperfect (rent granting marred workable competition). It is stuck at point R.

Russia was unable to reach point R from point S in the factor-production space (Figure A1) in 1985 because it lacked the Marshallian excess-price adjustment mechanism (competitive profit seeking) to do so. The introduction of markets has changed everything. Improvements in technology (due considerably to technology transfer) and competitiveness after 1985 have made it possible for the Kremlin to have more guns and butter, and distribute 2020 GDP in Figure A3 better from the consumer sovereignty perspective. Russia has been able to treat A more fairly by decreasing Z's share of national income and improving distributive efficiency, without unduly harming Z. The superscripts on Z's 2020 iso-utility curves illustrate the case where Z's utility in 2020 exceeds 1985 despite Z's smaller 2020 share of national income. A's utility at R is higher than at S because the pie increased and A has enhanced consumer choice (superior utilitarian options analogous the superior technologies fixing the production feasibility frontiers in Figure A2). Although Putin's economy is imperfectly competitive, Russians are indisputably better off than they had been under Soviet communism.

---

[27]This is the utility possibilities frontier generated from guns and butter produced in the 2018 segment of the factor-production space depicted in Figure A1.

Transfer Space

Factors of production should earn the value of their marginal products in competitive theory, and recipients in Figure A3 should use their income to the purchase guns and butter produced at point E in Figures A1 and A2. People are entitled to spend what they earn, charitably give their money away to others, or use the ballot box to instruct government to tax the community and transfer the proceeds to the deserving. Figure A4 illustrates these transfer possibilities as utility feasibilities frontiers (UFFs) and utility possibilities frontiers (UPFs). The UFFs and UPFs derived from the utilities of A and Z generated from points S and E in Figure A3. They depict the effects of tax transfers (including public programs) from one individual to another in ideal (UPF) and real (UFF) circumstances. Figure A4 shows that both A and Z are experiencing higher utility in 2020 at point R than they did in 1985 at point S, even though better options exist along the utility feasibilities and utilities possibilities frontiers from various points of view. This suggests that there is substantial scope for improving social justice from diverse perspectives in Putin's Russia that are going largely

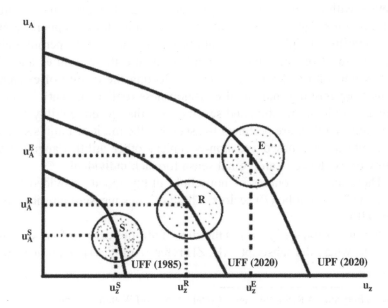

Figure A4 Transfer Space

324 Beleaguered Superpower: Biden's America Adrift

untapped.[28] The Kremlin can do much better, not only by enhancing competitiveness in the private sector, but in honing the government's skill at redistributing income.

Quality of Existence Space

Russia's workably competitive quality of existence depends on the per capita GDP (including Pareto imperfect transfers in cash and kind) examined in Figures A1–A4, plus non-pecuniary benefits (utilities generated by "democratic" Pareto imperfect cultural, social, ethnic, religious, class, family, community and political relations; institutions, rights, liberties, restrictions, obligations, income and wealth distribution and environmental policies). The main component of the quality of existence is utilities derived from consuming goods and services acquired through earnings and transfers (per capita GDP), but people also benefit or suffer from authoritarianism, conditions of labor, inequities, injustices, insecurities, illiberality, intolerance, discord, and environmental depredation. Job security, job quality, independence, cooperation, congeniality, team spirit, mutual support, and solidarity generate positive non-pecuniary workplace utilities. Political, economic, social, religious, and personal freedom, together with national and income security, psychological and spiritual health allow people to enjoy their incomes more fully. Supportive cultures, families, neighbors, communities, and compatriots permit richer lives. National income statistics neither capture these utilities and disutilities nor a host of virtuous factors affecting the quality of existence (gains from refining individual consciousness (enlightenment), wisdom, compassion, high morality, and sensibilities) that generate utility in their own right, but they are pertinent to assessing the merit of Putin's system. Per capita income-based and non-pecuniary other utilities augment the quality of existence in an ordinal sense for each individual.

There are two sources of household utility: goods provided by the private (H) and public (P) sectors. These utilities measure physical well-being (W):

$W = u_{AH} + u_{ZH} + u_{AP} + u_{ZP}$ is the sum of utilities derived from consuming GDP, where the subscripts AH, ZH refer to utilities (u) experienced by

---

[28] Abram Bergson, "A Reformulation of Certain Aspects of Welfare Economics," *Quarterly Journal of Economics* 52, no. 1, February 1938: 310–134.

individuals A and Z from consuming household goods and services (H), and subscripts AP and ZP denote the utilities that A and Z derive from government provided goods and services (P).

The quality of existence (QE) is sum of these utilities (W) and non-pecuniary other utilities (X):

$$QE = W + X$$

where $X = u_{AX} + u_{ZX}$.

The subscripts AX and ZX refer to utilities experienced by individuals A and Z from unpaid self and interpersonal services, and political, social, spiritual, and aesthetic experiences.

The highest quality of existence as individuals experience it is not necessarily best from all normative standpoints. The sum of utilities as individuals perceive them, and the community's assessment of their impact are likely to differ, and ethics vary.[29] Nonetheless, the utilitarian measure provides a sensible benchmark for gauging systems merit.[30]

It is reasonable to suppose that the stability of Putin's regime is highly correlated with Russian perceptions of the nation's quality of existence. Figure A5 shows why Russians in 2020 should have a greater QE than they had in 1985. The diagram arrays utility (U) on the ordinate and Russia on the abscissa at different moments in time. The lower segments of the vertical bars represent utility derived in household consumption

---

[29]There are three important contemporary schools of virtue ethics. Modern Stoicism, Kantian-deontology, and utilitarian consequentialist. Modern stoicism stress virtue ethics (Philippa Foot, Alasdair MacIntyre, and Martha Nussbaum). This means seeking personal gratification and validation by acting virtuously. Deontology means intrinsic virtue regardless of consequences achieved by adhering to categorical imperatives, or through karmic merit. Utilitarian-consequentialism counts utilities and disregards stoicism, idealism, and karmic calculus.

Rosalind Hursthouse and Glen Pettigrove, "Virtue Ethics," *The Stanford Encyclopedia of Philosophy* (Winter 2018 Edition); Edward N. Zalta (ed.), https://plato.stanford.edu/archives/win2018/entries/ethics-virtue/.

[30]Abram Bergson, "A Reformulation of Certain Aspects of Welfare Economics," *Quarterly Journal of Economics* 52, no. 1, February 1938: 310–134. Bergson famous welfare function is analogous to a utility indifference curve. The double tangency between Bergson welfare curve and the utility possibility frontier indicates a third party's view of the optimal point that treats individual choice as the highest good. Other third party judgments based on sentiment or ethics are also possible.

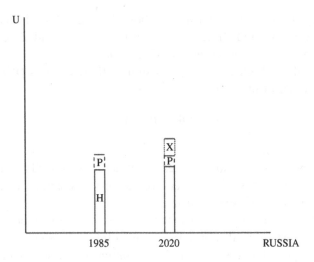

Figure A5 Quality of Existence Space

from private (*H*) and public (*P*) sources. The upper segments measures other non-pecuniary utilities. Russian per capita consumption indicated by Russia's lower bars in 2020 significantly exceeds the Soviet benchmark 1985. Russian public services are less than Soviet because defense spending has declined as a share of GDP. Russia has sharply increased the quality of existence too by introducing democracy, expanding civil liberties, cultural, economic, social and religious freedom in the *X* space while retaining much of the Soviet social safety net. It has significantly curbed terror, forced labor, excess deaths, and other forms of authoritarian oppression.[31] Russia's per capita consumption (well-being), and *X* utilities

---

[31] David Remnick, "The Historical Truth-Telling of Arseny Roginsky," *New Yorker* (December 2017), https://www.newyorker.com/news/postscript/the-historical-truth-telling-of-arseny-roginsky.

"'Russia today, for all its abysmal and authoritarian features, is not a replica of Stalin's Russia in the thirties. Things are bad enough, Arseny always made clear, but there was no need to lose one's head entirely. The year 1937 was above all about the murder of hundreds of thousands people and the sending of further hundreds of thousands to prison camps,' he said not long ago to a publication called Rights in Russia. 'It marked the final isolation of the country from the rest of the world, the start of life behind the Iron Curtain. Today the situation is completely different.'

all exceed the 1985 benchmark, contrary to the impression conveyed by most Western political commentators.

Walrasian Wage and Price Adjustment

The invisible hand has two aspects. The first is a price mechanism that reallocates labor and inventories to alternative use (Walrasian adjustment). The second is an output adjustment mechanism that alters factor supplies and outputs (Marshallian adjustment).

Figure A6 illustrates the Walrasian excess demand, price adjustment mechanism. When demand exceed supply measured by the horizontal

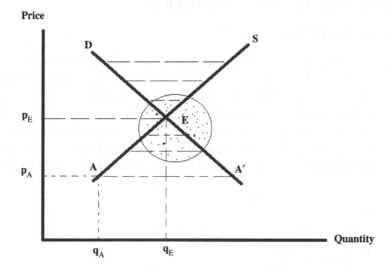

Figure A6   Price Adjustment Space

'Today our relatively sluggish authoritarianism is trying to turn into a strict authoritarianism. Today the regime is making more and more extensive use of anti-Western, Great Power rhetoric; this rhetoric is becoming the base for the ruling elite. It's hard to take and it's unpleasant, that's true,' he added. 'But not only is this not 1937, not mass state terror, it's also not life behind the Iron Curtain. There is no curtain and by all appearances you would no longer be able to lower one over Russia. This is not just a question of technical capabilities, the Internet and the like, but about the fact that real isolation would not hold out, it would fall apart. Yes, we live in a reactionary age, but becoming Burma or even the Soviet Union under Brezhnev is not something that can be done any more.'"

distance between points A and A', buyers try to acquire more goods from inventories, or labor by bidding up the product price or wage. If the disequilibria persists prices (wages) continue rising until equilibrium point E. If supply exceeds demand, the process operates in reverse.

Figure A7 illustrates the Marshallian excess price adjustment mechanism. When the demand price exceeds the supply price (marginal cost) measured by the vertical distance between points A and A', profit-seeking managers expand production. If disequilibrium persists, output continues expanding until equilibrium point E. If the supply price (marginal cost) exceeds the demand price, the process operates in reverse.

Marshallian Quantity Adjustment

Hierarchy of Purpose

Well-being and quality of existence are subjective. They measure individual ordinal utility and are unsuitable for computing ordinal interpersonal indexes. Moreover, any observer can render an independent judgment about the quality of Russia's existence in terms of his or her sentiments and ethics. Some Russians may feel that while life today is better than yesterday, the improvement is restricted primarily to the lower tiers (physiological and safety needs) of Abraham's Maslow's hierarchy

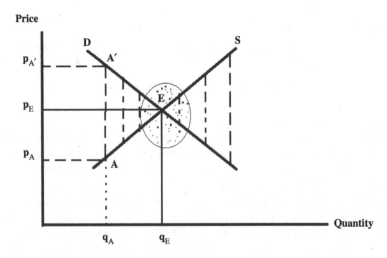

Figure A7 Quantity Adjustment Space

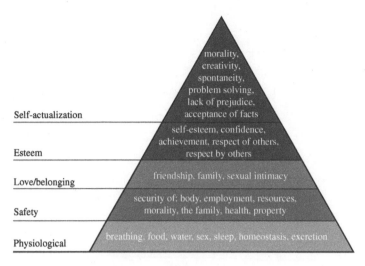

Figure A8   Maslow Hierarchy of Need

of purpose (need)[32] (see Figure A8). This however should not be so for most Russians because of improvements in X utilities associated with partial democratization and expanded civil liberties. Russians today enjoy the rights to own private property, engage in for profit business, act entrepreneurially, and travel abroad. They have broader social and religious freedoms, which provide QE benefits in Maslow's three top tiers (belonging, self-esteem, and self-actualization), while retaining much of the Soviet social safety net. Russia should not be teetering on the brink of political collapse because the quality of existence is stagnant or declining.[33]

---

[32] Abraham Maslow, "A Theory of Human Motivation," *Psychological Review* 50, no. 4, 1943: 370–396.
[33] Stephen Blank, "Can Russia Sustain Its Defense Buildup?," unpublished manuscript, January 2018.
   Many Western commentators feel confident that Russia is on the brink of collapse without thinking the matter through. Stephen Blank elaborates their position.

Bibliography

Abramovitz, Moses. "Catching Up, Forging Ahead, and Falling Behind." *The Journal of Economic History* 46, no. 2 (June 1986): 385–406.

Adomanis, Mark. "Russia's Foreign Trade is Collapsing." *Forbes* (March 2015). http://www.forbes.com/sites/markadomanis/2015/03/25/russias-foreign-trade-is-collapsing/.

AEI. "China Global Investment Tracker." http://www.aei.org/china-global-investment-tracker/?mkt_tok=eyJpIjoiWlRaa1pqVmpZalF5TXpkbSIsInQi OiIzcllESWpGNGhpQlBwVnlZR2lOaFBvN2xmelZCN0hGTmtoVEZCcUl 3ckJMMmNxY2hPckt2OUNVVFNiaWNkb1FwVXZMWmVMd2FxRGN VYndpdkhRYkNuM3M2NTBVTE41d2QxNUdBSVRZYm5sZjVKWEV vWWFWSldBVjI1YVdvVTdOUiJ9.

Akbarzadeh, Shahram, and Joshua Roose. "Muslims, Multiculturalism and the Question of the Silent Majority." *Journal of Muslim Minority Affairs* 31, no. 3 (September 2011): 309–325.

Akulov, Andrei. "Russian Iskander-M Missile System: Credible Deterrent." *Strategic Culture* (September 2016).

Allen, Susan Hannah. "The Domestic Political Costs of Economic Sanctions." *Journal of Conflict Resolution* 52, no. 6 (December 2008): 916–944, esp. 916–917.

Allison, Graham, and Robert Blackwill. "America's Stake in the Soviet Future." *Foreign Affairs* (Summer 1991): 77–97.

Alred, Lance, and Madina Rubly. "Russian International Relations: Russia's Power Revival and Engagement with the Global Community." In *Putin's Russia: Economic, Political and Military Foundations*, edited by Steven Rosefielde. Singapore: World Scientific Publishers, 2020.

332 *Beleaguered Superpower: Biden's America Adrift*

Amadeo, Kimberly. "Current U.S. Federal Budget Deficit." *The Balance* (September 2018). https://www.thebalance.com/current-u-s-federal-budget-deficit-3305783.

Ambinder, Marc, and D.B. Grady (David Brown). *Deep State: Inside the Government Secrecy Industry.* New York: Wiley, 2013.

Anderson, Collin, and Karim Sadjadpour. "Iran's Cyber Threat: Espionage, Sabotage, and Revenge." *Carnegie Endowment for International Peace* (January 2018). https://carnegieendowment.org/2018/01/04/iran-s-cyber-threat-espionage-sabotage-and-revenge-pub-75134.

Anderton, Charles H., and Jurgen Brauer. "Mass Atrocities and their Prevention." *Journal of Economic Literature* (still forthcoming).

Anderton, Charles H., and Jurgen Brauer. *Economic Aspects of Genocides, Other Mass Atrocities, and Their Prevention.* New York: Oxford University Press, 2016.

Andrei Tsygankov, Andrei. "Russia's the Turn to the East, 2012–2018." In *Putin's Russia: Economic, Political and Military Foundations*, edited by Steven Rosefielde. Singapore: World Scientific Publishers, 2020.

Antos, Joseph, and James C. Capretta. "National Health Expenditure Report Shows We Have Not Solved the Cost Problem." *AEI* (December 2017). http://www.aei.org/publication/national-health-expenditure-report-shows-we-have-not-solved-the-cost-problem/?mkt_tok=eyJpIjoiWlRBNVp qYzFNemxrT0RJeCIsInQiOiJKcGRxZEdjXC9PRUQ0Mm1ST0hqNlFP aGtodDRnZmw1cVFhU2xDb0MrSStyK0dGTzhGVGNGczVreDZIckJH WEdIM3lrS1JcL05OUStPUXpBcXdiVUs2VlloeWg2YitEMWI3QmVx SWpUM2RVbmtjRDRiSklGY1wvRjZYMWFDSGI3WHhjOCJ9.

Applebaum, Anne. "A KGB Man to the End." *Atlantic* (September 2020). https://www.theatlantic.com/magazine/archive/2020/09/catherine-belton-putins-people/614212/.

ARCGIS. "Public Health Agency of Sweden — Official Statistics." https://experience.arcgis.com/experience/09f821667ce64bf7be6f9f87457ed9aa.

Archibugi, Daniele. *The Global Commonwealth of Citizens: Toward Cosmopolitan Democracy.* Princeton: Princeton University Press, 2008.

Arms Control Association. "The Chemical Weapons Convention (CWC) at a Glance." (March 2018). https://www.armscontrol.org/factsheets/cwcglance.

Arms Control Association. "U.S. Nuclear Modernization Programs." *Arms Control Association* (March 2018). https://www.armscontrol.org/factsheets/USNuclearModernization.

Aron, Raymond. *The Opium of the Intellectuals.* Paris: Calmann-Levy, 1955.

Arrow, Kenneth, and Gerard Debreu. "The Existence of an Equilibrium for a Competitive Economy." *Econometrica* 22, no. 3 (1954): 265–290.

Ashenfelter, Orley. Robert F. Engle, Daniel L. McFadden, and Klaus Schmidt-Hebbel. "Globalization: Contents and Discontents." *Contemporary Economic*

Policy 36, no. 1 (January 2018): 29–43. http://onlinelibrary.wiley.com/doi/10.1111/coep.12237/full.

Aslan, Reza. *Global Jihadism: A Transnational Social Movement.* Saarbrücken: VDM (Verlag Dr. Müller), 2010.

Aslund, Anders. *How Russia Became a Market Economy.* Washington: Brookings Institution Press, 1995.

Aslund, Anders. "Why Has Russia's Economic Transformation Been So Arduous?" *Annual World Bank Conference on Development Economics* (April 1999). worldbank.org/INTABCDEWASHINGTON1999/Resources/aslund.pdf.

Aslund, Anders. *Building Capitalism: The Transformation of the Former Soviet Bloc.* New York: Cambridge University Press, 2001.

Aslund, Anders. *How Capitalism Was Built: The Transformation of Central and Eastern Europe, Russia, and Central Asia.* New York: Cambridge University Press, 2007.

Åslund, Anders. "Putin's Karabakh victory sparks alarm in Ukraine." *Atlantic Council* (November 2020). https://www.atlanticcouncil.org/blogs/ukrainealert/putins-karabakh-victory-sparks-alarm-in-ukraine/.

Aslund, Anders. *Russia's Capitalist Revolution: Why Market Reform Succeeded and Democracy Failed.* Washington: Peterson Institute for International Economics, 2007.

Aslund, Anders. "Russia's Neo-Feudal Capitalism." *Project Syndicate* (April 2017). https://www.project-syndicate.org/commentary/russia-neofeudal-capitalism-putin-by-anders-aslund-2017-04.

Aslund, Anders. "Making Sense of Russia's New Draconian Sanctions on Ukraine." *Atlantic Council* (November 2018). http://www.atlanticcouncil.org/blogs/ukrainealert/making-sense-of-russia-s-new-draconian-sanctions-on-ukraine.

Austin, Greg. "The US Will Win the Cyber War with China in 2017." *Diplomat* (November 2016). http://thediplomat.com/2016/11/the-us-will-win-the-cyber-war-with-china-in-2017/.

Baev, Pavel. "Russia Seeks to Rebuild Its International Respectability." *Eurasia Daily Monitor* 14, no. 117 (September 2017). https://jamestown.org/program/russia-seeks-to-rebuild-its-international-respectability/.

Baggott, Jim. *The First War of Physics: The Secret History of the Atom Bomb, 1939–1949.* New York: Pegasus Books, 2010.

Baldwin, Richard, and Javier Lopez-Gonzalez. "Supply-Chain Trade: A Portrait of Global Patterns and Several Testable Hypotheses." *The World Economy* 38, no. 11 (November 2015): 1682–721.

Balzer, Harley. "Can Russia Catch Up/Keep Up? Russian Science and Education in Putin's Fourth Term." In *Putin's Russia: Economic, Political and Military Foundations*, edited by Steven Rosefielde. Singapore: World Scientific Publishers, 2020.

334 *Beleaguered Superpower: Biden's America Adrift*

Barabanov, Mikhail. "Testing a 'New Look', The Ukrainian Conflict and Military Reform in Russia." *Centre for Analysis of Strategies and Technologies (CAST)* (December 2014).

Barfield, Claude. "Renewed Chinese Cyberespionage: Time for the US to Act." *AEI* (April 2018). http://www.aei.org/publication/renewed-chinese-cyberespionage-time-for-the-us-to-act/?mkt_tok=eyJpIjoiT1RZeVlqWm1 aVEptWmpSaSIsInQiOiJzY0ZmRklyNEg5Tm9SM2lWOFZ6ZE1ES3h uaWhPSUNZMDNcL1FTeGQweXlFN2FoZ0ZIM0k1cW8xTXJcL3FcLzl BUFlWWkNvVFpjVVhxK0prNitYeVwvaHNBblY5REpaZGg0b2NaZ0Vv ZDBUQkJrWjFRc1U1dEtLZFNybCtYc2Z3eHZzWmYifQ%3D%3D.

Barfield, Claude. "The Dual Goals of the Trump Administration's New Attack on Chinese Intellectual Property Theft." *AEI* (November 2018). www.aei.org/ publication/the-dual-goals-of-the-trump-administrations-new-attack-on-chinese-intellectual-property-theft/?mkt_tok=eyJpIjoiTVRrek9EVTJaR1Jt WldJMiIsInQiOiJuV0JDNGFsSEh0aHVpaENNZmtpODkxWTVNZn ZZeHgyZ0M1enJPRWw1Y2dPaDh4YVpZWjE5Y1BUY3ZnTHFJWS srNTNrbkxmYjFwU2lkRjRneGlJc0ZDS3p2ZTcxd1pMcnJuclJKR2laV m8yT3 pWQlZ2T3dpeHkwUnpOcGJGTkxIWSJ9.

Barnett, Thomas. *The Pentagon's New Map: War and Peace in the Twenty-First Century*. New York and London: Penguin, 2004.

Barro, Robert. "Cutting GDP to Counter the Coronavirus Pandemic." *National Review* (March 2020). https://www.nationalreview.com/2020/03/coronavirus-response-will-curbing-economic-activity-to-slow-virus-work/#slide-1.

Barry, John. *The Great Influenza: The Story of the Deadliest Plague in History*. New York: Viking, 2004.

Baumol, William. *Welfare Economics and the Theory of the State*. Cambridge: Harvard University Press, 1952.

Baumol, William. *Business Behavior, Value and Growth*. revised edition. New York: Macmillan, 1959.

Becker, Torbjorn. "Russia's Macroeconomy — A Closer Look at Growth, Investment, and Uncertainty." In *Putin's Russia: Economic, Political and Military Foundations*, edited by Steven Rosefielde. Singapore: World Scientific Publishers, 2020.

Beckley, Michael. "The Myth of Entangling Alliances: Reassessing the Security Risks of U.S. Defense Pacts." *International Security* 39, no. 4 (Spring 2015): 7–48. https://www.belfercenter.org/sites/default/files/legacy/files/IS3904_ pp007-048.pdf.

Belkin, Paul, Michael Ratner, and Cory Welt. "Nord Stream 2: A Geopolitical Lightning Rod." *Congressional Research Service* (August 2018). https://fas. org/sgp/crs/row/IF10943.pdf.

Belton, Catherine. *Putin's People: How the KGB Took Back Russia and Then Took On the West*. New York: Farrar, Straus and Giroux, 2020.

Bibliography 335

Bennett, Kirk. "What Gorbachev Did Not Hear." *American Interest* (March 2018). https://www.the-american-interest.com/2018/03/12/gorbachev-not-hear/.

Bergson, Abram. "A Reformulation of Certain Aspects of Welfare Economics." *Quarterly Journal of Economics* 52, no. 1 (1938): 310–334.

Bergson, Abram. "Soviet National Income and Product in 1937," Parts I and II, *Quarterly Journal of Economics* 64, nos. 2, 3 (1950), 208–241, 408–441.

Bergson, Abram. "On Inequality of Income in the U.S.S.R." *American Slavic and East European Statistician*, no. 3 (1951): 95–99.

Bergson, Abram. "Reliability and Usability of Soviet Statistics: A Summary Appraisal." *American Statistician* 7, no. 3 (1953): 13–16.

Bergson, Abram, editor and contributor. *Soviet Economic Growth: Conditions and Perspectives*. Evanston, Ill: Row, Peterson, 1953.

Bergson, Abram. "The Concept of Social Welfare." *Quarterly Journal of Economics* 68, no. 2 (May 1954): 233–252.

Bergson, Abram. *The Real National Income of Soviet Russia since 1928*. Cambridge, MA: Harvard University Press, 1961.

Bergson, Abram. "The Great Economic Race." *Challenge* 11, no. 6 (March 1963): 4–6.

Bergson, Abram. *The Economics of Soviet Planning*. New Haven, CT: Yale University Press, 1964.

Bergson, Abram. *Planning and Productivity under Soviet Socialism*. New York: Columbia University Press, 1968.

Bergson, Abram. "Development Under Two Systems: Comparative Productivity Growth Since 1950." *World Politics* 23, no. 4 (July 1971): 579–617.

Bergson, Abram. "Soviet Economic Perspectives: Toward a New Growth Model." *Problems of Communism* 32, no. 2 (March–April 1973): 1–10.

Bergson, Abram. "Social Choice under Representative Government." *Journal of Public Economics* 6, no. 3 (1976): 171–190.

Bergson, Abram. "The Soviet Economic Slowdown." *Challenge Magazine* 20, no. 6 (January–February 1978): 22–33.

Bew, John. *Realpolitik: A History*. London: Oxford University Press, 2015.

Biddle, Stephen. *Military Power: Explaining Victory and Defeat in Modern Battle*. Princeton, NJ: Princeton University Press, 2006.

Bidwell, Percy W. "Our Economic Warfare." *Foreign Affairs* (April 1942). https://www.foreignaffairs.com/articles/united-states/1942-04-01/our-economic-warfare.

Birman, Igor. *Ekonomika Nedostach* (The Shortage Economy). New York: Chalidize Publishing, 1983.

Blackwill, Robert, and Philip Gordon. "Containing Russia How to Respond to Moscow's Intervention in U.S. Democracy and Growing Geopolitical Challenge." *Council on Foreign Relations* (January 2018). https://cfrd8-files.cfr.org/sites/default/files/report_pdf/CSR80_BlackwillGordon_Containing Russia.pdf.

336 *Beleaguered Superpower: Biden's America Adrift*

Blanc, Jarret. "Trump's Iran Deal Decision: What Comes Next." *Carnegie Endowment for International Peace* (May 2018).

Blank, Stephen. "Baltic Buildup." *Jane's Intelligence Review* (May 2017): 6–13.

Blank, Stephen. "Imperial Strategies: Russia's Exploitation of Ethnic Issues and Policy in the Middle East." *Jamestown Foundation* (December 2017). https://jamestown.org/program/imperial-strategies-russias-exploitation-ethnic-issues-policy-middle-east/.

Blank, Stephen. "Making Sense of the Shanghai Cooperation Organisation." *European Security and Defense* (December 2017): 17–21.

Blank, Stephen. "Mission Impossible: Pursuing Arms Control with Putin's Russia." *Euroatlantic Policy Security Brief* (January 2018). https://www.europeanleadershipnetwork.org/policy-brief/mission-impossible-pursuing-arms-control-with-putins-russia/.

Blank, Stephen. "Moscow's Competitive Strategy." *American Foreign Policy Council* (July 2018).

Blank, Stephen. "Russia's Vostok-2018: A Rehearsal for Global War?, *RealClear Defense* (September 2018). https://www.realcleardefense.com/articles/2018/09/04/russias_vostok-2018_a_rehearsal_for_global_war_113764.html.

Blank, Stephen. "Whither the Russian–Chinese Alliance?" *European Security and Defence*, no. 4 (2018): 6–7.

Blank, Stephen. "Why Is the Sea of Azov So Important?" *Atlantic Council* (November 2018). http://www.atlanticcouncil.org/blogs/ukrainealert/why-is-the-sea-of-azov-so-important.

Blank, Stephen. "Can Russia Sustain its Defense Buildup?" In *Putin's Russia: Economic, Political and Military Foundations*, edited by Steven Rosefielde, Singapore: World Scientific Publishers, 2020.

Blank, Stephen. "Dealing with Russia: Bringing the Outlaw State to Justice," *The Hill* (September 2020). https://thehill.com/opinion/international/515251-dealing-with-russia-bringing-the-outlaw-state-to-justice.

Blumenthal, Daniel. "U.S. Policy in Asia: A Strategy for China's Imperial Overstretch." *American Interest* (March 2017). http://www.the-american-interest.com/2017/03/01/a-strategy-for-chinas-imperial-overstretch/.

Blumenthal, Dan. "It's Time to Reckon with What It Would Really Take to Deter North Korea." *AEI* (September 2017). http://www.aei.org/publication/its-time-to-reckon-with-what-it-would-really-take-to-deter-north-korea/?mkt_tok=eyJpIjoiT1dVMVpHTmhNVFl5TmpneCIsInQiOiIxa2wzK1BTS2E3bnJUVmpCakhFaFhvdHdvYk9ndGdVOXExUkVwSXB6d2lBXC96WHl0VzlyQ3hITE9XdWtJUlYwbWRraXhoSEJtYUI4UE9vazFNaDdObGh5UmJjSUVCR1wvU1wvUFRMQlZoWEhydXR4R4MWFETXAwcXF5WmlyM3JiYjdWYSJ9.

Bibliography 337

Blumenthal, Dan. "Trump Sets the Tone on China: America Will Not be Challenged." *AEI* (December 2017). http://www.aei.org/publication/trump-sets-the-tone-on-china-america-will-not-be-challenged/?mkt_tok=ey JpIjoiTldNM1pHUXhPVEV6WWpreSIsInQiOiJ3S0NhQnl0bjM4bHdOQk tmNWZJMWlja1IwblR6dHpBTUZsazJxNEt1Q3hiQ0xkcVRBK21oS0t vRUN0MVJQM3oxRmVOeW4zZTMzTkJIeVpoXC9SdG9OWkdDYklO OUVxUDkyRHV0Y3hxVkhhV24wY2lVS0daaHpFQ0J5bWVTV1wv RkxXIn0%3D.

Blumenthal, David. "Xi's 'Putinization' of China is a Massive Wake-Up for America." *AEI* (March 2018). http://www.aei.org/publication/xis-putinization-of-china-is-a-massive-wake-up-for-america/?mkt_tok=eyJp IjoiTTJGbU9HRmpZMlk0TUdZeCIsInQiOiJ4TjB2T3ZSY01KVl ZuQ0o2d0NaU1VUNTI1THRjZnZnVmFaRExLSzN0dGtzcEhgGWWN3 WFUxVExcL0xHS2Z2QlAyQUszZHpNcUpcL2l2RGw0UGdYV3Yzc 2dQdHdMUURCdHZBTU9cLzF2cVM0ZTBFWnBVQTZaUzR0Tmdvak wxMFViZkJJaCJ9.

Blumenthal, Daniel. *The China Nightmare: The Grand Ambitions of a Decaying State*. Washington, DC: AEI Press, 2020.

Bolling, Eric. *Corruption and Cronyism and How Trump Can Drain It*. New York: St. Martin's Press, 2017.

Bolton, John. "Brexit Victory is a True Populist Revolt." *AEI* (June 2016). http://www.aei.org/publication/brexit-victory-is-a-true-populist.

Bolton, John. "16 Years Later: Lessons Put into Practice?" *AEI* (September 2017). https://www.aei.org/publication/16-years-later-lessons-put-into-practice/?mkt_tok=eyJpIjoiTVRJell6Qm1ZVGcwTURreiIsInQiOiJmMXor N1hsRjZvRXU0WGEzY3pSZFJJVG5sWFA3VTZQdWR5T1ZVRFFsZH p0REFWVThiVWdxTDFQbWZWTm1uYkFWSnE5SFFHejRMcVNiZ2pl Y1RHN1lxZ3FrXC9lRjRlTEFvS3U1czY5U0p0V1d6dWV0SFdXbFp3b1J HQk13Ritka2IifQ%3D%3D.

Bolton, John. "FDR's 'Rattlesnake' Rule and the North Korean Threat." *AEI* (September 2017). http://www.aei.org/publication/fdrs-rattlesnake-rule-and-the-north-korean-threat/?mkt_tok=eyJpIjoiWTJRNVpXTNZVGM 0TnpZMCIsInQiOiJOWTdFbzRMZnNnZzRGRUVcL05WN05vaTN6Y XN2ZUhubEx6ZUxhRVpjb3VoWXRNZnExNzdRWE9CMmFnNmlOSjd PRkVCdUhueURtNkZXRG5XTUR2T215YmVhbm8zS1NBMGZLRnFhN 3NLRnlNMUptXC8yalY4S3Z6SUl6TFJoMFpEMlJmIn0%3D.

Bolton, John. "Iran Deal Devotees Try in Vain to Save a Sinking Ship." *AEI* (September 2017). http://www.aei.org/publication/iran-deal-devotees-try-in-vain-to-save-a-sinking-ship/?mkt_tok=eyJpIjoiWm1NMlpXWXlab VJoWTJOayIsInQiOiJmS01EWUtsUkptMjMrakR5Mnl0ZmVaYlYrNH A0R1JGSVdnY2JJNTNHdzZmM3g1YVJRa1BWV3E5U3pQakhPTWJ0

338 *Beleaguered Superpower: Biden's America Adrift*

cU5HXC90eFp5YjB4SXZzTEQ3cTVNYVBEUFJtRU1xVHhXQ2M5dk
ZRamdMbWVsZTBuYlA5XC9vVXpxa1pvUUZ5bmFIIn0%3D.

Bolton, John. "Expect America's Tensions with China and Russia to Rise in 2018." *AEI* (December 2017). http://www.aei.org/publication/expect-americas-tensions-with-china-and-russia-to-rise-in-2018/?mkt_tok=eyJpIjoiT0RjM01UY3dZV1U1TXpGayIsInQiOiJsU3NBQW h0bmYxczB5aFU1eEo3Q3VzWXVvXC9tQWlGZUNwNHVJXC94dCtq NXpIUWFKd1N4cFdQVitqclZUcldzb0dtODNxbzhBMFZMT21PRX NrV0VRV25RNlRTeHA2cGRUV202WmlXY2IxMTFhdmV2UkpWYzJy YUZWcGpmeGJlNjdxIn0%3D.

Boston, Scott, and Dara Massicot. "The Russian Way of Warfare A Primer." *Rand Corporation* (2017). https://www.rand.org/pubs/perspectives/PE231.html.

Brada, Josef, and Arthur King. "Is There a J-Curve for the Economic Transition from Socialism to Capitalism?" In *Stabilization and Privatization in Poland An Economic Evaluation of the Shock Therapy Program*, edited by Kazimierz Z. Poznanshki, 251–269. Boston: Kluwer Academic Publishers, 1993.

Brands, Hal. "China's Nuclear Buildup Changes Balance of Power." *AEI* (September 2020). https://www.aei.org/op-eds/chinas-nuclear-buildup-changes-balance-of-power/?mkt_tok=eyJpIjoiTWpNNE1EUXlNR1V4TW pjdyIsInQiOiJlWmhhb0FxRloyXC8wRHdEZ2l6MjRjVlYwXC9YZitYOD MrUWJZa3E0ME52OCtUbzNwQVpWajJJOVg3MjhibnFUVlVhT2FPd W5sanBhOUdwYlwvRkRJbGRHhSWZIRGdpWVZPWlh5bXhzZmQ3M mNqNVd2WFZUbVFHanpFMTBKdStuVFlUdiJ9.

Brennan, David. "Trump Won't Consider Palestinian 'Right of Return' in Peace Deal: Haley." *Newsweek* (August 2018). https://www.newsweek.com/trump-wont-consider-palestinian-right-return-peace-deal-haley-1094318.

Bunzel, Cole. "From Paper State to Caliphate: The Ideology of the Islamic State." *Brookings*, no. 19 (March 2015). https://www.brookings.edu/wp-content/uploads/2016/06/The-ideology-of-the-Islamic-State.pdf.

Bureau of Labor Statistics. "Labor Force Statistics from the Current Population Survey." (December 2017). https://data.bls.gov/timeseries/LNS11300000.

Butfoy, Andrew. "President Obama and Nuclear Disarmament." *Dissent* (August 2011).

Canto, Victor, Douglas Joines, and Arthur Laffer. *Foundations of Supply-Side Economics*. New York: Academic Press, 1983.

Cappola, Frances. "U.S. Sanctions On Russia Are Financial Warfare." *Forbes* (July 2014). http://www.forbes.com/sites/francescoppola/2014/07/18/u-s-sanctions-on-russia-are-financial-warfare/.

Carter, Ash., ed. "Shaping Disruptive Technological Change for Public Good." Belfer Center (August 2018). https://www.belfercenter.org/publication/shaping-disruptive-technological-change-public-good?utm_source=

Bibliography 339

SilverpopMailing&utm_medium=email&utm_campaign=TAPP_Ash%
20Carter_Shaping%20Disruptive%20Technological%20Change%
20for%20Public%20Good%20(1)&utm_content=&spMailingID=2022
7006&spUserID=NTQ3ODk4MzgxNTgS1&spJobID=1340856526&sp
ReportId=MTM0MDg1NjUyNgS2.

Carter, Ash. "Reflections on American Grand Strategy in Asia." *Belfer Center* (October 2018). https://www.belfercenter.org/publication/reflections-american-grand-strategy-asia?utm_source=SilverpopMailing&utm_medium=email&utm_campaign=Ash%20Carter%20China%20Paper%20-%2010-18%20(1)&utm_content=&spMailingID=20406637&spUserID=NTQ3ODk4MzgxNTgS1&spJobID=1361027524&spReportId=MTM2MTAyNzUyNAS2.

CDC. "1918 Pandemic (H1N1 virus)." *CDC*. https://www.cdc.gov/flu/pandemic-resources/1918-pandemic-h1n1.html.

CDC. "1918 Pandemic (H1N1 virus)." *CDC*. https://www.cdc.gov/flu/pandemic-resources/1918-pandemic-h1n1.html.

CDC. "Estimated Influenza Illnesses, Medical visits, Hospitalizations, and Deaths in the United States — 2018–2019 Influenza Season." https://www.cdc.gov/flu/about/burden/2018-2019.html.

Chang, Ha-Joon. *Bad Samaritans: The Myth of Free Trade and the Secret History of Capitalism*. London: Bloomsbury Press, 2007.

Charap, Samuel. "The Ghost of Hybrid War." *Survival* (December 2015–January 2016).

Cheang, Chris. "Russia's Interest in North Korea Crisis." *RSIS* (December 2017).

Childress, Ron. "'The Children's Crusade' — Namely the Needless American 'Humanitarian' Assistance to Post-Soviet Russia." *American Association for the Advancement of Slavic Studies* (September 1998).

"China Economic Transition." *Higher Education Press* 1, no. 2 (September 2018). http://journal.hep.com.cn/cet/EN/volumn/volumn_3317.shtml.

Christie, Edward H. "The design and impact of Western economic sanctions." *The RUSI Journal* 161, no. 3 (June/July 2016): 52–64.

Christie, Edward Hunter. "Does Russia Have the Fiscal Capacity to Achieve Its Military Modernisation Goals?" *The RUSI Journal* (2017): 4–15. https://doi.org/10.1080/03071847.2017.1406697.

CIA, "'Restructuring the Soviet Workplace': The New State Enterprise Law." (1987). https://www.cia.gov/library/readingroom/docs/DOC_0000499785.pdf.

CIA, *CIA World Factbooks*. 2017.

CIA. World Factbook: Iran. 2017.

Clark, John. "Toward a Concept of Workable Competition." *The American Economic Review* 30, no. 2, part 1 (June 1940): 241–256.

340 *Beleaguered Superpower: Biden's America Adrift*

Clark, John Maurice. *Competition as a Dynamic Process*. Washington: Brookings Institution, 1961.

Clinton, Bill. *My Life*. New York: Knopf, 2004.

Clinton, Hillary. "America's Pacific Century: The Future of Politics Will Be decided in Asia, Not Afghanistan or Iraq, and the United States Will Be Right at the Center of the Action." *Foreign Policy* (October 2011). http://foreignpolicy.com/2011/10/11/americas-pacific-century/.

Clinton, Hillary. "A National Security Reckoning How Washington Should Think About Power." *Foreign Affairs* (November/December 2020).

Cohen, Stephen. "Ukraine Revisited." *The Nation* (February 2017). https://www.thenation.com/article/ukraine-revisited/.

Cohen, Stephen. "Unverified 'Russiagate' Allegations, Irresponsibly Promoted by Congress and the Media, Have Become a Grave Threat to American National Security." *The Nation* (August 2017). https://www.thenation.com/article/unverified-russiagate-allegations-promoted-by-an-irresponsible-congress-and-media-have-become-a-grave-threat-to-american-national-security/.

Cohen, Stephen. "Russia is Not the 'No. 1 Threat'-or Even Among the Top 5." *The Nation* (November 2017). https://www.thenation.com/article/russia-is-not-the-no-1-threat-or-even-among-the-top-5/.

Collina, Tom and William Perry. *The New Nuclear Arms Race and Presidential Power from Truman to Trump*. New York: BenBella Books, Inc. 2020.

Conca, James. "The Iran Nuclear Deal Without the United States." *Forbes* (October 2017). https://www.forbes.com/sites/jamesconca/2017/10/17/the-iran-nuclear-deal-without-the-united-states/#8f346173c943.

Congress. "Coronavirus Aid, Relief, and Economic Security Act" or the "CARES Act," HR 748, 116th Cong., 2nd sess., Congressional Record 131 (March 19, 2020): S 3548, https://www.congress.gov/116/bills/s3548/BILLS-116s3548is.pdf.

Congressional Research Service. "The European Deterrence Initiative: A Budgetary Overview." (August 2018). https://fas.org/sgp/crs/natsec/IF10946.pdf.

Connolly, Richard, and Cecilie Sendstad. "Russian Rearmament: An Assessment of Defense-Industrial Performance." *Problems of Post Communism* (October 2016).

Cook, Sarah. "China's Party Congress Hints at Media Strategy for a 'New Era'." *The Diplomat* (November 2017). https://thediplomat.com/2017/11/chinas-party-congress-hints-at-media-strategy-for-a-new-era/.

Cooper, Julian. "The Russian Economy Twenty Years After the End of the Socialist Economic System," *Journal of Eurasian Studies* 4 (2013): 55–64.

Cooper, Julian. "Russia's State Armament Programme to 2020: A Quantitative Assessment of Implementation 2011–2015." *FOI* (March 2016).

Bibliography 341

Cooper, Julian "Russia's Invincible Weapons: Today, Tomorrow, Sometime, Never?" *CCW* (May 2018). http://oxford-ccw.squarespace.com/blog/2019/3/27/russias-invincible-weapons-an-update-by-julian-cooper.

Cooper, Marianne. "The False Promise of Meritocracy." *Atlantic* (December 2015).

Corbin, Michael. "Kennan Cable No. 33: A Russian Pivot to Asia? Russian Trade with Asia from 2006 to 2016." *Kennan Institute* (May 2018). https://www.wilsoncenter.org/publication/kennan-cable-no-33-russian-pivot-to-asia-russian-trade-asia-2006-to-2016?mkt_tok=eyJpIjoiT0dZd1lqWTVZakJpTURJMyIsInQiOiJhcllkXC9MM3RnZ0RNaW4wOWwxN2I0dFZVSzIwbzhaV2NcLzM3UlwvTWJ0YUJrRUx4S0VCdHJhZGV4WCtOZm44N25GOXFYeUlQYzR5bTJLMkw0UXNIaEVUcFpxOVlCWmVCWFdwUUczend3cjJmNWJ5XC9UZXo5bmhFNXNUeTljODhhcXoifQ%3D%3D.

Cordesman, Anthony. "Keeping the North Korean Threat in Proportion." *CSIS* (August 2017). https://www.csis.org/analysis/keeping-north-korean-threat-proportion.

Cordesman, Anthony, and Steven Colley. "Chinese Strategy and Military Modernization." *CSIS* (December 2015).

Cordesman, Anthony H., and Charles Ayers. "The Military Balance in the Koreas and Northeast Asia: Final Review Edition." *Center for Strategic and International Studies* (November 2016).

"Corporate Goliaths are Taking over the U.S. Economy. Yet Small Breweries are Thriving. Why?" *Atlantic* (January 2018). https://www.theatlantic.com/business/archive/2018/01/craft-beer-industry/550850/.

Dawisha, Karen. *Putin's Kleptocracy Who Owns Russia?* New York: Simon & Schuster, 2014.

Deshowitz, Alan. *Guilt by Accusation: The Challenge of Proving Innocence in the Age of #MeToo.* New York: Hot, 2019.

Deuber, Gunter. "Five Years of Financial Market and Banking Sector Sanctions — A 'New Equilibrium' Locally and Internationally." *Russian Analytical Digest*, no. 236 (June 2019). https://css.ethz.ch/content/dam/ethz/special-interest/gess/cis/center-for-securities-studies/pdfs/RAD236.pdf.

DIA, "Ballistic and Cruise Missile Threat." (2017). https://www.nasic.af.mil/LinkClick.aspx?fileticket=F2VLcKSmCTE%3d&portalid=19.

Doar, Robert. "Whose Recovery?" *AEI* (September 2018).

Donovan, Marie. "America Needs a New Strategy to Deter Iran's Destabilizing Behavior." *AEI* (October 2017). http://www.aei.org/publication/america-needs-a-new-strategy-to-deter-irans-destabilizing-behavior/?mkt_tok=eyJpIjoiT0RaalptTmhZemc1WVdaayIsInQiOiJTbjVQT1JyM0JLT2xYdjBOTHJYdkR3SEFYaW1hSXNjWVNaRzVSTlN5U1AxYnZZV3E0ZkZtVzlzV1dac3F0dFJYRWJkS0ZocXJpcV3h1VFZzRTJ5d0Y2WE1oYWZ3M25hMVpOQnZQSXBHeE9SWW1tV29oUkJTWGFtVVVd5TldHaUlCWiJ9.

342 *Beleaguered Superpower: Biden's America Adrift*

Doran, Michael, and Peter Rough. "What America Should Do Next in the Middle East." *Mosaic* (September 2017). https://mosaicmagazine.com/essay/2017/09/what-america-should-do-next-in-the-middle-east/.

Downs, Chuck. Over The Line: North Korea's: Negotiating Strategy. Washington: AEI Press, 1999.

Dueck, Colin. "Trump's National Security Strategy: 10 Big Priorities." *National Interest* (January 2018). http://nationalinterest.org/feature/trumps-national-security-strategy-10-big-priorities-23994?page=2.

Eaglen, Mackenzie. "Recommendations for a Future National Defense Strategy." *Senate Committee on Armed Services* (November 2017).

Eaglen, Mackenzie. "Repair and Rebuild: Balancing New Military Spending for a Three-Theater Strategy." *AEI* (October 2017). http://www.aei.org/publication/repair-and-rebuild-balancing-new-military-spending-for-a-three-theater-strategy/?mkt_tok=eyJpIjoiT0Raak5EWTVNalJpTkRBMyIsInQiO iJ1bGRCM3Uwenh1T2xhdnpDNjEyTCs0djhxbVdJYW9jQUVMM0ZLb0 hDQ2tuNWIrbHRaRldacjZaTndQNmVmcmkySWphbWpZalZVYlQ0UT ZoS3V1b3hiT01sd241S3gyK2ZxaFpBbXJ1Wm1UbnpydGx3M2p6MDA wOVZuYXI2SDlGZyJ9.

Eaglen, Mackenzie. "Defense Strategy and Priorities: Topline or Transformation?" *AEI* (March 2020). https://www.aei.org/articles/defense-strategy-and-priorities-topline-or-transformation/?mkt_tok=eyJpIjoiWVdZMVpqY zNNMkV6WW1ZMCIsInQiOiJldkJCUlZoaHdTZ3JrbEM4emt6MnZqY2 p4UFBLMzlnNFZlVlwvOU5UeG1PUnlqYVhraVBMdFo0dzBaYmVkZ DRKSk85akgxVFN2OCs5WVhWYW9GUGZzK3kzTmVtMnJHZXdwS zdaWHFEeHhJQkpaaHJRVVBoXC9iT2R0ZWExM3VESHlvIn0%3D.

Eaglen, Mackenzie. "What's in the $2.2 Trillion Stimulus for Defense?" *Real Clear Defense* (March 2020). https://www.realcleardefense.com/articles/2020/03/28/whats_in_the_2_trillion_stimulus_for_defense_115156. html?mkt_tok=eyJpIjoiWW1SaU9EWTNObU0zWkRFei IsInQiOiJoUm1XZlhrSkUyZXJLT1kxc1k3NTZHaWc3U1pI bFV5UEU5N0daaXlTWGhpOFRDSXo4MDN6aE9pOEo4VmMwdU 02VjJBT2dhXC9XRmR3bDE0WW1SVGRrZGxpbXZ6bWU3S3pFN jVRTnVKd1FSejA2SUMwQlZIdDYzcFlJZWp1dnV2QjEifQ%3D%3D.

Eaglen, MacKenzie. "What If the Pentagon Skipped 5G?" *Defense One* (May 2020). https://www.defenseone.com/ideas/2020/05/what-if-pentagon-skipped-5g/165277/?oref=d-river&mkt_tok=eyJpIjoiTURNM09EY3lNek5o TkRGaiIsInQiOiJGUTZzU0NzS3dHMmQrWEJ0SjR4ZVpSbWowWE4 yZXJJcFBudVhTN3NUcGw5aE44cytxSUNjOW5NSzJyQld4Wlc5d FVyTlpFV3BBQUNkSzNHY0UrRGFsMlVQYWZaNHZVaUhpd0JRUnlx M0RhTHozeXdGeG9GdFVmY0ViTWVcL0FmNVMifQ%3D%3D.

Eberstadt, Nicholas. "From 'Engagement' to Threat Reduction: Moving Toward a North Korea Policy that Works." *AEI* (January 2017). http://www.aei.org/

Bibliography 343

publication/from-engagement-to-threat-reduction-moving-toward-a-north-korea-policy-that-works/.

Eberstadt, Nicholas. "North Korea: Why do They Want Nukes?" *AEI* (August 2017). http://www.aei.org/multimedia/north-korea-why-do-they-want-nukes-in-60-seconds/?aei.org?utm_source=paramount&utm_medium=email&utm_campaign=Eberstadt-DPRK-in60seconds-mailing-082817.

Eberstadt, Nicholas. "Men Without Work." *AEI* (January 2018). http://www.aei.org/publication/men-without-work-2/?mkt_tok=eyJpIjoiTm1aall6UXlaVFpoWXpNdyIsInQiOiJsS3hlMmpNM09tNVJCQ2pXZkpiSXc3bUNoZTl2Yjl4OE12Nzh1ek05WXdsQ2pSOElzanhGQzVXV1IzRFVyZ1wvODF1SE1GRkNpeUZiamFMZ1paMThFMmtwU2M0aEt3K1E0K3MxMWVzVnBMVTZnTXFZU2E1czM4WExwSTc1QmZqXC9xIn0%3D.

Eberstadt, Nicholas. "Can South Korea Avoid Getting Played by the North?" *AEI* (January 2018). http://www.aei.org/publication/can-south-korea-avoid-getting-played-by-the-north/?mkt_tok=eyJpIjoiWkRnd01qQTVPVFF3TjJKbSIsInQiOiJWUE1YT1wvQ3lGOXZrQnZwQ0hKZnRvSkdaelNmRkNtdXU0SFJ4aG1TcGpMTlE4R1pEMEw0RzRXeXpZaytyUEpFRU5kbGhDYm9WQVZPcStMQ0FkQ2tTQjI3NUFiVVc1ajFpFpUnpWVHdoeEdkWUMwVDNwZTdjQ0xFMU5ieWdlaWFFZTmcifQ%3D%3D.

Eberstadt, Nicholas. "The Method in North Korea's Madness." *Commentary* (January 2018). https://www.commentarymagazine.com/articles/method-north-koreas-madness/.

Eberstadt, Nicholas. "North Korea's Phony Peace Ploy." *AEI* (April 2018). http://www.aei.org/publication/north-koreas-phony-peace-ploy/?mkt_tok=eyJpIjoiWlRBeVpqazNPRGd6WkdVMiIsInQiOiJBc2dxOFpBMHFKREJKU0tKZTBSK1Jnc1V4dGl6bCtWd00rd09hbXoxNEIwa1ZZU0RUalQwMVV6VTZPM1FjTFErNUZPRFZ5OXVtNFgwanNRK3U0SDRXdzZNZ2pCeUVVBKzluNGpDbWdRMUUrQkxOaWxlTTlxQVlqak9YOHVqUTlGdCJ9.

Eberstadt, Nicholas. "Big Government's Overlooked Americans: A Dearth of Data has Kept Suffering Hidden," AEI (December 2020). https://www.aei.org/articles/big-governments-overlooked-americans/?mkt_tok=eyJpIjoiWXpKbFFkyVXlNR1ZpWVRneCIsInQiOiJvQnRST2psemtjWCtEXC9KU1IwMjdXSHJvMG9PaUhwZVVRESmFhWnFzQXNYeXBFR3VsUTdHMmNIeFFVUDB5cUc5UDhtblo3NXRyyOE5pa1VheXlpc1U1Z010RHk5XC9KdjV6MkhqqVWo0eVBIWGdhT3ZMR3o2ZXIwOG5rM1hmZGFyN3NyIn0%3D.

Economist. "A Farewell to Arms Control — Old Deals to Limit Nuclear Weapons are Fraying: They May Not be Repaired — Politics and Technology Make Arms Control Harder than Ever." (May 2018). https://www.economist.com/news/briefing/21741537-politics-and-technology-make-arms-control-harder-ever-old-deals-limit-nuclear-weapons?mkt_tok=eyJpIjoiWm

pKallqUTNaR0UxWWpJeCIsInQiOiJYa3VGRkFaWitzWlVadkVFZUN
WQkhUOHJmalY2THdDXC95SXYwNEVmZkVzaWNGWENzTlUrRjh
FMWJtTit0eGh5Rm0yTFJrZzJXNGU0MFI0WVh3ZWhPOTFjT0RtV0
xXZ3B6QktEbkJHMmFQdDlTSHVNeGU0N2pRSFRIMmhKUFd1Sm4if
Q%3D%3D.

Economist, "North Korea Blows Up the South's *De Facto* Embassy: And With it, Detente on the Korean Peninsula." (June 2020). https://www.economist.com/asia/2020/06/18/north-korea-blows-up-the-souths-de-facto-embassy.

Elgindy, Kaled. "How the Peace Process Killed the Two-State Solution." *Brookings* (April 2018). https://www.brookings.edu/research/how-the-peace-process-killed-the-two-state-solution/.

Ellings, Richard, and Robert Sutter, eds. *Axis of Authoritarians: Implications of China-Russia Cooperation.* New York: NBR Books, 2018.

Ellison, Ralph Waldo. *Invisible Man.* New York: Random House, 1952.

Ellman, Michael. "Russia's Current Economic System: From Delusion to Glasnost." *Comparative Economic Studies* 18, no. 1 (2015): 1–18.

Engelbrecht, H.C., and F.C. Hanighen. *Merchants of Death.* New York: Dodd, Mead & Co, 1934.

Engvall, Johan, Gudrun Persson, Robert Dalsjö, Mike Winnerstig, and Carolina Vendil Pallin. "Conventional Arms Control — A Way Forward or Wishful Thinking?" *FOI* (May 2018). https://www.foi.se/rapportsammanfattning?reportNo=FOI-R--4586--SE.

Escribà-Folch, Abel, and Joseph Wright. "Dealing with Tyranny: International Sanctions and the Survival of Authoritarian Rulers." *International Studies Quarterly* 54, no. 2 (June 2010): 334–359.

European Central Bank (September 11, 2020). https://www.ecb.europa.eu/press/key/date/2020/html/ecb.sp200911_slides~d99f3020a8.en.pdf?f0e6377d091c1f1d633bb727cd429eee.

EUR-lex. "Council Regulation (EU) 833/2014 of July 31, 2014, Concerning Restrictive Measures in View of Russia's Actions Destabilising the Situation in Ukraine." (July 2014). http://eur-lex.europa.eu/legal-content/EN/TXT/PDF/?uri=CELEX:32014R0833&from=EN.

EUR-lex. "Council Regulation (EU) 960/2014 of September 8, 2014, Amending Regulation (EU) No 833/2014 Concerning Restrictive Measures in View of Russia's Actions Destabilising the Situation in Ukraine." (September 2014). http://eur-lex.europa.eu/legal-content/EN/TXT/PDF/?uri=CELEX:32014R0960&from=EN.

EUR-lex. "Council Decision (CFSP) 2017/1087 of June 19, 2017, Amending Decision 2014/386/CFSP Concerning Restrictive Measures in Response to the Illegal Annexation of Crimea and Sevastopol." (June 2017). https://eur-lex.europa.eu/legal-content/EN/TXT/?uri=CELEX%3A32017D1087.

Bibliography 345

EUR-lex. "Council Decision (CFSP) 2017/2426 of December 21, 2017, Amending Decision 2014/512/CFSP Concerning Restrictive Measures in View of Russia's Actions Destabilising the Situation in Ukraine." (December 2017). http://eur-lex.europa.eu/legal-content/EN/TXT/?uri=CELEX:3201 7D2426.

European Union, Council Regulation (EU) 692/2014 of June 23, 2014, "Concerning Restrictions on the Import into the Union of Goods Originating in Crimea or Sevastopol, in Response to the Illegal Annexation of Crimea and Sevastopol." (June 2014). http://eur-lex.europa.eu/legal-content/EN/TXT/PDF/?uri=CELEX:32014R0692&from=SV.

European Union, Council Regulation (EU) 825/2014 of July 30, 2014, Amending Regulation (EU) No 692/2014, "Concerning Restrictions on the Import into the Union of Goods Originating in Crimea or Sevastopol, in Response to the Illegal Annexation of Crimea and Sevastopol." (July 2014). http://eur-lex.europa.eu/legal-content/EN/TXT/PDF/?uri=CELEX:32014R0 825&from=SV.

European Council. "Russia: EU Prolongs Economic Sanctions by Six Months." (December 2019).

European Sanctions, "EU & US Extend Russia-Ukraine Sanctions by 1 Year." *European Sanctions* (March 2019). https://europeansanctions.com/category/latest-eu-measures/.

"Executive Order of March 2, 2018 on the President's Continuation of the National Emergency with Respect to Ukraine." *Code of Federal Regulations* (2018). https://www.whitehouse.gov/presidential-actions/executive-order-presidents-continuation-national-emergency-respect-ukraine/.

Ezrati, Milton. "Entitlements Threaten the Entire Federal Budget." *Forbes* (February 2018). https://www.forbes.com/sites/miltonezrati/2018/02/09/entitlements-threaten-the-entire-federal-budget/#f311a4258923.

Faltsman, Vladimir. "Importozameshchenie v TEK i OPK." *Voprosy ekonomik* (2015): 116–124.

Farley, Robert. "Should America Fear China's Nuclear Weapons?" *The National Interest* (August 2014). http://nationalinterest.org/feature/should-america-fear-chinas-nuclear-weapons-11046.

Farrukh, Maher, and Katherine Zimmerman. "President Saleh is Dead. What's Next for Yemen?" *Critical Threats* (December 2017). https://www.criticalthreats.org/analysis/president-saleh-is-dead-whats-next-for-yemen?mkt_tok=eyJpIjoiTmpJellUUmhaREU0WmpKaSIsInQiOiJjTUd4ak ZNQ251UjF2RXBiTVpCc3BHcWlzc1lpMjMzSEVub1U3UDRIRHNH dFpBbXhwYTVLWEtQUms1XC91WEZDS0RwSnVyYm5kbjJmbXd0VD F0alZCN0N1bkcrMnVPMEFhdEF2WHNNTlNGZ0c4c1huMUNtTjZ3 amhOdWhXN3BHaGoifQ%3D%3D.

346 *Beleaguered Superpower: Biden's America Adrift*

Felgenhauer, Pavel. "Moscow Clarifies Its Nuclear Deterrence Policy." *Jamestown Commentaries* 17, no.80 (June 2020). https://jamestown.org/program/moscow-clarifies-its-nuclear-deterrence-policy/.

Fischer, Joschka. "The New Fulcrum of the Middle East." *Project Syndicate* (December 2017). https://www.project-syndicate.org/commentary/israel-saudi-arabia-alliance-by-joschka-fischer-2017-12?utm_source=Project+Syndicate+Newsletter&utm_campaign=fee9988f36-sunday_newsletter_24_12_2017&utm_medium=email&utm_term=0_73bad5b7d8-fee9988f36-93559677.

Fisher, Irving. *The Theory of Interest*. New York: The Macmillan, 1930.

FitzGerald, Mary. "Marshal Ogarkov and the New Revolution in Soviet Military Affairs." *Center for Naval Analysis* (1987).

Fitzpatrick, Sheila. "New Perspectives on Stalinism." *The Russian Review* 45 (October 1986).

Fleisher, Belton, William McGuire, Xiaojun Wang, and Min Quiang Zhao. "Wages, Innovation, and Employment in China." *IZA Institute of Labor Economics* (April 2017). http://d.repec.org/n?u=RePEc:iza:izadps:dp10749&r=tra.

Fleming, Brian. "Hybrid Threat Concept: Contemporary War, Military Planning and the Advent of Unrestricted Operational Art." *United States Army Command and General Staff College* (May 2011).

FOI. "The End of the Second Karabakh War: New realities in the South Caucasus." *The FOI Russia and Eurasia Studies Programme* (December 2020).

Ford, John. "The Pivot to Asia Was Obama's Biggest Mistake." *The Diplomat* (January 2017). http://thediplomat.com/2017/01/the-pivot-to-asia-was-obamas-biggest-mistake/.

Fordham University. *Modern History Sourcebook: The Molotov-Ribbentrop Pact, 1939*. New York: Fordham University. https://sourcebooks.fordham.edu/mod/1939pact.asp.

Foreign Policy. "President Donald J. Trump's First Year of Foreign Policy Accomplishments." (December 2017).

French II, Robert, and Heewon Chang. "Conceptual Re-Imagining of Global 'Mindset': Knowledge as Prime in the Development of Global Leaders." *Journal of International Organizations Studies* 7, no. 1 (2016): 49–62. http://journal-iostudies.org/sites/journal-iostudies.org/files/JIOS-ReviewEssay_GlobalMindset.pdf.

Friedman, Uri. "What Is a Nativist? And is Donald Trump One?" *Atlantic* (April 2017). https://www.theatlantic.com/international/archive/2017/04/what-is-nativist-trump/521355/.

Friedman, Uri. "North Korea Says It Has 'Completed' Its Nuclear Program. What Does That Mean?" *The Atlantic* (November 2017). https://www.theatlantic.com/international/archive/2017/11/north-korea-nuclear/547019/?mkt_tok=e

yJpIjoiTlRKbVlUQTBNRGMwTUdOaiIsInQiOiJXU0RaMnZnTmJwSjF
vXC9hV2Z1NGsrb1NZY0pGV3BZTndzYm5Vd3R1ZE8wQzRzaGhwU
1hcLzdiTkpsWVhZeFIzMUVPTFFMdEtPbzd0aVVnaUhCR29Kb
Wd2QkRnNXdkeDdHaW9EVytQRUxrV0lzNE5zVXRuNW96bnR0ekZB
VUhqNHFaIn0%3D.

Fromkin, David. "Entangling Alliances." *Foreign Affairs* 48, no. 4 (July 1970): 688.

Gabuev, Alexander. "China and Russia's Dangerous Entente." *Carnegie Russia* (October 2017).

Gaddy, Clifford G. "Russia's Virtual Economy." *Brookings* (February 2008).

Gaddy, Clifford G., and Barry W. Ickes. "Russia's Virtual Economy." *Foreign Affairs* (September/October 1998): 53–67.

Gaddy, Clifford G., and Barry W. Ickes. *Russia's Virtual Economy*. Washington: Brookings Institution Press, 2002.

Gady, Franz-Stefan. "Russia to Launch Its Most Powerful Ballistic Missile Sub in November." *The Diplomat* (October 2017). https://thediplomat.com/2017/10/russia-to-launch-its-most-powerful-ballistic-missile-sub-in-november/.

Gaidar, Yegor. *The Economics of Russian Transition*. Cambridge: MIT Press, 2003.

Gaidar, Yegor, and Karl Otto Pohl. *Russian Reform*. Cambridge: MIT Press, 1995.

Gao, Yuning. *China as the Workshop of the World: An Analysis at the National and Industrial Level of China in the International Division of Labor*. London: Routledge, 2014.

Galbraith, James. "What Trump's Tax Cut Really Means for the US Economy." *Project Syndicate* (January 2018). https://www.project-syndicate.org/onpoint/what-trump-s-tax-cut-really-means-for-the-us-economy-by-james-k-galbraith-2018-01?utm_source=Project%20Syndicate%20Newsletter&utm_campaign=dc2ccb3349-op_newsletter_2018_1_19&utm_medium=email&utm_term=0_73bad5b7d8-dc2ccb3349-93559677&mc_cid=dc2ccb3349&mc_eid=a749d91574&barrier=accesspaylog.

GAO. "National Security: Long-Range Emerging Threats Facing the United States as Identified by Federal Agencies." (December 2018). https://www.gao.gov/assets/700/695981.pdf.

Geranmayeh, Ellie. "The Coming Clash: Why Iran Will Divide Europe from the United States." *European Council on Foreign Relations* (October 2017). http://www.ecfr.eu/publications/summary/why_iran_will_divide_europe_from_the_united_states_7230.

Gerschenkron, Alexander. *Continuity in History, and Other Essays*. Cambridge: Belknap Press of Harvard University Press, 1968.

Gerschenkron, Alexander. *Economic Backwardness in Historical Perspective: A Book of Essays*. Cambridge: Belknap Press of Harvard University Press, 1962.

348 *Beleaguered Superpower: Biden's America Adrift*

Gerschenkron, Alexander. *Europe in the Russian Mirror: Four Lectures in Economic History*. London: Cambridge University Press, 1970.

Gessen, Masha. *The Future is History: How Totalitarianism Reclaimed Russia*. London: Penguin Publishing Group, 2017.

Gigerenzer, Gerd, and Reinhard Selten. *Bounded Rationality*. Cambridge: MIT Press, 2002.

Giles, Keir. "Assessing Russia's Reorganized and Rearmed Military." *Carnegie Foundation for Peace* (May 2017). http://carnegieendowment.org/2017/05/03/assessing-russia-s-reorganized-and-rearmed-military-pub-69853?mkt_tok=e yJpIjoiT0dZMFlUWXpZalEzTWpKaSIsInQiOiJOdkVISXZcLzA4U khwNEZGaFROd0ZWSlllRjNVazBkVXM5dU12S05QZFlSWlhMZHZFV FRHQWtHTDJrWXdKM3FqaU5NYW9jcGVuZXVRT0tQUnZC MW1UemhyZXY1NXl2REdieXJFam1zSDdjMGtnN0lCRFI3ZWxnbV lvZ0tLMjhxRkUifQ%3D%3D.

Giles, Keir. "Russia Hostile Action Against Estonia." *AEI* (December 2017). http://www.aei.org/wp-content/uploads/2017/12/Russian-Hostile-Action-Against-Estonia-Military-Options.pdf.

Goldstein, Lyle J. "What Russia's Vostok-18 Exercise with China Means Moscow Knows What It is Doing and Washington Should Take Note." *National Interest* (September 2018). https://nationalinterest.org/feature/what-russias-vostok-18-exercise-china-means-30577.

Gollwitzer, Peter. "Action Phases and Mind-Sets." In *The Handbook of Motivation and Cognition: Foundations of Social Behavior* 2, edited by E. Tory Higgins and Richard Sorrentino, 52–92. New York: Guilford Press, 1990.

Gollwitzer, Peter. "Mindset Theory of Action Phases." In *Handbook of Theories of Social Psychology* 1, edited by Paul Van Lange, Ari Kruglanski, and E. Tory Higgins: 526–545. Thousand Oaks: SAGE, 2012.

Golts, Alexander. *Military Reform and Militarism in Russia*. Washington: The Jamestown Foundation, 2019.

Gómez, Paz. "Stakeholder Capitalism's Sleight of Hand." *Frontier Centre for Public Policy* (March 2020). https://fcpp.org/2020/03/13/stakeholder-capitalisms-sleight-of-hand/.

Gorbachev, Mikhail. *Perestroika: New Thinking for Our Country and the World*. New York: Harper and Row, 1987.

Gorshkov, Victor. "Finance." In *The Unwinding of the Globalist Dream: EU, Russia and China*, edited by Steven Rosefielde, Masaaki Kuboniwa, Satoshi Mizobata, and Kumiko Haba: 193–212. Singapore: World Scientific Publishers, 2017.

Gottemoeller, Rose. "Russia is Updating Their Nuclear Weapons: What Does that Mean for the Rest of Us?" *Carnegie Endowment for International Peace* (January 2020).

Bibliography 349

Gottemoeller, Rose, Thomas Graham, Fiona Hill, Jon Huntsman Jr., Robert Legvold and Thomas R. Picering. "It's Time to Rethink Our Russia Policy America's Current Mix of Sanctions and Diplomacy Isn't Working. An Open Letter on How to Reconsider Our Approach to Putin-And Whoever Comes Next." *Politico* (August 2020). https://www.politico.com/news/magazine/2020/08/05/open-letter-russia-policy-391434.

Government Offices of Sweden. "The Government's Work in Response to the Virus Responsible for COVID-19." https://www.government.se/government-policy/the-governments-work-in-response-to-the-virus-responsible-for-covid-19/.

Graeber, David. *Bullshit Jobs: A Theory*. New York: Simon & Schuster, 2018.

Graham, Loren. *What Have We Learned About Science and Technology from the Russian Experience?* Palo Alto: Stanford University Press, 1998.

Gramm, Phil, and Mike Solon. "Don't Be Fooled by 'Secular Stagnation'." (December 2017). https://www.wsj.com/articles/dont-be-fooled-by-secular-stagnation-1512171654.

Gray, Colin. *Strategy for Chaos: Revolutions in Military Affairs and The Evidence of History*. London: Frank Cass, 2004.

Gressel, Gustav. "Russia's Quiet Military Revolution, and What it Means for Europe." *European Council on Foreign Relations (ECFR)* (December 2015). http://www.isn.ethz.ch/Digital-Library/Articles/Detail/?id=195415.

Gricius, Gabriella. "The Danske Bank Scandal is the Tip of the Iceberg." *Foreign Policy* (October 2018). https://foreignpolicy.com/2018/10/08/the-danske-bank-scandal-is-the-tip-of-the-iceberg-money-laundering-estonia-denmark-regulation-financial-crime/.

Gurvich, Evsey, and Ilya Prilepskiy. "The Impact of Financial Sanctions on the Russian Economy." *Russian Journal of Economics* (2016): 1–27.

Gurvich, Evsey, and Ilya Prilepskiy. "Western Sanctions and Russian Responses: Effects After Three Years" In *Perspectives on the Russian Economy under Putin*, edited by Torbjörn Becker and Susanne Oxenstierna. London: Routledge, 2019.

Gvosdev, Nikolas K. "Moscow Has Used Its New-Found Influence in the Middle East to Thwart the U.S. Effort to Use Saudi Arabia as a Pressure Point Against the Russian Economy." *The National Interest* (September 2017).

Haass, Richard. "The Age of Nonpolarity: What Will Follow U.S. Dominance." *Foreign Affairs* 87, no. 3 (2008): 44–56.

Haass, Richard, and David Sacks. "American Support for Taiwan Must Be Unambiguous."

Foreign Affairs (September 2020). https://www.foreignaffairs.com/articles/united-states/american-support-taiwan-must-be-unambiguous.

350   *Beleaguered Superpower: Biden's America Adrift*

Hanham, Melissa. "China's Happy to Sit Out the Nuclear Arms Race While Putin and Trump Push for Bigger Arsenals, Beijing Has All the Nukes It'll Ever Need." *Foreign Policy* (January 2017). http://foreignpolicy.com/2017/01/30/chinas-happy-to-sit-out-the-nuclear-arms-race/.

Hansen, Alvin H. "Economic Progress and Declining Population Growth." *American Economic Review* 29, no. 1 (March 1939): 1–15.

Harknett, Richard, and Michael Fischerkeller. "Deterrence is Not a Credible Strategy for Cyberspace." *Orbis* (Summer 2017). https://www.fpri.org/article/2017/06/deterrence-not-credible-strategy-cyberspace/.

Harré, Rom. *The Philosophies of Science*, 2nd Edition. Oxford, GB: Oxford University Press, 1986.

Harre, and J. Arson and E Way. *Realism Rescued*. London: Duckworth, 1994.

Harre, Rom, and M. Krausz. *Varieties of Relativism*. Oxford: Blackwell, 1995.

Harré, Rom, and Paul Secord. *The Explanation of Social Behaviour*. Oxford: Blackwell, 1973.

Harré, Rom and Michael Tissaw. *Wittgenstein and Psychology*. Basingstoke, UK: Ashgate, 2005.

Harrison, Todd. "What Has the Budget Control Act of 2011 Meant for Defense?" *CSIS* (August 2016). https://www.csis.org/analysis/what-has-budget-control-act-2011-meant-defense.

Held, David. *Democracy and the Global Order: From the Modern State to Cosmopolitan Governance*. Palo Alto: Stanford University Press, 1995.

Hess, Frederick. "DeVos gets Title IX right." *AEI*. https://www.aei.org/education/devos-gets-title-ix-right/.

Hill, Christopher. "North Korea's Real Strategy." *Project Syndicate* (June 2017). https://www.project-syndicate.org/commentary/north-korea-nuclear-program-invasion-by-christopher-r-hill-2017-06?utm_source=Project+Syndicate+Newsletter&utm_campaign=2200ecc304-sunday_newsletter_25_6_2017&utm_medium=email&utm_term=0_73bad5b7d8-2200ecc304-93559677.

Hofer, Eric. *The True Believer: Thoughts on The Nature of Mass Movements*. New York: Harper and Brothers, 1951.

Hoffman, Frank. *Conflict in the 21st Century: The Rise of Hybrid War*. Arlington: Potomac Institute for Policy Studies, 2007.

Hollander, Paul. *The End of Commitment: Intellectuals, Revolutionaries, and Political Morality in the Twentieth Century*. Chicago: Ivan R. Dee, 2006.

Holloway, David. *Stalin and the Bomb: The Soviet Union and Atomic Energy 1939–1956*. London: Yale University Press, 1994.

House Permanent Select Committee on Intelligence. "Report on Russian Active Measures." (March 2018).

Bibliography 351

Howitt, Peter, and Philippe Aghion. "Capital Accumulation and Innovation as Complementary Factors in Long-Run Growth." *Journal of Economic Growth* 3 (June 1998): 111–130.

Howitt, Peter. "Endogenous Growth and Cross-Country Income Differences." *American Economic Review* 90 (September 2000): 829–846.

Hummel, Sarah, and Andrey Baklitskiy. "Nuclear Arms Control and U.S.–Russia Relations." *US–Russia Future* (May 2018). https://us-russiafuture.org/2018/05/10/nuclear-arms-control-and-u-s-russia-relations/.

Huntington, Samuel. "The Clash of Civilizations?" *Foreign Affairs* 72, no. 3 (1993): 22–49.

Huntington, Samuel. Clash of *Civilization and the Remaking of World Order*. New York: Simon and Schuster, 1996.

Huntington, Samuel, ed. *The Clash of Civilizations? The Debate*. New York: Foreign Affairs, 1996.

Huntington, Samuel. "The West: Unique, Not Universal." *Foreign Affairs* 75, no. 6 (Nov./Dec. 1996): 28–46. https://www.foreignaffairs.com/articles/1996-11-01/west-unique-not-universal.

Huntington, Samuel. "The Lonely Superpower." *Foreign Affairs* 78, no. 2 (March–April 1999): 35–49.

Hursthouse, Rosalind and Glen Pettigrove. "Virtue Ethics." *The Stanford Encyclopedia of Philosophy* (Winter 2018 Edition), Edward N. Zalta (ed.). https://plato.stanford.edu/archives/win2018/entries/ethics-virtue/.

IAEA. "IAEA, Iran Sign Joint Statement on Framework for Cooperation." (November 2013). www.iaea.org.

ICS Press. *Military Burden*. San Francisco: Institute for Contemporary Studies, 1990.

IMF. "World Economic Outlook Reports." http://www.imf.org/external/ns/cs.aspx?id=29.

Institute for Science and International Security (ISIS). "Iran's Nuclear Fuel Cycle." www.isisnucleariran.org.

International Institute for Strategic Studies. "Military Balance." *International Institute for Strategic Studies* 115, no. 12015.

Intriligator, Michael. "The Concept of a Peace Dividend." In *Economics of Peace and Security*, edited by James K. Galbraith, Jurgen Brauer, and Lucy Law Webster. Oxford: EOLSS Publications, 2009. http://www.eolss.net/sample-chapters/c13/E6-28A-02-04.pdf.

IP Commission, "The Theft of American Intellectual Property: Reassessments of the Challenge and United States Policy." *National Bureau of Asian Research* (February 2017). http://ipcommission.org/report/IP_Commission_Report_Update_2017.pdf.

Iwashita, Akihiro. "Bested by Russia: Abe's Failed Northern Territories Negotiations," *Wilson Center*, 2020. https://www.wilsoncenter.org/publication/

352 *Beleaguered Superpower: Biden's America Adrift*

kennan-cable-no-60-bested-russia-abes-failed-northern-territories-negotiations.

Izyumov, Alexei, Leonid Kosals, and Rosalina Ryvkina. "Defense Industrial Transformation in Russia: Evidence from a Longitudinal Survey." *Post-Communist Economies* 12, no. 2 (2001): 215–227.

Izyumov, Alexei, Leonid Kosals, and Rosalina Ryvkina, "Privatisation of the Russian Defense Industry: Ownership and Control Issues." *Post-Communist Economies* 12, no. 4 (2001): 485–496.

Jervis, Robert. "The Dustbin of History: Mutual Assured Destruction." *Foreign Policy* (November 2009). http://foreignpolicy.com/2009/11/09/the-dustbin-of-history-mutual-assured-destruction/.

Jones, Bruce. "Russia Pressures Ukraine with Naval Build-Up in Sea of Azov." *Jane's Defense Weekly* (June 2018). https://janes.ihs.com/Janes/Display/FG_952221-JDW.

Jones, Bruce, and Craig Caffrey. "Putin Signs New State Armaments Programme." *Jane's Defence Weekly* (February 2018). http://janes.ihs.com/Janes/Display/FG_749810-JDW.

Joravsky, David. *The Lysenko Affair*. Chicago: University of Chicago Press, 2010.

Kaempfer, William, and Anton Lowenberg. "The Theory of International Economic Sanctions: A Public Choice Approach." *American Economic Review* 78, no. 4 (December 1988): 786–793.

Kaempfer, William, Anton Lowenberg, and William Mertens. "International Economic Sanctions against a Dictator." *Economics and Politics* 16, no. 1 (March 2004): 29–51.

Kagan, Frederick. "The Future of the Iran Deal, Explained." *AEI* (October 2017). http://www.aei.org/publication/confusion-over-the-iran-deal/?mkt_tok= eyJpIjoiTVRNNU1tUTNNamxpTjJVNSIsInQiOiIxVm9QWTRZRDN QSXBaK2FhbGJ4cGpMTFZUaU0xbTdTMUt5cWtEUVdoZW9sWDh6a XdJaTVMMXBhZVwvTnJaVFZPWmJMZXd2eG1JXC9pQnpZSXBuakd pZ3lrb2IrSnZQN21aNHNMV1RxR2hTZEF2OFNDMjBzTkJ0UUV2O WtLZVZZEXC91MyJ9.

Kahneman, Daniel. "Maps of Bounded Rationality: Psychology for Behavioral Economics." *The American Economic Review* 93, no. 5 (2003): 1449–1475.

Kaine, Tim. "A New Truman Doctrine: Grand Strategy in a Hyperconnected World." *Foreign Affairs* 96, no. 4 (July–August 2017): 36–45.

Kantorovich, Leonid Vitaliyevich. *The Best Use of Economic Resources*. Cambridge: Harvard University Press, 1965.

Keating, Joshua. "Russia Resurgent." *Slate* (January 2017). http://www.slate.com/articles/news_and_politics/cover_story/2017/01/how_vladimir_putin_engineered_russia_s_return_to_global_power.html.

Kelton, Stephanie. *The Deficit Myth: Modern Monetary Theory and the Birth of the People's Economy*. New York: Public Affairs, 2020.

Bibliography 353

Kennan, George. "The Sources of Soviet Conduct." *Foreign Affairs* 25, no. 4 (July 1947): 566–582.

Khanin, Grigorii. "Ekonomicheskii Rost: Alternativnaia Otsenka." *Kommunist* 17 (1988): 83–90.

Khodzhaeva, Ekaterina, Irina Meyer (Olimpieva), Svetlana Barsukova, and Iskender Yasaveev. "Mobilizing Patriotism in Russia." *Center for Security Studies (CSS)* (2017).

Khrushchev, Nikita. "On Peaceful Coexistence." *Foreign Affairs* 38, no. 1 (October 1959): 1–18.

Kim, Jinwung. *A History of Korea: From "Land of the Morning Calm" to States in Conflict.* Bloomington: Indiana University Press, 2012.

Kim, Saeme. "Moon Jae-in Is Serious About Inter-Korean Cooperation: Moon is Intent on Pushing Ahead with North-South Cooperation, But He Needs to Remain Cognizant of the Risks." *The Diplomat* (January 2020). https://thediplomat.com/2020/01/moon-jae-in-is-serious-about-inter-korean-cooperation/.

Kipp, Jacob. "Putin's Ukrainian Gambit." *Conference on Challenges to the European Union, University of North Carolina, Chapel Hill* (September 2014).

Kissinger, Henry. *On China.* New York: Penguin, 2011.

Klinger, Bruce. "South Korea: Taking the Right Steps to Defense Reform" *Heritage Foundation* (October 2011). http://www.heritage.org/asia/report/south-korea-taking-the-right-steps-defense-reform.

Koestler, Arthur. *Darkness at Noon.* London: Macmillan, 1940.

Kogan, Eugene. "Russian Aerospace Forces and the Syria Campaign: An Assessment." *The European Geopolitical Forum* (May 2018).

Kogan, Eugene. "Russian Military Capabilities." *Georgian Foundation for Strategic and International Studies* (2016).

Kogan, Eugene. "Russian–Iranian Relations: A Mixed Bag." *European Security and Defense* (December 2017): 12–15.

Kovach, Matthew. "Twisting the Truth: Foundations of Wishful Thinking," *Theoretical Economics* 15 (2020): 989–1022.

Kramer, David. "Biden has a Clear-Eyed View of the Threat Posed by Russia — But a Lot of Bad Advice to Ignore." *Foreign Policy,* (November 2020). https://foreignpolicy.com/2020/11/13/biden-putin-russia/.

Kramer, Mark. "The Myth of a No — NATO — Enlargement Pledge to Russia." *The Washington Quarterly* 32, no. 2 (April 2009): 39–61.

Kramer, Mark. "Exclusive: Sanctions and Regime Survival." *Ponars Eurasia* (March 2015). http://www.ponarseurasia.org/article/sanctions-and-regime-survival.

Krasner, Stephen. "Sharing Sovereignty: New Institutions for Collapsed and Failing States." *International Security* 29, no. 2 (2004): 85–120.

354 *Beleaguered Superpower: Biden's America Adrift*

Krauthammer, Charles. "The Unipolar Moment." *Foreign Affairs* 70, no. 1 (1990/1991): 23–33.

Krauthammer, Charles. "The Unipolar Moment Revisited." *The National Interest* 70 (2002/2003): 5–17.

Krepinevich, Andrew. "CSBA: Why AirSea Battle? Center for Strategic and Budgetary Assessments (CSBA) — Scenarios." *CSBA* (2010). http://csbaonline.org/uploads/documents/2010.02.19-Why-AirSea-Battle.pdf.

Kristensen, Hans. "Non-Strategic Nuclear Weapons." *Federation of American Scientists* (May 2012). https://fas.org/_docs/Non_Strategic_Nuclear_Weapons.pdf.

Kristensen, Hans. "Russia Declared in Violation of INF Treaty: New Cruise Missile May Be Deploying." *Federation of American Scientists* (July 2014).

Kristensen, Hans, and Robert Norris. "Status of World Nuclear Forces." *Federation of Atomic Scientists*. https://fas.org/issues/nuclear-weapons/status-world-nuclear-forces/.

Kristensen, Hans, and Robert Norris. "North Korean Nuclear Capabilities, 2018." *Bulletin of Atomic Scientists* (January 2018). https://thebulletin.org/2018/january/north-korean-nuclear-capabilities-201811409.

Kristensen, Hans, and Robert S. Norris. "Russian Nuclear Forces, 2018." *Bulletin of the Atomic Scientists* 74, no. 3 (2018): 185–195.

Krugman, Paul. *The Return of Depression Economics and the Crisis of 2008.* New York: WW Norton Company, 2009.

Kuboniwa, Masaaki. "Weapons Growth." In *Putin's Russia: Economic, Political and Military Foundations*, edited by Steven Rosefielde. Singapore: World Scientific Publishers, 2020.

Kuhn, Ulrich. "With Zapad Over, Is It Time for Conventional Arms Control in Europe?" *Carnegie Endowment for Peace* (September 2017). http://carnegieendowment.org/2017/09/27/with-zapad-over-is-it-time-for-conventional-arms-control-in-europe-pub-73242?mkt_tok=eyJpIjoiTkRJeE1qTTN Oamt6TmpaayIsInQiOiI4V3ZMVFRTczdPWVUyNH pNSDBzbINBYWJnak5KTTF2SHZmZ2F6SnISVVwvS m9EVUlDZnY5cnZPN1dRWm83RGtMTDNkVkgrd1NpckJ2NWlx cll4T1JEd1gwY3ZGUk83Tm92em5ldWpkc0tVbCtkQjdBcTJiY2RsaU JaQkZSSGs0QkYifQ%3D%3D.

Kupiec, Paul H. "Democrats Lamenting Trump Policies Now See Dodd–Frank's Problems." *AEI* (December 2017). http://www.aei.org/publication/democrats-lamenting-trump-policies-now-see-dodd-franks-problems/?mkt_tok=eyJpIjo iWW1JNU1HTTVZelExTTJFMSIsInQiOiJZVURSVllMbWR1OXc0W WNObFBablF5YnE4UkdEN1ZjSjFqV29HN0tDZ0JNYmhQcnJiWkp cL1wvZDZOVjNxNTk0QmhlaHFSSUZJR3pFaUpmQUtxejVxOExoV 3JnajUrQVwvNEJEZmlnbnNPNDEwUGtGV3BaYUlGbmZLclwvZFF 1NHplZGYifQ%3D%3D.

Lachman, Desmond. "Congress' Deficit Hawks Seem to Have Gone Missing in Action." *AEI* (December 2017). http://www.aei.org/publication/congress-deficit-hawks-seem-to-have-gone-missing-in-action/?mkt_tok=eyJpIjoiTkR Ga01ETTVNR1ZpT0RrMSIsInQiOiJHYzBJR3VNd0U2MGdIYUVtVkc zZHNJUkFYMmk0aDZxY05YZE9xUmdyV2tnVWVNWTBuTXgzbH B4UTZGMUpneHNrd3NHXC9tS0dWU0VGNUw2bmthaGx3 3Y 095aU9xZDFyZXZVOGx1QmRvQVBPc3NPc2lqVDc3SHRcL3U2dH FjWVdNRWpqIn0%3D.
Lachman, Desmond. "Bubbles Pervade World Economy." *AEI* (January 2018). http://www.aei.org/publication/bubbles-pervade-world-economy/?mkt_tok=eyJpIjoiWkRnd01qQTVPVFF3TjJKbSIsInQiOi JWUE1YT1wvQ3lGOXZrQnZwQ0hKZnRvSkdaelNmRkNtdXU0SFJ4 aG1TcGpMTlE4R1pEMEw0RzRXeXpZaytyUEpFRU5kbGhDYm9WQV ZPcStMQ0FkQ2tTQjI3NUFiVVVc1ajFpUnpWVHdoeEdkWUMwVDNw ZTdjQ0xFMU5ieWdlaWFZTmcifQ%3D%3DIn.
Lachman, Desmond. "Golden Fleece Awards for the Worst Global Bonds." *AEI* (January 2018). http://www.aei.org/publication/golden-fleece-awards-for-the-worst-global-bonds/?mkt_tok=eyJpIjoiWlRFNE16RmlaV05qWlRGaSI sInQiOiJhQndNT2lnYkR3R040R1Rrbk8rTnFrZ3ZSQ2kyTlwvc2pkNUF jdDh6VkcwQ0JlcnpRdXJZVk5zelJzSFhpeTdPdGR4STV2XC9WWEN MVGFscFkzaHMrREhUdmpOQ3pHYnFMWktOZHMwZk04QzFYdlJmZ WRlUjJ0SXk4cCs0dmhMT0JqIn0%3D.
Langner, Ralph. "Defending Cyber Dominance." *Brookings* (March 2014). https://www.brookings.edu/on-the-record/defending-cyber-dominance/.
Lardy, Nicholas. "Issues in China's WTO Accession." *Brookings* (May 2001). https://www.brookings.edu/testimonies/issues-in-chinas-wto-accession/.
Lardy, Nicholas. "China: Forced Technology Transfer and Theft?" *PIIE* (April 2018). https://piie.com/blogs/china-economic-watch/china-forced-technology-transfer-and-theft.
Layne, Christopher. "The Unipolar Illusion Revisited: The Coming End of the United States Unipolar Moment." *International Security* 31 (2006): 7–41.
Leamer, Edward. *The Heckscher–Ohlin Model in Theory and Practice.* Princeton: Princeton University Press, 1995.
Lee, Chung Min. "The Case of Moon Jae-in." *ASAN Forum* (January 2020). http://www.theasanforum.org/the-case-of-moon-jae-in/.
Lee, Chung Min, and Kathryn Botto. "Korea Net Assessment: Politicized Security and Unchanging Strategic Realities." *Carnegie Endowment* (March 2020). https://carnegieendowment.org/2020/03/18/korea-net-assessment-2020-politicized-security-and-unchanging-strategic-realities-pub-81230?utm_source=carnegieemail&utm_medium=email& utm_campaign=announcement&mkt_tok=eyJpIjoiWTJZeFlqZz

356 *Beleaguered Superpower: Biden's America Adrift*

JaR1F5TURoaCIsInQiOiJmdkZHMTNQcmhnN3VibzVjVUNKeE5EcH
BXYTFVRWVRU1BQaFQ5OWYzR2ZwcjZvQkRkbnJyQTJLdVNocHE1
R3c4VmJVRWMwMUg3c01WNm1wam50VytKZFJMZmdaenRNSVdyaH
hTamRtMDJYWFFjVk1EMERBbjBqUDFiMm1Ga0JSYiJ9.

Lee, Kyung-hwa. "김정은 정권의 통일전략 (Kim Jong Un's Unification Strategy)." *Ministry of Unification* (2016): 4. Ministry of Unification (North Korea Information Portal). "화해협력정책 (Engagement Policy)."

Lektzian, David, and Mark Souva. "An Institutional Theory of Sanctions Onset and Success." *Journal of Conflict Resolution* 51, no. 6 (November 2007): 848–871.

Lemoine, Françoise, Grégoire Mayo, Sandra Poncet, and Deniz Ünal. "The Geographic Pattern of China's Growth and Convergence within Industry." *CEPII* (February 2014). http://www.cepii.fr/PDF_PUB/wp/2014/wp2014-04.pdf.

Lemon, Jason. "Trump's National Security Adviser, John Bolton, Says 'So-Called State of Palestine,' Uses Air Quotes." *Newsweek* (October 2018). https://www.newsweek.com/trump-national-security-advisor-john-bolton-says-so-called-state-palestine-1151344.

Lewis, Jeffrey. *Paper Tigers: China's Nuclear Posture.* London: Routledge, 2015.

Lider, Julian. "The Correlation of World Forces: the Soviet Concept." *Journal of Peace Research* 17, no. 2 (June 1980): 151–171. http://jpr.sagepub.com/content/17/2/151.abstract.

Lindsey, Brink, and Steven Teles. *The Captured Economy: How the Powerful Become Richer, Slow Down Growth, and Increase Inequality.* London: Oxford University Press, 2017.

Lippman, Walter. *The Good Society.* New York: Grosset & Dunlap, 1943.

Liu, Yiyi, and Steven Rosefielde, "Public Private Partnerships: Antidote for Secular Stagnation?" In *The Unwinding of the Globalist Dream: EU, Russia, China* edited by Steven Rosefielde, Masaaki Kuboniwa, Satoshi *Mizobata, and* Kumiko Haba. Singapore: World Scientific Publishers, 2017.

Lomborg, Bjorn. *False Alarm: How Climate Change Panic Costs Us Trillions, Hurts the Poor, and Fails to Fix the Planet.* New York: Basic Books, 2020.

Lowrey, Annie. "Millennials Are the New Lost Generation: They're Facing a Second Once-In-A-Lifetime Downturn at a Critical Moment." *Atlantic* (April 2020). https://www.theatlantic.com/ideas/archive/2020/04/millennials-are-new-lost-generation/609832/.

Lucas, Robert. "On the Mechanics of Economic Development." *Journal of Monetary Economics* 22 (January 1988): 3–42.

Lukyanov, Fyodor. "Gorbachev's Abandoned 'European Home'." *Russia in Global Affairs* (March 2010). http://eng.globalaffairs.ru/redcol/n_14661.

Bibliography 357

Lüthi, Lorenz. *The Sino-Soviet Split: Cold War in the Communist World.* Princeton: Princeton University Press, 2008.

Lynch, Allen. *The Soviet Study of International Relations.* Cambridge: Cambridge University Press, 1989.

Mackinnon, Amy, and Reid Standish. "Putin Fires His Puppet Master: Vladislav Surkov, Who Stage-Managed Russia's Involvement in Ukraine, is Replaced." *Foreign Policy* (February 2020). https://foreignpolicy.com/2020/02/21/putin-fires-vladislav-surkov-puppet-master-russia-ukraine-rebels/.

Maddison, Angus. "The World Economy: Historical Statistics." *OECD* (2003): 643.

Maddison, Angus. *Development Centre Studies: The World Economy: A Millennial Perspective.* Paris: OECD, 2001.

Mahadeva, Prem. "Maritime Insecurity in East Asia." *Center for Security Studies* (2013). http://www.css.ethz.ch/content/dam/ethz/special-interest/gess/cis/center-for-securities-studies/pdfs/Strategic-Trends-2013-EastAsia.pdf.

Majumdar, Dave. "The U.S. Navy's AEGIS Missile Defense vs. Russia's Supersonic Kh-31 Cruise Missile: Who Wins?" *The National Interest* (December 2016). http://nationalinterest.org/blog/the-buzz/the-us-navys-aegis-missile-defense-vs-russias-supersonic-kh-18662.

Maldonado, Monique M. "As North Korea Rattles Saber, The F-35 Jet Fighter Is Now Combat-Ready." *Homeland Security* (September 2017). http://inhome-landsecurity.com/f-35a-combat-north-korea/.

Mallaby, Sebastian. "The Reluctant Imperialist: Terrorism, Failed States, and the Case for American Empire." *Foreign Affairs* 81, no. 2 (March/April 2002).

Malmlöf, Tomas. "A Case Study of Russo-Ukrainian Defense Industrial Cooperation: Russian Dilemmas." *Journal of Slavic Military Studies* (2016): 1–22.

Marinov, Nikolay. "Do Economic Sanctions Destabilize Country Leaders?" *American Journal of Political Science* 49, No. 3 (July 2005): 564–576.

Markovits, Daniel. *The Meritocracy Trap: How America's Foundational Myth Feeds Inequality, Dismantles the Middle Class, and Devours the Elite.* New York: Penguin, 2019.

Marx, Karl, and Friedrich Engels. *Communist Manifesto.* London: 1848.

Maslow, Abraham. "A Theory of Human Motivation." *Psychological Review* 50, no. 4 (1943): 370–396.

Mathur, Aparna. "Monthly Jobs Report: Beyond the Headlines." *AEI* (December 2017). http://www.aei.org/multimedia/monthly-jobs-report-beyond-the-headlines/?mkt_tok=eyJpIjoiTm1ZMk1tTmlOREZrT1dNeiIsInQiOiIrajRB VzNWYm05cXc1a1wvcUgrd0dZRHJCVmp3Q2xSTTNaQmVlNk1qcX cyRHAxdHpVYmludit0cTlmWUJadEdieFhTNUxKeGRHcEpnR1RCZn

RPemlORHR2MVJcL2tYQXlxYXhSWDFnZDA2TURrRlkwTW4yNlpIR
WZFbWxwZTQzNHlpIn0%3D.

Mathur, Aparna. "Income Inequality Isn't as Bad as You May Think." *AEI* (January 2018). https://www.aei.org/publication/income-inequality-isnt-as-bad-as-you-may-think/?mkt_tok=eyJpIjoiTVRJeU56TmlORFl5 T0RsayIsInQiOiI4TkNuUlFsb3R4VFBsamVFUkV4N3IyQVhUVU9EQ 05SM1NjZFY0UUV0ZVlhTk9kejFENTlaK1dFWEI4YnJjZFQrUFVLSX dyWk1GckdRTEtFV25UXC9vcDA2bGJPNWVNa2FyZW5TdDRWV240 ZzVqR3dzaGZcL05Ib0paRkJKTHJEK0gxIn0%3D.

McAuley, James. "After Trump Says U.S. Will Withdraw from Iran Deal, Allies Say They'll Try to Save It." *Washington Post* (May 2018). https://www.washingtonpost.com/world/backers-of-iran-nuclear-deal-wage-last-ditch-blitz-seeking-to-sway-trump/2018/05/08/9b15e3f0-523e-11e8-a6d4-ca1 d035642ce_story.html?noredirect=on&utm_term=.0118ed4c7a01.

McDermott, Roger. "Russia's Electronic Warfare Capabilities to 2025: Challenging NATO in the Electromagnetic Spectrum." *International Centre for Defense and Security* (September 2017). https://www.icds.ee/publications/article/russias-electronic-warfare-capabilities-to-2025-challenging-nato-in-the-electromagnetic-spectrum/.

McInnis, J. Matthew. "Understanding Tehran's Defense Acquisition and Research and Development Decision-Making." *AEI* (April 2017). https://www.aei.org/wp-content/uploads/2017/04/Building-the-Iranian-Military.pdf.

McNamara, Robert, and Brian VanDeMark. *In Retrospect: The Tragedy and Lessons of Vietnam.* New York: Times Books, 1995.

Meade, James. *The Controlled Economy: Principles of Political Economy Volume III.* Albany: State University of New York Press, 1972.

Meade, James. *Wage-Fixing.* London: Unwin Hyman, 1982.

Metz, Steven, and James Kievit. "Strategy and the Revolution in Military Affairs: From Theory to Policy." *US Army War College* (June 1995).

Mills, Quinn. *Not Like Our Parents: How the Baby Boom Generation Is Changing America.* New York: William Morrow, 1980.

Mizobata, Satoshi. "State-Led Innovation and Uneven Adaptation in Russia." In *Putin's Russia: Economic, Political and Military Foundations,* edited by Steven Rosefielde. Singapore: World Scientific Publishers, 2020.

Mizokami, Kyle. "Russia Has a Super Torpedo That Kills Submarines at 200 Miles Per Hour (And America Can't Match It)." *The National Interest* (January 2017). http://nationalinterest.org/blog/the-buzz/russia-has-super-torpedo-kills-submarines-200-miles-per-hour-18917.

Monaghan, Andrew. "The Vertikal: Power and Authority in Russia." *International Affairs* 88, no. 1 (January 2012): 1–16. https://doi.org/10.1111/j.1468-2346.2012.01053.

Bibliography 359

Movchan, Andrew. "Sanctions and Retaliation: Where Russia–U.S. Relations are Headed." *Carnegie Moscow Center* (April 2018). https://carnegie.ru/commentary/76120?mkt_tok=eyJpIjoiWmpVM09HWXpNelJtTldNNSIsInQiOiJhd2VzaCs2N2NIZHlEa2p6T0wwbWJoOUhkVndRXC9IU29Sam5pYjNFWm8xNTFwXC9uMmZKcVpNMlhDZDRtRWVoT0RxTXo1b09VUlJLQnAzQ2FlS1BDaUVtYW0tbnRDWERbZGRIeCJ9. dnE5dmRcL3FYbkNYQ3NOQis2VWNZaEZiRGFldDRIeCJ9.
Myers, B. R. *The Cleanest Race*. Brooklyn: Melville House, 2010.
Myers, B. R. *North Korea's Juche Myth*. Sthele Publishers, 2015.
National Bureau of Asian Research. "IP Commission Report, The Theft of American Intellectual Property: Reassessments of the Challenge and United States Policy, Update." (February 2017). http://ipcommission.org/report/IP_Commission_Report_Update_2017.pdf.
National Intelligence Council. "Global Trends: Paradoxes of Progress." January 2017. www.dni.gov/nic/globaltrends.
Nelson, Rebecca M. "U.S. Sanctions and Russia's Economy." *Congressional Research Service* (February 2017).
Newsweek, "A Grand Bargain: Aid for Arms Control." *Newsweek* (September 1991). https://www.newsweek.com/grand-bargain-aid-arms-control-203408.
Nelson, Rebecca M. "Proposals to Impose Sanctions on Russian Sovereign Debt." *Congressional Research Service (CRS)* (August 2018). https://fas.org/sgp/crs/row/IN10946.pdf.
Nordhaus, William. "Projections and Uncertainties about Climate Change in an Era of Minimal Climate Policies." *American Economic Journal: Economic Policy* 10, no. 3 (2018): 333–360.
Norris, Guy. "Classified Report on Hypersonics Says U.S. Lacking Urgency." *Aviation Week and Space Technology* (February 2017).
Norris, Guy. "China Takes Wraps Off National Hypersonic Plan." *Aviation Week and Space Technology* (April 2017).
Norris, Guy. "U.S. Air Force Plans Road Map to Operational Hypersonics." *Aviation Week and Space Technology* (July 2017).
Novshek, William, and Hugo Sonnenschein. "General Equilibrium with Free Entry: A Synthetic Approach to the Theory of Perfect Competition." *Journal of Economic Literature* 25, no. 3 (September 1987): 1281–306.
Nozick, Robert. *Anarchy, State, and Utopia*. Oxford: Blackwell Publishers, 1993.
NRDC. "From Mutual Assured Destruction to Mutual Assured Stability Exploring a New Comprehensive Framework for U.S. and Russian Nuclear Arms Reductions." (March 2013). https://www.nrdc.org/sites/default/files/NRDC-ISKRAN-Nuclear-Security-Report-March2013.pdf.
NTI. "Iran's Nuclear Timeline." (June 2020). https://www.nti.org/learn/countries/iran/nuclear/.

360 *Beleaguered Superpower: Biden's America Adrift*

Nye Jr., Joseph. *Bound to Lead: The Changing Nature of American Power*. New York: Basic Books, 1990.

Nye, Joseph. "A Time for Positive-Sum Power." *Wilson Quarterly* (November 2018).

O'Hanlon, Michael. "America Is Not in a Zero-Sum Contest with Iran." *Mosaic* (September 2017). https://mosaicmagazine.com/essay/2017/09/what-america-should-do-next-in-the-middle-east/.

OECD. "OECD Interim Economic Assessment, Coronavirus: The World Economy at Risk.*" OECD Library*, no. 2 (March 2020). https://www.oecd-ilibrary.org/economics/oecd-economic-outlook/volume-2019/issue-2_7969896b-en.

Office of the Historian. "Kennan and Containment, 1947." https://history.state.gov/milestones/1945-1952/kennan.

Office of the Secretary of Defense. "Annual Report to Congress: Military and Security Developments Involving the People's Republic of China 2016." (April 2016).

Office of the Secretary of Defense. "Military and Security Developments Involving the Democratic People's Republic of Korea 2015." *A Report to Congress Pursuant to the National Defense Authorization Act for Fiscal Year 2012* (January 2016).

Office of the Secretary of Defense. "Annual Report to Congress: Military and Security Developments Involving the People's Republic of China 2020."

Office of the Secretary of Defense. "Annual Report to Congress: Military and Security Developments Involving the People's Republic of China 2019." (May 2019). https://fas.org/man/eprint/dod-china-2019.pdf.

Office of the Secretary of Defense. "Annual Report to Congress: Military and Security Developments Involving the People's Republic of China 2020." (August 2020). https://media.defense.gov/2020/Sep/01/2002488689/-1/-1/1/2020-DOD-CHINA-MILITARY-POWER-REPORT-FINAL.PDF.

Office of the United States Trade Representative. "Section 301 Report into China's Acts, Policies, and Practices Related to Technology Transfer, Intellectual Property, and Innovation." https://ustr.gov/about-us/policy-offices/press-office/press-releases/2018/march/section-301-report-chinas-acts.

Ogarkov, N. V. *Vsegda v golovnosti k zashchite Otechestva*. Moskva, 1982.

Ogarkov, N. V. *Istoriya Uchit vditel'nosti*. Moskva, 1985.

Orwell, George. *Nineteen Eighty-Four*. London: Harcourt, 1949.

Owen, Robert. *A New View of Society: Or, Essays on the Formation of Human Character, and the Application of the Principle to Practice*. London, 1813.

Oxenstierna, Susanna. "Russian Defense Spending and the Economic Decline." *Journal of Eurasian Studies* No. 1 (2016): 60–70.

Bibliography 361

Oxenstierna, Susanne. "The Western Sanctions against Russia. How Do They Work?" In *Putin's Russia: Economic, Political and Military Foundations*, edited by Steven Rosefielde. Singapore: World Scientific Publishers, 2020.

Oxenstierna, Susanne, and Per Olsson. "The Economic Sanctions against Russia: Impact and Prospects of success." *FOI* (September 2015).

Paine, Thomas. *Rights of Man, Common Sense, and Other Political Writings*. London: Oxford University Press, 1995 [1791].

Paul, T. V. "ASEAN and Soft Balancing: South China Sea as Zone of Peace?" *RSIS* (May 2018).

Perrigo, Billy. "'Already Dead to Us': Why the Trump Administration Has a Problem with the International Criminal Court." *Time* (September 2018). http://time.com/5393624/john-bolton-international-criminal-court/.

Persson, Gudrun. "On War and Peace: Russian Security Policy and Military-Strategic Thinking." In *Putin's Russia: Economic, Political and Military Foundations*, edited by Steven Rosefielde. Singapore: World Scientific Publishers, 2020.

Perry, William. "North Korea Called Me a 'War Maniac.' I Ignored Them, and Trump Should Too: Smart Diplomacy Backed by the Threat of Force, Not Twitter Bluster, Is the Way to Deal with Kim Jong-un." *Politico Magazine* (October 2017). http://www.politico.com/magazine/story/2017/10/03/north-korea-war-maniac-donald-trump-215672?mkt_tok=eyJpIj oiWVRjd09EbGlNVGc1TWpOaCIsInQiOiJ1MllqTmdKMG1vNUx0 VERFR216ZXJpWjkzRDBjSk1XS1NtR1R2RG1rTE1rRWxuekdOeC tYaTBIUmJWdFwvR2c4ZzNHQkI0ZHFCTUpPZnFYYQm9jUlorWnR6 K3Z6c3lyYlwvQnBZRUlPbmtJckQrQXdzczAyT0VnYYU1wTUtuOENDW nV6In0%3D/.

Persio, Sofia Lotto. "Did the U.S. Really Pay North Korea 'Extortion Money' for 25 Years? Fact-Checking Trump's Tweet." *Newsweek* (August 2017). http://www.newsweek.com/did-us-really-pay-north-korea-extortion-money-25-years-fact-checking-trumps-657177.

Persio, Sophia Lotto. "North Korea and the U.S. Are on 'Brink of Large-Scale Conflict,' Putin Warns." *Newsweek* (September 1, 2017). http://www.newsweek.com/north-korea-and-us-are-brink-large-scale-conflict-putin-warns-658580.

Persio, Sofia Lotto. "South Korea 'Blackout Bombs' Can Take Down Pyongyang Without Firing a Shot." *Newsweek* (October 9, 2017). http://www.newsweek.com/south-korea-builds-blackout-bombs-take-down-pyongyang-without-firing-shot-680465.

Pethokoukis, James. "Maybe Wealth Inequality Isn't as Dramatic as We Think." *AEI* (April 2020). https://www.aei.org/economics/maybe-wealth-inequality-isnt-as-dramatic-as-we-think/.

362 *Beleaguered Superpower: Biden's America Adrift*

Pethokoukis, James. "The Slump That Never Ends: Does the US Face 'Secular Stagnation'?" *AEI* (November 2013).

Pethokoukis, James. "Americans Might Really Like the Trump Tax Cuts. What Will Democrats Do Then?" *AEI* (December 20, 2017). http://www.aei.org/ publication/americans-might-really-like-the-trump-tax-cuts-what-will-democrats-do-then/.

Pethokoukis, James. "December Jobs Report: Maybe America's 'Great Stagnation' Isn't So Bad." *AEI* (January 5, 2018). http://www.aei.org/publication/december-jobs-report-maybe-americas-great-stagnation-isnt-so-bad/?mkt_tok=eyJpIjoiTUdaak9HUTJNVFE0TURKaCIsInQiOiJYZWRMMkp0T3lLa0U1QVByT2RoeVlBMkJWSzRhcm9PdCtLeG5lXC9ha25rNUthQmMZbVkzU1p0QVwvSUJZSDdNK3RGSVRkRkw5U3JOb1VtbFN3Z0hSQkNiZ3pJdm91QzZNoejFDOU01NGFZMTI5UXYzSnlsbmYwdnVxd2wxalRJUjdGIn0%3D.

Petro, Nicholas. "The Russian Orthodox Church." In *Routledge Handbook of Russian Foreign Policy*, edited by Andrei P. Tsygankov, 217–232. London: Routledge, 2018.

Piattoni, Simona. "Institutional Innovations and EU Legitimacy after the Crisis." In *Crises in Europe in the Transatlantic Context: Economic and Political Appraisals*, edited by Bruno Dallago and John McGowan, 119–136. London: Routledge, 2016.

Pifer, Steve, and Oliver Meier. "Are We Nearing the End of the INF Treaty?" *Arms Control Today* 48 (January/February 2018). https://www.armscontrol.org/act/2018-01/features/we-nearing-end-inf-treaty.

Pifer, Steven. "A Realist's Rationale for a World without Nuclear Weapons." *Brookings* (2016). https://www.brookings.edu/wp-content/uploads/2016/06/A-Realists-Rationale-for-a-World-without-Nuclear-Weapons.pdf.

Piketty, Thomas. *Capital in the 21st Century*. New York: Belknap, 2015.

Piketty, Thomas. *Chronicles: On Our Troubled Times*. New York: Viking Press, 2016.

Piketty, Thomas. *Why Save the Bankers? And Other Essays on Our Economic and Political Crisis*. New York: Houghton Mifflin Harcourt, 2016.

Piketty, Thomas. *Top Incomes in France in the Twentieth Century: Inequality and Redistribution, 1901–1998*. Cambridge: Harvard University Press, 2018.

Piketty, Thomas, and Emmanuel Saez. "Inequality in the Long Run." *Science* 344, no. 6186 (May 2014): 838–843.

Piketty, Thomas, Li Yang, and Gabriel Zucman. "Capital Accumulation, Private Property and Rising Inequality in China, 1978–2015." *IZA Institute of Labor Economics* (April 2017). http://d.repec.org/n?u=RePEc:nbr:nberwo:23368&r=tra.

Piper, Watty. *The Little Engine That Could*. New York: Grosset & Dunlap, 2001.

Bibliography 363

Pollack, Kenneth. "Iraq: Finding Calm After the Storm." *AEI* (September 2017). http://www.aei.org/publication/iraq-finding-calm-after-the-storm/? mkt_tok=eyJpIjoiTlRjeFpqUm1PRGc0TVRKayIsInQiOiI5STFZZ2 ZFdXhJT1diZUh4amU5YzV2VVYzUWh5Y3EzQXVsRkZnRWhDSHph QUJ0ZVg2MWxCWUZVcnBkekc0TERDWEtkQ3JVaEp0MmFUc0pFbk pxWEVzTUVrM0NMWHV0OHhObG1haXc4eTFia0xjWHB6UUwxNHEr c1lrVHUwOHRcL1YifQ%3D%3D.
Ponnuru, Ramesh. "Trump's Strong Start on Policy." *National Review*, December 26, 2017, http://www.nationalreview.com/article/454927/donald-trump-strong-first-year-report-card.
Popper, Karl. *The Open Society and Its Enemies*. Princeton: Princeton University Press, 1966.
Popper, Karl. *The Poverty of Historicism*. London: Routledge, 1957.
Pradt, Tilman. *China's New Foreign Policy: Military Modernisation, Multilateralism and the "China Threat."* London: Palgrave Macmillan, 2016.
Pravo. "Poslanie (2014) Poslanie Prezidenta RF ot 04.12.2014 (O polozhenii v strane i osnovnykh napravleniyakh vnutrennei i vneshnei politi gosudarstva)." (April 2014). http://kremlin.ru/acts/bank/39443.
Pregelj, Vladimir N. "The Jackson-Vanik Amendment: A Survey." *CRS Report for Congress*. (August 2005). https://fas.org/sgp/crs/row/98-545.pdf.
Psaki, Jen. "United States Expands Export Restrictions on Russia." *US State Department* (April 2014). www.state.gov/r/pa/prs/ps/2014/04/225241.htm.
Quester, George H. *Deterrence Before Hiroshima: The Airpower Background of Modern Strategy*. New York: John Wiley & Sons, 1966.
Rand. "The US-China Military Scorecard: Forces, Geography and the Evolving Balance of Military Power." (2015). http://www.rand.org/content/dam/rand/pubs/research_reports/RR300/RR392/RAND_RR392.pdf.
Rand, "An Interactive Look at the U.S.–China Military Scorecard." (2017). https://www.rand.org/paf/projects/us-china-scorecard.html.
RAND. "Overextending and Unbalancing Russia." RAND (May 2019). https://www.rand.org/pubs/research_briefs/RB10014.html.
Ratnam, Gopal. "White House Unveils Call for 'Strategic Patience'." *Foreign Policy* (February 2015).
Rawls, John. *A Theory of Justice*. Cambridge: Belknap Press, 1971.
Reddaway, Peter. *Russia's Domestic Security Wars: Putin's Use of Divide and Rule against His Hardline Allies*. Cham: Palgrave Macmillan, 2018.
Redlawsk, David, Andrew Civenttini, and Karen Emmerson. "The Affective Tipping Point: Do Motivated Reasoners Ever 'Get It'." *Political Psychology* 31, 4 (2010): 563–593.
Reichlin, Lucrezia. "Avoiding the Japanification of Europe." *Project Syndicate* (August 2020), https://www.project-syndicate.org/commentary/eu-fiscal-monetary-coordination-institutional-reform-by-lucrezia-reichlin-2020-08.

364 *Beleaguered Superpower: Biden's America Adrift*

Reinhart, Carmen. "Recovery is Not Resolution." *Project Syndicate* (August 2017). https://www.project-syndicate.org/commentary/advanced-economy-recovery-vulnerable-by-carmen-reinhart-2017-08?utm_source=Economics%20readers%20from%20Mather&utm_campaign=ba317fda52-lehman_10_year_anniversary_mailing&utm_medium=email&utm_term=0_991b581537-ba317fda52-106454839&barrier=accesspaylog.

Reinhart, Carmen, and Vincent R. Reinhart. "The Crisis Next Time: What We Should Have Learned from 2008." *AEI* (September 2018). http://www.aei.org/publication/the-crisis-next-time/?mkt_tok=eyJpIjoiWlRkbFltSXpOR014T0RCailsInQiOiJjN1wvTndzUWVEZE5scGNNUU5wc1lqSnpTT0VLSndvTlVtZUhVVmxXSndRUmZKcmFLOWlndVI0ZElPRlwveWlHdlVLUm9UaGFPZm5hQzVUUWDR5SXlEYUUrY2lvTVhSUzJcL3k3ajB3MdWRvU2trOFdObHFGeXRIT1lPWkUxYk9UQUc4diJ9.

Remnick, David. "The Historical Truth-Telling of Arseny Roginsky." *New Yorker* (December 2017). https://www.newyorker.com/news/postscript/the-historical-truth-telling-of-arseny-roginsky.

Renz, Bettina. "Russian Military Capabilities after 20 Years of Reform." *Survival* 56, no. 3 (June–July 2014): 61–84.

Rhodes, Benjamin. *The World as It Is: A Memoir of the Obama White House*. New York: Random House, 2018.

Rhodes, Richard. *The Making of the Atomic Bomb*, New York: Simon and Schuster, 1987.

Rice, Condoleezza. *Democracy: Stories from the Long Road to Freedom*. New York: Hachette Book Group, 2017.

Ricks, Thomas. "Hybrid War's Sword Arm: The Russians have Found Good Tactical Innovations." *Foreign Policy* (June 2017). http://foreignpolicy.com/2017/06/14/hybrid-wars-sword-arm-the-russians-have-found-good-tactical-innovations/.

Ritter, Scott. "The U.S.–Russia Nuclear Arms Race is Over, and Russia has Won." *Newsweek* (April 2017). http://www.newsweek.com/us-russia-nuclear-arms-race-over-and-russia-has-won-581704.

Rodrik, Dani. "In Defense of Economic Populism." *Project Syndicate* (January 2018). https://www.project-syndicate.org/commentary/defense-of-economic-populism-by-dani-rodrik-2018-01?utm_source=Project+Syndicate+News letter&utm_campaign=bf05d082c0-sunday_newsletter_14_1_2018&utm_medium=email&utm_term=0_73bad5b7d8-bf05d082c0-93559677.

Rogovoy, Aleksandr V., and Keir Giles. *A Russian View of Land Power*. Cambridge: Conflict Studies Research Center, December 2014.

Rolland, Nadège. "China's National Power: A Colossus with Iron or Clay Feet?" In *Strategic Asia 2015–16: Foundations of National Power in the*

Asia-Pacific, edited by Ashley J. Tellis, Alison Szalwinski, and Michael Wills. http://nbr.org/publications/element.aspx?id=836.

Rolland, Nadège, ed. *An Emerging China-centric Order: China's Vision for a New World Order in Practice.* The National Bureau of Asian Research (August 2020). https://www.nbr.org/publication/an-emerging-china-centric-order-chinas-vision-for-a-new-world-order-in-practice/.

Romer, Paul M. "Endogenous Technological Change." *Journal of Political Economy* 98 (October 1990): S71–S102.

Rosefielde, Steven. "Operational Economic Theory in the Excluded Middle between Positivism and Rationalism." *Atlantic Economic Journal* 4, no. 2 (May 1976): 1–8.

Rosefielde, Steven. "International Trade Theory and Practice under Socialism." *Journal of Comparative Economics* 1, no. 1 (March 1977): 99–104.

Rosefielde, Steven. "Post Positivist Scientific Method and the Appraisal of Nonmarket Economic Behavior." *Quarterly Journal of Ideology* 3, no. 1 (Spring 1980): 23–33.

Rosefielde, Steven. "A Comment on David Howard's Estimate of Hidden Inflation in the Soviet Retail Sales Sector." *Soviet Studies* 32, no. 3 (July 1980): 423–427.

Rosefielde, Steven. *False Science: Underestimating the Soviet Arms Buildup.* Rutgers: Transaction Press, 1987.

Rosefielde, Steven. "The Soviet Economy in Crisis: Birman's Cumulative Disequilibrium Hypothesis." *Soviet Studies* 40, no. 2 (April 1988): 222–244.

Rosefielde, Steven. "The Illusion of Material Progress: The Analytics of Soviet Economic Growth Revisited." *Soviet Studies* 43, no. 4 (1991): 597–611.

Rosefielde, Steven. "The Grand Bargain: Underwriting Catastroika." *Global Affairs* (Winter 1992): 15–35.

Rosefielde, Steven. "What is Wrong with Plans to Aid the CIS." *Orbis* 37, no. 3 (Summer 1993): 353–363.

Rosefielde, Steven. "Premature Deaths: Russia's Radical Economic Transition in Soviet Perspective." *Europe-Asia Studies* 53, no. 8 (2001): 1159–1176.

Rosefielde, Steven. "The Riddle of Postwar Russian Economic Growth: Statistics Lied and Were Misconstrued." *Europe-Asia Studies* 55, no. 3 (2003): 469–481.

Rosefielde Steven. "An Abnormal Country." *The European Journal of Comparative Economics* 2, no. 1 (2005): 3–16.

Rosefielde, Steven. *Russia in the 21st Century: The Prodigal Superpower.* Cambridge: Cambridge University Press, 2005.

Rosefielde, Steven. "Tea Leaves and Productivity: Bergsonian Norms for Gauging the Soviet Future." *Comparative Economic Studies* 47, no. 2 (June 2005): 259–273.

Rosefielde, Steven. "The Illusion of Westernization in Russia and China." *Comparative Economic Studies* 49 (2007): 495–513.

Rosefielde, Steven. *Russian Economy from Lenin to Putin*. New York: Wiley, 2007.

Rosefielde, Steven. "Russia's Aborted Transition: 7000 Days and Counting." *Institutional'naya ekonomika razvitie* (2010).

Rosefielde, Steven. "China's Perplexing Foreign Trade Policy: Causes, Consequences and a Tit for Tat Solution." *American Foreign Policy Interests* 33, no. 1 (January–February 2011): 10–16.

Rosefielde, Steven. "Communist Asia." In *The Economics and Political Economy of Transition: Handbook*, edited by Paul Hare and Gerard Turley, 445–455. London: Routledge, 2012.

Rosefielde, Steven. "Export-led Development and Dollar Reserve Hoarding." In *Two Asias: The Emerging Postcrisis Divide*, edited by Steven Rosefielde, Masaaki Kuboniwa, and Satoshi Mizobata, 251–266. Singapore: World Scientific Publishers, 2012.

Rosefielde, Steven. "The Impossibility of Russian Economic Reform: Waiting for Godot." *US Army War College, Carlisle Barracks* (2012).

Rosefielde, Steven. "Postcrisis Russia: Counting on Miracles in Uncertain Times." In *Russian Defense Prospects*, edited by Carolina Vendil Pallin and Bertil Nygren, 134–150. New York: Routledge, 2012.

Rosefielde, Steven. *Asian Economic Systems*. Singapore: World Scientific Publishers, 2013.

Rosefielde, Steven. "Russian Military, Political and Economic Reform: Can the Kremlin Placate Washington?" *U.S. Army War College, Carlisle Barracks* (May 2014).

Rosefielde, Steven. *China's Market Communism: Challenges, Dilemma's Solutions*. London: Routledge, 2017.

Rosefielde, Steven. *The Kremlin Strikes Back: Russia and the West after Crimea's Annexation*. Cambridge: Cambridge University Press, 2017.

Rosefielde, Steven. "Rising Red Star." In *The Unwinding of the Globalist Dream: EU, Russia, China*, edited by Steven Rosefielde, Masaaki Kuboniwa, Kumiko Haba, and Satoshi Mizobata, 237–244. Singapore: World Scientific Publishers, 2017.

Rosefielde, Steven. "Salvaging the European Union: The Inclusive Multi-Track Supranational Option." *Holistica — Journal of Business and Public Administration* 8, no. 1 (2017): 7–18.

Rosefielde, Steven. *Trump's Populist America*. Singapore: World Scientific Publishers, 2017.

Rosefielde, Steven. "EU Reform: Two Speed or Inclusive Multi-Track?" *Contemporary Economics* (2018).

Bibliography 367

Rosefielde, Steven. "Putin's Muscovite Economy." In *Putin's Russia: Economic, Political and Military Foundations*, edited by Steven Rosefielde. Singapore: World Scientific Publishers, 2020.

Rosefielde, Steven, ed. *Putin's Russia: Economic, Political and Military Foundations*. Singapore: World Scientific Publishers, 2020.

Rosefielde, Steven. "Russian Military Industry." In *Putin's Russia: Economic, Political and Military Foundations*, edited by Steven Rosefielde. Singapore: World Scientific Publishers, 2020.

Rosefielde, Steven. "New Millennial Economic Systems: Paradox of Power and Reason." *Foresight and STI Governance. Journal of the National Research University of Higher School of Economics, Moscow*, forthcoming, 2021.

Rosefielde, Steven. "Stakeholder Capitalism: Progressive Dream or Nightmare?" Holistica — Journal of Business and Public Administration, forthcoming 2021.

Rosefielde, Steven, and Bruno Dallago. *Transformation and Crisis in Central and Eastern Europe: Challenges and Prospects*. London: Routledge, 2016.

Rosefielde, Steven, and Bruno Dallago. "The Strange Fate of Brexit and Grexit and the Eurozone Integration and Disintegration." *Contemporary Economics* (2018).

Rosefielde, Steven, and Bruno Dallago. "New Principles for a Better EU." In *100 Year of World Wars and Postwar Regional Collaboration and Governance in the EU and Asia*, edited by Kumiko Haba and Satoshi Mizobata. Berlin: Springer, 2020.

Rosefielde, Steven, and Bruno Dallago. "New Principles for a Better EU." In *100 Year of World Wars and Postwar Regional Collaboration and Governance in the EU and Asia*, edited by Kumiko Haba and Satoshi Mizobata. Berlin: Springer, 2020.

Rosefielde, Steven, and Bruno Dallago. *Post Brexit European Integration*. Berlin: Springer, 2020.

Rosefielde, Steven, and Stefan Hedlund, *Russia Since 1980: Wrestling with Westernization*. New York: Cambridge University Press, 2009.

Rosefielde, Steven, Masaaki Kuboniwa, Kumiko Haba, and Satoshi Mizobata, eds. *The Unwinding of the Globalist Dream: EU, Russia, China*. Singapore: World Scientific Publishers, 2017.

Rosefielde, Steven, and Jonathan Leightner. *China's Market Communism: Challenges, Dilemmas, Solutions*. London: Routledge, 2017.

Rosefielde, Steven, and Yiyi Liu. "Sovereign Debt Crises: Solidarity and Power." *The Journal of Comparative Economic Studies* 12 (2017): 101–112.

Rosefielde, Steven, and Quinn Mills. *Democracy and its Elected Enemies: American Political Capture and Economic Decline*. New York: Cambridge University Press, 2013.

368 *Beleaguered Superpower: Biden's America Adrift*

Rosefielde, Steven, and Quinn Mills. *Global Economic Turmoil and the Public Good*. Singapore: World Scientific Publishers, 2015.

Rosefielde, Steven, and Quinn Mills. *The Trump Phenomenon*. Singapore: World Scientific Publisher, 2017.

Rosefielde, Steven, and Quinn Mills. *Populists and Progressives*. Singapore: World Scientific Publishers, 2020.

Rosefielde, Steven and Ralph W. Pfouts. *Inclusive Economic Theory*. Singapore: World Scientific Publishers, 2014.

Rosenblum, Morris Victor. *Peace Through Strength: Bernard Baruch and a Blueprint for Security.* New York: Farrar, Straus and Young, 1952.

Roubini, Nouriel, and Brunello Rosa, "The Makings of a 2020 Recession and Financial Crisis." *Project Syndicate* (September 2018). https://www.project-syndicate.org/commentary/financial-crisis-in-2020-worse-than-2008-by-nouriel-roubini-and-brunello-rosa-2018-09?utm_source=Project+Syndicate+Newsletter&utm_campaign=cb8165502d-sunday_newsletter_16_9_2018&utm_medium=email&utm_term=0_73bad5b7d8-cb8165502d-93559677.

Rouvroy, Claude Henri de. the Comte de Saint-Simon. *On the Reorganization of European Industry*. 1814.

Rowen, Henry, and Charles Wolf Jr. *The Impoverished Superpower: Perestroika and the Soviet Military Burden*. San Francisco: Institute for Contemporary Studies (ICS Press), 1990.

Rubin, Michael. "The Real Scandal of the Declassified Osama Bin Laden Trove Implicates Obama and the CIA." *AEI* (November 2017). http://www.aei.org/publication/the-real-scandal-of-the-declassified-osama-bin-laden-trove-implicates-obama-and-the-cia/?mkt_tok=eyJpIjoiTkRCa1pHTXhOamt5TWpoayIsInQiOiIyM3NkV3JEUFMwa3Z1M3JqY0dTbGtKTzBTNlJyMVRZczVKUTM2Y1VQY2twSHhEU1hIOVRVSEYzZTV0QkFNVWJ2b0VuQlcrYTZRdGxDVXc0MG82dlNhTDdpdk54R2FCWVFwQ3hseEN6ZXgyb01hYXd2WlczXC9cL0d3MXJKdVZ6QjZoIn0%3D.

Rubin, Michael. "The Iran Nuclear Deal Weakness That Even Republicans Ignore." *AEI* (November 2017). http://www.aei.org/publication/the-iran-nuclear-deal-weakness-that-even-republicans-ignore/?mkt_tok=eyJpIjoiWTJJM05HSTFOamc1WmpKaiIsInQiOiJyRGF2SGRLNEZuZlo0RXpzemZyNWx0dE9lekZcL1RMclJVVEdwcFJSQzgxcFIwT2E5RWlnZ2hTNGd2V0NldFwvcHVYQ05ZmVlVDVVWFM3ZlFnMEsxaUdjYUNwc3crT09FWCtJWnpBMnBBPZGZ1NmljYm1KbjVXTHBCWE1zRzVzRjVBIn0%3D.

Rubin, Michael. "6 Things You Need to Know About the Iran Protests." *AEI* (January 2018). http://www.aei.org/publication/968232/?mkt_tok=eyJpIjoiTVRSbE56RXhOOak0xTXpreiIsInQiOiJMaEdWZHBkRFIxbUNiSkc2QktOSm93OUFKd1MzN09ydk9hM0sxY2c0cXIrQWVsTWF1Qm

Voc1V0U0xWTklCZlwvSCsrSjBWTVdrNmpcLzZGQlAwMGp3VDd3b
zl0Q2dcL01uTGRyOXRuVE5TUFZcLzVFdzhJak0zRVJtWmdFaXRJTktn
b3YifQ%3D%3D.

Rubin, Michael. "How Did the US Get It So Wrong on Iran's Nuclear Program?" *AEI* (May 2018). http://www.aei.org/publication/how-did-the-us-get-it-so-wrong-on-irans-nuclear-program/?mkt_tok=eyJpIjoiTVdFNFkySXdNemRq WWpnMyIsInQiOiJVY1lBSDFWVEZEVWIwamh1ekFzTWpoSSsxalN sZWc3eHlid1grYVR2VVltaDFaTnA0MENrTzZpUWxyT2FHUXI0bG w1a2k4eXlRMmJPNnFmV01HbFZRZVFWOFNJWncyVVRPY2dPWn RBV3V5UzBhY0ZCU0pSN05vclp0TFdHRDNhKyJ9.

Rubin, Michael. "Statement before the Committee on Oversight and Government Reform, Subcommittee on Nation Security On 'Protecting America from a Bad Deal: Ending U.S. Participation in the Nuclear Agreement with Iran', Putting American Security First in the Post-JCPOA Order." *AEI* (June 2018). http://www.aei.org/wp-content/uploads/2018/06/2018-06-Rubin-Testimony.pdf.

Rubin, Michael. "The Middle East Strategic Realignment Reverberates through South Asia." *AEI* (September 2020). https://www.aei.org/op-eds/the-middle-east-strategic-realignment-reverberates-through-south-asia/?mkt_tok= eyJpIjoiTkRSaFltWTNNemcyT0dKbSIsInQiOiJjbTFwaE9Bb2lFdkhM WkxhZm5tc21CdU1paUIrNG5DR2UzNlc3cUMzM29CZWU5YlhWRz B5aTdkdVhnT01INGpmWnowa1RsRHhZeWJ1RW1XMGRzeERBd0V5e UtRWDJrNHhuTlgwUDJqclpcL1ZrUXRFU01idVBMR05oa2drMXJoVjYi fQ%3D%3D.

Rubinstein, Ariel. *Modeling Bounded Rationality*. Cambridge: MIT Press, 1998.

Rumer, Eugene. "A Farewell to ... Arms Control." *Carnegie Endowment for Peace* (April 2018). https://carnegieendowment.org/2018/04/17/farewell-to-arms-.-.-.-control-pub-76088.

Rumsfeld, Donald. "Transforming the Military." *Foreign Affairs* 81, no. 3 (May/June 2002): 20–32.

Ryan, Kevin. "After the INF Treaty: An Objective Look at US and Russian Compliance, Plus a New Arms Control Regime." *Russia Matters* (December 2017). https://www.russiamatters.org/analysis/after-inf-treaty-objective-look-us-and-russian-compliance-plus-new-arms-control-regime.

Sachs, Jeffrey. "New Approaches to the Latin American Debt Crisis." *Essays in International Finance*, no. 174 (July 1989). https://www.princeton.edu/~ies/IES_Essays/E174.pdf.

Sachs, Jeffrey. "Denuclearization Means the US, Too." *Project Syndicate* (May 2018).

Salam, Reihan. "Is Kim Jong-Un a Rational Actor?" *National Review* (September 2017). http://www.nationalreview.com/corner/451578/north-koreas-kim-jong-un-rational-actor-or-madman.

Sandel, Michael. *Justice: What's the Right Thing to Do?* New York: Farrar, Straus and Giroux, 2009.

Sandel, Michael. *The Tyranny of Merit: What's Become of the Common Good?* New York: Macmillan, 2020.

Sasse, Gwendolyn. "Crimea Annexation 2.0." *Carnegie Europe* (November 2018). https://carnegieeurope.eu/strategiceurope/77828?utm_source=ctw& utm_medium=email&utm_content=buttonlink&mkt_ tok=eyJpIjoiWTJNNE5qQTJNamt6TlRCaSIsInQiOiJKdV wvdndwVFlPTjUzRThEaDZMUVY2ZXNJMlU1Mm0rZW93UnB KSVluYlZDVVJmenNQcDVVM2hoTFhaSzJSZDZVNnVFamFq Y3BBdVJMODJKS2dvTUxHS09vVjJFOXJOWTZuTmQ3dE8rY mM1akM2ejdVbWZCcVN0QnM0cmFGMXhzV1UifQ%3D%3D.

Satel, Sally. "The Public-Health Establishment Has Diminished Its Credibility." *AEI* (June 2020). https://www.aei.org/articles/the-public-health-establishment-has-diminished-its-credibility/.

Schmitt, Gary J. "Trump, Taiwan: Calling China's Bluff." *AEI* (December 2017). http://www.aei.org/publication/trump-taiwan-calling-chinas-bluff/? mkt_tok=eyJpIjoiWkRaaE9HRTRZVEZtTkRjeSIsInQiOiJBZW JvRVF1MVwvRGgwUDRvT3d6dE1CdDlYdEFGaWZPMFVmMHV lWkNYVzNrOGpDWURNUEhQUXlkV29wRHQ3V3BZNmN6RkZq VmFoWlN0eVwvNHRreDhtWHd3ckhnM1U0QXphbThNTmc1NG ZpTFhiT0Q2QmROT0NjbmszczFCU1drNDlVIn0%3D.

Schmitt, Gary. "Good (Defense) News from London." *AEI* (November 2020). https://www.aei.org/foreign-and-defense-policy/good-defense-news-from-london/?mkt_tok=eyJpIjoiTm1WaVl6WTVabU15TldFMylsInQ iOiJ1dkxSRDRMNlZwcEhXUDZUbFBHVkRRZSt3YVlSMDhrN2FrUE hyVUtqYlRlQThES3R0YnZCa1hCbU1SVTVFTEcyQWwybmJwUXM5d 3hKcmVVQ0pUQ3l5NzcxblwvUHhCT2Y4NGx1OE5pamFqdXhJTFBH MXJtWDh6Z0w3MHVnSUdSUGYifQ%3D%3D.

Schmitt, Gary and Michael Mazza. "The End of 'Strategic Ambiguity' Regarding Taiwan: Here are the Steps the U.S. Can Take, and Why We Should Take Them," *Dispatch* (September 2020). https://thedispatch.com/p/the-end-of-strategic-ambiguity-regarding?mkt_tok=eyJpIjoiWkRoak56a zVNMkZqTURRMilsInQiOiI4dmVVM0RhWFQ0eVVOejhGZFFzWU54e k02Nlwvb1hOWXZETDdaY056aHBHQWtlbkNnQVJpSjQwa3JXUHB SaHRnQzJlZHBodHZaXC82YVdGS2x3eHNpUndVUTQ4ZDNLUm 9vSW1WbXNFcHAyaDJ1M29hXC82cUNycllXc1RFMkJ0a 2JuUyJ9Sep%2016.

Schroeder, Gertrude, and Imogene Edwards. "Consumption in the USSR: An International Comparison." *Joint Economic Committee of Congress* (1981).

Schwab, Klaus. *The Fourth Industrial Revolution*. New York: World Economic Forum, 2017.

Bibliography 371

Scissors, Derek. "45 Trillion Reasons Why China Can't Challenge America's Economic Might." *AEI* (October 2015). http://www.aei.org/publication/45-trillion-reasons-why-china-cant-challenge-americas-economic-might/.

Scissors, Derek. "America's Inconvenient Trillions." *AEI* (November 2017). http://www.aei.org/publication/americas-inconvenient-trillions/?mkt_tok=eyJpIjoiTnpSbU1UUTVOVFUwTURGaCIsInQiOiJLU2JQUXM5VXZSN09mZGhFYmF0SDRDaURtcmdmR0pPOUZWTEhZd0VGT0ltVnVMR050R3FFVzdERWRodnFhbFlGVFdySW9iTyswTHR4Mk9Zc2VLM0dLUEJZdFwvNjlMajI3NUlMVHNjaTl6d240TTkwTldJTXRBT0VVbzJVRGtqRkYifQ%3D%3D.

Scissors, Derek. "Sino-American Trade: We Know Where This is Headed." *AEI* (April 2018). http://www.aei.org/publication/sino-american-trade-we-know-where-this-is-headed/?mkt_tok=eyJpIjoiWVdJeVpETXlOV1U0WmpRNSIsInQiOiJCNGs0Szl3bkU3YVk3bzA5bjR4QXd3TW9iMnAxV3JLcjU5bXliYmFCYzdrODNvdDRDeXBrN2dwU3BPd2E0UStxZ1hKOUI0Wll0RGd1TlM0RVZKUDRNd09RSnpycmxqc0RLSFB4c3I5Wkt4VlpjZ1J5VWIxWnRRTUdBSDJaTzB2diJ9.

Scissors, Derek. "China Tariffs: Wrong Weapons, Right Result?" *AEI* (September 2018). http://www.aei.org/publication/china-tariffs-wrong-weapons-right-result/?mkt_tok=eyJpIjoiTWpVd1pqQmpPR0l6T0RZMSIsInQiOiJPbDE3VTZUcm1LMEdhYk5VWndSTFMxcHFiYmhndWYzWVwvWHFoKzhtZFNEc29wOUNaNERkMWtzRGF6dFhSUWgzMVlVSkk4TmNKOGhnN3NYTE1hYmJWcTlsb1VtdDlXVW9LREJiNHpuOGxMd3ZOa1FhTFRpYmt3MOEtPdkhMYkZOXC9rIn0%3D.

Scissors, Derek. "The Department of Commerce Ignores Congress," *AEI* (August 2020). https://www.aei.org/foreign-and-defense-policy/the-department-of-commerce-ignores-congress/?mkt_tok=eyJpIjoiTW1ReVpqQmxPVFppWkRaaaSIsInQiOiJvZGRmUUFsS1wvR2hmWXZcL0hpUlE5YTNjU1FXT25hWmF2SEJBclVcL1JDdm83Y3FncExpemJJNMGF3Sjl3QmNlT3BpdVh5UmtBS3NnNT3Npdm1pb0hYR2hXU29HMUFUUEtppZFpzNzFBTUlqaHI3UEhmSllXbmRuQlZrZ1p3a0U4XC8yYkQifQ%3D%3D.

Seals, Tara. "Russia, China's Cyber-Capabilities are Catastrophic." *Infosecurity* (January 2018). https://www.infosecurity-magazine.com/news/russia-chinas-cybercapabilities/.

Secrieru, Stanislav. "Have Sanctions Changed Russia's Behaviour in Ukraine." In "On Target? EU Sanctions as Security Policy Tools" (2015).

Sen, Amartya. *The Idea of Justice*. London: Penguin, 2010.

Schmitt, Gary. *A Hard Look at Hard Power: Assessing the Defense Capabilities of Key US Allies and Security Partners — Second Edition* (Carlisle, PA: US Army War College Press, 2020). https://press.armywarcollege.edu/monographs/921

Serhan, Yasmeen. "Why Europe Opposes America's New Russia Sanctions: Moscow Isn't the Only One That Could be Negatively Impacted." *Atlantic*

372   *Beleaguered Superpower: Biden's America Adrift*

(August 2017). https://www.theatlantic.com/international/archive/2017/08/why-europe-opposes-the-uss-new-russia-sanctions/535722/.

Shah, Syed Hasanat, Hafsa Hasnat, Steven Rosefielde, and Li Jun Jiang. "Comparative Analysis of Chinese and Indian Soft Power Strategy." *Asian Politics & Policy* 9, no. 2 (April 2017): 268–288.

Sharanstky, Natan. *Defending Identity: Its Indispensable Role in Protecting Democracy*. New York: Public Affairs, 2008.

Sherr, James. "Ukraine and the Black Sea Region: The Russian Military Perspective." In *The Russian Military in Contemporary Perspective*, edited by Stephen Blank. Carlisle: Strategic Studies Institute, US Army War College, 2016.

Sherr, James. "Russia's Strategy." *The Institute for Statecraft* (November 2017).

Shleifer, Andrei, and Daniel Treisman. "A Normal Country." *Foreign Affairs* 83, no. 2 (March/April 2004): 20–39.

Shleifer, Andrei, and Robert Vishny. *The Grabbing Hand: Government Pathologies and Their Cures*. Cambridge: MIT Press, 2000.

Shlykov, Vitaly. "Chto Pogubilo Sovetskii Soiuz? Amerikanskaia Razvedka ili Sovetskiskh Voennykh Raskhodakh." (What Destroyed the Soviet Union? American Intelligence Estimates of Soviet Military Expenditures), *Voenny Vestnik*, no. 8 (2001).

Shlykov, Vitaly. "Russian Defence Industrial Complex after 9–11." *Russian Security Policy and the War on Terrorism Conference, U.S. Naval Postgraduate School* (June 2003).

Shlykov, Vitaly. "Globalizatsiia voennoi promyshlennosti-imperativ XXI veka (Globalization of Military Industry: The 21st Century Imperative)." *Otechestvennye zapiski*, no. 5 (2005): 98–115.

Shlykov, Vitaly. "Nazad v budushchee, ili Ekonomicheskve uroki kholodnoi voiny (Back to the Future, or Economic Lessons of the Cold War)." *Rossiia v Global'noe Politike* 4, no. 2 (2006): 26–40.

Shlykov, Vitaly. "Nevidimaia Mobilizatsii (Invisible Mobilization)." *Forbes* no. 3 (March 2006): 1–5.

Shlykov, Vitaly. "The Military Reform and Its Implications for the Modernization of the Russian Armed Forces." In *Russian Power Structures*, edited by Jan Leijonhielm and Fredrik Westerlund, 50–60. Stockholm: Swedish Defense Research Agency, 2008.

SIGAR. "Corruption in Conflict: Lessons from the U.S. Experience in Afghanistan," *Special Inspector General for Afghanistan Reconstruction* (September 2016).

SIGAR. "Private Sector Development and Economic Growth: Lessons from the U.S. Experience in Afghanistan." *Special Inspector General for Afghanistan Reconstruction* (April 2018). https://www.sigar.mil/interactive-reports/private-sector-development-and-economic-growth/index.html.

Simon, Herbert. "A Behavioral Model of Rational Choice." In *Models of Man: Social and Rational-Mathematical Essays on Rational Human Behavior in a Social Setting*, edited by Herbert Simon. New York: Wiley, 1957.

Bibliography 373

Simon, Herbert. *Models of Man: Social and Rational — Mathematical Essays on Rational Human Behavior in a Social Setting.* New York: John Wiley and Sons, 1957.

Simon, Herbert. "A Mechanism for Social Selection and Successful Altruism." *Science* 250, no. 4988 (1990): 1665–1668.

Simon, Herbert. "Bounded Rationality and Organizational Learning." *Organization Science* 2, no. 1 (1991): 125–134.

Singal, Jesse. "The Reaction to the Harper's Letter on Cancel Culture Proves Why It Was Necessary." *Reason*, June 8, 2020. https://reason.com/2020/07/08/the-reaction-to-the-harpers-letter-on-cancel-culture-proves-why-it-was-necessary/.

Smith, Dan. "The Crumbling Architecture of Arms Control." *SIPRI* (October 2018). https://www.sipri.org/commentary/essay/2018/crumbling-architecture-arms-control.

Sokolsky, Richard. "The New NATO-Russia Military Balance: Implications for European Security." *Carnegie Endowment for Peace* (March 2017). http://carnegieendowment.org/2017/03/13/new-nato-russia-military-balance-implications-for-european-security-pub-68222.

Sokov, Nikolai. "Russia's New Conventional Capability: Implications for Eurasia and Beyond (Policy Memo No. 472)." PONARS *Eurasia* (April 2017).

Sokov, Nikolai. "The Russification of U.S. Deterrence Policy: After a Quarter-Century Monopoly on such Capabilities, the United States Finds Itself Essentially in the Same Predicament that the Russians or Chinese Have Faced Since the End of the Cold War." *The National Interest* (December 2017). https://nationalinterest.org/feature/the-russification-us-deterrence-policy-23785.

Solow, Robert M. "A Contribution to the Theory of Economic Growth." *Quarterly Journal of Economics* 70 (February 1956): 65–94.

Solow, Robert M. "Technical Change and the Aggregate Production Function." *Review of Economics and Statistics* 39 (August 1957): 312–320.

Statista. "U.S. National Health Expenditure as Percent of GDP from 1960 to 2018." https://www.statista.com/statistics/184968/us-health-expenditure-as-percent-of-gdp-since-1960/.

Steiner, Evgeny. *Stories for Little Comrades.* Seattle & London: University of Washington Press, 1999.

Stiglitz, Joseph. "Stagnation by Design." *Project Syndicate* (February 2014). https://www.project-syndicate.org/commentary/joseph-e--stiglitz-argues-that-bad-policies-in-rich-countries--not-economic-inevitability--have-caused-most-people-s-standard-of-living-to-decline?barrier=accessreg.

Stiglitz, Joseph. "The Myth of Secular Stagnation." *Project Syndicate* (August 2018). https://www.project-syndicate.org/commentary/secular-stagnation-excuse-for-flawed-policies-by-joseph-e-stiglitz-2018-08?utm_source=

374 *Beleaguered Superpower: Biden's America Adrift*

Project+Syndicate+Newsletter&utm_campaign=58788e9f11-sunday_newsletter_2_9_2018&utm_medium=email&utm_term=0_73bad5b7d8-58788e9f11-93559677.

Stiglitz, Joseph. *People, Power, and Profits: Progressive Capitalism for an Age of Discontent.* New York: W.W. Norton, 2019.

Strain, Thomas. "Next Task for GOP: Spend Less and Help the Poor." *AEI* (December 2017). http://www.aei.org/publication/next-task-for-gop-spend-less-and-help-the-poor/?mkt_tok=eyJpIjoiTldNM1pHUXhPVEV6WW preSIsInQiOiJ3S0NhQnl0bjM4bHdOQktmNWZJMWlja1IwblR6 dHpBTUZsazJxNEt1Q3hiQ0xkcVRBK21oS0tvRUN0MVJQM3oxRm VOeW4zZTMzTkJIeVpoXC9SdG9OWkdDYklOOUVxUDkyRHV0Y3hx VkhhV24wY2lVS0daaHpFQ0J5bWVTV1wvRkxXIn0%3D.

Strain, Michael. "The Paycheck Protection Program: An Introduction." *AEI* (April 2020). https://www.aei.org/research-products/report/the-paycheck-protection-program-an-introduction/?mkt_tok=eyJpIjoiTXpJelptVXhPREl 3WldabSIsInQiOiJ6ZXpyS2VQa0VhM1RnK0duQ3htUkRrO TdsOHF3eDNMeWhWNnFjU01kcG1PUlV0NkhhdTZXUVV3YUlOQzF mamFEVWNOK2V6Yk02SXpoblA2Q1wvTjZzM1ByWGx1dEVUa3pCY 0FwZ2J3Rlp0VTNGT3VqK0lOcmR5NmhLNDBZamY5UnMifQ%3D %3D.

Strange, Luke. "A Troubling Outlook for Future Defense Spending." *AEI* (November 2018). http://www.aei.org/publication/a-troubling-outlook-for-future-defense-spending/?mkt_tok=eyJpIjoiTURobE1HWmhObU5oT1daaS IsInQiOiJhNnZyUkJ4SjVrNUNLSmlCUk8xUkhnSUU3Q2s1U1p2dUZJc nY3MVZSZDR5blpSSEFVSXl3NVVXSjAxbW5mUytmSGxwRjJhV 0g5WUJVdkxvc0JHNE4wS2FxQ2ZjVXJ3OVdHSFwvSExzdlwvR m56OWViZnNLOWdkSTJ3dkpXTVwvYjh3NiJ9.

Sun, Tzu. *The Art of War: The Oldest Military Treatise in the World*, Translated by Lionel Giles. London: Luzac, 1910.

Sutter, Robert. "China–Russia Relations: Strategic Implications and U.S. Policy Options." *NBR* (September 2018). http://nbr.org/publications/element.aspx? id=1000.

Sutyagin, Igor. "The Russian Military Build-Up: Features, Limits, and Implications for International Security." *Royal United Services Institute (RUSI)* (forthcoming).

Swaine, Michael. "Time to Accept Reality and Manage a Nuclear-Armed North Korea." *Carnegie Endowment for International Peace* (September 2017). http://carnegieendowment.org/2017/09/11/time-to-accept-reality-and-manage-nuclear-armed-north-korea-pub-73065?mkt_tok=ey JpIjoiTUdVNE9EWTBPRGRoT0dRMiIsInQiOiJCNDVSZmF1MzVu YmR0VWJlU1VOWW8xK25HXC9ldVVmQlVFTG95NllcL0t3T0pFV0 pkWFQ3RW00d3hLM1prTWMwbTZJb2JnNWxmdmFHWElBVVZQT1B

Bibliography 375

HSURjaGhKUDhaOXF2KzNVTTNEVUQxWm16eWlaajY3OUNmY3g5 UnVHaTlCM2JGIn0%3D.

Swan, Trevor. "Economic Growth and Capital Accumulation" *Economic Record* 32 (November 1956): 334–361.

Talbott, Strobe. "America Abroad: The Birth of the Global Nation." *Time* (July 1992). http://channelingreality.com/Documents/1992_Strobe_Talbot_ Global_Nation.pdf.

Talbott, Strobe. *The Great Experiment: The Story of Ancient Empires, Modern States, and the Quest for a Global Nation.* New York: Simon and Schuster, 2008.

Taleb, Nassim. *The Black Swan: the Impact of the Highly Improbable*, 2nd ed. London: Penguin, 2010.

Tellis, Ashley J. "Covid-19 Knocks on American Hegemony." *National Bureau of Asian Research* (May 2020). https://www.nbr.org/publication/covid-19-knocks-on-american-hegemony/.

Terry, Sue Mi. "North Korea's Strategic Goals and Policy towards the United States and South Korea." *International Journal of Korean Studies* 17, no. 2 (Fall 2013): 63–92. http://www.icks.org/data/ijks/1482461379_add_file_3.pdf.

The Department of Defense. "The DoD Cyber Strategy." *The Diplomat* (April 2015). http://thediplomat.com/2016/11/the-us-will-win-the-cyber-war-with-china-in-2017/.

The International Atomic Energy Agency. Implementation of the NPT Safeguards Agreement and Relevant Provisions of Security Council Resolutions in the Islamic Republic of Iran. (November 2011). www.iaea.org.

Thiessen, Marc A. "The Warmbiers are Right: North Korea Should be Back on the State Sponsors of Terror List." *AEI* (September 2017). http://www.aei. org/publication/the-warmbiers-are-right-north-korea-should-be-back-on-the-state-sponsors-of-terror-list/?mkt_tok=eyJpIjoiWVRJeU1EWmxOREJq TnpaayIsInQiOiI4dXFvUk9qRXY2dVRoNUR6eTVpRUF3RVEzYW 4rRW4wWXFZdEs5YW5nVEdPZFFKbkZEQ2RpcjJuNXRPYkN1dWZjS DNVQzFPc1hpSkFMZGxTOVwvQzc0Y1liRG0wRW1FSlJiNkErc3ZvZT BlM3U2YitZNlpGaGNSUFQ2aUhKWTFmM1cifQ%3D%3D.

Thiessen, Marc. "Trump's Little-Noticed War on Hidden Taxes." *AEI* (December 2017). https://www.aei.org/publication/trumps-little-noticed-war-on-hidden-taxes/?mkt_tok=eyJpIjoiWVRJeVpXSTVOV1poTXpSaCIsInQiOiJ rZ0tlemxyend6SllzSXF1Q1dcL0FkSmtHOXVwaE5wcWZJdDRqRz RLTHB5Z0tlU0QwSmg4MzhWYkJ0blZoalRyd3BYbnZreWlsT29zdmt wK1gzckpJRXR4S3ZzSEJlcFA2cUtGWUxSeEhWN1NabjVzaGlxVjh0eW pYS2s3bmxLTXMifQ%3D%3D.

Thiessen, Marc. "Obama Took Lying to New Heights with the Iran Deal." *AEI* (June 2018). http://www.aei.org/publication/obama-took-lying-to-new-heights-with-the-iran-deal/?mkt_tok=eyJpIjoiWVRVM01EazFNRFJtTjJW

376 *Beleaguered Superpower: Biden's America Adrift*

aiIsInQiOiJHZ2dMQmVFemdXaVc5cHhPYTdxa2RFQUdFeEs5aHFKcG sweU5KeHlYSG53bWthT2JpWGtLUkNQY1B1OUxtakRzK3p5UjE1 VHV4R1gwNDdPRFM2VnVncm1ZUXpTSUlVQURrVUFTeEVLNUhP OW1BOTZcL1pmaWZla2tGdGxzaVZwZGcifQ%3D%3D.

Thiessen, Marc. "Chaos or Not, Trump is Racking Up a Record of Foreign Policy Success." *AEI* (September 2018). http://www.aei.org/publication/chaos-or-not-trump-is-racking-up-a-record-of-foreign-policy-success/?mkt_tok= eyJpIjoiWXpaaE5tWTNNR0ZqTnpNeiIsInQiOiJoY2Yxb2ppY0JB d2pUUEVwK2NjNlMwWjh1ZFV2dmg2Wm5HWkhuVEF2NnRZTTlmW WtheTBaWUQyck9SZ3IzWVkyZXc2UUxaeENpUk00b3ErVzJPNFV4bz NiQTExN0lpR2Q5MEZKTlh3K084b1ZIdFFzakhWQXJkMU4yZH RjZm16OCJ9.

Thomson, Derek. "Corporate Goliaths are Taking Over the U.S. Economy. Yet Small Breweries are Thriving. Why?" *Atlantic* (January 2018). https://www. theatlantic.com/business/archive/2018/01/craft-beer-industry/550850/.

Thompson, Derek. "Craft Beer is the Strangest, Happiest Economic Story in America: Corporate Goliaths are Taking Over the U.S. Economy. Yet small Breweries are Thriving. Why?" *Atlantic* (January 2018). https://www. theatlantic.com/business/archive/2018/01/craft-beer-industry/550850/.

Thompson, Loren. "If America's Military Loses World War III, Low Readiness Will Likely Be the Reason." *Forbes* (November 2018). https://www.forbes. com/sites/lorenthompson/2018/11/15/if-americas-military-loses-world-war-iii-low-readiness-will-likely-be-the-reason/#5c61c91c6bae.

Thurow, Lester. *The Zero-Sum Society*. Lexington: Basic Books, 1980.

Tian, Nan, Aude Fleurant, Pieter D. Wezeman, and Siemon T. Wezeman. "Trends in World Military Expenditure, 2016." *Stockholm International Peace Research Institute* (April 2017).

Tisdell, Clem. *Bounded Rationality and Economic Evolution: A Contribution to Decision Making, Economics, and Management*. Cheltenham: Brookfield, 1998.

Toal, Gerard, John O'Loughlin, and Kristin M. Bakke. *Near Abroad: Putin, the West and the Contest for Ukraine and the Caucasus*. London: Oxford University Press, 2019.

Toeffler, Alvin. *Power Shift: Knowledge, Wealth, and Power at the Edge of the 21st Century*. New York: Bantam Books, 1990.

Toynbee, Arnold. *A Study of History*. London: Oxford University Press, 1987.

Tooze, Adam. *Crashed: How a Decade of Financial Crises Changed the World*. London: Penguin Random House, 2018.

Traub, James. "The United States of America Is Decadent and Depraved." *Foreign Policy* (December 2019). https://foreignpolicy.com/2017/12/19/ the-united-states-of-america-is-decadent-and-depraved/.

Bibliography 377

Treisman, Daniel. "Inter-Enterprise Arrears and Barter in the Russian Economy." *PostSoviet-Affairs* 16, no. 3 (July–September 2000): 225–256.

Trenin, Dmitri. "Russia and the United States: A Temporary Break or a New Cold War?" *Carnegie Moscow Center* (January 2015). http://carnegie.ru/2014/12/08/russia-and-united-states-temporary-break-or-new-cold-war/hxw4?mkt_tok=3RkMMJWWfF9wsRoluaXPZKXonjHpfsX56OsvXqGg38431UFwdcjKPmjr1YACTsV0aPyQAgobGp5I5FEIQ7XYTLB2t60MWA%3D%3D.

Trenin, Dmitri. "The New Cold War is Boiling Over in Syria." *Foreign Policy* (April 2018). https://carnegie.ru/2018/04/14/new-cold-war-is-boiling-over-in-syria-pub-76081?utm_source=ctw&utm_medium=email&utm_campaign=20180418&mkt_tok=eyJpIjoiWXpReE9EaGxaV0V3WmpWbCIsInQiOiJ3ajRxNXZHTUt1eVBvQVdJRTRiaW9vOURSNk16ZWFcL0ZXQ3dqU2s5S0p6YlwvdnR4MlQwSG9KVmlGVTF0NmNYVTlwRjF3ZUJ3TzNZRnFyYlFzVnRRVcFd0SFNkVVpZYm1lYXErVjZFXC91dTZiZjc5Y1RDOFwvVEU4UnNOZm5aWkw4QmhpT0NsOSt0bzNMc2IyRlwvvUm9nWHpOZz09In0%3D.

Trump, Donald, and Tony Schwartz. *The Art of the Deal*. New York: Random House, 1987.

Tse-tung, Mao. "U.S. Imperialism is a Paper Tiger." In *Selected Works of Mao Zedong*. July 1956. https://www.marxists.org/reference/archive/mao/selected-works/index.htm.

Tsygankov, Andrei P. "Gulliver at the Crossroads: America's Strategy During the Global Transition." *Journal of International Analytics* 11, no. 2 (2020): 28–44 (in Russian). https://doi.org/10.46272/2587-8476-2020-11-2-28-44.

Tsygankov, Andrei. "The Revisionist Moment: Russia, Trump, and Global Transition." *Problems of Post-Communism* (August 2020). https://doi.org/10.1080/10758216.2020.1788397

Turgenev, Ivan. *Fathers and Children (Отцы и дети)*. Leipsig: Wolfgang Gerhard, 1880.

Turley, Gerard, and Peter Luke. *Transition Economics: Two Decades On*. London: Routledge, 2010.

Twigg, Judy. "Russia Is Winning the Sanctions Game." *National Interest* (March 2019). https://nationalinterest.org/blog/skeptics/russia-winning-sanctions-game-47517.

Twigg, Judyth. "Russian Health and Demographic Trends and Prospects" in *Putin's Russia: Economic, Political and Military Foundations*, edited by Steven Rosefielde. Singapore: World Scientific Publishers, 2020.

Tzu, Sun. *The art of war: the oldest military treatise in the world*, translated by Lionel Giles. London: Luzac, 1910.

U.S. Congress. House. *An Act To amend the Internal Revenue Code of 1986 to Repeal the Excise Tax on High Cost Employer-Sponsored Health Coverage.*

HR 748, 116th., 2nd sess. January 3, 2020. https://www.congress.gov/116/bills/hr748/BILLS-116hr748enr.pdf.

U.S. Department of Defense. "Asia-Pacific Maritime Security Strategy: Achieving U.S. National Security Objectives in a Changing Environment Maritime Security Strategy." (2015).

U.S. Department of Treasury. "Treasury Designates Russian Oligarchs, Officials, and Entities in Response to Worldwide Malign Activity." (April 2018).

United Nations. "Treaty on the Non-Proliferation of Nuclear Weapons (NPT)." https://www.un.org/disarmament/wmd/nuclear/npt/.

United Nations. "UN Res. 68/262, Territorial integrity of Ukraine." (2014). http://www.un.org/en/ga/search/view_doc.asp?symbol=A/RES/68/262.

US Department of the Census. "US trade in Goods with China." (September 2018). https://www.census.gov/foreign-trade/balance/c5700.html.

USCYBERCOM. "Achieve and Maintain Cyberspace Superiority Command Vision for US Cyber Command." https://assets.documentcloud.org/documents/4419681/Command-Vision-for-USCYBERCOM-23-Mar-18.pdf.

Usmanov, Jaloliddin. "The Shanghai Cooperation Organization: Harmony or Discord?" *The Diplomat* (June 2018). https://thediplomat.com/2018/06/the-shanghai-cooperation-organization-harmony-or-discord/.

Varoufakis, Yanis. "Solidarity with the Germans." *Project Syndicate* (August 2020), https://www.project-syndicate.org/commentary/next-generation-eu-recipe-for-divisiveness-paralysis-by-yanis-varoufakis-2020-08.

Vasiliev, Sergei, and Yegor Gaidar. *Ten Years of Russian Economic Reform*. London: Centre for Research into Post-Communist Economies, 1999.

Vollrath, Dietrich. *Fully Grown: Why a Stagnant Economy is a Sign of Success*. Chicago: University of Chicago Press, 2020.

Vu, Cung. "The Fourth Industrial Revolution: Its Security Implications." *RSIS* (May 2018).

Wallison, Peter J. "Government Ignorance is No Excuse for Another Dreadful Financial Crisis." *AEI* (September 2018).

Walt, Stephen. "The Hell of Good Intentions: America's Foreign Policy Elite and the Decline of U.S. Primacy." *Kirkus Reviews* (October 2018). https://www.kirkusreviews.com/book-reviews/stephen-m-walt/the-hell-of-good-intentions/.

Wang, Zhikai. "Belt and Road Strategy." In *The Unwinding of the Globalist Dream: EU, Russia, China*, edited by Masaaki Kuboniwa, Kumiko Haba, and Satoshi Mizobata, 249–262. Singapore: World Scientific Publishers, 2017.

Webmd. "Coronavirus and COVID-19: What You Should Know." https://www.webmd.com/lung/coronavirus#1-2.

West, Bing. "Deter the Cyber Weapon from Being Employed." *Hoover* (September 2017). http://www.hoover.org/research/deter-cyber-weapon-being-employed.

Bibliography 379

Weyland, Kurt. "Latin America's Authoritarian Drift: The Threat from the Populist Left." *Journal of Democracy* 4, no. 3 (July 2013): 18–32.

White House. "FACT SHEET: The Prague Nuclear Agenda." (January 2017). https://obamawhitehouse.archives.gov/the-press-office/2017/01/11/fact-sheet-prague-nuclear-agenda.

Williamson, John. "Development and the Washington Consensus." *World Development* 21 (1993): 1329–336.

Wittgenstein, Ludwig. *Tractatus logico-philosophicus*. New York: Harcourt, Brace & Company, 1922.

Wohlstetter, Albert. "Is There a Strategic Arms Race?" *Foreign Policy* 15 (Summer, 1974): 3–20.

Wolf Jr., Charles, and Henry S. Rowen. *The Impoverished Superpower: Perestroika and the Soviet Military*. Palo Alto: ICS Press, 1990.

Wolfe, Thomas. *Radical Chic*. New York: Farrar, Straus and Giroux, 1970.

Wolfowitz, Paul. "Is China Pivoting to the Middle East?" AEI (September 2020). https://www.aei.org/articles/is-china-pivoting-to-the-middle-east/?mkt_tok=eyJpIjoiWVdNNFptVmxNbVptTnpOaSIsInQiOiJrWG04XC9LaDdET nNlUkprWGg0SWhcL0tIQWN6S1wvQlVvZXVkV29CQVNoRjVDQzRW UjRsUDltc2E0YUNrbU1yTHRmYm1xakhSeUFTNzdHazIrQXZPdlo rMXdkNTIzYlB6SXV5Y2xYUE53OUN4Z2JROUQ3aXFIaE1MdlREY XNXdVE3dCJ9.

Woolf, Amy F. "Nonstrategic Nuclear Weapons." *Congressional Research Service* (February 2017). https://fas.org/sgp/crs/nuke/RL32572.pdf.

World Bank. "Country Partnership Strategy (CPS) for the Russian Federation, Report No.65115-RU." (November 2011).

World Bank. *Russia Economic Report: Dawn of a New Economic Era?* (April 2015): 4, 31. https://www.worldbank.org/content/dam/Worldbank/document/eca/russia/rer33-eng.pdf.

World Bank. "Russian Economy Returns to Modest Growth in 2017, Says World Bank." (November 2017). http://www.worldbank.org/en/news/press-release/2017/11/29/rer-38.

Wright, Robin. "Trump to Let Assad Stay Until 2021, as Putin Declares Victory in Syria." *New Yorker* (December 2017). https://www.newyorker.com/sections/news/trump-to-let-assad-stay-until-2021-as-putin-declares-victory-in-syria.

Wyler Tom and Ashley J. Tellis. "Sustaining America's Role in the World Demands Renewal at Home." *Carnegie Endowment for International Peace*, (October 2020). https://carnegieendowment.org/2020/10/21/sustaining-america-s-role-in-world-demands-renewal-at-home-pub-83017?utm_source=carnegieemail&utm_medium=email&utm_announcementcampaign=&mkt_tok=eyJpIjoiWkdNeFpEVXhOVGxsTkRCbCIsInQiOiJhQmJLXC9 uRDU0UFFHK3loMEFndEdrdnVobHZQVVZhUjdRZm9HQSt1X

380   *Beleaguered Superpower: Biden's America Adrift*

C9OeHp1K0lCeThKY3U5VkdvbU12VzlIeDY4TUlUK0FqN1BYSzhC
cit5ekRDbTZlbUNYSzRCd29UQ1ZQRnNkbXlwU3FRY01jODJBVEZ0a
mZhT1RURHBcL0R0OCJ9.

Yang, Zi. "China is Massively Expanding Its Cyber Capabilities." *National Interest* (October 2017). http://nationalinterest.org/blog/the-buzz/china-massively-expanding-its-cyber-capabilities-22577.

Yavlinski, Grigori, Boris Fedorov, Stanislav Shatalin, Nikolai Petrakov, and Sergei Aleksashenko. *500 Days: Transition to the Market*. London: St. Martin's Press, 1991.

Yoo, John. "Military Use of Space is Coming, Trump Can Help America Prepare." *AEI* (December 2017). http://www.aei.org/publication/military-use-of-space-is-coming-trump-can-help-america-prepare/?mkt_tok=eyJpIjoi T1RnME16QXpOREF5TWpJeiIsInQiOiJUcEtkNFpFZng0VWtyYlY zXC9cL29wNzVIeHlOTitxWk9WcFJQM0VPQ2U4endFczVYd1V cL1pVME1uSEZUVWxmU2dLWFk3RDRyUWNvdVpPNldGZ1BwV VYrMm9kZDg0OGlJRzQ0Sndvb0JkUkxlY0ZuTXJmdU5SMTNrM 1NORHZNUStvRCJ9.

Yoo, John. "Executive Non-Enforcement in the Era of the Trump Presidency." *AEI* (July 2020). https://www.aei.org/op-eds/executive-non-enforcement-in-the-era-of-the-trump-presidency/?mkt_tok=eyJpIjoiTXpnM1l6ZzFNVGcy WlRZNSIsInQiOiIzdzk5VUtcL2FwSGRKYWJyZ2RYU2JLN 0l4K2w5bmJKU1VieIBNZWVKRkdxblU5Z1VtRkdUNFYzcVwvT 1BuUlFqV2d2WWpsb05BZDBEVnJic0FZRGVUTlo5QnNmczRZV2xza 2pxbVUzU3pheVNEa2tjRmNtMjgwbHdjR0V1d1VtQ3cxIn0%3D.

Zehr, Howard. *The Little Book of Restorative Justice*. Intercourse: Good Books, 2002.

Zhang, Wenhong, ed. *Prevention and Control of COVID-19*. Singapore: World Scientific Publishers, 2020.

Zhavoronkov, Sergey. "Two Lean Years: Russia's Budget for 2018–2020." *Russia File* (December 2017).

Zycher, Benjamin. "Joe Stiglitz Reviews Bjorn Lomborg's New Book." *AEI* (August 2020). https://www.aei.org/articles/joe-stiglitz-reviews-bjorn-lomborgs-new-book/?mkt_tok=eyJpIjoiTmpkaE1qUXpNbVJrTWprMiIs InQiOiJCWWFsQzRlYzlIRXdWUzNQcFVSanJxZkc1Y2hLdm1VND NZTEVmTmxKblBzeEhCOGRxdTJ5SHlSXC9cL2xqazVXV0ZtNm9P Q3oyeFlXY3l3TGFpeEdFQmw3TUdnNHRFSnJ0QmM1ZHowb0o5cF Fvc3lQbVwvY2V5VGdTMlpppT0NRZmlnSiJ9.

Zygar, Mikhail. *The Empire Must Die: Russia's Revolutionary Collapse, 1900–1917*. New York: Public Affairs, 2017.

Zysk, Katarzyna. "Escalation and Nuclear Weapons in Russia's Military Strategy." *The RUSI Journal* (2018). DOI: 10.1080/03071847.2018.1469267.

Lightning Source UK Ltd.
Milton Keynes UK
UKHW040704290721
387939UK00001B/156